THE BREAKDOWN OF THE ROMAN REPUBLIC

From Oligarchy to Empire

In this book, Christopher S. Mackay recounts the last century of the Roman Republic in a readable narrative treatment. Within this narrative he analyzes the breakdown of the traditional Republican form of government as a result of the administrative and political crises brought about by the Roman conquest of the Mediterranean basin in the Middle Republic. He also shows how the many reforms instituted by Augustus, which effectively created the new imperial form of government, were a reaction to the failings of the Republic. Illustrated with an extensive collection of coin images that document the changes in contemporary political ideology, this volume also focuses on the political significance of the key personalities, including Marius, Sulla, and Caesar, who played a large role in the events that led to the demise of the Roman Republic.

Christopher S. Mackay is a professor in the Department of History and Classics at the University of Alberta.

THE BREAKDOWN OF THE ROMAN REPUBLIC

FROM OLIGARCHY TO EMPIRE

Christopher S. Mackay
University of Alberta

CAMBRIDGE
UNIVERSITY PRESS

CAMBRIDGE
UNIVERSITY PRESS

32 Avenue of the Americas, New York NY 10013-2473, USA

Cambridge University Press is part of the University of Cambridge.

It furthers the University's mission by disseminating knowledge in the pursuit of education, learning and research at the highest international levels of excellence.

www.cambridge.org
Information on this title: www.cambridge.org/9781107657021

First published 2009
First paperback edition 2012

A catalogue record for this publication is available from the British Library

Library of Congress Cataloguing in Publication data
Mackay, Christopher S., 1962–
   The breakdown of the Roman republic : from oligarchy to empire /
   Christopher Mackay.
      p.   cm.
   Includes bibliographical references and index.
   ISBN 978-0-521-51819-2 (hardback)
   1. Rome – History – Republic, 265–30 B.C.   2. Rome – Politics
   and government – 265–30 B.C.   I. Title.
   DG254.M25   2009
   973′.05–dc22   2008048943

ISBN 978-0-521-51819-2 Hardback
ISBN 978-1-107-65702-1 Paperback

Kelliae meae
coniugi atque adiutrici
optime de me merenti

CONTENTS

– CONTENTS –

Illustrations of Roman coinage follow page 294.

ABBREVIATIONS

BMCRR: Grueber, *Coins of the Roman Republic*
OGIS: Dittenberger, *Orientis Graeci Inscriptiones Selectae*
RIC: Sutherland, *The Roman Imperial Coinage*
RRC: Crawford, *Roman Republican Coinage*
RS: Crawford, *Roman Statutes*

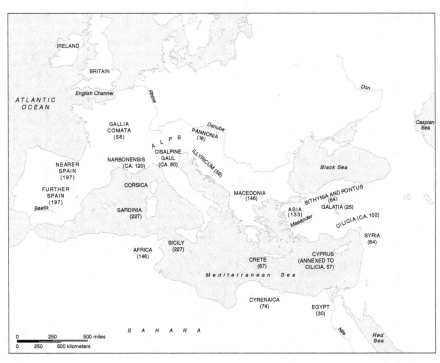

IRELAND

BRITAIN

English Channel

Rhine

Don

ATLANTIC
OCEAN

Caspian
Sea

GALLIA
COMATA
(58)

Danube

PANNONIA
(16)

A L P S

CISALPINE
GAUL
(CA. 80)

ILLYRICUM (59)

NEARER
SPAIN
(197)

NARBONENSIS
(CA. 120)

Black Sea

FURTHER
SPAIN
(197)

Baetis

CORSICA

MACEDONIA
(146)

BITHYNIA AND PONTUS
(64)

ASIA
(133)

GALATIA (25)

Maeander

CILICIA (CA. 102)

SARDINIA
(227)

AFRICA
(146)

SICILY
(227)

CRETE
(67)

CYPRUS
(ANNEXED TO
CILICIA, 57)

SYRIA
(64)

Mediterranean   Sea

CYRENAICA
(74)

EGYPT
(30)

S A H A R A

Nile

Red
Sea

| 0 | 250 | 500 miles |
| 0 | 250 | 500 kilometers |

Map 1. Major Provinces

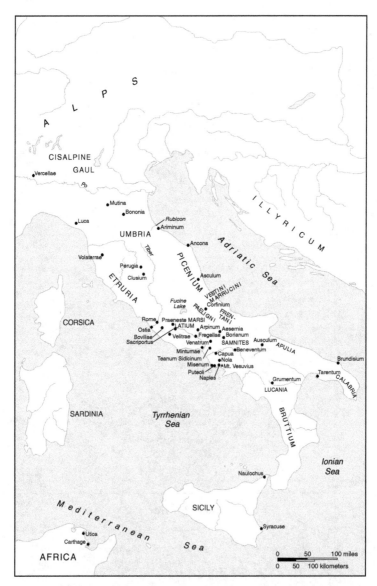

Map 2. Italy

Map 3. Western Europe

Map 4. Greece and the Near East

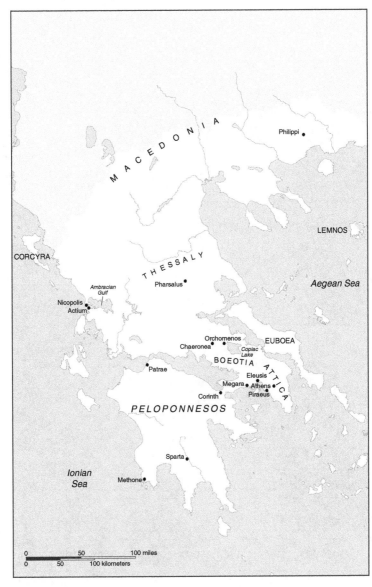

Map 5. Greece

THE BREAKDOWN OF THE ROMAN REPUBLIC

From Oligarchy to Empire

INTRODUCTION

I have no doubt that for most readers the origins and the immediately subsequent period will offer less pleasure, and that they will hurry on to the present events in which the strength of the dominant nation is wearing itself out. For my own part, I will consider it to be another reward of my labor that as I recollect those pristine times I can, for a little while at least, turn away from the sight of the evils which our generation has seen for so many years. Please, I bid everyone for his own sake to pay close attention to what way of life there was then and the sorts of men and virtues by which rule was acquired both at home and abroad. Then, as discipline declines, let him follow in his mind the sinking, as it were, of character, and next how character declined more and more and then began to collapse headlong, until the present time was finally reached, when we can endure neither our faults nor cures. What is particularly beneficial and fruitful in considering historical events is for you to view instances of every sort of example set out in an illustrious precedent, and from it you may select for yourself and your state what you should imitate and what you should avoid since it is foul from beginning to end. In any case, unless my love of the work that I have undertaken deceives me, there was never any state that was greater or more devout or one which was richer in good examples, nor was there any body of citizens among whom greed and high living arrived so late or so much honor was given to modest means and frugal living for so long. The fewer possessions there were, the smaller the avarice, but recently riches have imported greed, and plentiful pleasures have imported the desire to ruin everything and to be ruined with high living and lust.

(Livy, *From the Foundation of the City,* Preface)

The historian Livy began writing his monumental history of the city of Rome during the turbulent 30s B.C., when the Roman world was wracked by the final stages of the civil wars that marked the demise of the Republican constitution. In his introduction, Livy exhibits his disgust with the present situation and contrasts his own attitude with the one that he attributes to his audience, whose morbid curiosity he thinks will be drawn more to the calamities of their own times. For his part, Livy prefers the past, seeing his careful study of it as a way to ignore the unpleasant realities around him. Despite his desire to escape from his own period of time, he nonetheless imagines that he has an explanation for it.

In Livy's view, the troubles of the Late Republic were attributable to moral causes. In the early days of the Republic when there was little wealth, there was correspondingly less desire for it, and the upright men of those days used their moral rectitude to acquire an empire. Subsequently, however, increased wealth had two deleterious effects: material prosperity inspired greed, and the new decadent way of life resulted in a perverse desire for self-destruction. Livy is rather vague about the whole process, and he specifies neither when the change from the supposed virtue of the past began nor how exactly this putative decline in the moral tone of the national character resulted in this suicidal mania. Since Livy had little understanding of the exact nature of the problems in contemporary political life, much less what processes or developments had caused them, it is little wonder that the only solution he could find was to avert his eyes from the present and look longingly at the idealized picture he was drawing for himself of the good old days of the Early Republic. Livy was not the only man in the last days of the Republic to wonder how things had turned out so badly.

Writing perhaps a few years earlier and dealing with the political misfortunes that had taken place a few decades before, the historian Sallust had an explanation similar to Livy's:

After the Republic had expanded through hard work and justice, mighty kings had been conquered in war, fierce nations and huge peoples had been subdued by force, Carthage, the rival of the Roman empire, had been utterly destroyed, and all the seas and lands had been opened up, fortune began to rush about in havoc, throwing everything into confusion. Peace and wealth – things that are otherwise desirable – were an oppressive cause of misery for those who had easily endured hard work and danger and events both doubtful and dire. For this reason, there grew a greed first for money and then for rule, and these were like the raw material for all evils. For avarice overthrew good faith, honesty and all the other virtues, and in place of them it taught arrogance, cruelty, neglect of the gods, and the notion that everything was for sale. Self-serving ambition forced many men to become false, to have one thing closed up in their heart and another on the tip of their tongue, to consider their friendships and enmities not on the basis of fact but of advantage, and to keep their countenance good rather than their character. These things at first grew gradually and were occasionally punished, but when the contagion spread like the plague, the state was

changed: what had been the best and most just empire became a cruel and
unendurable one.

(Sallust, *Catilinarian Conspiracy* 10)

Here Sallust agrees with Livy in ascribing a perceived decline in the political situation of the Late Republic to moral causes that have to do with
increased wealth. Greed undercut the good character that had prevailed
in the earlier period when the Romans established their empire by defeating foreign kings and nations. Amidst the resulting wealth, greed sapped
the traditional morality, and the desire for political office led men to
abandon the objective honesty which had been the main Roman trait in
favor of concealment of one's inner thoughts in the interest of achieving
one's personal aims. Like Livy, Sallust characterizes this moral decline
as a disease, but he is somewhat more specific than Livy in giving a date
to this development. He states that it took place after the destruction (in
146 B.C.) of Carthage, Rome's first major overseas opponent, and elsewhere (*Jugurthine War* 41.2–3) he elaborates that while prior to the
destruction of Carthage the Romans' fear of that city had forced them to
remain virtuous, the removal of this fear through that city's overthrow
had allowed high living and arrogance to flourish unchecked. But even if
Sallust, unlike Livy, presents a chronological framework for this supposed
decline in personal morality, he has no clearer idea of how exactly this
decline resulted in the subsequent political troubles, nor does he have any
solution. Like Livy, he withdrew from involvement in the contemporary
world because of his disgust at it, and turned his attention to historical
writing as a consolation and distraction (*Catilinarian Conspiracy* 4.4).

Writing in the late 30s B.C., in the midst of ongoing civil wars, the poet
Horace viewed the situation in a similar, though vaguer, manner:

A second generation is now being worn down with civil wars,
and Rome herself collapses under her own strength.
The city which the neighboring Marsi or the Etruscan troop
of menacing Porsenna were unable to destroy,
which neither the manliness of rival Capua nor grim Spartacus
and the Allobrogan without faith in times of revolution
nor fierce Germany with her blue-eyed youth
or Hannibal, whom parents detest, conquered:
this city will we, an impious generation of accursed blood, destroy,
and the soil will again by inhabited by wild beasts.

(*Epode* 16.1–10)

While not as explicit in ascribing the ruin of the Late Republic to moral
decline, Horace resembles the historians in attributing the cause to a fault

in the Romans themselves, whom he conceives of as working out some sort of curse that has been placed upon them. Like Livy, he thinks that the very strength of the Roman state was being used to destroy it, and like Sallust he contrasts the self-destruction of the present with the military victories of the past. Again like them, he has no solution for the evils of his times, and suggests a literary escape. He proposes that the "entire accursed state or at least the part that is better than the common herd" (lines 36–37) should set sail for the fabled Isles of the Blessed, where a Golden Age of peace and plenty has been hidden for the pious by the god Jupiter. Since there is no such place, he presumably means that literature provides the only refuge from the turmoil and civil war that was engulfing the Roman world.

Clearly, men of the Late Republic found the world in which they lived (and died) an appalling one and were grasping for an explanation of what had gone wrong with their state, which had only a few generations earlier enjoyed seemingly incredible military success in conquering the Mediterranean basin. Their only explanation was based on considerations of personal morality: somehow the disastrous cause of civil discord was to be sought in the failings of contemporary Romans, who had apparently deviated from the integrity which they took to be such a notable characteristic of their forebears. Since the Romans tended to view wealth with suspicion and were quite conscious of the extent to which the riches that had poured into Rome after the conquests greatly surpassed the resources available in early days of the Republic, it is not surprising that they chose to connect the apparent decline in morality with this increase in wealth and to imagine that these developments were at the root of the problem, even if the exact mode of causality was left unclear.

It is to be noted that all three of these analyses of the political problems of the Late Republic were written by men who would have possessed far more wealth than most of the citizenry. It would be nice to know what the average citizen, whether in his capacity as voter or soldier, thought about the turbulent events around him, but for the most part our information comes from texts written by wealthy individuals. The great majority of Romans, with comparatively little or no wealth, have left no record of their thoughts. What follows, then, is the story of how the office-holding class lost control of the political situation in Rome as the result of both structural faults and external pressures, and how the resulting military chaos was eventually brought under control through the covert establishment of an autocracy.

Two millennia later, the question of why the Republican form of government, which had been so successful in conquering the Mediterranean basin in a series of overseas campaigns from the mid third to the mid second centuries B.C., rapidly fell apart in the century from the death of Ti. Gracchus in 133 B.C. to the battle of Actium in 31 B.C. continues to attract popular interest, as is attested by the large number of books on the subject that have recently appeared in print (not to mention various television treatments ranging from a fictionalized miniseries on HBO to straightforward narratives on the History Channel). These books are written by nonacademics and so rely on out-of-date academic work and the sort of moralistic biographical interpretations that appear in the ancient sources; this kind of analysis tends to concentrate on individual behavior and leave out of consideration the structural problems of the Roman political system. There are also academic works on the subject, but they often deal with the minutiae of the linguistic interpretation of the Greek and Latin sources and are of comparatively limited use (or interest) for nonspecialists. Nonetheless, a discussion of the nature of the sources should prove useful to the general reader.

We have some documentary evidence in the form of inscriptions, but such sources are comparatively rare for the Republic (epigraphy provides much more evidence for the Empire). Hence, our information about the Late Republic is skewed by the nature of our literary sources. While these sources do provide a large amount of information, the picture they provide is limited by a number of considerations.

To begin with, there is no complete annalistic history (i.e., one that provides a synoptic view of affairs on a year-to-year basis) that survives for our period. Some stretches of history (for instance, the 110s B.C. and the 70s B.C.) happen to be comparatively poorly attested. This in part results from the biographical perspective that pervades a large number of our sources. Many of these are strongly focused on the personalities of individuals, so that our knowledge of periods that were not dominated by the sorts of personalities that appealed to the moralizing biographical authors who provide much of our information largely depends on unsatisfactory passing allusions in later works. Furthermore, even for the periods that are better known, the emphasis of the sources on the activities of prominent individuals has a tendency to distort the overall picture by viewing events from the perspective of those individuals and underappreciating the activities of the less conspicuous actors of history. This sort of concentration on individuals further distorts the picture given in the ancient sources by highlighting the actions (and motives) of specific individuals and paying little or no attention to broader themes. For instance, while Caesar's campaigns in Gaul mean that we are given a good overview of his activities (especially since he wrote a self-serving account of his own that survives), the prolonged campaigns that brought the interior of the Balkans under Roman control are virtually unknown apart from the names and terms of office of the commanders, the dates of various defeats and victories, and some information about the triumphs in Rome that resulted from the latter. About the only ancient source that tries to paint a broader perspective is the five-book account of the *Civil Wars* written by Appian, who attempts to outline the role of violence in the political crisis of the Late Republic (an effort that is far from successful in that this obsessive interest in violence itself distorts the narrative).

A related consideration is the fact that the ancient sources with their fixation on important individuals have little sense of the broader social context of the events that they narrate. There are stray references to the interests and views of the lower strata of society, but these are few and far between. Basically, we are left in the dark about the attitudes of even the wealthy nonsenators in Rome, not to mention the small landowners of the Italian countryside or the landless rural population that eventually provided the soldiers whose depredations so demoralized Livy, Sallust, and Horace. Even in terms of the electoral process, something that should have been of some interest to the historical sources, the ancient authors provide little information about how voting was carried out and elections won (though the speeches and letters of Cicero go some way to make up this failing).

Even the stories told of the subjects of biographical interest are often determined more for the purpose of providing the reader with uplifting or salutary moral lessons than giving a thoughtful analysis of the historical significance of the events. In this regard, it is worthwhile to consider the words of Plutarch at the start of his biography of Alexander the Great. He overtly distinguishes the activity of a biographer from that of a historian, noting that a gesture or joke may say more about character than a major battle in which thousands died. Plutarch compares the biographer to a painter, whose aim is to give the viewer a sense of the subject's character through the subtle shading of detail rather than to give nothing but the outline of his features. (For a modern comparison, one might contrast a well-executed portrait with a casual snapshot.) Hence, much of the information that is provided by biographical and other moralizing sources cannot be taken at face value.

In connection with this, it is worth pointing out that most of the sources that we have are what would be called in modern terms "secondary sources." That is, they were not written by contemporaries but by later authors (often centuries after the fact) who had to rely on previous accounts to compose their own version of events. This means that writers under the Empire often had a weak sense of the political realities of the Republic, and in any case the tradition that survives in later authors often reflects a historical analysis that is based on a double form of distortion. First, the historical tradition was established by the well-to-do, and hence by definition tends to be pro-senatorial and hence hostile to those who were perceived (rightly or wrongly) as having acted against the senate's interests. Second, as the truism has it, history is written by the victors. While this is not entirely true, it is the case that for periods involving civil war, the ancient historical assessment was drawn up in favor of the victors. It is only the history of the period from the late 60s to the late 40s B.C., which is attested by the accounts of Caesar and the speeches, letters, and essays of Cicero, that largely rests on contemporary evidence. This is far and away the best attested period of classical antiquity (though even for it we have to make use of later works, and much remains unknown).

The preservation of a historical work from antiquity is determined by the literary tastes of Late Antiquity and the later vicissitudes of fate. In Late Antiquity, the older practice of writing texts on papyrus was replaced with the use of vellum (animal skin), and this change meant that virtually all texts that were not copied over in the new medium were lost. The new material was expensive, and for the most part only works that were esteemed for literary (aesthetic) reasons were copied over and hence preserved. Even if a work was copied, this did not guarantee that the text would be preserved through the Middle Ages until the dissemination of texts through printing began in the early modern period. The upshot is that much of the ancient literary tradition about the Late Republic has been lost for reasons that have little or nothing to do with the inherent value of those sources.

These considerations about the failings of the ancient sources may make it sound as if it is not possible to get any but a very limited sense of the history of the ancient world. While it is true that the limitations of the sources have to be borne in mind, the intensive study of these texts over many, many years has made it possible to overcome their deficiencies and to use them to answer questions that probably never occurred to the ancients. At the most basic level, the process of source criticism has been developed to sift through conflicting accounts and to determine the actual course of events (though this procedure can go only so far, since some events are related by only one source). On a more interpretive level, from the stray information provided by Cicero and others it is possible to reconstruct the general nature of the electoral system (even if the specifics are unclear and its operation in a given instance is mostly unrecoverable).

The present work is an attempt to answer the question that so puzzled the likes of Livy, Sallust, and Horace: why did the Republican form of government break down and come to be replaced by the military autocracy that became the Roman Empire? The answer is given largely in the form of a general narrative of the last century of the Republic that is dominated by the lives of the important individuals whose stories figure so prominently in the ancient sources. While the lives of these figures will by necessity play a very prominent role in the narrative, the tack taken here is more or less the exact opposite of that advocated by Plutarch. Whereas he preferred the sometimes seemingly insignificant personal details that illuminate character at the expense of the broader historical events because of which these men were important, here these lives enter the narrative only to the extent that they are relevant to the story of how the use of violence to attain political aims spiraled out of control and quickly made the old form of government unworkable. The personal quirks and proclivities, the sexual habits and physical appearance of the great men of the past – topics that fascinated the ancients – are not treated here.

A number of factors contributed to the breakdown of the Republican government. The use of violence in domestic politics first came to be considered appropriate in very narrow circumstances in 133 B.C., and by the end of the second century B.C., it was already widespread in the assemblies in Rome. The use of political violence took a more ominous turn when it was extended to the Roman military. Down to 107 B.C., the Roman soldiery was conscripted from landowners (however small their holdings), but after that the rural poor were the main source of recruits, and it turned out that generals could take advantage of their soldiers' interests to further their own objectives. The fall of the Republic would take many twists and turns, and a number of potential alternative developments were possible, but for the most part, once it became possible for military leaders to use the public forces of violence at their disposal for their own purposes, the old form of government was doomed. The military needs of the empire that the Romans had acquired were such that there was no way to avoid laying huge forces in the hands of certain generals, yet there was no institutional means of controlling the behavior of these generals, and it was inevitable that these forces would be used to further the ambitions of generals once the political restraints on the use of violence for personal ends fell by the wayside. The following narrative aims to make sense of these developments and to show how the (partially) concealed military autocracy that would be erected by the first Roman emperor was an effective way of bringing order to the bloody chaos into which the Republic had collapsed. In addition to the main narrative, the book contains a series of coin illustrations that give a visual representation of the process by which individuals usurped for themselves the state power that had previously been exercised in a collective manner by the senatorial oligarchy and eventually resulted in the personification of state power in the form of the first emperor.

Given the audience of general readers and introductory students for which the book is intended, I have eschewed extended argument with other interpretations of individual points in favor of giving a relatively unitary presentation of my own views. The reader should therefore be warned that there is hardly any point in this book which some scholar would not wish to dispute. Weighing the book down with large numbers of references to the views of others (often in foreign languages) would make it cumbersome to read without doing much to illuminate the intended audience. The purpose is to give the general reader not simply an outline of the events of the last century of the Republic but also an interpretive framework that analyzes the events in terms of the broader trends and developments that made the old system of government unworkable and necessitated its replacement with a veiled despotism. With this general interpretation and narrative in mind, the reader is strongly encouraged to read the ancient sources to see how they present the events and to read more detailed technical works to find out how these may elaborate, modify, or even contradict the views expressed here. To this end, a running list of ancient citations for the facts in the text is given at the end, and the bibliography should help the reader find further discussions of various topics. I hope that this book will prove to be useful both for those who are interested in Republican history in its own right and for those whose primary aim is to read some of the many ancient historical sources that were written during or about the fall of the Republic and wish to understand the underlying political realities of those tempestuous times.

To help the reader make sense of the broader significance of events, I have added at the end of each chapter a series of questions that should facilitate understanding of the relationship of the specific details of the chapter to the overall themes of the book. There is also an appendix at the end on the complicated system of Roman nomenclature. The reader may wish to peruse this before starting the main text, as the at times varying nomenclature used in the text presupposes a familiarity with the principles governing the use of Roman names.

Finally, all translations are my own.

1

HISTORICAL BACKGROUND

ORIGINS OF ROME

The Roman historical tradition held that the city of Rome was founded in the year 753 B.C. or thereabouts. Modern archaeology shows that there was no single date of foundation. Instead, the hills that were eventually included within the city were gradually occupied during the Iron Age beginning around 900 B.C. These early settlements were sparsely populated farming communities, but as in many other locations in Italy, Rome soon developed more advanced social and economic structures. These trends are marked by much more elaborate buildings that began to appear in the 600s B.C., and by the 500s B.C. Rome was ruled by a monarchy. In the last decade of that century, wealthy landowners overthrew the last king and established the form of government known as the Republic (this is traditionally dated to 509 or 507 B.C.). Under the Republic, the Romans would conquer first Italy and then the Mediterranean world, but while the institutions of the Republic were suitable for waging wars of conquest, they proved incapable of maintaining those conquests or of dealing with the problems that ensued from them.

POPULUS ROMANUS, *PLEBS*, AND NOBILITY

The Middle Republic was a period of comparative stability, and the political system that allowed the Romans to establish their hegemony over Italy and the Mediterranean basin was the result of the fourth-century settlement that put an end to the domestic unrest that had characterized the Early Republic.[1] In the half century after the foundation of the

---

[1] "Early Republic" refers to the period before the Romans began to write literary historical accounts. Though the later tradition preserves an account for this period, the

Republic (ca. 507–450 B.C.), the wealthy office holding families of the time secured for themselves a monopoly on the magistracies and were termed the patricians. The rest of the populace comprised a body known as the *plebs*, and the individual members of the plebs were known as plebeians. Most plebeians were poor and had economic disagreements with the patricians, and this situation worked to the advantage of the wealthier plebeians, who served as the spokesmen for the plebs. These spokesmen were called "tribunes of the plebs," and they acted to protect individual plebeians threatened by patrician magistrates and to advance the political and economic goals of the plebs. The tribunes were elected in the assembly of the plebs, their number eventually stabilizing at ten per year. The conflict between the plebs and the patrician-dominated senate is known as the Struggle of the Orders, and it was basically settled in a compromise reached in about 366 B.C. The plebeians were first given the right to hold the consulship, and in the next decades most of the public offices and priesthoods were opened to plebeians (the few obscure offices reserved for patricians provided one of the ways of telling in the Late Republic which families held patrician status). Soon, the wealthy plebeian families who were elected to high office gave up championing the economic complaints of the poorer plebeians and instead merged with the patricians to form a new ruling group, the "nobility." The Latin word *nobilis* means "prominent person," and as a technical term it signified anyone with an ancestor in the male line who had held the highest office (the consulship). This nobility that resulted from a fusion of long-standing patrician and wealthy plebeian families would lead the Romans in their conquest of the Mediterranean basin, and the nobles acquired vast wealth in the process.

At the same time that the wealthy plebeians were made an integral part of the senate, the corporate institutions of the plebs were also assimilated to those of the Roman People (the *populus Romanus*). Though the theoretical distinction between the plebs and the Roman People was maintained down to the end of the Republic (and gave rise to many of the peculiarities of the Roman constitution), the organs of the plebs were made a feature of the public life of the whole body politic.

accuracy of the details is open to question (the list of magistrates for the Early Republic is generally reliable, but virtually all the narrative details are subject to doubt). "Middle Republic" signifies the period from the late fourth to the mid second century. For this period, the historical tradition is much more reliable (though still not entirely accurate).

REPUBLICAN CONSTITUTION

The Roman Republic cannot be considered a republic in the modern sense of the word (that is, a representative democracy). The word "republic" derives from the Latin *res publica*, which means "the public property or affairs" and thus corresponds to the English "commonwealth." In ancient Rome, only the wealthiest citizens held office, and given the overwhelmingly agrarian nature of the ancient economy, this meant rule by landowners. The political control of the wealthy was not the result of any explicit legislation granting them a monopoly on office holding but instead reflected their dominant social and economic position and the fact that the constitution was constructed in such a way as to guarantee that the voice of the wealthy would prevail in elections. Thus, the Roman Republic would in modern terms be more properly called an elective oligarchy.[2] Since ex-magistrates were enrolled in the senate, which thus served as the collective body of the office holders and more broadly of the office-holding class, one can speak of a senatorial oligarchy (though in the Late Republic many members of that oligarchy would act against its interests).

The Roman Republic had no permanent bureaucracy or civil service, and thus the "state" in the abstract modern sense of the word did not exist. Rather, there were functions that were exercised by the various magistrates, and if no one filled those magistracies, then their functions simply lapsed. The personal nature of the exercise of public authority would become particularly problematical in the provinces distant from Rome. Given the nature of communications in antiquity, it could take weeks for news to travel to and from Rome. Hence, magistrates at a distance necessarily had to operate on their own. In the Early and Middle Republic, office holders had little inclination to act against the interests of the senatorial oligarchy, and in any case

---

[2] With his book *The Crowd in Rome in the Late Republic* (1998), F. Millar has argued that the "democratic" element in Roman politics was stronger than previously recognized, and this interpretation has inspired a certain number of works exploring the theme. While it is certainly true that Roman politics played itself out in a public setting, Millar's argument often boils down to one of shifting definitions, and in any case it does little to undermine the traditional picture of a very limited group of rich competitors for office dominating public life. Furthermore, as we will see during the course of the following narrative, a very real problem that would face the Republican form of government was the question of determining who exactly the "Roman People" were. The traditional Roman conception of the role of the electorate dated back to the Middle Republic and became increasingly untenable over the course of the first century B.C., as the right to vote in Roman elections was extended to the entire free population of Italy, while at the same time the voting process in Rome became increasingly subject to manipulation through violence. The situation was thus far more complicated than a simple distinction between an "aristocratic" and a "democratic" interpretation of how politics functioned in Rome.

they had no means of securing a military force to use against the oligarchy. The military needs of the Late Republic would change this situation.

The Republican constitution consisted of three disparate and unequal elements. First, the elective magistrates directly exercised public power. Second, these magistrates belonged to the senate, which was the collective body of the office holders. The senate's direct powers were comparatively limited, but its deliberations were very influential. Though magistrates could flout its decisions, most did not. The most prominent members of a small number of important families who provided the consuls over a number of generations to a large extent controlled the senate as an institution. A major role in the downfall of the Republican constitution would be played by a series of prominent individuals in the senate who used military power to further their own interests despite the opposition of the senate. Finally, the various assemblies of the Roman people had an array of powers that were theoretically extensive, but in practice the assemblies mostly complied with the wishes of the senate during the Middle Republic. This situation would change at the end of the second century, when the interests of the senate and those of many voters diverged, and certain members of the senate attempted to capitalize on popular discontent with the senate's management of public affairs for their own advantage.

Magistrates

Roman magistrates were grouped into various boards called "colleges." The members of each college had equal powers, and the objections of one member would prevent the action or proposal of another. This procedure was designed to thwart any attempt at tyranny, it being assumed that the rivalry among the magistrates would hold them all in check. This aspect of the system would break down in the Late Republic, when certain men attained sufficient power to allow them to shrug off any interference from colleagues. Another element in the system that was designed to restrain the power of the magistrates was that tenure of office was limited to one year for most magistracies, and a new board was elected each year. Though the magistrates could take on new tasks as necessary, normally the senate would choose in advance the tasks that were to be assigned to the new magistrates, and these were then distributed by lot.

Consuls and Imperium

Since the foundation of the Republic, the chief magistrates were the two consuls. The consulship marked the high point of a regular career, and the year was named after the consuls.[3] In the beginning, the consuls were the only magistrates of the Republic, and they operated by virtue of possessing the power called *imperium*. The etymological origin of this word is unclear, but the later Romans understood it to be the regal power of the kings, which had been handed over to the magistrates of the new Republic. Whatever its origin, imperium theoretically signified the power of life and death, but in terms of citizens this aspect was restricted from an early date. First, a magistrate with imperium was prohibited from exercising the power of life and death within the *pomerium* (the sacred boundary of the city of Rome).[4] Later, in the second century B.C., three laws prohibited its use anywhere – even outside of the pomerium – against Roman citizens who were not in military service. But a magistrate with imperium could always use it against noncitizens, a fact that would eventually become a strong motive for the non-Roman population of Italy to wish to acquire Roman citizenship. Most importantly, imperium was the power by which magistrates led Roman armies. The Romans had no professional generals. Instead, each Roman army was commanded by a magistrate by virtue of his imperium. The progression of a Roman politician's career guaranteed that the senior magistrates had gained extensive experience in warfare,[5] and to a large extent the ability to exercise military command was the primary (though by no means exclusive) function of the magistrates with imperium.

Praetors

Their role as military commanders often took the consuls away from Rome, and since this circumstance hindered their activities in the city, in 366 B.C. a junior colleague with imperium was provided to assist the consuls. The new magistrate was called the praetor,[6] and as more praetorships were created,

---

[3] For instance, the year called "133 B.C." according our reckoning would have been described by the Romans as "the consulship of L. Calpurnius Piso and P. Mucius Scaevola."

[4] The Roman historical tradition held that this restriction on the exercise of imperium within the city was one of the fundamental measures taken to establish the Republic at the time of the final expulsion of the Roman kings ca. 507 B.C. Modern scholarship frequently holds on the basis of historical plausibility that this restriction was implemented only at the end of fourth century B.C., and then anachronistically ascribed to the foundation of the Republic after the restriction came to be viewed as a basic principle of the constitution. The historically accurate dating of the restriction is not important for present purposes.

[5] Until about 100 B.C., ten years' military service as a soldier was a prerequisite for office holding.

[6] It would seem that the original term for the chief magistrates was "praetor," but by the time that the junior position was established, the two senior magistrates were called "consul," and the term "praetor" was restricted to the new magistrate.

the senior praetor was termed the urban praetor, and as his name implies he tended to legal and administrative matters in Rome. In about 244 B.C., a second praetorship was established, and while there is some dispute about the original reason for creating the position, the second praetor was designated the peregrine ("foreign") praetor and eventually dealt with legal matters involving non-Romans. After the establishment of the first permanent overseas provinces in 238 B.C., two more praetors were created to provide governors in 227 B.C., and, when the next two provinces were established in 197 B.C., yet another pair of praetorships was created, for a total of six. It is clear that this expansion in the number of praetors was viewed with alarm by the senatorial oligarchy: in the late 180s B.C., an attempt was made (by the *lex Baebia*) to alternate between years in which four and years in which six praetors were elected. Yet even the reduction of the average number of praetors to five per year was impractical because of the constant need for holders of imperium: in addition to functioning as provincial governors, praetors could oversee extraordinary legal matters and hold subordinate commands during wars. Why then, if the needs of public affairs dictated a higher number of magistrates with imperium, was the oligarchy disinclined to create further praetorships? With the number of consuls fixed at two – and it was literally inconceivable for the conservative-minded Romans to increase their number beyond the traditional two – every increase in the number of praetors above two per year guaranteed that there would be more ex-praetors whose ambition to hold the consulship would be thwarted, and it was thought that their attempts to gain the higher office, at whatever the cost, would threaten the stability of the oligarchy as a whole. For this reason, when two new provinces were created in 146 B.C., new praetorships were not created, and indeed their number would remain fixed at six for more than half a century. As time went on, the difficulty of finding enough magistrates to govern the increasing number of provinces and to take care of other administrative functions would only increase. Thus, there was an inherent conflict between the needs of the ruling oligarchy and those of the empire which the oligarchy had to rule, and the inability to find a way to govern the empire with the institutions provided by the traditional constitution would be one of the major causes of the Republic's downfall.

Prorogation and Promagistrates

The method by which the seemingly insoluble problem of finding a sufficient number of magistrates was dealt with under the old constitution was a procedure called prorogation. By the late 300s B.C., it had become obvious that if a successful consul was engaged in a long-term operation like a siege, it made little sense to replace him with a new and potentially inept consul before the operation's conclusion. At first, the old consul's command was extended by law, but soon the senate's decision (which did not have the force of law, as explained later) that such an extension was appropriate came to be considered sufficient (since the passage of the necessary law was never disputed, this cumbersome additional step was dropped). The old commander would be termed a proconsul (or propraetor in the case of a praetor whose command was prorogued) and continue to hold imperium until he crossed over the pomerium and thereby lost his imperium and returned to the sphere of civilian affairs in the city of Rome. Only commands outside of the city could be prorogued, and a new set of consuls and praetors was elected each year. Those who had held office in the city during their term as magistrates could now be assigned further duty as provincial promagistrates. While this system did not threaten the overall control of the senatorial oligarchy during the Middle Republic, when such assignments were of comparatively limited scope, the military needs of the Late Republic would necessitate the establishment of extraordinary proconsulships with massive responsibilities, whose holders were in a position to gain independent power that could be used against the wishes of the oligarchy in Rome.

Lesser Magistrates

Below the praetorship were various lesser magistracies, whose incumbents did not possess imperium. At the lowest level were various junior offices for minor legal, administrative, and military duties. These positions, which were held by young men, were never obligatory in a senatorial career. The lowest regularly held office was the quaestorship. The quaestors were young and aspiring senators, and one was attached as a close assistant to each magistrate with imperium. The tribunate of the plebs was the next office that a man could hold (if eligible), but this was not strictly speaking a magistracy of the Roman People and will be treated below. The aediles were originally market officials and also looked after roads, but increasingly the most prominent function of the office was to put on public entertainment in the form of chariot races and various other spectacles (like gladiatorial shows), and more and more lavish sums would be spent on these events. The censorship was a somewhat anomalous magistracy. Two censors were elected for an eighteen-month term every five years. Since the office was elected so infrequently and was normally held by ex-consuls (consulars), it was a higher honor than the consulship, but because its civil functions did not provide as much scope for glory as the consulship, the censorship was not really so prestigious. The office was first created in the later 400s B.C. to oversee the distribution of the citizens in the five census classes (see later in the chapter), and eventually the censors took over the task of updating the list of senators (because a member's inappropriate behavior was one criterion for expulsion, this function gave rise to the modern sense of the term). They also gave out public contracts.

Fixed pattern of office holding

Although it was always obvious that magistracies with imperium were more important than those without, there was not at first a fixed hierarchy of office holding (for instance, in the 200s B.C., men sometimes held the praetorship after the consulship). In the early second century B.C., laws were passed to regulate career patterns. In 180 B.C., the *lex Villia annalis* set up an overall framework for office holding: the quaestorship was established as the prerequisite for the praetorship and the praetorship for the consulship, and the ages of twenty-five, thirty-nine, and forty-two were fixed as the minimum ages at which the three offices could be held. In addition, repetition of the consulship was restricted: first, a law prohibited repetition within a ten-year period, and at some date after 153 B.C. any repetition at all was prohibited altogether. Previously, certain powerful individuals within the oligarchy had held repeated consulships, but this was contrary to the overall interests of the oligarchy. It was thought best to guarantee that every member of the oligarchy should have a reasonable chance of holding the most important office in Rome, but the possibility of this eventuality would be reduced if a small number of men repeatedly held the consulship. (The new fixed hierarchy of offices meant that the lower offices were not normally held more than once.) The history of the Late Republic would see much tension between the ambitions of many powerful (and talented) individuals who wished to win repeated or even consecutive consulships on the one hand and the desire of the oligarchy to prevent this on the other. (See Coin 1 for a visual example of the basically "collectivist" ethos of the senatorial oligarchy in the second century, and Coin 2 for an early attempt to express individuality through the images on the coinage.)

SENATE

Ex-quaestors at least would normally expect to be enrolled in the senate upon completion of their term of office.[7] Thus, the senate, which had

---

[7] The exact details of how and at what stage in their career ex-magistrates were enrolled in the senate in the Middle Republic is open to debate, but all the new quaestors were more or less automatically enrolled by the next pair of censors.

originated as the council of advisors to the kings (the word "senate" derives from *senex*, the Latin word for "old man"), was the collective body of all the office holders and provided such general oversight of the administration as ancient Rome possessed. Yet, as an institution, the senate was ill-suited to provide much control over the activities of the magistrates. It could meet only when summoned by a magistrate with imperium or a tribune of the plebs (see later in the chapter), and the presiding magistrate determined not only what topic was to be discussed, but also, more importantly, what question would be voted on.[8] In addition, a decree of the senate, a *senatus consultum* (literally, "consultation of the senate"), did not have the force of law, and the sole areas in which the senate's views were authoritative were orders for the disbursement of funds from the public treasury and the determination of what the provinces for the new magistrates would be (these would then be distributed among the incoming magistrates by lot), and which promagistrates in the provinces were to be replaced and which prorogued. Otherwise, the senate could do no more than "urge" magistrates to comply with its wishes. Nonetheless, since most magistrates wished to be respected members of the senate once their term of office was over, for the most part they submitted to the senate's will during the Middle Republic. But the great power that certain promagistrates acquired in the Late Republic would allow them to flout the senate's authority.

The senators were arranged hierarchically by the highest office held, so that first the ex-consuls (consulars) were asked their views, then the ex-praetors (praetorians), ex-aediles (aedilicians), ex-tribunes (tribunicians), and finally the ex-quaestors (quaestorians) (magistrates in office did not give an opinion in senatorial debates). Although occasionally a particularly confident and obstreperous junior senator would dare to disagree with his seniors, for the most part the first consulars to speak set the tone of the discussion, and most of the following speakers simply agreed with the preceding view. In a given group, the members were asked in order of seniority (i.e., the person who had been elected to the office first was asked his opinion first, and so on), except that the first consular

---

[8]   A senator could, when his turn to speak came, discuss whatever he pleased – famously, in the late 150s B.C., the senior senator Cato the Elder always ended his speech on any topic with the phrase "besides which, my view is that we have to destroy Carthage" – but only the most bold and confident would dare to ignore the proposed topic. In determining the question, the presiding magistrate would chose two senior senators whose opinions seemed to encapsulate the divergent views of the senate and bid the senators to show which option they preferred by moving to the side of the man whose opinion they supported.

to be enrolled by the censors in their review of the roll of senators held the rank of *princeps senatus* ("leading man of the senate") and would give his opinion first.[9] Thus, the proceedings of the senate were arranged in such a way that under normal circumstances, the consulars (including the new consuls of the present year) could control the senate.

There were no legal restrictions on who could run for office, and election to office was the sole criterion for enrollment in the senate. As a practical matter, however, only the wealthy would seek office (there was no pay, and in any case, the well-off electorate thought it unacceptable to vote for any but the wealthy). While the senatorial oligarchy was always open to allowing talented (and amenable) men from outside the senate to enter public life, the connections and wealth of older senatorial families made it much easier for them to gain high office in later generations. The higher the office, the harder it was for a "new man" (*novus homo*) who lacked senatorial forebears to succeed, and down to the end of the Republic, the scions of the nobility held a near monopoly of the consulship – except under extraordinary circumstances.

The hierarchical organization of the senate allowed the institution to be dominated by the senior consulars, and the leading families to which they belonged may be termed the "senatorial oligarchy" in contradistinction to the senate as a whole, which included large numbers of lesser ranking men who under normal circumstances had little influence in the workings of the senate and for the most part followed the lead of the dominant consulars. During the Middle Republic, the senatorial oligarchy was able to retain control of the political process in Rome without too much difficulty, and a significant part of the story of the breakdown of the traditional constitution during the Late Republic consists of the increasingly futile efforts of this oligarchy to retain its control in the face of challenges posed by powerful individuals within the senate.

Even if it had been possible to receive adequate information from distant provinces in sufficient time, the senate had no permanent organization of committees and the like to digest information and foresee events. Instead, the senate merely reacted to specific questions put to it by the presiding magistrate, and it had a rather parochial outlook determined by the interests of the consulars. For instance, it sometimes happened that when magistrates would arrange treaties with communities in Spain that were at war with the Romans, these treaties would then be rejected by the

---

[9] Sulla would later change the method of choosing the princeps senatus, so that the title was given to the first consular to be asked his opinion in the first session of the senate held by the newly elected consuls. Hence, a new princeps would be chosen every year.

senate in the interest of the incoming magistrates, who wished for their own purposes to continue the war. Just as there were tensions between the ambitions of the various magistrates and those of the oligarchy as a whole, the senate also found it difficult to reconcile the selfish interests of its favored members and the "public good" (especially if the aggrieved party consisted of non-Romans).

TRIBUNES OF THE PLEBS

The position of the tribunes of the plebs (*tribuni plebis*) in the constitution was an anomalous holdover from the early Struggle of the Orders. Not properly magistrates of the Roman People but only representatives of the plebs, the tribunes were nonetheless regular magistrates for all practical purposes, as the office had been given a place in the political system as part of the compromise that ended the Struggle in the mid fourth century B.C. The tribunes had the right to convene the senate and put issues before it and to lodge criminal accusations before the assemblies of the Roman People. In recognition of their origin as defenders of the plebs, the tribunes were allowed to prohibit the actions of a magistrate with the word *veto* ("I forbid") and were expected to make themselves available in public to hear complaints. In about 287 B.C., the legislation passed in the assembly of the plebs (*plebiscita* or "plebiscites") was recognized as having the validity of a law passed by the assemblies of the Roman People (previously, the plebiscites were binding only on the plebs), and this change had a major long-term significance. Once the plebeians were allowed to hold public office, young sons of the nobility began to hold the tribunate early in their career as a way to make a name for themselves among the general populace, and the senate fell into the habit of asking the tribunes to pass in the assembly of the plebs legislation that the senate desired.[10] In the period from the third to the early to mid second centuries B.C., this procedure caused the senate no difficulties, but it would turn out that the right to pass legislation was a potent weapon in the hands of a tribune who opposed the senatorial oligarchy.

---

[10] Passing legislation in the assembly of the plebs was easier because that assembly lacked the cumbersome religious procedures of the assemblies of the Roman People, and in any case the magistrates with imperium, who alone could convene the People's assemblies, were often occupied with other matters, such as presiding over the senate and waging war.

Assemblies and Elections

The assemblies at Rome had vast powers in theory but were organized in such a way as to ensure that the senatorial oligarchy could keep control of their decisions. In Roman elections, all votes were not counted together as a whole. Instead, the voters were arranged in various units containing unequal numbers of voters, and the majority of the voters in each unit determined the vote of that unit. Each unit then had a single vote, and the election was determined by tallying the single votes cast by the various units.

The centuriate assembly (*comitia centuriata*) elected magistrates with imperium, passed legislation, and conducted trials. Here, the voters were distributed into centuries on the basis of which census class they belonged to: each census class had a fixed number of centuries, and the voters of that class were distributed among those centuries. The wealthiest citizens in the first census class controlled eighty-eight out of 193 centuries, and thus had the predominant voice in elections.[11] Those citizens who did not meet the minimum property qualification for military service were lumped into a single century and thus had virtually no say in the elections of consuls and praetors.

In the assembly of the plebs (*concilium plebis*), which elected tribunes and passed plebiscites, and the tribal assembly of the Roman People, which elected magistrates without imperium and decided the outcome in minor trials, the voters were arranged by geographical districts called "tribes."[12] (Indeed, the title "tribune" may well derive from this term.) Supposedly, at the foundation of the Republic, there were four tribes in the city of Rome and sixteen in the outlying districts. As the Romans continued to annex territory in central Italy, they created new tribes. Eventually, the number of rural tribes reached thirty-one, the last two being created in 242 B.C. At the same time, the number of tribes for the city of Rome never changed. Even though the population of Rome increased greatly throughout the second and first centuries B.C., it was never granted any extra tribes, and since in elections, each tribe had a single vote determined by the votes of its members, this system heavily favored rural voters, who could be controlled by the landowners.

---

[11] These eighty-eight centuries included the eighteen special centuries controlled by the *equites Romani* (see following text).

[12] This geographic use of the word "tribe" should not be confused with the ethnographic use (e.g., "Indian tribes"), which derives from the use of this word in the Latin translation of the Bible to designate the "twelve tribes of Israel."

The Romans had a social institution called *clientela*, whose influence in the electoral process is hotly debated. The term *clientela* described the situation in which a hierarchically lower person ("client") sought help from a superior one ("patron") and thus became obliged to the patron. While the exact extent to which patrons actually controlled the votes of their clients is debated, there can be no doubt that in the Middle Republic the wealthy in general and the hereditary senatorial oligarchy in particular were able to influence the voters sufficiently to maintain their control of the electoral process. In particular, voting was conducted openly and verbally until the 130s B.C., which facilitated oversight by the influential. In any case, at least in the centuriate assembly, in which the voters were men of military age and selected the magistrates who would command them in the field, there was not much divergence of interests. In effect, the troops were choosing their captains. In the Late Republic, the interests of the electorate and the oligarchy began to diverge, and the ability of the oligarchy to control elections eroded.

Though the various assemblies of the Roman People could theoretically order whatever they pleased by legislation, in practice the assemblies had little power of initiative. Apart from the practices of voting by units and of open voting, which allowed the wealthy to control the outcome, an assembly could be convened only by an appropriate magistrate (a consul or praetor in the case of the assemblies of the Roman People, and a tribune in the case of the assembly of the plebs), and all the voters could do was to approve or reject the proposed legislation. Such legislation had to be displayed publicly ("promulgated") three Roman (eight-day) weeks in advance and could be debated informally in the interim, but unlike the assembly in a democratic city-state in the Greek world, a Roman assembly had no ability to modify or influence the legislation put before it.[13] Thus, so long as the magistrates who controlled the assemblies worked in the interests of the oligarchy, the oligarchy was safe. Troubles would arise in the Late Republic when magistrates began to act in opposition to the oligarchy.

NATURE OF ELECTORAL CONFLICT

In the ancient interpretation of the politics of the Late Republic two opposing groups were identified. The *optimates* ("optimates") or "supporters

---

[13] A magistrate could hold informal assemblies called *contiones* (singular, *contio*) to "sound out" (or manipulate) public opinion on any topic he wished, and in this way it was possible to determine in advance whether there was serious objection to a proposed bill before it was officially promulgated.

of the best men"[14] upheld the traditional dominance of the senate (and by extension the privileged position of the oligarchy), while those who opposed the senate and instead championed the "liberty of the Roman People," which in practice meant securing support for themselves through the assemblies, were called *populares* (sing. *popularis*) or "supporters of the People."[15] These groups were not permanent organizations with an identifiable membership and overt programs in the manner of modern political parties. Instead, these labels categorized the behavior of individual members of the political class, whose "allegiance" would vary with their careers. Generally speaking, populares were younger members of the oligarchy who wished to make a name for themselves at the start of their careers, and most populares tended to become more optimate in their policies as time went on.[16]

For the most part, the second century B.C. was one of comparative calm in the senatorial oligarchy, which was secure in its control of the political process. Yet, even here, popular discontent could force the hand of the senate. In the late 170s B.C., popular indignation led to the trials of certain praetors who were thought to have mistreated allies in Spain and Greece (though other magistrates of higher standing were let off the hook). In 147 B.C., discontent with the prosecution of the final war against Carthage led to rioting motivated by a desire among the voters that command in the war should be turned over to P. Scipio Aemilianus, who was the adoptive grandson of the man who had defeated Hannibal in the previous war with Carthage but who was only running for the aedileship (he was disqualified for the consulship both by virtue of his youth and by not having held the praetorship yet). In the face of this rioting, the senate had to allow Aemilianus to run for the consulship, which he won. A decade later, the inability of the commanders to conquer the city of Numantia in Spain led once again to a demand that Aemilianus be returned as consul despite any legal disabilities (by now repetition of the consulship was prohibited), and in 135 B.C. the senate was forced to allow him to run for the office in violation of the legal requirements. These events illustrate two factors

---

[14] In Greek political thought, aristocrats called themselves the "good men" in contradistinction to the common rabble, and this same conception was picked up by the Romans. In effect, the wealthy attempted to seize the moral high ground by giving a privileged position to the better education and more cultured way of living that they acquired through their wealth.

[15] To avoid confusion, the Latin adjective *popularis* will be used in this technical sense in place of the English derivative "popular," which has a more general meaning.

[16] For instance, L. Marcius Philippus, who as consul in 91 B.C. led senatorial opposition to the popularis activities of the tribune M. Livius Drusus, had himself proposed popularis (agrarian) legislation as a tribune in the turbulent year 104 B.C.

that would play significant roles in the political crisis of the Late Republic. First, popular hostility to the oligarchy was particularly acute at times of perceived military mismanagement: if a war was proceeding successfully, the abuses of commanders would be tolerated, but if it was thought that the regular magistrates were bungling things, the electorate did not care about the rules and regulations which the oligarchy had set up to govern the careers of its members. The voters would demand the man whom they considered to be the best-qualified commander, whether or not he was technically available. Second, at this time, even the highest members of the oligarchy were not above using popular discontent to further their own ambitions. Already in the 130s B.C., the existence of discontent among the voters with the control exercised by the oligarchy was exhibited by the desire to replace open voting with secret voting by ballot. A measure to introduce the ballot in the elections of magistrates was bitterly (but unsuccessfully) opposed by the oligarchy in 139 B.C., and use of the secret ballot was gradually adopted for all forms of voting in the following years (it was introduced for most trials in 137 B.C. and in the votes on proposed legislation in about 130 B.C.; for a later coin that may allude to the law of 137 B.C., see Coin 14). Nonetheless, though there were instances in which the interests of the senate and those of the electorate came into conflict during the Middle Republic, there was not yet a persistent divergence of interest that could be conceived of globally as a dispute between the senatorial oligarchy and its supporters (the optimates) and the advocates of the electorate in opposition to the senate (the populares) so that this divergence could be exploited by politicians for their own purposes. It would take the death of Ti. and C. Gracchus (see Chapters 2 and 3) to make the notion of popular opposition to the oligarchy an ongoing aspect of Roman political life.

Equites Romani

A special section of the nonsenatorial electorate calls for separate discussion: the *equites Romani* (sing. *eques Romanus*). Originally the equites served as the cavalry (the term itself signifies "horseman," and in the past was often translated as "knight," a rather misleading rendering). Because owning a horse was expensive, only the wealthy were in a position to serve as cavalrymen, and since service in the cavalry was physically demanding, the equites were generally young men of the first census class. In the later period, there was a monetary qualification for status as an eques Romanus, but it is not known what it was at the time of the Gracchi or earlier. In the distant Republican past, it had been decided that because service in the cavalry was hard on horses, certain men should be given a horse at public expense, and men so honored were enrolled in eighteen special centuries of equites Romani in the centuriate assembly. The Romans found out in the third century that their own cavalry was not very good and began to make increasing use of cavalry provided by their allies. Those Romans who had the money to qualify for the cavalry could then be used as officers, and the rank of eques Romanus came to be held by anyone who had enough money to qualify theoretically for the cavalry service, regardless of whether they actually did serve in this capacity. In this sense, the word simply signified a wealthy nonsenator, and these equites Romani were not socially or economically different from the senators but had simply chosen not to seek public office.

Since it was generally frowned upon for senators to engage openly in economic activity other than agriculture, it was left to the equites Romani to provide the Roman government with services such as the construction and maintenance of buildings and aqueducts in Rome and the delivery of military supplies. Contracts for such services were auctioned off by magistrates, and the equites formed partnerships to pool together the huge resources necessary to undertake these activities. A particularly important aspect of this sort of public business carried out by the equites was the collection of tribute owed in the provinces to the Roman People (those engaged in this business are called "publicans"). The partnerships would bid to collect the taxes and give a fixed sum at the start of the contract, then go to the province to collect the money, availing themselves of the powers of the governor in a case of dispute.[17]

The term equites thus had several different meanings in the Late Republic (and would only be formally defined during the Early Empire). In its broadest sense, it meant the wealthy Romans who met the census

[17] The procedure of bidding would theoretically guarantee that the winning bidder would pay to the treasury the highest percentage of the foreseen taxes while retaining enough to earn a profit. This system is often derided in modern literature, but it provided the Roman government with a number of advantages. Since there was no permanent civil service or bureaucracy, the task of providing the staff to manage the no doubt complicated financial transactions in the provinces was left to the winning partnership. In addition, the risk involved in collecting the tribute (which to a large extent was contingent upon the state of local agriculture) was thrown onto the publicans. There were obvious problems, of course. Once the amount paid to the treasury was set, it was in the publicans' interest to collect as much as possible since any sum collected beyond the cost of the contract and the expense of collecting the tribute was profit, and they therefore had every reason to extort money unjustifiably. Naturally, the governor was to oversee their activities, but having gained the goodwill of the influential publicans would be no small advantage for future electoral campaigns.

qualifications to service as "cavalrymen" (i.e., officers) in the army, a rather large group. It could also signify more specifically those honored with the "public horse," who comprised the eighteen equestrian centuries of the centuriate assembly. It would seem that the very wealthy equites who headed the largest partnerships of publicans dominated those centuries, and in terms of the political scene in Rome, the publicans represented the "order of the equites." These influential equites would later dominate C. Gracchus's panel of jurors, and the terms "publicans," "equestrian jurors," and the order as a whole were to some extent synonymous.

MILITARY EXPANSION

The ruling class of Rome, whether the old patricians or the later nobility, proved to be capable of providing a constant stream of competent commanders who would use Rome's ever expanding pool of manpower to wage war on a progressively larger scale. In political terms, victory in the field brought glory for oneself and prestige for one's descendants. More practically, a Roman general was in control of the resources that he could seize, and while he was expected to share his loot (in the form both of money taken from foreign communities and of enslaved foreigners who could be sold) with the soldiery (and the gods), the office holders made very large profits from their wars of aggression. At the same time, the Romans showed themselves to be astute in binding conquered foreign communities to them. Nonetheless, the conquests and victories of the Middle Republic would bring along with them unforeseen side effects that would destabilize the political situation in Rome.

CONQUEST OF LATIUM AND ITALY DURING THE EARLY REPUBLIC

Rome is the northernmost city in Latium, the area on the central western coast of Italy in which the Latin language was spoken. The first century and a half of the Republic was spent in establishing Roman domination over Latium, which was finally made permanent in about 338 B.C., when the Romans dissolved the Latin League. Some towns closest to Rome were annexed to the Roman state, while a few remained as independent communities that had no foreign policy of their own and were obligated to provide troops when requested. In the succeeding decades, the Romans set about subduing the other communities in Italy, all of which were more or less under their control by 270 B.C. By this point, the Romans had annexed a solid block of territory in central Italy; outlying areas retained their internal independence but as allies of the Roman People, they owed military units for Roman armies. The status of the Latin and the Italian communities was similar, but the Latins, who were very close in culture to the Romans (they all adopted the Roman form of Latin), held a favored position: Latins who moved to Rome could easily become Roman citizens, and those visiting the city were allowed to vote in a randomly chosen tribe.

ITALIAN ALLIES

At first, the Italian allies were reasonably content with their position. They profited (albeit on an unequal basis) from the rewards of the wars in which they fought and for the most part did not feel any need to rebel against their subordinate status. The only occasion when military circumstances led to revolts was in the mid 210s B.C. following a series of massive Roman defeats at the hands of the Carthaginian general Hannibal, and even then it was only a few more distant cities that revolted, with the majority remaining loyal. As the years went on, however, this loyalty began to change. The Italian peninsula contained a plethora of separate ethnic and linguistic groups, and prior to the Roman conquest, the term "Italy" had been merely a geographical term; Roman domination, however, brought about a new unity in Italy. Communities adopted Roman political practices, the Latin language spread, and everyone shared the common experience of service in Roman armies. It thus became a source of irritation that while the allies suffered equal losses in Roman armies (half of every army consisted of allied troops), the rewards were not equal, and the allies had no say in the selection of magistrates in Rome. Even worse, perhaps, was the increasing haughtiness of Roman magistrates. While in the years after the subjugation of Italy the Romans had at least found it a good idea not to offend their allies at a time when wars were being fought overseas, by the mid second century B.C., the Romans faced no serious enemies abroad, and the attitudes of the nobility toward the allies became more arrogant. Magistrates who were displeased even by trivial offenses in allied communities might with impunity have a leading citizen flogged or even executed. A desire to acquire Roman citizenship (and its protections against the abusive behavior of magistrates) arose among the allies, but the Roman nobility, who had learned how to control the present political arrangement, saw little reason to endanger their dominance through the enfranchisement of large numbers of foreigners. The dispute about whether to enfranchise the Italian allies would be one of the major destabilizing factors at the start of the Late Republic.

Conquest of the Mediterranean during the Middle Republic

In 264 B.C., the Romans undertook their first overseas war, and over the course of the next century, they defeated first the Carthaginians of North Africa (two Punic Wars, 264–241 and 218–202 B.C.), and the major Greek kingdoms of the Greek mainland and the Near East (a series of wars 200–167 B.C.).

During the course of the Second Punic War, the Romans threw the Carthaginians out of Spain,[18] and without much reflection they stayed. It soon turned out that controlling the comparatively primitive communities there would be a daunting task, and for decades the Romans had to undertake a series of hard-fought wars against various towns in Spain, suffering a number of major defeats in the process. By 134 B.C., however, the last major town opposing the Romans (Numantia) had been defeated, though comparatively minor revolts would continue for more than a century. Overall, the Roman commanders did not behave in a very upright manner in Spain. Whereas in the East, the Romans courted the good opinion of the culturally advanced Greeks, in Spain the Romans apparently felt no qualms about acting savagely and at times in poor faith. On several occasions, the senate rejected agreements that had been worked out with the locals by Roman magistrates.

In the East, the main Roman concern was winning glory and booty. In a series of wars, the Romans defeated the Macedonian (200–196 and 171–168 B.C.) and Syrian monarchies (191–189 B.C.). At first, the Romans wished to win support among the city-states of the Greek world by purporting to be the champions of Greek liberty. While there may have been some truth to the claim, more fundamentally the Romans were interested only in the profits to be made from warfare and had no desire to assume direct control of territory. In 167 B.C., they abolished the Macedonian dynasty and tried to set up four republics on the territory of the old kingdom to protect Greece against the tribes of the Balkans, but this expedient intended to avoid a permanent Roman commitment in the area proved to be a failure. In 148 B.C., a usurper who claimed to be a member of the old dynasty was easily crushed by the Romans, but at the same time certain city-states on the Greek mainland revolted in reaction against the increasingly haughty attitude of the senate. This revolt too was easily put down, and the Romans were forced to the recognition that their destruction of

---

[18] "Spain" is shorthand for the Spanish peninsula.

the major powers in the area necessitated a direct Roman presence, with the result that a new province was created in Macedonia in 146 B.C.

At the same time that the Romans had to suppress revolts in Greece, they had to deal with their own decision to destroy the city of Carthage during the final Punic War (149–146 B.C.). They had granted a fifty-year truce to the Carthaginians at the conclusion of the war with Hannibal back in 201 B.C. The Romans had been greatly embittered with the Carthaginians as a result of the severe depredations that Hannibal had inflicted on Italy during the decade and a half when he maintained an army there, and in addition, Carthage had quickly regained its prosperity during the decades since the end of the war despite the heavy indemnity they had been forced to pay every year to the Romans. Accordingly, the Romans were eager to renew the war as soon as their treaty obligations allowed them to. Whereas the unprofitability of service in Spain made it increasingly difficult to enlist soldiers for the prolonged campaigns there, the expectation was that victory in Africa would be both swift and remunerative for all concerned, so that a large army was quickly and easily enrolled. As it turned out, the cornered Carthaginians fought desperately, and the lack of quick victory resulted in violent demands in Rome that Scipio Aemilianus should be elected to the consulship despite his ineligibility. As already noted, rioting forced the senate to allow this, and the arduous task of capturing Carthage was soon carried out. At the end of the war, another new province (Africa) was established on the old territory of Carthage (corresponding to modern Tunisia).

Establishment of Overseas Provinces

The wars of the Middle Republic were basically motivated by the desire for glory and booty on the part of both the senatorial commanders and the soldiery. What the Romans did not particularly want was territorial annexations overseas, whose administration would impose increasingly unsustainable strains on the limited number of magistrates. In the late third and early second century B.C., the senatorial oligarchy was willing to increase the number of praetors to provide the necessary governors, but after 197 B.C., the senate refused to authorize any further increase in their numbers and even tried unsuccessfully to lower the number. This unwillingness to expand the Roman political system to meet the administrative needs attendant upon further territorial expansion goes some way to explain the Roman refusal to seize any land for themselves during the many victorious campaigns in the East in the first half of the second century B.C.

In 238 B.C., the Romans seized their first overseas territories. Having taken Sardinia and Sicily from the Carthaginians, they at first decided to act as overlords in those areas and to collect tribute from the local communities rather than obligate them to provide troops as the Romans did with their allies in Italy. This procedure necessitated a permanent Roman presence on the islands, and in 227 B.C. it was decided to create two new praetorships, one for each new "province."[19]

The Roman effort to throw the Carthaginians out of the Spanish peninsula resulted in a more or less unplanned permanent Roman presence there once the Carthaginians were defeated in 207 B.C. After a series of special magistrates sent out as governors on an ad hoc basis, two more praetorships were created in 197 B.C. to govern the provinces of Closer and Further Spain. The increase in the number of praetors was clearly perceived to be incompatible with the smooth operation of career patterns within the senate, since an attempt was made in the late 180s B.C. to alternate between four and six new praetors per year (explained earlier). The realities of the need for praetors soon brought this practice to an end, but no new praetorships were to be created until the late 80s B.C., despite the creation in 146 B.C. of two new provinces, in Africa and Macedonia. With the number of territorial provinces exceeding the annual number of praetors, the senate had no choice but to resort to the prorogation of old magistrates to find governors. In the coming years, the territory directly governed by the magistrates of the Roman People would only increase, and the senatorial oligarchy would find it more and more difficult to deal with the administrative burden of providing the necessary governors.

AGRARIAN CRISIS AND PROBLEMS
WITH CONSCRIPTION

The Roman military organization that made the military victories of the Middle Republic possible depended upon the small landowners whose property was valuable enough for these men to meet the minimum property qualification for the fifth census class. The original reason for this requirement was that the soldiers were obliged to provide their own weapons and armor, which only the propertied could afford. In the distant past, the higher census classes had been equipped with more elaborate (and

---

[19] Originally, the word "province" (*provincia*) signified the sphere of activity assigned to a magistrate (a meaning it continued to have throughout the Republic). Hence, a given magistrate's province could consist of management of the public treasury in Rome or command in a war.

expensive) equipment, but by the Late Republic, most troops had the same gear. The Roman army was originally a sort of militia. At the start of the campaigning season, the troops would be levied and divided into four units called legions, and at the end of the summer the legions would be disbanded and the discharged troops would go home. All this changed with the start of prolonged campaigning abroad. The troops raised for a given campaign would remain in the field until the army was brought back to Rome. The campaigns in the East sometimes lasted several years, but at the end the victorious (and enriched) troops would return with their last commander to Italy, where they would be discharged. The long campaigns in Spain against disparate enemies often did not have clear-cut conclusions, and the troops would have to remain on duty until a new army was sent out to replace them. According to the standard explanation, which is based for the most part on such ancient understanding of the problem as survives (Plutarch, *Life of Tiberius Gracchus* 8.1–2, Appian, *Civil Wars* 1.7; both accounts are based on a common source that has been lost), the military successes of the Middle Republic undermined the class of independent small farmers who provided the backbone of the armies in two ways. The physical absence of the troops was detrimental to their livelihood as farmers, and the wealth that poured into Italy also undermined these farmers.

With the male head of the household away on military duty, the economic viability of a small farm was seriously threatened. The situation would be restored if he eventually returned with a tidy sum from his campaigns, but the results could be dire if he died on service. Furthermore, enrollment in an army to be sent to the East promised lavish rewards, but service in Spain was both dangerous and unremunerative. While the consuls who raised an army in 149 B.C. for the final campaign against Carthage had no trouble recruiting troops because of the prospect of an easy and profitable expedition, by the 130s B.C. it was proving difficult to find troops for Spain. In 138 B.C., some of the tribunes issued an edict restricting the magistrates' activities in recruitment and went so far as to arrest a consul who ignored their decision. The perceived crisis in securing sufficient troops for the military needs of the empire was to play a major role in the political crisis of the Late Republic.

The wealth that accrued to both the office holders and other wealthy Romans who made money providing public services further undermined the viability of the smallholders. The landholding class had a prejudice against trade and commerce, and in any case land was the only sound form of long-term investment in antiquity (the possibilities for manufacture were severely limited, and trade was risky). The wealthy put pressure on the smallholders in two ways. First, they established large farming operations whose workforce was provided by the large numbers of slaves who were captured during the wars of conquest, and the smallholders found it difficult to compete against these comparatively efficient operations. Second, the wealthy wished to increase their landholdings by buying out the smallholders. If a farm was already in economic distress, the sale may have been voluntary, but the wealthy would also compel the unwilling to sell. To what extent the problem of raising armies was caused by rural depopulation rather than by simple disinclination to serve in Spain is not now clear (there would have been no statistical evidence even in antiquity), but certainly some people at the time thought that the slaves were at least in part responsible. It also appears that the minimum census qualification for the bottom census class (and thus eligibility for military service) was drastically reduced in the second century B.C. In any case, the now dispossessed smallholder would often move to Rome, increasing the city's population while at the same time decreasing the number of available soldiers.

There have always been objections to various aspects of this exposition of the agrarian situation of the second century B.C., and to some extent the validity of the entire analysis of the economic situation in the countryside has been called into question by recent scholarship. On the other hand, there is little other evidence to go by, and the theoretical considerations used to undermine the ancient interpretation are less than convincing.[20] In any case, the truth of the matter is of little consequence in the present context. What is important is not what was actually going on in the countryside but what the political class in Rome thought was going on. Whatever the exact cause, there was clearly something wrong with the

---

[20] For an extended criticism of the ancient interpretation, see Nathan Rosenstein, *Rome at War* (2004). First, he argues that the number of slaves in Italy has been overestimated and that they could not have been as detrimental to the smallholders as has been posited. Second, various demographic conjectures are used to argue that paradoxically the admittedly large military losses among the conscripted smallholders led to prosperity for those who remained, which in turn led to a large increase in population. It was this increase, then, that was the actual cause of the crisis, and the ancient interpreters misunderstood the demographic shift that was taking place. This interpretation is conceivable, but it is based on much hypothesizing in the absence of evidence and on doubtful theoretical constructs. Notably, a major premise in the argument is the claim that smallholders did not marry until their mid to late twenties and that therefore a large percentage of the conscripts (and hence the losses incurred during military service) were unmarried. This premise is based on urban inscriptional evidence from the Imperial period, which may well not be at all relevant to the demographic behavior of the large majority of the population who lived in the countryside and felt no need to leave any inscriptional record of themselves. Fundamentally, Rosenstein thinks that his theorizing allows him to understand what was going on in the Italian countryside better than contemporary observers whose main economic pursuit was agriculture did.

class of smallholders who provided the Republic's citizen soldiers, and the political crisis of the Late Republic began with Ti. Gracchus's proposal to do something about this situation.

Slave Unrest

By the 130s B.C., not only was it seemingly clear that the smallholders were being undermined as a class by the large estates cultivated with slave labor, but it came to be felt that the large numbers of slaves posed a threat in their own right. In around 135 B.C., 450 slaves were crucified in Minturnae south of Rome, and in about 133 B.C., 4,000 slaves revolted. The major disturbance, though, was in Sicily, where a major slave revolt broke out in 135 B.C. The slaves actually formed themselves into an army and defeated several Roman praetors. By 133 B.C., the matter was so serious that one of the consuls had to assume command there. Only in 132 B.C. was this revolt finally quashed by a second consul. These disturbances probably stirred up the poorer residents of Rome, since at the time the city's grain supply was largely provided from Sicily, and the result must have been a serious increase in the price of grain in Rome. It would have been clear that something had to be done about this problem too.

AGER PUBLICUS

The rich had another opportunity for investment in the form of public land (*ager publicus*). At the time of the revolts that broke out in southern Italy during the war with Hannibal, the Romans eventually reconquered all the rebellious towns and as a punishment would confiscate a portion of each town's territory. In this way, extensive tracts of land came into public ownership. As a result of the depredations of the war, large amounts of this land lay uncultivated in the early second century, so that the Roman officials were happy if it was brought back into production, and little attention was paid to the question of who owned it. By the middle of the century, a law existed stating that an individual could occupy no more than 500 *jugera* of it (a *jugerum* was about two-thirds of an acre).[21] The law was apparently still being obeyed in 167 B.C., but by

---

[21] The Roman historical tradition claimed that a limit of this size had existed in the fourth century B.C., but it would seem that here (as in numerous other instances) the writers of the later Republic anachronistically ascribed the situation of their own day to the poorly attested past. It is very hard to believe that such a large figure for permissible occupation could have been prescribed in the fourth century, when the holdings of the Roman state were much smaller than in the period after the war with Hannibal.

133 B.C., it was routinely ignored, there being no established procedure to enforce compliance.

Agrarian Crisis of the Late 130s B.C.

Thus, after the oligarchy had used the manpower resources provided by Roman domination of Italy to wage a series of highly remunerative campaigns in the second century B.C., these very successes brought in their wake a number of problems. The number of provinces that the Romans had been forced to govern directly exceeded the administrative capacity of the form of government that the oligarchy preferred. The Italian allies now wished to receive Roman citizenship as a reward for their role in maintaining Roman military superiority, but the oligarchy was unwilling to do so for fear that such large-scale enfranchisement would endanger their political control in Rome. Finally, the survival of the Roman small-holders who formed the backbone of the Roman military establishment was thought to be threatened by the economic competition of the owners of large-scale farms worked by slaves, and the presence of such large numbers of slaves was itself considered a menace to public safety. The oligarchy that controlled the Roman Republic would try to deal with these problems, but eventually the military needs of the empire would necessitate the end of the elective system of government and its replacement with a military autocracy. The violent process that resulted in this change in the system of government began with the attempts of Ti. Gracchus to find a solution to the plight of the smallholders.

Questions for Study and Reflection

1. Was the Roman Republic a democracy? What elements were democratic? Were there aspects of Roman public life that served to curb these elements?
2. What were the magistracies of the Roman Republic and what were their powers? What was imperium and which magistracies had this power? What institutional principles served to restrict and restrain the magistrates in the exercise of their functions?
3. What were the official qualifications for running for office? From what social group were the office holders drawn? What was the cause of office holding being restricted to this group?
4. What was a regular career pattern for office holders? What measures were passed to regulate office holding? What was the purpose of such regulations?

5. What were the Roman assemblies? What powers did they have? What features of their operation served to curb their freedom of decision? Were the assemblies democratic?

6. What was the difference between the populus Romanus and the Roman plebs? How were the collective institutions of the plebs incorporated into the Roman state? Did these institutions provide a democratic element in public life?

7. What was the senate? What were the qualifications for serving in the senate and how did one become a member? What powers did the senate have? How did it deliberate? What was the senatorial oligarchy?

8. What was the Roman nobility? What was their significance in public life? What was the relationship between the nobility and the senatorial oligarchy?

9. Who were the equites Romani? What were the qualifications for this status? What role did they play in public life? Who were the publicans and what was their relationship with the equites Romani?

10. Who were the Latins and the Italian allies? Why were the Italian allies not incorporated into the Roman state? What was the relationship between them and the Roman state? What obligations did the Italian allies have to Rome? What were the disadvantages to the state?

11. What provinces were conquered under the Middle Republic? What was the difference in status between the provincial subjects and the Italian allies? How did the Romans rule provinces? What problems were caused in Roman public life by the acquisition of overseas provinces?

12. How were Roman armies raised? Who served in them? Were there any difficulties in raising armies in the second century B.C.? Were there campaigns that encountered difficulties in conscription? What economic factors were thought to be the cause of these problems?

13. What was ager publicus and how had it been occupied by private individuals? What did this process have to do with the difficulties of the smallholders?

14. What does slave holding have to do with both the occupation of ager publicus and the problems of the smallholders?

2

TRIBUNATE OF TI. GRACCHUS

The tribunate of Ti. Sempronius Gracchus is important for a number of reasons.[1] As several ancient sources indicate, it marks the first time that blood was shed in Roman politics since the early days of the Roman Republic centuries before. The second century B.C. had been one of comparative domestic peace, and Ti. Gracchus's tribunate marks the beginning of the spiral of violence in the Late Republic that would eventually kill thousands and destroy the constitution. It was the "optimates" – the supporters of the ruling oligarchy – who felt so threatened by Tiberius that they resorted to this violence. Eventually, they would reap the rewards of this action, since they were to be the principal victims of the violence. They killed Tiberius because his use of the latent powers of the assembly of the plebs in the attempt to implement measures opposed by the oligarchy seemed to undermine the traditional form of government (or at any rate, the oligarchy's control of the government, which amounted to the same thing in the eyes of the oligarchs). Tiberius's tribunate thus represents the first major example of the use, by a member of the oligarchy, of popular discontent to further his own career. Tiberius stumbled into his conflict with the oligarchy unintentionally, but the Republic was to be destroyed by members of the oligarchy who quite consciously tried to advance themselves to the detriment of the Republican political system.

TIBERIUS'S EARLY CAREER

Because Ti. Gracchus is often characterized as a "revolutionary" (both in ancient and modern works), it is worthwhile to examine his background

---

[1]   Be sure to read the appendix on Roman nomenclature to understand the various forms that a Roman name may take. Ti. Gracchus will for the most part be called Tiberius to distinguish him from his brother C. Gracchus or Gaius (subject of Chapter 3).

and early career before turning to the events of his fatal tribunate. He belonged to one of the most prominent families of the senatorial oligarchy (the Sempronii Gracchi first attained the consulship during the Second Punic War, and Tiberius's father had the distinction of holding the consulship twice and being elected to the office of censor). Prior to his tribunate Tiberius himself had had an illustrious career that would have given every expectation that he would go on to reach the consulship as his father had.

At this period, a Roman had to serve ten years in the army before seeking major political office. In 147 B.C., Tiberius served on the staff of his cousin Scipio Aemilianus during the attack on Carthage and was given an award for being the first to mount the walls of a minor town being stormed. In 137 B.C., while serving as the quaestor of the consul C. Hostilius Mancinus, who had suffered a major defeat in Spain, Tiberius played a significant role that was reinterpreted after the fact by his enemies in light of his perceived antisenatorial policy. For nearly twenty years Rome had been trying to stamp out native revolts in Spain. One particular source of trouble was the town of Numantia, which provided leadership for the revolt of the Celtiberians. Mancinus managed to get his entire army surrounded in a valley, and was compelled to surrender to the Numantines. Capitalizing on his father's reputation for fair dealing, Tiberius negotiated the terms. When these terms reached Rome, the senate repudiated the agreement, and turned over Mancinus naked to the Numantines in atonement for the breaking of the agreement. (The Numantines thoughtfully refused the offer, knowing that the fault lay elsewhere: the senate, that is, those in the senate who favored continuation of war in Spain, had recently ruined several agreements made by commanders in Spain.) This turn of events was a personal humiliation for Tiberius, since his pledges of good faith to the Numantines had been made worthless by those who opposed the treaty at Rome. Some ascribed his later course of action in his tribunate against the leadership of the senate to a desire to avenge himself. It was commonplace in Late Republican Rome for the adherents of the senate to ascribe only personal motives to those who acted in opposition to the oligarchy. As we shall see, however, there is no reason to imagine that Tiberius thought he was doing anything but furthering the interests of the senate with his agrarian legislation.

TIBERIUS'S AGRARIAN PROPOSAL

As tribune for the year 133 B.C., Tiberius came to grief over his attempt at land reform. He wished to solve the problem of the apparent shortage of men willing to be conscripted for military service by increasing the pool of available smallholders. To do so, Tiberius proposed that the Roman People reclaim amounts of ager publicus that were held by individuals in excess of the legal limits. Tiberius's proposal would remedy the fact that the law imposing these limits lacked any mechanism for enforcement by establishing an elected board of three to survey public land and redistribute to landless citizens amounts held in excess of the previous legal limit.

Later (hostile) sources give various personal motivations for this proposal, but to assess his own sense of what he was trying to do it is necessary to view the matter as a contemporary would. We are explicitly told (Plutarch, *Life of Tiberius Gracchus* 9) that Tiberius had consulted some of the leading men of the senate in drawing up his proposal. Foremost was his father-in-law, the princeps senatus Ap. Claudius Pulcher cos. 143.[2] We know of two other supporters: P. Mucius Scaevola cos. 133 and Scaevola's brother, P. Licinius Crassus Mucianus cos. 131 (his name indicates that he was a Mucius who had been adopted by P. Licinius Crassus). Scaevola happened to be consul in 133 B.C. and could guide the discussion in the senate since his colleague was off putting down the slave revolt in Sicily. Mucianus would within a year be appointed as pontifex maximus (a particularly prominent position among the priests of the Roman state) and take advantage of this position to gain himself command of the war in Asia in 131 B.C. (discussed later in the chapter). Clearly any proposal backed by such men could not have been self-evidently revolutionary, and he may well have been attempting to implement a plan that had been urged upon him by one of his elders. Given the level of influential support that Tiberius enjoyed in his proposal, he probably did not anticipate much objection. If so, he was wrong.

The exact details of the proposal are somewhat confused in the inadequate sources. Fundamentally, it seems to have been an attempt to enforce the old limit of 500 jugera of ager publicus with the balance to be reclaimed by the state and then distributed to landless citizens. According to Appian (*Civil Wars* 1.9), the original proposal guaranteed possession of the 500 jugera and granted an additional 250 jugera for every child under a father's control. When Plutarch (*Life of Tiberius Gracchus* 9) discusses the law that was eventually passed, he mentions only the 500 jugera and indicates (10) that an earlier form of compensation had been withdrawn

---

[2] In modern scholarship, the practice is to identify Republican magistrates with the date of their highest office. The consulship is identified with the ancient abbreviation "cos." (in the early period, the "n" was pronounced weakly and so was omitted from the abbreviation). Those who did not attain the consulship may be identified as "pr." (for praetors) or "tr. pl." (for tribunes).

from the original version to the joy of the poor; it has been conjectured that the additional amounts for children were withdrawn from the final version (the poor would rejoice since this would increase the amount for distribution). To prevent the land from immediately returning to the rich, clear title to the distributed land was not given, so that resale was not permitted. A land reform law from two decades later seems to indicate that thirty jugera was the maximum amount that one could receive under the law (whether this was an average allotment is not known, but if it was, it was high by the recent standards of Roman land distribution, e.g., ten jugera back in 173 B.C.).

DID THE LAND DISTRIBUTION BENEFIT ONLY ROMAN CITIZENS?

There is some debate as to whether the Italian allies were given land under the Gracchan legislation. A bronze inscription (*RS* 2, Crawford, *Roman Statutes*; hereafter *RS*) preserves fragments of a law passed in 111 B.C. that affected the status of land distributed by the Gracchan land commission. This law repeatedly describes the people and the land covered by its provisions as follows: "And to the Roman citizen to whom a triumvir has given or assigned some of that land by lot on the basis of a law (plebiscite)" (l. 3) and "As for the ager publicus that existed in Italy during the consulship of P. Mucius and L. Calpurnius [133 B.C.], whatever of this ager a member of the board of three for assigning and granting land [granted or assigned?] to some Roman citizen by lot on the basis of a law (plebiscite)" (l. 15). These clauses apparently make it clear that land was distributed only to Roman citizens and not to the Italian allies. Such an interpretation would then be confirmed by Italian complaints in 129 B.C. that the land commission was now reclaiming ager publicus from them (if the Italian allies were also entitled to allotments of the reclaimed land, what right did they have to complain?), and by the appeal of M. Livius Drusus and M. Fannius (see Chapter 3) to the selfishness of the Roman electorate (what was the point of claiming that the extension of Roman citizenship to the allies would lessen the benefits to citizens, if the allies were already benefiting from the land redistribution, one of the major benefits granted to citizens?).

But there is a piece of evidence to the contrary, and a number of scholars have used it to interpret the land redistribution as benefiting the allies too (who had also been given lesser allotments in Roman colonies founded early in the second century B.C.). In his discussion of the agrarian background to Tiberius's proposal, Appian emphasizes (*Civil Wars*

1.7–8) that the main concern was the declining population of Italy. Since the corresponding passage in Plutarch (*Life of Tiberius Gracchus* 8.1–5) also mentions the general Italian situation, this concern about Italy is to be attributed to the common source of both passages. Appian ascribes this concern about Italy as a whole to Tiberius himself, who is said to have "spoken grandiloquently as tribune about how the Italian race was excellent at war but was gradually being worn down to poverty and how there was a shortage of males and no hope of correction" (*Civil Wars* 1.9.1), and to have considered with reference to his proposal that "nothing better or more splendid could be done for Italy" (*Civil Wars* 1.11.1). But this continuing emphasis on Italy is a false interpretation of Appian, since the legal text of 111 B.C. should be decisive. This is solid contemporary evidence, which fits in with the generally selfish attitude toward the Italian allies that can be perceived in Roman politics in the period from the Gracchi down to the outbreak of the Social War in 91 B.C. It is easy to imagine that Appian, who is prone to error through excessive abridgement, has here conflated the interests of the rural Romans at the time of Ti. Gracchus with the broader issue of the treatment of the Italian allies, a conflation that would have been all the easier for him to have made if the source that spoke of rural conditions discussed the condition of Italy as a whole. In addition, he attributes to Tiberius a policy (the promotion of the interests of the Italian allies) that was conspicuous among the later proposals of his brother Gaius. The procedure of attributing measures of Gaius to Tiberius is attested elsewhere (see n. 7), and given the extent to which Gaius would champion the demands of the allies (and give them places in his own colonial foundation in Carthage; see Plutarch, *Life of Gaius Gracchus* 9) and the fact that Appian himself is interested in the issue of the allies' demands, it would not be surprising if Appian gives a misleadingly broad interpretation of Tiberius's proposal.

OBJECTIONS TO THE LAW

Whatever the relevance of the law to the Italian allies, the effect of the proposal on Roman citizens led to immediate and vigorous opposition. Naturally the law was detrimental to the wealthy, but nonetheless, various arguments were made against it on the basis of fairness.

- It was argued that those whom the law harmed were the very men who governed the state, and that the law would thus undermine the prosperity of those upon whom the commonwealth had to rely for its continued well-being in the future.

- The retroactive aspects of the law were deemed unfair. The land had been brought under cultivation with no objection years, even decades, before, and its "possessors" had spent their own capital in improving it. It was hardly reasonable to turn around after such a long passage of time and ask for it back.
- The law was also inequitable. The ager publicus had been treated as private property and was inextricably entangled in the domestic affairs of those who possessed it. Some was given to daughters as dowries. Were they now to be stripped of their financial security? Furthermore, ager publicus had been divided among sons, not always evenly. What of the son who had inherited ager publicus while his brother received "private" property? Was he alone to be made destitute?

It was all very well to say that the land should not have been usurped in the first place, but reclaiming it after so long struck its possessors as a great injustice. They found a champion in a colleague of Tiberius, and the conflict between the two was to have very unfortunate consequences.

Promulgation

Ti. Gracchus entered office as tribune on December 10, 134 B.C.[3] Soon thereafter (presumably), he promulgated his agrarian bill. A bill had to be announced (promulgated) a *trinundinum* before it was voted on. The exact sense of trinundinum is disputed, but it is basically a period of three Roman eight-day weeks. (During this period a bill could be debated in public in *contiones* or informal meetings called by a magistrate to sound out and influence public opinion.) During the trinundinum after the promulgation of the proposal, one of Tiberius's colleagues became an outspoken opponent of the bill: M. Octavius. The Greek sources say his services had been bought by the "rich," but presumably he was the legitimate representative of those (rich) people who felt that they were being treated unfairly by the proposed repossession of ager publicus. It appears that there were heated exchanges between Tiberius and Octavius.

Veto

When the bill came to be voted on in the assembly of the plebs, the herald began to read out the text as a standard preliminary procedure. At this point, Octavius interposed his veto, forbidding the reading. This was the way in which a tribune quashed a colleague's proposal. Tiberius postponed

---

3   The tribunes anomalously entered office on December 10 for reasons that are lost in the darkness of early Roman history.

the reading for a week, apparently in the hope that the bill's manifest popularity among the voters would cause Octavius to change his mind. This did not happen, and when Octavius vetoed the bill a second time, a consular friend of Tiberius suggested that he bring the matter before the senate.

Senate Fails to Intervene

At this point, the matter could have been resolved peacefully. Both Tiberius and Octavius had clearly attached their personal prestige to their positions, and by the standards of Roman upper-class morality, neither could yield without suffering damage to his *dignitas* ("personal prestige"). There was, however, a traditional Roman practice that could have settled the disagreement peaceably. The word *concordia* designates the principle of resolving disputes through compromise in the interest of the broader good. The senate tended to work through consensus based on the opinion of the senior members, and if someone influential had spoken strongly in favor of compromise and carried the house, Tiberius and Octavius could conceivably have been persuaded to modify their positions. Certainly, a contentious matter had recently been settled through concordia.

In 139 B.C., a tribune had proposed a law to institute voting by ballot instead of orally. This proposal was strenuously opposed by the senators, who thought it would undermine their control of elections, and they enlisted the opposition of another tribune despite the obvious popularity of the measure. The conqueror of Carthage, Scipio Aemilianus, who himself opposed the bill, persuaded the tribune to give up his veto because of the obvious desire of the plebs to pass the bill. Thus, to some extent it was recognized that the oligarchy had to give in to very popular bills that it opposed, and perhaps such was the outcome that Tiberius wished for in the senate. The fact that Tiberius was willing to put the matter before the senate may indicate that he was also willing to compromise, though perhaps he simply expected his highly placed supporters to carry the day.

As for Octavius's supporters, in some time around 140 B.C., an agrarian proposal of Scipio Aemilianus's friend C. Laelius had been abandoned when it met significant opposition in the senate (the details are unknown), and perhaps the opponents of Tiberius's bill were equally intransigent. In any case, no efforts were undertaken to induce compromise – Aemilianus, who happened to be Tiberius's brother-in-law, was away on campaign subduing Numantia – and Tiberius, facing humiliation if his proposal was thwarted, turned to a drastic solution.

Removal of Octavius from the Tribunate

Tiberius now announced that in a week he would bring forward two measures: the agrarian bill and the deposition of Octavius from office as an opponent of the plebs' will. The latter was a completely unheard of step. Rome had no written constitution, merely the interpretation of the inherited system on the basis of precedent. Thus the "constitution" was fluid and could be reinterpreted at any moment, since what succeeded in being recognized as valid *was* "constitutional." There was no constitutional precedent for deposing a tribune, since such a thing had never happened, and it had never occurred to anyone that such a thing might happen. But if Tiberius succeeded, he would in effect change what was considered constitutional.

Tiberius apparently justified himself on three grounds (Plutarch, *Life of Tiberius Gracchus* 15; Appian, *Civil Wars* 1.51).

1. A tribune could be deposed if he committed heinous crimes like burning the temple of Jupiter Optimus Maximus on the Capitol or the naval dockyards.

2. A man ceased to be a real tribune if he blocked the will of the plebs. As their representative he must act on their behalf, and a tribune opposing their will should be deposed.

3. The tribunes were sacrosanct, and Tiberius had to counter the argument that the tribunes' sacrosancticity prevented their deposition. ("Sacrosancticity" meant that they were religiously inviolable on account of an oath supposedly sworn by the plebs to defend the tribunes' persons when the first tribunes were elected in the early fifth century B.C.) Tiberius replied that the consecrated last king had been expelled, and the Vestal Virgins (young priestesses who vowed chastity to the goddess Vesta) were subject to being buried alive if convicted of violating their oath of virginity. Thus, a tribune who violated his office was likewise stripped of its protection.

The last argument is not very convincing. The kingdom was overthrown rather than voted out of existence, and the Vestal Virgins were punished by the pontifex maximus (a senior official priest) in a proper legal procedure. The main argument is number two, which is related to number one. It was an accepted principle of the Roman constitution that the tribunes represented the interest of the plebs, and Scipio Aemilianus's argument in persuading the tribune in 139 B.C. to give up his opposition to the proposal on voting by ballot was based on the notion that a tribune should not obstruct the interests of the plebs. It is conceivable that the entire course of events would have been changed if someone with Aemilianus's prestige had tried to persuade Octavius to give up his veto. As it was, no one did, and Tiberius felt obliged to press on with the rash attempt to force his way around Octavius's perfectly legal veto by securing his deposition from office. But there was no constitutional precedent for claiming that a tribune's position obliged him to give in to a course that he opposed merely because it was popular. In the heat of the struggle to secure passage of the agrarian proposal, people who supported it may have paid little attention to the implications of Tiberius's arguments in favor of deposing Octavius, but Tiberius's opponents would later seize upon disturbing aspects of this action in the attempt to discredit him.

At the electoral assembly called to vote on the bill to depose Octavius, Tiberius continued to urge him to yield to the circumstances. When the first tribe to vote approved his deposition, Tiberius begged him to give up his opposition but he refused. After seventeen tribes (one short of a majority) voted for deposition, another unsuccessful appeal was made, and then the eighteenth tribe voted for deposition, thereby ratifying the bill as law. While the measure was of questionable legitimacy since such an act had never been done before, it was not inherently and self-evidently improper. At any rate, none of the other tribunes vetoed the vote. That Octavius did not impose his own veto on the proceedings is an unexplained mystery. Perhaps he did not recognize the validity of the proposal at all or perhaps he lost his nerve (presumably, violence was to be expected at the hands of the bill's supporters if Octavius vetoed the bill to depose him).

In any case, the agrarian bill was then passed without opposition into law as the *lex Sempronia*, and a replacement for Octavius as tribune was elected.

Agrarian Commission

The lex Sempronia provided for a board of three (*tresviri agris iudicandis adsignandis* or "three-man commission for judging on and assigning fields") to survey public land and to oversee the repossession of illegally held land and its distribution in small parcels to landless Roman citizens. Elected to the first board were Tiberius himself, his brother Gaius, and his father-in-law Ap. Claudius Pulcher cos. 143. Though there is no inscriptional evidence for the operation of the board at this time (we have later boundary stones with inscriptions that include the name of Tiberius's replacement among the board members), it must have begun the initial steps to reclaim land because the senate tried to impede its actions though its control of finances by granting it insufficient funding to carry out its duties. This obstruction led Tiberius to a countermeasure that would significantly weaken his support and could be characterized as "antisenatorial."

PERGAMUM

Just as Tiberius was being thwarted by the senate's refusal to grant adequate funds for the commission, news reached Rome that King Attalus III of Pergamum had died and left his kingdom by will to the Roman People. The practice by which kings in the East bequeathed their kingdoms to the Roman People may seem a bit odd at first, but in fact it was perfectly logical. If the king did not have a definite heir available within his dynasty, making a will leaving the kingdom to Rome was the simplest way to deter assassination attempts at the hands of those who wished to seize the throne, since such an act would be pointless if upon the death of the present king the throne would fall to the greatest military power in the Mediterranean. Such wills resulted in Roman acquisition of Pergamum (133 B.C.), Cyrene (96 B.C.), Bithynia (74 B.C.), and Cyprus (58 B.C.), plus a doubtful claim to Egypt.

Tiberius received news of the inheritance quickly: his father had been a patron of the kingdom, and for this reason the envoy bringing news of the inheritance actually visited the patron's son with advance news of this very important event. Tiberius realized that the inheritance would include the royal treasury, and he decided that he could use this turn of events to get around the senate's opposition to his agrarian scheme. By doing so, however, he would be encroaching on clear prerogatives of the senate in foreign policy and state finance, and this would lead to a hardening of senatorial opinion against him.

First, Tiberius proposed a bill before the plebs accepting the inheritance of the royal treasury to fund the agrarian commission. The money was to be used to provide the recipients of land with funds to start their farming operations.[4] The law also prohibited senatorial deliberation about the inheritance, though the senate ought to have discussed the implications of taking such a momentous move, which would entail the establishment of

---

[4] Such is the explicit statement of Plutarch (*Life of Tiberius Gracchus* 14). The late antique *epitome* ("summary") of Livy claims under the year 133 B.C. that since Tiberius had incited the plebs to expect more land distributions than the land available could reasonably accommodate, the money was to be distributed to those who were eligible under the lex Sempronia (but presumably could not actually receive land). This characterization of the situation is clearly anti-Gracchan and should be considered a misrepresentation. Since the land commission continued to operate for four more years, there clearly was land available, and Plutarch's sensible version should be accepted.

an entire new province. Tiberius also indicated that he would put forward another bill dealing with the status of the cities in the kingdom. Since Attalus had granted the cities freedom under the terms of the will, the implication was that Tiberius would ignore this provision, an act that would constitute bad faith. The inheritance was an extremely delicate matter to begin with, and to ignore the freedom granted to the cities was a very dangerous move. Once again, Tiberius was usurping the traditional role of the senate in foreign affairs (though it seems that the proposal about the cities never became law).[5] While his deposition of Octavius had been of dubious legitimacy, it was not self-evidently impermissible. The senate's control of foreign policy and state finances, however, was generally accepted, and it now became clear that Tiberius was willing to use his popularity among the electorate to usurp the senate's traditional prerogatives. It is not hard to see how members of the senate would have viewed this development in a very poor light and came to consider Tiberius a demagogue who was bent on overturning the senate's constitutional position.

Tide Turns against Tiberius

In terms of domestic policy Tiberius's action was very disturbing. He was in effect seizing the money from the inheritance and giving it to the People as an act of his own personal largesse. There were many examples in ancient history of men who set themselves up as tyrants after gaining popularity through largesse, and for many members of the oligarchy, who must already have harbored suspicions about Tiberius's motives, the lessons of the past could only have heightened their anxiety.

It is unlikely that Tiberius himself conceived of what he was doing as an attempt at establishing a personal domination over the state, but others

---

[5] An inscription (*OGIS* 435, Dittenberger, *Orientis Graeci Inscriptiones Selectae*; hereafter *OGIS*) preserves a decree of the senate ratifying the terms of Attalus's will en bloc and directing future governors of the province to uphold his enactments. It would be natural to assume that this decree was passed in 133 B.C., but the session of the senate that passed this decree was presided over by an otherwise unknown praetor (C. Popilius Laenas, presumably the brother of the consul of 132 B.C.). Since the urban praetor would normally preside over the senate in the absence of the consul, and as far as we know P. Mucius Scaevola cos. 133 spent his entire consulship in Rome, it has been proposed that the decree was passed later, perhaps in 129 B.C. as part of the final settlement of the province after the defeat of Aristonicus's revolt (see Chapter 8). If this were the case, however, it would be quite extraordinary for the decree to speak only of the king's will without any mention of subsequent events (and in any case, it is unlikely that no decision would have been made about the status of the king's provisions in the interim). It is preferable to assume that Scaevola was for some reason unable to preside, and Laenas was acting temporarily in his place.

did. We are explicitly told that his behavior concerning the inheritance changed attitudes (Plutarch, *Life of Tiberius Gracchus* 14). Everything he had done before was now given a sinister interpretation. The agrarian law, the deposition of Octavius, the election of his close relatives to the board – all these actions now seemed to be signs of an attempt to set up a *regnum* (the Latin word for "kingship").

Regnum is the pejorative term used metaphorically to describe the position of anyone who was thought to be dominating the political scene in an unacceptable manner, but it seems that in this instance it was believed literally of Tiberius. One consular reported that the envoy from Pergamum had been seen showing Tiberius the royal attire of the Attalid kings.[6] Another accused Tiberius of keeping a gang of thugs. One particularly telling incident involved the aged consular T. Annius Luscus cos. 153, who challenged Tiberius to defend himself in a sort of legal wager (*sponsio*) in which Luscus asserted that Tiberius had broken the law in deposing Octavius. Tiberius allowed Luscus to speak in a contio, expecting that he would receive a cold reception from the crowd. Luscus asked a simple question: If you harm me, and I invoke the assistance of another tribune, will you depose him? Tiberius was apparently flabbergasted by the question and dismissed the contio. The question brought out a serious implication of the deposition that had not been considered at the time. The ability of the tribune to depose an obstructionist colleague had no theoretical limit and basically violated one of the fundamental principles of the Republic, collegiality. No magistrate could do whatever he wished because he had colleagues who could prevent any illegal actions on his part. But if a powerful tribune could have a difficult colleague removed from office, what prevented the tribune from doing whatever he pleased, including setting himself up as tyrant? Tiberius's inability to answer Luscus's question shows that he had not considered the implications of the deposition. The move had merely been a tactical device to get rid of Octavius's obstruction, but now Tiberius found that he was forced to defend a course of action that did in fact have disturbing aspects to it.

Attempt at Reelection

One of Tiberius's leading opponents threatened to prosecute him after he left office. Magistrates were immune from prosecution during office,

---

6   This absurd claim is clearly a misrepresentation of the fact that Tiberius was informed by the embassy of the Pergamene inheritance in advance of any official announcement in the senate.

and it was one of the basic principles of the Republic that one could not go directly from one office to another (including immediate reelection to the same office) since this would grant permanent immunity from prosecution. Tiberius nonetheless decided to seek reelection as tribune. There was no absolute prohibition on direct reelection, but no one in the four centuries before Tiberius had ever sought such reelection. Thus, the move was literally unprecedented (a deplorable circumstance in the eyes of the conservative Romans, for whom the adjective *novus* or "new" had negative connotations such as "strange," "unheard of").

The two main sources are at variance. Plutarch (*Life of Tiberius Gracchus* 16–17) suggests that two assemblies were involved in Tiberius's last days. The first was an electoral assembly summoned to approve radical legislation, but this was dismissed because of lack of support.[7] Appian (*Civil Wars* 1.14–15) reports two assemblies, both electoral. In the first, after the first two tribes voted for Tiberius, the "rich" demanded a halt to the voting on the grounds that reelection was illegal, and when the presiding tribune, who had been chosen by lot, wavered, and Octavius's replacement demanded that the presidency of the election be given to him, the others insisted upon a new selection by lot. The assembly was then dismissed, and a second session was announced for the next day.

FINAL DAY

There is some dispute over the details of Tiberius's last day, but the general course of the events is clear. He had had his personal followers seize the site of voting (the Capitol, which was the religious complex on the top of the Capitoline hill) before dawn in an attempt to keep out his

---

[7] It has been argued that there was no proper election at all before Tiberius's death and that the entire matter on the Capitoline concerned an attempt to pass a law to legitimize the reelection, but this argument puts too much weight on the specific terminology of an ill-informed account written much later. Cicero, a highly knowledgeable source, leaves no doubt that it was actually an election when he says in describing the final misdeed that resulted in Tiberius's death that "he wished to be made tribune for a second time" (*iterum tribunus plebis fieri voluit*, *Catilinarian* 4.4; the verb "to be made" is a standard term for being returned in an election), and he gives no hint of any legislation. In any case, Plutarch indicates that the legislation that Tiberius supposedly had in mind concerned proposals designed to curry popular favor: a reduction in military service, the right of appeal against public courts, and the adding of an equal number of equites to senatorial jurors (the unreliable Dio Cassius makes similar claims: 24 fr. 83). While it is not inconceivable that Tiberius had some such plans, it seems far more likely that the later proposals of his brother Gaius were falsely ascribed to Tiberius (perhaps by a supporter of Gaius, or even Gaius himself) to lend legitimacy to Gaius's proposals as if they had been first conceived by Tiberius.

opponents. (Using force to seize control of the voting place became an increasingly common tactic in later events and would eventually undermine the legitimacy of the assemblies.) The resort to such a tactic of intimidation may have been prompted by the fact that it was summer and Tiberius's mainly rural supporters were too occupied with agricultural tasks to attend the assembly (apparently the poorer residents of the city were not very interested in land distribution). Octavius's successor now presided over the election, and the other tribunes left (or were forced out). In effect, Tiberius had seized control of the electoral assembly to guarantee the result he wanted. While this sort of tactic was soon to become commonplace, this was the first time it happened in the Late Republic, and it must have seemed shocking at the time. If he could secure reelection in this fashion once, what would prevent him from doing it indefinitely?[8] His opponents could reasonably feel that he was in fact seeking a regnum. (During the assembly, he apparently made some sort of gesture toward his forehead, which was taken as meaning that he sought the diadem that symbolized kingship in the Greek East. Whatever the truth of the matter, this interpretation shows what his opponents thought he was up to.)

As events proceeded ominously on the Capitol, the senate was summoned to the temple of Fides (the goddess representing "Good Faith" or "Dutifulness") by the consul P. Mucius Scaevola, one of Tiberius's senatorial supporters (initially at any rate). Word of disturbing events came down from the Capitol, and the appearance of the eight tribunes must have clearly indicated the nature of what was going on there. The denouement occurred through the action of P. Cornelius Scipio Nasica Serapio cos. 138, who was pontifex maximus (head of the college of pontifices and thus the leading priest of the state religion) and whose father had been cheated of the consulship in 162 B.C. through the actions of Tiberius's father. When Nasica asked what Scaevola planned to do about the situation, Scaevola replied that while he would not uphold any illegal actions, he would likewise take no step until something illegal had actually been done, and that he would not put citizens to death without a trial (which would be a clear violation of the law). In effect, Scaevola was saying that he would act to quash any illegality that Tiberius carried out, but only after the fact and within the scope of the regular legal system. (Since Scaevola was a well-known jurist, such a legalistic response is not surprising.) This answer was

---

[8] One might compare the position of Pericles during the Athenian democracy of the late fifth century B.C. He was elected as *strategos* ("general," a position of significant political influence) in twenty-nine of thirty consecutive years, which allowed him to dominate the city's politics.

not good enough for Nasica, whose view was that if Tiberius was allowed to get away with securing illegal reelection through manipulating the electoral process, the very legal basis of the state would be undermined, and that for this reason Scaevola's legalistic position was unacceptable. This was (to Nasica's mind) a dire emergency that demanded immediate "quasi" legal action. Nasica turned to the assembled senate and famously urged that anyone who wished the Republic to be safe should follow him. The exact words he used (*qui rem publicam salvam esse vult me sequatur*) are a direct quotation of the phrase traditionally used by a magistrate conducting a *tumultus*. (This was an emergency levy raised when there was an immediate danger to the city of Rome; the formula is quoted in Servius's late antique commentary on *Aeneid* 8.1.) By citing these words, Nasica made it very clear that he thought the situation up on the Capitol to be as much of a direct threat to the city's safety as the onslaught of a marauding squad of Gallic horsemen or a band of rebellious slaves (the normal reasons for declaring a *tumultus*), a threat that required drastic action *now*. In effect, Nasica was enlisting the senators in an ad hoc military unit to ward off what he conceived of as a dire emergency.

Nasica then led the senators up to the Capitol. In later decades, when the use of violence in domestic politics became commonplace, they would have been easily driven off, but on this first instance, when the mere sight of the senators was still enough to intimidate men of lower-class status, the crowd gave way before this onslaught of unarmed senators. Nasica had covered his head in the edge of his toga in the scheme called the *cinctus Gabinus*, which was adopted during sacrifice (the exact significance of this move is unclear, but at the least it must have added to the solemnity of the occasion). The senators began to attack Tiberius's followers with whatever was handy, and Tiberius himself was struck first with a bench plank by P. Satureius, one of his tribunician colleagues. Two to three hundred supporters of Tiberius were killed, and that night their bodies were dumped into the Tiber by the aedile C. Lucretius, whose family thereby earned the cognomen Vespillo ("undertaker").

From a legalistic perspective such as Scaevola's, this senatorial attack on Tiberius's assembly was a rash and uncalled-for step. After all, seeking reelection as tribune was not overtly illegal, and if control of the assembly place had been seized by violence, it would have been possible to prosecute the offenders later. On the other hand, the issue was not simply legal but also political. Whether or not the means by which Tiberius secured reelection were legal, it would have been difficult to prosecute him once he was recognized as tribune for the next year. As already stated, "constitutionality" was simply a question of whether a procedure was accepted in practice, and if Tiberius could get himself reelected, then whatever the means he used, the success itself would go a long way toward justifying his actions. In any case, such reelection did in fact pose a serious threat to the established order, and while in the present day it is easy to discount considerations of precedent in matters that are no longer of any immediate concern, Nasica no doubt considered the situation to be one of the utmost importance at the time. If Tiberius could be reelected once, why not any number of times? And if he could depose from office any magistrate who opposed him, how would this unassailable position differ from a tyranny? It is only in hindsight that we can see how dangerous a precedent Nasica himself was setting by introducing the use of violence into domestic politics.

ASSESSMENT

When Ti. Gracchus entered office, he endeavored to pass a bill on land reform that was supported by influential members of the senate. When promulgated, the bill aroused vigorous and not entirely unjustifiable opposition. When thwarted by one of his colleagues, Tiberius got his way by having the opponent removed from office, a step that was unprecedented. In effect, Tiberius put his own prestige in getting the billed passed before any other considerations. When his opponents used the senate's financial powers to hinder the implementation of the bill, Tiberius made another unprecedented move in ignoring the senate's traditional oversight of state finances and foreign policy by passing a bill to accept the inheritance of the kingdom of Pergamum to fund the implementation of his agrarian commission. This attack on the senate's privileges led to a hardening of opposition to him. In response, he attempted to seek an unprecedented second term as tribune, and was willing to use force to manipulate the electoral process to achieve his end. Clearly, Tiberius had little sense of proportion and was willing to undermine fundamental principles of the state to uphold his own prestige. He was accused of attempting to establish himself in a position of unassailable power (regnum), and a mob of senators killed him and several hundred of his supporters to thwart this attempt. While at the time it no doubt seemed acceptable to resort to violence to stop this illegality, the violence would by no means stop there.

POPULAR REACTION TO THE DEATH OF TIBERIUS

There was no single, clear-cut reaction to the death of Tiberius. Some commoners felt that he had been cut down while looking after their interests and formed a sort of Gracchan "faction." Things became so difficult for Nasica that to remove him from harm's way (i.e., an accusation before the People of murder), the senate sent him as an envoy to Pergamum to investigate the troubles there (see Chapter 8), and conveniently enough, he soon died.

Certain senators posed as upholders of the policies Tiberius had advocated, and it was now to become a common practice for some young senators to win popular acclaim for themselves by opposing the senate in the interests of the People. In particular, C. Papirius Carbo is attested as being strongly associated with Gracchan politics. After the death of L. Licinius Crassus Mucianus cos. 131, he was elected to the agrarian commission, and as tribune in 131 or 130 B.C., he took several steps that show his allegiance.

First, he embarrassed Scipio Aemilianus by publicly asking him, soon after his triumphant return from his conquest of Numantia, whether he approved of Tiberius's death. Aemilianus gave the ambiguous reply that Tiberius had been legitimately killed if he had intended to seize control of the state (a crafty answer, since its implications depended on whether or not the "if" clause was considered true). Supposedly, Aemilianus lost popularity because of his refusal to condemn the killing outright. Second, Carbo unsuccessfully attempted to pass a law that permitted reelection to the tribunate. Presumably, the intention was to lend retroactive legitimacy to Tiberius's efforts back in 133 B.C. Finally, Carbo passed a law mandating the use of the ballot in elections on legislation. The use of the ballot had been introduced in elections for magistrates in 139 B.C. and in most trials in 137 B.C., and while there is no report of intimidating those who voted for the Gracchan legislation in 133 B.C., the events of the next year may have suggested that it would be wise to thwart the possibility of such intimidation through secret voting. In any event, the images on certain coins and statements made in speeches by Cicero show that the secret ballot soon came to be viewed as an integral element in the "freedom" (*libertas*) of the Roman electorate. (For a reference to the libertas of the Roman People in coinage, see Coin 3.) Given this background, it is not surprising that Carbo would maintain this pro-Gracchan stance for the next decade (when he made a famous volte-face and tried to rejoin the senatorial oligarchy).

Prosecution of Tiberius's Supporters

in 132 B.C.

P. Scaevola cos. 133 had prevented any precipitous action being taken against Tiberius's supporters in 133 B.C., but the consuls of 132 B.C., P. Popilius Laenas and P. Rupilius, undertook to prosecute them (they must have been elected with this intention in mind), resorting to a novel use of their recognized powers to do so. The reason for this new procedure was that it was thought that these men could not be convicted in the regular mode of prosecution, and since the senatorial oligarchy thought that they had to be punished, the consuls were determined to find a way to get around the popular disinclination to do so. To understand the way in which the consuls used their traditional powers for this nontraditional purpose, it is necessary to examine the legal rights of Roman citizens.

According to a law dated by the Roman historical tradition to the first year of the Republic,[9] a Roman citizen could not be executed or flogged by a Roman magistrate within the sacred boundary of the city of Rome (the pomerium).[10] This right was based on the concept of appeal to the People (*provocatio*). In effect, any citizen threatened with such punishment could appeal to the People, and such appeals were automatic in that a capital sentence could only be passed in a trial conducted before an assembly of the People. Thus, only a sentence of the People could result in execution in the city. In the second century B.C., three *leges Porciae* (laws passed by someone called Porcius) extended this right to cover all citizens abroad (and not on military duty). Thus, in 132 B.C., a Roman magistrate could not flog or execute (i.e., pass capital sentence on) any Roman citizen (apart from a soldier) without authorization of the People. (For a visual representation of this procedure and its importance in the self-conception of the rights and liberties of the Roman People in the Late Republic, see Coin 4.)

The second century B.C. saw the start of a second method of prosecution, which would eventually give rise to a series of public courts in Rome. In the Middle Republic, magistrates would sometimes conduct investigations outside of the city called *quaestiones* (sing., *quaestio*). During the second century B.C., the procedure arose of authorizing magistrates by law to exercise capital sentence in certain situations where it would be impractical to try the matter before the People. (Such cases generally concerned people of low social standing who were accused of crimes far from Rome. Hence, it was considered both impractical and unnecessary to go to the bother of trying such cases through the cumbrous procedure involved in the traditional method of lodging accusations before the assemblies in

---

9 The literary historical tradition for the early years of the Republic is not terribly reliable; sources for this period were scarce, and when the Romans began writing histories of their distant past in the second century B.C., much fiction, often anachronistically based on contemporary practices, was written to fill in the gaps.

10 Many scholars hold that the right dates to a late stage in the Struggle of the Orders (see Chapter 1) rather than to the foundation of the Republic. Whatever the validity of this argument, the Romans of the Late Republic considered this right to be a fundamental aspect of Roman citizenship.

Rome.) Although a magistrate could conduct an investigation into anything he pleased, any sentence that was covered by the leges Porciae could
be meted out only with the prior authorization of the People.

It must have been perfectly obvious in 133 and 132 B.C. that the People
would neither convict Tiberius's associates if they were accused before
the People in the traditional way nor authorize a magistrate to investigate
their behavior in a quaestio and then impose a sentence. Accordingly,
the consuls of 132 B.C. attempted to circumvent this situation by using a
normally restricted power that was inherent to their office. This power,
which is called *relegatio*, was possessed by any magistrate with imperium,
and it allowed him to restrict a person to or forbid him from a particular
place. Relegatio was traditionally used only against those of recognized
immorality, and it was normally a temporary act that lapsed once the
magistrate who had relegated a given person left office.

If the consuls of 132 B.C. had simply relegated Tiberius's supporters in
the regular way, the supporters would have been able to return to the city
the next year. Such a relegation was clearly not meant to be a permanent
penalty, but the consuls tried to turn their relegations into criminal sentences by inflicting this punishment after the accused had been convicted
in a quasi-judicial procedure before the consuls' informal *consilium* (board
of advisors).[11] The use of legal procedure was intended to make the relegations permanent in that the relegation would not be a simple act of a magistrate's caprice that could be overturned at will by his successors (the use of
the consilium in the "trials" of the accused supporters would have had the
appearance of "due process"). Furthermore, since this punishment did not
involve execution, flogging, or fining, that is, the acts prohibited without the
People's authorization by the laws on provocatio, the right to provocatio was
not overtly violated. In effect, P. Laenas and his colleague were attempting to
introduce an unprecedented form of exile into the Roman legal system.

While theoretically any magistrate could have ignored these novel
relegations, most senators no doubt did favor the punishment of Tiberius's

---

[11] It was considered poor form in the collegial Roman oligarchy for decisions to be made
by a single man on his own. Instead, he would summon a consilium ("council of advisors") before whom an issue to be determined by the magistrate would be discussed
before he reached his decision. (This practice derives from Roman private life, where a
man would convene such a council of his relatives and friends to discuss an important
decision in his personal affairs.) The composition of the board was up to the magistrate, who was not bound by its decisions. (Generally, the advisors were members of
his staff, but he could summon anyone whom he deemed suitable.) Given his authority
and prestige, a determined magistrate could sway the board's decisions. Nonetheless,
this procedure was to some extent a check on the magistrate's ability to abuse his
powers, and a sensible magistrate would include on his consilium men who had some
experience with the issue at hand.

supporters, and "constitutionality" in Rome basically meant what was considered acceptable. If no one objected and the penalties were treated as valid, then over the years, they would assume the air of legitimacy. While this new procedure did not directly violate the letter of the right to provocatio, it did fundamentally undermine its spirit. At this time, a Roman citizen convicted of a capital offense was not actually executed under normal circumstances, but was allowed to go into exile in non-Roman territory. His literal life was not forfeited by conviction of a capital crime, but his life as a citizen was. This was apparently the result of the actions of the consuls of 132 B.C. – until a decade later, when Tiberius's brother C. Gracchus passed legislation that would retroactively invalidate the actions of Laenas and his colleague (see Chapter 3).

Later Activity of the Agrarian Commission

We are told explicitly (Valerius Maximus 7.2.6) that the senate did nothing to invalidate Tiberius's agrarian legislation. The opposition was thus to the man and his methods, not to the bill itself, which obviously had wide support. The agrarian commission continued to function until 129 B.C., when it apparently began to repossess land occupied by Rome's Italian allies, who sent a delegation to seek the assistance of Scipio Aemilianus. As a result of his intervention, the senate passed a decree that the power to adjudicate disputes over repossession should be transferred to the consul, who promptly left Italy to fight a minor war in Illyricum. At this point, the commission lapsed into inactivity. There is no way to know what exactly the motivation was in curtailing the activities of the land commission, but presumably sufficient land had been distributed in the four years since Tiberius's death that the senate felt it could attempt to bring the commission's operations to a close, which the complaints of the allies gave it an opportunity to do. From now on, the senate would seem to have automatically viewed any form of land distribution with distaste. In any case, the commission would remain in abeyance until Tiberius's brother Gaius endeavored to avenge his brother by reviving his aims and vindicating his methods.

Mucianus's Machinations to Secure the Command in Asia

There was discontent in Asia at the bequest of the Attalid kingdom to Rome, and soon rebellion broke out. This will be discussed in its own right later (see Chapter 8). For the time being, we will examine only a dispute in Rome about who should command the army sent to put down this rebellion. It was a regular phenomenon in Roman politics that senior senators held permanent priesthoods and manipulated religious procedures for their own benefit. P. Licinius Crassus Mucianus, who was the brother of P. Mucius Scaevola cos. 133 but had been adopted by a Licinius Crassus, was an initial supporter of Ti. Gracchus (discussed earlier). After the death of Tiberius's opponent P. Cornelius Scipio Nasica cos. 138, Mucianus replaced him as pontifex maximus. He was then elected to serve as consul in 131 B.C., and the suppression of the revolt in Asia had been selected by the senate as one of the provinces for the consuls of that year. The appointment fell by lot to Mucianus's colleague, who unfortunately held the position of *flamen dialis*, an archaic priesthood that was dedicated to the worship of Jupiter and circumscribed by a number of peculiar taboos. Among other things, the flamen dialis could not ride on horseback or look upon corpses, restrictions that were difficult for a general to comply with. In the past, a flamen dialis had been prohibited from assuming an overseas command, and now in his capacity as pontifex maximus Mucianus forbade his colleague to travel to Asia to take up his command. The details of the dispute are poorly recorded, but it would seem that tribunician intervention (presumably either to restore command to the flamen dialis or at least to thwart Mucianus) eventually resulted in a law being passed to authorize an election to choose the commander by popular vote in the tribal assembly (the assembly of the Roman People as a whole that was organized by tribe like the assembly of the plebs). Mucianus then won this election, the votes of only two tribes going to P. Scipio Aemilianus, who had recently won great prestige by finally ending the prolonged war against the city of Numantia in Spain. Though not often recognized as such, the election has all the indications of being a popularis measure (the populares were politicians who acted in opposition to the senate by championing causes popular among the general electorate – see Chapter 3). Although elections had been held at the end of the third century to choose commanders for Spain before the two new provinces were created there in 197 B.C., there had been no such elections for decades, and by this point it was the sole prerogative of the senate to determine provincial commands. In future decades, various popular generals would secure commands against the will of the senate by getting tribunes to pass laws providing for special elections to pick the commander, a practice that began here with Mucianus. He himself reaped little benefit from all his efforts to win the command in Asia for himself, since his inadequate preparations resulted in a crushing Roman defeat and his own death. (Consuls of 130 and 129 B.C. eventually put down the revolt, as will be discussed later.)

QUESTIONS FOR STUDY AND REFLECTION

1. What was Ti. Gracchus's motivation for introducing his agrarian legislation?

2. What was ager publicus (public land) and how did Tiberius's proposed agrarian legislation affect it? What innovations were to be instituted by the legislation?

3. What arguments could be given in favor of Tiberius's attempt to reclaim public land that was illegally in private hands and redistribute some of it to the landless? What arguments could be made against the legislation?

4. Was Tiberius antisenatorial in his aims and methods? Did his attitude change during the course of his tribunate?

5. What did "constitutionality" mean in Rome?

6. Why did Tiberius wish to depose M. Octavius? Was it constitutional to do so? What arguments were there in favor of and against the effort?

7. To what extent did opinions about Tiberius and his aims change over the course of his tribunate?

8. Was it constitutional for Tiberius to seek reelection?

9. What motivated the senators who attacked and killed Tiberius and his supporters? Were their fears justified? What alternative course of action was there? Were there any broader implications to their actions?

10. What was the attitude of the senate and of the general electorate toward Tiberius after his death? Did the senate make any distinction between Tiberius's methods and his policy?

3

TRIBUNATES OF C. GRACCHUS

CITIZENSHIP AND THE ITALIAN ALLIES

In the 120s B.C., discontent among the Italian allies began to be an important factor in Roman politics, and various issues relating to them would cause strife in Rome for more than a generation. At first, there were two grounds for this discontent, and the first involved ager publicus. Seemingly, all the ager publicus that was readily available for redistribution in Roman territory had been used up within a few years, and the agrarian commission then began to reclaim land held by the allies. In 129 B.C., the objections of the Italian allies to the activities of the Gracchan agrarian commission on their territory had led to a halt in its operations, and it seemed that the commission could not be revived until the allies' objections were overcome. Second, by the 120s B.C., the opinion had taken root among the allies that they should be enrolled as Roman citizens. Several attempts would be made in the next decades to achieve this end, but the Roman nobility as a whole successfully resisted the idea. Even after the outbreak of civil war forced the Romans to give citizenship to the allies, contention about the method to be employed in enrolling them in the body politic would cause strife for a further decade. Eventually, it turned out that the allies could be granted citizenship without harm to the constitutional order, but over the course of the decades during which their enfranchisement was disputed, this issue would play a major role in the process by which the use of violence in domestic politics came to be increasingly accepted and acceptable.

M. FULVIUS FLACCUS'S PROPOSAL ON CITIZENSHIP

A member of one of the great families of the plebeian nobility and a supporter of Ti. Gracchus, M. Fulvius Flaccus was elected to the land commission in 131 or 130 B.C. In 125 B.C., he was elected consul and attempted to resolve the Italian allies' objections to the operations of the land commission by offering them a form of Roman citizenship in return for acquiescence in the commission's repossession of Roman ager publicus occupied by the allies. Specifically, the Latins were to receive full citizenship, and the allies would in turn be given the old status of the Latins, that is, they would be allowed to vote in one tribe in tribal elections (but not in the centuriate assembly). This effort fell through when Flaccus had to go to Transalpine Gaul (southern France) to deal with threats by Celtic tribesmen against the allied city of Masilia (modern Marseilles) (see Chapter 8). That the desire for citizenship was strong among the allies is shown by the fact that the Latin colony of Fregellae actually went into revolt when the proposal failed, and the colony was destroyed by the praetor L. Opimius, whom we will meet again. (It is symptomatic of the spotty nature of our information about this period that we have no detailed information about this astonishing event.) C. Gracchus would revive the proposal in three years' time, with disastrous consequences.

C. Sempronius Gracchus

C. Gracchus was the younger brother of Tiberius (he was born 154 B.C., nine years after Tiberius). He was very loyal to his brother's memory and supported his policies (specifically the agrarian legislation and the legitimacy of seeking reelection to the tribunate). But whereas Tiberius stumbled into his image as a "revolutionary" through increasingly desperate and irresponsible efforts to uphold his agrarian proposal and thereby preserve his *dignitas* ("personal prestige"), Gaius entered into office as tribune with a fully thought-out program of reform. In his two tribunates, he passed or proposed more pieces of important legislation than most Roman politicians could dream of in a lifetime. He was also reputed to be an excellent speaker, and for this reason he is the only orator before Cicero from whose speeches reasonably large excerpts are preserved. These amount to no more than a few paragraphs, but they do give us direct access to the sort of public persona he tried to convey.

Early Life

At the time of his death, Gaius was married to Licinia, the daughter of P. Licinius Crassus Mucianus cos. 131, who along with his brother

Q. Mucius Scaevola cos. 133 was a supporter of Tiberius's land proposal.[1] This shows that he was part of the family group that initially supported Tiberius's agrarian proposal. Gaius served on the staff of his cousin and brother-in-law Scipio Aemilianus during the campaign against Numantia in Spain starting in 135 B.C. He was elected to the land commission in 133 B.C. and is attested as being denied permission to dispose of Tiberius's body, which indicates that he was already back in Rome before the return of Aemilianus in 132 B.C. This is the early career of a man who had high expectations for his senatorial career.

A story is recorded (Cicero, *On Divination* 1.56) that Gaius told many people that when he hesitated to run for the quaestorship, his dead brother appeared to him in a dream and told him that the same fate awaited both of them ("Delay as much as you want, you nonetheless must die the same death as I did"). Plutarch takes this to be evidence that until then he had pursued a quiet life, an idea that is obviously false. In addition to the evidence of his earlier activities, he gave a speech in 131 or 130 B.C. in support of Carbo's unsuccessful effort to pass a bill legitimizing the reelection of tribunes. A quotation from the speech proudly boasts of his connection with his brother: "The worst men killed my excellent brother Tiberius. Look how alike the two of us are!" In 126 B.C., he spoke against a proposed bill expelling non-Romans from Rome. Clearly, he had maintained a direct connection to his brother's policies and wished to retain the goodwill of his brother's supporters. As for the statement about the dream, this supposed hesitation was presumably a rhetorical ploy to win public sympathy, while at the same time – and perhaps more importantly– claiming fraternal authorization for his course of action.[2]

QUAESTORSHIP

In late 126 B.C., he secured election to the quaestorship in the next year. He was assigned to the consul L. Aurelius Orestes, who was given the task of subduing a revolt in Sardinia. Orestes' command was prorogued, so

---

[1] One source says he was married to the daughter of L. Junius Brutus Callaicus cos. 138. Presumably she was a first wife. Both marriages show that Gaius was well connected with the senatorial oligarchy.

[2] It would seem that Gaius was prone to making melodramatic attempts at gaining favor by alluding to his supposedly pathetic family circumstances. In a speech from the start of his tribunate, he says that since he and his child were the only descendants left of Scipio Africanus and Ti. Gracchus cos. 177, the People would no doubt have excused him from acting on their behalf in order to prevent the extinction of the family. It is noteworthy that this statement presupposes that he too could expect to die in pursuit of his brother's policies.

that two years later he and Gracchus were still on the island. In 124 B.C., Gaius returned to Rome to seek the tribunate while Orestes was still fighting in Sardinia, and he was accused before the censors of abandoning his commander. He pointed out that he had fulfilled his legal requirements of military duty since he was obligated to stay with Orestes for only a year. Since we hear of no complaint from Orestes (he would return to celebrate a triumph in 123 B.C.), Gaius presumably left with his permission (in the Roman conception the magistrate with imperium under whom a quaestor served was to be like a father to the quaestor).[3] Gaius was also accused of being implicated in the revolt of Fregellae in 126 B.C. His speech in defense of himself apparently humiliated his accusers, but the very fact that someone took the trouble to accuse this young senator shows how dangerous he was considered to be.

C. Gracchus's Election as Tribune

In 124 B.C., Gaius was elected tribune for the following year. His candidacy was extremely popular, and large crowds came to support him. Yet it also seems that the opposition to him was sufficiently strong that he was returned fourth instead of first (out of ten positions). However, even if his opponents could exercise this much influence in the voting of the assembly of the plebs, once he was in office, Gaius's oratorical skills and the inherent popularity of his proposals were such that initially he completely dominated the political scene in Rome. His first steps were acts of retaliation against the treatment of Tiberius and his supporters in 133 and 132 B.C.

Revenge against Octavius

Gaius proposed a law that anyone who had been removed from office by the People should be ineligible for any further office. This was obviously directed against M. Octavius (the tribune who had been deposed by Tiberius), since passage of this law implied that Octavius's removal from office had been legitimate. Gaius then gave up this proposal, claiming that his mother Cornelia had interceded with him on behalf of Octavius. While it may well be true that she did so, Gaius's readiness to drop the bill suggests that he bore no particular ill will against Octavius. Presumably,

---

3 In effect, the quaestorship served as a way of breaking a young aspirant into the ways of the senate. He was to be the dutiful assistant of his commander, who in turn could vouch for the young man's qualifications during his future electoral campaigns. The Romans compared the relationship of the quaestor to his commander to that of a son to his father.

the implicit threat was meant to intimidate anyone who might have been considering a repetition of Octavius's obstruction during Gaius's tribunate. At any rate, Gaius met with no such interference from his colleagues during his first term as tribune.

LEX NE DE CAPITE CIVIS ROMANI INIUSSU POPULI IUDICETUR

While Gaius was apparently not too worried about Octavius, he clearly was extremely hostile to P. Popilius Laenas cos. 132.[4] As discussed in Chapter 2, the consuls of 132 B.C. had used their power of relegation to sidestep the unwillingness of the Roman People to countenance any accusations against Ti. Gracchus's supporters. Gaius decided to pass legislation that would deny legitimacy to the proceedings used a decade earlier against his brother's associates – and in the process make Laenas subject to punishment for his actions.

Gaius's legislation did not deal directly with the proceedings of 132 B.C. Instead, his law provided "that no judgment should be passed regarding the *caput* of a Roman citizen without the authorization of the People" (*ne de capite civis romani iniussu populi iudicetur*), and it thereby quashed all unauthorized judgments of any kind that affected the life of a Roman citizen. The Latin word *caput* ("head") is used to express both the literal and metaphorical life of a citizen. By referring solely to the passing of judgment and not specifying the manner in which the legal procedure was conducted, any possibility of quibbling about the difference between relegatio and proper legal actions was precluded. The law was also written so that it retroactively covered prior offenses and provided that any accusations under it would be conducted before the People.[5] Since the crime was a capital offense, the centuriate assembly would decide cases brought under Gaius's law. This would seem to imply that Gaius felt that Laenas's conviction could have been secured even in the most conservative assembly (the centuriate assembly was dominated by the first census class).

Once the law was passed, there could have been no doubt what fate awaited Laenas if an accusation was lodged against him (as one undoubtedly would be). Without waiting to be brought to trial, he immediately

---

[4] Presumably, Gaius would also have been hostile to Laenas's consular colleague, but the man had died in the interim.

[5] In general, the Romans recognized that applying laws retroactively was unfair, but they thought it acceptable to penalize after the fact actions that in their minds were self-evidently wrong.

withdrew from the city and went into voluntary exile in the Campanian town of Nuceria; this withdrawal was then made official through the passage of an interdict.[6] By forcing Laenas's exile, Gaius had avenged his brother's supporters, and at the same time, this victory over such a high-placed enemy established his ascendancy in Roman politics.

GAIUS ASCENDANT

Once Laenas had gone into exile, Gaius reigned supreme in Rome. He clearly had much popular support and used it to pass an amazing amount of legislation. Before discussing the course of his two tribunates, it is convenient to discuss this legislation, which often cannot be firmly dated to one or the other tribunate. It seems that Gaius was self-consciously attempting to win widespread support among various segments of the electorate. Unfortunately, the episodic nature of the sources makes it impossible to determine what development may have taken place in the objectives for which he wished to enlist this support. Conceivably, he may at first have simply wished to court popularity for his future career, but eventually his main purpose was to gain support for the enfranchisement of the Italian allies. In any case, his efforts to seek favor consisted for the most part of legislation that can be seen as benefiting either the equites or the plebs, but other activities are also discernible. In addition, he passed legislation that dealt with the senate directly, and this will be examined later. Let us first consider the notion of gaining votes through bestowing governmental benefit, then discuss how Gaius benefited the equites.

PRACTICAL SIDE OF POLITICS

The ancient sources concentrate on "high" politics, that is, the activities of magistrates (especially electoral and military affairs). The sources also tend to view politicians as pro- or antisenatorial, and while it is true that the course of action that certain politicians proposed to take while in

---

[6] It was an accepted right of a citizen on trial to go into exile before conviction, and in that case a special act called an interdiction was passed against him. A person under interdiction could be legally killed if he returned to Roman territory, and thus the act was designed to make the withdrawal of the accused official and permanent, whether he was actually convicted or merely thought that conviction was likely. Otherwise, those under threat of conviction could simply leave temporarily and then return once they thought the danger was passed. Before the enfranchisement of all of peninsular Italy during the Social War, Roman nobles who left Rome for exile normally took up residence in a congenial allied town in Italy. In the later period it was necessary to leave Italy altogether.

office was known during electoral campaigns, it would seem that other, nonideological considerations normally swayed the voters – just the sorts of things unlikely to attract the attention of the sources. Among the upper classes, social relationships determined by blood and by the association of the voter with the candidate (either through personal relations or inherited relations with the candidate's ancestors) would under normal circumstances determine the vote of even the most conservative senators. Since the sources are most interested in the overtly ideological aspect of elections, a factor that must have been significant much of the time is seldom mentioned, namely, the extent to which a politician was being repaid for past benefits. For instance, in 65 B.C., Cicero related to his friend Atticus who his competitors in the consular elections in the following year were likely to be, and Cicero ascribed a high likelihood of success to one potential rival, Ser. Sulpicius Galba, on the grounds that the road whose rebuilding he was overseeing was about to be finished. Presumably, the equestrian-rank contractors were expected to canvass actively (and decisively) on Galba's behalf. As events turned out, Galba did not run for the office, but if a simple (and comparatively small-scale) building project like Galba's could be taken by a well-informed observer as capable of turning the tide in the consular elections, we can imagine the unknown effects that must have resulted from the plethora of financial dealings that went on between Roman magistrates and their contractors, dealings about which we are totally uninformed. Thus, what must have been an important practical aspect of the Roman electoral system is almost entirely hidden from us.

POLITICAL POSITION OF THE EQUITES

As noted in the introduction, the equites Romani were basically the non-political segment of the upper class. Pretty much by definition, the equites were the wealthy Romans who chose not to seek public office. But not holding public office was by no means the same thing as lacking interest in public policy. Since it was the equites who made money by providing various services to the state, they had a strong interest in how the senate exercised its functions. Indeed, when the equites thought their interests were being harmed, they could be a potent force. Back in 169 B.C., when the censors dealt with certain contracts in a way that annoyed the equites, the result was that a tribune accused one censor before the People, and it was only the intervention of his popular colleague (the father of the tribunes Ti. and C. Gracchus) that prevented his conviction. A stray anecdote preserves the memory of a law that seems to show that in the early 120s B.C., there was an endeavor to strengthen the equites' voice in electoral politics. In the previous period, the special eighteen centuries of the centuriate assembly that were reserved for the equites who were given a horse at public expense (see Chapter 1) frequently contained the young sons of the nobility, and these young men could influence the voting of the eighteen equestrian centuries on behalf of the senate. In 129 B.C., a law was passed that removed from the equestrian centuries anyone who entered the senate. It would be useful to know more about the motivation for this change, but presumably the removal of senators from the equestrian centuries represented an effort to bolster the equites' political independence. In any case, it would seem that C. Gracchus actively sought the support of the influential equites in Rome by promoting their material interests and by enhancing their political role through making them the jurors in his reform of the court that judged senators accused of provincial corruption. These jury panels would soon be extended to other courts that were to be set up, and the dispute over who should sit on the jury panels was to cause an artificial conflict between the senators and the equites, even though their basic community of interests ought to have led them to cooperate politically.

Gaius's Measures Benefiting the Equites

Law on Asian Tithes

It appears that Gaius passed a law affecting the way in which contracts were let out for the collection of taxes in Asia (for a discussion of this system, see Chapter 1). Previously, the bidding for these contracts was conducted in Asia by the governor. Gaius's law provided that the auctions were now to be carried out by the censors in Rome. The exact motive for the change is unclear, but the new procedure would seem to have favored the high-ranking equites resident in Rome. (These were also the men who would sit on the jury panel that Gaius established, as discussed later.)

Construction

Gaius was involved in some sort of extensive road-building project and in the construction of the granaries necessitated by his grain law.[7] We are explicitly told (Appian, Civil Wars 1.23) that Gaius thereby won the

---

[7] While one might not necessarily think that road building was a self-evident job for the tribunes, in fact there are several other examples of their involvement in the upkeep of roads.

support of the (equestrian) contractors and the workers. He would later be attacked for overseeing his own projects.

Control of Juries

In establishing a position for the equites on the jury panel for the court handling accusations of provincial corruption, Gaius was giving them a prominent public honor, though this would not have been his primary aim.

LEGISLATION BENEFITING THE COMMON PEOPLE

The ancient historical sources are almost exclusively interested in the activities of the senatorial class and give us very little information about the views, motives, and activities of wealthy nonsenators, much less those of the common people, who are generally lumped together in an amorphous mass (the plebs) when their views are mentioned at all. Yet, it is clear that apart from any other differences, there was a substantive distinction between the interests of the rural and the urban plebs. While the former had a strong desire for continued land distribution and were directly affected by matters relating to the conscription of soldiers, questions of the living conditions in Rome were of greater significance for the urban plebs. Gaius may well have remembered how the fact that his brother's support had been restricted mainly to the rural plebs had helped to weaken his position during his final days (see Chapter 2), and he seems to have solicited support from both groups though relevant legislation.

Agrarian Legislation

Gaius in some way revived his brother's agrarian commission, though the details are not clear. Conceivably the urban plebs may have also benefited, but land distribution was normally a matter for the rural landless, and certainly the urban plebs seem not to have been particularly interested in the reelection of Ti. Gracchus, whose main source of popularity was his land commission. In any case, Gaius expanded the scope of land distribution by passing legislation that authorized the establishment of Roman colonies in Italy. Colonies were self-governing communities of Roman citizens, and the sending out of colonies (mainly motivated by military considerations) had ceased by the mid second century. Now colonies were to be established for domestic purposes. First, older communities in southern Italy would be revived through the establishment of new colonies of Roman citizens nearby.[8] Second, the pressure for land among the poor was to be relieved by setting up entirely new communities for them. Gaius also proposed the establishment of an overseas colony to be called Junonia on the site where Carthage had been destroyed in 146 B.C., and he would encounter serious difficulties later because of this.[9] There is no evidence to show that any of his proposed colonies became permanent settlements (though the sources do indicate the initial stages of establishing Junonia were actually undertaken).

Military Legislation

Gaius passed a law regulating military service. Since conscription in antiquity was generally conducted in the countryside (the urban population was thought to be soft), this legislation was also aimed at the rural plebs and contained two provisions. First, deductions that were made against soldiers' pay for weapons and clothing were stopped. Apparently, the difficulties of finding willing recruits for the army from the class of smallholders meant that men were being enlisted who could not provide these things themselves as they were theoretically obliged to do.[10] Second, the conscription of recruits under the age of seventeen (the traditional minimum for service) was prohibited. The need to halt such practices shows how desperate the Roman levy had become in that the poor and underage were being drafted contrary to accepted usage. (The ongoing pressure to find new recruits continued nonetheless, and simply passing legislation against these abuses did not end the practical necessities that had led to them. Within two decades, the exigencies of a war in Africa would result in first the repeal of Gaius's restrictions on conscription and then in the complete abandonment of the traditional method of raising troops.)

---

[8] Capua in Campania and Neptunia by the site of the old Greek city of Tarentum are mentioned.

[9] As any reader of Virgil's epic the *Aeneid* knows, Juno, the wife of the chief Roman god Jupiter, was associated with Carthage, and the new colony was to be named after her (rather than the hated city of Carthage). (The practice of naming colonies after gods is attestable earlier in the century; the reason for this new custom is not known.)

[10] It would seem that the minimum property qualification for military service was lowered from 11,000 to only 3,000 sesterces toward the end of the second century. In the distant past, the troops had provided their own equipment, but the procedure had long since changed into one whereby the state provided the troops with their arms and the cost was deducted from their pay.

Grain Law (Lex Frumentaria)

Gaius was clearly acting on behalf of the urban plebs when he passed a grain law (*lex frumentaria*) that allowed all citizens to buy grain from the state at six and two-thirds sesterces per *modius* ("bushel"). This program was later converted into a free dole, but the strange figure established by Gaius's legislation indicates that he was imposing a maximum rate on the free market. So long as people could buy from private merchants at a lower rate, they no doubt would, but if the price in the free market were to rise above the prescribed sum of money, then people would turn to the state supplies.[11] There are earlier examples of efforts by magistrates to secure grain supplies from abroad, but now Gaius institutionalized this activity so that the common people in Rome would be safe against excessive prices in difficult times. In the future, the senate would come to oppose grain legislation on principle (because of the cost and the supposedly negative effect on the citizenry).

SENATORIAL LEGISLATION

While Gaius sought support from the equites and the plebs through his legislation, he also passed much legislation that regulated the functioning of the magistrates and of the senate as an institution. Later sources claim that he was antisenatorial, but it is clear from Gaius's legislation that what he opposed was not the senate as such but what he considered abuses in the behavior of the senatorial oligarchy. The content of his legislation shows that he was not aiming to destroy the senate's traditional guiding role in the state. Rather, his intention was to correct what he took to be an ingrained habit of the senators to act for their own self-interest (often greed) and not for the "public interest." To some extent, this policy was an attempt to curb the self-serving manipulation of the senate as a whole by the comparatively small number of wealthy and powerful families who dominated the consulship and controlled the proceedings of the senate for their own purposes. If, in the process, Gaius undermined the dominant clique, which had also caused his brother to come to grief, so much the better! The consulars, not unnaturally, tended to equate the senate as a whole with themselves and to speak as if any attempt to curb

---

[11] To put the figure into some sort of context, all it took was a few hundred sesterces to provide an adult with basic food for a year (a sesterce was a large copper coin). What the cost of living or a reasonable (or manageable) price for grain in Rome at the end of the second century B.C. would be cannot be determined, but presumably Gaius's figure represented what he took to be the maximum tolerable cost.

the reasonably clear abuses that were committed by the magistrates and the machinations that took place within the senate was an attack on the traditional role of the senate as a whole (an interpretation that is often echoed in the ancient sources). Thus, while Gaius's purpose was to reform the senate as he thought appropriate, his conception of senatorial propriety was at variance with that of the senatorial oligarchy, and his opponents represented him as attacking the senate itself.

In this way, the Roman political scene was beginning to harden into the binary opposition of two groups (whose composition changed on an ongoing, ad hoc basis): the populares, who supposedly championed the People against the abuses of the senate, and the optimates, who defended the traditional constitutional arrangements against the interference of those whom they characterized as rabble-rousing demagogues.

Lex de Pecuniis Repetundis

A prime example of senatorial behavior that could be taken to be in conflict with the public good was the acceptance of bribes by magistrates, and Gaius sought to curb such activity with the *lex de pecuniis repetundis*. This phrase literally means "law regarding the reclaiming of monies," and it was the standard term for a law covering provincial misconduct.[12] Since it was not possible in practical terms to curb the magistrates' use of imperium – it was the basis of their power to govern provinces and allowed them to kill any foreigner – the Romans had tried various methods to do away with the motive for which imperium was most commonly abused, namely, the acquisition of money. Earlier in the second century B.C., there had been various attempts to penalize such behavior, and the first permanent court was set up by the *lex Calpurnia* of 149 B.C. to provide a venue for prosecuting accusations. The procedure was basically the same as the one used in civil courts for reclaiming stolen property; the jurors who decided such cases were senators, with a praetor presiding over the trial. By the time of Gaius's tribunate, however, it was clear that the senatorial juries authorized to judge cases of provincial corruption involving money were unable or unwilling to convict, and Gaius introduced legislation to modify the procedure of this court.

---

[12] In scholarly works, the accusation of provincial extortion is often referred to as *repetundae*. This is an ungrammatical barbarism in Latin (the phrase *repetundarum* can be used adverbially to signify that someone has been accused "of extortion," but it cannot appear in this sense in the nominative *repetundae*) and should never be used. Cicero uniformly uses the phrases *lex* and *quaestio de pecuniis repetundis* ("law/court regarding the reclaiming of funds"), and it is best to stick with this terminology.

The details of Gaius's proposed reforms are hazy in the sources, but it appears that he made two separate proposals. It would seem that in the original proposal he simply changed the composition of the jurors while otherwise preserving the earlier "civil" procedure (i.e., the plaintiffs simply got their property back if a conviction was secured, and the defendant was not further penalized). In the older court, the so-called jury was actually the consilium or "board of advisors" of the magistrate who presided over the trial.[13] Whether the magistrate had been technically bound to follow the decisions of the members of his consilium is not clear, but presumably he was to be bound under the provisions of Gaius's proposal, which introduced equestrian members into the jury. In effect, the presiding magistrate would continue to use his authority to exercise the functions of the court, but the judgment in the case would be determined by jurors who were no longer exclusively senatorial. Some sources (Plutarch, *Life of Gaius Gracchus* 5.2; *Comparison of Agis and Cleomenes and the Gracchi* 2; *Epitome* of Livy 60) indicate that he proposed a jury board consisting of either half senator and half equites Romani or one third senators and two thirds equites Romani.[14] The reasons for the change in the composition of the jury are reasonably clear. The senators had shown that they found it hard to convict fellow senators. Given the hierarchic nature of Roman society, the equites Romani were the only other acceptable source from which to choose the jurors. While it is taken for granted in most ancient sources that Gaius's motives were antisenatorial, it is worth noting that he did not propose a more radical course of action. For instance, if his attitude toward the senate had been intrinsically hostile, he could have

---

[13] For the consilium, see Chapter 2 n. 11.

[14] Plutarch expressly states that 300 equites would be added to the 300 senators. The inaccurate account in the *Epitome* of Livy states that he passed a law enrolling 600 equites in the 300-member senate without referring this to the *lex de pecuniis repetundis*. This description is obviously some sort of confusion with M. Livius Drusus's proposal in 91 B.C. to enroll equites in the senate (see Chapter 5). Presumably, this confusion is to be attributed to the man who in Late Antiquity composed the summary of Livy (it is hard to imagine that Livy himself gave such an account, since there is no other evidence that Gaius wished to make such a drastic change in the composition of the senate). If so, it is conceivable that what truth lurks behind the version given by the *Epitome* is a tradition in which Gaius provided in his original proposal for a jury board of one-third senators and two-thirds equites. Methodologically, it would be better to prefer Plutarch's straightforward and sensible version to the garbled one in the *Epitome*, but one piece of solid evidence makes more sense with the proportions suggested by the latter. The law as eventually passed provided for an album of 450 equestrian jurors. This number makes little sense by itself, but it is easily explicable if in the original proposal the old senatorial panel of 300 potential senatorial jurors was replaced by so many equites, and to them one-half of the senate was added, for a total of 450.

attempted to set up some sort of popular jurisdiction over this crime (and in fact a system along exactly these lines was implemented in the early 80s B.C.; see Chapter 7). But he was not a revolutionary and was simply attempting to come up with a viable alternative to senatorial juries.

Gaius, it appears, quickly changed his mind and embarked upon a drastic reform of the court. The reason for this is arguably the acquittal of M.' Aquillius cos. 129, who is said to have received huge sums of money as bribes during the course of his settlement of Asia following the suppression of Aristonicus's revolt (see Chapter 8), and was acquitted under the lex Calpurnia. Though the exact date of his acquittal is not known, it could have taken place during the course of Gaius's tribunate[15] and thus provided a motive for his making a second, more stringent proposal. The new law was apparently passed as the *lex Acilia* under the name of one of Gaius's colleagues (which shows that he learned from his brother's mistake and sought to win the support of his fellow tribunes by associating them in his activities).[16]

Large amounts of this law (*RS* 1) are preserved on a broken bronze inscription (known as the *tabula Bembina* after its earliest owner), and it is thus possible to form a direct notion of Gaius's reform. The new court covered all magistrates elected by the Roman People and forbade them to receive any monies in a province in excess of a set amount (the exact sum is not preserved in the inscription). The jury was to consist exclusively of equites Romani (whose specific qualifications are likewise not preserved). Every year 450 equites resident in Rome were to be drawn up in a list by the praetor in charge of the court (this list is known as the *album*, which signified the whitewashed board on which the names of the panel members were publicly displayed). For a given trial, the prosecutors would select from this list 100 jurors; from these, the defendant would pick the fifty who actually decided the case. The trial could cover any accusation of taking money in the provinces that had occurred since any earlier trial; if acquitted, the defendant could never again be prosecuted for any prior misdeeds. Through this seemingly odd provision, the law encouraged the prosecutor to bring forward all previous misdeeds once a man was accused

---

[15] It is known that he returned to Rome in 126 B.C., when he celebrated a triumph, but it is possible that the accusation took a few years to be prepared and was not lodged until late 124 B.C., so that the acquittal took place soon after Gaius entered office.

[16] The name of the lex Acilia is given in Cicero (*Verrines* 1.51), and the equation of this with the Gracchan bill is generally agreed. That Gaius had tribunician colleagues pass some of his legislation is demonstrated by the fact that the law authorizing the foundation of a colony in Africa (a bill that must have meant much to him, since his later downfall is closely tied to this colony) was actually a lex Roscia.

but then granted him immunity from further prosecution for those deeds if he was acquitted. Conviction resulted in twofold restitution: the victims were given simple restitution and the state received the rest. (The procedure would ensure that if convicted, the defendant would be penalized for his theft without giving any encouragement of questionable prosecution, since the plaintiffs would receive back nothing more than what they had lost.) It would appear that conviction was not a capital offense, that is, those convicted were not obligated to go into exile to avoid (theoretical) execution.

Gaius's law thus represents a reasonable attempt in the Roman context to solve the problem of senatorial juries proving to be incapable of convicting fellow senators. Gaius manned the juries with equites Romani, the nonpolitical equivalents to the senators in social terms. What he did not realize at the time was that the respective interests of the senators and the equites might be divergent in this court, especially if the publicans who controlled the collection of the provincial tribute dominated the jury panel. It might be thought that the publicans would be naturally hostile to governors who tried to restrain them, but in fact it was only much later (in 92 B.C.) that the equites used their control of the extortion court to avenge themselves on such a senator, an outcome that Gaius could hardly be expected to have foreseen (see Chapter 6). Long before that event, an entirely different matter made control of the jury panels a bone of contention between the equites and the senate, when the equestrian jury panels exacted punishment from senators who were thought to have caused various military disasters in the last decade of the second century (see Chapter 4). The senators, who thought they were being persecuted, accordingly wished to regain control of the jury panel while the equites fought to retain it. (The juries for all courts that were subsequently set up were provided by the album of the court for provincial extortion.) None of these future developments could have been known (or even predicted) by Gaius. Presumably, in turning to the equites to man the courts, Gaius was also seeking their support by giving them such a public honor, but he was certainly not intentionally attempting to undermine the senate.

Law on Consular Provinces (Lex de Provinciis Consularibus)

Another law passed by Gaius clearly shows his intent to reform, not undermine, the senate. This is his "law on consular provinces," which concerns the selection of the provinces for the incoming consuls. The senate had the right to determine which magistrates would be prorogued in office and which provinces would receive new governors from either the outgoing urban magistrates of the present year (whose imperium would be prorogued) or from the newly elected magistrates, and whether a given province that was to receive a new governor would be of consular or praetorian rank. These posts would then be distributed by lot among the available magistrates. Although the generally poor nature of our sources for this period does not allow us to see examples, it would seem that the selection of the provinces for the consuls was affected by favoritism and influence once it was known who the new consuls would be. Gaius proposed to end this by making the senate choose the provinces for the new consuls before the elections, so that (in theory, at any rate) the determination would be based on an objective assessment of the situation rather than the desire to indulge (or harm?) the new pair of consuls. What is remarkable for interpreting the motives of the supposedly antisenatorial tribune is that this law prohibited tribunician veto of the senate's decision. Otherwise, anyone with an interest in the matter would simply get a friendly tribune to delay the decision until after the elections. It seems clear that Gaius's wish was that the senate should carry out its responsibilities properly, that is, in accordance with the public good and not for the benefit of the new consuls, and the prohibition of interference on the part of the tribunes shows that he was ready to curb the tribunes' powers in the interest of the broader public good.

Reelection and Plans for Enfranchising the Italian Allies

One of the astonishing things about Gaius's first tribunate is the ease with which he managed to secure reelection to a second term. His brother had been killed when he attempted this very thing, and in 131 or 130 B.C., a proposed law explicitly authorizing reelection had been defeated. The sources are not very interested in this surprising event and give rather spotty information. Plutarch (*Life of Gaius Gracchus* 8.1) tells us that he was not even a candidate but was elected because of the enthusiasm of the "people" (*demos* in the Greek, presumably meaning the plebs), while Appian (*Civil Wars* 1.21) explains the reelection by mentioning a law that allowed the voters to choose anyone they wished if there were not enough candidates. This law, of unknown date, was presumably intended to ensure that the comparatively high number of ten positions as tribune was always filled, even if there were not enough qualified candidates. But it is hard to see how Gaius's opponents (and any reelection would undoubtedly have met some objections) could not have ensured that the requisite number of candidates was available. If Plutarch's information is combined with Appian's, one can conceive of some sort of scheme designed to secure his reelection. Perhaps he did not openly announce his candidacy, but friendly tribunes conducting the election made sure to disqualify some of the candidates, thereby throwing the election open to anyone available, so that popular acclaim would then allow Gaius's candidacy at the last minute. Such a procedure would have avoided opposition by not giving any advance warning of the attempt at reelection and then presenting the senate with a (very popular) fait accompli.

Another unusual aspect of these elections is the return of M. Fulvius Flaccus cos. 125 as tribune for 122 B.C. It was unheard of for a consular to be elected tribune – the tribunate was an office for someone at a much lower stage in his career – so clearly there must have been a special reason for this unusual step. Flaccus had been a supporter of Ti. Gracchus and had unsuccessfully tried during his consulship to extend Roman citizenship to the Italian allies. Flaccus would be closely associated with Gaius in the attempt to secure citizenship for the allies during the tribunate of 122 B.C., and presumably his unusual decision to run for the tribunate as a consular indicates that he wished to work for passage of the bill on citizenship. If the reelection of Gaius was a well-thought-out, premeditated plan, then it was intended for the two of them to cooperate in agitating for citizenship, though the election of Flaccus could be interpreted differently. Perhaps Gaius's reelection was the result of fortuitous popular demands, and it was intended that Flaccus, with his great prestige as a consular, was meant to carry on the fight in 122 B.C. by himself. The sources really do not allow an answer to this question. In any case, the drive to give citizenship to the allies would lead to disaster for Gaius and Flaccus.

OPPOSITION TO THE EXTENSION OF CITIZENSHIP

Another colleague of Gaius in his second term was M. Livius Drusus. Presumably, he had not been elected as an opponent of Gaius, since the very fact of Gaius's reelection indicates great popular support (the evidence suggests that tribunician elections were normally held in July; seemingly, Drusus had changed his mind about Gaius by December). Drusus had an ally against Gaius in M. Fannius cos. 122. We are told (Plutarch, *Life of Gaius Gracchus* 8.1) that it was only through the electoral support of C. Gracchus that Fannius gained election. Whatever the exact extent to which Fannius associated himself with Gaius's activities in his electoral campaign (Gaius's support may have been motivated solely by personal considerations, and Fannius may not have campaigned as an associate of Gaius and his policies), Gaius certainly could not have considered Fannius in any way an opponent. If so, Gaius was to be bitterly disappointed, since as consul Fannius would work against him.

Drusus and Fannius set about using various arguments to undermine Gaius's popularity with the plebs. Drusus accused Gaius of self-interest, attacking him for carrying out the provisions of his own laws (that is, building roads and granaries and serving on the commissions establishing colonies).[17] Drusus also tried to replace Gaius in the plebs' affection by taking up Gaius's own proposals on their behalf and making them more generous. He proposed establishing more colonies than Gaius did along with an increase in the number of poor citizens to be enrolled as colonists. He also proposed doing away with the rent which under the Gracchan legislation was owed to the treasury by those to whom ager publicus had been distributed. Finally, to assuage the discontent of the Latins at least, he proposed that flogging them even on military duty was to be prohibited. In effect, Drusus was acting in a "demagogic" manner on behalf of the senate (a ploy that his son would repeat in 91 B.C.).

Fannius opposed the extension of citizenship, and a fragment is preserved of a famous speech before the People in which he made the point that if the number of citizens was increased, there would be less room at the public games. To some extent, this argument is silly, but it illustrates in a readily understandable manner an argument directed at the selfishness of the electorate: if there was only a fixed quantity of resources available for the benefit of the citizens, and the number of citizens was greatly increased, then the present citizens could only expect a decrease in the size of their own benefits. This shortsighted argument was quite successful in achieving the immediate goal of undermining Gaius's support among the plebs. On the other hand, the policy of denying citizenship to the allies would eventually provoke an unnecessary civil war.

The sources are not entirely clear, but it seems that toward the start of his second tribunate, Gaius attempted to put forward a bill regarding the extension of citizenship, and that Drusus vetoed it. Instead of tackling this setback head-on as his brother had done in similar circumstances, Gaius apparently decided to seek additional support for his proposal before making another attempt to get it passed. He must have been trying to avoid the confrontational methods of his brother, but the shift in tactics proved to be a disaster.

---

[17] Later legislation, passed most likely as a result of what Gaius did, prohibited the magistrate who passed a bill from carrying out functions enacted by that law.

Junonia and the Final Defeat
of the Bill on Citizenship

After his bill on extending citizenship was vetoed, Gaius made the remarkable decision to sail to Africa and personally oversee the foundation of Junonia, the new colony on the site of Carthage. Under normal circumstances, tribunes were not allowed to be absent from Rome for more than a day, so Gaius must have had strong reasons to do so (and he presumably secured dispensation from the senate). He apparently wished to increase the number of non-Romans among the colonists to strengthen their support of his citizenship bill. He left Flaccus behind to keep up the pressure for the bill during his absence.

The plan must have been that once the groundwork was laid by Flaccus, Gaius would return triumphantly from Africa and press on with the bill for citizenship. If so, things did not go according to plan. Flaccus was outmaneuvered politically by Fannius and Drusus, who continued to increase the electorate's hostility toward the proposal. Gaius was away for seventy days, and when he returned he found complete disarray. His enemies further undermined his popularity by alleging that there had been ill omens during the founding of the colony in Africa. It would seem that the tide had completely turned against him.

Upon his return, Gaius tried to have his citizenship bill passed. His enemies must have felt confident that it would be defeated, since this time they allowed it to be put to the vote. Though many Italians came to support the bill, the senate decreed their expulsion, and Gaius's prestige had dropped so low that he could not use his tribunician powers to prevent this. The bill was defeated.

Elections for 121 b.c.

In the tribunician elections in 122 b.c., Gaius tried to secure reelection for the following year but failed. Plutarch's pro-Gracchan source (*Life of Gaius Gracchus* 12.3–4) claims that he actually received enough votes, and it was only through the dishonesty of his colleagues that he was not returned. It is hard to judge the accuracy of this account.[18] Certainly, the

---

[18] Plutarch also claims that the sole reason for the hostility of Gaius's colleagues was that in a bid to gain popularity he had torn down the fence around a gladiatorial show they were putting on to allow free access for everyone. Given the extent to which his popularity had evidently sunk, one would imagine that the hostile tribunes would oppose him as a matter of policy. Most likely, the story about the gladiatorial show was put

defeat of the citizenship bill indicates a strong decline in support, though he may well have retained enough to win reelection. Even worse was the election in late 122 B.C. of L. Opimius as consul for the next year. Back in 125 B.C it had been Opimius who as praetor destroyed the Latin colony of Fregellae, which had gone into revolt after the failure of Flaccus's citizenship proposal in that year. Clearly, he was an opponent of citizenship for the allies and of Gaius.

Death of Gracchus and Flaccus

In early 121 B.C., Gaius's enemies worked quickly to overturn his legislation. One law to be repealed was the one that had authorized the foundation of Junonia. Gaius could apparently not tolerate this insult, and in the early morning, supporters and opponents of rescinding this bill gathered on the Capitol, where the vote was to take place. When an attendant of one of the consuls was carrying out the necessary pre-dawn sacrifices, he said something provocative to the Gracchans ("let the bad citizens make way for the good"),[19] and was stabbed to death by them with the styluses used for marking ballots. The assembly then broke up in chaos. It is noteworthy that Cicero would later characterize the circumstances under which Gaius met his fate as "trying to stir up the rustics" (*Catilinarian Oration* 4.4). This implies that despite the grain law he had passed on their behalf, Gaius had lost the support of the urban plebs and in the end had to rely on the rural citizens (presumably the people who most expected to benefit from the agrarian and colonial legislation).

The sources are a bit contradictory about the precise order of the events, but these seem to have been as follows. Gaius tried to explain away what had happened that morning, but made little progress. The senate was in session when the funeral procession of the murdered attendant was ostentatiously led past the senate house, whereupon the senate demanded an explanation from Gracchus. Gaius and Flaccus gathered their supporters during the ensuing night, and early the next morning, after arming themselves with the weapons that Flaccus had captured in Gaul during his victorious campaign in 125 B.C. and then used to decorate his house,

out by a pro-Gracchan source as part of an attempt to impugn the integrity of the other tribunes by ascribing their opposition to selfish personal motives (and at the same time portraying Gaius as acting on behalf of the interests of the plebs as a whole).

[19] In the immediate context, the words would signify that the Gracchan supporters should literally make way for him, but the words could be understood metaphorically to indicate that the wicked citizens (i.e., the Gracchans) should yield politically to the senate and its supporters (the "good" men).

Flaccus's and Gaius's adherents seized control of the Aventine hill (which was traditionally associated with the Roman plebs). Presumably, the intention of this move was to prevent any attempt to use violence against them as had been done to Tiberius and his supporters on the Capitol in 133 B.C.[20] From their fortified position, the Gracchans wished to bring the situation to an end through negotiation, but if they expected the consul Opimius to be willing to discuss terms, they misjudged their man. Determined to settle the matter by force, he refused to negotiate, and when Flaccus's younger son was sent to the consul to find out his terms for resolution, Opimius had him arrested. Instead, he had the senate pass a decree vaguely instructing that the consuls should "see to it that the Republic not be harmed" (this decree is discussed later in the chapter).

The city of Rome did not normally have any permanent police or military force at hand, and this circumstance would cause much trouble once the habit arose of using violence to get one's way. Conveniently for Opimius, just as the Gracchans showed their determination to resist any attempt to suppress them by violence, there was a military force outside the city that would allow him to use seasoned troops rather than simply rely on a gang of senators as Nasica had done back in 133 B.C. Q. Caecilius Metellus cos. 123, who had successfully subdued a revolt in the Balearic Islands, was about to celebrate a triumph, and the troops who were to participate in the procession were gathered outside the city at that very moment.[21] On the basis of the senate's decree, Opimius had these troops hastily brought forward to launch an assault on the Gracchan position. Flaccus led the final defense on the Aventine, but the Balearic veterans easily threw back the defenders, and 3,000 Gracchans (including Flaccus) were killed. Gracchus took flight to a nearby sacred grove, where he had a loyal slave kill him to prevent his capture.[22]

[20] Plutarch (*Life of Gaius Gracchus* 14.5–15.1) portrays Flaccus as an impetuous drunkard bent on violence, while the supposedly peaceable Gaius plays little role in the final encounter. This picture may well come from a pro-Gracchan source that wished to absolve Gaius of any blame for the debacle of 122–121 B.C. and to lay the responsibility squarely on Flaccus's shoulders.

[21] While the word "triumph" has a rather general sense in English, the Latin word from which it is derived had a very specific meaning. When a magistrate with imperium was about to cross the pomerium (sacred boundary of the city) to go on campaign, he first ascended to the Capitol (the precinct of Jupiter Optimus Maximus on the Capitoline Hill) to make a vow to share any booty with Jupiter if he should deign to grant victory. If the magistrate then won a victory in open battle, he could ask the senate to allow him to celebrate a triumph, that is, a ceremonial reentry into the city with his troops, ostensibly to deposit the booty in the Capitol.

[22] Opimius issued a decree stating that he would give its weight in gold to anyone who brought him Gaius's head. The man who did so (a low-born associate of Opimius)

Opimius later built a temple to the goddess Concordia (the personification of harmony). The intention was to encourage the populace to restore harmony in the state by obediently deferring to the senate.[23] This was the senatorial vision of harmony, but many commoners resented the apparent hypocrisy of a man who had just killed thousands of citizens on flimsy grounds talking of the promotion of concord.

"Final Decree of Senate" (*Senatus Consultum Ultimum*)

A decree of the senate instructing the magistrates to "see to it that the Republic not be harmed" was first passed in 121 B.C., and this eventually came to be accepted as a standard response to an immediate threat of violent disorder in the city. In discussing the passage of this decree in 49 B.C., Caesar (*Civil War* 1.5.3) states that "the well-known extreme and final decree of the senate (*extremum atque ultimum senatus consultum*) was resorted to," and from this passage it has been inferred that the phrase "*senatus consultum ultimum*" was an ancient technical term. Hence, it is sometimes designated in modern works with this name or the abbreviation *SCU* (from the Latin *senatus consultum ultimum*). While this term is a convenient way of referring to this momentous decree, it would appear that Caesar was merely describing the nature of the decree and not using a technical term. In any event, the passage of such a decree was a novelty in 121 B.C. While its legitimacy would still be a matter of debate in the 50s B.C. (see Chapter 18), the use of this sort of decree in times of civil unrest was mostly accepted after C. Marius had another such degree passed in 100 B.C. (see Chapter 5).

Aftermath of the Gracchan Period

The years after C. Gracchus's death saw a number of affairs that resulted from his tribunate. Unfortunately, no full narrative survives for these comparatively peaceful years when the senatorial oligarchy resumed reasonably uncontested control of the political scene, so we are dimly informed about the next decade or so and must rely on stray anecdotes to see how certain problems and issues relating to the Gracchi played themselves out.

---

snatched the head from someone else and was thought to have filled the skull with lead to increase the reward!

[23] The Romans worshipped goddesses representing various abstract notions, and a statement of policy could be indicated by building a temple to a suitable goddess.

Trial and Acquittal of L. Opimius

In 120 B.C., L. Opimius ceased to be consul and was tried before the People by a tribune in connection with the death of C. Gracchus. Opimius's advocate in the trial was the consul C. Papirius Carbo, seemingly an odd choice. Carbo had previously been a major supporter of the Gracchi (he was a member of Tiberius's land commission, and as tribune himself in about 131 B.C. he had proposed an unsuccessful bill allowing reelection to the tribunate), but he changed sides at some point before the final downfall of Gaius. Reaching the age for the consulship, Carbo must have wished to regain acceptability within the oligarchy, and in securing election as consul for 120 B.C., he had presumably enjoyed Opimius's support. As all of this illustrates, it was not expected that a Roman politician would hold to a fixed policy over the course of his career. Instead, even though someone may have espoused popularis causes in his earlier career, it would later be natural for him to seek accommodation with the oligarchy as he sought higher office.

As for the trial itself, the sources are sketchy, but it seems that while Carbo admitted Opimius's responsibility for Gaius's death, he argued that it was justified by virtue of the decree of the senate instructing the consuls to defend the state. The argument seems to have been accepted, since Opimius was acquitted. This could thus be taken as implicitly acknowledging the legitimacy of the "final decree of the senate," but it was a second use of the decree under rather different circumstances two decades later that would win general acceptance for the decree (and even then its legitimacy would still be then contested by some).

Trial of Carbo

As soon as Carbo ceased to be consul, he was himself prosecuted by the young nobleman L. Licinius Crassus in 119 B.C. Upon conviction, Carbo committed suicide. Crassus eventually became consul in 95 B.C. and was seen by Cicero as the greatest Roman orator before him. Since in 118 B.C. Crassus took part in a popularis land settlement in Gaul (discussed later), it is reasonable to see the attack on Carbo as a form of vengeance for his defense of C. Gracchus's killer.

Recall of Laenas

We know that Opimius took no action to recall P. Popilius Laenas cos. 132, who had gone into exile to avoid conviction under C. Gracchus's law against trying citizens without popular authorization. At some time soon after Opimius's consulship (and probably as a result of Opimius's acquittal), the interdiction that recognized Laenas's self-imposed exile was repealed.

End of the Gracchan Agrarian Legislation

The ancient evidence is rather meager and contradictory,[24] but within fifteen years of either the death of Ti. Gracchus or (more likely) C. Gracchus, the Gracchan agrarian legislation was gradually repealed. The allotments became full private property that could be sold, and apparently the process by which the wealthy took over the land of the smallholders resumed. In effect, the Gracchan attempt to establish a permanent class of smallholders through land distribution was at an end. Yet, the problem of finding sufficient recruits for the army from the hard-pressed smallholders remained unsolved and would only worsen.

Foundation of Narbo Martius

The meager sources for the decade after C. Gracchus's death give little hint that the senate's control was challenged, but a stray piece of information suggests that the demand for land distribution continued unabated. (It will be remembered that M. Livius Drusus undermined C. Gracchus's support by proposing even more settlements than he did, but these plans were apparently never carried out.) In 118 B.C., L. Licinius Crassus advocated a bill to found a colony in southern Gaul, and he and Cn. Domitius Ahenobarbus, son of the consul of 122 B.C. who had recently played a major role in establishing a new province there (see Chapter 8), were elected as commissioners to found the new colony, which the senate opposed. The details of these events are unknown, but it seems clear that this effort reflects a continuation of the Gracchan agrarian program. The town was called Narbo Martius, and this divine name ("Martius" is the adjective derived from Mars, the god of war) recalls the divine names of C. Gracchus's colonies (e.g., Junonia and Neptunia). While Romans had been settling in large numbers in Spain for some time on a private basis,

---

[24] Appian (*Civil Wars* 1.27) summarizes three laws passed to undo the Gracchan legislation, indicating that the process took place over the fifteen years following the passage of "Gracchus's law." This seems pretty clearly to refer to Tiberius, but parts of a law of 111 B.C. (preserved on a fragmentary inscription, *RS2*) seem to come from one of the laws mentioned by Appian, in which case Appian's dating starts with Gaius (whatever Appian himself may have thought).

the founding of Narbo Martius marked a major step in using territory outside of Italy to solve the Roman agrarian crisis. (In 123 B.C., there were settlements on the Balearic Islands, but these had less dramatic implications for the intrusion of Roman settlement into foreign territory.) Narbo Martius (modern Narbonne) gave its name to the Roman province in southern Gaul, which was called Gallia Narbonensis. It is also to be noted that Crassus and Ahenobarbus were, like the Gracchi, young members of important families who were attempting to win acclaim for themselves at the start of their careers by advocating policies opposed by the senate as a whole. They both would eventually become important members of the oligarchy, and no doubt Ti. Gracchus and perhaps C. Gracchus imagined that they too would follow the same course.

While there was doubtless dispute over these events, there was comparative calm in internal Roman politics until the military disasters of the last decade of the century produced popular resentment against the apparent incompetence and venality of the ruling oligarchy.

Importance of C. Gracchus

C. Gracchus undertook to implement a broad program of reform, by which he tried to remedy what he perceived to be problems in society, especially the inability of the senate to carry out its functions properly. While not inherently antisenatorial, his reforms were opposed by leading members of the senatorial oligarchy. He attempted to win enough support to extend Roman citizenship, but here his opponents cleverly played upon the anxieties and selfishness of the common Romans and completely undermined his support. The next year, his opponents provoked him into rash actions and gained the opportunity to kill him. Once again, opposition to reform resulted in bloodshed, which this time seemed to have received official justification through the *"senatus consultum ultimum"* (and its apparent validation as a result of Opimius's acquittal). While the oligarchy may have had narrow justification for using violence in 133 and 121 B.C. to defend the traditional constitution (and its own prerogatives), the senators would soon find that once the use of violence came to be accepted in the political arena, the sword could easily be turned against them. In any case, Plutarch tells us that statues of the Gracchi were venerated by certain plebeians with quasi-divine honors, and not only would the murdered brothers serve as a model for those who wished to stir up the plebs against the senate, but from now on the populares were a permanent (if fluid) element in Roman politics.

QUESTIONS FOR STUDY AND REFLECTION

1. What was C. Gracchus's attitude toward his brother? Was he antisenatorial?
2. What were Gaius's priorities upon first becoming tribune? How did the laws that he had passed fit into these priorities?
3. What was the purpose of Gaius's law about not trying a Roman without the authorization of the Roman People? What perceived abuses did it correct?
4. How and why did Gaius reform the procedure for trying provincial corruption? Was his law antisenatorial in intent? Why was the composition of the jury panel changed? What side effect did the creation of jurors of equestrian rank have?
5. In what way is it reasonable to view Gaius as having a program of reform? What exactly were his intentions? What groups did he benefit?
6. Why did Italian citizenship become such an important issue for Gaius? Why was his proposal rejected?
7. Why did Gaius lose support during his second term as tribune? What role did C. Fannius and M. Livius Drusus play in this?
8. What role did M. Fulvius Flaccus play in Gaius's second tribunate?
9. What was the legal force and validity of the "final decree of the senate"? What was the relevance of the trial of L. Opimius to this issue?
10. What was the fate of agrarian legislation in the years after the death of C. Gracchus? What was the effect of the legislation? Did it solve the problems it was meant to?
11. Did the way in which the senate reacted to the death of C. Gracchus differ from the situation after the death of Tiberius?

4

Numidia, Senatorial Failures, and the Rise of C. Marius

Situation in the Aftermath of C. Gracchus's Death

The senate managed to overcome the threat that the Gracchi posed to its domination of politics, but the underlying discontent that had allowed the Gracchi to attain prominence remained unresolved. Until the last decade of the second century B.C., the oligarchy continued in its monotonous control of the state with the regular succession of magistrates who have left little impression on the poor historical record for the years after C. Gracchus's death, but the frequent and at times disastrous failures of commanders sent by the senate to deal with military conflicts in Numidia and Gaul would soon create tremendous dissatisfaction among the electorate in Rome, and this tumultuous uproar would lead to the rise of a man who would challenge the oligarchy's control in a way that the Gracchi never had. In addition, the crisis of military recruitment would become intolerable, and this would lead to the adoption of new form of conscription that had ominous consequences for the Republican form of government.

Sallust's *Jugurthine War*

We know a great deal about the course of the war with Jugurtha in Numidia and its political consequences in Rome because C. Sallustius Crispus (known in English as Sallust) wrote a historical monograph on this topic (the *Jugurthine War*) in the 30s B.C. Sallust was a popularis senator who had taken Caesar's side during the civil war of 49–45 B.C. but retired from public life in (he claimed) undeserved disgrace. He then gave vent to his disgust with public life by writing several historical works, and the popularity of his mordent prose style led to the preservation of two: the *Jugurthine War* and the *Catilinarian Conspiracy*. His aim in the former was to show how this war led to the first occasion when the will of the oligarchy was thwarted through popular opposition (*Jugurthine War* 5.2). Unfortunately, in writing of these events many decades after the fact during the death throes of the Republic, Sallust presents a picture that is unsatisfactory in a number of ways. He has a great interest in moralizing, and for this reason he tends to paint an exaggerated picture of the senate's faults and to cast his hero C. Marius in an excessively favorable light. In telling his tale of the nobility's come-uppance, he is careless in matters of chronology and geography, and as an author he is more creditable for rhetorical flair than for historical interpretation. In particular, he analyzes events in terms of a simplistic opposition between the self-interest of Roman politicians and the "public good" that shows little understanding of how the Roman political system actually functioned. Nonetheless, the survival of his monograph gives us a far more detailed picture of the last decade of the second century than would otherwise be the case.

Dynastic Troubles in Numidia and the Rise of Jugurtha

One of the keys to the Roman defeat of the Carthaginians at the conclusion of the Second Punic War was the defection of Carthage's Numidian allies, which was brought about by the Numidian prince Masinissa. He was rewarded with control of all of Numidia (the area to the west of the Carthaginian territory, more or less corresponding to the northern part of modern Algeria). The Numidians were a nomadic people who excelled in horsemanship, but Masinissa attempted to make them adopt a settled agricultural way of life. Upon Masinissa's death in 148 B.C., the kingdom of Numidia was divided by the decision of Scipio Aemilianus. Aemilianus was not only in control of the Roman forces then attacking Carthage but he was also the adoptive grandson of Masinissa's patron Scipio Africanus, who had bestowed the kingdom on Masinissa back in 203 B.C. Aemilianus divided the kingdom among Masinissa's three sons, but two soon died, leaving Micipsa sole king. Micipsa brought into his household Jugurtha, the son of one of his brothers by a concubine. When Micipsa sent forces to assist Aemilianus in his attack on Numantia in 134 B.C., he put Jugurtha in charge of them. In this capacity, Jugurtha not only won the approbation of Aemilianus but became familiar with many men who were to be prominent Roman senators in the years to come. Jugurtha also became skilled in Roman methods of warfare.

Jugurtha entered Micipsa's household when Micipsa was childless, but the king soon fathered two sons, Adherbal and Hiempsal. Micipsa adopted Jugurtha, and made him joint heir with his own sons. When Micipsa died in about 118 B.C., there were plans to divide the kingdom again, but Jugurtha had other ideas. He soon had Hiempsal assassinated, and the kingdom was riven with strife between the supporters of Jugurtha and Adherbal. Adherbal enjoyed more support as the natural heir of the late king, but Jugurtha attracted the bolder spirits. Adherbal's forces were completely defeated, and he fled to Rome, which now became directly involved in the conflict. (Since Rome had long since become the undisputed military power in the Mediterranean basin, it was natural for the senate to be called upon to intervene in the domestic disputes of allied states.) Jugurtha for his part sent envoys to plead his side. The stories told by either side are hard to assess for accuracy, but Jugurtha's envoys used effusive bribery to secure the support of important senators. Some leading members of the senate who noted this supported Adherbal simply as a reaction against the perception of undue influence on Jugurtha's part (or so Sallust would have us believe), but a compromise was reached. The notorious L. Opimius cos. 121 was sent at the head of a commission of ten senators to divide the kingdom between Jugurtha and Adherbal, who respectively received the west and east.[1]

Jugurtha's Conquest of Adherbal's Territory

The chronology of what happened next is uncertain, but the general course of events is clear. Jugurtha attacked Adherbal's kingdom, and a junior senatorial commission was sent to tell him to stop. He ignored this order and besieged Adherbal in his capital, Cirta. In light of this contumely, the

---

[1] It was standard policy during the Middle Republic to send out commissions of senators to deal with important situations in the field. In effect, the senate was not in a position to render a decision at a distance about some complicated matter of foreign policy and so it would delegate its authority to a group of senators (generally numbering ten), who were trusted to make a sensible decision on the spot. Sometimes they were to see to the implementation of a senatorial decision by foreign states (as happened several times during the dynastic struggles in Numidia); sometimes they were to assist Roman magistrates in drawing up the terms that would make a permanent settlement after a war. Such commissions were a reflection of the solidarity of the senatorial oligarchy as a whole during the Middle Republic. Even when an individual magistrate had achieved victory during the war that he had conducted with sole responsibility by virtue of his imperium, the final peace arrangements were settled through the cooperative efforts of the senate as a whole. It is a sign of the trend by which powerful magistrates came to exercise public authority by themselves without reference to the senate that little is heard of such commissions after the Social War of 90–89 B.C.

senate sent a much more prestigious commission headed by M. Aemilius Scaurus cos. 115, who was now the princeps senatus.[2] Jugurtha was summoned to the Roman province of Africa and told to stop, but once more, he ignored the decision of a senatorial commission and pressed home his attack. Adherbal relied on the resident Italian traders as his main troops in the defense of the town, and when these Italians decided that they had had enough of fighting, Adherbal was forced to surrender. The Italians imagined that because of the senate's protection Jugurtha would not dare harm Adherbal, much less themselves. In this they were mistaken: not only did Jugurtha torture Adherbal to death, but he also put his Italian defenders to the sword. This slaughter took place in 112 B.C., before the consular elections.

M. Aemilius Scaurus

A man whom we will see several times playing a prominent role in the late second and early first centuries B.C. is M. Aemilius Scaurus. Although Scaurus possessed the distinction of patrician birth, his family had been unsuccessful for several generations (Sulla would later have to overcome a similarly deficient patrician background). In fact, Scaurus supposedly served as a common soldier and was at first uncertain about pursuing a political career. Nonetheless, despite such a huge disadvantage, through hard work, talent, and good luck, he managed to reach the consulship in 115 B.C. and to marry into the powerful family of the Caecilii Metelli. From then on, he led the dominant group in the senatorial oligarchy and held the position of princeps senatus for more than two decades until his death in about 90 B.C. The exact nature of his control over senatorial deliberations is unclear, but it was presumably based on his ability to manipulate his relations with other senators behind the scenes (one might compare the influence that M. Licinius Crassus would exert in the 60s B.C.). On account of this ability to influence senatorial proceedings, Cicero called him a man "at whose nod the world shook" (*In Defense of Fonteius* 24), words that recalled a phrase used by Homer to describe the power of Zeus, the king of the gods.

L. Bestia's Campaign

When news of Jugurtha's massacre of the Italians reached Rome, the result was an outburst of popular indignation. Numidia was assigned

---

[2] For the importance of the princeps senatus, see Chapter 1.

as a province (area of operation) to one of the consuls of III B.C., and the lot fell to L. Calpurnius Bestia, who engaged the services of the princeps senatus Scaurus as a legate, that is, subordinate commander.[3] Presumably, Bestia wished to take advantage of Scaurus's experience, but given Scaurus's earlier association with the commissions to Numidia, Bestia's use of Scaurus would later contribute to the belief that Bestia received bribes from Jugurtha. In any case, Bestia invaded Jugurtha's territory but soon reached an agreement with him. When the terms became known at Rome, however, they were considered too lenient, and the indignant electorate was abuzz with rumors that bribery was the cause of Bestia's supposed mildness. C. Memmius, who was one of the tribunes, then took the surprising step of passing a law ordering one of the praetors to fetch Jugurtha under safe-conduct. The astonishing proposition that a foreign leader against whom the Roman People were at that moment waging war should be brought to Rome to give evidence against some of the most prominent members of the senate shows how far public distrust of and dissatisfaction with the senatorial oligarchy had gone. In the event, when Jugurtha was brought before a contio to reveal those whom he had bribed, the veto of another tribune prevented him from speaking. Before leaving Italy, Jugurtha had one of his retainers arrange an assassination attempt on one of Jugurtha's cousins, who was a claimant for the Numidian throne. The assassins were caught and Jugurtha's role revealed. Needless to say, this attempted skullduggery further blackened Jugurtha's reputation, and no doubt helped to increased public indignation at the members of the oligarchy who were thought to be acting in cahoots with him.

Sp. Postumius Albinus's campaign

As a result of the popular indignation, Bestia's agreement with Jugurtha was repudiated, and the war resumed. The command fell to Sp. Postumius Albinus, one of the consuls of IIO B.C. He had not achieved much in

---

[3] The term "legate" (*legatus*) has two distinct but related meanings. Literally signifying someone "bound" (i.e., to carry out a task), it referred to senators who were dispatched by the senate on commissions. In a process whose origins are unclear, magistrates with imperium began to use such legates as senior military subordinates. (Otherwise, the only other obvious choice for selection as a senior officer was the quaestor, who was comparatively young, and in any case each magistrate had only one.) In this sense of the word, the legate was appointed by the senate, but the senate normally did so at the request of the magistrate, who could thereby gain the services of men whom he trusted to act as his direct subordinates.

Numidia before he had to return to Rome in the fall to preside over the consular elections, leaving his brother Aulus in charge. Aulus so bungled an attempt to capture a Numidian town (his intention was supposedly to seize plunder) that when his camp was surrounded, the Roman army was forced to surrender, and Aulus agreed to withdraw from Numidia within ten days. Whatever the truth about Aulus's motives, his manifest incompetence, following on the heels of his brother's failure to make any noticeable headway against Jugurtha, seemed to provide even more proof that the senate could not carry out its most basic function, that is, provide able commanders for the Roman military.

REACTION IN ROME

All hell broke loose when news of this debacle arrived, and the tribunes of 109 B.C. were the conduit for popular outrage at the incompetence of the senate's handling of affairs in Numidia. Disapproval of the senate was heightened by military failure elsewhere. In 113 B.C., Cn. Papirius Carbo, the governor of Macedonia, had provoked a battle against a Germanic tribe called the Cimbri, and his army was totally destroyed (see Chapter 8). By 109 B.C., the Cimbri had migrated into Gaul, where the consul M. Junius Silanus suffered another catastrophic defeat at their hands. It seemed as if the ruling oligarchy was no longer capable of producing effective magistrates, and the rumors of bribery seemed to provide the explanation of this incompetence.

ASSESSING SENATORIAL "BRIBE TAKING"

Sallust bases his account of Jugurtha's interactions with various members of the Roman senate over the years upon a straightforward contrast between the personal relations between the Numidian king and individual Romans on the one hand and the supposedly objective "public good" on the other, presenting the former as an immoral activity by which the latter was subverted. In effect, Sallust thought that any decisions based on personal relations (which in his mind necessarily involved bribery) were inherently suspect, and he subscribed fully to the widespread view current in 109 B.C. that Jugurtha had been managing to get his way through bribery – first when the intervention of several senatorial legations failed to restrain him and then when the Roman war effort did not result in quick victory. Sallust's contrast of personal influence and public good is a facile conception, however, and it flies in the face of all that we know of the way in which public business was conducted under the Republic.

The reality was more complicated than Sallust's simplistic moralizing would suggest. In the first place, while Jugurtha may well have used his personal connections for his own benefit, there is no evidence that the legates acted in bad faith (and of course it was easy to make accusations of bribery after the fact). Rather, Jugurtha used the negotiations as a means of thwarting Roman interference in his plans for as long as possible. Fundamentally, it was only through the use of force that the senate could impose its will upon a recalcitrant Jugurtha. But it naturally took several years before it became obvious that Jugurtha was unwilling to comply with the senate's decisions and eventually the use of force is exactly what was resorted to.

As for the war itself, it is hard to imagine that any Roman commander would have thought any bribe more valuable than the prestige that was to be won through victory in the field. No doubt Jugurtha's friends were happy to receive a monetary token of his appreciation, but that is not the same thing as saying that they were consciously subverting the public good as a result of Jugurtha's favors. Since we do not know the terms that Bestia granted, it is impossible to assess their supposed leniency, but the rejection of those terms could well have been engineered on behalf of the next year's consuls, who would have wanted a share in the glory for themselves and thus had an interest in making sure that the war continued (such machinations are amply attested earlier in the century, when the senate rejected peace agreements made by retiring commanders in Spain). As for the military disaster of 110 B.C., this seems to be attributable merely to the incompetence of A. Postumius Albinus. The charges of bribery and venality, then, are likely to be the result of popular frustration with the conduct of the war.

Basically, the senators were interacting with Jugurtha in the way that they would deal with any Roman ally, and this was considered a fault once Jugurtha's headstrong behavior resulted in a military conflict that could not be brought to a swift and victorious conclusion. This is not to say that there was no failure in the execution of Roman policy, but it was frequently the case that the ultimately successful wars of the Middle Republic began in a bumbling fashion (notably the Third Macedonian and Third Punic Wars), and that it took a few elections (and years without victory) until a competent commander was chosen.

QUAESTIO MAMILIA

The tribune C. Mamilius had a law passed authorizing a special court or *quaestio* to investigate charges of bribery (the *quaestio Mamilia*). Three presiding magistrates (heads of the courts) were to be chosen by election to preside over various trials in this court, and it is remarkable that one of those elected was M. Aemilius Scaurus, the princeps senatus. This seemingly peculiar circumstance shows that matters were not clear-cut. Since he had headed one of the senatorial commissions disregarded by Jugurtha and then had actually participated in the war on Bestia's staff, Scaurus ought to have been a prime target of suspicion, but support for him was strong enough to win him a place presiding over the very court before which he might have been haled. In any case, the jurors were chosen from the album of the jurors for the *quaestio de pecuniis repetundis* (provincial extortion court), that is, the equestrians first enrolled under C. Gracchus's legislation. In light of the people who were convicted – these included L. Bestia cos. 111, who as tribune in 120 had passed legislation recalling P. Popillius Laenas cos. 132 from exile, Sp. Albinus cos. 110, and L. Opimius cos. 121, the killer of C. Gracchus – Cicero (*Brutus* 128) called these jurors "Gracchan jurors" (*Gracchani iudices*, with the Latin adjective suggesting adherence to a political faction), which suggests that they were motivated by a spirit of revenge. This seems to be a simplistic explanation. These jurors may well have received some satisfaction at the downfall of Gracchus's opponents, but there is no sign of an antisenatorial attitude on the part of the jurors before this time. It seems much more likely that the motivation for the convictions was simply popular dissatisfaction with the perceived military incompetence of oligarchy.

Q. Metellus in Numidia

Even as the quaestio Mamilia was ostensibly wreaking vengeance on those who had brought about the previous failure to subdue Jugurtha by arms, the war against Jugurtha was resumed under the command of one of the new consuls for 109 B.C., Q. Caecilius Metellus. The Caecilii Metelli had been prominent since the First Punic War, and large numbers of this consul's brothers and cousins were reaching the consulship at the end of the second century. As consul, Metellus invaded Numidia and soon won a battle against Jugurtha. This victory showed the difficulties of the campaign. Jugurtha escaped to raise another army, so mere victory in the field was of limited value. Jugurtha's ability to wage war had to be circumscribed, and final victory in the war would only be achieved once he was eliminated. Hence, in order to achieve the first goal, Metellus spent the rest of his consulship seizing and occupying towns in Numidia. Metellus's command was prorogued for the next year (108 B.C.), when he continued his methodical and gradual subjugation of the country. He again defeated Jugurtha, who withdrew to the south, raised another army, and secured the reluctant cooperation of his father-in-law Bocchus, the king of Mauretania (the area along the North African shore to the west of Numidia). It is at this point that Metellus's legate C. Marius sought permission to return to Rome to run for the consulship.

IMPORTANCE OF C. MARIUS

The career of C. Marius illustrates a number of the trends that would lead to the fall of the Republic. He was a novus homo (man without senatorial forebears) from the Italian countryside who came to prominence in Rome through military competence and whom the oligarchy had a hard time assimilating into the "system." He was given unprecedented power at Rome to deal with a military emergency, a situation that led to the bending of accepted constitutional practice. Finally, he instituted a military reform that ended the raising of troops only from those who owned land. In the long run, this reform would entirely change the relationship of the troops to the state, which would be an important factor in the subversion of the Republican political order.

MARIUS'S EARLY CAREER

Marius was born ca. 157 B.C. in the town of Arpinum in southern Latium. The town had been conquered by the Romans in the late fifth century and was given Roman citizenship without voting rights. Only in 188 B.C. did the town receive full citizenship, and his family, which was of equestrian status, had ancestral connections with the nobility in Rome. While his family was important locally, it was of no prominence at all in terms of the electoral system in Rome, and the problems faced by Marius in his early career there illustrate the difficulties that faced a "new man" who embarked on a political career.

Prior to 135 B.C., Marius began his military service in some capacity in the army that became demoralized in the war with Numantia, and his bravery brought him to the attention of Scipio Aemilianus. It would seem that from an early time Marius was interested in pursuing a political career in Rome. He ran for election as one of the twenty-four special military tribunes of the first four legions who were elected (the rest were appointed by the magistrate who raised the legion). Sallust tells us (*Jugurthine War* 63.4) that he was unknown by sight to the electors but was returned by all the tribes on the basis of his accomplishments.

We next learn that he ran for the quaestorship after losing a local election in Arpinum. This is hard to interpret. (His earlier military tribunate shows that he already was interested in Roman politics before the quaestorship, so it is unclear why he should have been continuing to seek office back home.) Nothing is known of what he did as quaestor.

In 120 B.C., Marius was returned as tribune of the plebs for the following year. It appears that he had already lost an earlier attempt (in 121 for 120 B.C.?). He won with the support of a Caecilius Metellus, who was his hereditary patron (that is, Marius's ancestors had been clients of the Caecilii Metelli). During his tribunate, Marius pursued a popularis line. He passed a law that restricted the interference of the wealthy in elections. In the 130s B.C., voting by ballot had been introduced in elections, but the wealthy continued to try to influence the voting by inspecting ballots. To counter this, Marius's law provided for the narrowing of the passages down which voters passed to cast their votes in order to prevent outsiders from accosting the electors. In the passage of this law, Marius alienated the Metelli, who opposed it.

Soon thereafter, Marius ran for the curule aedileship, and after losing he ran unsuccessfully for the plebeian aedileship.[4] In 116 B.C., he was the last candidate to be returned as praetor for 115 B.C.[5] He was promptly accused of *ambitus* (electoral corruption) and barely managed to secure an acquittal. After he spent an uneventful year as praetor in Rome, Marius's imperium was prorogued for 114 B.C., and he was sent to govern Further Spain, where he won success suppressing brigands (that is, armed gangs in the countryside, an occupation that was considered acceptable to some of the natives but not to the Romans).

Marius received no triumph on his return and did not run for the consulship. At about this time, however, he did contract a prestigious marriage with Julia, the aunt of C. Julius Caesar (the famous Julius Caesar).[6] The Julii Caesares were a patrician family, but at this period they seem to have found it hard to advance above the praetorship (only once in the second century B.C. was a Julius Caesar consul, back in 157 B.C.). Marius had apparently achieved some substantial position by this point, to judge by

---

4   At this time, the office of aedile alternated between two curule aediles one year and two plebeian ones the next. Originally, only patricians could hold the curule aedileship, but by this time anyone could run for the office.

5   The order in which the winning candidates were returned was noted, and throughout their term, the colleagues in a given magistracy position would be listed in the order in which they were returned, from first to last.

6   Since Marius's son must have been born in 109/08 B.C., the marriage probably took place in about 110 B.C.

this marriage, but given his unspectacular career so far, Marius could not have reasonably expected any further advancement. The course of events in Numidia, however, would allow him to advance his career in a way that no one could have foreseen.

Legate to Metellus

As previously noted, the Marii were the hereditary clients of the Caecilii Metelli, and a Caecilius Metellus had aided Marius's campaign for the tribunate. Although he seems to have had a break with the Metelli as a result of his tribunate, the rupture was not permanent, since Q. Caecilius Metellus cos. 109 took Marius with him as his legate (subordinate commander) on his campaign against Jugurtha. (The rupture of 119 B.C. may have been exaggerated after the fact in light of his later, much more serious disagreement with Metellus about Numidia.) Clearly, Metellus must have had confidence in Marius's military abilities and trusted his loyalty.[7] For his part, Marius's intention may have been to strengthen his position as a candidate for the consulship, though it is more likely that he had no such plans before the start of the campaign. In any case, Marius and Metellus were to have a falling out over Marius's consular ambitions.

Marius's Run for the Consulship

After serving successfully as Metellus's legate for a year in Numidia, Marius decided in 108 B.C. to run for the consulship. He apparently sought permission from Metellus to go to Rome to do so, and Metellus urged him not to, supposedly advising him to wait until he could run in conjunction with Metellus's son. Since this son was only twenty, the proposed joint bid for the consulship would not take place until twenty years later, and it is hard to interpret this remark (if correctly reported) as signifying anything but irony or insult. Marius did not acquiesce, and he is said to have spent the summer of 108 B.C. ingratiating himself with the troops by relaxing military discipline and with the local Italian traders by claiming that he could capture Jugurtha in a few days with half of Metellus's forces. Both

---

7 It was natural for noble families to make use of the important small-town families that were associated with them. We have another example of such a relationship from Arpinum. Cicero's family belonged to the group of leading families that also included the Marii. In the late second century Cicero's grandfather was on close terms with M. Scaurus cos. 115, who praised him for resisting local legislation to institute the secret ballot, and the elder Cicero served on the staff of M. Antonius cos. 99 when he was sent as praetor in 102 B.C. to deal with pirates in Cilicia (see Chapter 8).

groups then wrote home in praise of Marius, insisting that unlike Metellus he could end the war quickly. In fact, Metellus's policy of methodically subduing the countryside was a rational course of action that had been drawn up in light of previous experience, but it did not promise the quick solution that was desired back in Rome. Eventually, Metellus gave in to Marius's request to return to Rome, realizing that it was counterproductive to have a resentful subordinate.

MARIUS WINS THE CONSULSHIP, SECURES COMMAND IN NUMIDIA

Under the circumstances, it is not difficult to understand why Marius was triumphantly elected consul in late 108 for 107 B.C. He was campaigning against Metellus's apparent lack of decisive action against Jugurtha, and given the repeated military debacles from 113 to 109 B.C. and the accusations that the oligarchy was open to flagrant bribery, it was natural for the electorate in Rome to look favorably upon the virtuous new man who had with difficulty worked his way up the ladder of offices as an alternative to the apparently inept and corrupt nobility.

The senate had a trick up its sleeve to thwart the ambitions of the new man (and the apparent popular will). The provisions of C. Gracchus's lex Sempronia on consular provinces prescribed that every year the senate was to determine the consular provinces for the next year before the elections (see Chapter 3), and the senate decided not to make the war against Jugurtha one of the provinces and instead prorogued Metellus in Numidia. Thus, while the senate was in no position to prevent Marius's election, they could refuse to give him the command in Africa on account of which he had been elected. (And in any case, a man as prominent as Metellus had a great deal of influence in the senate, and naturally he and his associates would have striven to keep him in command.) Marius got around the senate's decision by using a ploy that had previously been used by the consul Crassus Mucianus in 131 B.C. In that year, there was a prolonged dispute as to who should command the war against Aristonicus in Asia, and in the end a tribune had passed a law to settle the matter through popular decision by authorizing an election to select the commander (see Chapter 2). A similar tribunician law was passed on Marius's behalf in 108 B.C., and Marius was voted the command by the People in this special election. Not surprisingly, Metellus was embittered when he learned that his command was to be taken away from him through popular vote and given to a man whom he clearly considered his social and political inferior (and whom he refused to meet again when Marius arrived in Africa). Upon his return home, the senate showed its support of Metellus by granting him a triumph and bestowing upon him the title Numidicus ("conqueror of Numidia"; see Appendix on Roman names). Strictly speaking, Metellus was entitled to neither, since he had not ended the war in Numidia, but the intention was to snub Marius, since Metellus's awards implied that it was he who had really conquered the area as a result of his methodical campaigns of 109 and 108 B.C. This was just the first in a number of instances where the senate refused recognition to the outsider Marius, whose resentment would many years later play a major role in the first outbreak of open civil war in Rome.

Change in Recruitment Policy

Marius needed more troops, and to conduct the levy he made a change in the procedure used for recruiting them. This change would have grave consequences for the future, but undoubtedly Marius was totally unaware of these momentous implications. All of the Gracchan agrarian reforms had been premised on the traditional Roman levy, which excluded from service those whose property fell below the minimum qualification for the fifth census class. The Gracchi had tried to restore the smallholders who would constitute the majority of those qualified to serve. The repeal of the Gracchan land legislation did nothing to change the military crisis that gave rise to that legislation. It seems that the minimum qualification for the fifth census class (the lowest one eligible for military service) was lowered from 11,000 to 3,000 sesterces of property, and already in 109 B.C., the consuls had had to seek suspension of C. Gracchus's restrictions on the levy (see Chapter 3) to find enough conscripts. In 107 B.C., Marius cut the Gordian knot by deciding to ignore the census qualification altogether and conduct the levy with no inquiry into the property of the potential soldiers. From now on, Rome's legions would largely consist of poor citizens whose future after service could only be assured if their general could somehow bring about a land distribution on their behalf. This new circumstance resulted in a fundamental change in the relationship between the common soldiery and the political system.

Previously, the electoral decisions of the centuriate assembly, which chose the magistrates who possessed imperium, that is, the commanders of the armies, had been determined by the landowners large and small who would serve in those armies. In effect, the political system in Rome could be viewed as a comfortable mechanism by which the smallholders who provided the regular soldiery cooperated with the major landowners who provided the magistrates in assuring competent commanders for the armies. Thus, the old smallholders/soldiers had had a clear stake in the efficient functioning of the senatorial oligarchy. The new class from which the soldiery was to be raised from now on would have no interest in the traditional privileges of the senate or the electoral system in Rome (by definition, the class of voters from which the soldiery would now be selected was lumped into a single century in the centuriate assembly and had no influence whatsoever in elections carried out in that assembly). This situation would only become worse with the expansion of Roman citizenship to all of Italy as a result of the Social War. The newly enfranchised rural poor who lived at a great distance from Rome undoubtedly seldom if ever took part in the electoral process there.

Instead, the new soldiers wanted to be given a plot of land upon discharge. In the absence of any system of pensions, a plot of land was the only feasible way in antiquity to ensure an income in one's old age, and just as in the past the victorious magistrate had been expected to share the booty with his troops, in later years the soldiery would expect their commander to provide them with land. In effect, this new sort of personal self-interest made the soldiery far more loyal to their commander, and this circumstance would eventually overcome whatever theoretical allegiance they felt for the traditional constitutional order. On the other hand, as a result of its experience with the Gracchi, the senatorial oligarchy developed an ingrained hostility on principle to any schemes of land distribution and thus would attempt to thwart land grants for veterans. Furthermore, even if such grants were not viewed as inherently suspect, it was feared that the general who made such distributions would acquire an inordinate degree of support from those whom he thereby benefited, which would threaten the equilibrium of the oligarchy. Thus, the soldiers had a very strong personal interest in supporting their general against both the senate (i.e., the oligarchy) and the "public interest" (which was often equated with the senate). Marius did not avail himself of this potential source of support (and probably did not even understand the long-term implications of his innovation), but in less than two decades Marius's ex-quaestor Sulla would use it against Marius – with disastrous consequences for the Republican political order.

VICTORY IN THE WAR IN NUMIDIA

Once Marius took over operations in Numidia, he found that it was not as easy to end the war as he had claimed. He arrived comparatively late in 107 B.C., and in that year and the next he forced Jugurtha to the south and west toward Mauretania. Marius's quaestor in 107 B.C. had been L. Cornelius

Sulla, the son of a patrician family that had fallen on hard times. Marius was supposedly unhappy at receiving this dissolute young man as his subordinate, but Sulla proved a competent military leader. By 105 B.C., King Bocchus of Mauretania, Jugurtha's father-in-law and reluctant ally, was worried about the approaching Romans. After receiving word that an accommodation with them was possible, Bocchus insisted that Sulla make the hazardous journey to his capital. There, Sulla induced Bocchus to betray Jugurtha, who was duly handed over to Sulla, and this brought the war to a close. The fact that the war was caused by nothing more than Jugurtha's ambitions is shown by the settlement after his death. No territory was added to the Roman province of Africa, Numidia was given to Jugurtha's brother, and Bocchus was left undisturbed in Mauretania. Clearly, the Romans were happy enough with the territorial arrangements as they stood before the war.

There would later be dispute about who should be credited for ending the war, but there was really no doubt about the matter from a technical point of view. Since Marius held the imperium and Sulla was acting under his auspices,[8] the honor of capturing Jugurtha belonged strictly to Marius, but Sulla had clearly been the immediate agent of the capture (he had a signet ring made for himself commemorating the event). The issue was not contested at the time, but Sulla would later claim that the credit for ending the war was his, and this would cause a feud between him and Marius that was to have dire consequences in the late 90s B.C.

If this were all there was to the story of Marius, his unexpected rise to the consulship against the will of the oligarchy would have been remarkable enough but not an event of long-term significance. As it was, Marius was now the hero of the day, and yet another major military disaster brought about by a member of the senatorial oligarchy would shatter the oligarchy's control of the state (temporarily at any rate) and bring Marius to a level of personal power that was unheard of.

QUESTIONS FOR STUDY AND REFLECTION

1. What was Jugurtha's ambition? What was the senate's reaction? How did the senate attempt to impose its will on him? How did he thwart the senate?
2. Why exactly was war declared against Jugurtha?

---

[8] The "auspices" (*auspicia*) signifies the exclusive right of the holder of imperium to consult the will of Jupiter. Strictly speaking, the auspices were taken through the observation of the behavior of birds, but other (more convenient) sorts of divination had long since been adopted.

3. Was there anything illegal or immoral in senatorial dealings with Jugurtha? What consequences did popular perceptions of senatorial malfeasance have in Rome?
4. What was the purpose of the quaestio Mamilia? Was there anything antisenatorial in the behavior of its equestrian jurors?
5. What was Metellus's strategy in Numidia? Was it a successful one? What was Marius's strategy?
6. Why was there such discontent in Rome with the senate? How did this contribute to Marius's first election as consul?
7. What were Marius's origins? What relations did he have with the Metelli?
8. In what way was Marius's election to the consulship remarkable? How did the senate react to it? What was unusual in the way that Marius received command in Numidia? What precedent was there for this?
9. How and why did Marius change the method of conducting the levy? Why did the reforms of the Gracchi fail to solve the problems relating to conscription? What were the long-term implications of the new method of conscription?

5

ASCENDANCY OF C. MARIUS

DEFEATS AT THE HANDS OF THE CIMBRI AND TEUTONI

At the same time that mismanagement in foreign affairs and the failure to secure victory in Numidia were undermining the senate's political position in Rome, a situation arose in Gaul that would lead to even more trouble for the oligarchy. A major source of disturbance in the late second century B.C. were the Germanic Cimbri and the associated tribe of the Teutoni (or Teutones). The Cimbri apparently came from Jutland (Denmark), from which they emigrated in the second century B.C. Eventually, they reached the territory of the Celtic Boii in central Europe, by whom they were forced to move southward. By 113 B.C., they appeared in western Illyricum, where they were thought to pose a threat to Italy, so the consul Cn. Papirius Carbo (brother of the onetime Gracchan C. Carbo cos. 120, who defended L. Opimius against the charge of murdering C. Gracchus in 120 B.C.) was dispatched to the area. Carbo then needlessly attacked the Cimbri (they had offered to withdraw) and was rewarded for his troubles with a severe defeat at their hands in the battle of Noreia (a town in Noricum, in the area of modern Austria). They then migrated westward in the company of another Germanic tribe, the Teutoni, and after passing through what is now Switzerland, they had reached Gaul by 110 B.C., where they threatened the Roman province of Narbonensis to the south. In the next year, their complete defeat of the consul M. Junius Silanus resulted in unrest among the Celtic tribes recently conquered by the Romans in southern Gaul. In 107 B.C., the consul L. Cassius Longinus suffered a major defeat at the hands of a local tribe (the Tigurini) cooperating with the Cimbri and Teutoni, and the senior surviving officer (C. Popillius Laenas, son of C. Gracchus's enemy,

P. Laenas cos.132) managed to save what was left only by surrendering half the baggage and submitting to the humiliation of having the army "march under the yoke." Once again, perceived ineptitude on the part of senatorial commanders resulted in legal action. When Laenas returned to Rome in 107 B.C., he was accused before the People of *perduellio* (the old-fashioned charge of treason) and rather churlishly convicted. He argued that it was better to lose some baggage than an entire army, and since he was only a legate, one could hardly blame him for extricating the army he took over from the disastrous position into which the now dead consul had put it. Since a number of the men convicted by the quaestio Mamilia had acted in various ways that could be taken as anti-Gracchan (see Chapter 4), it is conceivable that hostility toward Laenas's father had something to do with his conviction, but it is more likely that the jurors were giving vent to the general anger felt about the defeat against the only person available. In any case, the Cimbri would soon inflict a far worse defeat on the Romans, in circumstances that would bring the senate into even greater disrepute.

Senatorial Reaction and the
Lex Servilia Iudiciaria

By 107 B.C., the oligarchy was clearly under attack, with its commanders in Gaul suffering several defeats and the command of the war in Numidia transferred to the outsider Marius. It responded by securing the consulship of 106 B.C. for Q. Servilius Caepio, a man who was clearly intent on upholding the senate's position against those who were assailing it. The most important step that Caepio took was the passage of the *lex Servilia iudiciaria* ("Servilian law on courts"). It seems that the sole purpose of this law was to change the composition of the jury boards. When new quaestiones were established, their jurors were drawn from the album of the first quaestio with a fixed and permanent album, the quaestio de pecuniis repetundis set up by Gaius Gracchus in 123 B.C. (see Chapter 3). Hence, the jurors for the quaestio Mamilia in 109 B.C. were, as Cicero characterized them, *Gracchani iudices*, that is, jurors of equestrian rank who supposedly looked favorably on the man who first installed them in their position on the album. Whatever the truth about this charge, the equestrian jurors clearly had no qualms about convicting senators brought before them, and the senators of the time believed the courts to be biased for political reasons. Caepio seems to have tried to rectify the situation by instituting a mixture of senators and equites (the sources are divided about the exact composition of the new jury panels). The equites resented having control of the album of jurors taken from them and were thus hostile to Caepio. They would get the chance to avenge themselves on Caepio after his arrogance caused a massive Roman defeat in Gaul.

Disaster at Arausio

While still consul in 106 B.C., Caepio marched to Gaul and captured the disloyal community of Tolosa (modern Toulouse), where a huge sum of money was taken from shrines but mysteriously vanished while being transported to Massilia. Caepio was prorogued into the next year, when one of the new consuls, Cn. Mallius Maximus, also operated in southern Gaul. Mallius was a new man like Marius, and he and the noble Caepio found it impossible to cooperate. At this time, the Cimbri and the Teutoni appeared along the Rhône River, and Caepio, who was encamped on the west bank, refused to come to the aid of Mallius on the other bank. Eventually the senate persuaded a reluctant Caepio to cooperate, but even when he crossed the river to help the threatened Mallius, he refused to join forces and kept his own a fair distance away. The result of Caepio's obstinate haughtiness was a massive Roman defeat near the town of Arausio, since the unnecessarily great distance between the two Roman camps meant that when the Germans attacked the separated armies, the Romans were unable to render assistance to each other. The Germans first routed Caepio, then destroyed Mallius's army on October 6, 105 B.C. Since the Romans fought with the river at their back, flight was not possible and the number of deaths reportedly amounted to 80,000. The losses in the preceding decade had been bad enough, but this defeat, apparently caused by the arrogance of the nobility and its refusal to cooperate with talented non-nobles, was the last straw. Not only had huge numbers of Romans lost their lives, but Italy itself was now exposed to invasion from barbarian hordes. Popular dissatisfaction with the oligarchy reached its pinnacle.

Reaction to the Defeat at Arausio

In Rome, reaction to the disaster at Arausio was swift. Already in 105 B.C., the People passed a law abrogating (canceling) Caepio's imperium. This act shows the depth of popular dissatisfaction with this defender of the oligarchy: it was an unprecedented move to take away the imperium of an unsuccessful commander. The hostility toward Caepio would continue the following year in the form of further tribunician agitation.

The tribune L. Cassius Longinus (not to be confused with the consul of 107 B.C.) passed a law in 104 B.C. expelling from the senate anyone whose imperium had been abrogated. Another action taken against Caepio was the establishment of a quaestio to investigate the mysterious disappearance of the plunder that had gone astray after the capture of Tolosa back in 106 B.C. Since Caepio was still around to be tried again the following year, it would seem that he either escaped conviction (perhaps not impossible given his own lex iudiciaria, which put senators on the album for the jurors) or conviction in this court was not capital. Since others were convicted, it is hard to imagine that Caepio was not.

It is noteworthy that those most responsible for the agitation in 104 B.C. were members of the high nobility: L. Cassius Longinus, Cn. Domitius Ahenobarbus (son of the consul of 122 B.C. who defeated the Gauls, and one of the popularis founders of Narbo Martius in 118 B.C.), and L. Marcius Philippus (who proposed an agrarian bill in this year but was to be a major defender of the oligarchy as consul in 91 B.C.). These men were clearly not riff-raff but junior members of the oligarchy, who championed popular discontent to further their own ends. Specifically, they were opposed to the dominant faction within the senate that was centered around the Caecilii Metelli. In effect, these men belonged to a group outside of power that wanted to bring down those who controlled the senate.

One can see this especially clearly in the behavior of Ahenobarbus. He was rejected for membership by two major priesthoods of the state religion (augurs and pontiffs), and in retaliation he unsuccessfully charged M. Aemilius Scaurus cos. 115 (the princeps senatus) with neglecting his priestly duties. Finally, he passed a law removing from the priestly colleges the right of coopting new members themselves, replacing this procedure with popular election (he himself gained election under the new system). Ahenobarbus also unsuccessfully prosecuted (presumably for treason) M. Junius Silanus, who as consul in 109 B.C. had suffered a disastrous defeat at the hands of the Cimbri. Unlike C. Gracchus with his carefully thought-out program of reform, Ahenobarbus was using the popular resentment caused by the string of military defeats for the basically selfish purposes of attacking his enemies within the oligarchy and furthering his own career. In the next year, L. Appuleius Saturninus and his supporters would carry on a more thoroughgoing assault on the senatorial oligarchy.

Marius's Repeated Consulships

The consular elections for 104 B.C. had been conducted in the fall of the previous year after news of the debacle at Arausio reached Rome. Though at that time Marius was still serving as proconsul in Numidia, he was elected consul for a second time both because of his military success and because he was known to be an outsider who had already reached the highest position in the state by his own merits – despite the hostility and opposition of the senatorial oligarchy. Election in absentia was unusual enough, but by 135 B.C. a law had been passed prohibiting second consulships altogether. This law must have been repealed in 105 B.C., since the crisis caused by threat of the Cimbri and Teutoni resulted in Marius being elected to an unprecedented five successive consulships (104–100 B.C.). It was felt that a new man was needed to counteract the perceived incompetence of the military commanders drawn from the senatorial nobility, and Marius's continued successes led to his repeated reelection – much against the will of the senatorial oligarchy. He had returned to Rome by January 1, 104 B.C., when he celebrated his triumph over Jugurtha, who was first led in the procession, then strangled in the public prison. (For a possible reference to this triumph on the coinage, see Coin 5.)

Preparations for a Showdown

with the Germans

As Marius prepared an army to face the Cimbri and Teutoni, they conveniently allowed him time to train his new forces (a task already started in the aftermath of Arausio by P. Rutilius Rufus, Mallius's colleague as consul in 105 B.C.). While the Cimbri marched into Spain, the Teutoni milled around in northern Gaul, which allowed Marius to avoid the dangers of engaging in battle with a newly raised and unseasoned army. This long period of training goes some way to explain the apparent ease with which Marius's forces defeated the Cimbri and Teutoni. (Incidentally, one of Marius's legates was his old quaestor L. Sulla, which shows that at this time there was no ill will between them.)

In 104 B.C., Marius was returned as consul again for 103 B.C. Though he could have continued to operate as proconsul, it seems that holding a consulship would make his position as commander unassailable and avoid any problems with the new consuls that wmight arise if he was only a proconsul. After all, the proconsul Caepio had caused the disaster at Arausio by refusing to cooperate with the novus homo consul Cn. Mallius: how much more likely would a similar conflict be if the roles were reversed, with the proconsul being a new man and the consul a member of the nobility? The People were eager to give Marius whatever he wanted, and it even seems that his support determined who the People would elect as his colleagues (his choice was supposedly determined on the basis of their malleability). In 103 B.C., the Cimbri continued their depredations in Spain, and Marius's colleague opportunely died, so Marius himself had to return to Rome to oversee the elections, in which he was returned once more as consul.

In 102 B.C., the Cimbri finally returned to Gaul from Spain, and they and the Teutoni decided to invade Italy. The Teutoni were to head south and advance toward Italy along the Mediterranean coast, the Cimbri were to attempt to enter Italy from the northwest by the Brenner Pass through the Alps, and the Tigurini (the Celtic tribe who had defeated the consul Longinus in 107 B.C.) were to cross the Alps from the northeast. Such a division of forces may have been necessary because it would have been difficult to find sufficient supplies along the way if everyone followed the same path, but this course of action proved to be disastrous. The division made each contingent manageable for the Romans, who could use their shorter lines of communication to concentrate their forces at will against the individual contingents and defeat them piecemeal.

Battle of Aquae Sextiae

First, Marius had to deal with the Teutoni, who were in the province of Narbonensis marching toward the Alps. Refusing to give battle where they wanted, he withdrew to Aquae Sextiae, which blocked their path into Italy. The leading contingent of the Germans, the Ambrones, foolishly attacked the Roman position without waiting for reinforcements, and 30,000 were killed. Marius then hid 3,000 troops in ambush, so that when the main German contingent finally attacked, the concealed Roman troops could fall upon them from behind. In the ensuing defeat, the Teutoni were completely annihilated, supposedly to the number of something over 100,000. Regardless of the exact numbers, Marius had finally managed to halt the string of defeats that had been inflicted upon Roman armies by the Germans. That this improvement in Roman fortunes had been brought about by a man from outside the senatorial oligarchy must have been as galling to the nobility as it would have been pleasing to the enemies of the senate.

Battle of Vercellae

Marius's colleague, Q. Lutatius Catulus cos. 102, did not enjoy the same success. He botched the job of holding the Brenner Pass, which allowed the Cimbri to advance into northern Italy in late 102 B.C. By now, Marius was in Rome, and after securing reelection yet again as consul for 101 B.C., he deferred his triumph over the Teutoni and marched north to join Catulus, whose command was prorogued into 101 B.C. Finally, in the summer of 101 B.C., a battle was fought at Vercellae in Cisalpine Gaul. Once again, Roman discipline was able to overcome larger numbers of less disciplined tribal forces. At least 65,000 Cimbri were killed (again perhaps as many as 100,000) and all the remainder enslaved. The Tigurini gave up their efforts to enter Italy from the northeast and went home. Catulus and Marius celebrated a joint triumph, but in popular thinking all the credit went to Marius. Catulus became alienated from Marius and would later act as one of his chief opponents. Once more, the outsider Marius had achieved victory when the magistrates belonging to the senatorial oligarchy had failed. As a sort of reward for his victories (the danger was now gone), Marius was returned as consul yet again, for 100 B.C. This year would not go well for Marius.

L. APPULEIUS SATURNINUS

From 103 B.C. on, Marius enlisted the services of L. Appuleius Saturninus, who belonged to a praetorian family (that is, a family that had attained the praetorship in the past but never managed to reach the consulship). Saturninus enacted a number of important pieces of legislation on Marius's behalf but also worked for himself, in the process earning the ill will of Marius, who was in the end responsible for Saturninus's death. Unfortunately, we have no full, reliable narrative for these tumultuous years but instead have to make use of short, inconsistent, and contradictory notices in various late sources. The general outline of events is clear enough, but the details are often quite uncertain.

What we can be sure of is that Saturninus was tribune in 103 B.C. and 100 B.C., and after being reelected for 99 B.C. he died at the end of 100 B.C. in connection with disturbances at the consular elections. The other events have to be fitted into this overall chronology.

SATURNINUS'S TRIBUNATE IN 103 B.C.

If Q. Servilius Caepio cos. 106 thought the year 104 B.C. was bad, the next year was certainly worse. The attack on the senate was led not by the young sons of prominent senatorial families, as had been the case in 104 B.C., but by Saturninus. The sources characterize his initial motive as resentment of his treatment as quaestor. In this capacity, he had been assigned the task of overseeing the importation of grain at Ostia (Rome's port), but in a time of crisis was replaced by the princeps senatus M. Aemilius Scaurus cos. 115 (Diodorus 36.12; Cicero, *Response of the Haruspices* 43, *Speech for Sestius* 39). This story is hard to assess. If the situation was so dire as to warrant the intervention of a man of Scaurus's stature, it must have been very serious. On the other hand, Saturninus may well have felt that he could have handled the matter – and earn the People's gratitude in the process. This quaestorship is often dated to 104 B.C., but normally one could not run for a second office when holding another, and the quaestors of 104 B.C. should still have been in office at the time of the elections for the tribunes of 103 B.C., so perhaps he was quaestor in 105 B.C. In any event, this sounds like another example of the senatorial habit of taking those considered antisenatorial as being driven by petty motives of revenge. The truth is more likely that Saturninus wished to take advantage of popular discontent with the senate to advance his career more quickly than would otherwise have been possible.

The tribunician activity of 103 B.C. can be divided into three categories.

Trials

Vengeance now overtook those responsible for the disaster at Arausio in 105 B.C. Saturninus himself prosecuted Cn. Mallius for perduellio (treason) before the centuriate assembly. Mallius was defended by M. Antonius (later cos. 99), who had connections with Arpinum and was apparently a friend of Marius, but to no avail. He went into exile.

Another tribune, C. Norbanus (a man with a noticeably non-Latin cognomen), prosecuted Q. Servilius Caepio cos. 106. Two tribunes vetoed the procedure and were driven off by stoning. During the fray the princeps senatus M. Aemilius Scaurus was hit in the head. (Quite a change from the days when the pontifex maximus could lead a mob of unarmed senators in a successful attack on Ti. Gracchus's last assembly!) Caepio claimed that the defeat was the result of bad luck (*fortuna*) but was condemned. It seems that hostility toward him was so strong that it was intended to impose the actual death penalty instead of allowing him the customary withdrawal into exile, but a tribune who had close inherited bonds of friendship with Caepio's family released him from jail and accompanied him into exile in the Asian city of Smyrna.

Lex de Maiestate (Minuta)

Saturninus also passed the *lex Appuleia de maiestate (minuta)* ("Appuleian law on [lessened] majesty"), which established a new permanent quaestio.

It had become clear that the cumbersome procedure of lodging tribunician accusations of perduellio before the People had disadvantages. Such proceedings could be vetoed by a colleague (even if obstructionist tribunes could be driven off by stoning, such behavior looked bad for popular tribunes), and in any case losing a battle was not necessarily treason. On the other hand, there could be no doubt that losing a battle did damage the prestige of the Roman People, and that is the sense of *maiestas minuta* (literally "reduced greatness"). In effect, the substance of the new charge was not the subjective issue of the intentions of the accused but the objective fact of his defeat. The new quaestio thus set up a permanent venue for accusing unpopular figures who could in some way be conceived of as having harmed the prestige of the People. That this new charge was basically a tactical device implemented for immediate purposes is shown by the fact that while the court did continue to exist in later years, charges were not lodged in it very often.

Land for Veterans in Africa

Saturninus passed a law providing for the distribution of land to Marius's veterans in Africa. (As consul in 104 B.C., Marius used against the German threat the new levies raised by the consuls of the preceding year, leaving his veteran troops in Numidia.) This law was vetoed by another tribune, who was then driven off by stoning. A late source claims that the size of the allotments was 100 jugera (this would be very large, considering the thirty-jugera limit on Gracchan allotments in Italy). Two towns in Africa bore the title "Marian" under the Empire, and an Imperial inscription preserves a dedication to C. Marius as the *conditor coloniae* (founder of the colony). Whether these are inaccurate generalizations or records of direct action by Marius is unclear. In any case, this act illustrates clearly how the troops would now be dependent upon their commander's political success if they wished to receive land as a reward for their service. While Marius did not take direct advantage of this powerful bond between general and soldiery, others soon would.

CENSORS OF 102 B.C.

The censors in 102 B.C. were Q. Caecilius Metellus Numidicus cos. 109 and his cousin Q. Caecilius Metellus Caprarius cos. 113. Saturninus somehow came upon a man called L. Equitius, whom he put forward as the son of Ti. Gracchus. (The sources claim that he was of freedman origin.) When the censors refused to enroll this man under the name of Gracchus, rioting broke out, in which Numidicus at least was stoned and forced to flee to the Capitol (some equites Romani came to his rescue). At some point during this tempestuous episode, Gracchus's sister (the widow of Scipio Aemilianus) was dragged into public (in a contio?) but could not be compelled to recognize the pseudo-Gracchus. Numidicus decided to act against Saturninus and his associate C. Servilius Glaucia by removing them from the rolls of the senate but was prevented by his colleague (who probably feared the consequences of such action). In any case, the attempt to establish Equitius as the son of Ti. Gracchus indicates that Saturninus and his associates were determined to use the memory of Gracchus (and his brother) to advance their plans (whatever exactly these were).

REELECTION OF SATURNINUS AS TRIBUNE

In 101 B.C., Saturninus was brought to trial on the grounds of having violated the immunity of the envoys of an eastern king, but the threats of a large crowd led to his acquittal. It is said that "senators" voted to acquit (Diodorus 36.15), which presumably means a trial before some sort of special quaestio that used the senatorial jurors of Caepio's legislation, but nothing further is known of the composition of the court. At the very least, the trial shows senatorial hostility toward Saturninus, which is hardly surprising.

In any case, he was elected in the same year to be tribune in 100 B.C. This result was brought about through murder, though the details are not certain. One not terribly reliable source (Valerius Maximus 9.7.3) says that when nine tribunes had already been elected and one space was left, there were two candidates, Saturninus and a certain A. Nunnius, and that Nunnius was murdered to guarantee Saturninus's election. Appian (*Civil Wars* 1.28.4–5) says that Nunnius spoke ill of Glaucia and Saturninus during the campaign and was murdered after his election, and that the next morning, before full cognizance could be taken of the murder, a hasty election was held to fill the vacancy and Saturninus was returned. Appian also says that Glaucia presided over the election as praetor. This cannot be true, since praetors (magistrates of the populus Romanus) never presided over plebeian elections (tribunes did this), and in any case he was certainly praetor the next year. A possible solution is that Glaucia was tribune in this year.[1] It is hard to believe that Saturninus could have been

---

[1] He should not have been eligible for election as a praetor for the following year, but perhaps the elections were postponed until after December 10 when the new tribunes came into office, and in any case since Glaucia sought to be elected consul while praetor, he was hardly scrupulous about constitutional niceties.

so unpopular as to be reduced to worrying about being returned in the last place, whereas Appian's account that Nunnius attacked both Glaucia and Saturninus seems implausible if he was so insignificant a figure as to be one of the last candidates to win election (he certainly was not of prominent birth, as nothing else is known of him or his family). In any case, the murder killed two birds with one stone. It got rid of a clear opponent and allowed Saturninus to be elected surreptitiously without any drawn-out arguments about the permissibility of holding a second tribunate. This use of straightforward murder during the electoral process marked a new low in the increasingly frequent and open use of violence in domestic politics.

The *epitome* of Livy tells us that Marius aided Saturninus's election, Nunnius being killed by troops of his. This indicates that Marius was determined to secure Appuleius's election as tribune. Given the fact that Saturninus had passed legislation for Marius's troops in 103 B.C. and was to do so in 100 B.C., it is hard to escape the conclusion that in 101 B.C. Marius intended to make use for a second time of Saturninus's violent ways to pass legislation for his veterans from the war against the Germans.

LEX SERVILIA DE PECUNIIS REPETUNDIS

Closely associated with Saturninus was C. Servilius Glaucia, who belonged to a once prominent family that had fallen on hard times. Glaucia was praetor in 100 B.C., and as we have seen may have been tribune in 101 B.C. At an unknown date, he passed a law reforming the quaestio de pecuniis repetundis. The new law made changes in several regards.

- Hitherto, jurors could vote that they were not sure about the charges, and if a majority voted this way, the case was retried in its entirety. This procedure was apparently abused as a way to wear out those jurors who wished to convict the defendant. A majority could vote for retrial in good conscience without violating their oaths as jurors, and if the case was repeatedly retried, the jurors wishing to convict would eventually give in and vote for acquittal (it is said that one case was retried eight times before the eventual acquittal of the defendant). Glaucia's law now prescribed a double presentation of the case (called *comperendinatio*) after which the jurors had to vote either to convict or to acquit.
- A provision termed *quo ea pecunia pervenerit* ("in whose hands the money wound up") was added to the definition of the crime. This allowed the prosecution of anyone who ultimately gained possession of the extorted money. Previously, since the lex de pecuniis repetundis covered only elected magistrates, once the extorted funds came into the possession of nonmagistrates, there was no way to reclaim it under the statute. Now it was no longer possible to exploit this provision to conceal sums that had

been taken in violation of the law by transferring them to someone not subject to the law.

• The album of jurors was again to be drawn solely from equites Romani, and the senatorial jurors introduced by the *lex Servilia iudiciaria* of Caepio in 106 B.C. were eliminated. Since the album of the quaestio de pecuniis repetundis provided the jurors for the other courts, the change of its composition necessarily changed the jurors in all the other quaestiones. Whatever other permanent quaestiones may have existed at this time, this measure would have affected the juries that decided cases under Saturninus's new treason law.

It is conceivable that Glaucia passed his law as praetor, but rather unlikely. Praetors were normally occupied by activities other than the passing of legislation, and this sort of demagogic law would have been more appropriate for the assembly of the plebs than the centuriate assembly. In any case, though no tribunate is attested for Glaucia, it is hard to imagine that he never served as tribune. When Appian (not the most reliable source for details) recounts Numidicus's attempt as censor in 102 B.C. to remove Glaucia and Saturninus from the roll of senators, he calls Saturninus an ex-tribune and Glaucia only a senator. Since Appian's account of Saturninus's election with Glaucia's complicity in 101 B.C. seems to be correct, Glaucia was probably tribune in 101 B.C. and passed his lex de pecuniis repetundis then.

SATURNINUS'S SECOND TRIBUNATE

As tribune in 100 B.C., Saturninus intended to pass a major piece of agrarian legislation for Marius. He seems to have followed C. Gracchus's lead in attempting to win support for his main intention by passing other legislation to benefit various segments of the electorate.

Grain Law

It seems that before this date, the grain law of C. Gracchus had been repealed, and it is only indirectly that we learn about Saturninus's attempt to revive it. In 100 B.C., Q. Servilius Caepio, a close relative of the consul of 106,[2] was urban quaestor (in charge of the treasury). He argued before the senate that the state could not afford the expense of subsidizing the price of grain, and the senate passed a decree stating that anyone proposing such a bill was acting against the public good. (For an allusion

---

[2] For the relationship, see Chapter 6, n. 3.

on the coinage to Caepio's dispute with Saturninus, see Coin 6.) When
Saturninus proposed his bill anyway, ignoring (as always!) his colleagues'
vetoes, Caepio led an attack of "good men" on the proceedings. This is
the only notice about the law that we have, and it is reported to us in connection with the later accusation of Caepio under Saturninus's treason
law in 95 B.C. (Caepio was acquitted). Since Sicily was a major source of
Rome's grain supply and a major slave revolt broke out there in 101 B.C.
(see Chapter 8), this circumstance may have contributed to the need to
reintroduce Gracchus's grain law. Presumably, the grain law was passed
in 101 B.C., assuring Saturninus of the support of the urban plebs – in the
short run at any rate.

Agrarian Law

Now, having apparently secured support in the city, Saturninus went on
to pass the agrarian legislation for Marius. We are not very well informed
about the details, but they are sufficient to show why Marius expected
strong opposition and wanted Saturninus, whose skill in passing legislation
despite opposition was clear, to implement it. The law authorized settlements in Gaul, Sicily, Achaia (mainland Greece), and Macedonia (and perhaps also in Africa). It was common enough for generals to settle troops in
the areas they conquered (this had been going on in Spain for decades, and
in 123 B.C. Q. Caecilius Metellus Balearicus settled troops in the Balearic
islands), so the settlements in Gaul and Africa are easy enough to explain.
But what of Sicily and Greece (Macedonia and Achaia)? Marius's colleague as consul in 101 B.C., M.' Aquillius (son of the consul of 129 B.C.
who made the final settlement in Asia), had just suppressed a major slave
revolt in Sicily, and the praetor T. Didius was at this time subduing territory near Thrace as governor of Macedonia. In effect, under the pretext
of benefiting his own veterans, Marius was authorized by Saturninus's
legislation to interfere in provinces that were none of his business. The
fact that the settlements in Africa later looked upon Marius as their founder shows the extent to which Marius could reap personal benefit from
this legislation (even at the expense of those who had actually subdued
the areas). The law also provided for the establishment of colonies. To
avoid financial complications, the law dictated that the money reclaimed
by the quaestio investigating the loss of the money taken in Tolosa by
Q. Servilius Caepio should be used to fund the land distributions.

Whether the law included distributions to non-Romans is not directly
stated, but this is probable. More land would be readily available overseas than in Italy, and Marius is known to have been open-minded about

granting Roman citizenship to worthy Italians. It would appear that despite the grain law, the urban plebs were strongly opposed to the legislation, and men from the countryside were brought to the city to force its passage through violence.

EXILE OF NUMIDICUS

The agrarian law contained a provision that within five days the senators were to swear an oath to uphold it (at this time, laws that it was thought the senate would oppose frequently carried such a provision). Marius as consul immediately called the senate and said he would not swear, supposedly opposing the provision as an insult to the senate. Numidicus spoke in approval of this stance, and Marius dismissed the senate. Five days later, when Saturninus summoned the senators to the forum to take the oath, Marius now claimed that he could not make a definitive decision about the oath, which he proceeded to take. Of the senators, only Numidicus refused, on the grounds that the law had been passed through violence and was therefore invalid. If he could get away with this, it would be an admission that the law had in fact been passed illegally, and so if the bill was to be upheld, it was necessary for him to be convicted for refusing to swear. He withdrew into exile, and a law of interdiction was passed to ratify this move and prevent his return.[3]

REELECTION OF SATURNINUS AND THE
ATTITUDE OF MARIUS

In the summer of 100 B.C., Saturninus was returned as tribune for the next year along with the pseudo-Gracchus, L. Equitius. Saturninus was clearly up to something, though exactly what is not known. Marius apparently had Equitius arrested, but he was broken out of jail by his supporters. Whether this was the start of the hostility between Marius and Saturninus is not clear, but certainly now that Marius had gotten what he wanted (land for his veterans), he was ready to sacrifice his disreputable and troublemaking associates. What Marius wanted now was respect in senatorial opinion, and he tried to make himself acceptable in their eyes. (Pompey would later do the same and find them equally unwilling to embrace him; see Chapters 16 and 18.) Marius was the "savior of the nation" (*conservator patriae*), as Cicero called him, and wished to enjoy

---

[3] For the interdict, see Chapter 3 n. 6.

the prestige of this position. He certainly did not want to rule the state literally (as Sulla would in two decades). As part of this "make over," he was ready to throw his old assistants overboard. They would not go without a fight.

Glaucia's Consular Candidacy
and More Electoral Murder

With the military emergency to the north now over, Marius was finally ready to give up the consulship. There were three major candidates for the consulship of 99 B.C. One was M. Antonius. He was a new man and a great orator, who was just returning from a victorious campaign in Cilicia (see Chapter 9). Antonius was later an enemy of Marius and supporter of the oligarchy, but various pieces of evidence indicate that at this stage he was a supporter of Marius.[4] The second candidate for the consulship was C. Memmius, the tribune who had been prominent in the attack on the nobility as tribune in 111 B.C. (see Chapter 4). Finally, Saturninus's associate C. Servilius Glaucia wished to run, even though as praetor in 100 B.C. he was ineligible for candidacy (on the principle that no one was allowed to seek a new office while already holding one).

The candidacy of Glaucia was definitely opposed by Marius. If Saturninus was tribune the next year with his associate Glaucia as consul, there was no telling what they might get up to. We do not know what their plans were, but clearly Marius had no desire to see Glaucia as consul. On the advice of a council of leading senators that he convened, he ruled (correctly) that Glaucia's candidacy was invalid.

At this point, Saturninus and Glaucia had two options. They could either accept this decision with good grace or use violence to press on with their plan despite Marius's obstruction. Not surprisingly, given their recent intemperate (not to say illegal and violent) behavior, they chose the second course. During the elections in the fall, Antonius was returned, but a riot broke out and one of Saturninus's minions murdered Memmius. Whether Memmius too was returned is not known, but certainly if he was not already, he was about to be. The uproar that resulted from the murder halted the election, and Saturninus and Glaucia acted to take advantage of the situation.

---

4   For example, he had close ties to the aristocracy of Marius's hometown of Arpinum including Cicero's family, his son married a daughter of the Julii Caesares, who were the family of Marius's wife, and Antonius himself later defended M.' Aquillius, Marius's colleague in 101 B.C., against accusations of provincial malfeasance.

Marius's Suppression of Saturninus
and Glaucia

The urban plebs were hostile to Saturninus and Glaucia, but men from the countryside supported them and seized the Capitol. Presumably the intention was to pass legislation, which would almost certainly have been a law authorizing Glaucia's eligibility for the vacant position of consul while still praetor. The murder of Memmius thus resembles that of Nunnius the preceding year, which had allowed a questionable candidate to be returned in a subsequent election. Marius had done nothing then, but what about now?

In 133 B.C., the pontifex maximus P. Scipio Nasica had led a mob of senators to kill Ti. Gracchus to preserve the state against what was perceived to be an attempt to subvert the constitutional order. In 121 B.C., a decree of the senate had authorized the consul L. Opimius to take measures to protect the state under similar circumstances, and by virtue of it, Opimius had killed thousands in violation of the normal legal protections of Roman citizens (see Chapter 3). The legitimacy of this "final decree" was implied by the acquittal of Opimius on a murder charge in 120 B.C., but the matter was still open. Now Marius, the popular novus homo who embodied the success of personal virtue over senatorial privilege, would finally legitimize this use of force in contravention of the law and in the interest of the senatorial oligarchy, whose esteem he now sought. It was not clear at the time, however, that Marius would take such drastic action. First, the suppression of Saturninus and Glaucia would basically serve the interests of his enemies in the senate, and second, it was one thing to kill rioting private citizens in 121 B.C. and quite another to kill a senior magistrate of the Roman People (the praetor Glaucia) and the sacrosanct person of a tribune (Saturninus). But if Saturninus and Glaucia counted on Marius's acquiescence in their use of murder in the consular elections (as had been the case in the tribunician elections of the preceding year), Saturninus and Glaucia made a (literally) fatal miscalculation.

When Saturninus and Glaucia seized the Capitol with their supporters, Marius had the senate pass the so-called final decree. First, he distributed arms among the urban plebs, and he next cleared the forum of Saturninus's supporters and then besieged them on the Capitol. Marius had the support of all the tribunes and praetors apart from Saturninus and Glaucia. It was a blazing hot day, and Marius had the pipes bringing water to the Capitol cut. As the propraetor Antonius was outside the city waiting to celebrate his triumph over pirates in Cilicia, his troops were available to enforce the "final decree" just as those of Metellus Balearicus had done back in 121 B.C., but before Antonius could bring his troops forward, Saturninus, Glaucia, and their supporters surrendered on terms to Marius. Once Marius had showed himself to be willing to invoke the emergency decree of the senate against them, they must have realized that continued resistance was pointless. Marius apparently gave his word that they would not be harmed, but in the event, his word proved to be of little value. Saturninus and some others were held in the senate house, while Glaucia was allowed to go to a senator's home. At this point Marius acted discreditably. A crowd broke into the senate and stoned those inside to death; Glaucia was dragged from the house in which he was lodged, and then his neck was broken. While Marius disclaimed responsibility, it is hardly credible under the circumstances that such force could have been used without his complicity.

Now the suppression of the laws and the use of force in the interest of a "higher" law by virtue of the final decree of the senate were finally given the aura of legitimacy through the use of that decree by the great popular leader Marius. (When the decree was passed against Caesar much later in 49 B.C., it was not its inherent validity but the appropriateness of passing it at that moment that he would dispute.) The oligarchy no doubt believed that its interests were secured. Yet once the principle was admitted that the laws could be broken for the sake of the "greater good," it was not long before it became clear that it was force alone that would determine this greater good – ultimately to the detriment of the oligarchy. The use of violence to determine political issues was now fully accepted (and acceptable), and over time it would only become more frequent and brutal.

Aftermath

Even with the death of Saturninus, a major issue remained concerning the exile of Metellus Numidicus. Not surprisingly, Marius and his supporters continued to thwart any effort to recall him for the remainder of his consulship after the death of Saturninus. More surprisingly, the consuls of 99 B.C. did nothing about the matter despite the agitation of the large clan of the Metelli and their adherents, and it was only in 98 B.C., when a relation of Metellus was consul (Q. Metellus Nepos, son of Numidicus's first cousin Q. Metellus Balearicus cos. 123), that the necessary legislation passed allowing Numidicus to return to Rome. Prominent among the advocates of reform was Numidicus's son Q. Metellus, who earned the additional name (*agnomen*; see Appendix on Roman Names)

Pius ("the dutiful") for his efforts (he was to be the most prominent member of the family in the next generation).

As for Marius, it turned out that his decision to abandon his allies Saturninus and Glaucia to curry favor with the senate did him no good at all. His reputation among the electorate as a whole suffered badly from his violent suppression of such popular figures, and the senate felt no gratitude toward the man who had recently done so much to undermine the political control of the oligarchy. About a year later, he took a journey to Asia Minor (see Chapter 9), supposedly to make good on vows that he had made to eastern gods during his campaigns (the trip may have been an excuse to get away from Rome). When he returned, he did not even bother to run for the censorship of 97 B.C. His popularity in Rome was not entirely undermined, however, as is shown by his being elected as augur during his absence. He would lapse into a sullen retirement for most of the 90s B.C., only to emerge again as a military commander during the Social War, when he would be treated shabbily by the senate.

Questions for Study and Reflection

1. What grounds did the senate have for feeling that the equestrian jurors were persecuting them? Was this a valid view? What did Q. Servilius Caepio cos. 106 do in response?
2. What caused the defeat at Arausio and what effect did this defeat have in Rome?
3. What was remarkable about Marius's second and subsequent consulships?
4. Why did Saturninus set up a quaestio to handle the new charge of maiestas?
5. How and why did Glaucia change the procedures of the court de pecuniis repetundis?
6. How did L. Saturninus resemble C. Gracchus or differ from him in his methods and aims?
7. What was the purpose of murdering A. Nunnius and C. Memmius? How do these killings represent a new form of violence in domestic politics?
8. What was the relationship between Saturninus and Glaucia on the one hand and Marius on the other? What did each side want from the other?
9. What was the significance of Marius's use of the final decree of the senate?

6

THE ITALIAN ALLIES, M. LIVIUS
DRUSUS, AND THE SOCIAL WAR

SURREPTITIOUS ENROLLMENT OF ITALIAN ALLIES
AS CITIZENS THWARTED

After the death of Saturninus, the early and mid 90s B.C. were a time of
comparative domestic calm. The major disquieting note took place during
the consulship of L. Licinius Crassus (the great orator, who had secured
the conviction of C. Papirius Carbo in 120 B.C. and founded Narbo
Martius in 118 B.C.) and Q. Mucius Scaevola (son of P. Scaevola cos. 133,
whose unsatisfactory response to Scipio Nasica's question had led to the
lethal assault on Ti. Gracchus). As consuls in 95 B.C., they jointly passed
a law that instituted a quaestio whose purpose was to strip Roman citizenship from Latins and Italian allies who had usurped Roman status and
to restore them to their original peregrine (i.e., non-Roman) status. While
this law was completely unobjectionable from a purely legal point of view,
it had disastrous political consequences. Many non-Romans who desired
to become Roman citizens had been allowed to do so on the sly by surreptitiously enrolling themselves in the Roman census, but it was now clear
to the non-Roman inhabitants of Italy that the senatorial establishment in
Rome was completely unwilling or unable to extend Roman citizenship to
the rest of Italy. There would be one last attempt on the part of a Roman
politician to enfranchise the Italian allies, and his failure would lead to a
major revolt against Rome. This final attempt was part of a major effort
to reform many perceived faults in the state, and was motivated by the
conviction of P. Rutilius Rufus in 92 B.C.

P. Rutilius Rufus

The taxes owed to the Roman People in the province of Asia were collected by publicans (tax farmers; see Chapter 1). Equites in Rome formed companies that would bid in auctions held in Rome under the lex Sempronia of C. Gracchus for contracts to collect the taxes. Though the Roman governors of Asia theoretically should have ensured that the locals paid no more than what they owed, in practice it was both easier and more advantageous for them to cooperate with the politically influential publicans in oppressing the provincials (and of course these same equites, and their friends, sat on the juries for the quaestio de pecuniis repetundis in Rome). By the 90s B.C., it was clear that the excessive demands of the publicans had made a mess of the province, and Q. Mucius Scaevola was sent to clean up the situation. Scaevola's conduct was so irreproachable that he became the paragon of an upright governor – when Cicero later governed Cilicia he overtly modeled his behavior on Scaevola's – and he made numerous rulings against the practices of the publicans. (The date of Scaevola's term is disputed, but he probably served after his consulship.)[1]

Scaevola stayed in Asia for only nine months. He was assisted by P. Rutilius Rufus cos. 105 (as consul Rufus had raised the army that Marius would lead to victory against the Germans). When Scaevola returned to Rome, he left Rufus in charge as *legatus pro praetore* (that is, the legate who acted in place of an absent governor). In this capacity Rufus was subject to the lex de pecuniis repetundis, which normally covered only elected magistrates, and in 92 B.C. the annoyed equites haled him rather

---

[1] Asconius, the ancient commentator on Cicero's speeches, mentions in connection with Scaevola's activities as consul that he "had declined a province." It is sometimes held that this refers to a position as governor after the consulship. This would mean that he served in Asia during or after his praetorship, which fell at the latest in 98 B.C. (because of the provision providing for a two-year interval between offices). It is true that in this period consuls were not normally appointed as proconsuls if they had served their term of office in Rome. This would suggest that Scaevola acted in Asia after his praetorship, but since Scaevola served as governor for only one year, it is odd that the resulting trial took place at such a later date, in 92 B.C. (though sometimes prosecutions were taken up at a later date). In addition, it would be rather out of place for the consular P. Rutilius Rufus to have served as legate to a mere praetor, and when this consideration is combined with the date of the trial, it becomes a much more likely interpretation that Scaevola went to Asia in 94 B.C. after his consulship, and that he declined a province after his praetorship. As for the unusualness of a consul being sent out as a proconsul after a consulship spent in Rome, the appointment in Asia was clearly an unusual one, which would also explain the presence of the very senior Rufus as Scaevola's subordinate.

than Scaevola before the quaestio de pecuniis repetundis. While it was accepted practice for those accused before Roman courts to cry and plead for mercy, Rufus, who was clearly not guilty, refused to stoop to such behavior. In fact, being a man of Stoic inclinations in philosophy, he self-consciously modeled his behavior after that of Socrates, who had courted his own conviction in 399 B.C. through adopting an insultingly provocative attitude toward the jurors (at least as Plato presents his defense in the *Apology*).[2] The jurors duly convicted Rufus, who went into exile in Smyrna, a major city in the very province that he had been convicted of despoiling.

Outrage ensued at this vindictive violation of justice by the jurors. It was felt that the equestrian jury members had abused their power by convicting an honest governor who had stood up to the equestrian publicans and tried to curb their abuses. It is this event that was later "read back" into history, when C. Gracchus was accused of having intended this result from the start (see Chapter 3). In fact, it had taken thirty years for the equites to abuse their power in this way. (Of course, to a senator it may have seemed that the equites were acting vindictively during the many political cases that they had decided a decade earlier in the various extraordinary quaestiones of the last decade of the second century.)

Q. Caepio's Attack on Scaurus

Another accusation in the public courts led to the feeling that something had to be done about the exclusively equestrian composition of the album. This accusation was made by Q. Servilius Caepio, who may have been the son of the consul of 106 B.C. and in any case was certainly a close relation.[3] This man was apparently of a tempestuous disposition, having opposed Saturninus's grain law by force while quaestor in 103 B.C. (for which he was unsuccessfully prosecuted under Saturninus's law about minuta maiestas in 95 B.C.; see Chapter 5). Although the elder Caepio had been a staunch defender of the senate, and M. Scaurus, the princeps

---

2 Stoicism was a school of Greek philosophy that appealed to Roman aristocrats because of its emphasis on strict adherence to moral principles. Socrates was not a Stoic, but his supposedly unbending attitude in court would have appealed to a Stoic.

3 We are told (Strabo, *Geography* 4.1.13) that the consul of 106 B.C. left only daughters as heirs, which would seemingly exclude the possibility that this Caepio of the next generation was his son. But since we are not told of the date of the elder Caepio's death (all we know of his later life it that he went into exile at Smyrna after being convicted in 103 B.C.), he may have survived the death of the younger Caepio in 90 B.C. Nonetheless, the Caepio active in the 90s B.C. may have been a nephew or cousin (there were a number of consular Servilii Caepiones in the mid second century).

senatus, had been wounded in a riot defending Caepio against turbulent tribunician legislation, the younger Caepio had a falling out with Scaurus and his allies, the Caecilii Metelli. The grounds for this rupture are not now recoverable. It is known that the younger Caepio and M. Livius Drusus (son of the tribune of 122 B.C. and a member of the group associated with the Metelli) had been close personal friends, each marrying the other's sister, but some sort of personal dispute led to a total severing of friendship between the two brothers-in-law, and perhaps this had something to do with Caepio's alienation from the dominant senatorial faction that was centered around the Metelli. At any rate, around the start of M. Drusus's tribunate in 91 B.C., the younger Caepio indicted the old princeps senatus under the quaestio de pecuniis repetundis. The exact charge and the circumstances of the accusation are unknown, but we are told that the accusation was made "on account of enmity felt against the legation to Asia" (Asconius 21C) and that Caepio was "excessively devoted to the equestrian order" (Cicero, *Brutus* 223). Presumably, these statements are related to the activities of Rutilius Rufus, but how exactly Scaurus was involved is not clear. What we do know is that Scaurus extricated himself (he lodged a counter-accusation against Caepio and managed to get this case heard before his own) and "also advised M. Drusus the tribune of the plebs to change the courts" (Asconius 21C).

M. LIVIUS DRUSUS

M. Livius Drusus was the son of the man who had outmaneuvered C. Gracchus in 122 B.C. and then reached the consulship in 112 B.C. His father was associated with the Metellan group in the senate, and this connection was continued by the son. The younger Drusus was a very wealthy and influential member of the highest nobility, and as tribune in 91 B.C., he decided that he would solve all the problems of the state in one fell swoop. While the initial motivation was the perceived need to do something about the equestrian control of the quaestio de pecuniis repetundis because of the conviction of Rutilius Rufus and the accusation of M. Scaurus, Drusus attempted to include land distribution and citizenship for the Italian allies in his reforms. Apparently, Drusus's overall purpose was to preserve the position of the senate within the state, but he aroused vehement opposition from within the oligarchy. He claimed to be acting as the patron of the senate, but unfortunately, many senators did not want to be beholden to another (rather junior) senator. In particular, the leading consulars have thought it presumptuous for a mere tribune – even one of great wealth and prominent lineage – to adopt such an attitude.

Drusus's Proposals

Drusus proposed a number of measures, which were seemingly intended to gain for him the support of all the various groups who could exert political pressure in Rome.

- Grain law. Like C. Gracchus and L. Saturninus, Drusus proposed a grain law to win over the urban plebs. The details are not known.
- Coin devaluation. Drusus passed a measure that tampered with the silver content of the coinage (the details are disputed). It is not known who this measure was intended to benefit, but in the event it just caused more trouble. At any rate, confusion in the value of the currency ensued, and the urban plebs were extremely grateful to the praetor who in the mid 80s B.C. issued an edict to rectify the situation (see Chapter 10 n. 3).
- Land law. Drusus apparently wished to establish in Italy and Sicily a number of colonies that had been voted on in the past but not actually set up. His father had proposed such colonies to undermine C. Gracchus's support, and the laws of L. Saturninus, which had not been repealed, also provided for such colonies. This measure was designed to ensure support from the rural plebs.
- Equites and the quaestio de pecuniis repetundis. The problem with the quaestio de pecuniis repetundis seemed to be that the equestrian jurors were using their control of the court to further their own (financial) interests. Drusus sought to remove this conflict by enrolling the top 300 equites in the 300-member senate, and then selecting the album of jurors from the members of this enlarged senate. Thus, the problem of the irresponsible use of the courts by the equestrian jurors would be at an end.
- Citizenship. The final element of Drusus's reform was to grant citizenship to the non-Roman Italians. He appears to have had connections with the nobility of the towns of the Italian countryside, who came to Rome to support his measures.

As it turned out, Drusus's attempt to secure the passage of his bills by giving something to everyone backfired. The support of those who benefited was limited, while the resistance of opponents was vigorous. The senate resented the proposed inclusion of equites as senators. After all, the present senators had gained their prestigious position through the toil of the electoral process and were disinclined to share this status with men who had not run for any office at all. For their part, the equites were hardly thrilled at the prospect of gaining senatorial status. They had intentionally refrained from the trouble and expense (not to mention potential dangers) of public office, and while they enjoyed the influence that they exercised through control of the album of the juries, they were content with their literally irresponsible position and had no desire to become subject to the provisions of the lex de pecuniis repetundis, from whose operation they had previously been exempt. As usual, the urban plebs were not interested in the agrarian concerns of the rural voters, and the electorate as a whole was opposed to the enfranchisement of the allies. Thus, Drusus's efforts at building a grand coalition for reform simply resulted in widespread hostility toward his overall program.

Drusus Struggles to Get His Legislation Passed

While Drusus was acting, as he claimed, in the interest of the senate, not everyone was convinced. He was forced to use violence in passing his laws and faced vigorous opposition from the consul L. Marcius Philippus and from Q. Servilius Caepio (Drusus's estranged brother-in-law). This conflict was of a very direct and personal nature: Philippus got a bloody nose in one battle, and Drusus threatened to hurl Caepio from the Tarpeian Rock (an ancient form of tribunician punishment). Drusus's major supporter in the senate was none other than the great orator L. Crassus, who as consul in 95 B.C. had passed the law to halt the usurpation of Roman citizenship (discussed earlier). We do not know if Crassus had come to regret his actions of a few years earlier, but it would seem that he had reached the conclusion that citizenship had to be granted legally to the Italian allies. In addition, Crassus had, since at least 106 B.C., advocated an end to equestrian control of the album of jurors. At this time, Crassus supported Drusus's efforts and spoke vigorously on his behalf in the senate. After a particularly heated exchange with Philippus in the senate on September 13, Crassus was carried home ill and died six days later. It is an indication of the powerful influence that could be exerted on the deliberations of the senate by a strong personality that the death of Crassus caused Drusus's support in the senate to collapse. Seemingly, Drusus himself lacked the *auctoritas* – the power of suasion based on personal standing and prestige – necessary to maintain his position on his own, and once Crassus was removed, he could no longer resist the opposition led by Philippus. The consul had the senate pass a decree declaring that Drusus's laws had been passed in violation of the auspices (presumably either bad omens had been reported and ignored or the reporters of the omens had been driven off by violence) and were therefore invalid. Drusus himself refrained from vetoing this decree, which presumably shows that while he realized that he could no longer uphold his program in the senate, he was not willing to use violence to uphold his laws as the Gracchi and Saturninus had done.

ASSASSINATION OF DRUSUS

Apart from not wanting to get himself killed, Drusus apparently felt that the passage of the citizenship law was not out of the question and continued to press for it. He must have considered that if he did get such a bill passed, the gratitude of the new citizens would outweigh any loss of prestige that he suffered through the invalidation of his previous legislation. As a man of high standing who was attempting to pass important (contested) legislation, he received many visitors in his house, and one day toward evening he was suddenly stabbed in the upper thigh or groin by one of these visitors and soon died an unpleasant death. The killer escaped without being identified, and while Philippus and Caepio were suspected of planning the assassination, it was never discovered who committed the crime, much less who had instigated it. As he lay dying, Drusus supposedly asked his friends and relatives who were present when the state would again have a citizen like him. If by this question he meant another member of the ruling oligarchy who would attempt as tribune to reform the state through legislation, the answer was never. His death was to lead to the events which introduced the Roman military as the determining factor in the politics of the Late Republic and ultimately subverted the nobility's control of the state.

Upon the news of Drusus's death, which meant the failure of the third attempt to secure Roman citizenship for the Italian allies through legislation (in 125, 122, 91 B.C.), the Italian allies rose in revolt against Rome. It must have seemed that the Romans could never be persuaded by peaceful means to make the Italians their equals and that the only alternative was to compel them by force.

ARMING OF ITALY AND OUTBREAK OF REVOLT

Even before the death of Drusus, the Italian allies seem to have been gearing up to use force to compel the Romans to grant them citizenship. At the forefront of this movement was Q. Poppaedius Silo of the Marsi (an ethnic group in central Italy), an associate of Drusus who was present in Rome to lobby for the enfranchisement of the Italians. He was apparently talked out of a proposal to send 10,000 Italians to Rome under arms to demand citizenship. There had been a plan to kill the two consuls of 91 B.C. at the beginning of the year when they took part in an ancient religious ceremony to the south of Rome, but Drusus got word of the plot and warned the consuls. Already by the time of Drusus's death, some cities were forming a conspiracy, and the situation in rural Italy was so tense that the senate sent around legates and magistrates to investigate and restrain the unrest. A Roman magistrate (probably a praetor, but his exact status is uncertain) was informed of an exchange of hostages (to guarantee loyalty in war) among conspirators at the town of Asculum in Picenum (an area to the northwest of Rome on the Adriatic), which was holding a festival. When the magistrate threatened the conspirators, he was killed along with a legate, and the other Romans in the town were then slaughtered. This event, which marked the outbreak of armed conflict, took place very late in 91 B.C. or early in 90 B.C., and the war broke out in earnest in 90 B.C.

SOCIAL WAR

The war with the Italian allies is now known as the Social War (from *socius,* the Latin word for "ally"). This is a term of the Imperial period (first used by the author Florus in the second century A.D.). The Romans of the time called it the Marsic War (specifically designating it after the people directly to the east of Rome who would manage to defeat and kill two consuls) or the Italian War. It is worth noting that with one small exception (Venusia in distant Apulia), the Latin communities did not defect. The revolt began with and was mainly fought by the communities of Italy that were most martial and closest to Rome both geographically and culturally. These were peoples who spoke Oscan languages (a group of languages closely related to Latin) and consisted of two blocks. Located to the east of Rome on the other side of the Apennines were the Marsi, Paeligni, Marrucini, Vestini, Ferentini, and (to the northeast) the Picentines, while the Samnites lived in the southern Apennines (the mountainous spine of Italy). The Samnites were a mountain-dwelling people whom the Romans had conquered in the late fourth and early third centuries B.C., and who had never become completely reconciled to the Romans. The peoples to the east of Rome had been conquered at about the same time as the Samnites but seem to have been more fully integrated into the Roman system. They provided one of the most important allied contingents in the Roman army, and it was said that no Roman general had ever celebrated a triumph over the Marsi or without them (that is, the Romans had never defeated them in pitched battle before their conquest, and later the Marsi never revolted and instead formed a crucial element in successful Roman armies). The revolt did eventually spread to certain other areas (e.g., Apulia in the far south, and to a small extent Etruria and Umbria to the north of Rome), but this was only after major Roman setbacks, and these areas were clearly not the driving force in the revolt.

AIMS OF THE ITALIAN REBELS

It would appear that the leading members of the rebellious communities were completely frustrated at their inability to participate in Roman politics. At the same time, the revolt must have enjoyed wide popular support. Presumably lower-class members of these communities resented their inferior treatment in the distribution of booty and land. Both groups must have disliked being completely at the mercy of the imperium of Roman magistrates and wished to acquire the protections that Roman citizens enjoyed against the capricious use of violence by the magistrates. (For a visual image of the contradictory aims of the rebels, see Coin 7.)

POLITICAL ORGANIZATION OF THE REBELS

The attitude of the rebellious allies was that if the Romans would not let them play the game on equal terms, they would go off and create their own game. At any rate, they made a confederation that mimicked the Roman state. They chose as their capital a town in the territory of the Paeligni called Corfinium, to which they gave the significant new name *Italia*. They created (or intended to) a 500-member senate and elected two annual magistrates like the Roman consuls along with twelve praetors.[4] There is evidence from inscriptions that after their long familiarity with Roman institutions, the towns of Italy were assimilating themselves to the Romans (adopting such peculiarly Roman institutions as the censorship and tribunate). Feeling rejected by the Romans, the rebels – that is, the Italians who felt closest to the Romans – now wanted to set up their own version of Rome without Rome, and in the process they took a major step toward turning the concept of Italy into more than just a geographic term.

For the year 90 B.C. the Italian rebels elected as their chief magistrates Q. Poppaedius Silo, who was the military leader in the north, and C. Papius Mutilus of the Samnites, who held overall command in the

---

[4] The size of the senate and number of praetors is some indication of the general recognition at this time of the inability of the Roman government with its 300-member senate and six praetors to run the empire. Why the Italians themselves thought they needed so many praetors is not clear, but the foreseeable military necessities of the revolt may have played a role in setting the number so high.

south. In each area, junior magistrates (presumably praetors) held command in various towns.

While the extent of anti-Roman feeling should not be underestimated, it should also be borne in mind that most communities remained loyal, and even in the rebellious communities many individuals stood by Rome and rendered valuable services to the Romans in the suppression of the revolt. "Italy" existed only in opposition to Rome and its political system, and the confederation was doomed to failure from the start. The Italians were never united in their hostility toward Rome or ultimate aims, and once the war forced the Romans to make concessions, the rebellion quickly crumbled. But it took major Roman defeats in the field to make the senate and electorate in Rome realize the folly (and ultimate futility) of having thwarted the enfranchisement of the Italian allies for the past thirty-five years.

CAMPAIGN OF 90 B.C.

The consuls of 90 B.C. were P. Rutilius Lupus (not to be confused with P. Rutilius Rufus!) and L. Julius Caesar (a distant cousin of the future dictator's father, who had died as propraetor in 91 B.C.), and they divided the military campaigning into two areas: a northern theater of operations (which actually lay to the east of Rome) and a second one to the south. Lupus was to subdue the eastern rebels in the Apennines and the plains of Picenum to the northeast along the Adriatic, while Caesar attacked the Samnites in the south. The coming struggle was clearly going to be hard, and to symbolize the gravity of the situation, the magistrates refrained from wearing the symbols of their office, the citizens took off their togas (the symbol of one's role as citizen in peacetime), and all legal business (with one important exception to be discussed later) was suspended.

Northern Campaign

Lupus had as his legates a number of important men, including Q. Servilius Caepio, the enemy of M. Drusus who was perhaps not yet praetor in the late 90s B.C.,[5] and the great C. Marius (a relative), who had retired from public life after the unfortunate events of his last consulship in 100 B.C.

---

[5] There is no direct attestation of the praetorship, and while one might expect the legates in the war to be of this rank, it is circular reasoning to argue that he must have been at least an ex-praetor since he was a legate. Nonetheless, a recent praetorship is likely.

Marius advised Lupus to wait until he had trained his newly raised troops,[6] but Lupus ignored this sensible advice (apparently thinking that it had been given in bad faith), with disastrous consequences for his campaign to subdue the territory of the Marsi, the first mountainous people due east from Rome. First, one legate suffered a major defeat and was removed from command (his troops were given to Marius). Next, while crossing a river in June, Lupus was defeated in an ambush, in which the consul was himself numbered among the many Roman dead (his funeral at Rome was so depressing that the senate decreed that henceforth commanders killed in battle should be buried in the field). Marius, who was camped downstream and learned of the defeat from the bodies floating in the current, then attacked and defeated the Italians. It is a measure of the extent to which the senatorial oligarchy disliked him that when young Caepio won a minor victory, he was given a command equal to Marius's (a snub all the more galling if Caepio was not even of praetorian rank). Caepio then showed that he was not Marius's equal in war by falling into an ambush in which he too was killed along with many of his men. Marius now assumed full command of this operation and routed the Italians again.

Meanwhile, Cn. Pompeius Strabo, son of a comparatively new consular family (going back only to 141 B.C.), was sent as Lupus's legate to subdue Asculum in Picenum (the place where the revolt had started). After suffering two defeats himself, he eventually managed to inflict a major defeat on the Italians and began the siege of Asculum, which turned out to be a nasty, protracted affair. As a mark of his success, the magistrates in Rome resumed wearing the insignia of their office.

Southern Campaign

The town of Aesernia lies on the road connecting Corfinium (that is, Italia, the confederation capital) and Beneventum, the major town in Samnite territory. Thus, Aesernia controlled communications between the two major areas of revolt, and the Italians needed to seize it. After the town was placed under siege, the consul L. Julius Caesar led his army to its defense but was routed. After a long siege, during which the defenders were forced to eat dogs, the town eventually capitulated, despite other Roman efforts to save it.

Next, an Italian army invaded southern Campania (the area to the south of Latium), which had remained loyal to Rome. After an initial

---

[6] After all, one of the reasons for Marius's ability to inflict overwhelming defeat on the Cimbri and Teutoni had been his having sufficient time to train his raw recruits.

success (Nola was captured through treachery), a number of towns went over to the rebels. L. Caesar led a new army, reinforced with Gallic and Numidian auxiliaries, to oppose C. Papius Mutilus, the Italian "consul" and commander in Campania. The Numidians went over to the Italians in such numbers that their units had to be disbanded, but eventually Caesar defeated Mutilus. He was hailed *imperator* by his troops.[7] This event was the first major Roman success in the war, and it was considered such good news in Rome that the mourning attire that had been adopted at the start of the war was now officially given up.

The Italian onslaught in Campania had cut off a Roman army in the far south. It was penned up in Grumentum, and Apulia generally joined the revolt.

LEX JULIA

Toward the end of 90 B.C., the surviving consul, L. Caesar, returned to Rome to oversee the elections. He also passed a law that in effect granted to the Italians what they had always been seeking – Roman citizenship. Those allies who had never taken up arms were immediately granted citizenship, and it seems that it was also given to those rebels who laid down their arms. While there was certainly resentment against Rome and doubtless those who were deeply implicated in the war genuinely did seek independence, the whole notion of "Italia" was inherently artificial, and the major grounds for the war were now removed. A few laws passed in the following year clarified matters, including one passed by the consul Cn. Pompeius Strabo in 89 B.C. that gave Latin status to Cisalpine Gaul (the area north of the Po River and south of the Alps).

MILITARY ARRANGEMENTS FOR 89 B.C. AND

THE SENATE'S SNUB OF MARIUS

The consuls for 89 B.C. were Cn. Pompeius Strabo, who had placed Asculum under siege as Rutilius Lupus's legate in 90 B.C., and L. Porcius Cato. It is a further indication of how much rancor the oligarchy felt toward Marius that even though it was Marius who had saved the day following Lupus's defeat at the hands of the Marsi, his command was turned over to the consul L. Cato. (Plutarch says that Marius resigned on

---

[7] The title imperator, signifying "victorious general," was given to a general by the acclamation of his troops after a victory in open battle, and such an acclamation was a prerequisite for seeking authorization from the senate to celebrate a triumph.

grounds of ill health, but this may simply have been a face-saving device.) Cato even boasted after an initial victory that he had accomplished more than Marius, though his eventual death in battle showed how fatuous this claim was. Even more galling from Marius's point of view was the fact that L. Sulla, who had taken over command of the armies in Campania after the return of L. Caesar to Rome in 90 B.C., was allowed to continue in command there as a legatus pro praetore. Sulla, who had served as Marius's quaestor during the war against Jugurtha and had recently (at a disputed date in the 90s B.C.) operated successfully as praetor in Cilicia (see Chapter 9), was looking forward to a run for the consulship. Apparently it was felt that it was time to slight the aged Marius in favor of the up-and-coming Sulla. Thus, according to the new arrangements, both consuls of 89 B.C. were to serve in the north, and as a result of this decision the propraetorian Marius was relieved of command while the propraetorian Sulla was allowed to retain control of the Roman forces in the south. If the transfer of command from Marius to Cato was intended as a direct insult to Marius, the senate would soon find that Marius's resentment would have disastrous consequences.

CAMPAIGN OF 89 B.C.

The North

L. Cato took over Marius's army and continued the drive into the territory of the Marsi, where the consul Lupus had met with disaster the preceding year. After an initial victory, Cato was defeated near the Fucine Lake (close to the Italian capital at Corfinium) and killed. The degree of the bitterness caused by his appointment is shown by the fact that Marius's son was accused of surreptitiously killing Cato during the battle. In any case, the other consul, Cn. Strabo, assumed direct command of Cato's army while he continued the attack on the Marsi through legates.

Meanwhile, as the siege of Asculum went on, the Italians gathered a huge army to relieve the city. In the ensuing battle, the Romans are said to have had 60,000 troops, the Italians 75,000 (very large numbers). Strabo defeated this relief force and then finished off the remainder in a mountain pass. The fate of Asculum now was sealed, and the town surrendered in November. The officers were flogged and beheaded, the citizens were forced from the town without possessions, and their property was sold (Strabo kept the proceeds for himself). This broke the back of the revolt in the north; Italia, the rebel capital, was abandoned, and Q. Poppaedius

Silo fled southward to Samnium. On December 25, 89 B.C., Strabo entered Rome in triumph.

The South

Sulla continued to command the Roman armies in Campania. After defeating the Italians in a battle in the spring of 89 B.C., he began to retake various towns in Campania during the late spring and early summer. He then turned to Samnite territory, where he invaded by an unexpected route and took Bovianum, the southern capital of the revolt. Sulla then returned to Rome, where he was elected consul for the next year, while his legates continued to reconquer Samnium.

WINDING DOWN THE WAR

The campaign in the south would continue the next year (88 B.C.). Silo breathed some life back into the revolt in Samnium and even recaptured Bovianum. Various Romans operated in the south, in particular Q. Caecilius Metellus Pius (later cos. 80), who as propraetor finally defeated and killed Silo in battle. This pretty much ended the war (a few remaining rebellious towns were also retaken in Campania). In the meanwhile, the praetor Q. Cosconius reconquered the far south.

LEGAL AFFAIRS IN ROME

Quaestio Varia

The revolt of the allies resulted in a number of legal complications. One of the tribunes of 91 B.C., Q. Varius, passed – as so often now, in disregard of tribunician veto! – a law authorizing a quaestio to try those who were thought to be culpable for instigating the revolt. This measure appears to have been a move directed by the equites against the senate. Drusus was considered to have been acting with the nobility in his attempt to gain citizenship for the allies, and it was thought that the nobility could be blamed for the resulting revolt, as if the cause had been the attempt of M. Drusus and his supporters to solve the problem of the allies' discontent rather than the persistent refusal in Rome to do anything about the issue for more than thirty years. The quaestio Varia was thus intended to have results similar to those of the quaestio Mamilia in 109 B.C. This special quaestio was the only one to remain in session in 90 B.C. when the regular courts were closed because of the war. There were a large number of accusations (including one against the ubiquitous, and now aged, princeps senatus, M. Aemilius Scaurus cos. 115), but the number of convictions is not clear.[8] In 89 B.C., a reaction against such prosecutions seems to have set in, and ironically Q. Varius himself was haled before his own court and convicted. If nothing else, this shows how the criminal accusations and verdicts were often made for political reasons that had little to do with the actual legal issues.

Lex Plautia Iudiciaria

Yet another reform of the juror panels of the quaestiones was instituted in 89 B.C. by the *lex Plautia iudiciaria* ("Plautius's law on law courts") of the tribune M. Plautius Silvanus. The panels of the quaestio Varia had once again seemingly shown the equestrian hostility toward the senatorial order, and Silvanus made an interesting attempt at reform by introducing an entirely new method of appointing jurors. His law provided that each of the thirty-five electoral tribes was to elect fifteen jurors, for a total of 525. This mode of selection would theoretically end the squabble between the senators and equites for control of the juries (and would also result in senators sitting on the juries, which the equites had exclusively controlled for more than a decade since the lex Servilia of Glaucia). Some people below the equestrian census qualification even got elected. This method of selection was used only during the turbulent 80s B.C., but it was abolished at the end of the decade when Sulla restored the juries to the senate after his victory in civil war. Hence, we have no way of knowing whether this novel procedure of involving the electorate in the management of the album of jurors would have been an effective method in the long run. (Given the extent to which the assemblies soon came to be completely intimidated through the use of violence – a practice that had already been developing for several decades – one may doubt that jury selection through voting would have been a viable alternative for long.)

QUESTIONS FOR STUDY AND REFLECTION

1. Why was P. Rutilius Rufus convicted? What did this conviction say about the attitude of the equestrian juries?

---

[8] Prosecuted by Varius himself, Scaurus was famously acquitted after asking the jurors, "Q. Varius from Spain makes without evidence the accusation that I, M. Aemilius Scaurus, the princeps senatus, incited the allies to revolt. Who do you believe?"

2. What was M. Livius Drusus's intention in his tribunate? How did he try to fulfill his plan? What opposition did he meet?

3. How do Drusus's aims and methods compare to those of Ti. and C. Gracchus and of L. Saturninus?

4. What were the immediate and the broader causes of the outbreak of the Social War? What were the main areas of revolt, and what made these areas in particular more prone to rebellion? Why did the Italian allies want to become Roman citizens? Why had the enfranchisement of the allies been opposed for decades in Rome?

5. What role did Marius play in the war, and how was he treated by the senate? What was the senate's attitude toward Sulla?

6. How does the quaestio Varia resemble the earlier quaestio Mamilia?

7. What was the purpose of the judicial reform implemented by the lex Plautia iudiciaria? Would it have succeeded in its aims?

7

SULLA, MARIUS, AND CIVIL WAR

RIVALRY BETWEEN SULLA AND MARIUS

As soon as the Romans had finally put an end to the revolt of their allies, political life in Rome became even more violent as the result of a civil war provoked by the rivalry between C. Marius, six times consul, and his ex-quaestor, L. Cornelius Sulla. Although many other issues were involved in the outbreak of the civil war, the personal relations of these two men were a major element. Sulla belonged to a patrician family that had fallen on bad times. Sulla was Marius's quaestor in 107 B.C., and it was into Sulla's hands that Jugurtha was delivered by Bocchus in 105 B.C. (see Chapter 4). Though credit for ending the war became an issue between them at a later date, it seems not to have been at the time, since Marius was confident enough of Sulla to employ him as a legate during his war against the Germans. In the early 90s B.C., Sulla ran once unsuccessfully for the praetorship, but after eventually winning the office, he served first as urban praetor and then as proconsul in Cilicia the following year (see Chapter 9).

Just before the outbreak of the Social War, Sulla undertook a provocative move to help his anticipated campaign for the consulship. He had his friend King Bocchus of Mauretania erect a monument on the Capitol showing Sulla receiving Jugurtha from Bocchus. Such an image was clearly an insult to Marius, implying as it did that it was Sulla in fact who was responsible for the victorious conclusion of the Numidian war. This monument would have had to be approved by the senate, and presumably it was felt that it was expedient to help Sulla attain the consulship at the expense of the aged and (to the oligarchy) unpalatable Marius. Marius was preparing to have his partisans tear the thing down through violence, and only the outbreak of the Social War prevented the matter from coming to a head.

During the war, Marius's yeoman duty in saving the situation after P. Rutilius Lupus's defeat in 90 B.C. was ignored, and he was not continued in command in 89 B.C., while Sulla was retained as commander in the south (having taking over as legate from the consul L. Caesar). The oligarchy was getting back at the pushy new man Marius, but his resentment of this shabby treatment would redound to the detriment of the oligarchy.

Sulla's Consulship

Sulla was elected consul for 88 B.C. with Q. Pompeius Rufus (a distant cousin of Cn. Pompeius Strabo cos. 89 and son or grandson of Q. Pompeius cos. 141, a new man). Sulla entered into an alliance with Rufus, marrying his daughter to his colleague's homonymous ("same-named") son. Sulla also became at this time a major figure in the faction in the senate that centered around the Metelli. He married Caecilia Metella, the niece of Q. Metellus Numidicus cos. 109 and the widow of M. Aemilius Scaurus cos. 115, the old princeps senatus, who had recently died. Sulla was thus closely associated with the group of men over whose objections Marius had risen to prominence. (It was apparently said by some in the oligarchy that Sulla was unworthy of marrying Metella. This means that the rise of Sulla to prominence from a family that had been insignificant for some time was resented by some. This is worth remembering in assessing Sulla's later claim to be the champion of the senate.)

Issues in 88 B.C.

The Italian allies had won Roman citizenship under the lex Julia of 90 B.C., but the issue was not over. The nobility that had been thwarting every attempt to enfranchise the allies for a generation was not about to concede the issue, and they devised a plan to undermine the value of the new citizens' votes by placing them in a limited number of tribes. The sources are not clear on the details. It seems that eight new tribes were to be created for the new citizens, who could thus be outvoted by the thirty-five tribes already existing. In addition, the voting procedure in the centuriate assembly was based on the tribes, so that the restriction of the new citizen to a small number of new tribes would also have drastically reduced the influence of the wealthier new citizens in the election of the magistrates possessing imperium.[1]

---

[1] In the first census class, the seventy voting centuries consisted of two centuries from each of the thirty-five tribes (one century for men over the age of forty-five, one for the younger voters). If the same procedure had been carried out in the other four census

The other issue concerned the war with King Mithridates of Pontus (see Chapter 9). It was by this point clear that a major war would have to be fought with him, and that the command of this war in the next year offered great potential for glory. Before the consular elections in 89 B.C., the senate had already decided, in accordance with the lex Sempronia on consular provinces (see Chapter 3), that one of the consular assignments for the following year would be the province of Asia and the war against Mithridates. This command duly fell by lot to Sulla, and during the summer of 88 B.C. he was busy enrolling an army in Campania before crossing over to attack Mithridates's forces (which by now had overrun Asia and reached Greece). The aged Marius, however, had other plans. He saw in the war an opportunity to regain the glory that he had won through his defeat of the Cimbri and Teutoni (this reputation had been tarnished in the view of some as a result of the debacle involving Saturninus and Glaucia in 100 B.C.). And if in the process Marius could get back at the invidious senate and his previous quaestor and current enemy Sulla, so much the better! Unfortunately, the effort to secure the Eastern command for himself would result in a bitter and prolonged civil war.

P. SULPICIUS RUFUS

One of the prime movers in the events of 88 B.C. was the tribune P. Sulpicius Rufus. Like M. Livius Drusus tr. pl. 91, he was a protégé of L. Licinius Crassus cos. 95. Rufus seems to have resembled Drusus in acting as a defender of the oligarchy but getting carried away with himself (in the opinion of the oligarchy at any rate). He first opposed C. Julius Caesar Vopiscus, the younger brother of L. Caesar cos. 90. Vopiscus was aedile in 88 and wished to be (illegally) elected directly to the consulship, passing over the praetorship. Vopiscus clearly sought this premature consulship

classes, each class would also have had seventy centuries. In fact, the other four classes had only thirty or forty centuries each, so a process was devised to reduce the number of the total of seventy units based on the tribes to the number of centuries assigned to that class. For each class, the names of the tribes were selected by lot so that the voters from two or three tribes were randomly grouped together as a single "voting" century. This peculiar procedure had been posited in the nineteenth century by the great German historian Theodor Mommsen to explain why ancient discussions of the census seemed to indicate that the division of the citizenry into tribes had some role to play in the centuriate assembly. His proposal met with a certain amount of skepticism, but an inscription discovered in 1947 that set up a novel form of voting in the time of the emperor Augustus (see Chapter 24) attests exactly the sort of procedure as the one hypothesized by Mommsen. Hence, creating only eight additional tribes for the new citizens would mean that in every sort of electoral assembly they would have less than a quarter of the influence of the old citizens.

in order to receive command in the war against Mithridates. Naturally, Marius was equally opposed to the candidacy, wanting the command for himself.

Sulpicius Rufus came to oppose the senate for what seems to be a comparatively trivial reason. At first, he resisted the proposal of a colleague to bring back from exile "those who had not been allowed to defend themselves" in an unnamed quaestio. Next, Rufus made a similar proposal of his own, but for his part he described those who were to be restored as "those who had been driven out by force." Perhaps this amnesty referred to those who had been exiled as a result of the proceedings of the quaestio Varia. At any rate, the efforts of the senate to thwart the proposed restoration of exiles led Rufus to embark on a policy of attacking the senate.

As an associate of Drusus, Sulpicius Rufus was interested in the fair treatment of the allies and wished to pass legislation to distribute them evenly in the existing thirty-five tribes. To garner support for this measure, he proposed at the same time that freedmen (ex-slaves who gained Roman citizenship upon manumission) should also be evenly distributed instead of being confined to the four urban tribes as was the traditional practice. Rufus was willing (like a good tribune) to use violence to get his laws passed and entered into a personal quarrel with the consul Q. Pompeius Rufus (an old friend). In the effort to gain more support, Sulpicius Rufus enlisted the aid of the embittered savior of the country, C. Marius, who was among other things the darling of the equestrian order. In exchange for his own efforts (and those of the equites, whom he could sway) on behalf of the bill to distribute the new citizens evenly in the tribes, Marius wished to be given the command against Mithridates.

RIOTING IN ROME

The consul Sulla now returned to the city from his military preparations to cooperate with his colleague Q. Pompeius Rufus in opposing Sulpicius Rufus's bill about the distribution of new citizens. They declared an official suspension of public business (iustitium), which Sulpicius Rufus ordered them to rescind as illegal. He then promulgated a vote on his proposal and had his supporters come to the assembly armed. When the two consuls spoke against the bill, a riot broke out. Q. Rufus managed to escape, but his son of the same name (Sulla's son-in-law) was murdered, and Sulla was eventually forced to seek refuge in Marius's house to escape the same fate. There, a momentous meeting took place between Sulla and his old commander. It is clear that a deal was struck between them (though Sulla later denied this). He was allowed to leave unharmed and to retain the consulship, but he gave his word (presumably on oath) to rescind the iustitium, apparently on the understanding that Sulpicius Rufus would then have his legislation passed.[2] Sulla was released, and after lifting the iustitium he fled to his army in Campania. While the faith that Marius and Sulpicius Rufus placed in Sulla's word is touching, it was misplaced: he had no intention of honoring it.[3]

Transfer of Command to Marius

After the passage of the law on distributing the new citizens, it was time to repay Marius. As consul, Sulla had already received the command against Mithridates by the traditional method of selection by lot, but there was no reason why a constitutional ploy already used once before in Marius's interest could not again be used to give him this command – a law ordaining an election to pick the commander by popular vote (see Chapter 4). Accordingly, Sulpicius Rufus proposed an election to decide the command against Mithridates. There was nothing inherently unconstitutional about this, but once the law was passed (presumably by violence), there could be little doubt as to who would win the election: the command was duly transferred to Marius.

Sulla Redux

Sulla reacted to this setback with an action that was to have momentous consequences for the later history of the Republic. He returned to his army in Campania, and pointed out to the troops that if Marius took over, he was going to replace these troops with others raised by himself, and (most importantly) that if this happened, the spoils of the lucrative campaign in the East would go to the new soldiers and not to those enlisted by Sulla. When legates came from Rome to take over the army on behalf of Marius, the newly elected commander, they were driven off by stoning. Sulla then led his army against his enemies in Rome. While Sulla could (and no doubt did) claim that his enemies were acting illegally and that all he was doing was freeing the state from political oppression at

---

[2] We know that the deal took place because while Sulpicius Rufus took no action against Sulla afterward, he had a law passed abrogating the imperium of Sulla's colleague Q. Rufus, who had not agreed to give up his obstruction. Sulla was sufficiently embarrassed by this turn of events that he later denied having fled to Marius's house, and claimed instead that he had gone there voluntarily to discuss Sulpicius's activities.

[3] To be fair, Sulla may have felt that an oath given under compulsion was not binding (though to a legalistic Roman mind, an oath was an oath, regardless of the circumstances).

the hands of a narrow faction, this move was to be fatal for the oligarchy (and the Republican institutions upheld by it). The Roman army of poor soldiers established by Marius now showed that in the final analysis they gave their loyalty to their commander, from whom alone they could expect rewards, and that the commander of an army could make use of this loyalty to wage war on the government in Rome to secure his own aims. Significantly, while in 88 B.C. only one officer remained loyal to Sulla (his quaestor L. Licinius Lucullus), when Caesar was to lead his army against Rome four decades later in 49 B.C., only one officer would refuse to follow him (see Chapter 19). Thus, Sulla was the first general to avail himself of the possibilities inherent in Marius's method of recruiting the army from the poor and to use the army under his command for his own political purposes (the proconsul Cn. Pompeius Strabo also got the message but Sulla beat him to the punch in putting it into practice). Sulla eventually claimed to be the defender of the oligarchy against Marius and his cronies, and after his ultimate victory in civil war, it was in the interest of many to uphold this myth. It is clear, however, that in 88 B.C. Sulla started out by defending his own personal interests through the troops under his command, and that his actions were initially frowned upon by the oligarchy.

Sulla's move was completely unexpected in Rome. Sulpicius Rufus and Marius were astonished to find that the legislation they had had passed by violence was worthless in the face of an army that disregarded it. For its part, the senate was by no means pleased by Sulla's use of independent military force against the city. To carry out violence in accordance with a decree of the senate was one thing, to march against Rome on one's own initiative was quite another! M. Antonius cos. 99 suggested that both sides should lay down their arms, but the majority demanded that Sulla stop. Two praetors were sent to inform him of this decision, and his troops replied by stoning them. Sulla's opponents then fled before his military force, and he seized the city. First, he had the senate decree that twelve prominent leaders opposed to him (including P. Sulpicius Rufus, C. Marius, and C. Marius's son) were military enemies (*hostes*) of the Roman People because of their assault on the consuls. In effect, they were declared to have forfeited their citizenship and for this reason could be killed with impunity. Sulpicius Rufus was betrayed by a slave and executed,[4] but Marius junior escaped to Africa. The elder Marius

---

[4]   In an act typical of the sometimes absurd sense of legalistic scrupulousness to which the Romans were prone, the slave who revealed Rufus's location was first rewarded with manumission for betraying his master, then executed for the same act of disloyalty!

fled south but found no popular support (he had no veterans in the area). He was caught hiding in a swamp near Minturnae (a town in Latium to the south of Rome) but escaped when the public slave sent to execute him turned out to be a captive from Marius's war against the Germans who could not bring himself to overcome his awe of the old victor. Eventually, Marius made it to Africa, but he found little welcome either there or in Numidia, and he wound up on the island of Cercina off Africa, where some veterans of his had been settled.

Sulla's Actions in Rome

After taking the city, Sulla had Sulpicius Rufus's legislation repealed on the grounds that it had been passed through violence. He also had certain laws passed, though the details are not certain (this legislation is confused by the sources with the legislation he would later pass in 81 and 80 B.C.). He seems to have prohibited the passage of legislation that had not already been approved by the senate and also ordained that only the centuriate assembly could pass laws (this would have abrogated the *lex Hortensia* of about 287 B.C. that had made plebiscites binding on the People as a whole). Sulla also had legislation passed about Cn. Pompeius Strabo's imperium (discussed later in the chapter).

Sulla then held the consular elections for 87 B.C. Even though he had seized the city by force, he apparently was unable or unwilling to exert his will over the centuriate assembly. At any rate, because of Sulla's unpopularity (a circumstance worth noting), one of his favored candidates was defeated by L. Cornelius Cinna, who was openly opposed to Sulla and had to swear a public oath on the Capitol that he would uphold Sulla's enactments. Sulla then returned to his army, and finally in the spring of 87 B.C., he crossed over the Adriatic with his troops to Greece.

Cn. Pompeius Strabo

After his triumph in late 89 B.C., Cn. Pompeius Strabo cos. 89 returned to his army in Picenum as proconsul. Following Sulla's capture of Rome, a law was passed giving this army to Sulla's consular colleague Q. Pompeius Rufus, who attempted to take the army over later in 88 B.C. Strabo received him in an appropriate manner and pretended to depart, but since he wished to retain control of the army to help get himself reelected as consul, he had laid plans to foment revolt among the soldiers, who duly mutinied and murdered Rufus. Strabo then returned and resumed command of the army. This happened while Sulla was still in Italy. Sulla's attitude to this treacherous (and treasonous) treatment of his colleague (and the father-in-law of his daughter) is not known, but there are several instances recorded of him acquiescing in the murder of subordinates. In any case, it would seem that since he was in no position to do anything about the matter, he ignored it. While Sulla has the "honor" of being the first commander to take advantage of the implications of Marius's new form of recruitment by using his army against the state, Strabo appears to have been already prepared to do so.

BREAKDOWN OF LEGITIMACY

Down through the second century B.C., it would have been literally inconceivable for a Roman commander to lead his troops against Rome. No matter how much a commander disagreed at that time with a decision to recall him, there was absolutely no possibility that he could have appealed to his troops against the decision taken in Rome. The situation was obviously different in 88 B.C., when Sulla marched his troops to Rome, and Cn. Pompeius Strabo incited his troops to murder his legitimate replacement (the consul Q. Pompeius Rufus). Two factors contributed to this change. First, the frequent use of violence in the assemblies meant that laws passed in them could not be viewed as the self-evident will of the Roman People (however interpreted). Thus, Sulla could make a perfectly reasonable argument that the law and the resulting election that had taken away the command against Mithridates from him and given it to Marius were in fact illegitimate, since the elections had been marred by violence, while he himself was the legitimately elected and appointed consul (Marius's supporters would no doubt have rejected such an interpretation, but the argument was plausible enough). Second, the fact that Sulla and Strabo both retained command by virtue of their personal standing among the troops – whatever constitutional excuses may have been cited in justification – marks the start of an issue that would become increasingly problematical as the old norms of political behavior broke down in the final decades of the Republic: if the troops were loyal to their commander, on what basis did they owe their allegiance to him? Sulla certainly made a direct reference to his soldiers' self-interest (greed) in appealing to them to support him against the assemblies in Rome, but what would happen if someone else made a better offer? In several later instances, Roman commanders found it necessary to use money to maintain the loyalty of their troops. At the same time, however, the soldiery sometimes felt uncomfortable about acting selfishly, and in any case such behavior could only lead to chaos in the long run.

Thus, one of the major causes for the breakdown and replacement of the Republican form of government was its inability to provide a central institutional focus for the soldiers' loyalty, and ultimately the only solution to the problem would be the establishment of a military autocracy.

POLITICAL DIVISIONS BECOME PERSONAL

As a result of the consulship of Sulla, two inherently distinct issues – the method of enfranchising the Italian allies and the personal rivalry between Marius and Sulla – had become intertwined and confused. On the one hand, those who supported generous treatment of the new citizens were now associated with Marius and Sulpicius Rufus and opposed to Sulla, who had repealed their legislation. Although the later sources tend to personalize the issues involved and to lump all these various groups together as "Marians," one could certainly favor this side in the political dispute without being simply a follower of Marius. Furthermore, while Marius may have retained a great deal of personal prestige as the earlier "savior of the fatherland," it was L. Cinna who acted as the leader of this group in his capacity as consul in 87 B.C. On the other hand, the more restrictive attitude toward the new citizens was supported by the senate (more specifically by its leadership), and adherents of this policy were naturally opposed to Marius and Sulpicius Rufus. Such people may have harbored doubts about Sulla's actions, but for the time being, while he was off campaigning in the East, this problematical issue could be ignored, and the leadership of the group fell to Cn. Octavius, the other consul of 87 B.C. Thus, the political scene in 87 B.C. was divided into two camps on the basis of interlocking conflicts of policy and personality.

L. CORNELIUS CINNA

When L. Cornelius Cinna became consul in 87 B.C., he soon proved that he would not abide by his oath to uphold Sulla's enactments (Sulla was even indicted for treason by one of the tribunes, presumably with Cinna's acquiescence, but he paid no attention to this). The sources are poor for this period, and since Cinna's reputation was later blackened by Sulla's supporters, it is to some extent difficult to get a good picture of the man and his aims and methods. Nonetheless, there is enough information to rescue something of his policies from the posthumous vilification. Cinna belonged to a patrician family that had not been successful recently, but he had served as the legate of one of the consuls during the Social War.[5] Presumably, he was a respectable member of the oligarchy, and it is not entirely clear what Cinna's attitude at the time was. At any rate, the fact that he had to swear an oath about his future behavior suggests that there was already some doubt on the question. In any case, it was only after Cinna took up the consulship in 87 B.C. (and Sulla had withdrawn to his army in Campania) that he openly declared himself the champion of the newly enfranchised citizens, announcing that he would try to have them enrolled in all the tribes (in effect reviving the policy quashed by Sulla's invalidation of Sulpicius Rufus's legislation). Like many other members of the oligarchy, Cinna tried to advance his own career by championing causes that were opposed by the dominant elements of the senate. As it turned out, Cinna was an energetic and competent leader, and while he held together the anti-Sullan coalition, he was a moderating figure (it is to be regretted that the hostility of the surviving sources leaves him such a shadowy figure).

BELLUM OCTAVIANUM

Cinna's efforts on behalf of the new citizens were resisted by his colleague Cn. Octavius, and the resulting violence is known as the *bellum Octavianum* ("Octavius's war"). Octavius's opposition is hardly surprising given his family background. He was son of Cn. Octavius cos. 128, whose brother was the M. Octavius who had opposed the agrarian legislation of Ti. Gracchus back in 133 B.C. In addition, the brother of the consul of 87 B.C. (another Marcus) had, as tribune in the early 90s B.C., passed some sort of reduction of the cost of Saturninus's grain dole in Rome.

When Cinna brought in new citizens to help pass his legislation (and repeal Sulla's), rioting broke out; in the short run, the senatorial party led by Octavius prevailed, and Cinna was driven from the city. Declaring him to be a public enemy (*hostis*), the senate decreed that he was no longer consul, and L. Cornelius Merula was elected in his place as a suffect (replacement) consul. Since Merula was flamen dialis (an ancient priesthood with many taboos attached to it; see Chapter 2), he was effectively

---

5   He is attested (*epitome* of Livy 76) as subduing the Marsi in 89 B.C. after the death of the consul L. Cato. The context in Livy and the situation suggest he was operating under the auspices of Cn. Strabo, but it is possible that he owed his original appointment to Cato. In this campaign, he was apparently cooperating with Q. Metellus Pius, which suggests a further connection with the leadership of the senate allied with Sulla, though perhaps not much should be made of wartime collaboration.

ruled out of military command. Presumably this choice was intentional, the purpose being to allow Octavius to operate alone.

In the meanwhile, Cinna withdrew to Campania, where he took over a legion that had been left near Nola by Sulla under the command of an ex-praetor to deal with the last vestiges of resistance remaining from the Social War. The troops were easily convinced that Cinna was still consul (and may have been irked that Sulla was not going to take them along in the campaign against Mithridates), and as he marched toward Rome, Cinna raised large forces from among the new citizens. In the meanwhile, Marius had gained control of Africa, and upon Sulla's departure, he returned to Italy with a military force that he had raised among his veterans on the island of Cercina. He first landed in Etruria (the area north of Rome), where he raised more troops among his veterans, then went on to capture Ostia, the port of Rome. Cinna now joined forces with Marius, and they marched on Rome together. Their forces were sufficiently large that they could be divided into four armies. Cinna and Marius each commanded one contingent, and the other commanders were Cn. Papirius Carbo and Q. Sertorius (both were to be important opponents of Sulla). In addition, to secure support for their efforts, Marius and Cinna came to terms with the rebellious Samnites to the south.

Octavius had been the first to resort to force, but he evidently had not learned the lesson of Sulla's actions the preceding year. He appears to have thought that he could rely on the support of the senate to maintain his position and did not marshal a military force as efficiently as Cinna did. Q. Caecilius Metellus Pius, who was finishing off the war in Samnium, was instructed to end it on terms, but the senate rejected the demands of the Samnites, and they went over to Cinna. Metellus's army was recalled to Rome but took a while getting there. At this point, Octavius's only possible source of support was the army of Cn. Pompeius Strabo in Picenum. Strabo was cagey, parleying with both sides in his quest for a second consulship (he needed this to protect himself against prosecution for the murder of Q. Rufus cos. 88). It would seem that he was most interested in joining forces with Cinna and becoming consul with him in 86 B.C. (familiarity with Cinna is suggested by the cordial relations between Strabo's son and certain men who cooperated with Cinna in the mid 80s B.C.). Eventually, however, Strabo marched toward Rome to lend support to Octavius. Marius had in the meanwhile marched up from Ostia and captured the Janiculum, a hill on the right bank of the Tiber opposite Rome. Octavius dislodged the Marians, but Strabo refused to let Octavius remain on the attack, hoping to extort a second consulship for himself. The Cinnan forces captured several important towns around

Rome, and the loyalty of Octavius's troops was undermined. The decisive factor was the death of Strabo, who was carried away by a plague that broke out among the armies. With Strabo now out of the way, the forces of Cinna and Marius proceeded to seize Rome.

MARIAN SLAUGHTER

Cinna entered the city and revoked Sulla's law against Marius and the other exiles. When Marius entered, he wreaked bitter vengeance upon his many enemies. The consul Octavius was killed (misguided trust in a favorable horoscope prevented his escape, the first example in politics of the increasing popularity of astrology among the Roman upper classes). The head of the consul was hung up on the rostra (the speaker's platform in the forum), another infelicitous first. The heads of L. Caesar cos. 90 and his brother C. Caesar Vopiscus (who had served as an agrarian commissioner in Marius's interest in 100 B.C.), and of M. Antonius cos. 99 also wound up on the rostra. L. Cornelius Merula the suffect consul and Q. Lutatius Catulus, Marius's colleague in the consulship of 102 B.C. and the triumph over the Cimbri, were driven to suicide by criminal indictments (Merula had already resigned from his consulship when Cinna captured the city). In total, some fourteen senators are known to have been killed. While by later standards the number of deaths was small, those killed were among the most prominent senators, and such slaughter was unprecedented. The driving force behind the violence was the embittered old Marius (one man supposedly pleaded for his life in front of Marius, who enjoyed watching him be killed), and Cinna did what he could to restrain the carnage. (Carbo may have been responsible for the death of Antonius, whose prosecution of Carbo's father, Cn. Papirius Carbo cos. 113, after his defeat at the hands of the Cimbri had resulted in the father's suicide.) The oligarchy was now beginning to feel the violence which they had themselves unleashed forty-five years before with the killing of Ti. Gracchus.

Marius and Cinna were elected as consuls for 86 B.C. Much to the relief of Cinna, Marius died soon after taking up his seventh consulship, and L. Valerius Flaccus was elected suffect consul in his place. Some semblance of peace and order was restored over the next few years under Cinna's leadership, but during this period the question of what to do with Sulla – and his ultimately victorious army – remained a source of disquiet and dispute.

Sulla would eventually lead his troops to victory in the East and then return with them to seize control of Italy in civil war. This would mark the first time that the military needs of the empire had allowed a commander to impose his will in Rome by force, but before tracing the story of Sulla's deeds in the East, this is a convenient time to leave the history of domestic politics, which is more or less dominated (in the ancient sources at least) by the story of prominent individuals, and to examine the great increase in territorial commitments overseas that had taken place in the four decades since the death of Ti. Gracchus.

Questions for Study and Reflection

1. What were the two proposals for enrolling the Italian allies in the Roman body politic? What was the purpose of the different methods?
2. How did the rivalry of Marius and Sulla affect the situation? On what was their rivalry based?
3. Why did Marius feel aggrieved? Why did he seek the command in the East? Why did the senate seem to favor Sulla?
4. What was P. Sulpicius Rufus's aim? How and why did he attempt to enlist Marius's support?
5. What happened when Sulla and Q. Pompeius Rufus attempted to thwart Sulpicius Rufus's legislation?
6. Why did Sulla march with his troops on Rome? Was this action legal? On what grounds would Sulla have justified this step and Marius rejected it? What did the senate think of it? Why did the troops follow Sulla?
7. What did Sulla do upon taking Rome?
8. Why did Cn. Pompeius engineer the murder of Q. Pompeius Rufus? What does this murder say about the attitude of the soldiery at this point?
9. Who was L. Cornelius Cinna and what was his attitude toward Sulla's actions? How did Cn. Octavius react? What do his actions show about his understanding of the use of force in domestic politics?
10. What was the attitude of Cn. Pompeius Strabo toward the two sides during the bellum Octavianum? What was his ultimate goal?
11. How did Marius behave upon capturing Rome? Why did he act this way? What was Cinna's attitude?

8

ROMAN TERRITORIAL EXPANSION BEFORE THE FIRST MITHRIDATIC WAR

TERRITORIAL EXPANSION AND THE ROMAN STATE

Marius's election as consul for 107 B.C. to rectify perceived deficiencies in the senate's conduct of the war in Numidia was by no means a unique example of popular interference with normal senatorial politics under such circumstances. Within recent memory, Scipio Aemilianus had twice been illegally elected consul (in 147 and 135 B.C.) as a result of popular discontent with the course of military affairs. In any case, Marius's first election as consul (and his somewhat irregular election as commander) did not have any further effect on the workings of the political system: once he was given the command, Marius simply continued with the prosecution of the war, while electoral politics in Rome returned to normal. Such was not the case with his repeated reelection to consulships in the period 104–100 B.C. For the first time since new regulations for office holding had been established in the early second century B.C., the administrative and electoral system in Rome was distorted by the military needs of the overseas territories controlled by the Roman People. In the case of Marius, this situation was brought about by the threat posed by the Cimbri and the Teutoni, but soon the Roman administrative system would suffer from long-term strains imposed by the strategic needs of the ramshackle collection of Roman provinces, which had to be looked after in a more coherent way than could be routinely provided for by the fundamentally ad hoc nature of the Republican system of administration. This sort of broad analysis is lacking in the ancient sources, which concentrate on the policies and activities of prominent individuals and give little thought to long-term trends. The following account lays out the external expansion of the Roman state at the very time when the domestic troubles were undermining the senate's previous control of the political system in Rome. These two trends would then converge in the figure of Sulla, who used the military forces entrusted to him for a foreign war to establish his personal domination of the political scene in Rome.

The extra-Italian empire influenced affairs in Rome in two ways. First, there was a more or less constant series of wars that had to be fought for a number of reasons. Some, such as the war against Numantia in the 130s B.C. or the campaign of L. Aurelius Orestes in Sardinia in 126– 124 B.C., were straightforward attempts to suppress rebellious groups within already established Roman provinces. Others, such as Marius's campaigns against the Cimbri and the Teutoni, were efforts to ward off external aggressors from territory claimed by the Romans. Finally, certain wars like the campaigns in the interior of the Balkans or the war against Jugurtha may be characterized as attempts to maintain peace in areas that were not directly administered by Rome but were within the Roman sphere of interest. These wars sometimes had direct political consequences in Rome, especially if the campaigning did not fare as well as was hoped in Rome. In such instances, the surviving ancient sources give more or less detailed information if the wars directly related to the careers of individuals in whom ancient historiography was especially interested (e.g., the life of Marius gives rise to numerous discussions of the wars against Jugurtha and the Cimbri and Teutoni). Other wars and prolonged campaigns, which may have been of much greater long-term importance than the ephemeral conflict with Jugurtha (such as the continuing small-scale rebellions in Spain and the wars with Balkan tribes to the north of Macedonia) have left virtually no record. In this regard, the loss of Livy's annalistic (i.e., year-by-year) account for the period after 167 B.C., is particularly regrettable.

The second effect of the empire was the strategic imperative that would bring about the more or less unintentional establishment of further provinces. It seems reasonably certain that in the Middle Republic the Romans were militarily aggressive, but not imperialistic in the sense of being motivated by the desire to seize foreign territory. To the contrary, the Romans often showed themselves to be actively averse to acquiring new territory outside of Italy even when the opportunity arose. Rather, their wars of the early to mid second century B.C. (apart from the suppression of revolt in already existing provinces) were for the most part large-scale raids for the purpose of gaining glory and plunder. To some extent, the year 133 B.C. is of little significance in this regard, and the story of the empire's development is a continuous tale that goes back a century further to the decision to establish the first provinces back in 238 B.C. Nonetheless, there was a perceptible change in the situation in the mid second century B.C., when the continuous wars in Spain and the decision to create new provinces (Africa and Macedonia) without new praetorships in 146 B.C. began to strain the traditional constitution. The previous Roman provinces (Sardinia, Sicily, and the two in Spain) were more or less self-contained and did not abut on areas that could influence them, so that apart from maintaining internal order (which was itself often a difficult task) these provinces did not entail further territorial commitments. This was hardly the case with the new provinces, with the establishment of Africa leading to involvement in neighboring Numidia, and various governors of Macedonia waging wars in the interior of the Balkans. Furthermore, not only had the Romans defeated all the major military powers of the Mediterranean basin by the mid second century B.C., but their collection of provinces scattered across the shores of the Mediterranean necessarily involved them in the affairs of assorted neighbors, so that new conflicts and annexations were unavoidable. Both strategic necessity and the ambitions of magistrates would soon lead to the establishment of a number of new provinces, which imposed ever increasing strains on the administrative apparatus in Rome. In broad terms, the traditional constitution was hard-pressed simply to provide sufficient magistrates to govern them, and in any case it was incapable of determining and implementing any sort of long-term policy to oversee the greatly expanded empire. The inherent dynamic of this situation would eventually place in the hands of certain individuals powers that were totally unprecedented and allowed them to wield a degree of influence in Rome that would previously have been inconceivable.

Unfortunately, the loss of Livy's text for this period means that many of the details of foreign policy in the half century between the tribunate of Ti. Gracchus and the civil wars of the 80s B.C. are completely lost, and we are left only with inadequate hints of the relevant developments. The wars with Jugurtha and the Cimbri and Teutoni have already been treated because of the way in which those conflicts are intimately tied up with political events in Rome, but it is convenient to bring together in a single chapter other notable events in foreign affairs for the period down to the outbreak of the First Mithridatic War, when the nature of the source material begins to improve somewhat.

Pergamene Inheritance

One of Rome's allies in the Greek East since the late third century B.C. was the kingdom in western Asia Minor, which was ruled by the Attalid dynasty from their capital city of Pergamum. In the late third and early second centuries B.C., this dynasty had urged Rome to war against the Antigonid dynasty in Macedon and the Seleucid in Syria, and it had benefited from Rome's victories. The last king of the dynasty, Attalus III, bequeathed his kingdom to the Roman People in 133 B.C.

The king did not simply pass on his full royal powers untrammeled, but he specifically granted the cities in his realm freedom (i.e., internal autonomy) and immunity from tribute. Presumably, this provision was intended to secure local acquiescence in the transfer of power. The king's arrangements were eventually upheld in Rome, but not before Ti. Gracchus proposed accepting the inheritance but using revenues collected from the cities to fund his agrarian activities (see Chapter 2). Under such circumstances, it was highly irresponsible to give any indication that Rome would not uphold the immunity granted by Attalus in his will, as it soon became clear that there would be opposition to Roman rule.

Revolt in Asia and Establishment of a New Province

The bequest was not well received among certain of the kingdom's subjects, and a revolt was started in 132 B.C. by Aristonicus, the illegitimate son of Attalus's predecessor. Dynastic loyalty may have played some role in this rejection of Roman rule, but Aristonicus also seems on the whole to have enjoyed the support of the poor. Presumably, the example of Macedonia and mainland Greece made it clear enough that Roman rule meant the preservation of local oligarchies controlled by the wealthy. The city governments, on the other hand, tended to remain loyal to Rome.

The possibility of trouble was already clear in 132 B.C., when P. Cornelius Scipio Nasica cos. 138, who was unpopular among the general public because of his leadership of the attack on Ti. Gracchus the preceding year, was dispatched to Asia to investigate the situation (and get him out of harm's way in Rome). Once there was no doubt that force would have to be used to restore order, it was decided that one of the consuls of 131 B.C. would be sent, and after a prolonged dispute as to the choice, L. Licinius Crassus Mucianus (C. Gracchus's father-in-law and a member of the Gracchan land commission) secured the command for himself (see Chapter 2). He brought a hastily raised force to the East, where he soon suffered defeat at the hands of the rebels and died in the battle.[1] M. Perperna cos. 130 took over command of the war and killed Aristonicus in battle in 130 B.C. The settlement of the province fell to M.' Aquillius cos. 129, who remained there until 126 B.C.

Wealth of the Province of Asia

In the final settlement, some of the distant areas were given to local kings, and the province of Asia was established in Ionia (western Asia Minor). Cities that had stayed loyal during the revolt – and most had – retained their freedom, and tribute was imposed on the cities that had supported Aristonicus. The new province, which had rich farmland and many prosperous cities, was far wealthier than any of the previous ones, and this wealth would prove a great temptation to its governors. More immediately, Aquillius apparently made very large sums of money out of the many decisions that had been made regarding the settlement of the province in general and the consequences of the revolt in particular. While the Romans understood in theory that bribery was wrong, in practice it was not considered absolutely wrong to receive gifts of "thanks" from grateful provincials, so that even honest governors would leave their provinces with cash on hand.[2] The Republic would institute various measures intended to curb the rapaciousness of provincial governors, but these efforts would prove to be of little avail.

Administrative Implications

The establishment of the province of Asia represented the third time (after Macedonia and Africa in 146 B.C.) that a new province was set up

---

[1] It is a not uncommon phenomenon of the Late Republic that newly raised armies would be defeated by a veteran force, whether of foreigners or of other Romans during a civil war. Even though these new armies would have in them many conscripts with previous military experience, it took months of practice and training for the troops to become familiar with one another and for the competent leaders to become known. The failure of the Republic to keep a trained military organization on permanent duty would lead to numerous initial defeats for this reason (once set in proper order, the Roman army would normally prevail in the end).

[2] Cicero made a very conscious effort to act in an exemplary manner as governor of Cilicia in 51–50 B.C., but even so, by the time he returned home, he had acquired three million sesterces and needed to decide what to do with it as civil war loomed (he eventually decided to contribute it to Pompey's war chest, much to the annoyance of his subordinates, who thought it should have been distributed among them!).

without the creation of a corresponding new praetorship. Clearly, it was now accepted as a matter of course that the number of provinces would exceed the number of annual praetors, and that the praetors of previous years would have to be prorogued regularly to provide the requisite number of provincial governors. This situation would soon deteriorate even further, when the establishment of new judicial functions for praetors in Rome (as the presiding magistrates in the permanent quaestiones) made further claims upon the six annual praetors.

Another problem was caused by military considerations. A little over a decade earlier, the senate had accepted a major permanent military commitment in Macedonia, whose governor would have to deal with the threat posed by various tribes to the north in the interior of the Balkans. It may have been thought in 133 B.C. that the acceptance of the Attalid inheritance in Asia Minor did not entail a similar commitment. Internally, Aquillius's settlement of 129–126 B.C. must have resulted in the establishment in the local city-states of oligarchic governments that could be relied upon to remain loyal to Rome, and the external situation was much less threatening than in Macedonia. The western end of the province abutted on the Aegean Sea, on the other shore of which lay Roman-controlled Greece. To the east in the interior of Asia Minor lay various local populations and kings, none of whom posed any threat at the time. Hence, there was no immediate need for a permanent Roman garrison in Asia. Instead, the Roman governors (normally of praetorian rank) relied upon the forces of the local city-states to maintain internal order. This assessment of the situation was clearly valid at the time, and for nearly four decades the province was controlled adequately enough with these meager military resources. In the late 90s B.C., however, military disaster would show the inadequacy of these arrangements.

GAUL

The late 120s B.C. saw the establishment of yet another territorial commitment, this one in Gaul (the area delineated by the Alps and the river Rhine on the east, the Atlantic on the west, and the Pyrenees mountains on the south, which is more or less equivalent to modern France and the Low Countries). The region was mainly occupied by speakers of Celtic languages. For a long time the Romans had been militarily active in southern Gaul, but for decades they resisted any permanent commitment.

In the early second century B.C., the Romans conquered the area between the Po River and the Alps, and southern Gaul was the natural path for Roman armies to take when marching from Italy to Spain. In this area, the Romans had an ally in the Greek colony of Massilia (modern Marseilles);

in the 150s B.C., the Romans defeated some Celtic tribes on behalf of Massilia, but they did not become directly involved in governing the area. In 125 B.C., the consul M. Fulvius Flaccus had to abandon his efforts to extend citizenship to the Italian allies (see Chapter 3) in order to campaign against Gallic tribes threatening Massilia. Though he won a triumph in 123 B.C., three more consuls (C. Sextius Calvus cos. 124, Cn. Domitius Ahenobarbus cos. 122, and Q. Fabius Maximus cos. 121) operated in the area and directly conquered a number of tribes. Somewhat surprisingly, Domitius not only continued to operate in Gaul after Fabius's arrival, but he even remained there after Fabius's departure and oversaw the construction of a road (via Domitia) from the Rhône to the Pyrenees. The exact date at which the area became a permanent Roman province (that is, a fixed geographical area to which a governor was regularly assigned) is disputed. This was certainly the case by the 90s B.C., and may well have taken place much earlier (it is often argued that Domitius himself established the province, but there is no direct evidence for this). In any case, the Gallic area to the north of the Po and south of the Alps known as Cisalpine Gaul ("Gaul this side of the Alps") would sometimes be associated with Gaul to the west (Transalpine Gaul), though the latter was sometimes granted to a governor of Nearer Spain. In any case, the Romans now had a fourth province for which to provide a governor without any corresponding increase in the number of praetors (in addition to Africa, Macedonia, and Asia).

This area was comparatively quiet for more than a decade after its establishment, and the foundation of a large colony at Narbo Martius in 118 B.C. seems to have formed part of the aftermath of the Gracchan agrarian reforms (see Chapter 3). The more Romanized area of Transalpine Gaul in the south came to be called Narbonensis after this town, and this area was then distinguished in the first century B.C. from the rest of Transalpine Gaul, which encompassed the territory to the north that was not directly controlled by the Romans.

By 110 B.C., the Cimbri and Teutoni appeared to the north of the Roman province (after having inflicted a major defeat on the governor of Macedonia in 113 B.C.), and the need to keep them at bay caused a number of governors of Gaul to seek them out in battle. The defeats suffered by these governors in the period 109–105 B.C. were then the cause of Marius's repeated consulships (see Chapter 5).

SLAVE REVOLT IN SICILY

A major slave revolt in Sicily in the years 135–133 B.C. may have played a role in Ti. Gracchus's attempt to strengthen the smallholders of Italy against the perceived threat posed by the large slave-operated estates. In any case, the slaves had defeated a number of Roman magistrates before being subdued, and in 101 B.C. yet another major uprising broke out. M.' Aquillius, Marius's colleague as consul in 101 B.C., was dispatched to the island and successfully quelled the uprising. The two slave rebellions in Sicily show how easily an ungarrisoned area that held a large slave population in the countryside could be overrun if the slaves got out of hand, and also how quickly such slaves, who had presumably only recently been reduced to slavery during Roman wars in comparatively primitive areas (for example, Spain or the Balkans), could form themselves into militarily effective units and rout hastily raised Roman forces. As an island, Sicily was isolated, and for this reason the rebellions there were of limited influence elsewhere (except perhaps to the extent that Rome's grain supply was affected), but the great Italian revolt led by Spartacus twenty-five years later would make the consequences of employing so many rural slaves felt much closer to Rome.[3]

CILICIA

Since the end of the third century B.C., the Greek island of Rhodes off the southwestern coast of Asia Minor had been a reliable Roman ally, providing much assistance to the Romans with its large navy. During the Third Macedonian War, the Romans had been disgruntled by what they took to be lukewarm support for their cause on the part of the Rhodians, and in 167 B.C. the Romans opened a free port on the Aegean island of Delos to punish the Rhodians. This ruined the economic prosperity of the Rhodians, who largely depended for their revenues on the transit charges they made on the commerce that passed through their busy port. The Rhodian navy had previously suppressed piracy in the eastern Mediterranean, but the short-sighted Roman decision to undermine the Rhodian economy changed this. The Rhodians could no longer maintain their fleet, and in the absence of any other force to keep piracy in check, pirates became an increasing problem in the eastern Mediterranean. In

---

[3] In the course of his settlement of the province, Aquillius was guilty of flagrant corruption just as his father had been in Asia during the early to mid 120s B.C., and he was tried for extortion in the early 90s B.C. He was defended by M. Antonius cos. 99, who used the (in)famous ploy of tearing open Aquillius's clothing before the jurors to show the wounds he had received in battle as a token of personal valor. Aquillius's bravery in battle was no doubt laudable, but that was beside the point. Nonetheless, Aquillius was acquitted despite his manifest guilt. This shows the difficulties that Roman juries faced in convicting of corruption generals who had otherwise benefited the state.

102 B.C., M. Antonius was given a special command as praetor to subdue the home territory of the pirates in Cilicia (the southeastern coast of Asia Minor). By 100 B.C., Antonius returned to celebrate a triumph and run for the consulship of the next year (this conveniently made troops available for the suppression of Saturninus and Glaucia after their disruption of the consular elections; see Chapter 5).

There is some doubt as to when Cilicia became a fully formed province, but to some extent this is a matter of definition. Some provinces were defined as a geographically fixed area when the decision was made to send out a (pro)magistrate to govern the area on a regular basis, and in certain instances the magistrate who first organized the province would issue a decree know as a law (*lex*) that explicitly laid out the privileges and obligations of the recognized *civitates* ("states") of the province.[4] The example of Cyrenaica, which was bequeathed to the Roman People in 95 B.C. but not set up as a province for which a (pro)magistrate had to be provided as its governor every year, shows that an area could fall within the Roman sphere of influence without needing a regular governor. Conceivably, Cilicia was at first an ad hoc provincial assignment, receiving a Roman magistrate only when the need for one was felt, but even if this is so, various strategic considerations soon ensured that a governor had to be sent there on a regular basis.

In the first place, there is clear evidence of a Roman commitment to suppress piracy in Cilicia throughout the 90s B.C. and later. The Roman system of employing regional governors with limited capacity would prove incapable of dealing with the problem of piracy, which spanned the entire eastern Mediterranean, and eventually the solution to the problem would force the Romans to create a military command of unprecedented scope in the early 60s B.C.

Furthermore, the Roman decision to take responsibility for Cilicia entailed the need to maintain order throughout eastern Asia Minor. Much of this activity consists of the sorts of events that tend to be ignored in the ancient sources with their emphasis on important individuals, but the later fame of L. Cornelius Sulla ensured that his activities as propraetor in Cilicia in the early to mid 90s B.C. are preserved. Not only was he forced to deal with the affairs of certain kingdoms in the interior of Asia Minor to the north of Cilicia (see Chapter 9), but he is also attested

---

4   For instance, M.' Aquillius cos. 101 established a *lex Aquillia* for Sicily that was cited by Cicero in 70 B.C. during his prosecution of the governor C. Verres, and the *lex Pompeia* by which Pompey established Pontus and Bithynia in 64 B.C. was still cited as being in full force in the early second century A.D.

as the first Roman magistrate to treat with the Parthian kingdom. The Arsacid dynasty of Parthia was based in the Iranian plateau, but the western end of their realm included Mesopotamia, which lay to the southeast of Cilicia. Sulla reached an agreement with them as to the border between Roman and Parthian territory on the upper Euphrates River (an area that would be the scene of conflict for centuries). It is indicative of the inadequacy of the Republican system of provincial government that a major decision like this had to be made on the spot by the local governor without any further consultation with Rome. Other such decisions would have to be made in the following decades by various powerful individuals in a basically ad hoc manner, but if the increasing number of Roman possessions was to remain under control, a more rational basis of overseeing them would have to be found. In any case, the situation in Cilicia illustrates how the strategic considerations of preexisting Roman territory (i.e., Asia proper) first led to involvement in Cilicia, which in turn brought about yet more involvement in surrounding areas. In effect, within a generation, the decision to accept the Attalid inheritance brought in its train a Roman commitment to oversee all of Asia Minor. In 91 B.C., a seemingly minor dispute over an insignificant border would reveal both the extent of Roman commitments in Asia Minor and the lack of preparation on the Roman side to deal with these.

WARS IN THE BALKANS

The Balkan peninsula abuts on the Mediterranean and Black Seas on the east, south, and west and extends up to the Danube in the north and the Alps in the west. With the creation of the province of Macedonia in 146 B.C., the Romans not only assumed control of the Greek cultural area in the south of the peninsula but necessarily had to protect this area against the more primitive inhabitants to the north. The interior had long been inhabited by Illyrians to the northwest in the area once occupied by modern Yugoslavia, and by Thracians to the northeast in the area of modern Bulgaria and European Turkey. Though the Romans are attested as interfering in Illyricum (the territory of the Illyrians) as early as the late third century B.C., they seem to have been content to leave the area alone as long as nothing disturbed the peace across the Adriatic in Italy. For unknown reasons, L. Caecilius Metellus cos. 118 waged a successful campaign against the Dalmatians, a tribe in Illyricum, earning himself a triumph (and the title Delmaticus). There would also be some activity in the direction of Thrace, but the main cause of trouble in the Balkans came from the Scordisci, a Celtic tribe who had been settled in the area of modern Serbia since the late third century B.C. and who repeatedly attacked neighboring regions. There had already been troubles in 141 and 135 B.C., but toward the end of the century the situation was grave enough to require the presence of various consuls for several years. After that, the Balkans continued to be the location of intermittent campaigning until the emperor Augustus undertook the major task of extending direct Roman control up to the Danube.

The major troubles began in 119 B.C., when the praetor or propraetor Sex. Pompeius was defeated in battle by a Celtic tribe (most likely the Scordisci). By 114 B.C., the consul C. Porcius Cato was assigned Macedonia, where he suffered defeat at the hands of the Scordisci in the direction of Thrace (and as a result he was convicted in the court for provincial corruption for a trivial sum the next year – this again shows that convictions in this court were far more likely if the accused governor was militarily unsuccessful). In 113 B.C., C. Caecilius Metellus Caprarius operated in Thrace, where he earned a triumph. M. Livius Drusus, C. Gracchus's tribunician opponent, went to Macedonia as consul in 112 B.C. and resumed the campaign against the Scordisci. He remained there until 110 B.C., earning a triumph (and, it would seem, much booty). M. Minucius Rufus cos. 110 took over from Drusus, waging war against the Scordisci and other tribes until 106 B.C., when he triumphed over the Scordisci. By the end of the decade, the situation was sufficiently under control that Macedonia became a praetorian province, and in the last years of the century, the praetor T. Didius continued to harass the Scordisci (also subdueing an area of Thrace). Despite all of these campaigns, however, there was no territorial expansion apart from the small region annexed to Macedonia by Didius. For the most part, the Romans were content to keep the Scordisci and Thracians at bay.

LAW ON PRAETORIAN PROVINCES (*LEX DE PROVINCIIS PRAETORIIS*)

A Roman law (*RS* 12) has been preserved on two fragmentary inscriptions, one on the Aegean island of Delos, the other in the city of Cnidos on the Aegean coast of Asia Minor. The two inscriptions preserve separate (presumably, locally produced) Greek translations of the same law, but unfortunately much of the law's content has been lost. A major element of the law overtly concerns the perceived need to ensure safe sailing in the East and to halt the depredations of pirates. Large amounts of text are devoted to instructing the senior consul to dispatch letters to eastern kings to enlist their assistance in these efforts, and the law in some way directed that envoys from the island of Rhodes, which had a traditional interest in the suppression of piracy, were to be brought before the senate to make some plea about the matter. The law regulated a large number of administrative matters in the East relating to the provinces of Asia, Macedonia, and Cilicia. Among other things, it seems to have established Cilicia as a regular praetorian province. It also canceled a dispatch of troops who were to have been sent to Macedonia under the terms of an earlier law. In addition, it dictated how the recently conquered area in Thrace was to be made part of the province of Macedonia by the latter's governor and how frequently future governors were to visit it. The law seems to have been passed late in 101 B.C., and if this is so, it is hard to imagine that the law could have been passed without Marius's acquiescence at the least.[5] Unfortunately, the very fragmentary state of the text makes the interpretation of many details problematical, not to mention the overall thrust of the document. When only the copy of the text from Delphi was known, the apparent content of those fragments led to the law being designated informally as a "law on pirates." Since the dissemination of the text from Cnidos, the law has generally been known as a "law on praetorian provinces" (*lex de provinciis praetoriis*), it being commonly assumed that the law in its full form dealt with all the praetorian provinces. But there is absolutely nothing in the law to suggest that it covered any but eastern affairs, and accordingly it is best to conceive of it as a sort of omnibus regulation of the military and political activities of the eastern governors. The phraseology of the letters that were to be sent to monarchs to enlist their cooperation speaks clearly about the Romans' obligation to maintain peace and order throughout the eastern Mediterranean, which shows a clear awareness of the imperial obligations that Rome had acquired as the dominant power in the area.

One provision of the law underscores how poorly informed we are about the details of foreign affairs. This provision states in passing that the law was not to be taken as affecting the assignment of Lycaonia as a

---

[5] The law refers overtly to the consulship of C. Marius and L. Valerius Flaccus, which fell in 100 B.C. Thus, the law must have been passed after the consular elections of late 101 B.C., and while it could conceivably have been passed in 100 B.C. (as many scholars hold), its provisions seem to make more sense if they were supposed to regulate the provinces that would subsequently be chosen by lot for the praetors of 100 B.C. rather than rearrange these matters after a preceding selection that had already been carried out after the elections of 101 B.C. In any case, the year 101 B.C. seems the appropriate time to provide for a permanent position as governor of Cilicia, since M. Antonius was going to return the following year after his successful campaign there.

province to the man who held the province of Asia. Lycaonia is an area on the southern coast of Asia Minor, and in the previous piece of information we have about the area in the literary record, it had been given to one of the sons of the king of Cappadocia, who had died during the war with Aristonicus (presumably, M.' Aquillius made this grant as part of his settlement of Asia in the early to mid 120s B.C.). It is totally unknown what exactly this province of Lycaonia (and perhaps also of neighboring Pamphylia, which is mentioned in a very fragmentary section of the law) signified, though presumably the governor was conducting some sort of campaign in the area in conjunction with M. Antonius's suppression of piracy in Cilicia to the east.

The law is clearly a piece of tribunician legislation, and it directly interferes with the senate's traditional assignment of provinces. It also undertook to regulate the activity of provincial magistrates by specifying in detail certain actions which they had to take. It is sometimes inferred that the law specified who the governors were to be, but there is no direct evidence for this (and such a provision seems unlikely). It is disheartening that even in a period of time that is comparatively well attested because of the activities of Marius and Saturninus, the literary sources have absolutely nothing to say of this law. At the very least, this law indicates an attempt to use popular legislation to force the senate's hand in eastern affairs. Seemingly, it also indicates an effort on someone's part to undertake some sort of overall review of policy in the East, which makes it all the more unfortunate that it is so difficult to be sure of the details and that the identity of the legislator and the circumstances that gave rise to the law are completely unknown.

While the law might be taken as showing how actively the Roman People, duly convened in their assemblies, could be involved in provincial matters, it instead shows the opposite. The law was approved in a popular assembly, but the very detailed provisions were drawn up by some specific magistrate. He may well have had the public good, as he saw it, in mind (the law refers to the People's obligation to keep the seas safe for the sake both of Romans, the Latins, and Italian allies and of the foreign nations in a state of friendship with Rome), but there was no way that the voters could have influenced the law's content, and the provisions no doubt benefited certain magistrates. In effect, the Roman People could pass laws that concerned such administrative minutiae, but there was no method of proper deliberation on these matters, and eventually the assemblies would be manipulated (at times through violence) by magistrates who wished to use the assemblies' powers for their own ambitions. This was no rational way to administer the vast expanse of territory now under Rome's sway.

CYRENAICA

Cyrene was a Greek settlement in what is modern Libya, and the surrounding area is known as Cyrenaica. In the second century B.C., a junior branch of the Ptolemaic dynasty of Egypt was given control of Cyrenaica, and in 96 B.C. the last king of this line followed the precedent of Attalus III of Pergamum in bequeathing his kingdom to Rome. Though the Romans had accepted the inheritance, for familiar reasons (not enough praetors) they did not establish a proper province. Instead, they took over the royal estates and gave the Greek cities their freedom (i.e., allowed them to govern their own affairs without direct Roman supervision). Seemingly, it was thought that since the region was of no broad strategic importance (deserts to the west separated it from Roman Africa and it posed no threat to Egypt to the east), it was good enough if the local cities recognized Roman supremacy, and thus there was no cause to install a Roman governor (which would occupy yet another praetorship). This situation is comparable to the arrangements made in Greece after the destruction of the kingdom of Macedonia in 167 B.C., when the Romans were content to interfere in local affairs without assuming any direct administrative responsibility. If so, the Romans would find that this sort of indirect hegemony was untenable, and by the mid 70s B.C. the strife of the local city-states would compel the senate to establish yet another province (see Chapter 12).

QUESTIONS FOR STUDY AND REFLECTION

1. Why did Attalus bequeath his kingdom to the Roman People? Why was this decision not uniformly popular among his subjects?
2. What criteria were used to determine whether a new province would be created? What factors influenced the decision and who made it?
3. What resources were available to maintain order in the new provinces and to protect them against invasion?
4. What effect did the creation of new provinces have on politics in Rome and the Roman administrative system?
5. What were the strategic implications of the creation of the province of Macedonia? Of Asia? Of Gaul? Of Cilicia?
6. How does the law on praetorian provinces show the inability of the assemblies in Rome to exercise any meaningful oversight of foreign policy?
7. Why was no province created in Cyrenaica? What are the implications of this decision?

9

FIRST MITHRIDATIC WAR

MITHRIDATES

Pontus is the mountainous area of northeastern Asia Minor, and a kingdom was set up in this region by a Persian nobleman in 302 B.C. during the upheavals following the death of Alexander the Great. Over the years the dynasty became heavily (if perhaps superficially) Hellenized. In 121/0 B.C., Mithridates VI Eupator established himself as sole king upon the death of his father, murdering his brother and mother and marrying his sister in the process. Mithridates proved to be an extremely energetic and competent ruler and caused the Romans many years of trouble.

The events of his reign before the 90s B.C. are poorly attested. He established his control over the Greek colonies on the Crimean peninsula (now in the southern Ukraine), which were weakened by tribes to their north. He also took over the western Caucasus (modern Georgia and Armenia). These areas, along with Pontus itself, formed the heartland of his kingdom.

CAPPADOCIA

In the first few decades after the creation of the province of Asia, the Romans were more or less content to leave the interior of Asia Minor to its own devices.[1] This attitude changed with the establishment in 100 B.C. of the province of Cilicia in the southeastern corner of Asia Minor (see

[1] This is not to say that the rulers of Asia Minor did not seek to use Roman power to their advantage. A large fragment of a speech of C. Gracchus concerns the bribery used by a king of Bithynia to secure the passage of a favorable piece of legislation (whose content is completely unknown), and in 102 B.C. L. Saturninus acted insolently toward envoys of Mithridates, who had supposedly come to Rome with large amounts of money to bribe senators. Nonetheless, while the Romans may have been happy enough to influence events to the east of the province of Asia, they had no desire at this time to administer the region directly.

Chapter 8). Directly to the north of the new province lay the kingdom of Cappadocia, which Mithridates sought to bring under his control, not by openly annexing it but by manipulating, intimidating, and (at times) replacing its kings. This suggests that while he wished to expand his influence into the interior of Asia Minor, he also intended to avoid a direct confrontation with Roman power. The exact chronology of his early dealings there is hard to pin down, but the general course of events is clear enough. Soon after 100 B.C., Mithridates's interference in Cappadocia resulted in the demise of the old dynasty, and in its place he attempted to install a young son of his (he had many), though it was claimed that this boy king belonged to the old royal line. The king of Bithynia, who had his own disputes with Mithridates, feared this increase in his rival's power and set up his own contender, who likewise made false claims of descent from the old line. At an unspecified point in the early 90s B.C., Marius took a trip to Asia Minor to thank a local divinity to whom he had made vows during the German campaign, and during this visit Marius met Mithridates in Cappadocia, where he told him either to prepare to get the better of the Romans or to do what he was told. The later tradition read this in light of subsequent events as an attempt to stir up trouble, but presumably Marius meant that unless Mithridates thought himself militarily superior to the Romans (which there was no reason to believe at the time), he should not disregard decisions of the senate. (This situation seems reminiscent of the attempts to make Jugurtha behave himself in the 110s B.C.) In any case, both sides to the dispute sought confirmation from the senate in Rome, which was apparently disgusted with the situation and decided to bring foreign intervention to an end by declaring that both Cappadocia and Paphlagonia (a disputed region between Bithynia and Pontus) were to be "free." Similar declarations of freedom had been made for Greece in 196 B.C. and for Macedonia in 167 B.C. In those instances, the point had been to free the regions from royal interference and to have the local city-states govern their own affairs under the overall hegemony of Rome. In this case, such freedom was inappropriate since there was no tradition of self-government by city-states, and soon an embassy of Cappadocian nobles arrived to ask the senate to allow them to choose a king. (Apparently, making decisions in Rome about distant and little understood regions was harder than it seemed!) With the senate's permission, a local nobleman named Ariobarzanes was elected, but adherents of Mithridates soon forced him to flee to Roman territory. The senate then instructed L. Sulla, who had received Cilicia as his province after serving as urban praetor, both to force Mithridates to withdraw from Cappadocia and to install Ariobarzanes as king. This task Sulla was able to carry out with a small Roman force plus levies that he gathered from local Roman allies. It is sometimes thought that Sulla's activities should be placed in the late 90s B.C., but careful analysis of the evidence suggests that he was praetor in 97 B.C. and the installation of Ariobarzanes took place the following year. In any event, while Mithridates may have given way when faced with force, he was hardly finished with his attempts to subvert Cappadocia, and his next move would unexpectedly result in a major war with Rome.

Conflict with Rome

The conflict began in 91 B.C. – the date is uncertain because the initial steps, which are undated in the sources, have to be calculated back from later, datable events – when Mithridates engaged in two plots that threatened Roman interests. First, he supported the overthrow of Nicomedes, the new king of Bithynia and ally of Rome, by Nicomedes' brother Socrates. At the same time, Mithridates also engineered the expulsion of Ariobarzanes of Cappadocia by local forces. Though Mithridates was once again eager to avoid direct involvement, his machinations resulted in the replacement of kings loyal to Rome with ones more to Mithridates' liking. Since this posed a threat to two Roman provinces (Asia and Cilicia), the senate decided to send a commission under a senior consular to inspect the situation firsthand and browbeat Mithridates into undoing his actions.

M.' Aquillius as Legate

In late 91 or 90 B.C., the senate sent out a three-man senatorial commission led by M.' Aquillius cos. 101. This took place at the beginning of the Social War, and while it may not yet have been realized how perilous the situation was, it is clear that Aquillius's brief went no further than trying to induce Mithridates through diplomacy to cooperate in the restoration of Nicomedes in Bithynia and Ariobarzanes in Cappadocia. In 90 B.C. this was done. Since Mithridates was not directly involved in their overthrow, he still retained the title of "friend of the Roman People."

At this point, Aquillius (in conjunction with Q. Oppius the governor of Cilicia) appears to have incited Nicomedes to wage war on Mithridates. It is not clear whether this was in late 90 or 89 B.C. The motive is alleged to have been that since Nicomedes had promised large bribes to important Romans (presumably including Aquillius) and had contracted large debts in Rome, Aquillius wished Nicomedes to raise the funds needed to repay his creditors by raiding Mithridates' territory. Under the circumstances, with Italy engulfed in the Social War and very few Roman forces stationed in Asia Minor, this turned out to be a very rash step, especially since Aquillius had no authority from the senate to precipitate a war. To make his actions seem rational (if not excusable), it has to be remembered that at the time he would not have realized how potent Mithridates's military force was – or how feeble were the resources available to use against Mithridates if he refused to back down. Aquillius presumably thought that Nicomedes would be able, with a bit of Roman support, to defeat the forces of Mithridates's barbarous little kingdom (and in the process make a bit of money for Aquillius and his friends). To be fair to Aquillius, he may well have felt on the basis of Sulla's success in forcing his wishes upon him back in 96 B.C. that Mithridates would not put up a fight. As things turned out, Aquillius got more than he bargained for.

When Nicomedes' forces ravaged the western part of his kingdom, Mithridates sent an envoy to complain to Aquillius, pointing out that he, Mithridates, was still a friend of the Roman People and asking Aquillius to halt Nicomedes's incursion. Aquillius equivocated by saying that since both kings were friends of the Roman People, neither should suffer harm, and he did nothing. In retaliation, Mithridates invaded Cappadocia, replacing the Roman-supported king Ariobarzanes with his own candidate.

FULL-SCALE WAR AND ROMAN DISASTER

By his rash actions, Aquillius had provoked Mithridates into open war with Rome's allies, and in 89 B.C. he was forced to defend them with very inadequate forces. C. Cassius, the proconsul in charge of Asia, had a small Roman force under his command, which was presumably also the case with Q. Oppius, the proconsul in Cilicia.[2] The Romans quickly raised emergency troops among their allied cities in Asia.

The Roman commanders decided on a three-pronged invasion of Mithridates's territory. Aquillius was to help Nicomedes attack from the west and Cassius was to lead his forces from the south through Galatia (in central Asia Minor), while Oppius subdued Cappadocia. The campaign went disastrously wrong. Nicomedes's army was completely destroyed, and in the retreat he joined his forces with those of Aquillius. This army

---

[2] Both governors were ex-praetors, but propraetors generally held the title of proconsul in the Late Republic, that is, they had proconsular imperium even though they had only been praetors in the city.

was in turn wiped out by Mithridates, and a general retreat of the Romans ensued. Aquillius fled to the coast of the province of Asia, and Nicomedes joined Cassius, the two of them retreating to the southwest.

At this point, all resistance to Mithridates in the field collapsed, and he swept into the Roman province of Asia. Bithynia likewise fell to him, and he gained control of the Bosporus (the channel between Europe and Asia), allowing his fleet to emerge from the Black Sea into the Aegean. He treated all the local levies in kindly fashion when they surrendered to him, hoping to win their support for his cause. In this he was partially successful. While the Romans were not entirely popular in Asia and a number of communities went over to Mithridates, it is likewise clear that many remained loyal to Rome and opposed Mithridates. (To what extent loyalty to Rome should be attributed to genuine favor or to a rational calculation that the Romans were more likely to emerge victorious from the conflict cannot be determined.) Aquillius was seized by the Greek town of Mytilene while he was fleeing to Rhodes and turned over to Mithridates. Aquillius was taken to Pergamum (capital of the province of Asia), and after being humiliated he was executed by having molten gold poured into his mouth, a punishment that symbolized his rapacity. The proconsul Q. Oppius was also betrayed to Mithridates by the town of Apamea, but unlike Aquillius he was treated civilly in captivity, which suggests that Mithridates had some particular animus against Aquillius.

In order to cement the loyalty of the cities of Asia, which had gone over to him voluntarily or by force by 88 B.C., Mithridates decreed a general massacre of the resident Romans. A command was issued in every city on the same day that this massacre was to take place immediately (this ruse would prevent any stalling by the locals or escaping by the victims); 80,000 were massacred, often in violation of the rights of sanctuary. After this slaughter, the implicated cities would obviously not be very eager to see the Romans return.

REACTION IN ROME

The phenomenal success of Mithridates in 89 B.C. and the precipitous collapse of the Roman position in Asia Minor must have been equally surprising to the Romans and to Mithridates himself. Having been forced into military operations against Rome by the actions of Aquillius, he suddenly (and presumably unexpectedly) found himself the master of Asia. In accordance with the lex Sempronia on consular provinces (see Chapter 3), the senate declared in 89 B.C. that the province of Asia and the war against

Mithridates would be assigned to one of the incoming consuls, and this command fell by lot to Sulla. He first had to raise an army and was then prevented by civil strife in Italy from heading east until the spring of 87 B.C. (see Chapter 8). By that time, the situation had deteriorated as a result of Mithridates's campaign of 88 B.C.

CAMPAIGN OF 88 B.C.

Once it had become clear in 89 B.C. that his forces could get the better of the Romans (even though he had not met a proper army of Roman legionaries), Mithridates decided to take the offensive. He first turned his attention to the island of Rhodes, to which the proconsul C. Cassius had fled, and conducted a protracted campaign against it. At first, the Rhodian fleet defeated Mithridates's ships; he eventually managed to land his army on the island, but its assault on the city's walls failed. Finally, after the failure of another assault involving a massive tower carried on ships, he abandoned the effort. At this point – some time well into 88 B.C. – he decided to send a force against Greece. Supposedly, Mithridates was so disheartened by his setback at Rhodes that from then on he ceased to exercise direct command in the field and instead sent a number of generals to command expeditions against Greece. One might also imagine that he had his hands full with administering the many newly conquered cities of the prosperous province of Asia.

ARCHELAUS'S INVASION OF GREECE

Mithridates's general Archelaus swept across the Aegean with a fleet and landed in Athens. At this point, much of southern Greece went over to him. Another force under Metrophanes crossed over to central Greece. This force met with less success, though it did capture the island of Euboea, which became a major base. The lack of success on the mainland is attributable to the fact that now there was actually a proper Roman army to face it, namely, the force stationed in Macedonia to guard against the Illyrian tribes to the north. The governor there (C. Sentius) sent his legate Q. Braettius Sura south with a large force. Sura threw Metrophanes out of central Greece and met Archelaus in battle at Chaeronea in Boeotia (the region north of Attica, which was the territory belonging to Athens). After three days' fighting, Archelaus withdrew to Athens in late 88 B.C. Meanwhile, he received reinforcements from his new Greek allies in the Peloponnesus, which deterred Sura from pressing on. Sura then spent the winter in Boeotia.

SULLA ARRIVES

In the spring of 87 B.C., Sulla was finally ready to bring his army over to attack Mithridates's forces in Greece. First, he sent his quaestor L. Licinius Lucullus ahead to order Sura to withdraw to Macedonia, since the war against Mithridates was Sulla's by virtue of the decree of the senate in 89 B.C. It was just as well that Sura returned to Sentius in the north, as Mithridates was about to launch an attack on Macedonia, which was apparently beaten off successfully by Sentius and Sura around the time of Sulla's arrival.

Lucullus then gathered the Roman garrisons in Boeotia, and most of the towns, being stripped of Roman troops, went over to Mithridates (the Romans had never been very popular in Boeotia). Sulla appears to have decided that it was best to marshal all the forces he could to defeat Mithridates's armies, after which the towns of Boeotia could be recovered at will. Sulla had arrived with five legions (and presumably no allied troops), but he needed all the forces he could get his hands on. Given his relations with Rome (where Marius and Cinna had recently seized control after Sulla's departure), he obviously could count on receiving no reinforcements from Italy – he was on his own.

ATTACK ON THE PIRAEUS AND ATHENS

Sulla decided that it was best to try and stamp out the main Mithridatic outpost on the mainland – Athens and its port, the Piraeus. He launched an immediate assault on the Piraeus, but this proved to be a disaster, and he had to withdraw to Megara (a large town to the southwest). There, he prepared proper siege equipment and sent subordinates throughout areas of Greece controlled by the Romans to secure funds. Upon returning to Attica, he placed Athens under siege and went back to assaulting the walls of the Piraeus. This proved to be an extremely difficult enterprise (for one thing, Archelaus could bring in supplies and reinforcements by sea). Sulla continued his unsuccessful attacks throughout the rest of 87 B.C. until he withdrew from the Piraeus to Eleusis (a town to the west of Athens) for the winter. The siege of Athens went on. In the meanwhile, Sulla sent Lucullus to raise a fleet among Rome's allies in Egypt and Syria.

In the spring of 86 B.C., Sulla resumed his massive operations against the Piraeus. Good news came on March 1 when Athens capitulated, though the citadel (the Acropolis) held out. The town was sacked, which was doubtless good for the troops' morale and loyalty. Sulla continued the incessant assaults on the Piraeus's fortifications, and eventually Archelaus decided that it was not worth the effort to continue defending the port. He withdrew by sea, and Sulla burned the Piraeus upon its capture.

Roman Loss of Macedonia

One reason Archelaus decided to give up the Piraeus may have been that Macedonia had finally been overrun in late 87 or early 86 B.C. by yet another Mithridatic army, which would make possible a broad attack on Sulla's position. In any event, Archelaus joined this new army and took over command upon the death of the commander of the force from Macedonia. This new Mithridatic army was something like three times larger than Sulla's Roman troops and Greek allies.

Battle of Chaeronea

In 86 B.C., the new army under Archelaus's command marched south through Thessaly into Boeotia, where Sulla moved to meet it. After some maneuvering for position, Archelaus seized some high ground near the Boeotian town of Chaeronea, which dominated the routes of entry into Attica. Sulla was now finally forced to give battle, since Archelaus was threatening to cut him off in Boeotia. The Romans were greatly outnumbered and came close to being overwhelmed by Archelaus, who was a competent general, but the now seasoned Roman troops did not break as Sulla hurried about, moving his troops to support weak areas and taking advantage of opportunities. Eventually, Archelaus's left flank gave way, and a general rout ensued. Only 10,000 men out of an army that had numbered many more managed to escape with Archelaus to the island of Euboea. Sulla was now hailed by his troops as imperator ("victorious general") and his position in Greece at least was secure.

Battle of Orchomenos

After his victory, Sulla learned that an army sent out from Rome to fight Mithridates in Asia was passing eastward across Macedonia along the *via Egnatia* (see discussion later).[3] Sulla moved his army north to Thessaly to keep an eye on this force. In the meanwhile, Archelaus gathered another large force on Euboea with the intention of renewing the attack on the

---

[3] The via Egnatia was the road the Romans built to allow the passage of armies across the Balkans. The road began at Dyrrachium, which was the port at which Roman armies arrived in the Balkans, and then passed eastward into Macedonia and continued to Byzantium, which was the port from which one crossed over into Asia Minor.

Greek mainland. When Archelaus crossed over to Boeotia, Sulla moved south to meet him near the town of Orchomenos. While Sulla was having his troops dig trenches around his flanks to protect them against cavalry, Archelaus attacked. Once again the battle was hard fought, but Roman discipline and Sulla's dexterous movement of troops led to another complete debacle for Mithridates's forces. The mainland was now completely abandoned to Sulla, who began to build a fleet to cross over to Asia (nothing had yet been heard of Lucullus's mission to raise a fleet). He also entered into negotiations with Mithridates, who was having to suppress unrest in Asia, where his putative supporters were beginning to suspect that they had backed the wrong horse.

Flaccus's Arrival with an Army from Italy

As already mentioned, Sulla had marched his army northward during the interval between the battles of Chaeronea and Orchomenos to keep an eye on a force that had arrived from Italy. A few days after entering his seventh consulship in 86 B.C., C. Marius had died, and L. Valerius Flaccus was elected as suffect consul in his place (see Chapter 7). Flaccus was then given the task of taking an army to Asia. Although Sulla had been declared a public enemy (*hostis*) and later Sullan propaganda claimed that Flaccus's army was directed against him, it is clear from the course of action he took that Flaccus was not actually operating against Sulla and that the faction around Cinna in Rome had decided not to confront Sulla at this moment. Flaccus took the overland route through Macedonia in order to cross over into Asia at Byzantium. Furthermore, while Sulla had five legions under his command, Flaccus brought only two, which hardly seems an adequate force if he was to confront Sulla directly.

Fimbria's Murder of Flaccus

Mithridates's forces at first opposed Flaccus in Macedonia, but once Flaccus captured Philippi, Mithridates's commander withdrew across the Bosporus into Asia Minor. Flaccus then began to ferry his army over to Bithynia on the Asian side. At this point, a rebellion against his authority was started by his subordinate C. Flavius Fimbria (son of Marius's consular colleague in 104 B.C.).[4] Flaccus and Fimbria did not get along,

---

4   The tradition based on Livy suggests that Fimbria's title was legate, but Strabo, a not unreliable source from the age of Augustus, describes him as quaestor, which may well be correct. If so, his disloyalty is all the more heinous, given the close relationship that was expected between the senior magistrate and his quaestor (see Chapter 3 n. 3).

and it seems that Fimbria indulged the troops' desire to engage in loot-
ing, which Flaccus curbed. As the army crossed over, Flaccus relieved
Fimbria of command in another dispute and sent him back to Rome.
At Byzantium, Fimbria seized control of the garrison left there, and
when Flaccus returned to Byzantium to stop this, the troops completely
rebelled, and he fled back across the Hellespont. Fimbria pursued him to
Nicomedia, where Flaccus was betrayed and killed. (Since Flaccus is still
called consul at this point in the sources, it would appear that his death
took place in late 86 B.C.) Fimbria now took over command of the entire
army. Flaccus's reputation was later blackened by Sullan propaganda,
which portrayed him as greedy and incompetent. It appears, however,
that he was guilty of trying to restrain his troops, and the troops' dissatisfaction with his discipline was taken advantage of by a treacherous subordinate. The ease with which Fimbria undermined the troops' loyalty to
their lawful commander shows how quickly the inherent claim to legitimacy of a duly elected magistrate had broken down in the short period
of time since the outbreak of civil war in 88 B.C. It would seem that by
this point one could not go wrong playing on the greed of the troops.
(Fimbria's treachery brings to mind the willingness of Cn. Strabo's troops
to stand by him and murder Q. Pompeius Rufus cos. 88, but now the
treachery went even further. Whereas in 88 B.C. the situation involved
an established commander refusing to hand over his command to his
successor, we now have a subordinate seizing command from his own
general.) In any case, Fimbria was not to enjoy the fruits of his treachery
for long.

Fimbria's Campaign in Asia

In 85 B.C., Fimbria began to attack Mithridates's forces in Asia. He first
inflicted a major defeat on an army commanded by one of Mithridates's
sons, and then marched on Pergamum, where Mithridates himself was
located. Abandoning the city, Mithridates fled to Pitane on the coast,
and now that it seemed the Romans would prevail, many cities went over
to Fimbria. When Fimbria began to besiege Pitane by land, Mithridates
summoned reinforcements from the sea. At this point, Sulla's quaestor
Lucullus happened by, finally bringing up the fleet that Sulla had sent him
to collect and reestablishing Roman control over the islands off the Aegean
coast of Asia Minor. Fimbria asked Lucullus to cut off Mithridates by sea,
pointing out the glory that would fall to the man who brought about the
capture of Mithridates. Would Sulla's man cooperate in the capture of
a king who had on his hands the blood of tens of thousands of Roman

citizens (including the consular legate M.' Aquillius)? Certainly not, since Sulla wanted to cut a deal with Mithridates, preferring to make peace with the king and then have a free hand to deal with his enemies in Rome. Accordingly, Lucullus refused to intervene and allowed Mithridates to escape to Mytilene on the island of Lesbos.

Peace of Dardanus

While Fimbria was working to restore the Roman position in Asia, Sulla negotiated personally with Mithridates at Dardanus in the Troad (the northwestern coast of Asia Minor). Mithridates's position was desperate. While Fimbria was retaking the cities of Asia, and Lucullus's fleet was capturing the Aegean islands, he was losing all support in his new acquisitions. He therefore agreed to Sulla's terms, which under the circumstances were extremely mild. The king was to

- give up all his conquests
- surrender his prisoners (including the proconsul Q. Oppius)
- provide a fleet of seventy ships plus supplies for Sulla's army
- pay a large indemnity (2,000 or 3,000 talents).

In return Mithridates would

- be guaranteed possession of his ancestral kingdom
- regain the title of "friend of the Roman People."

In effect, Sulla was allowing Mithridates to return to the situation that had prevailed before the war in return for providing Sulla with the means to prosecute his own war against his domestic enemies back in Italy. Sulla's troops were a bit sulky at this lenient treatment of Mithridates, but he would show that he knew how to win their loyalty.

End of Fimbria

After the escape of Mithridates, Fimbria had marched to the southeast into Phrygia. After his agreement with Mithridates at Dardanus, Sulla brought his army over to Asia from Thrace and pursued Fimbria to his camp at Thyatira. At first, Fimbria was contemptuous of Sulla, but it soon became clear that he could not count on the loyalty of his troops (some began to desert and most refused to fight). Sulla then began to dig fortifications around Fimbria's camp. Once Fimbria had lost all confidence in his troops, he gave up. The exact circumstances of his death are unclear, but Fimbria committed suicide, and Sulla took over his army.

SETTLEMENT AND VENGEANCE IN ASIA

Sulla now restored the kings of Bithynia and Cappadocia to their thrones. He also set about "restoring" the province of Asia. To solidify the loyalty of his troops after his less than complete triumph over Mithridates, he billeted them in the disloyal cities and allowed them to extort large sums from the locals. He also punished the province by imposing on it a 20,000 talent indemnity for the costs of the war and for five years' lost taxes. Under the circumstances, raising this sum from local resources was impossible, and the cities contracted huge debts, which would prove to be a ruinous burden.

After having bought himself the loyalty of his troops, the question was, what would Sulla do with it?

QUESTIONS FOR STUDY AND REFLECTION

1. What was Mithridates's attitude toward Roman power in Asia Minor?
2. Why did Aquillius provoke war?
3. Why did the Roman position in Asia Minor and Greece collapse so quickly? What was the attitude of the locals toward the Romans? What motives led them to remain loyal to Rome or to take Mithridates's side?
4. What was Sulla's strategy in prosecuting the war against Mithridates's forces in Greece? How was he viewed by the men controlling Rome, and how did this affect the options available to him?
5. What was Flaccus's intention in bringing an army to Greece? What was his attitude toward Sulla?
6. What allowed Fimbria to undermine Flaccus's authority and what does this tell us about the loyalty of the soldiery?
7. What sort of peace did Sulla impose upon Mithridates? Why were the terms not harsher?
8. What did Sulla do to ensure the continued loyalty of his troops?

10

SULLA'S VICTORY IN CIVIL WAR

CINNA'S "TYRANNY"

The period in Rome between the death of Marius in early 86 B.C. and the outbreak of civil war in 83 B.C. is hard to assess because of later reinterpretation. Once Sulla had won this war, he justified his actions on the grounds that the faction controlling the government in Rome had been tyrannical and that as a result of oppression, many nobles had fled the city to seek refuge in Greece with Sulla, who was the (self-proclaimed) defender of the senate. For their own part, those who belatedly joined Sulla found this a convenient fiction, and both exaggerated the "tyrannical" aspect of the situation and ignored their own (and others') participation in public life in Rome during Sulla's absence. In particular, since some men did go over to Sulla after Cinna's death in 84 B.C., and at the very end of the period before the outbreak of civil war there was some use of violence against those considered likely to do so, it was easy to conflate these events with the violence that marked Marius's earlier capture of the city in 87 B.C. and pretend that such violence against the senate had characterized the entire period of Sulla's absence. This misleading picture then became the standard ancient interpretation of the period. The known facts about the period between the death of Marius and the return of Sulla do not agree with the ancient image of "Cinna's tyranny" (*dominatio Cinnae*).

Cicero notes (*Brutus* 308) that "for a three-year period the city was generally without arms," which must refer to the years 86–84 B.C. Once Marius died and Cinna brought an end to the (limited) violence that followed their capture of the city during the bellum Octavianum, all the major figures that we know of stayed in Rome and indeed took part in public life. For instance, L. Marcius Philippus, who had opposed M. Livius Drusus as consul in 91 B.C., was elected censor in 86 B.C. Furthermore, it would seem that one of the major elements in the cause of Marius and

Cinna – citizenship for the Italian allies – was sacrificed in the interest of domestic harmony. At any rate, the *epitome* of Livy indicates that the vote was granted to the new citizens only in 84 B.C. This would seem to indicate that the censors of 86 B.C. had not yet enrolled them (small wonder with Philippus as censor), and it was only when Sulla's return posed an immediate threat that the earlier grant of citizenship was finally implemented in practical terms.[1] Thus, to avoid problems with senatorial opponents and to attempt to restore concordia (see Chapter 2) in Rome, even Cinna abandoned one of his major sources of support. So much for Cinna's "tyranny."

It should not, however, be thought that Cinna and his associates had given up their popularis program in order to reach an accommodation with the conservatives in the senate. In particular, L. Valerius Flaccus, Marius's successor as consul in 86 B.C., passed a law that allowed debtors to pay off their creditors with only one-quarter of the principal. Debt was a major issue at this time. Back in 89 B.C., the praetor L. Sempronius Asellio had been giving favorable rulings to debtors as urban praetor, and this so enraged creditors that a mob led by a tribune had attacked him while he was sacrificing in the forum and killed him. (Despite a senatorial offer of rewards for information, no one revealed the perpetrators.) This shows how high emotions were about this issue, and not surprisingly, Valerius's law was severely censured among the wealthy. Measures such as these would certainly have done nothing to lessen the opinion in the senate that Cinna and his associates were simply popularis troublemakers. Nonetheless, they held office legitimately and would have to be tolerated as Marius had been – for the time being.

DEALINGS WITH SULLA

Ultimately, the major problem facing the new regime in Rome after the bellum Octavianum (see Chapter 7) was what to do with Sulla.[2] He was declared a public enemy (hostis), but no concrete action was taken in

---

[1] Remember that until the new citizens were officially enrolled in a tribe and registered in a census class they would not be able to vote. The eventual method adopted for incorporating the newly enfranchised territories into the Roman state was that the various Latin and allied communities were each assigned in their entirety to a tribe, so that each tribe, which had previously had a compact and contiguous territory, was made up of communities scattered across Italy, which was now a patchwork of the various tribes.

[2] Of course, there was no "regime" in the modern sense of a government, and this term is simply a convenient shorthand for the control of the political institutions in Rome that was exercised by Cinna and his supporters.

connection with this. His new wife Caecilia Metella was not obstructed in leaving Italy to join him in Greece. As we have seen (in Chapter 9), Marius's replacement as consul in 86 B.C., L. Valerius Flaccus, took an army east, ostensibly to reconquer the province of Asia (in the eyes of the regime, Sulla's abrogation of the lex Sulpicia and of the law that transferred the eastern command to Marius was itself invalid, and Flaccus was sent out in place of the now dead Marius). By the time Flaccus crossed the Adriatic, Sulla had defeated Archelaus at Chaeronea, and Flaccus considered it prudent to leave Sulla alone in Greece, moving on through Macedonia to Asia. (Presumably he would have acted against Sulla if circumstances had warranted such a move.)

In 85 B.C., Cinna was reelected consul along with Cn. Papirius Carbo (son of the consul of 113 B.C. who was defeated by the Cimbri and nephew of the consul of 120 B.C. who had betrayed his Gracchan allegiance and defended Opimius against the charge of murdering C. Gracchus). In light of Sulla's victory over Mithridates and despite (or perhaps because of) his defeat of Fimbria's army, the regime in Rome agreed to enter into negotiations with Sulla. The first move came from Sulla, who must have felt the need to find some way to secure his return to Rome. The ancient sources inform us of the terms that he proposed: he would punish his enemies, but no one else need fear him, including the new citizens. These terms seem to have been made up in light of later events and are presumably a misrepresentation put out by Sulla himself, who later published an account of his life. Whatever the actual events, the princeps senatus L. Valerius Flaccus cos. 100 (not the father of the suffect consul of 86 B.C. but perhaps his uncle) gave a speech in the senate urging a peaceful solution to the problem, and envoys were sent to negotiate with Sulla.

At the same time, it would seem that Sulla was acting cooperatively with the regime in Rome. There is clear though spotty evidence that he was allowing new officials elected in Rome to operate in his sphere. Certainly, L. Cornelius Scipio Asiagenus, who would later oppose Sulla as consul in 83 B.C., is attested as the praetorian governor in the recently liberated province of Macedonia. Furthermore, new governors were even sent out to Sulla's immediate sphere of activity in Asia Minor. A new proconsul seems to have been appointed in Cilicia, and by the time of his invasion of Italy, Sulla had acquired a new quaestor (to act in place of the trusty Lucullus, who was then operating in an independent capacity). Perhaps most tellingly, either a legate of Sulla or a relative of the legate was elected praetor and took over Asia. All of these magistrates could only have received office in Rome. Not only was Sulla accepting in his area men elected by the "tyrannical" regime in Rome, but that regime was allowing (arranging?) the election of men who would be amenable to Sulla.

Clearly, neither Sulla nor Cinna and his supporters were burning any bridges yet. These acts of accommodation must date to 85 and early 84 B.C. Then, an event took place in 84 B.C. that would completely change the situation and lead Sulla to decide to return to Italy by force.

DEATH OF CINNA

Cinna and Carbo were reelected as consuls for the year 84 B.C. Never before had both consuls been reelected, and one of them must necessarily have presided over his own reelection, a circumstance that no doubt brought the regime into further disrepute with its opponents.[3] These reelections no doubt contributed to the image of Cinna's regime as a tyranny, but given the circumstances – and Marius's precedent – they are understandable. One should also bear in mind the dangers entailed in giving up the consulship to an unknown quantity during perilous times, as Sulla himself had found out in 87 B.C.

While the Cinnan regime was negotiating with Sulla, it was also making military preparations, which included the raising of troops and money in Italy. There is of course no way that we can be sure of the motives of either Cinna's supporters or of Sulla. Since neither side knew the future, they presumably had to take precautions even if they were negotiating in good faith.

---

[3] Another irregular election that took place at about this time involved M. Marius Gratidianus. A member of the Gratidii family of Arpinum, he had been adopted by the elder brother of C. Marius cos. 107 and hence was closely associated with his famous uncle. As praetor in about 86 B.C. he had issued a highly popular edict that clarified the uncertainty that affected the currency in light of M. Drusus's debasement (see Chapter 6). The importance of this legislation is shown by the fact that it was worked out in common by a meeting of the entire colleges of praetors and tribunes (a very unusual circumstance). They had all agreed to issue the edict jointly later in the afternoon, but Gratidianus stole the glory for himself by immediately rushing to the forum and issuing it in his name alone. This act won him such extreme popular acclaim that statues were actually raised to him by the plebs (these were later torn down by Sulla). Gratidianus is said to have duped his associates in this way in order to help a prospective run for the consulship. He never did run for that office, but he took the unusual step of holding the praetorship a second time. Unfortunately, neither office can be securely dated (perhaps 86 and 83 B.C.), but it would seem that while the need to reserve the consulship for more prominent members of Cinna's faction prevented him from seeking the highest magistracy, it was still felt that his services could not be dispensed with, and the solution was to give him imperium through the very unusual method of repeating the praetorship.

In any case, Cinna decided to lead an army against unruly tribesmen in Illyricum. Though long under Roman hegemony, the area was not directly administered by the Romans and for the most part was left to its own devices. At the least, this campaign would teach the newly conscripted troops to work together and give them some seasoning before any showdown with Sulla. Furthermore, on the other side of the Adriatic, they would be in a position to act against Sulla if the opportunity arose. From a strategic point of view, then, this Illyrian expedition made sense. Unfortunately, things went wrong – disastrously so. The passage across the Adriatic was undertaken early in the spring, and the seas were rough. Some of the troops who had not yet crossed balked at embarking, and when Cinna insisted, they rebelled and stoned him to death. There is now no way to know why exactly the soldiers adopted such a mutinous attitude. Perhaps they really did object to nothing more than seasickness. It is possible, however, that their presumption in killing a consul was motivated by a disinclination to move against Sulla (a not unreasonable calculation given the fate that had befallen Mithridates and Fimbria). In any event, the soldiery showed once again that they were no longer in any awe of even the chief magistrate of the Republic if they were disinclined to obey.

Cinna is a bit hard to read as a personality. We know nothing of his activities and allegiances before his election to the consulship of 87 B.C. What is clear is that he was the man who held together the opposition to Sulla in Italy. For whatever reason, his colleague Carbo was unable to maintain Cinna's dominance in Roman politics. Once Cinna's death became known, waverers began to act circumspectly and to prepare the ground for going over to Sulla. At this time, certain envoys from Sulla were returning to Rome with the senatorial delegation that had gone east for negotiations at the urging of the princeps senatus, but upon learning of Cinna's death when they reached Brundisium in southern Italy, they immediately turned around and journeyed back to Sulla. With Cinna dead, the whole situation was changed, and the old negotiations were now irrelevant.

This new situation increased the chances that an invasion of Italy by Sulla would turn out successfully (perhaps he was influenced by the apparent recalcitrance of the troops in Italy to serve against him as indicated by the mutiny against Cinna), and he brought his army across the Aegean to Athens. The soldiers had spent more than a year fattening themselves on the plunder of Asia and were now completely loyal to their commander, who alone could assure their safe return to Italy. It is noteworthy that Sulla took with him to Italy only the five legions that had come over with him in the spring of 87 B.C., leaving behind in Asia the two legions that he had taken over from Fimbria. Presumably, he mistrusted the loyalty of the troops raised by his enemies, and the problem of loyalty and legitimacy faced by a commander who was seeking to usurp the personal allegiance of his troops for his own purposes was already becoming acute.

Attitudes in Italy at the Time of Sulla's Invasion

The consuls for 83 B.C. – L. Cornelius Scipio Asiagenus (descendant of P. Scipio Africanus's brother Lucius, who had defeated Antiochus the Great at the battle of Magnesia back in 190 B.C.) and C. Norbanus (a colleague of L. Saturninus as tribune back in 103 B.C.) – prepared to meet Sulla's impending invasion. The fact that Carbo was not reelected as consul can be taken in two ways. Perhaps this merely indicates how much lower his prestige was compared to Cinna's. On the other hand, given that Asiagenus had recently been tolerated by Sulla as governor of Macedonia, the consular elections for 83 B.C. may reflect an attempt to choose men thought to have a chance of coming to terms with Sulla (unlike Carbo, who was too deeply implicated in the bellum Octavianum). In any case, the effectiveness of the new consuls would be put to the test that spring, when Sulla crossed over with a large fleet and landed in southern Italy at Brundisium and Tarentum.

At this point, the legal situation would not have been entirely clear, except to those directly committed to one side or the other. From the point of view of the regime in Italy, Sulla's command was illegal, and any hostile actions taken by him would have been considered totally unjustified. To some extent, this would have been the automatic position of anyone in Italy who was not a partisan of Sulla. Certainly, all of the lawfully elected magistrates had been chosen under the Cinnan regime and shared its outlook. Thus, at the start of the war, one might term the regime's forces the "loyalists," and they would have had first claim to the citizens' allegiance. Everyone who fought against Sulla was by no means a "Marian" or "Cinnan," and whatever one's views about the desirability of enfranchising the allies or the conflicts between Marius and Sulla, many would have considered it their patriotic duty to take up arms against the invasion from the East. Sulla's ultimate victory would make this a very unfashionable point of view (and one that many were happy to disown after the fact).

On the other hand, those who favored the traditional senatorial oligarchy (the "good men") and upheld its policies (such as the disinclination to redistribute land or enfranchise the allies) would have been tolerant at best of Marius and his adherents; their natural inclination would have been to consider Cinna, Carbo, and the like as Marius's henchmen and to judge both them and the regime in Rome accordingly. Such opponents of Marius and his successors would no doubt have taken Sulla to be the lawful commander in the East, and the Marian murders at the end of the bellum Octavianum would have gone a long way to erase any unease with Sulla's methods back in 88 B.C. In such quarters, there would have been a distinct lack of enthusiasm for the loyalists, and any sign that Sulla would prevail was likely to impel first the loyalist regime's opponents and then the undecided and uncertain to go over to the invaders. (For two coins minted by Sulla's forces that illustrate his self-representation during the invasion, see Coins 8 and 9.)

MILITARY CONSIDERATIONS

The ensuing civil war would show that the loyalist forces raised in Italy to oppose Sulla were outclassed by his legions. Two points are especially noteworthy. First, while on several occasions loyalist troops would betray their commanders, this problem seems not to have troubled Sulla. His victorious troops, who had spent years subduing the forces of Mithridates and reconquering the East, were devoted to their leader (and the wealth that he had showered upon them in Asia no doubt helped assuage any qualms they may have felt about the legitimacy of his actions). They were bound to Sulla by close ties of affection and interest, ties that were lacking in the relations of the loyalist commanders and their troops. Second, though some of Sulla's victories in Italy were close-run affairs, and it was by no means a foregone conclusion that he would prevail in the end, his veteran legions clearly had a distinct superiority over the newly raised forces of the loyalists. The practical experience and esprit de corps won through years of service in the East proved to be decisive advantages in the field. Exactly the same conditions would hold true at the outbreak of the next civil war in 49 B.C., and the outcome would likewise be the same: the victory of the seasoned invaders.

OPENING MOVES IN THE WAR

The consul Norbanus first came south with an army to meet Sulla. He was defeated at Canusium, a town that blocked Sulla's path to the north, and then retreated to Capua, where Sulla defeated him again. Meanwhile, the other consul, Scipio Asiagenus, came south with his own army. After Norbanus's second defeat, Sulla negotiated with Asiagenus at the town of Teanum Sidicinum to the north of Capua. In an anecdote related many years later, Cicero, who was an eyewitness, implies that Sulla was not acting in good faith and tried to undermine the loyalty of Asiagenus's army (*Philippics* 12.27). Certainly that is what happened. The consul's army abandoned him and went over to Sulla (it must have been clear to the troops that whatever their willingness to fight, they had little chance against the veterans from Asia). Sulla apparently bore Asiagenus no ill will and let him go unharmed after the two of them agreed on some sort of settlement. Asiagenus immediately broke his agreement, however, and Sulla apparently took this betrayal very badly. He later made a declaration that he would forgive those who had opposed him before Asiagenus broke the agreement but would pursue to the end those who continued to fight against him after that date. And a bitter end it would be.

REACTION TO THE INVASION

Many who had been biding their time now went into open and vigorous support of Sulla. In Africa, Q. Caecilius Metellus Pius (who apparently still held propraetorian imperium that dated back to his military service during the Social War) led an unsuccessful revolt against the (presumably pro-Cinnan) governor and then joined Sulla in Italy, where he became a major supporter of Sulla (who was married to Pius's first cousin). Cn. Pompeius (generally known under the Anglicized form "Pompey"), the son of Cn. Pompeius Strabo cos. 89, raised an army among his father's dependents in Picenum, even though he had held no senatorial office yet. (Pompey had reason to demonstrate his supposed loyalty to Sulla since he had been defended by Carbo during the mid 80s B.C. and presumably had been in Cinna's good graces.)[4] Many others also now went over to Sulla, as the weakness of his opponents became clear.

After his release by Sulla, the consul Scipio Asiagenus moved north with more troops to oppose the force raised by Pompey in Picenum. There, Asiagenus was once again abandoned by his troops and forced to flee.

DESPERATION IN ROME

The year 82 B.C. was a desperate one for Sulla's opponents. Needing to shore up their support, they not only reelected Cn. Papirius Carbo to his

---

4 In this regard, it is worth noting that Cinna apparently served as legate under Cn. Strabo in 89 B.C. during the Social War.

third consulship but had C. Marius, the twenty-six-year-old son of the great general, elected as his colleague. The loyalists were clearly eager to regain the prestige of young Marius's father, as the new consul's age was sixteen years below the normal minimum requirement for the consulship. After further victories were won by Sulla in 82 B.C., certain senators remaining in Rome were suspected of wanting to go over to him, and at a meeting of the senate summoned by the urban praetor L. Junius Brutus Damasippus, a slaughter of such men was carried out. (Prominent victims were Q. Mucius Scaevola cos. 95, the pontifex maximus and son of the consul of 133 B.C., and a homonymous cousin of the consul Cn. Carbo. It was this sort of partisan carnage that was later projected back into the peaceful years of the mid 80 B.C.)

CAMPAIGN OF 82 B.C.

The consuls of 82 B.C. divided Italy in two, Carbo operating in the north, Marius in the south. First, the praetor C. Carinnas attempted to attack Pompey's forces in Picenum from the north, but he was defeated and withdrew. Carbo then took over and retreated northward to Ariminum after learning of Marius's defeat at Sacriportus. As Pompey and Metellus subdued the north and northeast of Italy, Carbo withdrew to Etruria. (For a coin that illustrates the lack of a clear leader or rallying cry on the part of the loyalists, see Coin 10. For a coin minted at this time by Metellus Pius, a prominent supporter of Sulla from the highest levels of the senatorial oligarchy, see Coin 11.)

Meanwhile, C. Marius the younger took the field in the south against the old quaestor of his father. The Samnites, feeling that their agreement with Cinna's regime would not be honored by Sulla, supplied troops for Marius's army. At Sacriportus in central Latium, Marius fought a long and hard battle with Sulla, finally suffering defeat when five of his cohorts went over to Sulla. Marius then withdrew to Praeneste, which Sulla proceeded to put under siege.

After leaving his legate Q. Lucretius Afella in charge of the siege, Sulla himself moved north to oppose Carbo in Etruria (on the way Sulla took Rome, which his opponents had abandoned upon learning of his march). An indecisive battle was fought at Clusium, and there was other action in Etruria. Sulla could not achieve a decisive victory, but Carbo fled to Africa after receiving further bad news. In Cisalpine Gaul, the loyalist forces under C. Norbanus cos. 83 collapsed when the commander of one legion killed all the others apart from Norbanus (who escaped) and went over to Sulla; and in the south, attempts to relieve Marius in Praeneste also failed.

Sulla's Victory

The remaining loyalist commanders in the north (mainly praetors) joined forces and attempted to relieve Marius in Praeneste (three previous efforts had already failed). They cooperated with a very large force of Samnites under Pontius Telesinus (a rebel commander in the Social War), who had already tried unsuccessfully to break the siege. This new force was repulsed yet again by Sulla, who had moved south to check them, and they in turn moved north toward Rome. Sulla hastened north in pursuit, and a decisive battle was finally fought on November 1 outside of Rome near the Colline Gate. The battle was long, and Sulla, commanding the left, was pushed back to the walls of the city. On the right, however, his forces drove back the enemy, and with this the entire enemy line broke. The complete defeat of their last army in the field broke the back of the opposition.

The next day, Sulla summoned a meeting of the senate to make the new situation clear to all. The session was held in the temple of Bellona (the goddess of war) in the Campus Martius, so that Sulla would not lose his proconsular imperium by crossing the pomerium into the city. While he was speaking, 3,000 or 4,000 Samnite prisoners who had been gathered nearby were executed. When the attendant bedlam caused consternation among the senators, Sulla told them to pay no attention to the punishment of a few malefactors and listen to his speech. The message was clear. The power of life and death was in the hands of Sulla, and all who opposed him could expect nothing but death.

Meanwhile, the siege of Praeneste went on. Sulla had the head of Brutus Damasippus (the praetor who had slaughtered senators of dubious allegiance earlier in the year) thrown into the city as graphic proof of Sulla's victory at the Colline Gate. Marius tried to escape through a tunnel, but when he realized the futility of this attempt, he had a slave kill him. When the city surrendered, all those of senatorial rank were executed (some immediately, some later). There are two traditions about the treatment of the 12,000 common soldiers who were captured. One says that first Sulla tried them individually, then tired of the business and had them all executed. Another has him release the Roman citizens after telling them off but execute all the Samnites and the Praenestine men (the women and children of the city were left alone).

Young Pompey's Command

Pompey had performed well despite his youth (he was only twenty-four in 82 B.C.), and Sulla sent him to subdue the loyalist areas to the south that were still holding out. Pompey first conquered Sicily, which the consul Carbo had entered from Africa. Carbo was taken alive, and the equestrian Pompey put the consul to death despite his pleas. Then, in early 81 B.C., Pompey went on to conquer Africa, where he put Cn. Domitius Ahenobarbus (Cinna's son-in-law) to death. Such brutality earned Pompey the nickname "teenage butcher" (*adulescentulus carnifex*). For his own part, Pompey, whose family normally did not sport a cognomen (presumably, his father's cognomen "Strabo," which means "squinty eyed" in Greek, refers to a problem with his eyesight), adopted the name "Magnus," which means "Great" and could be taken as "the Great." His opponents in the ranks of the oligarchy would generally avoid this name, which hinted not so subtly at a comparison with Alexander the Great. In any case, now that Sicily and Africa were safely under control and his main opponents wiped out, Sulla could feel secure in his possession of Italy.

Pompey would soon teach Sulla that he had no respect for anyone. Upon his return to Italy, he asked Sulla to let him celebrate a triumph, even though he had no claim to the honor since he lacked imperium. When Sulla refused, Pompey implied that he would use his army for his own purposes. Sulla gave in, presumably thinking that it was not worth the trouble to oppose the headstrong young man, who was after all simply following in Sulla's own footsteps. Throughout the 70s B.C., Pompey would continue to make use of military force under his control to extort for himself honors to which he had no legal claim.

Questions for Study and Reflection

1. What was Sulla's legal position when he served as proconsul during the war against Mithridates? How was he viewed in Italy?
2. What was the nature of Cinna's regime in Italy? How exactly was it associated with Marius? Was it the legitimate government in Italy? What is the view of the ancient sources, and where did this view come from? Is the ancient view valid?
3. How did the Cinnan regime treat Sulla? What was Sulla's attitude toward the magistrates elected in Rome?

4. What were Cinna's intentions in undertaking his Illyrian expedition? Why did his troops mutiny? What effect did Cinna's death have on Sulla's plans?

5. What was the intention of the anti-Sullan party at the start of the civil war? Who constituted the legitimate government at that time? How were the loyalist magistrates and Sulla viewed by various segments of the Italian population when war broke out? How did attitudes change as the war progressed?

6. Why did Sulla prevail in the civil war?

7. What role did Pompey play in the war? How constitutional were his actions?

11

SULLA'S SETTLEMENT

SULLA THE DICTATOR

By late 82 B.C., the state was, following the deaths of C. Marius and Cn. Carbo, without consuls. Under such circumstances, the consular elections were normally conducted by an official called the *interrex*.[1] As interrex, the princeps senatus L. Valerius Flaccus cos. 100, passed, at Sulla's request, a rather unusual law, which authorized the election of a dictator, an office that had not been held for more than a century (it was no longer needed after the military crisis of the war with Hannibal), and in the ensuing election Sulla was duly returned. This was a new kind of dictatorship. His position was officially described as dictator "for arranging the Republic" (*rei publicae constituendae*), a specification of the duties of a dictator that had never been made before. In this way, it was overtly indicated at the creation of the office that Sulla was to be a novel kind of dictator. A further innovation was that while the regular position of dictator was held for only six months, Sulla's appointment provided for no fixed date of termination. In effect, Sulla would continue to be dictator for as long as he wished.

Flaccus also passed legislation (probably in the law establishing the dictatorship, though conceivably in a separate enactment) granting Sulla extraordinary powers. Not only was he given immunity from prosecution for any acts that he had taken in the past but was authorized in advance to

---

[1] The archaic office of interrex dates back to the kingdom, and literally means "in-between king." Presumably, the interrex was in origin some sort of temporary official who was appointed upon the death of the previous king to exercise the royal authority until the king's successor was chosen. Under the Republic, the interrex took over when there were no consuls (whose imperium supposedly derived from the power of the kings). Only patricians could serve as interrex, and the right to hold the office was one of the privileges that marked a family as having patrician status.

kill, confiscate, distribute land, and found colonies. Thus, by virtue of this provision, Sulla was made not simply above the law, but his very decrees were given the force of law. It remained to be seen how he would exercise this unprecedented power.

Sulla's Position in the State

In his capacity as dictator, Sulla had two consuls elected to serve under him in 81 B.C. One (M. Tullius Decula) is a complete nonentity of whom nothing is known. The other (Cn. Cornelius Dolabella) was a not particularly prominent patrician. These men clearly would not cause Sulla any trouble. At the time of these elections, Q. Lucretius Afella, the man whom Sulla had left in charge of the siege of Praeneste, tried to run for consul despite not having been quaestor. When he ignored Sulla's order to desist, Sulla had him killed in the forum. Apparently no one, not even his most active supporters, could disregard the will of the dictator without paying the consequences.

While still dictator, Sulla was elected consul for the year 80 B.C. along with Q. Caecilius Metellus Pius. In 79 B.C., after instituting his reforms, he finally restored the Republic. Refusing a third consulship, he first oversaw the election of the consuls for 78 B.C. (including one candidate whom he opposed) and then resigned the dictatorship. He withdrew to Puteoli (a port in Campania) where he died in 78 B.C. of an unpleasant disease (perhaps the gods had tired of their favorite).

Sulla the "Fortunate"

In addition to being elected permanent dictator, Sulla was granted the title Felix ("the Lucky") by the senate at the time of the death of C. Marius cos. 82. He apparently believed that the gods were favorable to him (and under the circumstances who could doubt this?). He had developed this belief in the East, where he used the title *Aphrodisius* ("belonging to Aphrodite," the Greek equivalent of the Roman goddess Venus, who had associations with good fortune), and already in 86 B.C. he gave the names Faustus and Fausta (basically male and female versions of "Lucky") to his children by Caecilia Metella. There is some precedent for his adoption of the agnomen Felix in that the branches of certain noble families had distinguished themselves with hereditary additional names, and various generals had in the past received special names after victories, but there is no example of a senatorial grant under circumstances like these. Note in particular that while Sulla's own modified name – L. Cornelius Sulla Felix – would seem distinctive but not unheard of, that of his son – Faustus Cornelius Sulla – had a *praenomen* that was at complete variance with normal practice.

The divine associations of Sulla's new name also added to the notion that he was in some way superior to mere mortals, a trend that would become far more pronounced after the next civil war. In effect, Sulla was marking himself off as a special individual, and as such he headed a faction or "party" known as the *Sullani* ("supporters of Sulla"). Political divisions in Rome had frequently had a personal and familial aspect to them, but now factions were forming around extraordinary individuals who would then found dynasties. As it turned out, Faustus would not be a favorite of the gods as his father had been, but eventually the cooperative oligarchic system of the senate would be replaced by a dynastic autocracy. (For a coin issued in the 50s by Faustus that celebrates his father the dicator, see Coin 15.)

VENGEANCE

By the time Sulla fought his way back to Italy, he was clearly a vindictive man. He was also a strong believer in the ancient adage that one should help one's friends and hurt one's foes. Whether his earlier efforts at reconciliation had been completely fraudulent cannot be known, but it is perhaps not likely that they were. As already noted, he seems to have taken very badly the betrayal of the agreement that he had worked out with L. Scipio Asiagenus cos. 83 (see Chapter 10). In any case, following his victory, he would take vigorous steps to obliterate those whom he considered his opponents. He acted with posthumous rancor against his old commander Marius, whom he presumably saw as the driving force behind all his troubles starting in 88 B.C. He had Marius's physical remains scattered into the river Anio (a tributary of the Tiber). Cicero notes (*Laws* 2.57) that Sulla was the first patrician Cornelius to want to be cremated and suggested that this was through fear of the same fate befalling him. He also had Marius's victory monuments in Rome dismantled and buried (as dedications to the gods they could not be destroyed). A more satisfying form of vengeance could be wreaked upon his surviving opponents.

PROSCRIPTION

Beginning with his victory at the Colline Gates, Sulla began a slaughter of his enemies. Some of this was rather gruesome. M. Marius Gratidianus, nephew of C. Marius cos. 107 and second cousin of Cicero, had been a prominent supporter of the Cinnan regime, and he was tortured to death "one limb at a time" as a funerary offering to Marius's consular colleague and later enemy Q. Lutatius Catulus cos. 102, who had committed suicide at the time of Marius's entry into Rome in 87 B.C. The seemingly indiscriminate killing soon caused much uncertainty, and it was suggested that a list of authorized victims should be drawn up (the ancient sources give quite detailed and completely incompatible versions of who suggested the procedure and under what circumstances). A law was then enacted that provided for the publication of lists of Sulla's enemies, who could then be killed with impunity (the word "proscription" refers to the public display of these lists). Their property was confiscated, and their children were prohibited from holding office in future (this would later cause much strife). In practice, when the property was sold at public auction, it was won at cheap prices by Sulla's associates (who would be stupid enough to bid against them?). (Sulla supposedly freed 10,000 confiscated slaves, who as citizens received the nomen Cornelius and presumably cherished the memory of their benefactor and namesake.) The law of authorization ordained that the proscription lists were valid until June 1, 81 B.C.

The first proscription list involved comparatively small numbers, encompassing the prominent loyalist magistrates who remained among the living (including both consuls of 83 B.C., L. Cornelius Scipio Asiagenus, who was eventually killed at Massilia, and C. Norbanus, who would commit suicide in Rhodes). Soon, the lists were expanded to include large numbers of rich equites. Eventually, many other names were entered. It seems that Sulla's cronies got personal enemies (even those who had fought for Sulla!) entered on the lists. The sources are hopelessly contradictory about the numbers included.[2]

SULLA'S SETTLEMENT IN ITALY

The victory at the Colline Gate did not bring a complete end to the war in Italy. The cities of Nola in Campania and Volaterrae in Etruria did

---

[2] There was apparently a first list containing 80 (or 40) names, which seems to have been restricted to magistrates, and then over the next two days two more lists containing a further number approaching 500 (equites?) were added. Sulla apparently stated in public that these were all the opponents he could think of at the time and reserved the right to add more. Appian claims 1,600 equestrian victims, and two late sources based on Livy give a total of 2,000. The Early Imperial writer Valerius Maximus goes so far as to claim a total of 4,700. Seemingly, at least 500 initial victims were involved, and perhaps Appian's 1,600 could be added to this for a total of about 2,000, but since the exact basis of the various figures is not known (there were clearly several different lists, and the preserved figures may go back to incompatible figures in earlier sources), it is not possible to be more precise.

not finally surrender until 80 B.C. Particular devastation was wrought in Samnium. When Sulla invaded Italy in 83 B.C., he apparently agreed to respect the newly won rights of the Italian allies but excluded the Samnites. They had still been at war with the Romans when the Cinnan faction came to power, and Sulla refused to recognize an agreement that had been reached between Cinna's regime and the Samnites. Sulla seems to have loathed the Samnites and slaughtered Samnite prisoners taken during his battles (the men slaughtered during the meeting of the senate on November 2, 82 B.C., were Samnites). His troops devastated Samnium, some towns being reduced to the level of villages and others completely destroyed.

Once warfare ceased, Sulla punished the cities that had opposed him. He confiscated territory from many and even passed laws stripping the Roman citizenship from others (some courts later refused to recognize the validity of this action). These confiscations gave him the opportunity to solve a pressing issue: what to do with the troops who had served him so loyally? Sulla is said to have disbanded twenty-three legions, and he founded many colonies of his veterans in Italy on the sites of towns that had opposed him. Colonies were established throughout Etruria and Campania, and the validity of these grants would later be questioned. In any case, the recipients were not always successful farmers, and some later would support efforts to overthrow the government in Rome (in the hopes of profiting from new confiscations).

Sulla's "Constitution"

As dictator, Sulla implemented a large number of reforms. These were intended to

- restore the supremacy of the senate
- regulate the functions of the magistrates and promagistrates
- curb the power of the tribunate
- regulate provincial administration
- regularize the court system.

Put together, these reforms drastically changed the operation of the governmental system in Rome, and they may be referred to as the Sullan constitution (though Rome of course had no formal constitution). The new system was modified in various ways before the regular Republican government came to a halt in 49 B.C., but it was in the framework established by Sulla that the Republic functioned for its last three decades, and to a large extent the course of politics was determined during those decades by the opposing policies of those who advocated either the maintenance or the abolition of Sulla's reforms.

Senate

The bloody years from 90 B.C. on had led to the deaths of a large number of senators. Sulla himself was said to have been responsible over the years for the deaths of 105 (the nominal total was only 300). As part of his effort to restore the senate's political control, Sulla had to replenish its numbers, so he enrolled many new senators, raising the total to 600. These new senators were mostly of equestrian status. The larger total was necessary for manning the large jury panels, which were turned over exclusively to the senate (discussed later in the chapter).

Up until this date, the senate list had been revised every five years by the censors, who generally enrolled all the new junior magistrates who had been elected since the last revision of the list. Sulla now passed a law prescribing that all quaestors should automatically become senators. The theoretical total of 600 senators could then be maintained on the assumption that the twenty new quaestors each year would enter the senate at the age of thirty and live on average another thirty years.[3]

Magistrates

Sulla increased the number of praetors from six to eight and the number of quaestors to twenty (exactly how many there had been before is not known). While in the past the quaestorship had been held at a younger age, thirty years now became the minimum for holding the office. The old rule that ten years had to intervene between the repetition of an office was reinstituted (this mainly pertained to the consulship, since the lower offices were not normally repeated). To accommodate the large number of magistrates to be elected, the time fixed for the election of the magistrates of the

---

[3] That is, 20 × 30 = 600. How valid this system was there is no way of knowing, but presumably the calculation was based on some sort of rule of thumb about the life expectancy of a young senator. (If an ex-praetor eventually gained office only after the passage of a number of years since he became eligible, this would not affect the total of thwarted ex-praetors, since his victory would necessarily deny a position for another of the newly eligible praetors.) We do not know whether this scheme was based on empirical observation or was from more or less arbitrary, preconceived notions of life expectancy, and we have no way to assess its statistical validity (apart from circular arguments based on the application of modern estimates of life expectancy in premodern societies, whose relevance to the ancient world is unknown). At any rate, it must at least have seemed a plausible estimate.

Roman People was moved from its old date in the last few months of the year to July (the number of hours of sunlight may have been the factor).

The increased number of magistrates allowed a new pattern of office holding, which was intended to take care of the many urban responsibilities that had to be carried out by magistrates with imperium, while at the same time providing a sufficient number of governors for Rome's many provinces. It was still possible for the consuls and praetors to operate abroad during their regular office if necessary, but from now on they all normally served in Rome: the consuls would oversee all the important business that had to be handled in the senate, and the praetors were all occupied with presiding over the public courts (quaestiones) and supervising civil suits. After their year in office, all the magistrates then left the city to govern a province as promagistrates. Since there were now ten provinces – the two Spains, Transalpine Gaul (Narbonensis), Cisalpine Gaul, Sardinia and Corsica, Sicily, Africa, Macedonia, Asia, and Cilicia – theoretically there was one promagistrate for each province every year. This system did not entirely work in practice (even in the comparatively peaceful late 70s B.C. C. Verres governed Sicily as a propraetor for three years), but this was the general pattern down to the late 50s B.C., when yet another reform was necessary to try and find enough governors for the ever increasing number of Rome's provinces.

Provincial Administration

Sulla attempted to regulate the behavior of governors in their provinces, writing a number of new provisions into his modified version of the treason law (lex de maiestate minuta). Governors now needed the authorization of the senate or People to

- leave their province
- wage war
- enter an allied kingdom.

Also, the old governor had to depart within thirty days of the arrival of his replacement. These measures were meant to curb the independence of the imperium-holders in the provinces. The most obvious motivation for these measures is perhaps the irresponsible behavior of M.' Aquillius in Asia in the late 90s B.C., though other examples can be cited. Basically, the governors were to be subordinated to the central authority of the senate and any legislation passed at its behest. It would soon turn out that mere laws were unable to restrain a determined governor with the will to use military force, as Sulla himself should have foreseen.

Tribunate

Sulla imposed a number of restrictions on the power of the tribunate, an office that had seemingly been at the heart of the civil discord (and supposedly antisenatorial agitation) since 133 B.C.

- Anyone who held the tribunate was prohibited from being a magistrate of the Roman People. This effectively barred anyone with senatorial ambitions from holding the office.
- The right to pass legislation was taken away. (The sources are not entirely clear on this point; some modern scholars have argued that the tribunes could pass laws with the senate's authorization, but this view seems mistaken.)
- While the tribunes did retain their original power of intercession (the right to veto the actions of a magistrate), even here Sulla placed some restrictions (we do not know what they were).

Sulla clearly wished to eviscerate the political power of the tribunate, which was based on the right to pass legislation, and to make holding the office unpalatable to senators. One of the major popularis issues in the 70s B.C. was the campaign to restore the powers of the tribunate, which was finally accomplished in 70 B.C.

Courts

Sulla began his reform of the public courts with a general court law (*lex iudiciaria*), according to which the album of the jurors for the public courts (quaestiones) was to be selected exclusively from members of the senate. The available senators were divided into panels (*decuriae*) for hearing different cases, but the details of this procedure are elusive.

Sulla also reformed the laws that authorized three specific permanent courts (quaestiones). Before his time, three quaestiones are definitely known to have existed:

- The quaestio de pecuniis repetundis instituted first in 149 B.C. and given its later form by C. Gracchus in 123 B.C. (as modified by Glaucia ca. 100 B.C.)
- The court of treason (maiestas minuta) instituted by Saturninus in 103 B.C.
- The murder court, which an inscription shows to have existed as a permanent court in the mid 90s B.C. (thus having been established at some unknown date after 123 B.C.)

Sulla passed new laws authorizing these courts and set up five other courts for

- parricide (killing a relative)
- electoral corruption (*ambitus*)
- embezzlement of public funds (*peculatus*)
- use of violence in private life (*iniuria*)
- forgery (*quaestio testamentaria, nummaria*).

The last court is known to be an innovation. The others had existed before, though whether there were permanent quaestiones for these crimes in the period before Sulla is not known for sure. Since it was the tribunes who in the past had made accusations before the People, Sulla's major reduction of the power of the tribunate meant that a new system for trying important crimes had to be created. Once the tribunate was later restored, prosecutions occasionally took place before the People under very unusual (political) circumstances, but Sulla's system was the normal mode of enforcing criminal law until the Early Empire.

As we have seen, the eight praetors now normally spent their year in office presiding over legal matters in Rome. The urban and peregrine praetors continued to oversee the civil law system, and the remaining six praetors were left to preside over the eight quaestiones. Even if there was only one case in the docket of each quaestio (and there were often more), there were still not enough praetors to go around. To solve this problem, Sulla continued an earlier practice whereby the praetor who was in overall charge of a quaestio could delegate the power to preside over a given trial to a senator of aedilician rank (i.e., someone who had been aedile but not yet praetor).

Importance of Sulla's Actions as Dictator

When Sulla resigned the dictatorship in 79 B.C. and allowed the regular offices of the Republic to return to full operation, he must have thought that he had ensured the continued control of public life by the senatorial oligarchy. Two factors soon militated against this happy outcome.

In the first place, Sulla had acted in such a bloody, vindictive manner that large numbers of people were left bitterly opposed to everything he stood for and eager to overthrow his arrangements. All manner of people ranging from those dispossessed of their land to the children of the proscribed could dream of nothing but the revocation of everything ordained by him. Even some like Cicero, who thought that the totality of Sulla's arrangements had to be defended since the abrogation of one could cause the whole system to unravel, felt somewhat uneasy about the situation. The eventual "received opinion" about Sulla came to be that while his victory over his opponents was desirable, the way in which he exercised power afterward was deplorable. Thus, his constitutional arrangements had an aura of "original sin" about them.

Second, the civil war had had a deleterious effect on the senatorial class. One result was a sort of negative process of selection. While many of his associates were respectable members of the senatorial oligarchy who did not engage in unseemly behavior (though even they could make a profit out of the situation), a number of his supporters – especially young men whose main experience as adults consisted of the recent discord and violence that were plaguing Roman politics – proved to be greedy, murderous thugs. For example, C. Antonius (the son of M. Antonius cos. 99 who would later be Cicero's colleague as consul in 63 B.C.) and L. Sergius Catilina pr. 68 were thoroughly corrupted by the experience of civil war during their youth, which they spent murdering people, seizing property, and squandering their ill-gotten gains (which then had to be recouped through means of dubious propriety). Among the members of the aristocracy who went over to Sulla and then became the bulwark of his system, those who were not themselves corrupt were certainly guilty by association.

It is hard to overestimate the importance of Sulla's deeds as dictator for the final thirty years of the functioning Republic. The acts of vengeance that he inflicted on his enemies and the sometimes questionable favors that he bestowed on his friends would still be disputed twenty years later. The senatorial oligarchy came to be identified with the Sullan "constitution," and given the ancient tendency to personalize political disagreement, attacking Sulla's acts and attacking the oligarchy were to some extent synonymous. The person of Sulla continued to cast a baneful shadow over Roman politics long after the man himself ceased to be. (For coins that tried to take advantage of the positive view that some later held of Sulla, see Coins 15 and 16.)

Apart from the continuing ramifications of his acts of reform and vengeance, Sulla's career had another effect, which was much more harmful to the well-being of the Republic. It is a truism of modern scholarship that Sulla could not undo the precedent which he himself had set. He had shown that it was possible to use violence to overthrow the "legitimate" government and that those who assisted such an attempt would make vast sums of money in the process. Many learned the lesson about violence, but most failed to note that it was ultimately Sulla's veteran legions that secured his success. There would be several unsuccessful efforts in the next two decades to use "private" violence to overthrow the state, but it was only with Caesar's willingness in the year 49 B.C. to lead his Gallic legions against Rome that Sulla's example would finally destroy the Republican form of government.

Questions for Study and Reflection

1. What was Sulla's constitutional position after his victory in civil war? What was traditional and what was novel in his dictatorship?
2. What was the ancient interpretation of Sulla's dictatorship?
3. How did he treat his friends and enemies?
4. What were the proscriptions? In what way did they resemble or differ from earlier forms of political violence in Rome?
5. What governmental reforms did Sulla introduce? What was their overall purpose?
6. What effect did Sulla's acts and reforms have on the later course of events? What attitude did the senate and its supporters have toward Sulla? Why did others vilify him?
7. Was Sulla a beneficial or harmful figure? Did his career hurt or help the reestablishment of constitutional (legitimate) government?
8. How else could Sulla have established his authority? Could he have gone about his reforms in a different manner?

12

THE 70S B.C.

Attacks on the Sullan Regime and the Rise

of Pompey

THE DECADE AFTER SULLA

The 70s B.C. are characterized by turmoil resulting from the Sullan settlement. Many people, like the disenfranchised children of the proscribed and those who had lost land, wished to overturn his arrangements. On the other hand, these arrangements were supported not only by those who had directly benefited from them but also by those who considered them to be inextricably intertwined with the permanent establishment of senatorial control. The ultimate result of the developments of this period was that Cn. Pompeius (Pompey) rose to become the leading personality in public life. (For a coin of disputed date that aggrandizes Pompey, see Coin 12.)

The evidence for this decade is comparatively scanty, because apart from Q. Sertorius no major figure whose life was treated extensively in antiquity was at the high point of his career during this period (though some were starting out).

M. AEMILIUS LEPIDUS

The attack on Sulla's constitution had already begun during his lifetime. While still dictator in 79 B.C., he presided over the consular elections for the following year. Both men elected were apparently supporters of Sulla's arrangements. Q. Lutatius Catulus was definitely a Sullan man. His homonymous father had been Marius's colleague as consul in 102 B.C. and committed suicide in 87 B.C. after Marius's capture of Rome; in 82 B.C. the son (that is, the later consul of 78 B.C.) had had M. Marius

Gratidianus, Marius's nephew, tortured to death as a funerary offering to his father. Like his colleague, M. Aemilius Lepidus also belonged to a prominent patrician family. Lepidus had been in Rome during the 80s b.c., when he was married to a relative of L. Saturninus. He went over to Sulla at the time of his return to Italy, divorcing his "Marian" wife. He may well be the Aemilius Lepidus who is attested as a legate of Sulla during the civil war, and in any case he became praetor under Sulla's regime. He had also made large sums of money during the proscriptions. Thus, there was every reason to expect that he would, like Catulus, uphold Sulla's arrangements. This was not the path that he chose to follow, however. Instead, his behavior is reminiscent of L. Cinna's: both were patrician consuls who tried to advance their careers by championing discontent with the oligarchy.

During the course of 78 b.c., Sulla died an unpleasant natural death. There is slight evidence that already before Sulla's death Lepidus was acting in a way that Sulla frowned upon. Certainly right from the moment of Sulla's death, Lepidus began to pursue a policy of opposition to Sulla's legacy. Sulla's supporters wished to have his body brought to Rome and given a public funeral. While Catulus supported the proposed funeral, Lepidus opposed it. Sulla's supporters won out, and he was cremated in a huge ceremony. From this point on, there was constant discord between the consuls.

Initially at any rate, Lepidus was not opposed to the new constitutional arrangements. When the tribunes sought the restoration of their powers, he was the first to assert in a contio that this was not a useful move. He then went on to pass a grain law, presumably to gain support among the urban plebs. He also made proposals to rescind certain measures of Sulla that affected individuals:

- Restoration of exiles
- Cancellation of acts made by Sulla during the war
- Revocation of Sullan land grants
- Restitution of confiscated property

It seems that later he actively supported the restoration of the tribunate.

Not unexpectedly, Catulus opposed all of these measures. There was uproar in the city, but what Lepidus planned for the long run is not clear. He had received Cisalpine Gaul (the area between the river Po and the Alps) as his province and was administering it through a legate, M. Junius Brutus (father of the man who would later lead the conspiracy to assassinate Caesar the dictator). An ancestor had played a large part in settling the area a century before, so Lepidus had a large inherited clientele there.

Lepidus apparently thwarted any elections for the following year, so that 77 B.C. began with an interrex.[1]

The matter reached the point of open warfare in 78 B.C., when Lepidus championed a spontaneous uprising in Etruria. Sulla had caused much destruction there in 82 B.C., and after confiscating a large amount of land, he had settled many veterans on it. When the locals at Faesulae made an attack on the Sullan settlers, the senate ordered the consuls to suppress the uprising. Lepidus was given the task, but instead of suppressing the rebels, he joined forces with them and summoned to his side the children of the proscribed (who had been barred from political life by Sulla). This apparently happened late in the year, since it was an interrex who proposed in 77 B.C. that the senate should pass the senatus consultum ultimum (see Chapter 3). This it did, entrusting Q. Lutatius Catulus (now proconsul) with the task of suppressing Lepidus.

Lepidus marched on Rome, hoping to win a second consulship. Catulus in the meanwhile sent Pompey north as his legate to attack Lepidus's legate Brutus in Cisalpine Gaul. Brutus fell into Pompey's hands; the sources are uncertain as to whether Brutus betrayed his army or vice versa. In any case, Pompey treacherously had Brutus killed. When news of the outcome reached Rome, Lepidus's resolve (or support) collapsed, and he fled to Sardinia, where he soon died of natural causes. This was not the end of the troubles, as one of Lepidus's supporters, M. Perperna Veiento, son of the consul of 92 B.C. and grandson of the consul who defeated Aristonicus back in 130 B.C. (see Chapter 8), took the remnants of Lepidus's forces to Spain, an area under the control of Q. Sertorius, who had been opposing Sulla since the civil war. Although the lesson would not be grasped by everyone, the Lepidus episode showed the futility of using rural discontent to supply the means for seizing Rome by violence. Only command of properly organized military units would suffice for such purposes.

SPAIN AND SERTORIUS

Under Q. Sertorius, Spain remained a center of anti-Sullan activity long after Sulla's death. Sertorius was a man of equestrian background from Umbria (an area to the northeast of Rome). Having served with distinction in the German wars of Marius and in Spain, he was elected quaestor in 90 B.C. In 87 B.C., he adhered to the anti-Sullan side during the bellum Octavianum, when he fled Rome with the consul L. Cinna, and then commanded one of the four contingents that captured Rome (see Chapter 7).

---

[1]   For the position of interrex, see Chapter 11 n. 1.

Sertorius supposedly opposed Marius's violence, and in private he urged moderation on Cinna. He was elected praetor for 83 b.c. and assisted the consuls Scipio Asiagenus and Norbanus in their unsuccessful campaigns against Sulla. He had been given Nearer Spain as his province and went there in late 83 or early 82 b.c. Not surprisingly, Sertorius figured on the first proscription list in late 82 b.c.

In 81 b.c., Sulla sent an army against Sertorius, who had given a subordinate the task of guarding the Pyrenees. The subordinate was assassinated, and when the Sullan army crossed into Spain, Sertorius fled across the Mediterranean to Mauretania in North Africa. In 80 b.c., he was summoned back to Spain by the Lusitani, a large ethnic group in Further Spain. Sertorius defeated a subordinate of the Sullan governor at sea and the governor himself on land. At this point, the senate decided to send Sulla's consular colleague Q. Caecilius Metellus Pius cos. 80 against Sertorius.

Things did not go at all well for Metellus. In 79 b.c., both a legate of Metellus and the governor of Nearer Spain were defeated in battle and killed by Sertorius. Metellus summoned the governor of Transalpine Gaul to his assistance, and he too was defeated.

Sertorius's "State"

Sertorius now set himself up as an alternative to the Sullan regime in Rome, and he gathered around him those who were unable or unwilling to come to terms with Sulla. He established a senate of 300, which elected quaestors and praetors, and his position was further strengthened in 77 b.c. by the arrival of the remnants of Lepidus's army under M. Perperna (discussed earlier).

Sertorius also realized that he needed the support of the natives, and he enlisted this in two ways. First, he trained the native troops in Roman methods, and he summoned the sons of local leaders and gave them a Roman education (they served as hostages, too). Second, he cleverly played upon native sensibilities (he had a domesticated white fawn that was taken to be a mark of divine favor) and maintained a body of troops who were pledged to serve him loyally to the death (a native custom).

Fundamentally, all this Roman and native support depended on Sertorius's own personal prestige and charisma. The story of the decline of the Republic revolves around the issue of how a military leader could establish a new form of legitimacy once the traditional system broke down. Sertorius's somewhat odd attempt to combine Roman and native forms of legitimacy was an idiosyncratic solution to the problem that was forced upon him by his specific circumstances. For the most part, Roman commanders would rely only on Roman elements in their efforts to gain legitimacy, though Mark Antony would later make another attempt at melding Roman and foreign elements in justifying his position.

POMPEY EXTORTS A COMMAND

In 78 B.C., Pompey had caused the collapse of Lepidus's attack on Rome through his defeat of Lepidus's legate Brutus in Cisalpine Gaul. After this victory, the proconsul Catulus, under whose auspices Pompey was operating as a legate, commanded him to disband his troops. With various excuses Pompey put off complying. His aim was to extort a command from the senate. Since things were going badly in Spain, he wished to be sent there as a proconsul. Both consuls had refused to go to Spain, and L. Marcius Philippus cos. 91 made the quip that in his proposal to give the command to Pompey he was sending him not *pro consule* (literally "in place of the consul," the technical term for holding a command equivalent to the imperium of a consul) but *pro consulibus* ("in place of the consuls"). This joke cannot conceal the fact that the appointment was totally unconstitutional, since Pompey had not yet won even the quaestorship and he held no imperium of his own (under normal circumstances it could be acquired only through popular election to an office possessing it or through delegation from someone who possessed it through election). Nonetheless, given the military situation, the senate had no choice. Pompey thereby succeeded where death had cut short his father Cn. Pompeius Strabo cos. 89, that is, in using an army to extort a command for himself (see Chapter 7).

POMPEY'S AND METELLUS'S CAMPAIGN AGAINST SERTORIUS

The year 76 B.C. did not go well for Pompey. He was defeated in Nearer Spain, and he and Metellus withdrew to the Pyrenees for the winter, leaving Sertorius in control of all of Spain. The years 75 and 74 B.C. were again spent in indecisive combat and sieges. Pompey proved himself to be a less than stellar commander (he seems to have performed no better than Metellus), though ultimate victory gave him the reputation of being one. Pompey also continued to use intimidation in his relations with the senate. In 74 B.C., he coerced the consul L. Lucullus into sending supplies to Spain by threatening that otherwise he would return to Italy with his army, presumably implying that his return would not be a peaceable affair.

The end came in 73 B.C., not through victory but treachery. Sertorius seems to have become tyrannical toward the end, and Perperna felt threatened. He entered into a conspiracy with ten other prominent supporters of Sertorius, and they assassinated him at a feast. Perperna assumed command, but he lacked Sertorius's prestige (his position was further undermined when Sertorius's will named Perperna as an heir, which seemed to heighten the ingratitude of the assassination). Pompey lured Perperna's army into a trap, and after defeating it, he captured Perperna, who offered him Sertorius's correspondence. Though these letters supposedly incriminated many prominent men in Italy, Pompey burned them and had Perperna executed. Pompey then remained settling affairs in Spain until 71 B.C.

Italy after Lepidus

The 70s B.C. after the defeat of Lepidus were marked by continued agitation against the Sullan settlement (this period is particularly poorly attested apart from the slave revolt of Spartacus). Perhaps the most prominent issue was the restoration of the tribunate, and in 75 B.C. the prohibition against tribunes holding other political office was repealed by a consular law. On the whole, however, the Sullan arrangements remained in place down to 70 B.C. One practice of Sulla's that was openly challenged was his having allowed certain people not to pay to the treasury the sums they had bid for the property of the proscribed. Nothing came of this: though a consul in 72 B.C. proposed a law to force repayment, it was apparently not passed.

Foreign Affairs

In the late 70s B.C., a number of important developments took place in the East.

Inheritance of Bithynia and War with Mithridates

In 74 B.C., King Nicomedes of Bithynia died, leaving his kingdom to the Roman People. It was clear that acceptance of the inheritance would lead to another war with Mithridates, and the consuls, who had received unimportant provinces under the lex Sempronia before their election in 75 B.C., contrived to be given commands in the East. One, M. Aurelius Cotta, received the task of establishing Bithynia as a province (in this he could expect to make much money), and the other, L. Licinius Lucullus (Sulla's quaestor and right-hand man), received Cilicia in expectation of military glory against Mithridates. (This war will be described in Chapter 13.)

Cyrenaica

In 96 B.C., the king of Cyrene had likewise bequeathed his kingdom to Rome; while the inheritance was accepted, no province was created, and the local cities were left to manage their own affairs (see Chapter 8). By 74 B.C., however, it was clear that local autonomy had resulted in chaos as a result of disputes between the cities and that a properly constituted province had to be established, so the senate sent a quaestor to carry out this task. (It is not known why such a junior magistrate was given this important assignment.)

When Sulla had raised the number of praetors to eight only a few years earlier, there was an equal number of provinces and magistrates with imperium. Now, only five years after his death, the demands of the empire were beginning once again to outstrip the resources available to administer it.

M. Antonius's Campaign against the Pirates

Already in 102 B.C., M. Antonius had been sent during his praetorship to subdue the pirates operating out of Cilicia in southeastern Asia Minor (see Chapter 8). The turmoil of the First Mithridatic War had led to an upsurge in their depredations. From 78 to 75 B.C., P. Servilius Vatia cos. 79 operated in Cilicia as proconsul, subdueing much of the south coast of Asia Minor. He received the title *Isauricus* for subdueing the Isaurians (a troublesome group of mountain dwellers) and was granted a triumph. All good and well, but the broader problem of piracy remained unsolved. In 74 B.C., the praetor M. Antonius (son of M. Antonius cos. 99 and father of the famous Marc Antony) was given the unprecedented task of subdueing the pirates throughout the Mediterranean with proconsular imperium extending some miles inland from the coast of every province. To some extent, this novel command overcame the problem caused by the geographically restricted provinces, namely, that if a Roman magistrate operated against the pirates in one area, they could simply sail off somewhere else. Antonius's personal presence was still needed for operations, however, and this restricted his effectiveness. In 74 B.C., he operated among the islands of the western Mediterranean, but in later years he turned his attention to the large Greek island of Crete, where piracy was a traditional occupation. In 72 or 71 B.C., he suffered a major defeat at their hands and actually had to make a treaty with them. He died soon afterward in 71 B.C. without returning to Rome. Despite his defeat he was given the title *Creticus*. The problems with the pirates went on unabated, however, and they even attacked the coast of Italy. It would take several more years of their depredations before a novel solution could be found, a solution that would further demonstrate the inadequacies of the traditional consitution.

SPARTACUS

In the third century B.C., the Romans picked up a taste for gladiatorial spectacles, probably from the Samnites. Gladiators were captives who were to fight to the death as a funerary offering. Under the Republic, gladiatorial shows were never put on by magistrates in an official capacity, but magistrates would offer such shows privately as a way of gaining popularity. Soon the numbers of gladiators presented swiftly increased, and schools (*ludi*) were established for training slaves (often military captives) as gladiators. Campania was a favorite site for such schools, and in 73 B.C. a revolt broke out at one of these. It began with seventy-four prisoners at a *ludus* in the important city of Capua, and was led by two Gauls and a Thracian called Spartacus. The rebels spread out into the countryside, and large numbers of rural slaves joined them (gangs of workers on large estates were kept in barracks called *ergastula*), raising their numbers to the tens of thousands. Since many of these rural slaves had only recently been taken captive during various Roman campaigns against warlike tribes, they contributed materially to the military effectiveness of the rebel forces. Augmented in this way, the rebels took possession of Mt. Vesuvius, and a praetor was sent against them. He besieged them, but they put him to flight and seized his camp. The victorious slaves then moved into south Italy, where their numbers increased further and they spent the winter.

The ability of the rebels to win so many victories illustrates once more how difficult it was to raise a Roman military force from scratch. Just a decade earlier, the failed opposition to Sulla's invasion had demonstrated the inherent unreliability of hastily raised troops. As was often the case, the Romans would eventually prevail against the rebels once there was sufficient time for the troops to be trained and organized properly and for competent officers to be placed in command, but in the short run defeats were suffered even at the hands of impromptu armies of slaves who had no experience of working together and came from quite varied origins (but obviously had a strong motivation to succeed).

In 72 B.C., the slave army was large enough to divide in two, one contingent under the command of the Gaul Crixus, and the other under Spartacus. Spartacus realized that in Italy defeat was inevitable, and he wished to escape across the Alps. Crixus, on the other hand, stupidly refused to give up plundering southern Italy. The Romans reacted energetically, if not always competently. The propraetor Q. Arrius, who was supposed to take over Sicily, destroyed the force under Crixus. Things were not so easy with Spartacus, who was moving north. First, he defeated the consul Cn. Cornelius Lentulus Clodianus. Next, he defeated the other consul, L. Gellius, and Q. Arrius as well. By now he was in the far north, where he defeated the proconsul of Cisalpine Gaul (C. Cassius Longinus cos. 73) and another praetor (Cn. Manlius). At this point, when so close to escaping from Italy, the slave army foolishly insisted, against Spartacus's advice, on turning back south. There is one claim that Spartacus was aiming at Rome, but this is hard to believe. Whatever his intentions, he wound up in the far south, trying unsuccessfully to persuade Cilician pirates to ferry his force over to Sicily.

After the defeat of the consuls, the senate ordered them out of the war, and it was turned over to M. Licinius Crassus, who had been praetor the preceding year (73 B.C.). Crassus's exact status as commander is difficult to determine, and perhaps the command against Spartacus was granted through a special election. In any event, he managed (with some difficulty) to bring the war to an end in six months between late 72 and early 71 B.C. After a minor defeat was suffered by one of his subordinates, he punished a cohort through the traditional practice of decimation, by which every tenth man was executed. Thus bolstered in discipline, his army dug a trench across the entire toe of Italy (thirty-seven miles) to hem Spartacus in, but this failed and Spartacus moved into open country in southern Italy. He tried to escape by sea at Brundisium, but a Roman army returning from Macedonia cut off retreat in that direction, and he had to go north again. The rebel force split in two once more, and the German/Gallic contingent was wiped out by Crassus. Spartacus wished to retreat, but his army forced a battle and it was too destroyed. Spartacus died in the battle, and all that remained now was to round up the fugitives. Pompey, who had recently returned from Spain, aided in this task, and to Crassus's great annoyance, he claimed that it was he who had finished off the slave war. (This would not be the last time that Pompey tried to usurp someone else's glory.) As a mark of victory, Crassus had the 6,000 slaves who were captured after Spartacus's defeat crucified on the Appian Way between Rome and Capua.

Spartacus is often taken as a symbol of revolt against oppression, but he was not opposed to slavery as an institution. He simply did not want to be a slave himself, and if his followers had listened to him, he could have led them back to the Balkans. In any case, the success of his revolt pointed out the danger of not having any permanent military force in Italy and the potential risk inherent in using such large numbers of recently captured slaves in agriculture.

M. Licinius Crassus

M. Licinius Crassus is a hard personality to interpret, as the ancient sources are hostile to him, and he would later be overshadowed by his associates Pompey and Casear. Of an important patrician family, Crassus, like Pompey, emerged as an energetic young supporter of Sulla at the time of his invasion of Italy. Indeed, it was he who led Sulla's right flank to victory at the battle of the Colline Gate and thereby saved the day. Not surprisingly, he greatly improved his financial situation through buying up at auction the property of proscribed individuals. One might, therefore, expect him to be a steadfast supporter of the Sullan establishment. In the 60s b.c., however, he would make his great wealth available to troublemakers and thereby incurred the suspicion of more staid members of the oligarchy. Whatever his stance in the later stages of his career, there is no reason to think him anything but a respectable member of the establishment at this point, and he had every reason to resent the upstart Pompey, who had so notably attempted to steal Crassus's glory.

Return of Pompey and His Consulship
with Crassus

In 71 b.c., after settling affairs in Spain, Pompey and Metellus returned to Italy. Pompey received approval from the senate for a plan to give land to his veterans, but this was not actually carried out on the grounds that the state was too poor (and that the soldiers had received enough money from the Spanish booty). Pompey already had great prestige from his victory in Spain, and this was only enhanced by his claim (whether legitimate or not) to have ended the slave war. By the time the consular elections were held (presumably in July), both Pompey and Crassus were still in command of their forces, and they ran successfully for the consulship. While Crassus was legally eligible, Pompey, as an eques Romanus who had not even held the quaestorship, much less the praetorship (both legal prerequisites for holding the consulship), and who was six years below the legal minimum age, had to be absolved of the legal requirements by a decree of the senate. As consul designate, he indicated that he would restore the tribunate. On the day before he entered office, Pompey celebrated a triumph with Metellus Pius.

The consuls designate clearly did not like each other (not surprisingly, Crassus resented Pompey's attempt to claim credit for defeating Spartacus), but they made a public reconciliation. By the time they entered into office, however, their enmity had reasserted itself, and they generally thwarted each other. Their only achievement was the abrogation of Sulla's law curbing the powers of the tribunate, which thereby regained its traditional place in the constitutional order.

RESTORATION OF LEPIDUS'S AND SERTORIUS'S SUPPORTERS

In about 70 B.C., a tribunician law restored the citizenship of those who had followed M. Aemilius Lepidus cos. 78 during his rebellion and then adhered to Sertorius. Nothing is known of the exact circumstances under which this measure was passed, but it would seem that the citizenship of those who had gone with Perperna to Spain after the collapse of Lepidus's revolt had been taken away. This bill was apparently proposed with the consent of the senate, so it presumably formed part of the effort to settle affairs after the defeat of the rebels in Spain. (The dating is affected by a number of complicated and interrelated chronological issues, but 70 B.C. is the most plausible date and cannot be off by more than a year.)

PROSECUTION OF VERRES AND COURT REFORM

The year 70 B.C. saw yet another change in the composition of the jury panels, which had been in the hands of the senators since Sulla's victory. There were many accusations in the air that the senatorial jurors had been open to bribery (perhaps not surprising given the men put in the senate by Sulla). In this atmosphere, Cicero made a name for himself with his prosecution of C. Verres, who had been urban praetor in 74 B.C., and then served as governor of Sicily in 73–71 B.C. By any standard, Verres's extortion and misbehavior as governor was outrageous, but he expected to escape prosecution through the influence of important friends. Cicero, who had been quaestor of Sicily in 75 B.C., was asked by the Sicilians to prosecute Verres.[2] Though Cicero preferred on principle not to act as prosecutor, he accepted (in fact, this is his only prosecution). (Generally, young men of the nobility brought prosecutions against enemies of their families as a way to make a name for themselves; the new man Cicero normally steered clear of giving offense in this way.) Cicero accused Verres of stealing 40,000,000 sesterces, quoting him as having said that the proceeds of the first year were reserved for his (senatorial) protectors, those of the second for the jurors (in the extortion trial that he anticipated), and those of the third for himself. Throughout the preserved speech, Cicero points out to the jurors the dangers of acquitting Verres, since in that case there would be no doubt of the venality of senatorial jurors, which would lead to the jury panels being taken away from the senate yet again. Cicero's initial presentation of the case (see Chapter 11 for the procedure) was so damning that Verres did not even wait for the obligatory second presentation of the case and went into exile. One of Verres's defenders in the case (Q. Hortensius, consul designate for the next year) had previously been considered the greatest orator in Rome, but with the oratorical skill that he demonstrated in his prosecution of Verres, Cicero won this distinction for himself.

The conviction of Verres did no good for maintaining senatorial control of the juries. The praetor L. Aurelius Cotta passed a law dividing the jury panels evenly between senators, equites, and a category of men called *tribuni aerarii* ("tribunes of the treasury"). (The tribuni aerarii had earlier been involved in tax collection, but what exactly the title signified at this time is unclear. At any rate, they apparently had the same census qualification as the equites.) It says something of the inability of the consuls Pompey and Crassus to cooperate that this popular measure was passed by a praetor. In any case, this compromise in the composition of the jury panels seems to have largely lulled the dispute over control of the courts that had raged so bitterly in the decades since C. Gracchus's introduction of equestrian jurors. At any rate, the public courts would operate under this system for the last two decades of the functioning Republic (until Caesar the dictator removed the tribuni aerarii).

---

[2] By this time the procedure in the quaestio de pecuniis repetundis had been modified so that the foreign victims of theft at the hands of Roman magistrates were no longer allowed to conduct the case themselves. Instead, they had to secure the services of a prominent Roman to lodge the accusation and prosecute the case on their behalf.

CENSORS OF 70 B.C.

In 70 B.C., there were censors for the first time since 86 B.C. It used to be thought that Sulla had curtailed the office, but there is no evidence for this apart from the fact that the office was not filled in 76 B.C. (civil war prevented their election in 82 B.C.). One of the major tasks of the censors was to revise both the census rolls and the list of senators. There was now no need to enroll new members of the senate, since Sulla's reforms had directly enrolled newly elected quaestors in it. The censors still retained the right to expel those whom they deemed guilty of unacceptable behavior, however, and the new censors, L. Gellius and Cn. Cornelius Lentulus (both cos. 72), were noted for their severity in purging the ranks of the senate. They expelled sixty-four members, or something like 10 percent of the entire senate. These included a number of the disreputable characters who had entered the senate from Sulla's entourage, such as C. Antonius, who would be Cicero's colleague as consul in 63 B.C. (after regaining senatorial status by winning the praetorship for 66 B.C.) and P. Cornelius Lentulus Sura, who had been consul only the preceding year (he too would hold the praetorship a second time in 63 B.C. in order to secure reentry into the senate, and would be executed that year for his role in the so-called Catilinarian conspiracy; see Chapter 15). While the censors could remove some of the more egregious creatures of Sulla, they could not revoke the baneful influence of his legacy.

The need to distribute the citizenry among the tribes and centuries must have been pressing, as this task (which was necessary for the proper functioning of the electoral system) had not been carried out properly in two decades. In the previous census conducted back in 86 B.C., the newly enfranchised Italian allies had not been counted as citizens (see Chapter 10), and the number of citizens recorded at that time amounted to only 463,000. Now, with the allies in Italy enrolled, the total reached 900,000.[3] It would seem, then, that the enfranchisement of Italy had doubled the number of Roman citizens, and conceivably it was a continued disinclination to implement the outcome of the Social War that had led to the failure to elect censors six years before. Whatever the cause of that, the new census must have had a significant effect on the electoral process.

It is doubtful that the poorer new citizens who lived at a great distance from Rome would have bothered to come to Rome for elections. There is clear evidence, however, that the votes of wealthy citizens in

---

[3] Though the evidence is not unequivocal, it seems that the census figures refer to adult males.

Cisalpine Gaul were solicited for consular elections, so they at least did take the trouble to travel all the way to Rome for the regular elections, where their votes would have had a significant influence in the centuriate assembly. Since there is no substantive data about election returns and there were only two decades left for the electoral system to function, it is difficult to assess the overall effect of this large expansion of the electorate. In the short term, at any rate, it did nothing to threaten the nobility's virtual monopoly of the consulship, but the lack of anything like a full list of the lower magistrates makes it impossible to determine what influence the new voters had on the election returns. What is clear is that in the last decades of the Republic large numbers of men from the towns of Italy began to run for office in Rome. The death of the Republic cut short the developments that would have resulted from this situation, but these "new men" would assume an important position in the senate of the Early Empire. (For a coin that may have been minted around this time and alludes to the reconciliation of Rome and Italy in the aftermath of the Social War, see Coin 13.)

Questions for Study and Reflection

1. What attitudes were held about Sulla immediately after his death?
2. What was the attitude of M. Aemilius Lepidus cos. 78 to the Sullan settlement? How did he intend to take advantage of dissatisfaction with Sulla's arrangements? Why did his revolt fail?
3. What was unconstitutional about Pompey's behavior in 77 b.c.? How does his activity fit into the broader pattern of generals using their troops for their own political advancement?
4. What was Q. Sertorius's long success based on? What allowed him to hold out for so long against Metellus Pius and Pompey? How effective a commander did Pompey show himself to be in action against Sertorius?
5. What were the aims of the slaves who rebelled and their leader Spartacus? Why did they enjoy so many successes against Roman armies? How did the Romans finally prevail over them? What role did Pompey play in their defeat?
6. What was unusual about Pompey's consulship? Why did he and M. Crassus quarrel?
7. What aspects of the Sullan "constitution" were overturned in the 70s b.c.?
8. In what way was the question of the jury album finally settled?
9. What effect did the final enrollment of the Italian allies have on the electoral process?

13

Third Mithridatic War, War with the Pirates, and the Ascendancy of Pompey

Second Mithridatic War

The terms of the Peace of Dardanus, which Sulla had imposed upon Mithridates at the end of the First Mithridatic War, restored the territorial situation that had prevailed before M.' Aquillius provoked war back in 91 B.C. While Mithridates retained his ancestral kingdom of Pontus in the northeast of Asia Minor, the Romans continued to administer the provinces of Asia in the west and of Cilicia in the southeast directly, and held the southern coast and the interior under their hegemony.

In 83 B.C., L. Licinius Murena, whom Sulla had left behind in Asia when he invaded Italy, took it upon himself to resume the war against Mithridates, in violation of the agreement between Mithridates and Sulla. In the following year, Murena suffered serious losses and (perhaps in 81 B.C.) Sulla ordered him to stop (fobbing him off with a hardly deserved triumph). This less than glorious event is grandiosely named the Second Mithridatic War.

Roman acceptance of the inheritance of Bithynia upon the death of its king in 74 B.C. (see Chapter 12) changed the situation. Not only would this increase the area under direct Roman rule, but disputes over control of territory between Pontus and Bithynia would clearly lead to another war with Mithridates. Although it could not have been foreseen at the time, within a decade the large series of military campaigns and annexations that followed from the Third Mithridatic war would cause a drastic upheaval in the Near East, and Rome's territorial control and military obligations would in turn be greatly expanded.

Third Mithridatic War and Lucullus

The consuls of 74 B.C., L. Licinius Lucullus and M. Aurelius Cotta, got new provinces for themselves in the East in the aftermath of the inheritance. Cotta contented himself with the lucrative business of setting up the new province of Bithynia, while Lucullus took Cilicia in anticipation of marching north into Pontus. The consuls are still attested in Rome in late 74 B.C., and the Third Mithridatic War began with the spring of 73 B.C. While Cotta's role would be comparatively restricted, Lucullus, who had gained much experience in campaigning in Asia Minor from his days as Sulla's quaestor in the 80s B.C., was to enjoy spectacular initial success, though he would prove unable to bring the war in the East to a conclusion.

After Cotta and Lucullus were already in their provinces, Mithridates attacked Bithynia, shutting Cotta up in the town of Chalcedon and besieging the important port of Cyzicus on the Bosporus (Mithridates had established naval superiority and needed a base in the west). Lucullus marched north to help, and forced Mithridates to lift the siege by cutting off his supply lines to Pontus, thus achieving a strategic victory without open battle.

In the spring of 72 B.C., Mithridates was still at Nicomedia in Bithynia, when a great Roman naval victory at Lemnos in the Aegean made Mithridates's position untenable, and he withdrew into Pontus. Two obstacles stood in the way of pursuing Mithridates. First, the major town of Heraclea (on the Black Sea coast of Asia Minor) blocked the Romans' path into Pontus. Cotta spent two years besieging it, returning to Rome in 71 B.C. after it eventually capitulated. Second, Mithridates still had a fleet in the Aegean, and it was only after a legate (C. Valerius Triarius) destroyed it at the battle of Tenedos that Lucullus was able to prosecute the war further to the east (and at an unclear date was also given command of the province of Asia). The decision to move eastward in 72 B.C., which implied a great expansion of Rome's commitments, was made by Lucullus without consulting the senate.

By late 72 B.C., Lucullus had reached Amisus and put it under unsuccessful siege during the winter. In the spring of 71 B.C., Lucullus moved a little further east to Cabira, where he and Mithridates watched each other for a while without joining battle. Mithridates tried to attack Lucullus's supply trains, but after two failures he decided to retire further east. This decision proved a mistake. The Mithridatic army lost cohesion as it withdrew, and Lucullus destroyed it. He then set about subduing Pontus and Lesser Armenia, with Mithridates retaining control only of the Crimea and Colchis (in the western Caucasus). Lucullus was kept busy with sieges and campaigns against various eastern tribes until 70 B.C.

WAR WITH ARMENIA

After his disaster at Cabira, Mithridates fled to King Tigranes of Armenia (his son-in-law). In about 96 B.C., Tigranes had come to the throne of a small Armenian kingdom and was the vassal of the Parthian kingdom to the south and east. In the early first century B.C., both the Parthian ruling house and the Greek Seleucids of Syria fell into dynastic chaos, and Tigranes took advantage of the situation to seize northern Mesopotamia and northern Syria, adopting the eastern title "king of kings." Thus, Mithridates's son-in-law was the most important king to the east of Asia Minor.

In 70 B.C., with the conquest of Pontus complete, Lucullus sent his legate Ap. Claudius Pulcher, the patrician son of the consul of 79 B.C., to demand that Tigranes either turn over Mithridates or face war (it was thought that the war would not be properly finished until Mithridates was dead). Strictly speaking, Lucullus had no authority to wage war against Tigranes, but justified himself by treating Tigranes as Mithridates's ally, even though Tigranes had made no hostile move against the Romans. In any case, this step shows the extent to which Roman generals now felt comfortable about acting without any consultation of the senate (not a surprising attitude from Sulla's quaestor!).

In 69 B.C., Lucullus invaded Armenia. To force Tigranes into battle, Lucullus invested his newly founded capital, Tigranocerta. Lucullus won a decisive victory, but it did him little good, as Tigranes (and Mithridates) simply withdrew into mountainous northern Armenia. Lucullus destroyed the capital, and many vassals of Tigranes made their submission to the victorious Roman general. Lucullus also enlisted the assistance of the Parthian king.

In 68 B.C., Lucullus invaded northern Armenia, but Tigranes refused to give battle and harassed Lucullus's supply lines. The early onset of bad weather in the mountains forced Lucullus to give up his campaign, and he withdrew to the south, seizing Nisibis in northern Mesopotamia, where he spent the winter of 68/67 B.C. Tigranes then returned to southern Armenia and threw out the garrisons that Lucullus had left behind. Thus, while Lucullus retained overall military superiority, he could not bring the war to a conclusion. The situation is similar to the campaign against Jugurtha, in which it turned out that victory in the field was not enough to end the war, and a protracted campaign of occupying the countryside had to be undertaken in order to subdue the enemy. Unfortunately for Lucullus, he did not have the necessary resources for this, and fortune in her unpredictability did not smile upon his endeavors.

Meanwhile, Lucullus's position was undermined by events in Pontus. In 68 B.C., Mithridates took advantage of Lucullus's withdrawal to the south to move an army into eastern Pontus, where the locals welcomed his return. Lucullus had left two inferior legions behind to hold the territory, and Mithridates won a victory over a legate. C. Valerius Triarius brought reinforcements from Asia and assumed command. The Romans then spent the winter in the stronghold of Cabira, but in 67 B.C. Mithridates threatened a Roman base and thereby forced Triarius to abandon his easily defended position and come to the base's aid. The resulting battle of Zela was a Roman debacle.

Lucullus had already started marching to Triarius's relief but arrived too late. His troops met the shattered remnants of Triarius's army. They were clearly annoyed at the tight rein that Lucullus kept on them (preventing indiscriminate plunder) and were now stirred up by P. Clodius Pulcher (brother of the legate who had demanded that Tigranes surrender Mithridates, and also Lucullus's brother-in-law), so that when Lucullus proposed to march back east into Pontus, they mutinied. They insisted on withdrawing southwest into Cappadocia, where they refused to go over to the offensive, but they did agree to prevent any Mithridatic attack toward the west.

This was the end for Lucullus. His position of great power in the East was viewed with resentment in the senate, and efforts had already been undertaken to curtail it. In 69 B.C., Asia was taken from him, and in 68 B.C. Cilicia was assigned to Q. Marcius Rex, consul of that year. Finally, in 67 B.C. the tribune A. Gabinius passed a law assigning Pontus and Bithynia to one of the consuls of the year (M.' Acilius Glabrio, son of the man who had, as C. Gracchus's colleague, passed the reform of the quaestio de pecuniis repetundis). The revolt of his troops meant that Lucullus would have no opportunity to finish the war before Glabrio arrived in 66 B.C. As it turned out, command against Mithridates would go not to Glabrio but to Pompey, who was in the area to deal with the pirate situation (discussed later in the chapter).

Assessment of Lucullus

Lucullus is a transitional figure in the military commands of the Late Republic. He was born of a prominent noble family (he was a nephew of Q. Metellus Numidicus cos. 109), and his career soon became closely associated with that of Sulla. After serving under Sulla in the Social War, he was assigned to Sulla as his quaestor in 88 B.C. In this capacity, he was the only senatorial officer who remained loyal to Sulla in his march on Rome, and then became Sulla's most trusted lieutenant during the many years of campaigning in the East. With Sulla's conquest of Italy came suitable rewards, including the right to hold office in quick succession to make up for time lost in the East. After the death of Sulla, Lucullus became one of the standard-bearers of the new senatorial regime and a staunch defender of Sulla's enactments.

To some extent, Lucullus can be viewed as the last of the major senatorial commanders of the traditional kind. He received his command as the result of holding a regular consulship without any interference in the form of popular agitation or legislation. He then operated as a regular proconsul until his recall, when he duly turned over his forces to his legitimate successor. His conservative politics undoubtedly made it inconceivable for him to do otherwise, and the poor relations between him and his troops, which were a major cause – along with the inadequacy of his forces for his extensive campaigns – of his ultimate failure, are largely to be ascribed to his refusal to purchase their loyalty by bestowing large amounts of plunder on them, as any general who was determined to lead his troops in civil war would have been bound to do. On the other hand, the very nature of his command was inherently different from the comparatively limited campaigns waged by the famous generals of the Middle Republic. Instead of simply attempting to prevail over a specific foe (and win plunder), Lucullus (on his own initiative) had undertaken a fairly open-ended campaign of conquest in areas that stretched far beyond any place where any Roman armies had previously campaigned. Accordingly, he had to use his own judgment in making much more important strategic decisions than would have been the case with earlier commanders.

Lucullus's initial victories are impressive, and if he had managed to find a way to bring his wars to a successful end (and had had the unscrupulousness, charisma, and luck necessary to retain his troops' loyalty), he could have been as famous a figure as Caesar would soon become. As it was, for many years his enemies thwarted his richly deserved triumph, which he finally celebrated in 63 B.C. He largely withdrew from public affairs and led a life of private luxury that became a byword for sybaritic decadence. Pathetically, he lapsed into dementia before dying in about 58 B.C.

LEX GABINIA AND THE COMMAND AGAINST THE PIRATES

By 67 B.C., the situation with the pirates had become intolerable. In 71 B.C., M. Antonius Creticus's special command had ended with his failure in Crete (see Chapter 12). The consul of 69 B.C., Q. Caecilius Metellus (second cousin of Metellus Pius and grandson of C. Metellus Caprarius cos. 113, who was censor with Numidicus in 102 B.C.), continued the campaign in Crete, but elsewhere the pirates were out of control. They not only sacked various small islands but even attacked Ostia, the port of Rome itself, and took many prominent Romans (even legates) captive. Clearly, the ad hoc solutions employed until now were unsatisfactory, and in 67 B.C. the tribune A. Gabinius (whose grandfather had enacted the first ballot law back in 139 B.C.) proposed a completely novel form of command, promulgating a law that would authorize a special election to fill this new position.

One of the major problems of normal Roman commands was their geographical restriction. Though M. Antonius had been given *imperium infinitum* (unlimited imperium) in 74 B.C., it still basically had to be exercised by him in person (his legates derived their use of imperium from his, possessing none of their own). Under the *lex Gabinia*, Pompey was empowered to appoint fifteen legates who had their own imperium and were entitled *legati pro praetore* ("legates in place of a praetor"). This title was derived from an older usage, but its application here was novel in that previously a *legatus pro praetore* could by definition come into existence only in a province where the regular governor was absent (through death or departure). Now, legates with subordinate imperium were to exist alongside an elected holder of imperium, who was thereby enabled to control a province far greater than had normally been the case up to this point. In effect, the People were delegating to an individual their exclusive right to bestow imperium. (This administrative principle would eventually allow the emperors to control numerous provinces through legati pro praetore; see Chapter 24.) This procedure was necessary because in order to deal with the pirates, whose marauding encompassed the entire Mediterranean, the lex Gabinia gave the commander of the pirate war a vast province with correspondingly vast resources. His imperium was to be equal to that of all provincial governors to a distance of fifty miles from the coast, and he was given the power to raise huge numbers of troops (over 100,000) and large sums of money for the purpose. This command was to last three years.

While it might be concluded that the lex Gabinia was a means of exerting popular control over the administration, the electorate had no say in the provisions of the bill, and it was drawn up specifically for the benefit of a single man. In effect, the natural implication of the procedure was the need for a single individual to control the empire's military resources. In any case, such a broad command was fundamentally incompatible with the basic principles and traditions of Republican administration. Not surprisingly, it was bitterly resisted by the leading members of the senatorial oligarchy (prominent opponents were Q. Lutatius Catulus cos. 78, whom Pompey had served as legate back in 77 B.C. when he refused to relinquish command, and C. Calpurnius Piso, who was consul in 67 B.C.). In the first place, if Sulla had been able to win his way to power through the use of only seven legions stationed in Asia, what was the potential for tyranny inherent in this unprecedented command? In any case, it was obvious that the man who would be elected to fill the position was Pompey, whose ascent to the consulship had been totally irregular. Not surprisingly given Pompey's great popularity among the electorate, the oligarchy's opposition was unavailing: the bill passed and Pompey was promptly elected to the post.

As it turned out, once Roman resources were coordinated, the pirates could be dealt with in a much shorter period of time than was anticipated in the law. Within forty-nine days, Pompey and his legates swept the Mediterranean from west to east in a coordinated campaign, and the pirate threat was finally ended with a major naval victory off Cilicia. Thus, Pompey was now conveniently available in 66 B.C. when the full extent of Lucullus's setback in Asia became known in Rome.

LEX MANILIA

In 66 B.C., the tribune C. Manilius proposed a law transferring the provinces of Asia, Cilicia, and Bithynia and Pontus to Pompey, giving him vast resources to continue the war against Mithridates and the express right to act at his own discretion. This law represents a further step in the process by which the authority of the popular assemblies was used to force the hand of the senate. Whereas previously laws had been passed to set up elections to appoint commanders (e.g., in 131, 107, and 88 B.C.), now a (highly unusual) provincial command was to be bestowed through legislation without even the pretense that it was open to anyone competent to seek the position in an election. The lex Manilia was simply a means for

Pompey to use his great popularity to acquire yet another military command for himself.[1]

Once again, there was senatorial opposition to giving such a huge command to one person, but since Pompey's prestige had risen even further as a result of his astonishingly swift victory over the pirates, the bill (supported by the praetor M. Tullius Cicero in a surviving speech) was passed overwhelmingly.

POMPEY IN ASIA

Pompey soon took over in Asia Minor. The groundwork of restoring order had been laid by Glabrio (to whom the eastern command had been assigned in 67 B.C.). Pompey quickly marched from Bithynia into Pontus. Though Mithridates still had much money in his treasuries, he could not translate this into troops, and for once he was outnumbered by a Roman army (Pompey's force amounted to six to eight legions). A battle was fought at Dastira, where Mithridates's army was annihilated. (Pompey later founded the city of Nicopolis – Greek for "City of Victory" – on the site). Mithridates retreated eastward into Lesser Armenia with his remaining troops. Finding Tigranes unwilling to receive him, he passed on to Colchis in the north. In 65 B.C., he moved to the Crimea, where he spent the next two years trying to expand his influence in the region. In 63 B.C., he proposed a campaign that his army opposed, and the now aged king, who had been fighting against Rome for so long, was finally assassinated by one of his many sons.

Pompey made no serious effort to pursue Mithridates – and earned some criticism for this – but he had other plans in mind: the establishment of a permanent Roman presence in the Near East.

ARMENIA AND THE CAUCASUS

In late 66 B.C., Pompey advanced toward Armenia. Realizing that it was pointless to resist, Tigranes met Pompey in his royal attire, and after placing his diadem (the ancient equivalent of a crown) at Pompey's feet, he performed obeisance (prostrating himself on the ground, a ceremonial act performed in the East as a sign of submission to a king). Pompey then helped Tigranes to his feet and replaced the diadem on his head.

---

[1] It could have been argued that he was now in a position to use the imperium that had been granted to him by the lex Gabinia, but the fact remains that it was unprecedented simply to assign a province to a specific magistrate by name.

Thus, instead of demanding unconditional surrender (*deditio*), Pompey was giving his permission for a foreign ruler's assumption of royal power. Theoretically at any rate, Tigranes was now a client king, that is, one who owed his crown to the Roman People and could be replaced at their will. Rome was entering into a new phase of foreign relations. For a century and a half, the Republic had been able to destroy any king it chose to. Now, the Romans were coming into permanent relations with states on their boundaries that they were not in a position to occupy and annex. Pompey left Tigranes in control of his "ancestral kingdom" (just as Sulla had done with Mithridates at the end of the First Mithridatic War), but on behalf of Rome he laid claim to Tigranes's conquests in Mesopotamia, Cilicia, and Syria.

Pompey then spent the year 65 B.C. marching into the Caucasus, advancing almost as far as the Caspian Sea. His aim was not to conquer these places permanently but to make them subordinate to Rome through a display of force. In this he was successful: the inhabitants never threatened Roman territory in Pontus and regularly helped the Romans against the Parthians.

SETTLEMENT OF PONTUS AND WESTERN ASIA MINOR

By 64 B.C., Pompey was back in Pontus, busy organizing the new territory. The Pontic kingdom had been ruled autocratically through royal governors, which thwarted the growth of civic institutions among the Greek cities. Since Roman administration normally rested on the cooperation of such cities, Pompey established a system of eleven Greek-style city-states, dividing the countryside among them. In effect, he knew full well that the Republican form of provincial administration, with its complete lack of any sort of permanent bureaucracy, was incapable of exercising the heavy-handed administration that had been practiced by the previous regime, and he therefore had to create the sorts of local civic institutions that cooperated with the Roman administration in governing provinces like Sicily and Asia.

Pompey also established permanent relations with a number of local dynasties in the primitive upcountry of central and eastern Asia Minor.

ANNEXATION OF SYRIA

In late 64 B.C., Pompey appeared in northern Syria. (Ancient Syria was the area bounded by the Tarsus mountains in the north, the Mediterranean in the west, the desert west of the River Euphrates in the east, and the Sinai peninsula in the south. The ancient region is thus much more extensive than the modern country named after it.) This area was theoretically under the control of what was left of the Seleucid dynasty, but since 129 B.C. there had been no powerful king. As dynastic chaos took hold, the local cities quarreled with one another, and the area was threatened by nomads from the desert and by the Arabian kingdom of Nabataea to the south (it was in the far northwest of the Arabian peninsula). Previously, both Lucullus and his replacement as governor of Cilicia had intervened in the Seleucid dynastic disputes, but Pompey, for reasons not clearly known, decided to end the Seleucid dynasty altogether and establish a Roman province of Syria. With some technical justice, the last king complained that while Tigranes, who had waged war against the Romans, was now their "ally," he, the Seleucid king, was now to be dethroned even though he had received, and still deserved, that title. Presumably, Pompey felt that this wealthy area could not be left in a power vacuum, with the Parthians and Nabataeans ready to move in and disturb the newly established Roman settlement in neighboring Asia Minor.

POMPEY IN JUDAEA

Pompey was distracted from his new administrative tasks in Syria by troubles to the south. The mainly Jewish area of Judaea had achieved independence (with Roman support) in a revolt against the Seleucids in the mid second century B.C., and the Hasmonean dynasty combined the offices of king and high priest. In 67 B.C., the succession was disputed, and the contenders appealed to the Romans. After various complicated events, Pompey met the two of them in Damascus in 63 B.C. He decided not to give his judgment until finishing a campaign against the Nabataeans. When one contender for the throne refused to cooperate with Pompey and seized Jerusalem, Pompey lost patience, and after a three-month siege he captured Jerusalem in October.[2] Pompey entered the *sanctum sanctorum* ("holy of holies") of the great temple of the Jewish god Yahweh, where only the chief priest was allowed to set foot on a single day each year to make a special sacrifice for the nation. (Pompey was disappointed to find

---

[2] In this siege, Pompey took advantage of the Jewish reverence for the sabbath. He found that on that day the Jews would defend themselves if directly attacked but scrupled to respond to activities that were only indirectly threatening. Accordingly, the siege works could be advanced toward the walls on the sabbath without risk of encountering countermeasures from the defenders, and no action was undertaken during the other six days of the week. His soldiers must have enjoyed this leisurely stratagem.

the room empty, Yahweh having no fondness for the sort of sumptuous dedications that pagan gods favored.) Pompey now recognized the other contender as king and imposed a payment of tribute on him.

No War with Parthia

In 64 B.C., the Parthians went to war with King Tigranes of Armenia, who had encroached on their territory in northern Mesopotamia. Since Tigranes was now a Roman ally, Pompey could have decided to extend the war further to the east. He declined to take this step, perhaps thinking that he should not press his luck as Lucullus had done. He may also have thought that the vast new territorial acquisitions in Asia Minor and Syria constituted enough expansion for the moment and that it was unwise to launch any new wars before the administration of the new provinces was established on a permanent basis. In any case, Pompey offered to arbitrate and gave most of Mesopotamia back to the Parthians.

Wealth from the Campaign

The areas conquered by Pompey were very wealthy, doubling the income of the Roman state. Pompey was said to have recovered from the Mithridatic treasures 36,000 talents.[3]

The exact total is not known, but Pompey himself emerged from this war with vast sums in his pocket. He distributed 96,000,000 denarii to his troops. In accordance with the traditional Roman practice by which the well-to-do officers were rewarded at a much higher rate than the common soldiery, 25,000,000 was divided among his quaestors and legates, while the troops received 1,500 denarii apiece. If he followed Caesar's practice of giving a double share to centurions and a quadruple one to military tribunes, it can be estimated that 45,000 troops received this largesse.

Long-Term Significance of Pompey's Settlement

With his administrative settlements, Pompey basically determined the eastern limit of Roman territory. Although there would be various attempts

---

[3]   A talent weighed nominally about 80 pounds and was worth 6,000 drachmas (= 6000 denarii = 24,000 sesterces). To give some sense of the value of a talent, it took about two talents to finance the operation of a warship for a year.

to attack the Parthians, the Euphrates served as the eastern border for the next two centuries. Even when the Romans became more aggressive in the second century A.D., they merely annexed northern Mesopotamia (and even that was fleeting). Before the Third Mithridatic War, direct Roman control was limited to the western and southern shores of Asia Minor. Now the Romans were directly responsible for all of Asia Minor, establishing the provinces of Pontus and Bithynia in the north and setting up a complicated system of subordinate kingdoms in the interior and east. In addition, the Romans assumed direct control of northern Syria and now faced the Parthians with four legions and two proconsuls in the immediate area (in Cilicia and Syria). Thus, the decade between the outbreak of the Third Mithridatic War and Pompey's settlement saw the entire situation in the Near East change dramatically. This huge new area of direct rule would need a permanent garrison, but the Republican form of government was not set up to maintain such a large-scale military establishment, and the need to keep control of the military organization necessitated by the empire of the Roman People would be a prime reason for replacing the old elective oligarchy with a military autocracy.

Questions for Study and Reflection

1. What was the relationship between Mithridates and Rome in the immediate aftermath of the Peace of Dardanus?
2. What was the cause of the outbreak of the Third Mithridatic War? How did the course of this war differ from the First Mithridatic War?
3. In what way did Lucullus's campaigns in the East resemble the wars of the Middle Republic and in what way were they different? What prevented Lucullus from bringing the war to a conclusion?
4. What was the constitutional innovation of the lex Gabinia? In what way were the new propraetorian legates incompatible with normal constitutional practice? How did the situation involving the pirates necessitate this innovation? What aspect of the lex Manilia was an innovation?
5. What strengths did Pompey exhibit as a military leader in his eastern campaigns?
6. Why was the senatorial oligarchy opposed to Pompey? Why was he so popular among the electorate?
7. How did Pompey change Roman administrative responsibilities in Asia and the Near East? Why did he refrain from expanding the war into Armenia or Parthia?

14

THE 60S B.C.

Rome in the Absence of Pompey

POLITICS IN THE MID 60s B.C.

The decade of the 60s B.C. is the last one in which the Republican constitution came anywhere near to functioning as it was intended to. Even at this time, the problem that was to destroy the constitution menaced over it, namely, the vast military force that had to be placed in individuals' hands because of the military exigencies of the empire. The old popularis versus optimate conflict continued, but it took a new form by being connected with the career of Pompey. To a certain extent, the main problem of the 60s B.C. was Pompey. His command of first the pirate war and then the war against Mithridates had given him virtually unprecedented powers, and toward the end of the decade a major question would be what to do with the new victor in the East.

Pompey's career was anything but traditional, and he received his various commands despite the objections of the oligarchy set up by Sulla. Hence, in terms of traditional labels, he could be seen as a popularis. Yet, despite the fact that he restored the tribunate during his consulship back in 70 B.C. and that later he often received the support of various popularis tribunes, he was in no meaningful sense a popularis. While people like the Gracchi and Saturninus attempted to advance themselves by championing popular discontent about various issues, Pompey was only interested in promoting his own political position and did not have a political program of his own or any interest in satisfying any popular causes.

Given the path of Pompey's career, the senatorial oligarchy was clearly (and not unreasonably) opposed to his "unconstitutional" commands in the 60s B.C. Tribunes friendly to Pompey almost stripped one consul of 67 B.C. (C. Calpurnius Piso) of his office because of his obstruction of Pompey's exercise of his extraordinary powers. In 66 B.C., the Cretans, who were being subdued by the proconsul Q. Caecilius Metellus cos. 69, preferred to surrender to Pompey (who was in the province of Cilicia), and only the fact that Pompey chose instead to proceed to the East to take up the command of the war against Mithridates after the passage of the lex Manilia prevented a major conflict between the two. In effect, by interfering in Crete, Pompey was trying to use the lex Gabinia to steal someone else's glory, just as he had done to Crassus at the end of the Slave War in 70 B.C.

Once it became clear in the mid 60s B.C. that Pompey was quickly finishing off the war against Mithridates and Tigranes, everyone in Rome had to wonder what he was going to do upon his return (would he act like another Sulla?), and this uncertainty overshadowed all decisions. While the senatorial leadership viewed everything about him with suspicion, his success enhanced his already great popularity, and his huge military campaigns led him to employ the services of large numbers of important senators, who both benefited directly from the profits available in the East and would seek to advance their own careers in Rome by promoting the interests of Pompey, who was expected to promote theirs in turn. Thus, even in his absence, the figure of Pompey dominated the political scene in Rome.

INCREASING ELECTORAL CORRUPTION

From the 60s B.C. onward, so-called corruption becomes an extremely serious problem in the functioning of the electoral process. While the Romans always understood that the outright purchase of votes was unacceptable, the practice of "rewarding" one's supporters was expected, and in particular it was always assumed in legislation that it was legitimate to show one's goodwill to the members of one's own tribe with various sorts of gifts. But the line between an acceptable and a corrupt form of seeking the voters' favor became a dispute that resulted in much legislation and litigation in the last two decades of the Republic.

Although there had been previous laws governing electoral practices, at some point between the creation of the first permanent quaestio in 149 B.C. and the year 119 B.C. when Marius was charged with ambitus ("improper solicitation of votes") in connection with his run for the tribunate, a permanent quaestio may have been set up to deal with such accusations; if so, however, the details are unknown. A later lex Cornelia apparently prohibited those convicted of electoral corruption from seeking office for the next ten years. This law was unavailing, as is shown by C. Calpurnius Piso, who is said to have used much bribery in securing the consulship during the elections conducted in 68 B.C. and managed to avoid being prosecuted by successively bribing prospective prosecutors into not indicting him.[1] This was the background to the activity of C. Cornelius, a tribune in 67 B.C., who attempted to pass various anti-oligarchic proposals, including a new law on electoral corruption. To forestall this bill (which seemingly was never passed), the senate instructed the consuls (the bribe-giving Piso plus M'. Acilius Glabrio, who would temporarily replace Lucullus as commander of the Mithridatic War before the arrival of Pompey) to pass their own (weaker) revision of the statute against electoral corruption. By the terms of the ensuing *lex Calpurnia Acilia*, those who were convicted of electoral corruption had to pay a fine, and in addition to losing their office they were expelled from the senate and permanently debarred from seeking further office. Even this was insufficient to deter violators, and in 63 B.C. Cicero would be forced to increase the penalties even further by imposing a ten-year period of exile upon conviction. The increasing size of the penalties merely illustrates the inability of the legal system to curb the practice, as outrageous instances of bribery in the later 60s B.C. and especially in the 50s B.C. would bring the electoral system into great disrepute.

Consuls Designate Convicted
of Electoral Corruption

The new lex Calpurnia would soon be put to the test when the consuls returned in the elections of 66 B.C. for the following year were accused of electoral corruption. P. Cornelius Sulla was the son of the dictator Sulla's older brother and had not only been a partisan of his uncle during the civil war but had also made great profits from the auctioned-off property of the proscribed. Little is known of the background of P. Autronius Paetus, who was a coeval of Cicero's and served as a legate in Greece, most likely in connection with M. Antonius pr. 74's campaign against the pirates in the late 70s B.C. (see Chapter 12). Upon their election to the consulship, they were prosecuted by L. Manlius Torquatus, young son of one of the defeated candidates, and by the other candidate, L. Aurelius Cotta (who as praetor in 70 B.C. had passed the law by which the equites and tribuni aerarii were placed on the album of jurors). Despite the use of violence to disrupt the legal proceedings, both consuls designate were convicted and stripped of their office. As a reward, the prosecutors received the insignia of office

---

[1] It must be remembered that there were no public prosecutors, and accusations were lodged by private individuals, who then themselves presented the case to the jurors.

of the convicted, and in the new elections for the consulship, Torquatus and Cotta were returned. This incident shows the extent to which flagrant bribery was being used to secure office, and the two convicted candidates would soon turn up again in another attempt to secure power through illegitimate means.

Tribunate of C. Cornelius

One of the tribunes of the year 67 b.c. was named C. Cornelius, and after the senate rejected a proposal of his (he wanted to curtail the granting of loans in Rome to visiting foreign embassies, presumably to prevent their use as bribes), he decided to attack senatorial privilege. In turbulent legislative activity, he passed two laws that were intended to thwart the abusive practices in the senate. First, over the years, the senate had acquired the right to exempt individuals temporarily from regulatory (rather than criminal) law, and such exemptions were often passed in thinly attended sessions of the senate. To avoid this sort of influence that was exercised by the few, one law dictated a quorum of 200 for the passage of such exemptions. Second, the urban praetors regularly issued at the beginning of their term an edict listing the special formulas that they would use in the administration of civil law, but they would then deviate from their own edict if personal considerations relating to one of the parties to a case made it preferable to use a different formula. Both proposals met with senatorial disfavor, but we are told that no one had any arguments against the bills that they were willing to make in public. Clearly, then, these attempts to bring "transparency" to the legal process and to undercut the use of influence with important senators as a way to circumvent what we would call the "due process" of law were widely popular, and the apparently spontaneous violence that broke out when attempts were made to block the passage of the legislation reflects the strong support that certain segments of the electorate felt about this attempt to establish "justice for all." It would be very helpful if we knew who exactly resorted to violence to ensure the bills' passage. Presumably, not the poor, who would not be affected by the sort of influence that the legislation aimed to stamp out. One can only imagine that it was primarily affluent men of business who made use of the civil courts, and there was apparently widespread support for the notions that the written regulations should be adhered to and that it was inappropriate for certain men to take advantage of their senatorial contacts to attain some deviation from written procedure for their own benefit. This reflects the sort of popular, nonsenatorial opinion that is seldom mentioned in the literary sources.[2] It can also be conjectured that these were also the sort of men who reacted so hostilely to the apparent senatorial bungling at the time of the Jugurthine War and supported C. Marius as the competent "new man" who would receive the consulship because of merit and not birth and save the day (see Chapters 4 and 5). (Ultimately, this sort of use of influence was inevitable because of the social system in Rome, and the erection of an "objective" legal system was impractical. In the long term, it would be the Roman emperor who, as the embodiment of the state, would be the conduit through which such influence was exercised.)

MACHINATIONS OF M. LICINIUS CRASSUS

At the same time that Cicero was using his oratorical skills to advance his career, M. Licinius Crassus, the victor over Spartacus and Pompey's colleague in the acrimonious consulship of 70 B.C., was using money and intrigue to further his own ends. We are informed that he had inherited 300 talents, but by the time of his death was worth 7,100 talents.[3] He used this money as a means of exerting influence in the senate, being ready to help out anyone who needed cash. In addition, Crassus was an "operator" in the senate, who could "get things done" in behind-the-scenes machinations that are hard for us to grasp now.[4] In 65 B.C., he was elected censor with L. Lutatius Catulus cos. 78, the leading upholder of the Sullan

---

[2] The only reason we know anything about the tribunate of C. Cornelius is the survival of the commentary by Asconius on a (now lost) speech that Cicero gave the next year to defend Cornelius when he was brought to trial for the use of violence.

[3] The first augmentation of his inheritance came from buying up the property of the proscribed after Sulla's victory, and after that he took a keen (some thought unseemly) interest in increasing his wealth. A famous anecdote has it that Crassus built a slave force of firemen, who would put out the fire only after Crassus had bought the property at a very low price from its owner, who would otherwise suffer a complete loss. Much is made in the ancient sources of Crassus's supposed greed, but for the most part this can be attributed to the vilification he suffered after his disastrous campaign against Parthia (see Chapter 18). He was probably no more avaricious than Pompey or Caesar, and his reputation would have emerged less tarnished if he had met a more edifying death.

[4] M. Aemilius Scaurus cos. 115, who was princeps senatus at the end of the second and beginning of the first century, seems to have had the same ability to influence the senate's proceedings; and in the 70s B.C. a similar position of influence was enjoyed within the senate by P. Cornelius Cethegus, who had joined Sulla at the time of his invasion of Italy and then profited from the proscriptions. Though Cethegus did not have much of a career of his own, he is said to have arranged the assignment in 74 B.C. of command in the impending war with Mithridates to the consul M. Lucullus and of the command against the pirates to the praetor M. Antonius (both magistrates having supposedly solicited the intervention of Cethegus's mistress!).

establishment, who thwarted Crassus's plans (enrolling the residents of Cisalpine Gaul as citizens and imposing tribute on Egypt, which had been bequeathed to Rome in 80 b.c. under dubious circumstances), and they both resigned from office.

Though Crassus avoided any direct involvement, he was implicated in a number of questionable schemes in the 60s b.c. Seemingly, he was willing to lend financial support in case something panned out, but he took no active part in order to avoid complicity if things went wrong. He was presumably attempting to find some sort of counterbalance to Pompey's power, but this sort of behavior did nothing to enhance his reputation among defenders of the Sullan establishment. Crassus would eventually combine his influence with Pompey's when the latter returned from the East – with disastrous consequences for the Republican order.

CATILINE

A major figure in the late 60s b.c. is L. Sergius Catilina (known in English as "Catiline"). Like Sulla, Catiline was from a patrician family that had fallen upon hard times. He himself was a degenerate individual, embodying the worst traits that characterized the sorts of people promoted by Sulla. It was Catiline who had tortured M. Marius Gratidianus to death one limb at a time to the shades of Q. Lutatius Catulus cos. 102 (see Chapter 11), and he had made large sums of money in the proscriptions (and then squandered it through extravagance). Though many of the accusations made against him by his enemies are no doubt malicious (for example, the claim that he poisoned his own son to convince a certain noblewoman to marry him), there is no doubt that there was little to commend him.

After holding the praetorship in 68 b.c., he was an avaricious governor of Africa (67–66 b.c.). Upon his return to Rome, he wished to run for the consulship of 65 b.c., but the presiding consul, after reviewing the matter with a consilium of the most important senators, refused to allow him to do so because of the imminence of his indictment for provincial extortion. This prohibition was not strictly necessary since only an actual indictment prohibited someone from running for office, and the decision shows the extent to which he was distrusted. The eventual trial was still in progress at the time of the elections in July 65 b.c., and for this reason he was once again prevented from running. He was eventually acquitted through bribery. Before the verdict, Cicero wrote in a letter that the jurors could acquit only "if the sun doesn't shine at noon" (*Letters to Atticus* SB 10 [1.1] 1). Seemingly, Catiline had spread around enough money to affect jurors' vision!

"First" Catilinarian Conspiracy

As we have seen, the consuls designate for 64 B.C., P. Autronius Paetus and P. Cornelius Sulla, were stripped of office and expelled from the senate for electoral bribery. It was later alleged that they then entered into a conspiracy with the thwarted Catiline to assassinate the new consuls on the day they assumed office (supposedly Crassus was in on the scheme). There is no contemporary proof of the existence of such a plot (it was almost certainly concocted later to serve as an accusation against Catiline), but the fact that such an accusation could plausibly be made shows the poisonous atmosphere in Roman politics. In any event, Catiline would soon become involved in a real plot to overthrow the established order.

Questions for Study and Reflection

1. In what way was Pompey a popularis figure? Was there a difference between being a popularis and being popular in the modern sense?
2. What concerns were there about Pompey in the aftermath of his victorious eastern campaigns? What actions could he have taken upon his return to Italy? What would his previous career lead one to suspect about his intentions?
3. What form did electoral corruption take? What steps were taken to deal with this problem? Were they effective? What effect would such corruption have on the political system?
4. What measures did the tribune C. Cornelius propose? What was the intention of these proposals, and how do they fit into the overall program of popularis reform? In what sense were his measures antisenatorial? In his efforts to make administrative decision making more "objective," what realities of Roman social life did Cornelius run up against?
5. What do the activities of the consular candidates P. Autronius Paetus, P. Sulla, and L. Catilina say about the well-being of the electoral process in Rome? What led to their electoral failure?

15

Consulship of Cicero

Expansion of Information

Starting from the mid 60s B.C., and especially from the time of Cicero's consulship in 63 B.C., the contemporary evidence provided by the speeches and letters of Cicero and by the historical accounts of Caesar make the next two decades the best-known period of ancient history. In addition, the subjects of a large number of Plutarch's extensive biographies fall within these years and the final decade of the Republic before the battle of Actium in 31 B.C. This plethora of information means that the final phase of the breakdown of the Republican form of government, when the electoral competitions of the past gave way to the contests of rival warlords, can be described in much greater detail than is possible for the earlier stages of political crisis of the Late Republic. While it is unfortunate that our knowledge of earlier events like the revolt of M. Aemilius Lepidus cos. 78 is comparatively meager, the literary tastes of the Roman Empire are to be congratulated for preserving so many works relating to the demise of the Republic.

Cicero's Family Background
and Early Career

As an individual if not as a politician, M. Tullius Cicero is the most important figure of the Roman Republic and deserves a treatment of his own. He was born on January 3, 106 B.C., to a family that belonged to the local nobility of the town of Arpinum, which had been promoted to full Roman citizenship only in 188 B.C. (previously it had held second-class citizenship, which gave no voting rights). His family participated in local politics and had close associations with the Roman nobility. When

Cicero's grandfather (Marcus) had opposed the introduction of voting by ballot in local elections in 115 B.C., he was congratulated by M. Aemilius Scaurus cos. 115, the princeps senatus himself. The bill was proposed by M. Gratidius, one of whose sisters was married to Cicero's grandfather and another to the great C. Marius cos. 107, who also came from Arpinum. Any rancor over the issue seems not to have been long lasting, since both Gratidius and Cicero's uncle L. Cicero served on the staff of M. Antonius when he went to Cilicia as praetor in 102 B.C.

As a boy, Cicero was taken by his father to Rome, where he received the best literary education and made the acquaintance of a number of children of the nobility. His best friend was the equestrian T. Pomponius Atticus (hundreds of Cicero's letters to him survive). As he grew up, Cicero took after his grandfather in his political allegiance (his father is a shadowy figure), and in his heart he became a firm supporter of the senate (though other considerations sometimes put him at variance with its leaders). He could have taken a quite different path, as he was closely connected to C. Marius. Cicero's first cousin once removed, the son of the M. Gratidius whom Cicero's grandfather had opposed, was adopted by Marius's brother, taking the name M. Marius Gratidianus. This man was a prominent figure in the Cinnan regime of the 80s B.C. and an implacable opponent of Sulla during the civil war (it was he who was tortured to death by Catiline at the tomb of Q. Lutatius Catulus cos. 102). There was an even closer connection in that Marius himself had been married to a sister of Cicero's grandmother. Despite these family bonds, Cicero much preferred the Sullan establishment, and during his long career he never attempted to court popular favor through his relationship with Marius (as we will soon see, Caesar the dictator would adopt exactly the opposite attitude). It says a great deal about Cicero's sensibilities that he never sought the office of tribune of the plebs.

During the Social War, Cicero served on the staff of Cn. Pompeius Strabo cos. 89. Military matters did not appeal to Cicero, and he performed no more military service until he was forced to become proconsul of Cilicia in 51 B.C. Cicero instead preferred to advance himself through his oratorical skills. He seems to have done nothing to make use of his Marian connections during the Cinnan regime, and he joined Sulla at the time of his invasion of Italy (he was an eye-witness to the colloquy between Sulla and the consul L. Cornelius Scipio Asiagenus in 83 B.C.; see Chapter 10). In 80 B.C., he made his first major impression as an orator when he defended the wrongly proscribed Sex. Roscius, tactfully managing to attack the method in which the proscriptions were carried out without saying anything critical about Sulla himself.

In the early 70s B.C., Cicero went to the Greek East to study rhetoric, and after his return he embarked upon a political career in Rome. Cicero was a completely "new man" (he had no ancestors who had ever held public office in Rome). As such, his chances of attaining the higher offices were doubtful. Yet, on the basis of his supreme oratorical talent and a certain amount of luck, he not only reached the consulship but was elected for every office at the earliest legal age (*suo anno* in Latin). For the most part, in legal cases Cicero would employ his oratorical skills only in defending the accused.

He first ran for the quaestorship, serving in 75 B.C. in Sicily. Because of this, the Sicilians sought to have him prosecute the ex-governor C. Verres on their behalf (see Chapter 12), and his success earned him the reputation as the best orator in Rome, which had previously belonged to Verres's advocate, Q. Hortensius cos. 69.

By bringing to justice a manifestly guilty member of the oligarchy, Cicero could win a "popular" name for himself. Yet, in the long run, his sensibilities lay with the senatorial oligarchy, and Cicero would constantly strive to win the acceptance of the nobility. Hence, as he advanced up the ladder, he attempted to downplay any popularis aspect of his career, which was mainly connected with the defense of Pompey's interests. A notable example of his attitude at this stage of his career is his surviving speech in favor of the lex Manilia in 66 B.C. when Cicero was praetor (see Chapter 13). Cicero does everything he can to play up Pompey's excellent qualifications in urging the audience to pass the bill, and he attempts to undermine optimate criticism without directly attacking the bill's opponents. By the time of his consulship, Cicero had definitely made the transition to acting as a defender of senatorial privilege. In his efforts to "join the club" in the senate, he met with limited success. While the oligarchy at various times had great need of his oratorical skills, he was never fully accepted by the leading oligarchs as "one of us," and after his consulship those skills became increasingly less important. The day was then ruled by military prowess and power, things of little interest to Cicero the orator.

As an individual, Cicero is not very appealing to modern tastes. He is assertive about himself in ways that today seem boastful (ancient propriety allowed self-promotion in ways that seem excessive today, but even under the Empire, Seneca the Younger said of Cicero that he praised himself "not without reason but without end"). His later policy of advocating *concordia ordinum* ("harmony of the orders of society") seems out of touch with reality, and certainly failed. His letters reveal him to be somewhat fickle and a bit prone to whining in adversity. Yet he had an amusingly sharp tongue that attracted many witty young men of the nobility to him, and there is no doubt as to the bravery (and futility) of his defense of the Republican constitution in the last year of his life. As for his speeches, while he at times belabors his points, there is no doubting the clarity and emotive power of his oratory. To judge by the surviving fragments of his predecessors, it is with good reason that they quickly fell into obscurity in Antiquity, and he established the standard for prose style against which all later Latin was judged.

Cicero's Election as Consul

In 64 B.C., three men ran for the consulship: M. Tullius Cicero, L. Sergius Catilina, and C. Antonius. In 65 B.C., Cicero had written to his friend Atticus of his hope to defend Catiline in his extortion case (see Chapter 14) and then to run with him for the consulship. By ancient standards, defending someone that you believed to be guilty could be considered an acceptable step, and Cicero and Catiline had apparently known each other in the past.[1] In any case, by 64 B.C. any hope of cooperation between Cicero and Catiline was gone, and Catiline worked to get himself elected with C. Antonius (the son of the consul of 99 B.C., brother of M. Antonius Creticus pr. 74, and uncle of the famous Mark Antony). C. Antonius was of exactly the same stripe as Catiline: as a young lout, he had supported Sulla's invasion of Italy and profited from the proscriptions; in 70 B.C. he was expelled from the senate for unseemly behavior. No good was to be expected from either of them, and the nobility supported Cicero as the best of a bad lot (from their point of view, at any rate). Cicero was returned triumphantly, with Antonius as his colleague. Cicero had to prevent his wicked but lazy colleague from cooperating with Catiline, bribing him by giving up his province of Macedonia in Antonius's favor (no great loss for Cicero with his complete indifference to military affairs). (Antonius was governor in 62–60 B.C., and upon his return he was convicted of flagrant extortion despite Cicero's now lost but apparently somewhat embarrassed defense speech.)

Rullus's Agrarian Bill

Cicero's first major task as consul was to deal with an agrarian bill promulgated by the tribune P. Servilius Rullus. This bill proposed the election for five years of a board of ten agrarian commissioners with

---

[1] They both served under Cn. Pompeius Strabo in 89 B.C., and when he was quaestor in Sicily, Cicero employed as a scribe a certain L. Sergius, who may well have been a freedman of Catiline's.

imperium who were to have broad rights to sell public land in order to make land distributions to citizens and to found colonies. Cicero gave a speech before the People against the bill, and it was actually defeated by voting. Cicero claimed in his speech before the People that the bill was directed against Pompey, but this is uncertain (Pompey's veterans would have benefited from the distributions). It is a measure of Cicero's oratorical skills that this is the only time an agrarian bill was rejected by the plebs, though it must be admitted that much of the argumentation in the preserved speeches is trivial, misleading, and disingenuous.

CATILINARIAN CONSPIRACY

Cicero presided over the elections for 62 B.C., in which Catiline was once more seeking the consulship. There was widespread use of bribery, but Catiline lost yet again. Now there was no hope of legal election to the consulship, and Catiline began to consider extralegal actions. Cicero later made out that right from the start Catiline meant to overthrow the state, but this is by no means clear. We are informed about the events of the conspiracy from the four surviving speeches that Cicero gave on the matter, and while these perhaps exaggerate the importance of the events, the affair deserves to be treated at length since it is so well known.

One night soon after the elections, someone delivered at the house of M. Crassus (for his influence, see Chapter 14) a group of sealed letters addressed to various important senators. Crassus opened the one addressed to him: it was anonymous and advised him to leave town to avoid an impending massacre of senators. Crassus took the letters to Cicero, who the next day in the senate had the addressees open their own letters, which said the same thing as Crassus's. The senate declared a *tumultus* ("military emergency") and authorized Cicero to track down the author of the letters. The massacre failed to take place, and the author never was found. Cicero was convinced that Catiline was behind the plot, but many senators disbelieved this (some even thought Cicero concocted the whole affair himself).

There was widespread rural discontent at this time. One might expect this to have arisen from those dispossessed by Sulla, but it seems to have been centered around his settlers, who had fallen into debt and were keen to have another civil war, with all the attendant opportunities for plunder. This discontent extended throughout Italy, but the outbreak of violence began in Etruria, where a certain C. Manlius, who had served as a centurion under Sulla, was reported to be stockpiling weapons and gathering troops. It is not clear what exactly the purpose of this activity was, but Cicero was again convinced of Catiline's involvement. When news reached Rome of what was going on in Etruria (it was said that open revolt would start on October 27), the senatus consultum ultimum (see Chapter 3) was passed on October 21. Once again there was no evidence connecting Catiline to these events.

On the night of November 6–7, Catiline called a meeting of the senators and equites who supported his plans. According to Cicero, Catiline divided up the regions of Italy among them as their spheres of command in the impending revolt. He also indicated that he could do nothing while Cicero was alive, and two equites volunteered to assassinate him the following morning while he was receiving visitors. The plot was revealed to Cicero, who thwarted it. The same day, Cicero convened the senate and accused Catiline of complicity. Still, Cicero had no proof of Catiline's involvement, and in his masterly *First Catilinarian* his aim was basically to implicate Catiline in the activities covered by the senatus consultum ultimum of October 27, even though that decree had nothing to do with him. Cicero sufficiently embarrassed Catiline that he left the city the next day, supposedly to go into voluntary exile in Massilia (modern Marseilles). As it turned out, he went to join Manlius in Etruria. Whatever his original involvement in the rural disturbances had been (probably marginal at best), now that his final hope of securing the consulship more or less legally was dashed, he decided to throw in his lot with the rural malcontents. This strategy is very similar to the one pursued in 78 B.C. by M. Aemilius Lepidus – and would prove to be no more successful.

Meanwhile, his fellow conspirators in Rome entered into a harebrained plot. A number of prominent senators (including P. Autronius Paetus, the ex-consul designate of 65 B.C., and two relatives of Sulla's) belonged to the conspiracy, the chief being P. Cornelius Lentulus Sura. Yet another disreputable protégé of Sulla's, Lentulus Sura had reached the consulship in 71 B.C. but was expelled from the senate by the censors of 70 B.C. (see Chapter 12). He had then secured election to the praetorship of 63 B.C. to regain his place in the senate. This move to rejoin the ranks of the senior magistrates was apparently part of an effort to collaborate with Catiline in his designs to gain power.

At this time, representatives of the Allobroges (a Gallic tribe in Gallia Narbonensis) were in Rome. Conquered back in the late 120s B.C., the Allobroges had fallen into debt, and the conspirators thought that the tribe could be impelled to give military assistance to their attempt to overthrow the state. After being approached, the tribal representatives thought it best to reveal the matter to their ancestral patron Q. Fabius Sanga (a descendant of Q. Fabius Maximus Allobrogicus cos. 121, who first conquered them), and he in turn revealed the matter to Cicero.

Cicero had the Allobrogan representatives press the conspirators to give them incriminating letters, which they foolishly did. On the night of December 3, the representatives were escorted out of the city by certain members of the conspiracy, and Cicero had these conspirators stopped and taken into custody. Other members were then arrested. On December 5, a session of the senate was convened to discuss this grave turn of events. First, Lentulus Sura was made to admit that the letter encouraging the Allobroges to revolt was his. Then, a debate was begun about the punishment of the conspirators. The consul designate, D. Junius Silanus, proposed death. This was agreed with by subsequent speakers until the praetor designate C. Julius Caesar (the famous Caesar) argued that the proposal was contrary to the law, and that the senatus consultum ultimum should not be invoked (it had been passed more than six weeks earlier under different circumstances). Instead, he proposed that a special quaestio to try cases relating to the affair be established by law, suggesting a penalty of permanent imprisonment (something unheard of in Antiquity). This opinion then found favor until the tribune of the plebs designate M. Porcius Cato (see Chapter 16) spoke vigorously in favor of the death penalty. Cato had a reputation for unbending probity, and he carried the day.[2] The senate voted for death, and Lentulus Sura resigned from his praetorship. That night, the conspirators were strangled in the public prison.

Meanwhile, forces were sent against the armed rebellion in Etruria and the south. The rebel forces were no match for regular troops, and early in 62 B.C., C. Antonius's legate M. Petreius annihilated the army of Catiline (though it was a hard-fought struggle). Catiline died in the battle, but Antonius took no part (he was supposedly suffering from gout, but he may have had no eagerness to suppress men who under other circumstances could have been his confederates).

Motivation for and Legality
of the Executions

The major remaining issue was the legality of the death penalty carried out on December 5. The senatus consultum of October 27 was by no means

---

[2] It is worth noting how far down the hierarchy the discussion went to allow the low-ranking Cato the opportunity to speak. Presumably, most senators simply indicated their agreement with the previous speaker. In effect, the consul designate set the tone by giving the first opinion, and it took a man of confidence and authority (such as Caesar and Cato) to offer a new view that contradicted the proposal of his hierarchical superiors.

relevant, and in any case there was no longer any immediate threat to the state at the time of the executions. It is hard to escape the impression that Pompey's impending return led to Cicero's (and other people's) great haste to secure the conspirators' execution and to suppress all signs of discord. It could not be known when exactly Pompey would arrive (late 62 B.C., as it turned out), and neither was it known what his intentions were. It was perfectly possible that if there was public chaos in Italy, he might seize the opportunity to return like another Sulla (after all, his father Cn. Strabo cos. 89 had used military force for political extortion back in 88–87 B.C., and so had Pompey himself in 77 B.C.). This was a possibility that the oligarchy had to make every effort to forestall. Thus, it was imperative for the Catilinarian uproar to be brought to an end as swiftly as possible. The idea that the conspirators might still be hanging around waiting for trial was fraught with danger (especially as Catiline was still in the field), so Cicero's prompt action is perfectly understandable. He quickly claimed the distinction of having saved the state while wearing the toga (i.e., not as a general), but it was soon evident that there was much resentment at this course of action. One of the new tribunes for 62 B.C. (Q. Caecilius Metellus Nepos cos. 57) prevented him from giving the customary address to the People at the end of his consulship (though Cicero received strong applause when he gave his oath that he had upheld the laws).[3]

Over the next six years Cicero would be harassed on account of his actions, and in later speeches he would deny direct responsibility for the executions, claiming that he had merely been carrying out the will of the senate as expressed in the vote of December 5. This was nothing but an evasion of responsibility (the senate gave advice but nothing obliged him to follow it in exercising his imperium), and he would eventually pay for his actions with exile.

More Corruption in the Consular Elections

Cicero presided over the consular elections in 62 B.C., and one of the victorious candidates, L. Licinius Murena, was accused of electoral

---

[3] One might expect that as a member of the powerful family of the Caecilii Metelli (his father had been consul back in 98 B.C.) and thus part of the leadership of the senate, Nepos would have favored the executions, especially if the purpose was to thwart Pompey, but Nepos had served as a legate of Pompey's in the East and was acting, as he thought, in Pompey's interest. This attitude illustrates how the imposing figure of Pompey could lead to dislocations in traditional loyalties, as would later be the case with Caesar.

bribery. Cicero, who had as consul passed a bill that yet again stiffened the penalties for conviction on this charge (see Chapter 14), defended Murena. In his surviving speech, Cicero avoids directly addressing the accusation, a procedure that always gives rise to the suspicion that the defendant was guilty. Instead, Cicero spends much time arguing that conviction of Murena would play into the hands of the supporters of the executed conspirators. If this interpretation is correct, then Cicero was acting in a way that would be characteristic of him: sacrificing the ethically correct position in the interest of some imagined greater good (in this case, defending the guilty because allowing conviction would endanger the public order). Cicero not infrequently abandoned principle in favor of expediency, and this failing would eventually lead to his death.

QUESTIONS FOR STUDY AND REFLECTION

1. What was Cicero's social and political background? Why did he not make any political use of his relations with Marius? What was Cicero's primary political allegiance? Was he in any sense a popularis?

2. To what did Cicero owe his successful career? How was he received by the senior members of the nobility?

3. What were Catiline's aims in the mid 60s B.C.? Why were people so suspicious of him? What was Cicero's attitude? Did it change?

4. What exactly was the "Catilinarian conspiracy"? When was it started? What were its purposes? Did these change over time? What was the connection between Catiline's purposes and the rural discontent in Etruria?

5. Why was there such a rush to end the matter of the conspiracy once it came to light? On what basis were the conspirators executed? Was the execution either politically justifiable or legally defensible?

6. Could Pompey have tried to become a second Sulla in his return from the East? What exactly could he have done to carry out such a plan? What reaction would have taken place in Rome? Would the nobility have gone along with such plans? Who would have opposed it?

16

CONSULSHIP OF C. CAESAR

IMPORTANCE OF CAESAR'S CONSULSHIP

Although this was by no means clear at the time, Caesar's consulship in 59 B.C. marks the beginning of the end of the Republic. From that date on, the normal form of government became increasingly unmanageable, and the issues arising from his consulship led directly into the civil war that followed a decade later. C. Asinius Pollio, a friend of Caesar's and an important political figure after his death, began his (now lost) history of the civil war with the year 60 B.C. since an account of that year was necessary to understand the consulship to which he dated the start of the Republic's demise.

CAESAR'S EARLY CAREER

Before his consulship, Caesar had not played a particularly important role in Roman politics, but it is worthwhile to examine the earlier stages of his career – these are preserved in some detail because of his later fame – in order to understand both how he became consul in 59 B.C. and why his actions tended to be directed against the senatorial establishment.

C. Julius Caesar was born on July 13, 100 B.C. (the sources are in conflict on the date and the years in which he held office are problematical, but this date seems the most likely). His father belonged to a less prosperous branch of a moderately successful patrician family (the Julii Caesares who held consulships of 157, 91, and 90 B.C. were not direct ancestors of Caesar). Caesar's father died with praetorian rank in the late 90s B.C., but more important for Caesar's political career was the fact that his father's sister was married to the great C. Marius cos. 107. When Marius and Cinna gained control of Rome in the mid 80s B.C., the young Caesar was clearly in their favor. He married Cinna's daughter and was to be given a prestigious priesthood.[1] His behavior at the time of the civil war is noteworthy. He did not attempt to go over to Sulla (as Pompey and Crassus did, for instance), and even at the time of the proscriptions that followed Sulla's victory, he did not disavow his Cinnan connections: when Sulla told him to divorce Cinna's daughter, he refused. As a result of this obstinacy, he had to go into hiding, but the intervention of high-placed relatives who were among Sulla's supporters ensured that no harm came to Caesar. This incident exhibits two aspects of Caesar's character that would remain constant throughout his career. He strongly associated himself with the Marian/popularis tradition, which he would often demonstrate in very public ways, and he placed great importance on his own personal *dignitas* ("prestige") to the exclusion of other considerations. Hand in hand with his affiliation with Marius and Cinna went a general hostility toward the Sullan establishment in the senate. The sources do not make it clear what exactly led Caesar to be so steadfastly devoted to his vanquished relatives and so hostile to Sulla (at first perhaps nothing more than family loyalty?), but this frame of mind determined the course of his later career. He clearly had no affection for the traditional position of the senate and chose to dissociate himself from its leadership, to which he could so easily have belonged. It is perhaps worth remembering that he reached adulthood in the turbulent 80s B.C. and thus had no familiarity in his formative years with the normal functioning of the constitution. In any case, the eventual result of his actions would be the destruction of the traditional Republican form of government.

Caesar went to the East in about 80 B.C. to serve as a military tribune, but hastened back to take part in the actions of M. Aemilius Lepidus in 78 B.C. (see Chapter 12). Deciding that Lepidus's grab for power was not going to succeed, Caesar refrained from involvement. He undertook two unsuccessful prosecutions of prominent associates of Sulla (a consul of 78 B.C. and the disreputable C. Antonius who would later be Cicero's consular colleague) and then returned to the East to pursue literary studies.[2]

He came back to Rome to be installed as a pontifex (member of one of the senior colleges or bodies of public priests). Since the selection of priests had been restored by Sulla to the priests themselves, this instal-

---

[1] It must be admitted that this priesthood, the post of flamen dialis, was hemmed in by taboos that rendered it a potential liability (see Chapter 2). Presumably, such was not the intention with Caesar.

[2] There he was captured by pirates, and after ransoming himself he raised a force to pursue them and had them crucified, something that in captivity he had jokingly promised to do. This anecdote is illustrative of both his personal drive and his sense of self-importance.

lation shows that his clearly anti-Sullan attitude did not affect his fellow aristocrats' attitude toward him. In 69 B.C., he became quaestor. That year saw the deaths of his aunt, the wife of Marius, and of his own wife, the daughter of Cinna. In praise of them, he gave famous public speeches in which he emphasized his connections with Marius and Cinna. As it was a novelty to give a funeral oration for a woman, Caesar clearly contrived these occasions to provide himself with the opportunity to make a very public display of his political allegiance to the memory of the regime that had been overthrown by Sulla (in his wife's funeral, Marius's death mask was shown for the first time since Sulla's victory). After a year's service as quaestor in Further Spain, he received permission from the governor to whom he was attached to return early to Rome, presumably in 68 B.C.

Back in Rome, Caesar got a new wife: Pompeia, the daughter of Q. Pompeius Rufus cos. 88 B.C. by Sulla's daughter. This is a very surprising move, since not only was his new wife the granddaughter of his enemy Sulla but her father had been killed through the malfeasance of Pompey's father Cn. Pompeius Strabo cos. 89 (see Chapter 7). Given the way that Pompey had been advancing his career in opposition to the Sullan establishment, this marriage would suggest a strongly anti-Pompey attitude, but if so, this was soon forgotten since in the mid and late 60s B.C. Caesar showed himself to be a strong supporter of Pompey, playing a leading role in the effort to pass the lex Gabinia in 67 B.C. As aedile in 65 B.C., he won popular acclaim for the splendor of his lavish games, and once more he emphasized his connections with Marius. He had replicas made of the victory monuments that Marius had erected in commemoration of his victories over Jugurtha and the Germans and that Sulla had had destroyed (see Chapter 11). Caesar had these replicas secretly erected one night so that they would be greeted in the morning with astonished acclaim by those who cherished the memory of Marius and with startled outrage by those who supported the Sullan settlement. This bold and elaborate act of thumbing his nose at the senatorial establishment won him great popularity and increased the suspicions of the conservatively minded. Soon afterward, as the presiding magistrate in the quaestio for murder cases, he accepted accusations against men who had committed murder by virtue of the Sullan proscription lists. (For illustrations of the way that the memory of Sulla was cherished by some, see Coins 15 and 16.)

In 63 B.C. Caesar won two elections. He was returned as praetor for the following year in the regular elections, and more importantly, when the pontifex maximus Q. Caecilius Metellus Pius cos. 80 died, he won the position by defeating men of much greater standing than he had (P. Servilius

Isauricus cos. 79 and Q. Lutatius Catulus cos. 78). Since the defeated candidates (as well as the previous incumbent) were closely connected with Sulla, Caesar's surprising victory must, to some extent at least, be ascribed to anti-Sullan feeling. As praetor designate, Caesar won further prestige by arguing vigorously against the execution of the so-called Catilinarian conspirators in the debate on December 5 (see Chapter 15). Catulus and C. Piso cos. 67 (both of whom were enemies of Pompey) vainly tried to get Cicero to denounce Caesar as one of the conspirators.

Immediate Aftermath of the Execution

of the Conspirators

As praetor in 62 B.C., Caesar continued to act as a strong supporter of Pompey. He attempted to take away from Q. Lutatius Catulus the prestige of having restored the temple of Jupiter Optimus Maximus on the Capitol. Catulus was at this point the leading consular defender of the Sullan order, and Caesar's ongoing hostility toward him was another element in his self-conscious efforts to honor Marius and attack Sulla (and by extension those who upheld his arrangements). The temple had burned down during the civil war, and Catulus, who was put in charge of rebuilding it, had by now finished construction. Caesar accused Catulus of embezzling money during the project and proposed a law to give the honor (as well as the dedicatory inscription on the temple) to Pompey. Caesar also helped Q. Caecilius Metellus Nepos, one of the tribunes of 62 B.C., in his violent actions on Pompey's behalf. Nepos, who had been a legate of Pompey in the East, attempted to take advantage of the uproar following the execution of the Catilinarian conspirators. He forbade Cicero to give the customary "farewell" speech on the day he left office (see Chapter 15) and proposed a bill to summon Pompey with his army to restore order in Italy (exactly the situation that Cicero hoped to avoid by executing the conspirators). This bill was vetoed by his colleagues (including M. Porcius Cato, whose speech had led to the execution of the conspirators and who had run for the tribunate to thwart Nepos), but Nepos was strongly supported by Caesar in his attempt to use violence to pass the law. The senatus consultum ultimum (see Chapter 3) was passed, and the senate also decreed that Nepos and Caesar should cease to act as magistrates. Caesar was no fool, and seeing that the circumstances did not really justify any intervention by Pompey, he (to everyone's surprise) gave up his troublemaking and was allowed to return to his duties. For his part, Nepos fled to Pompey in the East, presumably in the expectation that Pompey intended to return as a new Sulla. Caesar then served as proconsul in Further Spain in 61–60 B.C.

M. PORCIUS CATO

One of the leading figures of the last years of the Republic was M. Porcius Cato, who would frequently clash with Caesar and whose death would make his name a byword for opposition to autocracy. (He is known as Cato the Younger to distinguish him from his famous grandfather, and as Cato Uticensis after the place where he eventually committed suicide.)

Cato's father died before reaching the praetorship and was the grandson of the novus homo M. Porcius Cato cos. 195. Cato's mother was Livia, the sister of M. Livius Drusus tr. pl. 91 (see Chaper 6). After the death of Cato's father, Livia married her brother's friend (and later opponent; see Chapter 6), Q. Servilius Caepio, the relative of the homonymous consul of 106 B.C. (and Drusus in turn was married to Caepio's sister Servilia). Following Caepio's death during the Social War, Livia brought all her three children by the two marriages to the Livian household, where the half-siblings were raised together. Thus, Cato not only was well connected through his father's family but also had many influential relations through his mother's marriage to a Servilius Caepio. Given this background, it is hardly surprising that Cato grew up to be a steadfast supporter of the senatorial oligarchy.

Cato grew up to have a very strong personality. He had deeply held beliefs about proper moral behavior that were tinged with Stoic philosophy.[3] Already as quaestor (in 64 B.C.?) he had tried to clear up the shenanigans of the permanent staff of scribes, and in the process he stood up to and humiliated Q. Catulus cos. 78, the most prominent leader of the Sullan establishment, who tried (vainly) to use his own prestige to protect malefactors. This anecdote is very illustrative of Cato's character. He was completely uncompromising in what he perceived to be a matter of principle and paid no regard to feelings or attitudes of those whom he considered transgressors, even if they were friendly toward him. When Cato was obstructing any accommodation with the publicans (see later in the chapter), Cicero famously complained that Cato was acting as if he lived "in Plato's Republic rather than amidst Romulus's dregs" (Cicero, *Letters to Atticus* SB 21 [2.1] 8).

It was Cato's uncompromising speech on December 5, 63 B.C., that won the senate over to the execution of the Catilinarian conspirators (see

---

[3] For the appeal of Stoic philosophy to Roman aristocrats, see Chapter 6 n. 2.

Chapter 15), and he would be instrumental in thwarting Pompey after his return from the East. Cato could clearly bring others around to his views, but he was fundamentally shortsighted and his refusal to accommodate was ultimately disastrous. He was no doubt driven by the feeling that excessively powerful individuals like Pompey and (later) Caesar were dangerous to the Republican form of government (i.e., they threatened the traditional career patterns of the oligarchy, which tried to give a significant but limited role to the consuls, who were expected to return quickly to the senate as respected consulars once their term of office was over). His intransigent attitude, however, turned men who could have been won over as acceptable members of the senate through judicious compromise into active opponents of the established order. A traditional Roman virtue was the concept of concordia ("harmony"), which meant a refusal to destroy one's domestic enemies even when this was possible and instead advised the desirability of restoring tranquility through accommodation. Cicero advocated this policy under the names concordia ordinum ("harmony of the orders," which really meant the cooperation of the senatorial and equestrian orders in upholding legitimate government) and *concordia omnium bonorum* ("harmony of all good men"). Cato's personal preference for the strict and uncompromising application of principle thwarted the natural coalition of the well-to-do, and this attitude would drive away from the senate men who really would have preferred to work through that body rather than against it. In this way, he contributed to the circumstances that would bring about the downfall of the Republic that he wished to preserve.

BONA DEA AFFAIR

During the period of Caesar's absence in Spain, an incident took place that was not particularly important in itself but would have serious consequences for Cicero. One duty of the wife of the pontifex maximus (at this time Caesar) was to hold a special ceremony in honor of the obscure goddess Bona Dea (the "good goddess"). Only women were invited, but P. Clodius Pulcher, the son of Ap. Claudius Pulcher cos. 79, decided to play a prank (it would seem). He attended the ceremony disguised in drag, and when word of this leaked out, a great scandal ensued (the act was considered sacrilegious by the religiously inclined or those like Cicero who chose to view it as such, and in any case, such behavior was taken to be part and parcel of the the disregard of tradition that was characteristic of the urbane younger crowd). Caesar divorced his wife Pompeia, not because she was involved, but because of the mere possibility that she might have been ("Caesar's wife must be above suspicion"). One has to wonder if he did not take advantage of the opportunity to unburden himself of his wife's obvious anti-Pompeian associations.

Cicero was particularly upset by the affair, and when a special quaestio was set up the following year (61 B.C.) to investigate the incident, he gave testimony destroying Clodius's alibi. Clodius was nonetheless found not guilty (through the usual bribery), and Cicero's testimony earned him the undying enmity of Clodius, who would soon renounce his patrician status in order to become tribune and wreak vengeance upon Cicero.

RETURN OF POMPEY FROM THE EAST

Throughout 62 B.C., there was much anxiety about Pompey's intentions. When Pompey was about to return, M. Licinius Crassus, his earlier colleague as consul, actually fled the city. As it turned out, when Pompey landed with his army at Brundisium in December 62 B.C., he promptly dismissed his troops, apart from a small contingent to escort him into the city in his triumph (held on September 28–29, 61 B.C.). Fears to the contrary notwithstanding, Pompey clearly had no desire to act like Sulla, choosing at this time not to use his army to advance his career any further. Basically, he (like Marius before him) did not want autocratic power as a tyrant but respect and prestige as a senior member of the senate. Everyone was greatly relieved, and Crassus returned to the city.

Pompey tried to manifest his frame of mind with a suitable marriage, and after divorcing his old wife he sought a new one in Junia, the daughter of D. Junius Silanus cos. 62, who as consul designate had first proposed the death penalty for the Catilinarian conspirators and whose wife Servilia was the half-sister of Cato. Pompey also requested that Silanus's other daughter should marry Pompey's eldest son Gnaeus. Since Cato had already established a reputation as not just a man of unimpeachable morality but also as a staunch defender of the oligarchy, these marriages would have firmly allied Pompey with the "establishment." It was indicative of the reception that Pompey was to meet in the senate that these proposed marriage arrangements were refused.

Pompey not unreasonably expected that the senate would treat the victor of the East (who had been hailed there as a new Alexander) in a suitably accommodating manner, but he had not counted on the opposition that he had stirred up through his high-handed treatment of various important people. One vigorous opponent was Q. Caecilius Metellus Creticus cos. 69, whose command in Crete Pompey had been about to wrestle away from him by virtue of the lex Gabinia when he got a better offer from the lex Manilia. Another was L. Licinius Lucullus cos. 74, whose command in the East Pompey had taken over and whose decisions and rulings (*acta*) there he refused to uphold. The major leadership of the opposition came from M. Porcius Cato, who, as we have seen, was fearless and tenacious in upholding what he thought right and could sway others to follow his lead. It is hardly surprising that the new cognomen *Magnus* ("the Great") that he had adopted at the start of his career continued to be viewed with disdain in certain circles of the senate.

What Pompey wanted from the senate was simple:

- Acceptance in block of his acta in the East. Failure to secure such a decree of the senate would make it much easier to overturn his decisions. Not only had Pompey made a lot of money in making his decisions, but perhaps more importantly, his prestige would be undermined if they were rescinded.
- Acquiescence in a land law to give rewards to his troops.

Having dismissed his army, he found that he now had no leverage to force the senate to comply with his wishes and that he had won no gratitude on account of his peaceful return. Out of spite, Metellus Creticus and Lucullus demanded a line-by-line examination of his acta. For his part, Cato feared any man who had such vast power and prestige, and he wished to undermine Pompey's position on principle, as it were.

For a year and a half, Pompey tried to get his measures passed. The year 61 B.C. was frittered away in senatorial debates, and in 60 B.C. Pompey had the tribune L. Flavius attempt to pass an agrarian bill that would, among other things, give land to his veterans. There was serious strife over this bill, and by June Pompey gave up on the matter, being unwilling to apply the necessary level of violence to achieve his purpose. He then turned to Caesar for help.

DEMANDS OF THE PUBLICANS

Another major factor in the election of Caesar was a matter involving certain powerful publicans. Not realizing the extent of economic disruption caused by the Third Mithridatic War, these men had overbid on the contract for collecting the taxes in Asia, and now they wanted the senate to authorize the cancellation of their contract. Cicero, who advocated the cooperation of the senate and equestrian order (which strongly supported the demands of the publicans), spoke in favor of the cancellation, though he admitted in private that the request was outrageous. With perhaps more principle than sense, Cato opposed the cancellation and carried the day in the senate. The equites were now hostile to the senate and inclined to support anyone who would help them out. In particular, Crassus, who had also supported them in the senate, reaped the benefit of Cato's obstructionism. This situation would redound to Caesar's benefit in his run for the consulship.

Caesar's Return from Spain

In the summer of 60 B.C., Caesar returned from Spain, where he had put down a revolt sufficiently large to earn the grant of a triumph by the senate. Caesar arrived just at the time when he would have to enter the city to announce his candidacy for the consular elections that July. If he entered the city before the triumph, he would lose his imperium, and thus forfeit the right to the triumph, so he requested that the senate grant him an exemption from the need to announce his candidacy in person. The senate probably would have gone along with this, but when Cato's turn to speak came, he filibustered – that is, he continued to talk until the day was over – and since it was clear that he would repeat this as often and as long as necessary, the request was dropped. Cato imagined that Caesar would give up the consulship in order to celebrate his triumph, but he misjudged Caesar, who promptly entered the city to announce his candidacy. Cicero had thought that he could win over Caesar to the senate's side, but Cato's obstinate hostility drove Caesar into the opposition.

Caesar's Election to the Consulship

A conjunction of interests now led Caesar and Pompey to enter into an agreement. Pompey had gotten legates of his elected consul in 61 and 60 B.C., (M. Pupius Piso Frugi and L. Afranius) but they had proved to be ineffectual in pursuing Pompey's aims, as had L. Flavius, tribune in 60 B.C. Feeling himself compelled to seek the cooperation of an energetic consul to secure his aims, Pompey now agreed to help Caesar to the consulship if he promised to pass Pompey's bills into law, by whatever means. In effect, Pompey was, at least temporarily, abandoning his long-term goal of cooperating with the senate, and he turned to Caesar for the ruthlessness and violence that would be necessary to achieve Pompey's immediate needs. Thus, the situation is somewhat similar to the way in which Marius had availed himself of Saturninus's services in passing legislation for him. This time, however, the junior partner would not in the end allow himself to be cast aside in the way that Marius had disposed of Saturninus.

For the time being, Pompey's support was kept secret, as Caesar ran for the consulship together with his wealthy friend L. Lucceius, who carried out extensive bribery on behalf of the both of them. The optimates carried out, with Cato's grudging acquiescence, a plan of counter bribery on behalf of Cato's son-in-law M. Calpurnius Bibulus (Bibulus had been aedile with Caesar and disliked him because all the credit for the games that they put on at common expense was given to Caesar, who put on additional games privately). Caesar was returned with Bibulus, and the optimates thought that the election of Bibulus would prove to be a sufficient check on Caesar.[4] They were not counting on the unforeseen consequences of their own obstruction of Pompey.

FIRST "TRIUMVIRATE"

Caesar saw that to be successful he also needed to have some form of cooperation from the senate. He vainly tried to win over Cicero, who could not bring himself to act against the senatorial oligarchy. Caesar then sought the help of Pompey's old enemy M. Crassus cos. 70. Crassus had lent Caesar large sums of money over the course of his career, and they already had a relationship on that basis. Furthermore, Caesar offered to pass a law cancelling the contract of Crassus's friends, the publicans for Asia. By reconciling Pompey and Crassus, Caesar could count on the support of Pompey's veterans on the one hand and of the equites and Crassus's protégés in the senate on the other.

---

4 In Roman elections, a voter could cast votes for as many candidates as there were positions to be filled, and the fact that a majority of the voters in the centuriate assembly gave both their votes to two such seemingly incompatible candidates is sometimes taken as proving that the anticipated policies of the candidates played no role at all in the decisions of the electorate, who were swayed rather by personal and social considerations. Unfortunately, in the absence of any information whatsoever even about how the votes were distributed among the electorate, much less about what motivated individuals to vote as they did, it is virtually impossible to draw valid conclusions about the intentions of the voters and the overall behavior of the electorate. It should be noted, however, that while such a pattern of voting may seem illogical to someone used to a parliamentary system in which a single vote is cast on the basis of party affiliation, a pattern of vote splitting is common enough in the more complicated governmental system in the United States, where not infrequently one party receives control of the legislature while a member of the other party is elected as the executive officer. In the Roman context, it is easy enough to see that even if a voter was sufficiently swayed by Caesar's personal popularity and the prestige of his family to return him as consul, it would have been reasonable enough to vote at the same time for Bibulus as a means of providing Caesar with a more "reliable" colleague who would make sure that things did not get out of hand. There was no way to foresee at the time of the election how powerless Bibulus would be to control Caesar.

The combined influence of Caesar, Pompey, and Crassus could not be thwarted, and until Crassus's death in 53 B.C., their combined power allowed them to dominate the political scene, to the outrage of optimate opinion. This alliance is traditionally called the "First Triumvirate," a term that is incorrect and misleading. The "Second" triumvirate formed in 42 B.C. by Caesar's heir and two others was a proper (if unprecedented) magistracy authorized by law (see Chapter 21), while the "First" one, so named by analogy with the second, was an informal, private arrangement. Caesar, Pompey, and Crassus had no officially recognized title, and they controlled events on an ad hoc basis merely by virtue of their various forms of influence. Hence, their association would more properly be termed a "coalition." Furthermore, the title suggests a greater degree of unanimity than there really was. In 60–59 B.C., the interests of the three men happened to coincide, and their cooperation continued for some years. Yet each, while tied to his companions, was nonetheless basically willing to cooperate only to the extent that he found it convenient to do so. The limited nature of the coalition is shown by the fact that their agreement was couched in negative terms: they swore not to do anything opposed by one of them. Crassus in particular would at times act against Pompey. So long as the optimates were united in the opposition to the three, however, they would have to stick together. The death of Crassus would eventually lead to a reconciliation of Pompey and the optimates against Caesar.

Caesar and Pompey tightened the bonds between them with the marriage of Caesar's daughter Julia to Pompey in 59 B.C. Pompey and Julia seem to have been genuinely fond of each other, and the death of both Julia and her newborn child in 54 B.C. is a salient example of the intervention of fortune in historical events. The Roman Republic may well come to a very different end if Pompey's son had been Caesar's grandson.

CAESAR'S CONSULSHIP

On January 1, 59 B.C., the optimates had reason to feel confident about the upcoming year. Their man Bibulus ought to have been able to obstruct Caesar's efforts, and foreseeing Caesar's election the senate had, before the elections for 60 B.C., designated the *calles silvaeque Italiae* ("the hills and forests of Italy") as the provinces for the new consuls. The exact sense of this province is not known, but clearly it was some sort of domestic matter of land management that was designed to keep Caesar from any significant military command. The optimates' complacency would not last long.

Soon after coming into office, Caesar put forward for discussion in the senate an agrarian bill that was far from provocative. It provided for the distribution of the remaining public land in Italy (apart from Campania) and for the purchase at a fair price of additional land if necessary. Only the most dyed-in-the-wool reactionaries could object, and they did. Cato had no substantive objections to raise and was reduced to arguing that agrarian bills were not in the interest of the senate. He used the same delaying tactics as he had previously done at the time of Caesar's candidacy, and in annoyance and frustration Caesar had him arrested. When the senate showed itself to be under Cato's sway by trying to meet outside the prison so that Cato could take part in the deliberations, Caesar abandoned any hope of cooperation with the senate and took his proposals to the People.

Up until now, Crassus and Pompey had kept out of the matter. In fact, Pompey's personal involvement with Caesar was so inconceivable that a faithful adherent of Pompey spoke strongly in favor of Cato's obstruction. Then came the bombshell. Pompey and Crassus both spoke in favor of the bill, with Pompey in particular making threats (he stated that if anyone used the sword, he would raise his shield, clearly implying that he would respond to violence with violence). When the bill came to the vote, Bibulus was on hand to announce unfavorable omens to halt the proceeedings, and a bucket of dung was thrown on his head to persuade him to give up. From now on, Bibulus stayed at home, issuing feeble edicts about watching for omens as later grounds for invalidating Caesar's legislation. People joked that it was the consulship of Julius and Caesar (instead of "Caesar and Bibulus"). Violence won the day, and the bill was duly passed.

In the spring of 59 B.C., Caesar also passed one law reducing by one-third the amount owed by the publicans holding the Asian contract and another law ratifying Pompey's acta in the East. Now the consul had fulfilled his obligations to his supporters. Later in the year, it would turn out that the land available under the initial bill was insufficient and that a second bill was needed to distribute the public land in Campania. This bill demanded an oath of adherence from senators, and the domination of Caesar was so obvious that even Cato complied.

Clearly, organized violence could be used to control the operations of the assemblies in the absence of any regular police force to maintain order, and over the next decade, the violence employed in the electoral process would become more organized, as both the supporters and opponents of the coalition formed gangs to wage battles to control the political process in Rome. It would soon become apparent that the traditional practice of making public decisions through voting was impossible under such circumstances (this problem was aggravated by the increasing resort to electoral bribery).

LEX VATINIA

Caesar also made provision for himself through tribunician legislation passed through violence by P. Vatinius. Since the senate had not seen fit to vote Caesar a worthy province, the *lex Vatinia* gave him the provinces of Cisalpine Gaul and Illyricum for five years. (For more on the details and dating, see Chapter 18.) In April, Q. Caecilius Metellus Celer cos. 60, who had received Transalpine Gaul as his province, conveniently died, and the senate added this area to Caesar's command. Caesar initially governed these areas through legates, not leaving Rome until the spring of 58 B.C.

The transfer of this large command through legislation represents a further step in the decline of the senate's control over provincial assignments. Back in 67 B.C., the lex Gabinia had used earlier precedent to set up an election to grant a special province (the war against the pirates) to Pompey over the senate's objections. The following year, the lex Manilia had bestowed on Pompey the further task of conducting the war against Mithridates, this time without even the pretense of an election. Now, for no pressing public reason at all, a provincial assignment of a quite substantial scope was being granted through legislation for a long period of time (five years was much longer than a regular term as governor). There can be no doubt that like all the other Caesarian legislation, the lex Vatinia was passed through violence, and this meant that control of provincial assignments (and of the military force that went with such assignments) could be granted at the discretion of anyone who could muster the necessary force to coerce the assemblies in Rome. It would not be long before the military resources granted by legislation like this would be employed to exert control over the assemblies from outside Rome.

LONG-TERM POLITICAL CONSEQUENCES
OF CAESAR'S CONSULSHIP

The violence used by Caesar and his associates in passing their measures brought Caesar, Pompey, and Crassus into disrepute. Pompey in particular was unhappy about being associated with this violence, but he had no choice but to stand by Caesar, since his prestige was now bound up with Caesar's laws, several of which were passed in his interest. When his distress was most obvious, the alliance was solidified by Pompey's marriage to Caesar's daughter. In addition, Caesar helped secure his own position for the following year by marrying Calpurnia, the daughter of L. Calpurnius Piso Caesoninus, one of the candidates for the consulship.

For the next decade, one of the major questions would be how to view Caesar's laws. All this legislation had been passed under dubious circumstances, but if any single law was invalidated, this would provide the grounds for invalidating all of them. Thus, anyone who benefited from one of the laws had to support them all, and the hostility of the senate under the influence of Cato and others necessarily forced Pompey to continue to stand by Caesar.

Even though Caesar's present and later difficulties with the senate led to the conclusion that he was inherently opposed to it, this is clearly not so. In the spring of 58 B.C., before going off to seek glory in Gaul, Caesar stayed close to the city and offered to submit his own acta for the senate's approval. Once more he met with nothing but obstruction. Presumably, he felt that he would be able to secure acceptance of his measures as a whole, and his opponents blocked any discussion through fear of this outcome. Caesar eventually gave up and left for what turned out to be ten years of campaigning in Gaul. When he returned a decade later, he found the same obstruction, but this time his opponents forced him into actions that would finally end the free Republic.

QUESTIONS FOR STUDY AND REFLECTION

1. What was Caesar's family background? What family relations did he have with Marius and Cinna? What use did he make of these relations in his career? What was his attitude toward Sulla and the Sullan settlement?

2. What was Cato's relationship with the oligarchy? What was the basis of his influence? What was the general thrust of his policy?

3. What was the reaction in the senate to Pompey after his return from the East? What did he want, and how were his wishes thwarted? What steps did he take to achieve his ends?

4. What problems did the publicans for Asia have, and how did they wish to get out of their difficulties? What was Cato's attitude, and what consequences did this have?

5. Why did Pompey and Crassus decide to support Caesar's run for the consulship? What did they want in return? What was the nature of their coalition ("triumvirate")? In what way was Pompey's support of Caesar at variance with his long-term goals?

6. How did Caesar achieve his ends as consul?

7. What did Caesar get from the lex Vatinia? How was this law similar to previous laws bestowing commands, and how was it different?

17

CAESAR IN GAUL

CAESAR'S CAMPAIGNS IN GAUL

Q. Caecilius Metellus Celer cos. 60 had been assigned Transalpine Gaul (Gallia Narbonensis) as his province because of disturbances in the area (recall the presence of envoys from the Allobroges in Rome to deal with problems involving debt at the time of the Catilinarian conspiracy back in 63 B.C.). It seemed by the spring of 59 B.C. that the threat of war had died down, and Celer's hopes of glory were dashed. Upon Celer's death that spring, his province was added by the senate to the provinces of Cisalpine Gaul and Illyricum that had been granted to Caesar by the lex Vatinia. Caesar was not about to let any outbreak of peace stand in the way of his own ambitions. He turned out to be a very good general, and in the name of his own glory he spent the next decade waging war right and left with little justification. Caesar expanded the area of Gaul controlled by the Romans, which had previously been confined to the south, to include all the territory between the Pyrenees, the Rhine, and the Alps. In waging all these wars, Caesar did not consult the senate at all, and while his undeniable successes lessened some of the hostility that he had incurred in Rome, he remained a basically unacceptable figure to the senatorial oligarchy, which did not forget his high-handed behavior as consul and feared his return to Rome.

In his subjugation of Gaul, Caesar and his lieutenants made vast amounts of money from plunder and the sale of captives into slavery. Hundreds of thousands of people, if not more than a million, were killed, but because of the splendor of Caesar's fame and his undoubted literary talents posterity has paid little attention to them. It is worthwhile to dwell on the picture that Caesar presents of his conquest of Gaul since no comparable account survives of similar Roman conquests of areas like the Balkans and Spain. It should be noted in his defense that Caesar's actions were perhaps no more unjustified than those of many proconsuls, but his ten-year tenure in Gaul gave him more opportunity to behave in this way, and his extensive account makes it possible to follow his actions in great (and often uncomplimentary) detail.

CAESAR'S *COMMENTARII*

Caesar's campaigns in Gaul are so well known because he wrote a work telling us about them. This is a seven-book account (commonly known as the *Bellum Gallicum* or *Gallic War*) written in the ancient genre known as *commentarii* or "memoirs." Commentarii were accounts that statesmen wrote of their own activities (Sulla, for instance, is known to have written commentarii, which do not survive). Caesar would also write an incomplete account of the civil war that broke out in 49 B.C. (the *Bellum Civile* or *Civil War*). Commentarii were supposed to be pedestrian accounts of historical events written by major participants, who thereby provided the raw material for writers of literary histories (the usual lack of literary polish explains why such works normally did not survive antiquity). Cicero tells us that he highly esteemed the style of Caesar's commentarii, and Hirtius, a lieutenant who added an eighth book to cover the last year of Caesar's tenure in Gaul, notes that the excellence of Caesar's account was such that it precluded the need to convert it into a proper literary history.

The observation that Caesar's commentarii were equal to literary history brings up the question of their reliability. Being for the most part the sole surviving version of events, Caesar's account cannot be checked against external information. This is not the case, however, with Caesar's account of the civil war, for which contemporary evidence exists as a check in the form of Cicero's letters. In this instance, it is manifest that Caesar's account can be seriously misleading if not outright mendacious. C. Asinius Pollio, a partisan of Caesar's who lived into the reign of Augustus and himself became a historian, admitted to falsehoods in Caesar's accounts and claimed that Caesar would have corrected them if he had had the chance, an assertion of doubtful accuracy (quoted in Suetonius, *Life of the Deified Caesar* 56). In any case, Caesar clearly uses literary techniques like juxtaposition and the telling use of (infrequent) direct quotations to exalt himself and malign his enemies.

Famously, Caesar speaks of himself in the third person, which lends the account a specious semblance of objectivity. But it must be borne in mind that Caesar was an eloquent man whose self-serving account is designed to magnify his success and shift responsibility for failure onto others. In the *Gallic War*, he manipulates the narrative to make it seem that he is a man of peace who is persuaded by the pleas of the oppressed to come to their aid and in the process is compelled to wage defensive wars against haughty and unreasonable foes. A detached assessment of the situation generally calls this presentation into question, and it is clear that Caesar was intentionally provoking wars for his own purposes.

Caesar as Military Leader

In addition to being an excellent writer, Caesar turned out to be a first-class general. A number of factors explain his phenomenal success over the course of many years. In the first place, he was blessed with a large quantity of that prerequisite for victory, luck. On numerous occasions during his career, all seemed to be lost, yet Caesar's forces managed to prevail in the end. Second, he himself was simply an excellent tactician and strategist. On the battlefield, he was able to see weaknesses in his enemy's formation and take advantage of them. In the broader perspective, he had a keen mental eye for perceiving how best to marshal his forces to achieve the complete defeat of his foe. Once again, he was quick to exploit deficiencies in the disposition of the enemy forces. In his own accounts he emphasizes his "swiftness" (*celeritas*). He clearly thought it important to seize the initiative, and time and again in his many campaigns he acted quickly to throw his enemy off balance. On the strategic level, Caesar proved to be masterful at taking advantage of internal divisions among his adversaries and at modulating savagery and mercy as he used his comparatively small forces to conquer the much more numerous but disorganized forces of the various peoples of Gaul. Third, he was a charismatic leader. Though much of the evidence comes from his own account, the behavior of his subordinates and the external confirmation of other sources confirm that he had a flair for winning the loyalty of both officers and men. Caesar would perform theatrical acts like having his horse taken away at the start of the battle to show the troops that he was sharing their dangers. Sulla too must have inspired similar loyalty, though he seems to have promoted an image of himself as the recipient of divine favor, a course that Caesar chose not to follow. In any case, Caesar gives numerous anecdotes to show the extreme devotion that his troops felt for him. Finally, again like Sulla and unlike Lucullus, he secured the loyalty of his troops through granting them a large share in the booty that he won and giving them relatively free rein to seize their own. Naturally, Caesar does not refer to this in his account, but assorted pieces of external evidence show that he was very liberal with money, something that is easy to do with the property of people you have killed.

Helvetii

Caesar's first campaign was against the Helvetii, a Celtic people who lived in the area of modern Switzerland. Induced by overpopulation, they devised a plan to emigrate into western Gaul in the spring of 58 B.C., and when they requested permission to cross the Roman province, Caesar seized upon this situation as way of justifying a resort to war. He deceitfully told them to wait for his answer, using the time to bring up his troops. (He had one legion in Transalpine and three in Cisalpine Gaul, and hurriedly raised another two.) Upon his eventual refusal, they went through the territory of the Aedui, who were Roman allies. Caesar used the pleas of certain Aedui for help and the claim that the Helvetii might harm Roman territory as a specious excuse to attack the Helvetii. After a long pursuit, he met them in battle, and he emerged victorious from a hard-fought struggle. He sent the surviving 110,000 Helvetii (out of 368,000 who had set out a few months earlier) back home.

Ariovistus

Caesar then used the excuse of protecting Roman allies (the Aedui again) to wage war on the German leader Ariovistus, who had entered Gaul when the Sequani (a Gallic tribe) hired Germans to help them in their war with the Aedui some years earlier. As it turned out, the Germans liked what they saw and decided to stay, establishing their control over the neighboring Gallic tribes (including the Sequani). Caesar himself had had Ariovistus declared a friend of the Roman People by the senate during his consulship. Now, however, he abandoned this stance and demanded that Ariovistus withdraw across the Rhine, claiming that their victories in the 120s B.C. gave the Romans a paramount position in Gaul. Needless to say, Ariovistus did not share this view, and war resulted. Caesar won another major victory in the early autumn, and the Germans were driven across the Rhine with great losses. He put the legions in winter quarters in eastern Gaul, leaving his legatus pro praetore T. Labienus in charge, and spent the winter in Cisalpine Gaul administering justice.

T. Labienus

Following the precedent of the lex Gabinia (see Chapter 13), the lex Vatinia authorized Caesar to appoint a legatus pro praetore, and to this position he appointed Labienus, who had previously been associated with Pompey (serving as a turbulent tribune in 63 B.C.). Caesar came to rely on Labienus as his trusted right-hand man, and later he would bitterly resent Labienus's return (or, in Caesar's eyes, defection) to Pompey at the start of the civil war. As a result, Caesar would portray Labienus in a very unflattering light in his commentarii on the civil war.

Conquest of the North

In the spring of 57 B.C., Caesar raised two more legions (this brought the total to eight) in preparation for a campaign against the inhabitants of northern Gaul – the Belgae, a mixture of Gauls and Germans – who felt threatened by his victories of the preceding year. The tribe of the Remi joined Caesar and became a trusted ally. The Belgae collected a large and unwieldy army (supposedly numbering 240,000 men), which it proved to be impossible to maintain in the field. After failing to attack Caesar, this force broke up so that the contingents could return to their home territories. Most of the north was then easily subdued, but four tribes held out under the leadership of the Nervii. These were then defeated in battle, and they submitted to Caesar. The Atuatuci surrendered their main stronghold but treacherously attacked the Romans. In retaliation, Caesar sold them all (53,000 people) into slavery.[1] Meanwhile, P. Licinius Crassus, one of Caesar's legates (and the son of Caesar's associate M. Crassus), subdued the tribes of modern Brittany and Normandy. That winter, Caesar quartered his legions all over Gaul as garrisons to maintain Roman control.

Now the only parts of Gaul not under Roman control were two tribes in the extreme north and Aquitania (the area in the southwest between the river Garonne and the Pyrenees). It seemed as if the conquest of Gaul was secure, and on Cicero's motion the senate decreed a fifteen-day *supplicatio* (ceremony of thanksgiving to the gods). Traditionally, five days had been the largest number of days for such celebration, but ten had recently been voted in thanks for Pompey's eastern victories in 63 B.C.

Veneti

The major event of 56 B.C. involved the Veneti, a tribe on the southern coast of Brittany. They resisted Roman grain requisitions and had strongholds on promontories that were inaccessible by land. Caesar tried fruitless land assaults on them but was forced to await the fleet that he had ordered

---

[1] Caesar reports that the tribe was descended from people left behind by the Cimbri and Teutoni to guard their baggage at the time of the final descent upon Italy in Marius's day. This historical tidbit was presumably imparted to make the Roman reader pleased at the tribe's annihilation.

to be built on the Loire. Once it arrived, the Romans won a naval victory and seized the strongholds. As a penalty for mistreating the requisition officers (on the bogus claim that they held the status of sacrosanct ambassadors), the leading men were executed and everyone else sold into slavery. Caesar was again trying to intimidate potential opponents through the savage suppression of resistance. The same summer, P. Crassus subdued Aquitania. The Romans took up winter quarters between the Loire and Seine to keep an eye open for revolt in Brittany.

TREACHERY ON THE RHINE AND INVASION

OF BRITAIN

In the spring of 55 B.C., two German tribes, the Usipetes and Tencteri, seized land on the left (western) bank of the lower Rhine, and Caesar hurried north to meet them. As he approached, German ambassadors asked to be given land on the left bank or to be allowed to capture it for themselves. Caesar said there was no land available and told them to return across the Rhine. The ambassadors asked for three days to get an answer from their people and requested that Caesar not advance during this time. He asserts that this delay was merely a pretext to gain time for the return of their cavalry, which was off foddering, but there is no reason to believe this claim.[2] Caesar continued to advance and the Germans asked for three days to come to an agreement with the Germans on the right bank. A battle then occurred between the Germans and some of his Gallic cavalry (the Germans won). When the German leaders came the next day to ask for forgiveness, Caesar had them arrested (this from the man who wiped out the Veneti for not respecting the sacrosanct persons of Roman grain requisitioners!) and seized the opportunity to attack the Germans. Without leadership, they offered no resistance. As Caesar puts it in his elegant Latin, "The remaining throng of children and women... began to flee randomly. Caesar sent his cavalry to pursue them" (*Gallic War* 4.14.5). The tribe was wiped out (he claims that there were 430,000 of them, though that cannot conceivably be right).

When some Germans on the right side of the Rhine refused to surrender fugitives, Caesar used this as an excuse to make a demonstration of Roman power. In ten days, he built a huge bridge across the river

---

[2] This was of course exactly the stratagem that Caesar himself had used against the Helvetii. Was Caesar simply projecting onto the Germans the bad faith of which he himself had been guilty?

(a prodigious achievement) and then spent eighteen days reconnoitering on the other side. Seeing no one, he crossed back over the Rhine and had the bridge destroyed. Presumably, he decided that there was little opportunity for glory on the far side of the Rhine.

Thwarted in one direction, the redoubtable Caesar tried another, and that fall he conducted a reconnaissance expedition in Britain with two legions. The island was virtually unknown up to this point (it was erroneously thought that it might be wealthy). Caesar suffered losses at sea and found no enemies worth fighting. He sailed back to Gaul before winter, intending to return in force the next year.

When the report of his campaigns for the year was read in the senate, Caesar was voted a twenty-day supplicatio. Cato, on the other hand, fruitlessly proposed that he should be turned over to the Germans to atone for his treachery (and avert any divine retribution against the Roman state). Whatever the legal and religious merits of his actions (Cato was no doubt more interested in harming Caesar than upholding divine law), Caesar had spent the year in a vain attempt to provoke a major new war.

Return to Britain, Revolt in Gaul

In 54 B.C., Caesar returned to Britain. Though not exactly a fiasco, the campaign did not live up to expectations. The British forces refrained from battle, and Caesar could find no solid support. He decided against permanent occupation, which would have been hard to maintain across the channel all winter.

Meanwhile, there was discontent in Gaul. Caesar had to favor his allies, and their enemies naturally became anti-Roman. The harvest in 54 B.C. was poor, which forced Caesar to scatter his legions far apart in their winter quarters. Fifteen cohorts (one and a half legions) were stationed among the Eburones in the far north. Under the leadership of Ambiorix, the Eburones attacked the winter camp, which was commanded by two legates, Q. Titurius Sabinus and L. Aurunculeius Cotta. Ambiorix treacherously offered to allow the Romans to leave unharmed, and when they agreed, he attacked them on the journey, wiping them out. Caesar uncharitably pins the blame for the debacle on Sabinus. According to Caesar's unflattering account, Sabinus alone among the Roman leaders was intimidated by the Gauls, and when thwarted in his advice to accept the Gauls' terms, he used disreputable means to compel Cotta and the centurions to give in against their will (Sabinus supposedly drew the common soldiery into the deliberations of the senior officers, a violation of all military propriety in the eyes of the hierarchically minded Romans). Even if this slanderous portrayal is accurate (and while Caesar may have had the testimony of a few survivors, he could hardly have learned from them the elaborately detailed and presumably fictional account that he gives), he conveniently ignores the constitutional reality that the imperium was his and that he had full responsibility for the actions of his subordinates. If he was going to take the credit for the successes of his legates like Crassus and Labienus, then he was just as responsible for the defeat of Cotta and Sabinus, and his blackening of the dead Sabinus's reputation is both contemptible and typical of Caesar's basically selfish personality. In any case, after the defeat of the Roman garrison among the Eburones, the Nervii were induced to attack another Roman camp commanded by Cicero's brother (and Caesar's legate) Q. Tullius Cicero pr. 62. By now, Caesar was hurrying north with two legions and rescued Cicero from a long and perilous siege.

The rest of the winter was spent putting down revolts in the north and threatening various Gallic leaders. Caesar raised two more legions himself and borrowed a third from Pompey, which brought his total to ten. (Possession of the legion borrowed from Pompey would later become a bone of contention.) The year 53 B.C. was spent subduing the north; the territory of the Eburones was ravaged so thoroughly that they are never heard from again in history.

GREAT REVOLT OF THE GAULS

In 52 B.C., the Gauls finally united after a fashion to defend themselves against the Romans. As with Italy during the Social War, the dominant position of the Romans had brought together their diverse enemies in a sort of artificial unity – and the Gauls would be just as successful in opposing the Romans as the Italians had been. This revolt clearly was one of "national" feeling, as even those whom Caesar had favored were carried along by the anti-Roman sentiment. Though the revolt eventually encompassed most of the tribes of Gaul, the driving force behind it was centered on the tribes directly to the north of the old Roman province in the south (Narbonensis). Presumably, these tribes were most familiar with the Romans and the least inclined to fall under their sway.

The leader of the movement was Vercingetorix, a prince of the Arverni on the northern border of the old Roman province. He knew that he could not beat the Romans in open battle and instead adopted a policy of denying them supplies and forcing them to withdraw.

Early Moves

By the late winter of 53/52 B.C., the tribes of central Gaul were in revolt, and Gallic forces threatened the Roman colony of Narbo. Caesar thwarted this move with his troop deployments and raised another twenty-two cohorts (more than two legions). Caesar decided to try and take Avaricum, the capital of the Bituriges. Vercingetorix advised its abandonment, but the Gauls insisted on trying to hold it. When it fell to the Romans, its inhabitants (supposedly 40,000) were massacred. Caesar expected this move to cause the revolt to crumble, but since Vercingetorix had advised against the defense, no one blamed him.

At this point, Caesar decided to split his forces. With six legions, he himself attacked Gergovia, a stronghold of the Arverni, while Labienus marched against the Senones to the north with four legions. When Caesar arrived at Gergovia, a 10,000-man infantry force was on its way from the Aedui, one of the main tribes supporting Caesar, to reinforce him. The loyalty of this force was being undermined by certain leaders who resented Roman domination, and Caesar had to take four of his legions to make sure that it did not defect (its loss might have completely undermined his position among the Gauls). The Aeduan force did return to loyalty when he caught up with it, and it is a measure of the desperation of his situation that he took no action against the instigators of the sedition. In previous years, Caesar had often used the concentrated application of violence and savagery against a few to cow the remaining opposition, but at this time Caesar apparently felt that in light of his weakened position such a course of action would be counterproductive.

Caesar now returned to Gergovia, since any failure to take it would greatly lessen Roman prestige. He launched a desperate attack, which resulted in a major defeat. At this point, news arrived that the Aedui were threatened by the rebels, and Caesar allowed their force to return home to defend their territory. There it was learned that the Aedui had officially gone over to Vercingetorix. Caesar now abandoned the siege and moved north to join forces with Labienus.

Meanwhile, the Gauls assembled in the territory of the Aedui, where they elected Vercingetorix as their leader and adopted the plan of invading the old Roman province. The Gauls then set up their main base for this project at Alesia in central Gaul. As for the old province, it was held only with Gallic allies and the twenty-two newly raised cohorts. Caesar would get no reinforcements from Italy and hired some German cavalry. With his main force, he marched south to defend the province. When

Vercingetorix attacked his columns and was repulsed, Caesar took advantage of the Gallic defeat and marched on Alesia.

SIEGE OF ALESIA

Alesia was a very large site, and Caesar built a ten-mile circuit of siege works around it. Vercingetorix barely managed to get his cavalry out in time. Forty-three tribes united to send a relief force, and Caesar had to build an outward-facing circuit of fortifications around his original siege works to prevent the Gauls from breaking through to the city. After thirty days, food had run out in the city, but the Romans were in desperate straits as well. The Gauls attacked the Roman position from both inside and out for four days. The relief army finally scattered after a huge defeat in which seventy-four military standards were lost.

Vercingetorix rode up the next day to surrender. If he expected leniency, he was mistaken. He languished in captivity for six years until Caesar's massive triumph in 46 B.C., after which he was strangled in the public prison just as Jugurtha had been. (It is worth contrasting Caesar's attitude of hostility toward this foreign foe and clemency toward his Roman opponents with Sulla's diametrically opposite behavior.)

Since his position was still insecure, Caesar decided to treat the Arverni and Aedui mildly, and when they went over to the Romans, the revolt pretty much collapsed. The winter of 52–51 B.C. and the following summer were spent suppressing various holdouts of resistance. On the whole, Caesar continued to be lenient. The major exception to this was the stronghold of Uxellodunum. When it was captured, he had the defenders' hands cut off as a permanent warning to those who would oppose Rome. This brutality shows that Caesar was once again confident of his overall mastery of the situation and decided that it was now opportune to bring the Gauls to heel.

FINAL SETTLEMENT

By the fall of 51 B.C., Caesar had exhausted Gaul into submission, adding 200,000 square miles to the empire of the Roman People. The comparatively small amount of tribute he imposed on the conquered territory (40,000,000 sesterces) indicates how debilitated the area was after ten years of warfare. In his triumph, Caesar claimed to have killed 1,192,000 people, and Gaul was so exhausted that no tribe would revolt again until 46 B.C. He had seized so much gold that the value of the metal dropped by a quarter in Italy (when coined at the official rate, a pound would yield 1,000 sesterces, but on the open market it would fetch only 750). Apart from benefactions made throughout the Mediterranean, he paid 100,000,000 sesterces just for the land on which to build his new addition to the forum in Rome. For Caesar and his army at any rate, the years in Gaul had been very profitable.

CAESAR'S FUTURE

It cannot be emphasized too strongly that Caesar now had a completely loyal, highly efficient military force at his disposal. He also faced the same problem that Sulla had – namely, how a victorious general could manage to return safely to Italy when he was disliked and distrusted by those who controlled the senate and the electoral process in Rome. As Caesar considered his prospects, he must have known that the devotion of his veteran army, which had suffered such hardship with him and emerged victorious and wealthy, would give him a huge initial advantage if, like Sulla, he eventually decided to settle the matter through a military solution.

QUESTIONS FOR STUDY AND REFLECTION

1. What sorts of pretexts did Caesar use in his wars (e.g., those against the Helvetii and Ariovistus, his crossing of the Rhine, and his invasion of Britain)? What were his motives? Were his wars "justified"?
2. What sort of commander was Caesar?
3. How brutal was Caesar in his wars? How did he modulate his brutality to suit circumstances?
4. What circumstances allowed Caesar to conquer Gaul in such a short period of time? Why did his invasions of Britain and Germany lead to no permanent conquests?
5. What was the reaction in Rome to his many victories?
6. Why were Caesar's forces so loyal to him?

18

LAST DECADE OF THE FREE REPUBLIC

POLITCAL SUPREMACY OF CAESAR, POMPEY, AND CRASSUS

The 50s B.C. began with the formation of a coalition by Caesar, Pompey, and Crassus to implement certain policies during Caesar's consulship. The passage of Caesar's laws through the use of violence created a permanent bond between the members of the coalition: no single piece of legislation could be invalidated without implicitly invalidating the lot of them, so the members were forced to cooperate to uphold all of Caesar's acta. (Henceforth, the three will be referred to as the "coalition members.") Pompey was the weakest link in the chain, clearly being uncomfortable with the methods of Caesar's consulship and his own ensuing alienation from the oligarchy. Nonetheless, despite Pompey's unease and his basic incompatibility with Crassus, the three managed to thwart the opposition mounted against them by senior members of the oligarchy and to manipulate the political scene through their combined power, influence, and money. The death of Julia in 54 B.C. and of Crassus in 53 B.C. completely changed the dynamic of the situation, and Pompey gradually came to a reconciliation with the oligarchs that ultimately resulted in civil war. In the meanwhile, the normal functioning of the Republican government increasingly broke down during the 50s B.C. as a result of the use of violence in Rome and the interference of powerful individuals.

ATTEMPTS TO UNDERMINE CAESAR

During his consulship, Caesar had clearly acted in an unconstitutional manner. He drove his colleague Bibulus out of public life, seized control of the voting places to ensure passage of his laws, and ignored any tribunician interference. Hence, it would have been reasonable to argue for the invalidation of his acta on various grounds if the matter had ever been properly debated, but the coalition members obviously could not allow this to happen. Their opponents naturally undertook various efforts to undermine Caesar's legislation. Already in the winter of 58 B.C., while Caesar was still in Rome, the praetors C. Memmius and L. Domitius Ahenobarbus attempted to raise the matter in the senate. Caesar agreed to submit his acta for discussion, which shows that he was reasonably confident of securing approval, but he left for his province when it became clear that this effort would prove fruitless. One tribune attempted to try him before the People, but the other tribunes prevented this on the legally correct grounds that he was away on public business (Roman magistrates could not be prosecuted during their term of office). His quaestor was prosecuted, though with what outcome is not known. Caesar could rely in 58 B.C. on the protection of the two consuls, L. Calpurnius Piso Caesoninus (his father-in-law) and A. Gabinius (a protégé of Pompey's), and the tribune P. Clodius Pulcher.

P. Clodius

P. Clodius Pulcher played a prominent role in the political disorders of the 50s B.C. He belonged to a prominent family of the highest patrician nobility – his father Ap. Claudius Pulcher had been consul in 79 B.C. and his brother Appius would hold the office in 54 B.C. – but Clodius preferred to use the lower-class pronunciation of his name (with the simple vowel "ŏ" in place of the diphthong "au") and pursued his political career as a demagogue in the popularis tradition. He was hostile to Cicero for having ruined his alibi during the Bona Dea scandal in 61 B.C. (see Chapter 15) and was particularly keen to destroy him for his execution of the conspirators in 63 B.C. Clodius often cooperated with the coalition members but was happy enough to attack them when it suited him: Clodius was something of a loose cannon. His independence and readiness to resort to organized violence in Rome make him reminiscent of Saturninus. One gets the impression that he enjoyed causing trouble for its own sake.

In 60 B.C., Clodius had himself adopted by a plebeian (he nonetheless continued to use his famous birth name), but the consul of that year, Q. Caecilius Metellus Celer, refused to recognize the adoption on the grounds that certain archaic procedures had not been carried out, and he thwarted Clodius's attempt to run for the tribunate. In 59 B.C., there was still a question about his adoption into the plebs, but Clodius was eager to be allowed to run. Early in the year, Caesar was still trying to win over Cicero and for this reason he did not allow Clodius to go through the archaic procedures. In early spring, however, Cicero was defending his consular colleague C. Antonius on a charge of extortion relating to his governorship of Macedonia, and in his speech, he let fall an unfavorable comment about Caesar's consulship. This angered Caesar, who within three hours performed (with the assistance of Pompey) the adoption ceremony needed to make Clodius a plebeian. Clodius then won election for the tribunate of the plebs for 58 B.C., which could only spell trouble for Cicero.

At the start of his tribunate, Clodius passed four major bills.

1. The censors would be allowed to expel someone from the senate only after a properly conducted judicial investigation. This was presumably intended to thwart Clodius's own expulsion if a severe censorship like that of 70 B.C. (see Chapter 12) was carried out.

2. The second-century Aelian and Fufian laws (*leges Aelia et Fufia*), which governed the obstruction of legislation through the announcement of unfavorable omens, were repealed. This undercut the objections to Caesar's laws, since the old laws that had been violated during the course of passing his legislation would no longer be in operation (and, conveniently, such grounds would no longer be available for invalidating Clodius's own legislation).

3. A grain law did away with any cost to the recipient for state-provided grain. This was a huge expense to the treasury but naturally won Clodius much gratitude among the poor of Rome.

4. A law of 64 B.C. that had abolished all *collegia* apart from those that had long existed was repealed. Collegia were professional organizations based on a common religious cult, but they had come to be used as a means of organizing armed gangs for violent intervention in politics, which was the reason for their abolition. The repeal of the earlier law allowed these collegia to function once again as political gangs, and Clodius became one of the major leaders of such gangs.

Having laid the groundwork in this way, Clodius went on to propose a law about executing Roman citizens that was directed against Cicero. In order to secure the cooperation of the consuls, on the same day Clodius promulgated laws giving the consuls special commands (Piso received Macedonia and Gabinius Syria). Finally, in order to remove Cato from the scene, Clodius passed a law ordering him to go to Cyprus to seize the island from its king and convert it into a Roman province on the grounds that it had been bequeathed to the Roman People by the rather dubious will of an earlier king. Cato complied and did not return until 56 B.C. In this way, Clodius got rid of the one person with enough backbone and prestige to stand up to him.

Exile of Cicero

In 60 and 59 B.C., there had already been talk of Clodius's intention to prosecute Cicero as tribune, and Pompey and Caesar had told him not to. By late 59 B.C., though, Cicero's uncooperative attitude had made Caesar unfriendly, and in December of that year he spoke in public about the illegality of Cicero's actions. Clodius's new law punished with exile anyone convicted under it of having killed a Roman citizen who had not been legally condemned. This clearly meant Cicero, since the senate had no power to try citizens and the debate in the senate on December 5, 63 B.C., could not be interpreted as a proper condemnation. Cicero overreacted as if his safety depended on the bill not being passed. He pleaded with Pompey to help, but Pompey left town to avoid doing anything. Of the consulars, only Lucullus advised resistance, and all the others told Cicero not to use violence to thwart the bill's passage. Abandoned by his friends, Cicero decided not to oppose passage of the bill and withdrew from Rome when it was passed. Clodius immediately passed a bill ratifying Cicero's exile through interdiction and forbidding any discussion of the case in the senate.[1]

Cicero was eventually forced to take up residence in Thessalonica on the north coast of the Aegean, where he stayed until the summer of 57 B.C. He was miserable there, and his whining letters show him at his worst. He bitterly regretted listening to the malicious advice (as he took it) of his consular "friends."

Cicero's recall was the result (more or less) of a violent falling out between Pompey and Clodius over trivial matters in the East (Clodius's arrangements for certain matters there conflicted with Pompey's acta). When Pompey came to a meeting of the senate in August 58 B.C., Clodius arranged to have a slave of his drop a dagger and reveal that he had been told to assassinate Pompey. This was enough to make the conqueror of the East hide in his house for the rest of the year. Cicero's recall was brought about in 57 B.C. through the efforts of one of the consuls, C. Cornelius Lentulus Spinther (his colleague, Q. Caecilius Metellus Nepos, who had been Cicero's enemy as tribune back in 62 B.C., agreed not to interfere). Even Caesar grudgingly went along. Though no longer tribune, Clodius refused to give in and used his gangs to disrupt matters. Pompey decided that counter-violence was needed, and two tribunes of 57 B.C., who strongly supported the effort to recall Cicero, P. Sestius and T. Annius Milo, organized gangs of their own to fight Clodius on his own terms. Finally, in June the senate passed a decree asking for Cicero's recall

---

[1] For the interdict, see Chapter 3 n. 6.

(only Clodius voted against the decree), and the appropriate legislation was soon passed by Spinther.

Cicero interpreted the many efforts that went on throughout Italy on his behalf as a sign of his own popularity (Pompey organized a campaign in which the communities of Italy passed decrees calling for his recall), but while there undoubtedly was an element of personal favor in this, the matter had come to be symbolic. Cicero's exile was seen as a reflection of the violence prevalent in Roman politics, and the demands for his recall were indicative of a desire to see a return to normal conditions. Though Cicero was recalled, this desire was to go unfulfilled. For his part, Cicero himself conceived a strong sense of gratitude toward Pompey for his role in securing his recall, forgetting that Pompey himself had allowed the exile in the first place by abetting Clodius's adoption and doing nothing to prevent the passage of his bill about executing citizens.

CURA ANNONAE

By late 57 B.C., there was rioting in Rome (instigated by Clodius) as a result of a shortage of grain (there had been poor harvests for several years). In response, the consuls proposed a special commission for Pompey to deal with the grain supply of Rome (*cura annonae* or "management of the grain supply"). By this proposal, Pompey was to be granted imperium for five years and the right to appoint fifteen legates; Cicero spoke strongly in favor of this bill. A tribune proposed granting him an army, a fleet, control of the treasury, and imperium superior to that of regular provincial governors. Opinion was unfavorable to the tribune's more extreme proposal, but it shows that an attempt was being made to bestow upon Pompey as much power as possible on the pretext of this temporary crisis. As it was, the lesser proposal was passed, once more giving Pompey imperium.

CRISIS IN THE COALITION

The opponents of the coalition continued their efforts to bring an end to the three men's domination of the state. In 57 B.C., there was a dispute between Crassus and Pompey about the restoration of King Ptolemy of Egypt, who had been driven out of Alexandria in 58 B.C. and wanted to be officially restored to his throne. While he wished Pompey to do this, Crassus was opposed (eventually A. Gabinius cos. 58 carried out the task as governor of Syria). Crassus encouraged Clodius in his hostility toward Pompey, and the dissension between Pompey and Crassus was so great that Pompey even thought that Crassus wished to have him assassinated.

Clearly, Pompey was the least committed member of the coalition, and the optimates (especially Cicero) strove to detach him. In late 57 and early 56 B.C., an effort was made to use the state's need for money to pay for Pompey's grain commission as an excuse to overturn Caesar's second agrarian law, which had distributed the public lands in Campania. Since Pompey's veterans had been provided for by Caesar's first agrarian law, it seemed that it might be possible to do away with the second law without directly harming Pompey's interests. If it turned out that Pompey could be persuaded to go along with the measure, this might cause a breach between him and the other two members of the coalition. Accordingly, Cicero proposed on April 5, 56 B.C., that the senate should discuss the matter on May 15.

In addition to the efforts to undermine the agrarian legislation, there were direct attacks on Caesar. In speeches, Cicero emphasized the outrageousness of the lex Vatinia. In the elections for aedile in January 56 B.C. (they had been delayed since the preceding summer), Vatinius himself was defeated. Cato's son-in-law L. Domitius Ahenobarbus, an implacable enemy of Caesar who was going to run for consul in the summer of 56 B.C., stated that when elected he would seek to deprive Caesar of his command (set to expire in March 54 B.C.). Things seemed to be going well for Caesar's opponents, when he took action against them by arranging a meeting with his partners. (For coins that show the hostility felt by the circle of Cato toward the domination of the political scene by the coalition, which was taken to be a form of tyranny, see Coins 17 and 18.)

CONFERENCE AT LUCA

In April, when Pompey was in the north of Italy dealing with the grain supply, Caesar was still in Cisalpine Gaul conducting the winter assizes. Caesar summoned the other two coalition members to Luca, a conveniently located town in his province. The influence of the coalition is illustrated by the fact that 120 senators came along and 200 lictors were also present.[2]

The result was a renewal of the agreement of the three men to cooperate to secure their ends. It was decided that Pompey and Crassus would hold the consulship in the following year, and that during their term they were to see to it not only that Caesar's command was extended for a further five

---

[2] Lictors carried the *fasces* (bundles of rods that symbolized imperium), consuls having twelve fasces (and lictors) each, praetors six (as a sign of their hierarchical inferiority).

years but also that Pompey and Crassus would themselves receive similar commands. For his part, Crassus agreed to curb Clodius.

After the conference, Pompey had a talk with Cicero's brother Quintus, who was serving as his legate on the grain commission. Quintus then went to inform his brother of the decision made at Luca, and when the senate met on May 15, the eagerly awaited debate on the second agrarian law failed to materialize. Not only did Cicero have to swallow this, but in June he himself had to speak in the senate against voting for Caesar's replacement as governor of Gaul. Cicero's desire to promote the interests of his brother (who was now eligible for the consulship) and the devotion to Pompey that he had conceived because of Pompey's role in bringing about his recall from exile would lead him to support the coalition for the remainder of its existence, contrary to his general inclinations.

SECOND CONSULSHIP OF POMPEY AND CRASSUS

The consul who would preside over the consular elections in 56 B.C. was hostile to the election of Pompey and Crassus to a second joint consulship. Although already asked before if they wished to stand, they did not enter their names until after the official deadline and were thus refused as candidates. They then used this as an excuse to have a tribune forbid the elections until January 55 B.C. In this way, they could wait until an amenable interrex was in office.[3] Waiting until winter also allowed Caesar to send a thousand of his troops to Rome under the command of his legate P. Crassus, elder son of Crassus the coalition member. By election time, only Cato's brother-in-law L. Domitius Ahenobarbus remained in the competition, and the night before the election he and Cato went down to the Campus Martius to seek support. In order to prevent any unpleasant surprises, their party was attacked by the coalition's forces. Cato's torch bearer was killed, Cato himself wounded, and Domitius forced to seek refuge in his house. The next day, Pompey and Crassus were duly elected consuls and then presided over the election of the lesser offices. Their manipulation alone secured the election of Vatinius (Caesar's tribune back in 59 B.C.) as praetor and the defeat of Cato's candidacy for the same office. There was rioting during the aedilician elections, and when Pompey came home with blood on his toga, the shock of seeing him in this state caused Pompey's wife Julia, the daughter of Caesar, to have a miscarriage, an event that would have most unfortunate consequences.

---

[3] For the position of interrex, see Chapter 11 n. 1.

Once in office, the new consuls stood for law and order. Pompey passed a law designed to curb judicial corruption. The three classes of jurors (senators, equites, and tribuni aerarii) were no longer to be chosen by the urban praetor at his own discretion. Instead, the richest men from each class were to serve (on the sanguine view that the wealthiest jurors would be the least susceptible to bribery). Crassus also passed a law attempting to curb the abuse of the collegia for political purposes (discussed earlier in the chapter).

For the consuls' benefit, the tribunician *lex Trebonia* granted Crassus a five-year command in Syria, while Pompey received a similar command in Spain. Crassus clearly yearned for military glory (he had held no command since his defeat of Spartacus sixteen years earlier) and intended to wage war on the Parthians. Given the military prestige of Pompey and Caesar, he had to do something if he wished to continue as their equal, and he left for the East in November 55 B.C. Pompey, on the other hand, had no need for more glory and did not go to Spain himself. Instead, he chose to rule his provinces through legates while staying in Italy himself. (It was already common practice that when consuls were voted provinces, they governed the province through a legate during the consulship unless the situation demanded immediate attention; then they set off for their province as proconsuls in the following year, just as Caesar had done in 59–58 B.C. Pompey expanded this practice by ruling the Spanish provinces for years through legates without ever setting foot there. This novel method of governance was ultimately to be used on a much greater scale by the first emperor.) By their joint *lex Pompeia Licinia*, the two consuls extended Caesar's command in Gaul for another five years.

The consular elections were delayed until November and then did not go according to the wishes of the coalition members. L. Ahenobarbus was finally returned along with Clodius's brother Ap. Claudius Pulcher, and Cato likewise secured election as praetor. These elections showed that unless force was used, the coalition could not control the outcome of elections. Nonetheless, the coalition still reigned supreme in Rome, but the capricious hand of fortune would soon change this.

CRASSUS IN THE EAST

In November 55 B.C., Crassus wished to depart from Rome for the East to take up his position as governor of Syria. It was clear that Crassus intended to go to war with Parthia in order to gain a military reputation comparable to that of his coalition partners. Hostile tribunes tried to prevent his departure, and Crassus had to have Pompey come out in person to assist him. When he finally did leave, the tribune C. Ateius Capito first announced unfavorable omens. After Crassus ignored this, Capito solemnly cursed both Crassus and his army. (In 50 B.C. Capito was expelled from the senate by the censor Ap. Claudius Pulcher for causing the disaster. Cicero pointed out the illogical nature of the censor's reasoning. If the omens were contrived, then they could not have had any effect on the events in the East, and if they were valid, then the fault belonged to Crassus for not heeding them.)

Parthian Dynastic Politics

Recent events in Parthia suggested that this would be an opportune time to launch an invasion. In 58/7 B.C., King Phraates III was murdered by his sons Mithridates and Orodes. Mithridates first became king, but he was expelled by a conspiracy and took refuge with the governor of Syria (A. Gabinius), while Orodes became king. Gabinius was bribed to restore Mithridates to his throne, but the more lucrative prospect of restoring King Ptolemy to the Egyptian throne drew his attention, and Mithridates started a civil war in Parthia to regain his throne by himself. Crassus received the Syrian campaign while this civil war was still in progress, but in November 55 B.C., just as Crassus was setting off for the East, Mithridates was captured by his brother and executed. There would be no dynastic unrest when Crassus arrived.

Crassus's First Campaign

After crossing by sea from Brundisium to northern Greece (there were more unfavorable omens at the point of embarkation, but this was realized only after the fact),[4] Crassus and his army traveled overland, reaching Syria in the spring of 54 B.C. With the troops brought from Italy (including 1,000 Gallic horsemen supplied by Caesar and commanded by Crassus's eldest son Publius), Crassus had seven legions. His quaestor was C. Cassius Longinus (later one of Caesar's assassins). It remained to be seen how the Roman heavy infantry would fare against the powerful Parthian cavalry and what sort of commander Crassus would prove to be when faced with a proper opponent rather than a hastily assembled band of desperate slaves.

---

[4] It turned out that a man hawking figs by shouting "Caunians!" (*cauneas*, referring to a popular variety named after a town in Asia Minor) was in fact giving the colloquial pronunciation of the phrase "Make sure you don't go" (*cave ne eas*). If only the gods would enunciate their warnings more clearly!

In the summer of 54 B.C., Crassus invaded Mesopotamia but had not gotten very far when he decided to halt for the winter. He left two cohorts from each legion as garrisons and returned to Syria with the balance of his army. He then spent the winter extorting money out of local kings (which did not help his posthumous reputation in the ancient sources). He also plundered the great temple of Yahweh in Jerusalem.

Battle of Carrhae

In the spring of 53 B.C., Crassus resumed his attack. The garrisons left the preceding year proved to be a major hindrance in that the need to recover them would restrict Crassus's freedom of movement in his advance. King Artavasdes of Armenia, who had come with a large force to assist Crassus, advised a route along the foothills of southern Armenia, where the Parthian cavalry would be less effective. Crassus rejected this advice, and Artavasdes left with his troops. Instead, Crassus chose a direct march toward Seleucia (the Parthian capital on the Tigris in southern Mesopotamia), picking up the garrisons along the way. Cassius suggested a cautious path along the Euphrates, but when Abgarus, the ruler of Osrhoene (a kingdom in northern Mesopotamia), indicated that the Parthians were retreating, Crassus decided to set off across open territory.

At the town of Carrhae, Crassus was informed that a Parthian force was nearby. This consisted exclusively of cavalry under a young general called the Suren,[5] Orodes having taken his infantry north to attack Armenia. Crassus immediately sent his tired troops against the Parthian force in a broad, thin front with cavalry on the flanks. When the Parthians approached, the Romans formed a square, and when the Parthians then attacked, the Roman skirmishers and cavalry withdrew into the square. Now the Romans were surrounded, and the Parthians rained arrows in on them. Seemingly, the Romans had no adequate response to the Parthian bowmen, but the full extent of their powerlessness was not yet clear.

Crassus sent his son Publius out with a large force (about 4,000 men) to drive the enemy cavalry away. At first the Parthians retreated, but this was just a standard ruse of theirs. When Publius was a fair distance away from the main Roman force, the Parthians rounded back and drove him to a hillock. There the Romans were wiped out (only 500 were captured alive), and Publius and most of the Roman officers committed suicide. The Parthians cut his head off to display it to Crassus.

---

[5] "The Suren" was not a personal name but the title of the head of the powerful Suren clan. The personal name of the vanquisher of Crassus is not known.

Crassus had been about to come to his son's rescue, but he became dispirited and lethargic upon the news of Publius's death. Nightfall ended battle, and on their own initiative Crassus's officers ordered a retreat to Carrhae. Four thousand wounded were left behind, and the next day the Parthians slaughtered them along with all stragglers (including four cohorts that had gone astray). Crassus was doing nothing to extricate his troops from impending disaster, as he abandoned the initiative to the enemy.

Crassus decided to retreat to the Armenian foothills. One force under a legate named Octavius managed to arrive there safely, but Crassus was guided by a Greek who purposefully led him along a circuitous path to allow the Parthians time to catch up. The quaestor Cassius was disgusted with the whole situation and fled to Syria with 500 cavalry. Meanwhile, when Crassus was only a mile and a half from Octavius, the Suren came up with the Parthian army. Octavius dutifully left the safety of his position to come to Crassus's aid. The Suren then offered a truce to discuss safe passage. Crassus was unwilling to go but was forced to by the threats of his men. During the conference, a fight broke out as a result of some sort of misunderstanding, and all the Roman officers were killed. At this point, the Roman army broke up. Some surrendered on the spot, others tried (generally vainly) to fight their way back to Syria. Of 42,000 men, about half died, a quarter (12,000) made it back to Syria, and the remainder were taken alive by the Parthians. The Parthians settled them in Margiana on the far northeastern boundary of the kingdom, where they intermarried with the locals (decades later, some were still living there).

One can certainly feel sympathy for the emotional strain that Crassus suffered upon the death of his son. But it is often at times of the greatest stress that people show their true mettle, and it can only be concluded that once his army was landed in dire straits as a result of his own decisions, Crassus, so far from doing anything to rectify the situation, was paralyzed by the disaster that he had himself brought on, and did nothing to save the thousands for whom he was responsible (compare both the vigorous actions taken by Crassus's quaestor Cassius and Antony's very different behavior after a later Parthian campaign went awry; see Chapter 22). In antiquity, the manner of a man's death often colored the tradition about his life, and thus it is not surprising that Crassus has such a poor reputation in the ancient sources.

PARTHIAN THREAT

The Parthians did not do much to exploit their victory, though the threat of invasion gave rise to much anxiety in Rome. The Suren was put to death by

Orodes as a threat to himself, and this disrupted any plans for an invasion of Roman territory in 52 B.C. Meanwhile, as *quaestor pro praetore* (that is, "quaestor acting in place of the praetor"), Cassius had organized the defenses of Syria, and in 51 B.C. he beat back an ineffectual Parthian attack before the arrival of the new governor, M. Calpurnius Bibulus (Caesar's colleague as consul in 59 B.C.). The defeat of Crassus taught the Romans a lesson about the power of Parthian cavalry, and with the distraction of civil discord it would be some time before they undertook another invasion of Parthia.

BREAKDOWN OF ORDER IN ROME

Meanwhile, the breakdown of civil order continued apace in Rome. For all their hostility to the coalition, the consuls of 54 B.C., L. Domitius Ahenobarbus and Ap. Claudius Pulcher, could not accomplish anything. There were numerous trials motivated by political reasons, and the elections were marred by rampant corruption, which brought the political system into further discredit.

Surviving letters in which Cicero kept his friend Atticus and his brother Quintus (who was serving in Britain at the time with Caesar) apprised of political affairs back home give us detailed information about the electoral scandals of 54 B.C. C. Memmius and one of the other candidates had entered into a contract with the current consuls in which they agreed to remunerate the consuls if they failed to provide false senatorial witnesses to vouchsafe that legal technicalities, which would allow the old consuls to take up their provinces, had been duly carried out when they had not been (presumably this whole charade was a way for the new consuls to compensate the old ones for making sure that the consular elections they presided over went the "right" way). Not only did Memmius reveal this plot in the senate (his motives are not clear), but he even produced documentation in the form of account book entries in which the purpose of the spending was clearly laid out. In addition, the loans taken out by various candidates for electoral bribery were so great that interest rates doubled, and the astronomical sum of 100,000,000 sesterces was to be offered at the last minute to the voters of the influential "prerogative" century in the centuriate assembly if they returned the bribers.[6] (The prerogative century was the first century to vote

---

[6] It is remarkable that in response to rumors about his participation in a conspiracy of some of the candidates, Cicero denies this not because it would be wrong or illegal to engage in such practices but only on the grounds that he owed a personal obligation to one of the candidates who was excluded from the conspiracy. Not much of a stickler about principles, Cicero had apparently come to view such flagrant bribery as simply a necessary part of the electoral system.

in the first census class. This century was chosen by lot, and its vote, which was given before any other centuries cast their votes, was taken as an omen and influenced the subsequent voting.)

In the climate of outrage among the electorate at such flagrant electoral corruption, the candidates for the tribunate made an agreement among themselves to behave properly, and each left a large deposit with M. Cato, who was to declare it forfeit if he judged that the candidate had not adhered to the agreement. As Cicero remarks, the personal prestige of Cato was more influential than the legal penalties, but Cicero fails to note that like the laws, Cato was in no position to enforce regular electoral behavior unless all the candidates agreed to abide by the rules, which was clearly not the case with the consular candidates.

Chaos and rioting ensued after this almost comical scandal, and the year 53 B.C. began with another interregnum (i.e., no regular magistrates when the term of those from the preceding year expired). Though there were rumors that Pompey would be made dictator, nothing came of this. Finally, in July (!) of 53 B.C., the consuls for that year were elected under Pompey's presidency. It was at this point that news reached Rome of Crassus's debacle at Carrhae.

Clearly, the normal functioning of the governmental system at Rome was beginning to break down. While the postponement of the elections for nearly a year may not have much significance today, the results must have been extremely disconcerting at the time. Since the Romans conducted elections hierarchically, starting with the consuls and continuing down through the lower offices, the failure to carry out the consular elections meant that none of the other offices could be filled, and since there could be no promagistrates within the city, the failure to elect new magistrates meant that at the start of the new year, regular government (including the legal system) would come to a halt. Apart from these practical considerations, such unprecedented delays would have had serious consequences for the viability of the entire electoral system. It is known that well-to-do voters traveled hundreds of miles for the elections (there is evidence of Cicero and Caesar soliciting votes in distant Cisalpine Gaul), and while a small delay in the elections would have been tolerable for such men, they could hardly have been expected to hang around in the city for months until circumstances allowed the elections to be held. And if one could not have a reasonable expectation that the elections would be held in July as they were supposed to be, this would make it likely that many voters would not bother to undertake the potentially pointless trip at all. If this situation continued, what legitimacy could the elections in Rome be thought to have?

COOLING OF RELATIONS BETWEEN CAESAR AND POMPEY

In September 54 B.C., Pompey's wife Julia, the daughter of Caesar, died giving birth to a daughter (who soon died). Though Pompey wished to bury her on his estate, the crowd in Rome seized the body for a public burial near Rome. Evidently, there was much emotion at the loss of someone who represented a permanent bond between the two most powerful men in the state. Her death was an ill omen.

Caesar wished to arrange new marriages to renew the bond between him and Pompey. He proposed that Pompey should marry Octavia, the granddaughter of Caesar's sister, while Caesar would divorce the daughter of L. Piso Caesoninus cos. 58 and marry Pompey's daughter. Pompey refused. This was a bad sign, since it indicated a disinclination on Pompey's part to continue any association with Caesar. This failure to renew the marriage connection between Caesar and Pompey meant that when the number of dynasts in Rome was reduced to two by the death of Crassus in the next year, there was little to prevent the situation from deteriorating into a direct confrontation between Caesar and Pompey. In 52 B.C., Pompey would contract a new marriage that symbolized his increasing alienation from Caesar and his reconciliation with the senatorial oligarchy.

POMPEY'S THIRD CONSULSHIP

The (by now) usual bribery and violence disrupted the consular elections that should have been held in 53 B.C. to choose the magistrates for the next year, and January 52 B.C. began yet again with an interregnum. T. Annius Milo, who had organized the gangs that countered those of Clodius, was a consular candidate, while Clodius himself was running for the praetorship. By accident, the two met on the Appian Way near Bovillae south of Rome on January 18. A brawl ensued in which Clodius was wounded. When he was taken into a nearby tavern, Milo had him dragged out by his men and killed. When the body was brought back to Rome, rioting ensued, and the senate house was burned down when it was used as the place to cremate the body. The house of the interrex was also attacked. Rome was in chaos, and there were various proposals to deal with Milo.[7]

---

[7] One of the tribunes who stirred up trouble was Q. Pompeius Rufus, whose homonymous grandfather had shared the consulship with Sulla back in 88 B.C. and been killed the next year as a result of the machinations of Cn. Pompeius Strabo cos. 89 (Pompey's father) while Pompeius's father had married Sulla's daughter and been

Pompey, who was not getting along with Milo, was happy to see his candidacy ruined.

There was more talk of a dictatorship, but in late February M. Calpurnius Bibulus cos. 59 proposed, with the agreement of his father-in-law Cato, that Pompey should be elected sole consul. This would give Pompey ten months in office, a longer period than the six months of a traditional dictatorship (Sulla's precedent of an unlimited dictatorship was obviously unacceptable). Duly elected, Pompey quickly passed harsh retroactive laws on electoral corruption and the public use of violence. Because there was the threat of rioting from Clodius's supporters during Milo's trial on the charge of public use of violence, Pompey posted troops in the forum during the trial, but to no avail. When Cicero spoke in Milo's defense, he was unnerved by Clodius's supporters, whose shouting disrupted the proceedings despite the presence of Pompey's troops, and he gave a less than brilliant speech. Milo was condemned and went into exile at Massilia (modern Marseilles).[8]

POMPEY'S GROWING ALIENATION FROM CAESAR

By this point, Pompey was married to Cornelia, the daughter of the peculiarly named Q. Caecilius Metellus Pius Scipio. Born a Cornelius Scipio, he was adopted by the childless Q. Caecilius Metellus Pius cos. 80 and thus was one of the most prominent men in the senatorial oligarchy on both sides of the family. Pius Scipio was one of the candidates for the consulship in 53–52 B.C. and was now threatened with an accusation of electoral bribery. To save him, Pompey chose in the summer of 52 B.C. to have him elected as his colleague for the rest of the year.

There was some talk that Caesar should become Pompey's colleague in the consulship. For reasons that are not entirely clear, this did not happen (either Caesar did not wish to leave Gaul yet or Pompey did not want

---

killed during the rioting that resulted from the two consuls' attempts to thwart P. Sulpicius Rufus's legislation in 88 B.C. (see Chapter 7). It is an example of how difficult it is to predict the behavior of individual senators on the basis of their family background that someone who had such an impeccable Sullan heritage (for a coin of his celebrating both his grandfathers, see Coin 16) should have been working in cooperation with Clodius against the senate (and continued to do so after Clodius's death). (For what it is worth, it was his sister who had been Caesar's wife in the early 60s B.C.)

[8] When Milo later received a copy of the polished version of the speech that Cicero published, he sent Cicero a letter in which he drolly remarked that he was glad that Cicero had not actually given the published version during the trial, since this would have prevented him from being in a position to enjoy the excellent local seafood.

him as a colleague). Instead, Pompey had a law passed by all ten tribunes allowing Caesar the right to run for the consulship in absentia (it was normally necessary to declare one's candidacy in person in Rome). This piece of legislation would be very important in the arguments about Caesar's attempt to secure a second consulship.

LEX POMPEIA DE MAGISTRATIBUS

Later in 52 B.C., Pompey passed a law that dealt with the problem of the interrelated issues of electoral corruption and provincial extortion. The law was passed in accordance with a decree of the senate from the preceding year and was intended to curb corruption by providing a five-year interval between the tenure of office in the city as consul or praetor and the assumption of a provincial governorship. Candidates for high office had been borrowing money to win election on the understanding that they would use a provincial command to "acquire" enough money to pay off their debts (and no doubt have enough left over for themselves). This practice would be more difficult if the magistrates would not be able to pay off such loans for at least seven years (one in the city as magistrate, the five-year interval, and at least one in the province). The new procedure of assigning governors meant that for five years some sort of interim mechanism for appointing governors would have to be worked out, and magistrates from earlier years who had not held a provincial command were called upon to serve as governors until the present magistrates would become available to serve as governors in 46 B.C. This resulted in M. Calpurnius Bibulus cos. 59 becoming governor of Syria in 51 B.C., where Cassius had been acting since 53 B.C. in place of the dead Crassus, and in Cicero cos. 63 becoming governor of Cilicia in 51–50 B.C. (Cicero had given up his provincial appointment in favor of his colleague back in 63 B.C., and in light of his lack of military inclinations or talent, the urbane and eloquent consular had no desire to govern a barbarous neck of the woods like Cilicia.)

The new system of appointing provincial governors had very serious implications for Caesar's command, which would expire in 49 B.C. In addition, Pompey's new law prescribed running for office in person, and since it made no reference to the tribunician law that had recently been enacted for Caesar, it implicitly abrogated the earlier exemption.[9] When Caesar's friends pointed this out, Pompey claimed that he had only made a mistake, and he added the exemption into the final copy, a procedure of

---

[9] It was a regular principle of Roman law that a new enactment abrogated earlier provisions at variance with it.

dubious legal validity. It would seem that Pompey was not terribly eager to protect Caesar's interest, but at the same time he was not yet prepared for an open confrontation.

RECHTSFRAGE

In the two years between Pompey's third consulship in 52 B.C. and the outbreak of civil war in early 49 B.C., the major political issue was what was to be done with Caesar. His command was soon to expire, and if he could not manage to secure a second consulship before giving up his command, he was quite likely to be condemned in a prosecution based on his illegal activities as consul back in 59 B.C.[10] Sulla had reintroduced the old provision dictating a ten-year interval between offices, and thus Caesar was legally eligible for reelection in 49 B.C. to the consulship of the following year (though talk of a consulship in 52 B.C. shows that it would have been perfectly easy to secure an exemption if Pompey agreed).

Rechtsfrage means "legal issue" in German, and this term is used to describe the extensive scholarly dispute concerning the details of the termination of Caesar's Gallic command in the late 50s B.C. and his efforts to secure a second consulship. For once, there is if anything too much ancient evidence. Unfortunately, the sources do not clearly lay out the basic nature of the dispute but simply recount various details, taking the broader issue for granted. Modern scholars have been forced to make their own reconstructions of the overall dispute and fit the ancient evidence, which is itself often susceptible to more than one interpretation, into these. This is not the place for a lengthy treatment of the various hypotheses, which often depend upon very detailed arguments based on the niceties of Roman constitutional practice. Fortunately, the most important issue – when Caesar could be replaced in Gaul – is clear enough in broad outline.

The lex Vatinia of 59 B.C. initially gave Caesar command of Cisalpine Gaul and Illyricum for a five-year period. (At a later date in the same year,

---

[10] The only direct attestation of Caesar's main fear being the threat of prosecution comes from a comment he is said to have made after the battle of Pharsalus (quoted in Suetonius, *Life of the Deified Julius* 30), but the arguments sometimes made against accepting this statement are weak; it is perfectly plausible for Caesar to have anticipated that he would be gotten rid of through prosecution just as Milo had recently been. In particular, there could be no doubt that large-scale bribery was by now obligatory in the consular elections, and the consuls designate were clearly liable to being stripped of their office if convicted of electoral bribery. If Caesar's enemies were in control of the courts, there was every reason to imagine that even victory at the polls would be quickly nullified.

Transalpine Gaul was given to Caesar by a decree of the senate. It would seem that the extension of the command in 55 B.C. covered all three areas, since in subsequent discussion there was no talk of any separate treatment of them.) There is much dispute about the exact date of the passage of the law in 59 B.C., but we know that the lex Vatinia stipulated that Caesar could not be succeeded in command before March 1, 54 B.C. His command was then extended for a further five years by the lex Pompeia Licinia of 55 B.C. There is no agreement about when exactly this second five-year term expired or even how the second five-year period was to be determined. In particular, we know that the lex Pompeia Licinia forbade any discussion of Caesar's command before March 1, 50 B.C.[11] It is sometimes argued that this prohibition of senatorial discussion of his replacement was the sole protection granted to Caesar by the lex Pompeia Licinia, which in effect prevented his replacement before January 1, 49 B.C. Cicero, however, refers to a definite legal limit (dies legis, or "day determined by law"), which should refer to a specific terminal date comparable to the one provided by the lex Vatinia. The most straightforward way to phrase such a provision would be to specify that Caesar could not be replaced until the fifth calends of March after the expiration of his command under the lex Vatinia, that is, March 1, 49 B.C.

In his account of the civil war, Caesar claims that his sole desire in early 49 B.C. was to continue to enjoy the privilege, granted to him by the law of the ten tribunes in 52 B.C., of being allowed to run for the consulship in absentia, but this claim seems to be a red herring used by Caesar to distract attention from his real problem. The exemption had been granted in 52 B.C. as a fob for his not holding the consulship with Pompey. If Caesar had sought a second consulship prior to 49 B.C., he certainly would have needed such an exemption, and there was in fact some thought of adopting this solution.[12] In 51 B.C., when Caesar went to Cisalpine Gaul to support Mark Antony's candidacy for the augurate, we are told (Hirtius, Gallic War 8.50) that Caesar also intended to commend his candidacy in

---

[11] Such a provision did not appear in the lex Vatinia, and presumably the reason why it was added to the later law was to avoid the sort of acrimonious debates about Caesar's replacement that began in the senate as early as 56 B.C. Thus, the lex Pompeia Licinia prohibited such discussion until 50 B.C. when Caesar's provinces could finally be discussed in the senatorial debate about the provinces to be allotted among the consuls who would be elected in July, 50 B.C., for the following year (when Caesar's replacement was permissible).

[12] It is true that Sulla renewed the old prohibition of holding the consulship for a second time within a ten-year interval, but Pompey's third consulship in 52 B.C. after he had held the office for the second time in 55 B.C. shows that under the right circumstances it would have been possible to get around the ten-year rule.

the following year, which can only indicate a plan to run in 50 B.C., before the expiration of his command, for the consulship 49 B.C. As it turned out, this possibility was not pursued. We are not told why this plan was not implemented, but the failure to win reelection in 50 B.C. was a serious defeat for Caesar. Since it was permissible to replace Caesar in Gaul as of March 1, 49 B.C., and the consular elections would not be held until July at the earliest, then Caesar would be liable to prosecution as soon as his successor arrived in Gaul.[13] This he had to prevent at all costs, and at the start of 49 B.C., the hostility of both consuls left him with no choice but to thwart any senatorial decision about the provincial assignments through tribunician veto – or resort to war.

RUNDOWN TO CIVIL WAR

The basic issue was whether an accommodation would be reached with the proconsul in Gaul or an attempt would be made to crush him, and Pompey's attitude was the most important factor in determining which course would be followed in the senate. If he refused to cooperate with Caesar's many enemies (especially the group centered around Cato) in taking action against him, then those who were hostile to Caesar would, as always, be helpless. If, on the other hand, Pompey finally achieved a reconciliation with the oligarchs (as he had planned to do back in 62 B.C.) and followed the tendency indicated by his marriage to Pius Scipio's daughter, then any attempt to force Caesar's hand by ending his proconsulship before his election to a second consulship was likely to result in war unless Caesar was ready to acquiesce in his own destruction (an unlikely event). Well into 50 B.C., Pompey's attitude remained unclear (he probably was not so sure himself), but by late 50 B.C. he was determined to resolve the matter by war.

In 51 B.C., one consul, M. Claudius Marcellus, was strongly anti-Caesarian and worked for Caesar's replacement in Gaul in violation of the lex Pompeia Licinia of 55 B.C. He was opposed by his colleague and various tribunes. From now on, Caesar would be careful to have one of the tribunes in his pocket to make sure that no motion was passed that was prejudicial to his interests. In late 51 B.C., the senate passed a decree that on March 1, 50 B.C., the consuls should immediately put before the senate

---

[13] It has been argued that magistrates designate were exempt from prosecution, but this appears to be incorrect. Thus, even if he could secure reelection, he would probably still be exposed to prosecution for nine months, but even if he would gain protection from prosecution as consul designate, he would remain vulnerable during the months leading up to the election (normally held in July).

the issue of the consular provinces. The senate also directed Pompey to seek the return of the legion that he had lent Caesar back in 53 B.C. at the time of the great revolt in Gaul (see Chapter 17). Pompey agreed but refused to do so immediately.

Of the two consuls of 50 B.C., C. Claudius Marcellus (cousin of the consul of the preceding year and husband of Caesar's grandniece Octavia) continued the opposition to Caesar. The other, L. Aemilius Lepidus, was the son of M. Aemilius Lepidus cos. 78, and Caesar won him over by providing him with 36,000,000 sesterces to complete his restoration of a public building in the Forum that had been built by an ancestor. In addition, Caesar bought himself a tribune, C. Scribonius Curio (son of the homonymous consul of 76 B.C.), by agreeing to pay off his massive debts. Up until now Curio had been a vehement opponent of Caesar, and in February he used a minor dispute with the senate as a pretext to go over to Caesar. From this point on, Curio steadfastly vetoed any measure dealing with the provinces and put Pompey on the defensive by suggesting that he and Caesar should both give up their provincial commands (Pompey had in the meanwhile laid down his command in Spain under the lex Trebonia of 55 B.C. and been given a new five-year command on the basis of a decree of the senate). Unless Curio could be persuaded to relent, no change in provincial government would be possible, and the old governors (including Caesar) would remain in command in 49 B.C.

Various events went against Caesar in 50 B.C., no doubt strengthening his resolve not to yield. There was disquieting news about the Parthians, and the senate decreed that Pompey and Caesar should each send a legion to Syria. As his contribution, Pompey chose the legion that he had lent Caesar, who was thus obligated to give up two. Caesar complied, but he gave the departing legionaries a gift of 1,000 sesterces each (at a cost of more than 5,000,000 sesterces) and raised new levies to replace them. As it turned out, the eastern crisis soon dissipated, and the two legions remained in Italy, where they were now at Pompey's immediate disposal.

Worse news came with the consular elections of 50 B.C. Caesar's candidate, Ser. Sulpicius Galba (one of his legates in Gaul), was defeated, and two stalwart opponents of his, C. Claudius Marcellus (brother of the consul of 51 B.C.) and L. Cornelius Lentulus Crus, were returned. It would be less easy for Caesar to prevent action against him in 49 B.C. if both consuls were determined to act against his interests. Two of the tribunes returned for 49 B.C. were strong supporters, however. In particular, M. Antonius (son of the homonymous praetor of 74 B.C. and commonly known in English as Mark Antony) had served Caesar as quaestor in Gaul in 52 B.C.

By late 50 B.C., it was clear that Caesar's tribunes could obstruct any proposal in the senate to replace Caesar, and thus a political stalemate in Rome would result unless drastic action was taken. In December, the consul C. Marcellus attempted to take advantage of a dispute between Curio and the censor Ap. Claudius Pulcher to have Curio censured in the senate. Curio manipulated the event to put forward another proposal that both Pompey and Caesar should give up their armies, and it was carried by a vote of 370 to 22. The leading members of the oligarchy, who were under the moral leadership of Cato and thought that through their reconciliation with Pompey they had found a military commander to counter Caesar, wished to bring matters to a head, but the main body of senators was clearly not at all inclined to force the proconsul in Gaul into rebellion. They may well have thought this inappropriate given Caesar's phenomenal success there, and in any case the bitter memory of the last civil war no doubt made many leery of recklessly precipitating a new one. The hard-liners in the senate would not give up, however. Without senatorial authorization, the consul Marcellus went to Pompey the next day with the consul designate Lentulus and entrusted him with the defense of Italy by handing over to him a symbolic sword, which Pompey accepted. This little drama not only proclaimed the consul's expectation that war would soon break out but also served as a public demonstration of the oligarchy's reconciliation with Pompey, whom they recognized as their military leader in the coming confrontation with Caesar (though as it turned out, Pompey at first had some trouble controlling other commanders). Not surprisingly, a last-ditch proposal by Caesar that he would give up Transalpine Gaul and all but one or two legions was rejected by Pompey, supposedly on the advice of Cato. When Cicero, who had recently returned from Cilicia, saw Pompey on December 10, he saw no hope for compromise on Pompey's part, though he continued to try and negotiate an acceptable compromise. The stage was now set for the outbreak of the civil war in January 49 B.C.

QUESTIONS FOR STUDY AND REFLECTION

1. In what way was the question of the legality of Caesar's measures as consul a major issue in the 50s B.C.?
2. What exactly was the "coalition" formed by Pompey, Caesar, and Crassus? What were its purposes, and what effect did it have on politics in Rome? How effective was the coalition at controlling the political scene in Rome?

3. Why was Pompey the weakest link in the coalition? How did he and Crassus get along? What was Pompey's ultimate political goal? How did his attitude toward Caesar change during the course of the 50s B.C.?

4. What was P. Clodius's contribution to the breakdown of the political order in Rome? Why was he so hostile to Cicero? Why did the recall of Cicero become such a popular cause? What exactly did Clodius want himself?

5. What circumstances led to the meeting of Pompey, Caesar, and Crassus at Luca? What was its outcome, and what effect did it have?

6. What were the provisions of the lex Trebonia and the lex Pompeia Licinia?

7. What were Crassus's motives in seeking his Eastern command? What effect did his death have on the relationship between Pompey and Caesar?

8. What caused the electoral system to break down toward the end of the 50s B.C.? What effect did bribery and violence have on this situation?

9. What actions and events manifest Pompey's growing disaffection from Caesar in the years after Crassus's death?

10. What was at stake in the issue about the termination of Caesar's command in Gaul? What was Pompey's attitude toward Caesar's predicament? What was Caesar's goal? How did his opponents wish to take advantage of the situation? How did Caesar try to thwart them?

19

CIVIL WAR AND CAESAR'S VICTORY

SHOWDOWN IN THE SENATE

Whatever the technical details about the terminal date of Caesar's command in Gaul, it is clear that by the start of 49 B.C., Caesar was legally outmaneuvered. Under present legal circumstances, he could be replaced in his provinces before the elections that summer and would have to reenter the city and lose his imperium to run in those elections; even if he did win, he would be subject for months to prosecution on various counts until he could once more have immunity through holding office. With Pompey now reconciled to his enemies and both consuls hostile, there was no hope of securing some sort of new legal privilege to rectify the situation. (It is noteworthy that a constant theme in Caesar's proposals right before and right after the outbreak of armed conflict in January 49 B.C. was that he and Pompey should both give up their military commands. Caesar apparently felt that if he gave up his command while Pompey retained his troops in Spain, those troops could be used to back up any moves to destroy Caesar politically in Italy.) All Caesar could do was hope that the two tribunes favorable to him would block any action that threatened him, especially the appointment of his replacement in Gaul. Since his enemies were intransigent and intended to force him either to give in and face political ruin or to resort to war, the situation quickly came to a head.

The consul L. Cornelius Lentulus Crus presided over the senate in January 49 B.C. and immediately began discussion of Caesar's command in a way hostile to Caesar. If Caesar's account is to be believed, Lentulus Crus enjoined the senate to stand firm and berated those in favor of compromise. On January 6, the senate voted for the proposal of Pompey's father-in-law Pius Scipio that Caesar should disband his army in Gaul before some fixed date. It is suspicious that Caesar, who harps upon the claim that his sole wish was to retain the permission to stand for the consulship in absentia that had been provided for in 52 B.C. by the law of the ten tribunes, avoids stating what this "fixed date" was. Presumably it was the date established for the end of the command under the lex Pompeia Licinia, namely March 1 (the date obviously was not January 1, since that date had already passed). The probable reason why Caesar avoids stating this date is that it was fully in accord with the lex Pompeia Licinia, and the privilege of being allowed to stand in absentia was beside the point, since this privilege was of no use to him if he could not also maintain his command until he became consul. In any event, apart from the unobjectionable date, the proposal undercut Caesar's position by the clever use of the senate's recognized authority to make arrangments for the disposition of troops without dealing with the contentious issue of Caesar's replacement. What was there for him to complain about if he was not replaced but merely had to disband his army now that Gaul was finally subdued? From Caesar's point of view, this proposal would have removed the only thing keeping him safe against his enemies in Rome, so the two tribunes working on his behalf, M. Antonius and Q. Cassius Longinus, vetoed it. On the next day (January 7), the senate passed the senatus consultum ultimum (see Chapter 3), enjoining the magistrates and promagistrates (i.e., Pompey) to save the state. Caesar's two tribunes fled, though no action had actually been taken against them.[1] Once Caesar's tribunes were gone, the senate finally made arrangements for sending out new governors in accordance with the lex Pompeia de magistratibus of 52 B.C. The most important of these was that L. Domitius Ahenobarbus cos. 54 (Cato's son-in-law and Caesar's implacable enemy) was to replace Caesar in Gaul.

By the end of the previous December, it was clear that a political impasse could result in military conflict and that such a conflict was desired by many. Accordingly, both Caesar and Pompey had drawn up contingency plans, and the flight of the two tribunes to Caesar set these plans in motion. Their interaction would trigger a full-scale civil war.

Pompey's Intentions

Pompey's plans were more fixed. By December of 50 B.C., he was clearly determined to fight Caesar, and to induce his senatorial allies to go along with him, he claimed that he could stamp the ground to raise troops.

---

[1] Presumably, the purpose of passing the decree was to intimidate the tribunes. It is not self-evident how the decree, which had previously been passed during situations involving rioting, could have been utilized against tribunes who were peacefully exercising their accepted right of veto, but the senate could have voted that anyone thwarting the distribution of provincial commands was undermining the well-being of the state and thereby subject to the decree.

He apparently stated that he had ten legions ready; if so, he must have misleadingly included his troops in Spain. As it was, he had at hand in Italy only the two legions recalled from Caesar in 51 B.C. to reinforce Syria but never sent there (see Chapter 18). Under the circumstances, he must have known that Italy could not be held against Caesar's veteran legions, and his intended strategy had probably always been to abandon Italy for Greece and gather his forces there. But he could not tell this to his senatorial friends – they surely would not have gone along with the plans to drive Caesar to war if they had realized how precarious the military situation in Italy was – and it was rather a shock to them when he told them in January that it was impossible to defend Italy (an associate of Cato snidely told Pompey that now was the time to stamp the ground).

Knowing that his position in Italy was untenable, Pompey decided that it would be necessary in the event of war to withdraw to Greece, where he could use his control of the Republican fleet to marshal the resources of the East and then return to Italy like Sulla. According to Cicero, his policy was "Sulla could do it, why can't I?" Given the unprincipled and selfish nature of Pompey's earlier career, it is hardly surprising that he wished to act in a manner that seems to have been inspired by Sulla's bloody return to Italy. Such an attitude on the part of the informal military leader of the senatorial opposition to Caesar did not bode well for the future course of events.

CAESAR'S PLANS

Caesar's plans in early January 49 B.C. are much less easy to make out. Two factors tend to obscure his intentions. First, in his later account of the war (the *Civil War*), he purposefully obfuscates about the outbreak of open warfare in order to lessen his responsibility for the start of the fighting. Luckily, Cicero's surviving correspondence serves to correct Caesar's misleading and at times mendacious account. Second, it seems clear that during the course of January, Caesar's aims changed drastically under the influence of unfolding events, and for this reason there has been a tendency to read his later actions back into the early stages of the conflict. It would seem that at first Caesar merely wished to make a demonstration of military force, seemingly to show his enemies in the senate that he could not be gotten rid of without a fight. He then made certain demands, but unfortunately we do not know what these were. Presumably, they somehow guaranteed him protection from prosecution and allowed him to run for the consulship in safety. Even though the senate eventually agreed to what he asked for, he embarked upon a full-scale invasion of Italy all the same. This apparently contradictory set of circumstances needs to be explained.

At the start of 49 B.C. Caesar was waiting with one legion on the northern side of the river Rubicon, which separated his province of Cisalpine Gaul from Italy proper. The subsequent movements of his forces indicate that he had a number of legions stationed in southern Gaul. Clearly, he was prepared for the worst, but his failure to have all of his troops immediately available shows that he could not have been determined to fight a major war right away. When the two tribunes reached Caesar on about January 10,[2] he promptly proclaimed his cause to be the protection of the rights of the tribunes. On about the fourteenth, he crossed the river Rubicon and advanced as far as Ancona, where he halted.[3] At this point, he entered into negotiations – and awaited reinforcements.

REACTION IN ROME

When news of the advance reached Rome on about the seventeenth, there was general outrage in the senate at Pompey's perceived lack of preparation, and the magistrates fled south with him to Campania. Representatives were sent to Caesar to protest this action and find out exactly what he wanted. Basically, he agreed to give up his command in Gaul and run for the consulship in person so long as Pompey left for Spain. His terms were pretty much accepted by the senate. Cicero was disgusted by the concessions, and Cato made noises about causing trouble, but it would seem that Caesar's demonstration of force had convinced most people in the senate that it was preferable to reach an agreement with him, and the same embassy was sent back to tell him of the acceptance of his terms. It appears that by the time that Caesar received the second embassy in late January, he had changed his mind. Even though he continued to negotiate, he had decided to seek a military solution. This decision marked the demise of the Republic.

---

[2] The Roman calendar was seriously out of alignment with the sun through Caesar's neglect of his duties as pontifex maximus (see Chapter 20), and at this time it was about seven weeks ahead of the seasons.

[3] The crossing itself was a carefully staged piece of drama, and the famous quotation "the die is cast" is generally misunderstood. The standard English translation suggests that he meant that there was no turning back, but what he actually said probably means "Let 'er rip." The phrase is a quotation from a lost play of the Greek playwright Menander, and the Latin version that is preserved in Suetonius is transmitted incorrectly. The Greek verbal form (a perfect imperative) shows that the Latin translation should be *alea iacta esto* (not *est*). The point is not that the die has been thrown (and hence cannot be stopped) but that it should be in play (that is, a wish for the game of chance to be in operation).

Republican Countermeasures

When certain magistrates raised new levies to hold the towns bordering the area occupied by Caesar in his initial advance, Pompey told them not to. His advice was ignored, since the men to whom he was giving it were magistrates of the Roman People with imperium and he was simply a prestigious consular. Unlike Caesar, who was the undisputed leader of his side, Pompey's position was not constitutionally clear, and at times he had trouble getting the Republican military commanders to follow his lead. Furthermore, Pompey was apparently unwilling to make his decision to abandon Italy public knowledge, so that he could not spell out clearly why it was inadvisable for the magistrates of the Roman People to offer direct resistance to a proconsul who was clearly invading Italy. (For a coin minted by the consuls' authority at the start of the war, see Coin 19.)

It appears that military strategy was not the only thing the Republicans inherited from Sulla. Caesar clearly indicates in his account his opponents' intention to carry out a bloodbath if they won. He is obviously a biased witness, but Cicero harbored similar suspicions about the intentions of the leading Republicans. Such an attitude would not be surprising among those whose families had come to dominate the senate through their support of Sulla – and been rewarded for their support with the proceeds of his proscriptions.

Caesar's Full-Scale Invasion of Italy

In late January, Caesar suddenly resumed his military operations and quickly overran the positions that had been established by various magistrates around the area that he had initially occupied. When Cicero learned of this, he was astonished that Caesar took this action when his requests had been conceded by the senate.

Three considerations that became apparent only during the course of the negotiations may well have led him to change his mind.

1. His army was unflinching in its loyalty. Not only was this true of the troops but also of the officers. Whereas Sulla had been able to count on the loyalty of only one of his officers during his march on Rome in 88 B.C., only one of Caesar's officers failed to stand by him.[4] Caesar's military success and bribery had clearly won the devotion of his army.

---

[4] This was T. Labienus, who overtly espoused the cause of constitutional propriety but was an old adherent of Pompey's. His defection was hailed by Cicero and apparently rankled Caesar, who had praised Labienus as his right-hand man in his *Gallic War* but vilified him as an implacable and bloodthirsty opponent in his *Civil War*.

2. His march into Italy did not meet with disapproval from the local citizens. Caesar had certainly won great prestige from his Gallic conquests, and the fact that he was apparently not bent on plunder must have come as a pleasant surprise to the wealthy, who no doubt had the savagery of Sulla's return to Italy fresh on their minds (see below).

3. The lack of military preparedness on the part of Pompey and the magistrates would have become increasingly obvious. Whereas Caesar had a large army of loyal veterans to command as he wished, his opponents had comparatively feeble forces available and were disorganized.

Given these circumstances, Caesar must have decided that even though the senate had agreed to his initial demands, any possible reentry into regular Roman politics still left him seriously exposed to the machinations of his enemies. Hence, he decided that he could gain more by appealing to the arbitrament of arms. It is impossible to know when exactly in January he made the decision to reject a political settlement and resort to open war. Certainly, he awaited the arrival of reinforcements from Gaul before resuming operations, though what role the timing of their arrival played in his thinking cannot be ascertained. It seems that once Caesar decided upon the military option in mid to late January, his continuing negotiations were simply a ploy to string the senate along until he was ready to launch his assault without any warning (after all, he had used exactly this stratagem against the Helvetii back in 58 B.C.).

In the face of Caesar's onslaught, Pompey finally declared openly that Italy could not be held, and announced his decision to cross over to Greece. He also issued an edict declaring that anyone who was not with him was against him, a move that seemed to prepare the ground for a repeat of Sulla's proscriptions after the anticipated return from the East. Pompey withdrew his forces toward Brundisium with the intention of crossing the Adriatic from there, and Caesar pursued him, arriving at the port on March 1. He still tried to restore his relations with Pompey, but this negotiating was presumably just a ploy to hinder Pompey's departure. Caesar tried by force to prevent Pompey's ships from setting sail, but by March 17, Pompey had managed to escape with his remaining troops. Italy was now in Caesar's hands.

CAESAR SEEKS LEGITIMACY

Given Caesar's earlier associations with the Marian and popularis side of politics and the fact that he was waging war on the senate and magistrates, it would have been natural for people to assume the worst of him and expect an attack on the wealthy from him. Caesar did his best to allay such fears and to present himself as a defender of constitutional propriety who posed no threat to the social order.

- Caesar argued (rather implausibly) that he was the defender of the constitution. In addition to his claim to be upholding the violated rights of the tribunate, he pointed to the mechanics of Pompey's law on magistrates from 52 B.C. as an example of the other side's subversion of Roman traditions.[5] He also claimed that he was seeking nothing but the privileges of the law of the ten tribunes of 52 B.C., an assertion that was a rather inadequate description of the constitutional issues. In any case, these claims were meant to give a patina of propriety to what was basically a preventive effort to thwart his enemies' use of their control of the political institutions in Rome to destroy Caesar's political career.
- Numerous important Republicans fell into Caesar's hands, and these Caesar released. With this policy of clemency, he was consciously avoiding Sulla's bloody behavior, and the slogan "Caesar's clemency" went a long way to winning over the uncertain at the start of the conflict. As a result of both the favorable impression made by this policy and the obvious fact that he had a better force than Pompey, the towns of Italy generally went over to him voluntarily. (Caesar seems to have been genuinely disinclined to kill and certainly lacked Sulla's vindictiveness, but as the war dragged on and his opponents showed no sign of giving up – and sometimes even resumed fighting after being pardoned – even Caesar's clemency would eventually wear thin.)
- Along with his refusal to act vindictively toward his foes, Caesar also steered clear of the sort of attacks on private property that were feared by the wealthy. Though he would take (comparatively) moderate steps to deal with the excessive indebtedness into which many had fallen, he did nothing to threaten basic property rights, and this unanticipated moderation did much to cause the well-to-do to leave Caesar alone in his struggle with his enemies.

Nonetheless, even if Caesar had won the acquiescence at least of the non-political landowners of Italy, the fact remained that he was acting against the legitimate government in Rome and that the magistrates and leading senators were overwhelmingly opposed to him. (For coins that illustrate confusion in the messages associated with Caesar during the war, see Coins 20 and 21.)

---

[5] In the *Civil War*, Caesar makes out that appointing ex-magistrates as governors when their imperium had in the meanwhile expired – including, conveniently enough, the appointment of L. Domitius Ahenobarbus cos. 54 as his own replacement – was a violation of traditional practice. This it was, though he ignores the fact that the appointments were based on the lex Pompeia de magistratibus that Pompey had legitimately passed in his third consulship.

Caesar in Rome

Once Pompey and the Republicans had crossed over to Greece, Caesar marched on Rome to try and put his constitutional position on a more secure footing. Though most senators had fled with Pompey, a few remained. In particular, Caesar sought the cooperation of Cicero, who had not gone east and was uncertain of what course he should take. If Cicero could be persuaded to remain in Italy if not to come out in active support of Caesar, this would do much to legitimize Caesar's actions. In the end, Caesar could secure the assistance of a very small number of reputable senators, and after much hesitation Cicero crossed over to Greece – his desire to win and retain the approval of the leadership of the senate and his misguided sense of indebtedness toward Pompey won out over his doubts about their intentions (and competence).

Though the leading members of the senate and the mass of senators went into opposition against him, Caesar had many young members of the senatorial oligarchy serving under him as junior commanders. Increasingly, the refusal of senior senators to cooperate with him forced him to rely on his own resources, and this plus the success of his actions led to the abandonment of this "constitutional" stance and its replacement by a more autocratic attitude. As his prestige continued to rise as a result of his repeated victories in the field, the comparatively low rank of his subordinates would only enhance his own status as the preeminent leader of a faction based on loyalty to him alone.

The visit to Rome also showed that Caesar's defense of the rights of the tribunes was a fraud. He was forbidden by one tribune (L. Caecilius Metellus, son of the homonymous consul of 68 B.C. and nephew of Q. Metellus Creticus cos. 69) to set foot in the central treasury (which had been left behind in the precipitous flight of January 18). Caesar had soldiers cast the tribune aside and remove 15,000 bars of gold, 30,000 of silver, and 30,000,000 sesterces. He desperately needed these vast sums of money to defray the costs of a prolonged war, and constitutional propriety was not about to stand in his way. So much for the rights of the tribunes.

Caesar Conquers Spain

Pompey's abandonment of Italy left it in Caesar's control, and the question for Caesar was what to do next. Clearly an immediate invasion of Greece was out of the question (Caesar had no real fleet), so he decided to seize the opportunity to secure his rear by attacking Spain, where three legates of Pompey controlled seven legions. By April 19, Caesar reached

Massilia in Gaul, which had gone over to the Republicans and admitted L. Domitius Ahenobarbus cos. 54, who was the senate's replacement for Caesar in Transalpine Gaul and whom Caesar had captured and released in Italy back in January. After a few weeks of unsuccessful attacks on the town, Caesar left the siege in the hands of a subordinate (D. Junius Brutus, who would later be one of his assassins, and proceeded with most of his army to Spain.

Two of Pompey's legates, L. Afranius cos. 60 and M. Petreius, joined forces (five legions) to oppose Caesar. (Both had long served Pompey as legates. It was Afranius who had vainly attempted to aid Pompey as consul in 60 B.C., and Petreius had commanded the troops that defeated Catiline's army in early 62 B.C.) After initial operations in which Caesar's supplies were threatened, he outmaneuvered their army at Ilerda. The morale of the Pompeian troops was dubious, and when Caesar cut off their water supply, Afranius and Petreius capitulated, with the third legate soon following suit. In only forty days, Caesar completely undermined Pompey's position in Spain. He then disbanded Pompey's legions, releasing the men from service.

Caesar left Q. Cassius Longinus, one of the tribunes who had fled to him back in January, in charge of Spain. (This would prove to be a poor choice.) It is a sign of the breakdown of traditional constitutional practice and of the usurpation of public authority by powerful individuals that Caesar gave Longinus the meaningless title *tribunus plebis pro praetore* ("propraetorian tribune of the plebs"). This title indicates that even though as tribune of the plebs Longinus was not supposed to leave the city of Rome at all, Caesar was bestowing praetorian rank imperium on him by his own authority. Under normal circumstances, imperium could be acquired only through election in Rome, and a legitimate holder of imperium could delegate it to a subordinate only to a very limited degree (and certainly not for independent activity over the course of several years).

Caesar Back in Italy

In the meanwhile, Caesar was appointed dictator by a praetor in accordance with a specially passed law. As he returned to Italy, Massilia was captured and stripped of its own privileges as a punishment for defending itself against him in the name of his legitimate replacement as governor of the province. Back in Italy by late 49 B.C., Caesar had himself elected consul for the following year along with P. Servilius Isauricus, son of the consul of 78 B.C. under whom Caesar had served his early military duty. Caesar tried to get major disturbances in Italy under control with a plan for debt reduction (it had been feared that he would cancel debts altogether).

Curio in Africa

Before setting off for Spain in 49 B.C., Caesar put C. Scribonius Curio, who had defended his interests as tribune in 50 B.C., in charge of a four-legion force to subdue Africa. Cato had been placed in charge of Sicily by the senate back in January, but he abandoned it to Curio in order to avoid bloodshed. Curio then invaded Africa with only two legions, and disaster ensued. When the Republican governor cooperated with King Juba of Numidia, Curio's force was overwhelmed, and he was killed. (This whole campaign was comparatively unimportant, but Caesar played it up in his *Civil War* as a literary device to contrast the loyalty unto the death of his subordinates with the unseemly squabbling that he ascribes to Pompey's legates in Spain.)

Invasion of Greece

By 48 B.C., Caesar was firmly in control of Spain, Gaul, and Italy, and he decided that the time had now come to confront Pompey directly. In January, Caesar tried to ferry his army across from Brundisium in the face of Republican naval superiority. He managed to ferry half of it across to the south Illyrian shore, when bad weather cut short the operation, and it was not until April that he could get the rest over. In the meanwhile, he again entered into negotiations, proposing that both sides should disarm and resume the attempt at settlement in Rome. Since Caesar was now consul and controlled the magistracies in Rome, this would suit him perfectly well. The Republicans could not agree to this. (There was a notion that elections for new magistrates should be carried out in the army in Greece, but this highly unusual step was not taken, and the magistrates of 49 B.C. continued to serve as promagistrates.)

From April until July, there was a lot of counter-maneuvering and digging of trenches in the area of Dyrrachium (the port on the eastern shore of the Adriatic opposite Brundisium). Finally, in July, Pompey pierced Caesar's line in such a way as to render his position untenable. As usual, Caesar's luck held, and he managed to slip away before the hapless Pompey realized the full extent of his success. Caesar retreated into Thessaly, where his recent defeat led to an uncooperative reception. To mollify his troops and make the Thessalians toe the line, he had the town of Gomphi sacked and plundered. From Thessaly, Caesar could follow

DEVELOPMENT OF LATE REPUBLICAN COINAGE

The minting of coins under the Republic was normally carried out by a board of three magistrates known properly as the "three men in charge of smelting and striking bronze, silver, and gold" (*tresviri aere argento auro flando feriendo*) and informally as the "three men of the mint" (*tresviri monetales*). (Occasionally quaestors or aediles also issued coins for special expenditures that they were making.) These men were normally elected in their twenties, and while they were sometimes of comparatively minor background, junior members of the most important families in the oligarchy also held the office. Early Roman coinage had no direct indication of the identity of the moneyer (as the minting officials are known in English) – only symbols (with perhaps an initial or two from the moneyer's name) were used to indicate the workshop in which the coin was produced – but soon the names of individual moneyers began to appear on the coins, often in a highly abbreviated form. Presumably, this was originally intended to show which moneyer was responsible for a particular issue of coins, but eventually the moneyers began to use the images on the coins that were marked with their name for their own purposes.

The coinages of republics, which are issued in the name of the state as a whole, tend to be fairly static, with a limited number of designs that symbolize the state appearing year after year. The coinage of the Middle Republic follows this pattern (see Coin 1). In contrast, the coinage of the Roman Empire is characterized by a wide variety of frequently changing designs that advertise messages that the emperor (or at least his mint officials) wished to be disseminated. The process of change from a republican to an imperial style of coin design developed over the last century of the Republic. First, the moneyers began to introduce rather subtle allusions to the prestige of their own families on the coinage. (For instance, the important family of the Caecilii Metelli was founded by a consul of 251 B.C. who famously brought back to Rome a number of elephants captured in battle, and for this reason an elephant's head would be a suitable image for a descendant of his to display on a coin; see Coin 11.) At the same time, standard designs of no particular significance continued to be used by some moneyers for decades more, but as the years went on, the moneyer's allusions became more concrete and obvious and these began to refer to the moneyer himself and not just to his family. Finally, as the public functions of the state came to be controlled directly by military leaders, the coinage too not only was used to advertise their programs and successes but was even issued in their name and eventually displayed their portraits. A number of coins illustrate this process, and at the same time show the messages that the moneyers of a given moment thought it worthwhile to disseminate through their coinage.

It should be borne in mind that except for issues that can be directly associated with a specific historical event, the dates of issue are conjectures based mainly on the evidence of hoards (that is, the analysis of which coins appear in which proportion with which other coins in a group of coins intentionally buried together but never recovered in antiquity). Also, the exact identity of the moneyers is sometimes obscure for several reasons. The moneyers served early in their careers, and some died before becoming prominent enough to be noticed in the historical sources. Also, the repetitive nature of Roman names (especially if the cognomen is not used) sometimes makes it at times difficult even to pin down a given moneyer's specific family, much less his relationship within it. Finally, while some moneyers belonged to prominent families, others came from relatively obscure ones of which little or nothing is known.

Note: In the heading for each coin, its numbering in the relevant numismatic catalogue is given (a number after a slash indicates a subtype):

BMC: Accession number in the coin collection of the British Museum.
HCRI: David R. Sear, *The History and Coinage of the Roman Imperators 49–27 BC* (London: Spink, 1998).
RIC: C.H.V. Sutherland and R.A.G. Carson, *Roman Imperial Coinage*, vol. 1 (London: Spink and Son, 1984).
RRC: M.H. Crawford, *Roman Republican Coinage* (London: Cambridge University Press, 1974).
Sydenham: E.A. Sydenham, *Coinage of the Roman Republic* (London: Spink and son, 1952).

Coin 1 (RCC 233/1). Here we see a typical coin (minted in about 138 B.C. by P. Aelius Paetus) with Middle Republican imagery. On the obverse is a helmeted portrait of a goddess who appears frequently on Republican coinage but whose identity is uncertain. (Inconclusive legends suggest Roma, the divine personification of the city, but the same inscription appears with other designs, including one featuring King Philip V of Macedon, and the iconography that sometimes accompanies the goddess is normally associated with Diana.) On the reverse are the Dioscuri, the semi-divine twins (Castor and Pollux) who were thought to have aided the Romans during a battle with the Latin League a few years after the foundation of the Republic. This coin is virtually identical to any number of issues going back to the start of silver coinage in the late third century B.C., and the design would be reused on numerous designs over the next decades by more traditionally minded moneyers, even as others would experiment with the possibilities for more immediate references in the designs on the coinage. Courtesy Dr. Busso Peus Nachfolger.

Coin 2 (RIC 235/1c). This coin is an early example of the realization that the image on the coin could be related directly to the moneyer. While the obverse has the traditional goddess portrait, the reverse has the famous scene in which the herdsman Faustulus (on the left) comes upon the abandoned royal children Romulus and Remus as they were being suckled by a she-wolf (on the right). (He raises them as his own children, but eventually their royal origins come to light and they go on to found the city of Rome.) The reason for selecting this scene is that the moneyer's name was Sex. Pompeius Faustulus (which appears in the archaic form "Fostulus"). The reference to the moneyer's cognomen is emphasized by the fact that the figure of Faustulus actually intrudes into the letters of the name. (Unfortunately for the moneyer, the large device has forced the legend so far outward that because of the inaccuracy of the striking process, coins normally lose the cognomen on the left or the rest of the name on the right, as in our example.) Here, the relationship of moneyer and device seems to be little more than a sort of visual pun. Later designs would make much more of the potential to make a political statement with the coin's device. It should be acknowledged that in *RRC* "Faustulus" is taken to be merely a description of the scene, apparently on the presumption that the moneyer is the Sex. Pompeius attested as pr. 119. This circular reasoning is not compelling: our knowledge of the second-century Pompeii is hardly complete (i.e., the moneyer could well be someone otherwise unattested), a legend identifying the image is unusual on Republican coinage, and in any event, if the scene is not an allusion to the moneyer's cognomen, the reason for choosing the scene is mysterious and there is no obvious reason why only one of the figures should should be identified. At the very least, this uncertainty illustrates the subjective nature of interpreting coin types. Courtesy Numismatica Ars Classica.

Coin 3 (RRC 266/1). C. Cassius (Longinus), the moneyer of this issue of 126 B.C., is an unidentified relative of L. Cassius Longinus cos. 128. As tribune in 137 B.C., the later consul Longinus introduced the use of the ballot in most trials before the People (see Chapter 1), and the coin alludes rather subtly to this reform. On the obverse a voting urn has been added behind the standard head of Roma, and while a goddess in a triumphal chariot is a common design on reverses, here the usual image of Victory has been replaced by a personification of *libertas* ("Freedom"), as indicated by the implements she holds, which are symbolic of the manumission of slaves. In effect, standard designs have been slightly modified so that the moneyer can allude to the popularity of his relative's voting reform (and presumably thereby enhance his own electoral prospects). The coin further illustrates the high regard in which the Roman electorate as a whole held its supposed freedom to vote as they pleased and not be in the thrall of the senatorial oligarchy. In any case, one might wonder how noticeable such minor symbolism was to most users of the coinage. Later coins would be much more overt in the messages conveyed in their imagery. Courtesy Numismatica Ars Classica.

Coin 4 (RRC 301/1). This coin, minted ca. 110 B.C. by P. (Porcius) Laeca, is another example of a moneyer celebrating the achievements of an ancestor. The laws passed in the second century B.C. by three different men named Porcius extended the protection of Roman citizens against being flogged or executed by Roman magistrates outside of the pomerium. One of these legislators was Cato the Elder, and another must have been the ancestor of this moneyer. The obverse has the usual head of Rome, but the reverse illustrates very vividly the new right of the Roman citizen. In the center is a Roman magistrate with imperium dressed in military attire, who is gesturing in a threatening manner toward a Roman civilian (as shown by his toga) on the left, while on the right is the magistrate's lictor, who is preparing to flog the man. At the bottom is the legend *provoco* ("I appeal," i.e., to the Roman People), which is the verbal utterance by which the citizen invokes his right of provocatio as a defense against the magistrate's menace. (Later evidence shows that the normal phrase became *civis Romanus sum* or "I am a Roman citizen"). Courtesy Numismatica Ars Classica.

Coin 5 (RRC 326/1). Issued under unknown circumstances ca. 101 B.C. by the quaestor C. Fundanius, this coin has the usual head of Roma on the obverse and a Roman imperator riding in a chariot during a triumph on the reverse. The date suggests that this *triumphator* must be C. Marius celebrating his victories over the Cimbri and Teutoni at Aquae Sextiae and Vercellae (see Chapter 5), but this connection is only implicit. Note the young rider on the nearest horse. This may be Marius's young son (who would later oppose Sulla in 82 B.C.). If this identification is correct, then perhaps this detail would have made reference to Marius's recent triumph more obvious to contemporaries. Courtesy Fritz Rudolf Künker Münzenhandlung.

Coin 6 (RRC 330/1a). The design of this coin issued in 100 B.C. is an example of self-promotion. The minters were a pair of quaestors identified only as Piso and Caepio. The former must be a member of the powerful family of the Calpurnii Pisones and the latter probably the relative (son?) of Q. Servilius Caepio cos. 106, who would later be an opponent of M. Livius Drusus in 91 B.C. (see Chapter 6). On the obverse is the god Saturn, who presumably represents the public treasury, which was housed in the temple of Saturn in the Roman Forum, thereby indicating indirectly that two moneyers were the urban quaestors who were in charge of the treasury. On the reverse are two men with ears of grain on either side; the legend below reads *ad fru(mentum) emu(ndum) ex s.c.* ("for buying grain by decree of the senate"). Presumably, the two men are the minting quaestors themselves. In this year, Caepio very publicly objected to the expense of L. Saturninus's grain legislation and was several years later tried (and acquitted) under the lex Appuleia de maiestate for his violent attempts to thwart the voting on that legislation. The exact relationship of the purchase of grain commemorated on this coin and the opposition to Saturninus's bill is unknown, but clearly the imagery on this coinage (presumably produced specifically to purchase grain) is being used to promote some sort of alternative. (This is perhaps similar to the efforts of M. Livius Drusus and M. Fannius to undermine C. Gracchus's support by offering a senatorial legislative program; see Chapter 3.) Courtesy A. Tkalec AG.

Coin 7 (Sydenham 635). This coin illustrates the inherently contradictory nature of the revolt of the Italian allies in the Social War. The coin is issued in the name of C. Papius Mutilus, one of the two "consuls" of the Italian allies, and his name appears in non-Roman format (the father's praenomen is given by itself without any abbreviation for "son of," as a Roman name would have it) and is written in the Oscan variant of the alphabet. This much proclaims its non-Roman origin, but otherwise the devices are typical of mid- to late-Republican *Roman* coinage (see Coin 1 for a very similar coin and an explanation of the imagery). The Dioscuri on the reverse symbolize divine intervention in a Roman victory from the distant past, and whatever the exact identification of the goddess on the obverse, she was definitely a symbol of the Roman state. One could hardly ask for a more concrete illustration of the fact that the geographical area known as Italy had become a social and political entity solely through the influence of Rome and that despite the ostensible goal of the revolt being separation from Rome, the revolt's ultimate cause was frustration at the Roman refusal to incorporate the Italian allies into their state. Courtesy Classical Numismatic Group.

Coin 8 (RRC 359/2). The design of this coin, which was issued in connection with Sulla's invasion of Italy, dwells emphatically on the persona of Sulla himself. The legend – L. *Sulla imp(erator) iterum* "L. Sulla, twice imperator" – emphasizes Sulla's capacity as military commander, the symbols on the reverse (two trophies and two items associated with the augurate) refer to Sulla's public achievements, and on the obverse the portrait of Venus accompanied by her son Cupid holding a palm of victory (an image not traditional in previous Roman coinage) shows a goddess closely connected to the pious Sulla (in Greek inscriptions his Latin title *felix* or "lucky" is rendered with *Aphrodisios* or "man of Aphrodite," the Greek goddess equated with Venus). The exact interpretation of these images is open to some question, but whatever the details, the importance of this type in the development of Republican coinage is clear. It is only at the time of this civil war that the habit arose of issuing coinage in the name not of the junior magistrate who was responsible for the issue but of a senior military commander (several generals from both sides minted coins in their own name). While this very personal design was unique in the civil war of 83–81 B.C. and the regular coinage soon reverted to the previous pattern, this sort of coinage commemorating a warlord would reappear in the next civil war. Courtesy Gemini LLC.

Coin 9 (RRC 367/3). A rather different message from that of the preceding coin is conveyed by this one, which was issued by Sulla's proquaestor L. Manlius (Torquatus), who apparently replaced Sulla's old quaestor L. Licinius Lucullus (who was left behind to manage affairs in Asia when Sulla moved against Italy). Whereas Coin 8 trumpets the military success bestowed on Sulla by the gods and names him alone, this design is much less provocative. It does show Sulla celebrating his triumph on the reverse (cf. the similar scene of Marius's triumph on Coin 5), but the allusion is rather unemphatic, and the rest of the coin does not dwell on Sulla (the obverse has the standard portrait of Roma, and while the obverse legend mentions Sulla, it also has the name of the issuing junior magistrate). Thus, while the design does promote Sulla's image, it does so through more traditional means that seem to harken back to regular Republican practices. Courtesy Classical Numismatic Group.

Coin 10 (RRC 364/1d). This rather uninspired design, with a head of Jupiter wearing the laurel crown of victory on the obverse and the divine personification of victory in a triumphal chariot on the reverse, was issued by Q. Antonius Balbus, who held command against Sulla as a loyalist praetor in 82 B.C. Conceivably, this issue was minted in accordance with a decree of the senate that gold and silver dedications be taken from the temples in Rome and melted down. In any case, the images clearly signify victory in a rather general sense, and certainly lack the immediacy of Sulla's designs. (Balbus was eventually killed while defending Sardinia against a lieutenant of Sulla's.) This vagueness of imagery shows how the loyalist forces opposed to Sulla lacked a charismatic leader of their own. Note the serration at edge of this coin. The planchets (blanks) of a number of issues were treated this way before striking, but the purpose of this practice is unclear; one might conjecture that this was meant to hinder clipping of the edge of the coin, but not only were not all issues produced this way, but even in those issues that do exhibit serration, not all coins were serrated. Courtesy Classical Numismatic Group.

Coin 11 (RRC 374/1). This coin was issued during Sulla's invasion of Italy by Q. Caecilius Metellus Pius imperator, who was the son of Numidicus and became the leading member of the senatorial oligarchy after Sulla's victory (in 80 B.C. he held the consulship jointly with Sulla, the husband of Metellus's cousin Metella). Metellus minted the issue in his own name, and it alludes to him and his family, though in a much less direct way than is the case with Sulla's coinage. The goddess on the obverse is the personification of *pietas* "dutifulness," which refers to the agnomen that Metellus won for his dutiful efforts to recall his father from exile. The obverse portrays an elephant, which refers to the famous incident in which L. Metellus cos. 251 captured elephants in a victory over the Carthaginians and brought them back to Rome. Thus, the symbolism is only implicit, and however much Metellus may have been acting in a nontraditional way in minting coins by his own authority, the coin places his career in the context of his senatorial forebears. Courtesy Fritz Rudolf Künker Münzenhandlung.

Coin 12 (RRC 402/1b). This gold coin (*aureus*) was struck at the time of one of Pompey's triumphs. On the obverse is a personification of Africa (identified by her wearing an elephant skin; in front of her face is a *lituus*, a crook symbolizing the college of augurs to which Pompey belonged), and the reverse portrays Pompey's ride in a triumphal chariot. In keeping with the self-aggrandizement that characterized most of his career, he is referred to simply with the name Magnus, the cognomen which he adopted because of his victories but which was not recognized by his enemies (meaning "great" in Latin, it could be interpreted as comparing Pompey "the Great" to Alexander the Great), and the title *proconsul*. The dating of this coin is problematical. The image of Africa would prima facie associate the coin with the triumph that he celebrated after conquering the province for Sulla in 81 B.C., but he is attested in a late source as ranking at that time as a propraetor, and he seems to have adopted the name Magnus only later. The coin was most likely issued at the time of his return to Rome in 70 B.C. after subduing Spain by virtue of the command that he unconstitutionally extorted from the senate back in 77 B.C. Whatever the exact date of issue, the coin is clearly intended to promote the fame of Pompey in a very direct manner that has much more to do with Sulla's propaganda from the civil war than the more subtle messages of the regular coinage, a circumstance that is hardly surprising given the constant (and often selfish) ambition that Pompey exhibited throughout his career. The rider on the horse is presumably Pompey's eldest son Gnaeus (born in the first half of the 70s B.C.), who would take over leadership of the anti-Caesarian forces after his father's death during the civil war of the 40s B.C. Courtesy British Museum.

Coin 13 (RRC 403/1). This very interesting coin alludes to the reconciliation of Rome and Italy in the aftermath of the Social War. On the reverse, the image of Italy on the left holding a cornucopia shakes hands with one of Rome on the right holding the fasces that symbolize imperium. Presumably this scene is meant to reflect the peaceful harmony that had resulted from the admission of the Italian allies to Roman citizenship. On the obverse are overlapping busts of *honor* and *virtus*, divine personifications associated with C. Marius, who built a joint temple to them. Though the words can have varying connotations, it would seem that they refer to the high office (a common meaning of the Latin word *honor*) that could be attained by a man of virtue (*virtus*), a message that implicitly repudiated the traditional prerogatives of the senatorial oligarchy. Since Marius was a strong supporter of the fair and equal distribution of the allies among the electoral tribes after the Social War, and his conflict with Sulla could be interpreted as being caused by Sulla's opposition to this policy (see Chapter 7), it is hard to escape the conclusion that the message of this coin reflects hostility to the senatorial oligarchy in the years after Sulla's victory. Unfortunately, the dating is quite conjectural (it is generally agreed that the coin dates to around 70 B.C., but there are far too few examples in hoards to provide an exact date), and the moneyers are not well known. One may be (Q. Fufius) Calenus, who supported Caesar in the later civil war and was made consul by him in 47 B.C. (Calenus would later clash with Cicero in the momentous year 43 B.C. because of Calenus's support of Antony); the identity of Cordus, the other moneyer, is quite unknown (For the serration, see the text for Coin 10.) Courtesy Numismatica Ars Classica.

Coin 14 (RRC 413/1). This coin, which was minted by L. Cassius Longinus as triumvir monetalis in ca. 63 B.C., returns to the regular mode of promoting the moneyer's family background and refers to his homonymous ancestor, who was consul in 128 B.C. (see Coin 3), As tribune in 137 B.C., the elder Cassius had extended the use of ballots into voting on trials before the People, and this association is reflected very concretely in the scene on the reverse, in which a voter is dropping a ballot marked with a V into a voting urn. On the obverse is the head of the goddess Vesta, who is associated with another famous deed of the old consul. Having a reputation for justice, he was elected in 113 B.C. to preside over a famous tribunal set up to try accusations of immorality committed by certain Vestal Virgins (priestesses of Vesta). There is a problem with the interpretation of the reverse scene. The letter "V" was used to cast a positive vote in legislative elections (for *vti rogas* or "as you propose," with a negative vote being indicated by "A" for *antiquo* or "I reject"), while the normal letters used in trials before the People were "C" for *condemno* or "I convict" and "A" for *absolvo* or "I find not guilty." Hence, the scene is apparently one of voting in a legislative election, which is not the sort covered by the lex Cassia of 137 B.C. It is conceivable that the scene on the reverse is the tribune's later election to serve as president of the trial in 113 B.C., but this seems a rather convoluted and indirect way of interpreting the scene. It is perhaps more likely that at this late date, when trials before the People had become a rare event after the full establishment of the public courts by Sulla, the exact significance of the lex Cassia was ignored, and it was simply taken to be a step in the general establishment of voting by ballot, which is here represented by a legislative election. Our moneyer went on to serve Caesar in the civil war. Courtesy Classical Numismatic Group.

Coin 15 (RRC 426/1). This coin from the mid 50s B.C. was issued by Faustus Cornelius Sulla, the dictator Sulla's son, and shows how he hoped to gain the support of those who still revered his father's memory. (The bloody victor of the civil war is generally not well thought of in modern works, and it is worth remembering that many people – including but not limited to those who had sided with him or received benefits from him – continued to think well of him.) The obverse portrays Diana, a goddess who had answered Sulla's vows before one battle. (The lituus behind indicates that Sulla was an augur, though there is a major scholarly debate as to the exact significance.) The reverse portrays the famous scene in which King Bocchus of Mauretania handed Jugurtha over to Sulla (see Chapters 4 and 7). The name "Felix" on the reverse must refer to the dictator's agnomen (see Coin 8) and was perhaps meant to suggest that the old man's good fortune had been passed on. In the event, the gods did not prove to be so kind to the son, who had only reached the quaestorship by the time the next civil war broke out in 49 B.C. (see Chapter 11). He was granted propraetorian *imperium* in the emergency session of the senate that took place once Caesar's tribunes fled, and after serving Pompey in Greece and fleeing to Africa following the defeat at Pharsalus, he was killed while attempting to make his way to Spain in the aftermath of the Republican defeat at Thapsus in 46 B.C. Courtesy A. Tkalec AG.

Coin 16 (RRC 434/1). This coin was issued by Q. Pompeius Rufus, whose grandfather was Sulla's consular colleague in 88 B.C. and whose father had married Sulla's daughter as part of an alliance between the two consuls and had then been killed in the rioting that took place when the consuls tried to thwart the legislation of P. Sulpicius Rufus on behalf of the Italian allies (see Chapter 7). On this coin of the mid 50s B.C., the moneyer could hardly be clearer in referring to the events of 88 B.C., portraying both of his famous grandfathers. Rufus was something of a turbulent politician; he was attached to P. Clodius, and as tribune in 52 B.C. he stirred up trouble after Clodius's death at the hands of T. Milo (see Chapter 18). One suspects that neither granddad would have approved of such behavior, and in any case Rufus was prosecuted for the illegal use of violence the next year by Cicero's protégé M. Caelius Rufus and went into exile after conviction. Courtesy Classical Numismatic Group.

Coin 17.

Coin 18.

Coins 17 and 18 (RRC 433/1 and 2). In these two coins of the mid 50s B.C., M. Junius Brutus (to give the birth name by which he is best known; see Appendix on Roman Names) shows his early dislike of those he perceived to be tyrants, an attitude fostered by his mother's half-brother, Cato the Younger. On Coin 17, the obverse portrays the personification of Liberty, while the reverse bears a scene in which a Roman magistrate is surrounded by lictors bearing the fasces and preceded by another attendant. The man is identified simply as Brutus, which must signify L. Junius Brutus, who according to the Roman historical tradition played a major role in expelling the tyrannical last Roman king and establishing the Republic ca. 507 B.C. and became one of the first two consuls. The Junii Bruti of the late Republic claimed to be the descendants of the ancient consul. On Coin 18, this Brutus is again portrayed, while the reverse bears a portrait described as Ahala, which refers to C. Servilius Ahala, a senator of the mid fifth century B.C. who was credited with having slain Sp. Maenius, another senator who was trying to set himself up as a tyrant. With these images of the establishment of liberty (meaning the Republican political system) and the suppression of tyrants, these coins clearly proclaim Brutus the moneyer's support of the most extreme measures against those who threatened the traditional government as interpreted by the oligarchy. At the time of the coins' minting, this must have signified opposition to the domination of the state by the coalition of Caesar, Pompey, and Crassus, and it indicates the sort of sentiment that would eventually lead Brutus to become one of the driving forces behind the later conspiracy to assassinate Caesar, who had apparently succeeded in setting himself up in the position that Ahala had aspired to four centuries earlier. (Note that the two portraits are bearded because the Romans of the Late Republic were aware that unlike themselves their distant ancestors did not shave.) Coin 17 courtesy Lübke and Wiedemann KG; coin 18 courtesy A. Tkalec AG.

Coin 19 (RRC 441/1=HCRI 2). This rather subdued design was issued by the urban quaestor Cn. Nerius in the first year of the civil war started by C. Caesar in 49 B.C. The obverse portrays Saturn as a symbol of Nerius's position (see Coin 6), while the reverse has various military standards plus an unusual legend indicating the consulship of L. Lentulus and C. Marcellus (Republican coins did not normally give the consular date). The standards obviously refer to the military defense of the Republic against Caesar's attack, and the consuls are presumably mentioned as the representatives of the legitimate government (rather than the unofficial general Pompey). Courtesy Leu Numismatik AG.

Coin 20 (RRC 443/1=HCRI 9). This coin reflects something of the confusion in the self-portrayal adopted by Caesar in the early stages of the civil war. The obverse has various sacral items associated with the pontifices as a reflection of Caesar's tenure as pontifex maximus. The iconographic symbolism of the elephant trampling the snake on the reverse is so obscure that there is no agreement as to its exact meaning. The word "Caesar" below indicates that the image is symbolic of his actions, suggesting the violent suppression of some sort of underhanded, traitorous foe. Perhaps the obscurity was intentional, but the design does seem to indicate a low opinion of those who opposed Caesar, and apparently does nothing to convey the notion that Caesar was upholding the Republic against those who would violate it, as he argues in the *Civil War*. Courtesy Gemini LLC.

Coin 21 (RRC 449/4=HCRI 23). Unlike the preceding coin, this one, minted for Caesar by C. Vibius Pansa (who would later defend the Republic against Antony as consul in 43 B.C.), does attempt to associate Caesar's cause with the defense of the Republic. The obverse portrays Liberty (oddly described in the genitive case *Libertatis* or "of liberty"), while the reverse has a victorious figure of Rome sitting on a heap of arms and crowned with the laurel wreath by a flying image of Victory. Seemingly, the success of Caesar is equated with the restoration of liberty and the victorious world dominion of Rome. No doubt his opponents would not have agreed, but this coin must have been intended to mollify those who thought that Caesar's victory would undermine the traditional political order. Courtesy Dr. Busso Peus Nachfolger.

Coin 22 (RRC 470/1c=HCRI 50). Struck by the proquaestor M. Minatius Sabinus for Pompey's elder son Gnaeus during the Spanish campaign of 46–45 B.C., this coin illustrates the way in which the leadership of the anti-Caesarian side had become "personalized" after several years of warfare. Whereas Pompey's image had not appeared on coinage for the Republican side at the start of the civil war, by now the anti-Caesar side was clearly identified with Pompeian leadership, and so this coin bears the face of Pompey's eldest son Gnaeus, who (at least nominally) assumed control of the forces that escaped from Caesar's victory at Thapsus in 46 B.C. and established themselves in Spain. The obverse legend of the coin reads simply *Cn. Magnus imp(erator)*, but other versions add an *f.* (for *filius* or "the son") at the end of the title to emphasize the present leader's connection with his illustrious father. The reverse portrays a personification of the Spanish city of Corduba welcoming the arrival by a ship of the soldiery coming by sea from Africa. Clearly, their cause was no longer that of the Republic but of their Pompeian leadership. Courtesy Lütke and Wiedemann KG.

Coin 23 (RRC 480/10=HCRI 107). During the last months of his life, large numbers of coins were issued with Caesar's portrait. This one (issued by the otherwise unknown moneyer P. Sepullius Macer) bears the legend *Caesar dictator perpetuo* ("Caesar, dictator for life") and must have been designed in the last month of his life (though production may have continued for some months during the uncertain period that followed his death). The reverse has a rather undistinctive image of Victory plus the name of one of the many moneyers involved in this extensive issue. This coin shows the extent to which Caesar had abandoned any pretence of defending the Republic. Anyone who was doubtful about his intentions needed to do nothing more than look at a new coin to realize that Caesar was never going to restore the traditional form of government. Courtesy A. Tkalec AG.

Coin 24 (RRC 490/2=HCRI 132). This *aureus* (a gold coin probably minted for distribution to troops) neatly encapsulates the initial claim to political authority of Caesar's heir. He appears on the obverse with the legend *C. Caesar cos. pont. aug.* ("C. Caesar, consul, pontifex, augur"). This title illustrates a number of things. First, he did not himself use the form "Octavianus" by which he is generally known in modern sources. Second, the coin was minted in the short period between his seizure of the consulship in July of 43 B.C. and his abdication from the office in accordance with the terms of his alliance with Antony and Lepidus. Third, his lack of personal distinction at such a young age is indicated by the perceived need to mention the two priesthoods that he held, since apart from the illegally extorted consulship, the twenty-year-old had held no public office. On the reverse is shown a portrait of the assassinated dictator, with the legend *C. Caesar dict. perp., pont. max.* Growing a beard was a sign of mourning among the Romans of the Late Republic, who normally shaved, and this explains the beard sported by the assassinated dictator's heir. Courtesy British Museum.

Coin 25 (RRC 488/2=HCRI 123). This crude coin was struck at the time of the establishment of the triumvirate. On the obverse is a portrait of Antony, who is given the peculiar title *imp. r.p.c.*, which must be some sort of conflation of the titles *imperator* and *triumvir rei publicae constituendae* (apparently the exact titulature to be used with this unprecedented office was at first unclear). On the reverse is a portrait of Caesar, with the legend *Caesar dict*. There could be no clearer symbol of the extent to which Antony was trying to portray himself as the natural leader of Caesar's followers, a claim that was hard to maintain in the face of the counter claim of Caesar's own heir. Like young Caesar on the preceding coin, Antony manifests his grief at the dictator's assassination by growing a beard. Courtesy Baldwin's Auctions Ltd.

Coin 26 (RRC 493/1b=HCRI 133). This aureus commemorates the reconciliation of Antony and young Caesar by portraying them on opposite sides of the same coin (they both have titles as triumvirs). Presumably, the issue was coined by young Caesar during the period of his comparative weakness right after he was compelled to abandon the consulship of 43 B.C. At any rate, there is another issue that has him on one side and the other triumvir Lepidus on the other (*RRC* 495). Perhaps he felt that he needed to shore up support by advertising the new alliance. In any case, these issues make it clear that the triumvirs were nothing but dynastic warlords who make no pretence of representing any political cause apart from their personal ambitions. Courtesy British Museum.

Coin 27 (RRC 508/3=HCRI 216). This coin was issued for Brutus the tyrannicide in his capacity as governor of Macedonia by *L. Plaet(orius) Cest(ianus)*, who was presumably Brutus's quaestor. Brutus had no legal justification in seizing control of the province and capturing C. Antonius (the governor appointed in place of his brother Mark Antony), but with the bold military title *Brutus imp(erator)* the coin clearly marks out the ostensible defender of the Republic as just another warlord, thus illustrating the unconstitutional means used by Brutus (and Cassius) in defending the traditional constitution. The reverse proudly proclaims the assassination of Caesar. In the center is the *pilleus*, a special cap that symbolized the newly manumitted slave's freedom, and around it are two daggers and the legend *eid. Mar.* "Ides of March" (the loss of the case endings in the abbreviated form makes it unclear whether this is a programmatic statement in the nominative or the date "on the ides of March"). Thus, the full message of the reverse is that the assassination of Caesar on the Ides of March represented the liberation of the enslaved Republic. The design as a whole indicates that there was no possibility of reconciliation with the triumvirs, who for their part loudly announced their loyalty to the dead dictator on their coinage. Courtesy A. Tkalec AG.

Coin 28 (RRC 511/1=HCRI 332). This aureus reflects the status of Sex. Pompeius in the period after the defeat of the Republicans at Munda in 45 B.C. On the obverse he portrays himself, wearing the beard of mourning for the death of his father, and the legend gives him the grandiloquent title *Magnus Pius imp. iter.* or "The Great Dutiful One, two times imperator." Thus, it gives much prominence to his own position as warlord and marks out his lofty status with his unusual new nomenclature (see Chapter 22). The reverse has facing busts of Pompey the Elder on the right and his son the warlord on the left, which symbolizes the claim that Magnus was making to the loyalty of his dead father's adherents. The reverse legend continues with Magnus's titulature, calling him by the title that was bestowed on him by the senate in early 43 B.C. during the preparations for the campaign against Antony: *praef(ectus) clas(sis) et orae marit(imae) ex s.c.* ("praefect of the fleet and of the sea shore by decree of the senate"). Given the control over Rome exercised by the triumvirs, this was the only official position that Magnus was ever to receive. Ultimately, his association with the more or less discredited family of Pompey would not be enough to counterbalance his lack of official recognition, and his supporters began to go over to the triumvirs after the Treaty of Misenum in 38 B.C. (see Chapter 23). Courtesy British Museum.

Coin 29 (RRC 519/2=HCRI 339). This coin illustrates the uncertainty of the surviving Republicans in the aftermath of their defeat at Philippi. Cn. Domitius Ahenobarbus, the son of Caesar the dictator's inveterate enemy L. Ahenobarbus cos. 54, served as a fleet commander under Brutus. The bearded head on the obverse is presumably an ancestor of his who had won a naval victory in the past, while the prow and trophy on the reverse may allude not only to the ancestral victory but to Ahenobarbus's own victory in 42 B.C. over a triumviral admiral (Cn. Domitius Calvinus cos. 53). The obverse legend (Ahenobarbus) refers explicitly to the ancestor and implicitly to admiral, the rest of whose name (*Cn. Domitius L.f. imp.*) appears on the reverse. Thus, the coin was probably struck in the year directly after Philippi, when Ahenobarbus retained a sort of independent command. Such independence was basically unsupportable, and he soon went over to Antony. (As consul in 32 B.C., the ex-Republican Ahenobarbus would even try to defend Antony's interests against Imp. Caesar; see Chapter 23.) Courtesy Hess-Divo AG.

Coin 30 (RRC 534/3=HCRI 307). M. Agrippa was Imp. Caesar's childhood friend and trusted general. Realizing that he was nothing without his connection to the young Caesar, Agrippa was always self-effacing, and the present coin, which was issued in 38 B.C., illustrates both his prestige and deference. The obverse bears the facing busts of the dead dictator (*Divos Iulius* "Deified Julius") and his heir (*Divi f.* "Son of the Deified One"), while the reverse legend merely indicates Agrippa's designation for the consulship of the following year (*M. Agrippa cos. desig.*) without any design or portrait. At once, Agrippa's privileged status is marked out, but all prominence goes to his leader (and his adoptive father). The coin also illustrates Agrippa's embarrassment at his humble nomen, which he routinely omitted. Courtesy Numismatic Group.

Coin 31 (RRC 524/2=HCRI 341). Q. Labienus, son of T. Labienus (Caesar the dictator's one-time lieutenant and later his bitter opponent), was sent by the Republicans to seek assistance from the king of Parthia, but instead he returned at the head of a Parthian army with which he overran the Roman Near East in 40 B.C. (see Chapter 22), when he issued this very odd coin. The obverse has Labienus's own portrait with the legend Q. Labienus Parthicus imp., which suggests that he was portraying himself as a Roman imperator who had defeated the Parthians. Presumably, he was explaining away his use of Parthian troops by implying that they were the sort of auxiliaries that were commonly supplied to Roman generals by conquered races. The Parthian military assistance is alluded to in a rather vague and unthreatening manner by the riderless horse with saddle, bow, and quiver on the reverse (the main Parthian strength was in their cavalry). Presumably, the rider was omitted as a way of downplaying the foreignness of these troops. Courtesy Classical Numismatic Group.

Coin 32 (RRC 543/1=HCRI 345). By 32 B.C., Antony had become fully allied with Cleopatra, as is illustrated by this coin. On the obverse is a portrait of Antony with the rather stark legend *Antoni Armenia devicta* "Of Antony, after the conquest of Armenia," which refers to his campaign against Armenia in retaliation for its king's having left Antony in the lurch during the nearly disastrous Parthian campaign of 36 B.C. The lack of Roman titles is in marked contrast with other legends from this period, which in addition to his triumvirate list the numbers of his acclamations as imperator, the number of his consulships and designated consulships, and his position as augur. Those legends also give his Roman praenomen. Presumably, the present coin was intended to play down his Roman honors, though it is hard to imagine who the (Latin-speaking) audience intended for such a portrayal would have been. The reverse bears Cleopatra's portrait and gives her the grandiloquent legend *Cleopatrae reginae regum, filiorum regum* ("Of Cleopatra, queen of kings [and] of princes"). Presumably, she was being portrayed as a powerful monarch with pretensions to the titles of the old Persian kings. Seemingly, this issue was meant for the local population and was intended to portray Antony and Cleopatra as joint eastern potentates. It is not hard to see why certain Romans would have felt uncomfortable with this image of their leader, and chose to defect to Imp. Caesar. Courtesy Classical Numismatic Group.

Coin 33 (RRC 544/10=HCRI 373). This coin forms part of a vast issue that was presumably meant for personalized distribution to individual legions. These coins all share the same obverse with a ship on it and Antony's Roman titles: *Ant(onius) aug(ur) iiivir r.p.c.* The obverse design consists of military standards. There was a separate issue for each of his units, with the legend of each issue bearing the name of a particular unit; twenty-two legions plus his praetorian cohorts (see Chapter 24) and an elite cohort of scouts (*speculatores*) are recorded in legends (the present coin commemorates the Tenth Legion). This vast emission was so plentiful that it remained in general circulation for more than a century (the emperor Trajan finally withdrew the coins in the early second century A.D.). Like many an imperator since the time of Sulla, Antony was trying to buy the loyalty of his troops: just a glance at the coins they received would remind them of the person to whom they owed their good fortune. For the most part, the soldiery did remain loyal but gave in fairly readily once they were abandoned in Greece after the defeat at Actium. Courtesy Astarte S. A.

Coin 34 (RIC 267=HCRI 422). This coin illustrates the transitional period after the defeat of Antony and before the settlement of 27 B.C. The obverse simply shows the head of Imp. Caesar with no legend at all. After the suppression of Magnus Pius (Sex. Pompeius), Lepidus, and Antony, there was no need to specify the portrait, since there was no longer any other leader in the Roman world. The reverse shows the arch that was erected in the Roman Forum in commemoration of the victory at Actium (it was to be replaced by an even more impressive monument within a decade; see Chapter 24 n. 21). Courtesy Numismatica Ars Classica.

Coin 35 (BMC 1995–4–1–1). An example was only recently found of this very rare gold coin, which was issued in commemoration of the initial steps taken by Imp. Caesar in preparation for the settlement of January 27 B.C. The obverse bears the head of Imp. Caesar with the simple legend *Caesar cos. vi* ("Caesar, consul for the sixth time [28 B.C.]"). The legend is continued on the reverse with the words *leges et iura p(opuli) r(omani) restituit* ("[he] restored the laws and rights of the Roman People"). The reverse image shows Caesar sitting on a *sella curulis* (the special seat used by magistrates with imperium). He is holding a papyrus roll in one hand, and beside his chair is a *scrinium* (a sort of filing cabinet used to hold papyrus rolls). The exact significance of this scene is not known, but it presumably represents a specific act of Caesar's. Since he had the right to sit between the consuls on the sella curulis during sessions of the senate, a reasonable guess is that he is giving a speech in the senate in which he spoke of giving up all his unprecedented powers and restoring the pristine political order. The legend suggests that the documents he has at hand somehow signify the laws of the Roman People. In any event, the very monarchical conception of the obverse seems to contradict the message of the reverse (and the very fact that it was within Caesar's power to restore the traditional privileges of the Roman People also undercuts the claim that the People were once more in charge). Courtesy British Museum.

Coin 36 (RIC 345). This large copper coin proclaims the end of the civil wars and the return to normalcy under Augustus's leadership. The obverse portrays the large oak wreath that was granted to Augustus by the senate in the year 27 B.C. at the same time that he received the title Augustus (see Chapter 24). As the coin indicates, this award bore the inscription *ob civis servatos* ("for having saved citizens") and was an updated version of a similar award that used to be granted under the Republic to a soldier who had saved the life of a fellow citizen during battle. Now, this award, which was to be posted permanently outside Augustus's residence, served to commemorate his salvation of the entire Roman world by bringing the civil wars to a close. The reverse symbolizes the ostensible restoration of the Republic in that the main image is the large letters *S.C.* ("by decree of the senate"), which indicate that the issue had been authorized by the senate. Around the edge of the coin appears the name of the traditional moneyer (a number of different moneyers are attested on various similar issues). The dual nature of the restoration of the Republic is (inadvertently and only implicitly) indicated by the fact that the letters *S.C.* appear only on the insignificant copper coinage, while the silver and gold series continue to be issued only in the princeps' name and with his image. The moneyer of this example (17 B.C.) is C. Licinius Stolo. A distant ancestor of this man had been instrumental in opening up the consulship to plebeians in the early fourth century B.C., and himself held that office ca. 360 B.C. After that, the family lapsed into obscurity. The moneyer thus exemplifies Augustus's practice of dredging up members of famous families from the distant past as a way of showing off his restoration of the traditional Republic. (One of Stolo's colleagues was a Ti. Sempronius Gracchus, who must have counted among his ancestors one of the famous tribunes of the second century.) As it turned out, this man is not attested as progressing further, and his son became a minor senator under Tiberius. Courtesy Classical Numismatic Group.

Coin 37 (RIC 207). This silver danarius illustrates Augustus's dynastic pretensions. While the obverse bears the by now usual portrait and titles of the princeps (*Caesar Augustus Divi f. Pater Patriae* "Caesar Augustus, son of the Deified One, Father of the Fatherland"), the reverse portrays his adoptive sons C. and L. Caesar, who are described as consuls designate and *principes iuventutis* ("leaders of the youth"). The latter was a title that had been bestowed on them by the equestrian order and hinted at the greatness for which they were destined without giving them any official designation. After all, since Augustus did his best to conceal the nature of his powers, he could hardly have bequeathed these to anyone, yet he did his best to make it clear who was to inherit his position. In the event, the death of the young men (portrayed on the coin in togas to represent their coming of age) forestalled Augustus's plans for them. He took their deaths hard, and it seems that this issue continued to be minted long after the dynastic scheme commemorated on it had come to naught. Courtesy Leu Numismatik AG.

Pompey if he decided to march northward to threaten Italy by land, and if Pompey began to besiege the towns held by Caesar on the Aegean coast, Caesar could force him to stop by attacking his father-in-law Pius Scipio, who was entering Macedonia with an army that he had collected in the East. As it turned out, Pompey joined forces with Pius Scipio anyway and camped near Caesar's position at Pharsalus.

Battle of Pharsalus

The battle of Pharsalus can be taken as the deathblow of the Republic. There, the united forces of the legitimate government were gathered against those of the military leader Caesar. Never again would there be a military force that was loyal to the Republican government rather than to its general.

Pompey originally thought it best to refrain from open battle with Caesar's veteran army. Caesar himself claims that Pompey was persuaded against his better judgment to engage Caesar at Pharsalus. The battle took place on August 9, 48 B.C. Pompey (supposedly on someone else's advice) had ordered his troops to maintain their position and receive the assault of Caesar's forces with their formation undisturbed. Caesar criticizes this tactic on the grounds that it failed to take advantage of the enthusiasm that naturally comes over soldiers attacking at the run. When Caesar's troops saw that Pompey's would not rush forward to meet them, they actually paused for a time to regain their strength before resuming their attack. The Republicans withstood their assault, but the battle was decided on the Republican left. There Pompey had placed his cavalry, in which he was greatly superior to Caesar. To counter this, Caesar placed a special force of eight cohorts behind his third line on his own right. When this force beat off Pompey's cavalry, the Republican left flank became exposed and broke. Pompey's whole army then retreated in defeat, and the remnants surrendered the next morning. Fifteen thousand were dead, including Caesar's bitter opponent L. Domitius Ahenobarbus cos. 54. Pompey himself fled for Egypt. When Caesar saw the dead, he said (Suetonius, *Life of the Deified Julius* 30.4), "This is what they wanted. After such achievements, I, Gaius Caesar, would have been condemned if I had not sought assistance from my army." While not entirely unreasonable, this assessment does leave out of account the readiness with which he pursued the military option once his opponents had pushed him into a corner. After all, the worst that he faced upon conviction was exile, a fate that had recently been suffered by numerous prominent Romans like C. Antonius and T. Milo. Was Caesar's dignitas worth 15,000 lives? To Caesar it apparently was.

After the battle, Caesar generally continued his policy of clemency. No one officially surrendered on behalf of the Republican forces, and Caesar would have to find some sort of accommodation with the traditional ruling class (in the long run he never did manage to achieve this). He excluded from clemency only those whom he had already pardoned, such as L. Afranius and M. Petreius. The first person to take advantage of the clemency was Cato's nephew Q. Servilius Caepio Brutus (better known by his birth name of M. Junius Brutus), who would later lead the conspiracy against Caesar. Cicero, who had never been too keen on Pompey's allies (he made himself unpopular after he finally showed up in Greece with a stream of mordent jokes about the Republicans' failings), likewise returned to Italy. Many others, however, refused to yield to the victor and fled to Africa, which was still in Republican hands.

EGYPT

After the debacle at Pharsalus, Pompey decided to flee to Egypt. In the 50s B.C., he had seen to the restoration of Ptolemy XII Auletes as king, but that pharaoh died in 51 B.C. and was succeeded by his sixteen-year-old son Ptolemy XIII, who was married to his sister Cleopatra.[6] If Pompey was expecting any gratitude from the heirs (and he was still owed 60,000,000 sesterces for recognizing Auletes as king), he was mistaken – he was murdered as he landed. Meanwhile, Caesar was busy occupying Asia, and when he learned of Pompey's destination, he headed for Egypt with thirty-five ships and 4,000 men. Upon his arrival on October 2, he was presented (supposedly to his disgust) with Pompey's head and signet ring.

Caesar quickly fell in love with the twenty-one-year-old Cleopatra (he was probably fifty-two). He then became embroiled in local dynastic squabbles and was besieged by the people of Alexandria in the palace. Having sent Mithridates (a wealthy magnate of Pergamum who was an associate of his) to fetch help, he struggled to maintain himself in the interim. Ptolemy and another sister (this one named Arsinoë) took over the forces opposing Caesar. By March 25, 47 B.C., Mithridates was approaching the Nile with the relieving army. Ptolemy marched with his forces to meet it, and that night Caesar himself set out to join forces with Mithridates. The next day, Caesar stormed the royal camp, and Ptolemy drowned in the Nile during the retreat. Caesar now made Cleopatra

---

[6] The native Egyptians sometimes practiced sibling marriages, and the Ptolemies adopted this custom.

queen with her younger brother, Ptolemy XIV (he would be murdered by Cleopatra in 44 B.C.).

Caesar remained with Cleopatra in Egypt until June, despite the fact that there were serious problems to deal with. Italy had been in disorder for some time, and the Republicans were gathering their forces in Africa.

TROUBLES IN ITALY

At the end of 48 B.C. after the battle of Pharsalus, Caesar was appointed dictator for a year, and Italy was to be controlled by his *magister equitum* ("chief of cavalry," the traditional title for the assistant of a dictator), M. Antonius ("Mark Antony" in English). The debt problem, which Caesar had attempted to solve the preceding year, continued to fester, and Antony found it difficult to master the situation. M. Caelius Rufus (Cicero's protégé whose letters had kept him – and now us – informed in detail about the political situation in Rome when Cicero was governor of Cilicia) attempted to take advantage of the continuing economic distress to gain independent power for himself. Elected as a Caesarian praetor for 48 B.C., he first stirred up trouble by advocating the cause of suspending debt and rent payments and by interfering with the other magistrates on behalf of the indigent. This was exactly the sort of rabble-rousing that Caesar wished to avoid (he had decreed a much more moderate form of debt relief the previous year), and when Caelius persisted, he was suspended from office by the senate at the urging of Caesar's consular colleague P. Servilius Isauricus, who was attempting to thwart Caelius's activities. Caelius then summoned the old troublemaker T. Annius Milo, who had apparently tired of Massilian oysters (see Chapter 18), and the two of them tried to raise a rebellion in southern Italy in the name of Pompey. Their efforts petered out (they supposedly even resorted to an abortive slave rebellion), and they were killed by forces loyal to Caesar. Both Caelius and Milo seem to have entirely misunderstood the lessons of recent history. They apparently believed that it was possible to seize power in Rome by posing as champions of the poor – this despite the fact that both M. Aemilius Lepidus cos. 78 and Catiline and his associates had tried exactly this, and failed miserably. Furthermore, both Sulla and Caesar had already shown clearly enough what it took to seize power by force: control of the regular military establishment. Mere possession of the political process in Rome meant little by itself, and anyone with a loyal army could easily impose his will in Rome.

In 47 B.C., the debt crisis continued, with the cause of debtors taken up by the tribune P. Cornelius Dolabella (Cicero's son-in-law). Dolabella seems to have been a turbulent individual, having much in common with P. Clodius in terms of both policy and method. Though born a patrician, Dolabella had himself transferred to plebeian status in order to hold the tribunate, and in this office he both advocated radical debt relief and organized violence to get his way when thwarted. The opposition was led by his colleague L. Trebellius, and he and Dolabella fought each other repeatedly with their gangs. The whole situation sounds very similar to prolonged disturbances caused by the rivalry of Clodius and Milo just a few years before. In any case, Antony first took Dolabella's side, but it soon became clear that this would not defuse the situation, and he then backed Trebellius. Eventually, Antony was forced to have a senatus consultum ultimum passed to authorize the use of force to suppress the rioting, but even then it turned out to be impossible to curb the popular Dolabella. The city would remain riven with strife until Caesar finally got around to returning late in the year. Clearly, the regular political institutions could no longer maintain order in the city, and unless a charismatic figure was present who had both the personality to win over the general populace and sufficient force to compel obedience if necessary, the city would quickly degenerate into chaos.

While these disturbances went on in Italy, Caesar himself did nothing to intervene. In June 47 B.C., Cicero complained that despite all the turmoil, Caesar had not written to Italy since mid December 48 B.C. In fact, the dictator Caesar seems to have been having a grand time touring Egypt in the company of his young girlfriend (she bore him a child that summer). His inaction is seemingly indefensible and also rather surprising given his vigorous activity since the start of the civil war; perhaps he was simply exhausted. In any case, once he finally roused himself, he was back to his old self.

Trouble in Asia Minor

Caesar finally left Egypt around the end of June 47 B.C. The reason was a military crisis in Asia. At the time that Pompey overran Mithridates Eupator's kingdom in Pontus, he allowed Mithridates's disloyal son Pharnaces to retain his father's Crimean territories. In the fall of 48 B.C., after Caesar left for Egypt, Pharnaces landed on the north coast of Asia Minor and soon overran his father's old kingdom. In December, Cn. Domitius Calvinus cos. 53, whom Caesar had left in charge of Asia with very limited military resources, lost a battle at Zela, the site of the defeat of C. Valerius Triarius back in 67 B.C. (see Chapter 13). Pharnaces had marched as far as Bithynia, when news of a revolt in the Crimea forced him to halt. Caesar apparently decided to wait until the start of the campaigning season (June by the calendar was March by the sun) to put down this invasion.

On the way north, Caesar made arrangements in Judaea and Syria, favoring those who had supported him and extracting money from those who had backed the wrong side. He also indulged in the Hellenistic royal habit of accepting gold crowns as gift offerings. Various Republicans continued to seek pardon, including C. Cassius Longinus, Crassus's quaestor in Syria and the brother-in-law of Brutus (he would be the second leader of the conspiracy against Caesar's life in 44 B.C.).

Caesar quickly put together an army and met Pharnaces at Zela on August 1, 47 B.C. He completely routed the royal army in four hours. In writing back to Italy, he used the famous phrase "I came, I saw, I conquered" (*veni, vidi, vici*). He also made the snide comment that Pompey was lucky to have gained his reputation for military competence by waging war against such enemies.

CAESAR BACK IN ITALY

In late September 47 B.C., Caesar finally landed in Tarentum in southern Italy. When he reached Rome, his presence finally put an end to the troubles caused by Dolabella. Caesar was not happy with Antony's clumsy handling of the matter, and Antony fell into temporary disfavor. In settling the disturbance, Caesar generally stuck to his arrangements in 49 B.C. Oddly enough, he not only pardoned Dolabella but came to favor him (this troublemaker, who was responsible for all the ruckus, would eventually be appointed to the consulship for 44 B.C.).

Once order was restored, Caesar could take care of his financial situation by having the property of his fallen enemies confiscated and auctioned off (Antony was supposedly surprised at being forced to pay the amount that he had bid). He also accepted gold crowns from Italian communities and secured loans from the wealthy to support his expensive activities (in particular, his planned invasion of Africa.). While Caesar was no Sulla, he was clearly beginning to behave in a manner by no means in accordance with Republican virtues.

Caesar rewarded two of his followers with the consulship for 47 B.C. and had himself elected consul with another follower (M. Aemilius Lepidus, the son of the homonymous consul of 78 B.C. and later triumvir) as his colleague in 46 B.C. He also made sure of suitable appointments to the praetorship (he now had ten elected instead of the traditional eight). Caesar was beginning to take direct control of the electoral process, a further sign of his increasing disregard for the traditional constitution.

Discontent among Caesar's Troops

Caesar's army in Italy was now tired of fighting and wanted concrete rewards and discharge. After numerous subordinates proved incapable of restoring order, Caesar himself had to intervene. His personality alone sufficed to end the troop's complaints (he had had to quell a similar recalcitrance after the Spanish campaign). When he called them "citizens" (*Quirites*), the soldiers instantly repented and sought his forgiveness. This incident illustrates two things about the development of the political situation during the civil war. First, Caesar's side was clearly focused on his larger-than-life personality, to the exclusion of any political considerations, and only his presence could restore order. Second, while Caesar may have weathered this storm, the loyalty of even his soldiers was ultimately based on their own material interests. The force of Caesar's magnetic personality allowed him to overawe the soldiers' dissatisfaction on this occasion, but a leader with less stature would have been in serious trouble, and even one as impressive as Caesar would not have been able to retain the troops' long-term loyalty without giving them impressive material benefits. Something would eventually have to be done on an institutional basis to restrain the soldiery.

Caesar's Invasion of Africa

Once order was restored in his forces, Caesar sailed for Africa in December 47 B.C., and he managed to land at Hadrumentum. It proved to be impossible to persuade the local commander to join him, but eventually he did find a suitable port (Leptis Minor). Pompey's father-in-law Pius Scipio was in charge of the province and received support from King Juba of Numidia (who had helped crush Curio back in 49 B.C.). There was much indecisive maneuvering in early 46 B.C., and this did not favor Caesar, who needed a quick victory since his position in enemy territory was insecure. Eventually, Caesar induced the enemy to give battle by putting himself in a seemingly disadvantageous position while attacking the town of Thapsus. As usual, Caesar emerged victorious, defeating two armies commanded by Pius Scipio, King Juba, and L. Afranius cos. 60. His troops were in a bad mood, and when the Republican army tried to lay down their arms, they refused to accept the surrender and slaughtered 10,000 Romans.

The Republican leaders attempted to flee to Spain, where there was dissatisfaction with Caesar's representative Q. Cassius Longinus (the propraetorian tribune). Pius Scipio died when his ship was attacked, and M. Petreius and Juba committed suicide. T. Labienus and Pompey's sons

Gnaeus and Sextus managed to reach Spain. Caesar was generally clement, but Faustus Cornelius Sulla (son of the dictator) and L. Afranius (who had been captured and pardoned back in Spain) were put to death on Caesar's orders. He also had L. Julius Caesar, a blood relative, put to death. This was a bad omen for the behavior of future Caesars.

Death of Cato

Cato had escaped from Greece to Africa after Pharsalus, and he was in command of the town of Utica, to which Caesar now brought his victorious army. Though the town still had strong defenses, it was clear that resistance would be pointless. After helping the escape of those who did not wish to surrender, Cato committed suicide on the day that Caesar's army arrived. Caesar later lamented his death and claimed that he would have pardoned him. No doubt, but in Cato's eyes the whole point was the fundamental unacceptability of the very notion of Caesar's clemency. As Cato viewed the situation, Caesar had no business "pardoning" fellow aristocrats whose sole crime had been opposition to Caesar and defense of the traditional government against his subversion. There was no doubting Cato's integrity (even his enemies had to concede it), and his refusal to accept autocracy was to set a destructive pattern for the attitude later adopted by aristocrats toward the autocratic form of government that eventually replaced the Republic. As a result of this final act of opposition, Cato is known as "Uticensis" ("of Utica"). Caesar later wrote a pamphlet called the *Anti-Cato* against his memory, but this proved to be a very unpopular work. Even in death, Cato remained a thorn in Caesar's side.

Settlement in Africa

Caesar annexed Juba's kingdom as the province of Africa Nova. He also confiscated the property of local Romans who had served his enemies as centurions and imposed tribute on towns that opposed him. In June, he set sail for Italy, stopping in Sardinia to collect more fines from supporters of the Republican cause. While he was still no Sulla, Caesar's clemency was beginning to wear thin, and he was starting to act more like an autocrat.

Triumphs

Once he was back in Italy, Caesar began preparations for a vast quadruple triumph that would last ten days in celebration of his victories over

Gaul, Egypt, Pharnaces, and Juba. He passed over the campaigns against citizens in Spain and Greece in silence, but claimed that the Republicans in Africa were serving Juba. This allusion to the deaths of citizens was not received well in Rome (only victories over foreigners were supposed to be celebrated). Cleopatra's sister Arsinoë, Juba's four-year-old son, and Vercingetorix (leader of the last major revolt in Gaul; see Chapter 17) were led in the procession. (The first two were released afterward, but Vercingetorix was executed as a traitor.) After the triumph, the soldiers in attendance received 20,000 sesterces, the centurions twice as much, and the military tribunes and cavalry officers four times the amount. The citizen spectators received 400 sesterces as well as a distribution of free grain and oil. This largesse foreshadowed the vast sums that the emperors would later spend buying the loyalty of the army and the populace of Rome.

CAESAR'S DEFEAT OF THE REPUBLICANS IN SPAIN

In November 46 B.C., Caesar was forced to leave Rome for Spain. There, the Republican refugees from Africa had taken advantage of local discontent and seized Further Spain. When the subordinates to whom Caesar had delegated the task of dealing with them proved incapable of doing so, he had to take the field again himself. By this point, only the most inveterate Republicans continued to oppose Caesar. Cn. Pompeius, son of Pompey, was in nominal control, though he took advice from Caesar's old enemy T. Labienus (see Coin 22 for an illustration of how the anti-Caesarian forces were now fighting for Pompey and his family rather than the Republic; see Coin 12 for an early image of Gnaeus's association with his father's career). Caesar began to force his opponents back, and Pompeius decided to fight because he was beginning to lose prestige among his supporters. On March 17, 45 B.C., a fierce battle took place near the town of Munda. The Republicans fought desperately since Caesar had started executing those whom he captured as rebels. Things went so badly for Caesar that he was forced to join the fray to restore order, but this saved the day and 30,000 of his enemies died on the battlefield, including T. Labienus. During mopping up operations, Cn. Pompeius was killed, but Sextus survived to cause trouble for Caesar's heir.

With this victory, there was no more military resistance to Caesar. Now that the proponents of the old Republic had been repeatedly defeated and Caesar faced no further armed opposition, it remained to be seen on what basis he would try to establish some sort of political order.

QUESTIONS FOR STUDY AND REFLECTION

1. How did the political situation in the senate change at the start of January 49 B.C.? What measures did the senate take? In what way was Caesar boxed into a corner? Why did the two tribunes flee to Caesar?

2. What were Caesar's plans at the start of January 49 B.C.? What were his initial grounds for crossing the Rubicon? How did his plans change over the course of January?

3. What were Pompey's intentions at the start of the civil war? What plans did he have to win the war? What were the intentions of the leadership in the senate? Were their intentions the same as Pompey's?

4. On what grounds did the two sides claim legitimacy? What were their soldiers fighting for? How did the population in Italy react to Caesar's invasion?

5. Why did Caesar show clemency to enemies who fell into his hands? Did this policy change over the course of the war?

6. What was Caesar's constitutional position as the war progressed? What were his followers fighting for?

7. How did the Republican defeat at Pharsalus change the situation? What two courses were available for Republicans to take after the defeat? What were those who continued to oppose Caesar fighting for?

8. What was the cause of Caesar's string of victories? How did Caesar bring the war to an end?

9. What was the significance of Cato's suicide?

20

CAESAR'S DOMINATION AND ASSASSINATION

CAESAR'S AUTOCRACY AND REACTION TO IT

Already by the time of his arrival in Italy in September 47 B.C., it was clear that Caesar held greater power than anyone since Sulla. Changing expectations in the intervening thirty-five years meant that it was natural to grant Caesar honors that went far beyond Sulla's. The defeat of the main remnants of the Republicans at Thapsus the next year only heightened the sense that Caesar was far superior to any other mortal. He received completely unprecedented powers and honors, and his position began to resemble that of a Hellenistic monarch (including overtones of divine worship). In the process, he alienated not only many who had fought on the other side but even some of his own supporters. To some extent, it is anachronistic to conceive of the civil war as a struggle between Republicans and Caesarians. Those who supported Caesar were not overtly opposed to the Republic, and the later behavior of some shows that while they took Caesar's side during the (seemingly unavoidable) civil war, they were just as attached to the old ways as their opponents were and had not served under Caesar with the intention of winning dictatorial powers for him. These disgruntled men entered into a successful conspiracy against his life. The assassins thought that the murder of the dictator would be sufficient to ensure the revival of the Republic. What they did not realize was that the concept of personal autocracy was now irrevocable, and that even after his death, Caesar's prestige could be used by others to win a similar position for themselves.

CAESAR'S CONSTITUTIONAL POSITION

DURING THE WAR

Caesar began the civil war on the narrow grounds of defending the traditional rights of the tribunes, and throughout his life he never claimed to be doing anything but restoring the Republic. But it is perhaps symbolic of his own uncertainty as to what would come after his victory that he stopped working on his *Civil War* at the point of his arrival in Alexandria. For even before that time, he began to assume a quite unheard-of position in the state. When he spoke in the rump senate in March 49 B.C., he said that if the senate would not cooperate with him, he would run the state himself. And this is basically what he did. He assumed the right to grant imperium and was appointed as an annual dictator every year for the next four years (he also held the consulship in every year but 47 B.C.). Clearly, Caesar completely dominated the state, though on a rather informal basis. This would change with his return from Africa in July 46 B.C.

Honors after Thapsus

After his return from Africa, Caesar was voted a forty-day supplicatio, a dictatorship for ten years, control of morals (a novel form of power based on the functions of the censors) for three years, and the right to designate men to be elected magistrates by the People, to sit in a curule chair in the senate between the consuls, and to give his opinion first in any senatorial debate. A triumphal statue of Caesar was placed in the temple of Jupiter Optimus Maximus and was later removed at Caesar's command (the accuracy of this is open to question). Whereas Sulla had first given himself unlimited power but then laid it down in reasonably short order, it seems that Caesar wished to retain somewhat lesser powers on a semi-permanent basis.

Reforms

Beginning at this point and continuing after his return from Spain, Caesar began to implement a number of new policies. It is sometimes claimed that Caesar had some sort of plan to reform the state, but while it does seem that he took the opportunity to introduce certain innovations, for the most part these take the form of actions that were forced upon him by immediate circumstances, and in any case no long-term principles are evident.

Colonies

Caesar had some tens of thousands of veterans to reward with land. Many he settled in Italy, but he also established a large number of colonies in the areas where they had fought: Africa, Spain and Gaul, Greece, and Asia Minor. He also dealt with the problem of the poor in Rome by including them in his overseas settlements.

Grain Dole

Caesar maintained the policy of distributing a fixed quantity of grain for free in Rome but reduced the number of recipients from 320,000 to 150,000. This policy of granting a free grain allotment to a limited number of citizens in Rome would continue long into the Imperial period as a sign of the emperors' concern for the capital.

Legal Reforms

Caesar modified the laws establishing a number of permanent quaestiones in Rome, and abolished the role of the mysterious tribuni aerarii (see Chapter 12), restricting membership on the jury album to senators and equites.

Calendar

The old Republican lunar calendar of 355 days had recently fallen nearly three months out of alignment with the sun because of Caesar's failure since 54 B.C. to exercise his duty as pontifex maximus of announcing the extra month that had to be inserted every two years to make up the shortfall. The new 365-day calendar with an extra day added every four years was based on the Egyptian one and is still used today.[1]

RULER OF THE ROMAN WORLD AND
REPUBLICAN DISSATISFACTION

When Caesar was in Italy between the African and Spanish campaigns, there was a feeling that the Republicans could come to some sort of accommodation with him and that he would restore the Republic. Caesar "magnanimously" allowed the return to public life of certain men who had strongly opposed him in the late 50s B.C. and fought against him during the civil war, such as M. Claudius Marcellus cos. 51. Certainly, Cassius wrote to Cicero during the Spanish campaign to the effect that he much preferred Caesar and his well-known policy of clemency to Cn. Pompeius junior, whom he characterized as stupid, arrogant, vain, and

---

[1] The method of intercalating leap years was slightly modified by Pope Gregory XIII in 1582 to take account of the fact that the solar year is slightly less than 365 ¼ days long, and for this reason the modern calendar is called "Gregorian" rather than "Julian."

cruel (Cicero, *Letters to Friends* SB 216 [15.19.4]). In the end, however, it turned out that reconciliation was not really possible.

In late 46 B.C., Caesar read a philosophical dialogue by Cicero about old age (the *Laelius* or *On Old Age*), in which Cato the Elder appeared as one of the characters. In the work, Cicero praised Cato Uticensis, great grandson of the man in the work, as the paragon of Republican virtue. In anger, Caesar published a retort under the title *Anti-Cato* in which he impugned Cato's reputation for integrity, but this made a very bad impression among those of Republican sympathies. A reply to Caesar's work was written by M. Brutus, who was soon to form the conspiracy against Caesar's life. This shows that however much Brutus may have supported Caesar recently in the last stages of the civil war, he fundamentally expected a return to constitutional normality. This was not to be.

YET MORE HONORS FOR CAESAR

News about Caesar's victory at Munda reached Rome on April 20, 45 B.C., and a succession of even more un-Republican honors followed. Caesar received a fifty-day supplicatio, victory games (as had Sulla), annual sacrifices to commemorate his victories, the dedication of a temple to Liberty in his name,[2] and the construction of a huge house for him at public expense. He was allowed to use the title imperator permanently (it was normally given up after the triumph, though there was recent precedent for its use as a permanent title of courtesy), and he was to wear the laurel crown of victory at all times and the special triumphal attire on all public occasions. In May, it was decreed that an ivory statue of Caesar was to be carried among the images of the gods during the religious processions at public games and that a statue of him was to be placed in the temple of Quirinus (a god associated with Romulus, the deified first king of Rome) and among the statues of the Roman kings on the Capitol.

Toward the end of the year, more honors followed. Among other things, he was to be called father of the nation (*pater patriae*), his birthday was to be celebrated as a holiday, and the month of his birth and a tribe were to be named after him. An oath had to be sworn by all senators to defend his life and by all magistrates to uphold his acts before entering office. A special group of priests was set up to celebrate his family, and a priest was established specifically for him.

---

[2]   Amidst all the extravagant honors being piled on Caesar, such a dedication may seem a bit ironic, but this is a holdover from Caesar's early claim to be a defender of the constitution. These mixed messages reflect incoherence in the image that Caesar was trying to convey of himself. For a coin that also associates Caesar with liberty, see Coin 21.

These honors indicate clearly that Caesar had no intention of restoring the old Republican constitution and would retain all his extraordinary powers. Previously, it might have been plausible to justify such excesses (as those of Republican sentiment would have viewed these honors) on the basis of the war situation, but now that the Republican forces in Spain had been crushed, Caesar was in a position to restore the old constitution if so inclined. He may not have been king in name, but his honors raised him in status above everyone else in the senate, and his privileges would allow him to completely dominate public life.

KINGSHIP AND DIVINITY

It is clear that toward the end, Caesar began to be given the kind of divine forms of worship offered in the Hellenistic world to Greek kings, though the nature of the (mostly later) sources, which are given to generalizations and to attributing to Caesar the honors that the emperors would come to enjoy, makes it hard to determine exactly what honors he received. During the Hellenistic period, there was a strong tendency to treat rulers as equivalents of the gods and to grant them godlike honors. Since the early second century B.C., certain Roman magistrates who made a particularly favorable impression through their deeds in the Greek world had been treated in the same way (for example, games were instituted in the name of Q. Mucius Scaevola cos. 95 because of his reforms in Asia; see Chapter 6). The statue in the temple of Quirinus is supposed to have had an inscription referring to Caesar as a "hero" (i.e., a human being who receives divine worship after death), but this is preserved only in a Greek source, and no one knows what the Latin term for this would have been. Certainly, Cicero makes it clear that a flamen was set up for Caesar (a flamen was an archaic priest, and there was one each for Quirinus, Mars, and Jupiter as well as a number of minor gods). The emphasis Caesar placed on his supposed descent from the goddess Venus (through the mythological figures of Anchises and Aeneas) strengthened the feeling that he was in some way divine (he built a large temple to Venus Genetrix or the "Progenitor" in his expensive new addition to the forum). While Caesar did not have himself directly deified, the monarchical implication of these honors was unmistakable.

CAESAR DISREGARDS CONSTITUTIONAL PRACTICE

In October 45 B.C., Caesar celebrated a triumph over his Spanish enemies, and in connection with this, he demonstrated his indifference to constitutional niceties. After his own triumph, he allowed two of his subordinates, C. Fabius and Q. Pedius (his own nephew), to celebrate lesser triumphs of their own. Since they were merely legates to whom he had delegated his own imperium, they had no constitutional right to a triumph, which was an honor pertaining only to those who possessed their own imperium. But if Caesar could grant a tribune propraetorian imperium (see Chapter 19), then he could also grant triumphs to his legates.

After the Spanish victory, Caesar decided to undertake a war in the Balkans and then to march against the Parthians in order to avenge the defeat of Crassus. None of these projects were particularly pressing, and perhaps he resolved upon them as an excuse to get away from the intractable problem of finding a permanent framework for public life that would be acceptable to the senatorial class as a whole. In any case, in connection with these plans, Caesar took a number of actions that made it quite clear that he had no intention of allowing a return to constitutional normalcy and was going to retain control of the electoral system for the foreseeable future.

A law was passed authorizing him to make constitutional arrangements for the years 43–41 B.C. (the anticipated period of his eastern campaigning). First, at the end of 45 B.C., he had C. Fabius (the legate who had celebrated the triumph) and C. Trebonius elected consuls for the remaining months of the year. In 44 B.C., he would hold the consulship with Mark Antony (with whom he had become reconciled after Antony's ineptitude in controlling Italy in 47 B.C.), and after setting out for the East in 44 B.C., he planned to give up the consulship and give it to the disreputable ex-patrician and tribune P. Cornelius Dolabella, who was not yet thirty. In December 45 B.C., he had two of his supporters (A. Hirtius and C. Vibius Pansa) elected consuls for 43 B.C., and in March 44 B.C. he held the elections for 42 B.C. (D. Junius Brutus and L. Munatius Plancus, two more lieutenants from the civil war, were returned as consuls). This completely unprecedented procedure of holding elections years in advance was nothing but a ploy to control the state in the future by making sure that reliable men held office in his absence. Considering the problems that Sulla had had in ensuring reliable successors for the consulship in 87 and 78 B.C., one can see the problem that Caesar was trying to deal with, but his solution was obviously unacceptable to anyone who adhered to the traditional constitution. In a further effort to control the electoral process, the tribune L. Antonius (Antony's brother) passed a bill in December 45 B.C. giving Caesar the right to appoint half of all the magistrates below the consulship. There were now to be sixteen praetors and forty quaestors – the new political situation finally nullified the difficulties inherent in increasing the number of praetors without increasing the number of consuls. Since the problem basically involved the electoral system, this consideration had ceased to count for much given that the elections for the consulship were no longer free. Caesar also disregarded the senate's recognized right to regulate provincial appointments by assigning provincial governors himself (abrogating the traditional appointment by lot). This procedure ensured that the important provinces were in the hands of men he could count on and that even if anyone hostile to Caesar did gain office, he would be in no position to cause trouble.

The point of all of these manipulations of the electoral and administrative system was to make sure that Caesar could retain overall control of the political scene in Rome, while at the same time enough "freedom" was left in the electoral process that he could avoid being viewed as openly abrogating the old constitution in its entirety. In effect, Caesar the dictator stood irremovably at the top of the system, where he could both place his own men in the important positions and prevent those who opposed him from gaining any significant power.[3] For anyone who cared about tradition, this was definitely not how the Republic was supposed to function.

An incident from the last day of 45 B.C. neatly illustrates Caesar's contempt for the normal functioning of Republican government. He was holding elections in the tribal assembly when news reached him that one of the consuls had died. Caesar immediately changed the assembly to the centuriate form without any of the necessary formalities and had a friend elected consul for one day. Cicero took this to be an act of derision directed against constitutional government.

Finally, on February 15, 44 B.C., as he was continuing his preparations for the Parthian campaign, Caesar was declared dictator for life. At this point, anyone who cherished the old system of government could only conclude that a return to free elections was impossible under Caesar. (For a coin portraying Caesar as permanent dictator, see Coin 23.)

PERSONAL ATTITUDES

In addition to accepting so many unheard-of honors and privileges, Caesar became increasingly intolerant of criticism. The triumph that he celebrated for his Spanish victory was not well received as a commemoration

---

[3] This situation was similar to the constitutional position of the Athenian tyrant Pisistratus of the late sixth century B.C., who did not supplant the preexisting elective constitution but held a permanent position "above" the elective offices that allowed him to control the political system.

of the defeat of Roman citizens (normally triumphs were celebrated only for foreign victories, though Pompey had celebrated a triumph for his conquests of Sicily and Africa after the last civil war). One of the tribunes, L. Pontius Aquila, refused to stand as Caesar's triumphal chariot passed him. Caesar was outraged, and for sometime afterward he would snidely add, whenever he proposed some measure, "provided Aquila permits it."

Caesar remained ambivalent about divine honors. In early January 44 B.C., someone put a diadem (a Hellenistic symbol of kingship) on the head of a statue of Caesar in the forum, and two tribunes, C. Epidius Marullus and L. Caesetius Flavus, had it removed without provoking any comment from Caesar. On January 26, when he returned from a religious ceremony, Caesar was hailed as king (*rex*) but replied with the pun that he was not a Rex (the cognomen of a noble family) but a Caesar. However, when Marullus and Flavus had the man who started the cry arrested, Caesar objected; when the tribunes then claimed that the tribunate was being violated, Caesar lost his patience. He demanded that the senate strip them of their office, and it promptly complied. Caesar even went so far as to demand that Flavus's father disinherit him but did not pursue the matter when he refused. Clearly, Caesar was getting fed up with people who were unwilling to defer to his exalted status, even if they held the sacrosanct office of tribune.

On February 15, 44 B.C., the day he became permanent dictator, he appeared in public at a religious ceremony wearing the traditional clothing of Rome's kings. Antony, who was participating in the ceremony as consul, placed a diadem on Caesar's head. Caesar took it off and dedicated it to Jupiter Optimus Maximus, noting in the official records that he had refused the kingship. What exactly this presumably staged event was meant to signify is unknown. Perhaps, he wished the crowd to thrust the kingship upon him but adroitly put a different "spin" on the situation when his wearing of the diadem was not greeted with popular acclaim. In any case, the clear tendency toward kingship and Caesar's permanent domination of the state must have been obvious to everyone.

Brutus and Cassius

The conspiracy that ended Caesar's life eventually encompassed a large number of senators, but two men provided its driving force: M. Junius Brutus and C. Cassius Longinus.

Brutus was supposed to be a descendant of the L. Junius Brutus who helped expel the last Roman king ca. 507 B.C. In terms of his immediate background, on the maternal side he was descended from the conservative

Servilii Caepiones.[4] In particular, his mother's half-brother was Cato, whose Republican ideology had a very strong influence on him. His father, on the other hand, had been a popularis tribune and had held Cisalpine Gaul for M. Aemilius Lepidus cos. 78 during his abortive uprising (see Chapter 12). Despite the fact that after surrendering to Pompey in 77 B.C. Brutus's father had been treacherously executed by him, Brutus's adherence to the idea of the Republic was powerful enough to outweigh this very personal motive for enmity with Pompey and to allow him to serve under Pompey at the start of civil war. Brutus had been pardoned after Pharsalus, and already in late 47 B.C. he governed Cisalpine Gaul for Caesar. Soon, however, his attitude began to change. In 45 B.C., Brutus married Cato's daughter (widow of M. Calpurnius Bibulus cos. 59, Caesar's consular colleague and bitter opponent), and, as already noted, he wrote a reply to Caesar's attack on Cato. Clearly, Brutus identified with Cato's principles and was fed up with Caesar's obvious disinclination to restore the Republic. (For coins that illustrate Brutus's hostility to the establishment of tyranny back in the 50s, see Coins 17 and 18.)

C. Cassius Longinus belonged to a prominent family of the plebeian nobility that had first held the consulship in the early second century B.C. Cassius had made a name for himself as Crassus's quaestor through his energetic actions in the aftermath of the defeat at Carrhae, when he had rallied the surviving Roman forces and defended Syria against any threat from the victorious Parthians (see Chapter 18). An anti-Caesarian tribune in 49 B.C., he had followed Pompey to Greece and served as a fleet commander for the Republican forces. Like Brutus, he had eventually reconciled with Caesar in the aftermath of the defeat at Pharsalus, and he served him as a legate in the years 47–46 B.C. He sat out the last stages of the war, though he preferred Caesar to Pompey's son. Like Brutus, his patience wore out when Caesar showed no signs of setting aside his extraordinary powers, even after his defeat of the Republicans at Munda.

Both Brutus and Cassius were appointed by Caesar as praetors in 44 B.C., but they decided to convert their exasperation with Caesar into a conspiracy against his life. In the event, they would become the leaders of the last attempt to restore the Republic. Brutus was a man of literary and philosophical inclinations, while Cassius was the superior military leader.

---

[4] Brutus's mother was the daughter of the Q. Servilius Caepio who had become a bitter opponent of M. Livius Drusus tr. pl. 91 (see Chapter 6), and his close companion was the son of his mother's brother (both the friend and his father were named Q. Servilius Caepio). After Brutus was adopted by this uncle, he was properly known as Q. Servilius Caepio Brutus but seems to have been generally known by his birth name.

CONSPIRACY

Caesar's monarchical tendencies were obnoxious to anyone who even remotely favored the underlying principles of the Roman state. The last king had been expelled 450 years before, and the Republican political system was based on the principle that competition for office was open to all eligible (i.e., wealthy) individuals. It was completely unacceptable for one man to assume as much power as Caesar had. It seemed that the only solution was to kill the tyrant, and the conspiracy begun by Brutus and Cassius found ready adherence among a large number of senators. Eventually sixty men were involved in the plot, including not only Republicans but also many longtime adherents of Caesar who had been willing to support him against his enemies during the civil war but were opposed to his monarchical ambitions after it. Cicero was not among the conspirators. Though he later complained of this, the conspirators were undoubtedly right to consider him unreliable, and his earlier attitude during the civil war shows him to have been both indecisive and by no means an enthusiastic supporter of the Republican side. It was only in the period after Caesar's death that he proved to be a vigorous advocate of firm action (and even here his policy would be misguided, as we shall see).

It was decided at Brutus's urging that only Caesar was to be killed and not his consular colleague Antony. (This would prove to be a mistake.) Caesar received hints of a conspiracy, but he refused to take precautions, fatalistically trusting in his good fortune. The ides of March (the Roman term for March 15) was chosen for the assassination attempt because it was known that he would attend a meeting of the senate that day. When he at first did not wish to go, he was persuaded to attend by D. Junius Brutus, who was a relation of the other Brutus and had served as Caesar's legate throughout the civil war. The conspirators met him as he entered the meeting place as if to petition him, and he died after being stabbed twenty-three times.

ASSESSMENT OF CAESAR

Like any good Roman aristocrat, Caesar thought his own dignitas (personal prestige) more important than anything else and started the civil war intending nothing more than to maintain his position. He originally posed as a defender of constitutional norms, but the refusal of the senatorial class as a whole to cooperate forced him to rely on his own resources; soon enough his almost preternatural success elevated him far above his supposed peers. It was not unnatural for him to receive unprecedented honors, and to some extent these went to his head. He clearly became autocratic toward the end, and he probably would have liked to have been "urged" to become king through public acclaim. Yet, he would not force the issue, and there was a large degree of hostility to the idea, especially among the traditional ruling class without which it was inconceivable to run the state. Caesar was thus in a quandary, and he presumably was happy enough at the prospect of escaping from Rome to wage war in the East. His assassination shows that hostility toward his thinly veiled autocracy was even greater than he suspected. It would take the cunning of his heir and the brutal experience of another thirteen years of war to reconcile the ruling class to the inevitability of abandoning the Republican constitution and establishing a permanent (though concealed) autocracy.

QUESTIONS FOR STUDY AND REFLECTION

1. How did Caesar's constitutional position change as the civil war progressed?

2. What extraordinary honors was he granted? What effect did these have on his political position? In what way was he treated as a god, and why?

3. Did Caesar want to become king? If so, why did he not simply assume the position?

4. What steps could Caesar have taken to establish his authority on a permanent basis? Was it possible for him to have accommodated Republican sensibilities?

5. How did Caesar manipulate the electoral process and the system of appointing governors? Why? In what way could the traditional constitution be considered operative in his final year?

6. Why was a conspiracy formed against him? What triggered the decision to kill him?

7. Why did certain men who had been important lieutenants of Caesar during the civil war nonetheless join the conspiracy to assassinate him?

21

TURMOIL AFTER THE IDES OF MARCH

SITUATION AT THE DEATH OF CAESAR

On the morning of March 15, 44 B.C. C., Julius Caesar was assassinated in the senate. The assassins acted on the assumption that the person of Caesar was the sole obstacle to the restoration of the function of traditional Republican government. In this they were wrong, for a number of reasons.

- The quasi divine honors granted to Caesar were to some extent a recognition of a widely held belief in his godlike stature. The image of Caesar was a very potent one, and anyone who could manipulate that image would be in a position to exert a great influence on the course of events. More specifically, there were large numbers of Caesar's veterans in Italy, and the man who could acquire and retain their loyalty would have a strong force.
- Caesar's arrangements would have had to be revoked for the Republic to revive. As it turned out, too many people benefited from his acta and plans, and his decisions were quickly ratified. This thwarted any return to normal government for at least several years.
- The surviving consul and virtually all provincial governors were men who owed their position to Caesar. While it seemed for a time that some sort of accommodation could be reached between Caesar's men (those who maintained allegiance to his memory) and the Republicans (that is, those who supported his assassination, including a number of men who had been "Caesarians"), it was inherently unlikely that such an arrangement could last long, and as it turned out, any permanent accommodation was out of the question.

In fact, the resumption of regular constitutional practice in Rome quickly proved to be impossible. A number of men decided to use military force for their own purposes, and once some began to appeal to arms, everyone was forced to adopt the same course. The situation would quickly degenerate into a series of contests between rival warlords.

General Developments in the Year after Caesar's Death

For some months after the assassination, the most important consideration was a person's attitude toward the defunct dictator. The consul Antony tried at first to rise above the fray, striving not to offend the assassins and their Republican supporters too much while at the same time using his official powers to retain a position of dominance among the "Caesarian" faction. This situation would change with the arrival of Caesar's heir, whose championing of the memory of Caesar forced Antony to become more extreme in this regard himself. This change in attitude brought Antony into conflict with the Republicans, who then determined to take military measures against him. While M. Brutus and C. Cassius seized provinces in the East and D. Brutus held out against Antony in Cisalpine Gaul, the Republicans in Italy cooperated with Caesar's heir against Antony. Eventually, Antony and Caesar's heir chose to enter into an alliance with each other against the Republicans, and this alliance marked the final demise of the Republic.

Immediate Aftermath of the Assassination

After killing the hated dictator, the assassins seized the Capitol. The next day, they descended to the Forum, where they were coolly received by the populace.[1] On March 17, Antony summoned the senate and urged the passage of both a general amnesty and a ratification of Caesar's acta. He invited the assassins to come down from the Capitol and entertained them at dinner. He also allowed the consulship of the dead dictator to be assumed by P. Cornelius Dolabella, an aristocrat of dubious character whom Caesar had marked out for the consulship upon his own departure for the projected war in the East.[2]

---

[1] It is a mark of popular outrage at the assassination that the tribune C. Helvius Cinna was murdered by an incensed mob, who mistook him for the assassin L. Cornelius Cinna (son of the consul of 87 B.C.), who was praetor in 44 B.C.

[2] This appointment had been made despite Antony's objections. Not only had Dolabella caused Antony no end of trouble as tribune back in 47 B.C. (see Chapter 19), but Antony had divorced his wife on account of her adultery with Dolabella.

The funeral of Caesar, at which Antony roused indignation against Caesar's assassination at the hands of those who had sworn to protect him, led to violent demonstrations against the conspirators, and they fled to towns around Rome. In line with his policy of accommodation, Antony secured from the senate a dispensation for M. Brutus, who as urban praetor was not allowed to leave the city for more than ten days. Antony also attempted to assuage Republican opinion with various proposals:

- The office of dictatorship was to be permanently abolished.
- M. Aemilius Lepidus (son of the consul of 78 B.C. and brother of the consul of 50 B.C.), who had been Caesar's last magister equitum (dictator's assistant) and was now governor of both Gallia Narbonensis and Nearer Spain, should attempt to make peace with Sex. Pompeius (Pompey's son who survived the battle of Munda and was in revolt in Spain).
- Only Caesar's acta and not his plans were to be ratified.

Antony also used violence to suppress popular agitation in memory of Caesar. Around this time, the senate assigned Macedonia to Antony and Syria to Dolabella as their provinces. In late April, Antony left Rome to attend to land distribution for Caesar's veterans in Campania. He was away for about a month, but by the time he returned the situation had completely changed with the arrival of Caesar's heir.

Antony's Background and Earlier Career

M. Antonius (or Mark Antony in the traditional English form) was the son of the homonymous praetor of 74 B.C. and grandson of the consul of 99 B.C., and his uncle Gaius had been Cicero's unreliable colleague as consul in 63 B.C. Antony himself was born around 83 B.C., and his mother Julia was the sister of L. Julius Caesar cos. 64, a distant cousin of Caesar the dictator. After the death of Antony's father, she married P. Cornelius Lentulus Sura cos. 71, the man who held the praetorship in 63 B.C. and was executed by Cicero as the leading Catilinarian conspirator (see Chapter 15), which made Antony this man's stepson. Antony first married his own cousin (daughter of C. Antonius cos. 63), but he divorced her in 47 B.C. for having an affair with P. Dolabella and married Fulvia, the widow of P. Clodius, Cicero's nemesis as tribune in 58 B.C. Hence, Antony had a number of personal connections with people who were disagreeable in Cicero's eyes.

From 57 to 55 B.C., Antony served as a junior officer in the army of A. Gabinius cos. 58 in Syria. Since Gabinius had allowed Clodius to exile Cicero, this service was another mark against Antony in Cicero's estimation. In 54 B.C., he began to serve under Caesar in Gaul. Caesar was apparently pleased with Antony since after being elected quaestor in 52 B.C. Antony was assigned to Caesar without the usual assignment by lot. In 51 B.C. Caesar supported his candidacy for the augurate, and in 49 B.C. Antony was to be one of Caesar's key supporters as tribune of the plebs. In 49 B.C., Caesar left Antony in charge of Italy while he subdued Spain and did so again in 47 B.C. Caesar was not entirely pleased with Antony's handling of the situation, but clearly no major break was caused by this, as is shown by the grant of the consulship in 44 B.C. (he never held the praetorship). Thus, Antony was a trusted subordinate of Caesar's when the dictator's assassination suddenly thrust him into prominence as the chief magistrate of the "liberated" Republic.

ANTONY'S INITIAL INTENTIONS AFTER CAESAR'S DEATH

We have no direct contemporary information about Antony's aims at this early period but perhaps he expected that he could take advantage of his powers as consul to assume the leadership of the Caesarian party and at the same time assume the dominant position in the state as a whole after reconciling the Republicans. Cicero later lamented the failure to assassinate him along with Caesar and claimed that from the start Antony intended to gain Caesar's position for himself. This seems unlikely. He apparently made a genuine attempt to reconcile the assassins when they had no military force to speak of, and he even seems to have attempted to get along with Cicero. If this was his plan, he did not count on opposition from Caesar's heir.

C. OCTAVIUS, CAESAR'S HEIR

At the time of his death, Caesar had three comparatively close male relations (there were also a number of other Julii Caesares who were fairly distant senatorial cousins). Two were the sons of his elder sister by two marriages. Caesar seems not to have thought much of them (though one, Q. Pedius, had served him as legate), and they received a quarter of the inheritance between them. They must have agreed with his assessment, since they declined their inheritance in favor of Caesar's main heir, their own first cousin once removed and Caesar's great-nephew.

Caesar's younger sister married M. Atius Balbus, a rather obscure senator from the Italian countryside. Their daughter Atia married C. Octavius, an energetic new man from Velitrae, a minor town in Latium. After holding the praetorship in 61 B.C., Octavius became governor of Macedonia, but his death there in 59 B.C. forestalled his hopes for the consulship. This man's son, likewise named C. Octavius, was Caesar's heir.

Born on September 23, 63 B.C., Caesar's great-nephew served with him during the Spanish campaign in 45 B.C. and was at Apollonia on the Adriatic coast of the Balkans (in modern Albania) when Caesar was assassinated. Caesar apparently thought highly of his great-nephew, leaving him three-quarters of his estate and adopting him posthumously. By traditional Roman nomenclature, he thus became C. Julius Caesar Octavianus. He himself never used the name Octavianus, which drew attention to his own rather unassuming origins, and at first styled himself simply C. Julius Caesar. Cicero did use the proper addition of Octavianus, and he is generally called Octavian in modern works to avoid confusion with his adoptive father. To make clear his extreme dependence on his (adoptive) paternal name at the start of his career, we will call him "young Caesar" for the time being (his nomenclature would eventually change as he gained independent stature of his own).

The elder Caesar seems to have been a good judge of character. After thirteen years of civil war, young Caesar was to become the undisputed master of the Roman world by defeating all his opponents. He surpassed his adoptive father by reconciling Republican sentiment to the establishment of a permanent autocracy and was to become the first Roman emperor under the name Caesar Augustus.

In the beginning, however, no one could have expected this future for the nineteen-year-old youth from Velitrae. In late March, his mother informed him of the assassination and asked him to return to Italy. At Brundisium, he received an enthusiastic welcome from the troops there and a letter from his mother and stepfather (L. Marcius Philippus cos. 56, son of the homonymous consul of 91 B.C.) urging him not to accept the inheritance. He rejected this advice and decided to pose as the avenger of his adoptive father. He spent April marching slowly through Campania, as he communicated with Caesar's old associates and met with his veterans. By early May, he reached Rome and officially accepted his inheritance. He also proclaimed his intention to uphold his new father's memory, insisting that he himself would put on the games in commemoration of the victory at Thapsus (the men in charge had not done so out of fear of the Republicans). Basically, all young Caesar had going for him in his bid for power was the memory of his adoptive father, and he was very skillful in playing upon this memory to gain support among his father's old adherents.

Maneuvering

In May, Antony returned to Rome after learning of the support that young Caesar was finding. They had a meeting, which did not go well. Antony's actions could only be undermined by this new person on the scene, who threatened his aspirations to lead the Caesarians. To help maintain his position, on June 1 Antony had a law passed giving him command in Cisalpine Gaul and Gallia Comata[3] for five years in exchange for Macedonia, whose legions he nonetheless kept. There were several procedural irregularities in the passage of this (apparently tribunician) law, which also guaranteed Dolabella a five-year term as proconsul of Syria, and because of this Cicero would later argue that it was invalid.

To maintain support among Caesar's soldiers, Antony also passed laws that allowed centurions to serve on the jury boards at Rome regardless of whether or not they possessed the necessary census qualification, and he distributed more land to veterans in Campania. To get the assassins Brutus and Cassius out of the way, in early June Antony had the senate authorize them to oversee the grain supply in Asia and Sicily. As a measure to thwart young Caesar's growing popularity, Antony had a friendly tribune forbid him to display emblems of his new father at official games.

Antony's new attitude in June did him little good. It alienated the Republicans, who now believed that Antony was trying to dominate the state with his new province (after all, from Cisalpine Gaul he and the legions that he would take from Macedonia could descend upon ungarrisoned Italy just as Caesar had done). As for young Caesar, he borrowed large sums of money to celebrate the games in honor of Caesar's victory in late July. During these games, the supernatural intervened. A comet became visible during the day, and the crowd took this as a sign that Caesar's spirit had been received among the gods in heaven.

At this point, it seemed that a major rift between Antony and young Caesar was possible. Brutus and Cassius, who had not left for their minor overseas commands, had issued some sort of edict indicating their terms, and Antony had replied favorably in public. During the games for Caesar's victory, however, the soldiery demanded an end to the quarreling among the supporters of the dead dictator, and Antony and young Caesar entered into a public reconciliation. Antony on the one hand and Brutus and Cassius on the other issued edicts complaining about each other, and in

---

[3] "Long-haired Gaul," that is, the areas conquered by Caesar to the north of the province of Narbonensis – a term used because of the comparatively primitive way of life outside the old area of Roman rule.

early August Antony had the senate vote them respectively the provinces of Crete and Cyrene as a means of getting them to finally leave Italy.

In the meantime, Cicero, who had hoped to reach an accommodation with Antony but was disillusioned by his changed attitude in general and his laws of June 1 in particular, decided in late July to head for Greece. Contrary winds drove him back several times, and in early August he received a letter indicating that Antony might again be accommodating, so he decided to return to Rome. On the way he met Brutus, who encouraged him to return to public life.

On September 1, Antony held a session of the senate in which he proposed some honors for Caesar. Cicero refused to attend, but he did come the next day to attack Antony in a famous speech (the *First Philippic*). Clearly, there was now a serious breach between Antony and the men of Republican sentiment. Antony's relations with young Caesar were no better. A tribune of the plebs had died around this time, and young Caesar wished to be elected in his place. Antony opposed this clearly illegal move (the Caesars were patrician and thus ineligible for the tribunate). Around this time, Antony also claimed to have discovered a plot by young Caesar to have him assassinated. No one knows the truth of the matter.

By early October, Antony had had enough of Rome. His colleague Dolabella had already departed to take over Syria, and on October 9, Antony himself set out for Brundisium; here he would pick up four legions that had sailed over from Macedonia and use them to claim his new province of Cisalpine Gaul, which had been granted to him by one of the laws of June 1. Under the arrangements made by the dictator just before his death, the province was to go to D. Junius Brutus, a relative of M. Brutus and one of Caesar's supporters in the civil war who joined the conspiracy to assassinate him. In April, D. Brutus had taken over the province, and he refused to recognize his replacement as governor by Antony as provided for by the law of June 1. It was now Antony's intention to take the Macedonian legions and drive D. Brutus out of Cisalpine Gaul.

YOUNG CAESAR'S ABORTIVE COUP D'ÉTAT

In the meanwhile, young Caesar decided to take military action himself. To this end, he sent agents to Brundisium to undermine the loyalty of Antony's legions that had recently arrived from Macedonia, while he himself went to Campania, where his lavish rewards allowed him to enlist several thousand troops from his father's veterans. He also entered into negotiations with prominent senators, most notably Cicero. Deciding not to attack Antony directly, young Caesar marched on Rome, arriving on

November 10. Here his plans fell apart. None of his senatorial supporters would come out for him openly, and as many of the veterans had served under Antony, they refused to march against him. To make matters worse, after having had to use a certain amount of violence to restore order among his troops from Macedonia, Antony was now marching on Rome himself. Realizing that his attempt at a coup d'état had failed, young Caesar withdrew northward into Etruria with the troops who remained loyal to him.

Antony entered Rome in mid November, but he was quickly distracted by disloyalty among his troops, with two of the legions transferring their allegiance to young Caesar late in the month. He did manage to make the arrangements for the praetorian provinces for the next year, stripping Brutus and Cassius of theirs and appointing his own brother C. Antonius as the new governor of Macedonia. He then set off for Cisalpine Gaul with his remaining troops, and by the end of the year he was in Cisalpine Gaul, where he besieged D. Brutus in the town of Mutina (modern Modena).

Cicero's Attitude

Cicero played a leading role in the last months of the Republic, and because of his speeches and letters we have a very detailed picture of the events of 44 and 43 B.C. In 44 B.C., he attended the senate only twice after the assassination, but he appeared repeatedly in 43 B.C., constantly urging war against Antony and battling (with partial success) against the many attempts at moderation on the part of other senators. He advocated supporting D. Brutus's claim to the governorship of Cisalpine Gaul against his legal successor Antony. The position of D. Brutus was analogous to that of Caesar in 49 B.C., which makes Cicero's support of him all the more striking. Cicero also advocated the recognition of young Caesar's position as the leader of an army that he had raised both through conscription on his own behalf without public authorization and by undermining the legions of a legitimate magistrate of the Roman People (Antony). In addition, Cicero strove to have the position of M. Brutus and Cassius legitimized after they seized provinces in the East. In effect, Cicero was supporting the private usurpation of public authority, which is what Catiline had attempted in 63 B.C. Clearly, Cicero was acting in a very immoderate fashion, and while claiming to be the defender of Republican government against the tyranny of Antony, he was actually abetting the very lawlessness that was at the heart of the crisis of the Republic.

This policy was fundamentally based on a deep-seated and seemingly irrational hatred of Antony, which is clearly revealed in both his letters and speeches. Back on September 2, 44 B.C., Cicero defended himself in a senatorial speech against an attack made on him the previous day by Antony. In response to further attacks from Antony, Cicero composed an extended pamphlet of abusive denunciation in the guise of a senatorial speech (the *Second Philippic*). Starting in late December, he began to deliver a large number of speeches both before the People and in the senate advocating his position of implacable hostility toward Antony. All these speeches were published in a collection (fifteen are preserved) under the title *Philippics*, which is a self-conscious reference to a series of speeches delivered in the mid fourth century B.C. by the Athenian politician and orator Demosthenes to rouse the Athenians to oppose the attempts of King Philip II of Macedon (hence the name) to dominate the Greek world. Cicero was thus comparing the situation of contemporary Rome to the time when Greek liberty was threatened by a barbarous king (as Demosthenes viewed the situation). Once Cicero conceived the situation in these terms, he seems to have found it impossible to think any other way – disregarding all indications that young Caesar posed a much greater threat to the Republican form of government than Antony did.

Why did Cicero adopt this stance, which seems on the surface to be so opposed to his normal constitutional stance? One argument has it that Cicero felt he could finally fulfill his desire to play the role of the sage advisor to the man of action. Cicero was basically an intellectual man of words and had tried to assume the role of advisor to Pompey and Caesar, with little success. Now, he would finally be able to act this way in guiding the young (and presumably malleable) Caesar. If this was his intention, he was doomed to further disappointment.

Another way of looking at Cicero's intentions is from a personal perspective. He had basically reached the pinnacle of his career nearly twenty years earlier during his consulship; after that he had had a rather minor role while military power dominated events in Rome. Hence, he had a long-standing frustration with his inferior political position, and now he finally found a role for his oratory by using it to champion opposition to the monster he saw in Antony. At the same time, Cicero suffered a number of personal losses that made him a loner and perhaps contributed to his reckless attitude.[4]

---

[4] In the early 40s B.C. he divorced his wife of many years, whom he suspected of cheating him financially (and a later marriage to a young heiress was brief and unsuccessful). During the previous civil war, there was a rift in his relations with his brother, whose career he had previously supported in a somewhat condescending manner. (Quintus and his son had apparently denounced Cicero before Caesar after the battle of Pharsalus; the details are unclear.) Though the two brothers later reconciled, their relations never were the same again. Finally, Cicero's beloved daughter Tullia died in

Thus, by late 44 B.C., when young Caesar was clearly ready and willing to oppose Antony (and had been suitably flattering the ego of the old statesman), Cicero threw himself into the battle with full vigor. Perhaps it was the pointlessness of it all – in effect, Cicero was advocating the destruction of the principles of the Republic in the supposed attempt to protect it – that explains the vehemence of his hostility to Antony, with whom he had previously been on good terms despite Antony's connections with a number of people uncongenial to Cicero. While there is no doubting his courage, Cicero's final actions certainly lacked moderation and good sense – how could anyone expect that in the long term Caesar's heir would support the restoration of the Republic if that meant reconciliation with the murderers of his adoptive father? – and Cicero would eventually pay for this policy with his life.

ISSUES IN EARLY 43 B.C.

On January 1, 43 B.C., the two new consuls, who had been elected under Caesar back in 45 B.C., entered into office. C. Vibius Pansa and A. Hirtius were both new men from the municipalities of Italy. They had no senatorial prominence but had served Caesar well. (Hirtius in particular had acted as a kind of political operative for Caesar, managing his affairs in Rome during his long absence. He also finished Caesar's incomplete *Gallic War* by adding an eighth book narrating Caesar's final year in Gaul.) How they would behave as consuls was a bit uncertain since they lacked much authority of their own and were definitely Caesarian men in that they owed their position to the dead dictator. As it turned out, they were moderate Caesarians who were both to die in battle defending the Republic. (For a coin issued for Caesar by Pansa during the civil war, see Coin 21.)

The major issue on New Year's day was the status of D. Junius Brutus and of young Caesar. D. Brutus continued to maintain his position as governor of Cisalpine Gaul that had been given to him by the dead dictator, despite the law of June 1, 44 B.C., by which it was transferred to Antony, and he needed senatorial legitimacy for his continued opposition to Antony. Meanwhile, young Caesar remained in Etruria with the troops that he had either raised himself without public authority or enticed away from Antony, and he too needed senatorial authorization to legitimatize his position.

---

45 B.C., and his grief plunged him into a serious bout of depression. (Cicero did have a young son, but he was rather a disappointment, and Cicero did not feel the same affection for him that he did for his daughter.)

In the senate, Cicero argued that Antony's laws were invalid because their passage had been marred by violence and other irregularities, and if this was so, then Antony had no right to replace D. Brutus as governor of Cisalpine Gaul. Accordingly, Cicero proposed that Antony should be declared a public enemy (hostis) and that D. Brutus's and young Caesar's positions should be regularized. There was a certain amount of opposition from those who either supported Antony or at least were unwilling to proceed directly to open warfare, but the senate did adopt measures detrimental to Antony's interests. It authorized public payment of the sums promised by young Caesar to his troops and gave him unprecedented honors. He was allowed to hold the consulship ten years below the minimum age requirement (i.e., when he reached the age of thirty-two – thirteen years from now!) and was made a senator with the rank of an ex-praetor. This last honor was completely unconstitutional. The senate had no right to select senators, who were supposed to enter the body after being elected to the quaestorship by the People. Cicero failed to get the senate to agree to declare Antony a public enemy. Instead, an embassy was to be sent demanding that he give up his recourse to arms and submit to the senate's authority.

While the embassy went north, preparations for war proceeded. When the envoys returned in early February, they brought Antony's response: he was willing to give up Cisalpine Gaul but wished to retain his five-year command in Transalpine Gaul. This offer was rejected by the senate, which passed the senatus consultum ultimum, though the senators still refused to declare Antony a public enemy. The consuls now prepared to take the field. Before the campaigning, however, important news came from the East.

Brutus and Cassius Seize the East

In February, word arrived in Rome that M. Brutus and C. Cassius, the leading assassins, had seized provinces in the East. Both had been praetors in 44 B.C. by Caesar's appointment, and Antony had tried to get rid of them by appointing them first as grain commissioners (June) and then assigning them the peaceful (i.e., ungarrisoned) provinces of Crete and Cyrene (August). In late 44 B.C. they hesitated to take their provinces, but after they eventually left Italy, their paths diverged.

Brutus first went to Athens to study philosophy, but when the governor of Macedonia, Q. Hortensius (son of the homonymous consul of 69 B.C., who had been Cicero's old oratorical rival; he was a relation of Brutus's) left the province, he gave command of it to Brutus (at this point mainland Greece was looked after by the governor of Macedonia). Brutus also persuaded the quaestors of Asia and Syria, who were returning to Italy with their governors' funds, to turn these over to him. Furthermore, the legions of Illyricum under P. Vatinius (Caesar's ally as tribune back in 59 B.C.) went over to Brutus. When Antony's brother C. Antonius, the praetor of 44 B.C. to whom Macedonia had been assigned after Antony exchanged it for Gaul the previous year, entered the province in January, he was quickly defeated and captured by Brutus.

Cassius meanwhile went to Syria, which he had saved in 53–51 B.C. as quaestor pro praetore in the aftermath of Crassus's defeat at Carrhae (see Chapter 18). At the present time, Caesarian generals with six legions were attacking a supporter of Pompey, who had one. All these troops promptly went over to Cassius. Four legions that were coming from Egypt to join the proconsul Dolabella in Asia also went over to Cassius, who now had a substantial military force under his control.

DOLABELLA IN THE EAST

In early March, more troubling news reached Rome from the East, where Cn. Cornelius Dolabella cos. 44 was to take up the proconsulship of Syria that been granted by the law of June 1, 44 B.C. On his journey to Syria with two legions, he overthrew the governor of Asia, C. Trebonius. Trebonius (a friend of Cicero) had taken Caesar's side during the civil war and was one of his most important generals, but after it became clear that the dictator would never give up his political control, Trebonius played a leading role in the conspiracy against the dictator (it was he who had taken Antony aside to prevent him from interfering with the attack). After Caesar's death, he promptly left Rome to take up the assignment as governor of Asia that Caesar had given him. Now, Dolabella had to pass through Trebonius's province on his way to Syria, and he decided to avenge the dictator by treacherously capturing Trebonius and torturing him to death. Cicero seized upon this news to have Dolabella (his ex-son-in-law) declared a public enemy, though Pansa the consul quashed Cicero's motion that Cassius (whose seizure of Syria was by now known in Rome) should be entrusted with the job of suppressing Dolabella. As it turned out, Cassius would have no trouble dealing with Dolabella on his own.

FAILURE OF NEGOTIATIONS WITH ANTONY

Meanwhile, though the preparations for war against Antony continued, the senate voted for another attempt at resolving the conflict with Antony peacefully. An embassy was supposed to visit him, but Cicero was chosen as one of the envoys and thwarted the move by refusing to go. The Caesarian governors of Transalpine Gaul also advised negotiation, but Cicero argued strongly against any compromise. Since February, Hirtius and young Caesar had kept their forces encamped in southern Cisalpine Gaul, while Antony continued his siege of D. Brutus in Mutina. In late March, Pansa left Rome to join his colleague and begin military operations against Antony.

WAR IN THE NORTH

When Hirtius and young Caesar arrived, Antony left his brother L. Antonius in charge of the siege and took units south to oppose Pansa and young Caesar, who were encamped separately near Bononia (modern Bologna), a town located a few miles to the southeast of Mutina, awaiting the arrival of Hirtius. On April 14, a confusing battle was fought at Forum Gallorum (a small town between Mutina and Bononia). Antony first defeated the army of Pansa (who was wounded), but toward evening Hirtius arrived with his troops and defeated Antony's victorious but disorganized army. Young Caesar also repelled an attack on his own camp. The three anti-Antonian leaders were hailed imperatores. Seven days later, Antony was decisively defeated at Mutina but managed to withdraw with his troops toward Transalpine Gaul. When news reached Rome, there was exhilaration, and a fifty-day supplicatio was voted. With the East mostly in Republican hands, it looked as if the Republic would be restored. But the victory had not been won without cost. Hirtius died in battle, and Pansa soon succumbed to his wounds. Now there were no consuls. Furthermore, it became clear that an attempt would be made to shunt young Caesar to the side. This was a fatal miscalculation on the part of the Republicans in the senate.

ALLIANCE OF ANTONY AND LEPIDUS

Antony meanwhile was withdrawing toward Transalpine Gaul after his defeat near Bononia. His reception there depended on the attitude of the two governors. The choices before them must not have been at all clear-cut. Antony had just been defeated by the Republican forces, but his army was intact, and the Republicans were leaderless after the death of the consuls. The two governors would have to decide in fairly short order what course of action it would be in their best interest to follow, but this decision must have been beset with much uncertainty.

Gallia Comata (the area of Gaul recently conquered by Caesar) was governed by L. Munatius Plancus, who was of a minor senatorial family.

His early career is unknown, but a brother (or cousin) of his had been instrumental in stirring up trouble after the death of Clodius back in 52 B.C. and was serving at this time under Antony. As for Plancus himself, he had been an important lieutenant of Caesar's during the civil war and was scheduled to hold the consulship the next year in accordance with Caesar's electoral arrangements. However, like many other supporters of Caesar in the civil war, he held Republic sentiments, and at this time he wrote to Cicero to affirm his firm allegiance to the Republic. In the event, it would prove that this was not an easy stance to maintain.

The other governor in Transalpine Gaul was a man of a different inclination. M. Aemilius Lepidus, who held both Narbonensis and Nearer Spain, was the son of the homonymous consul of 78 B.C., and during the civil war he had been a close supporter of Caesar, from whom he received the consulship in 46 B.C. Lepidus was the leading living consular (the civil war had been hard on prominent families), and it was obvious to him that if Antony was done away with, his turn would come next. Thus, he had good reason to reach an agreement with Antony.

As Antony retreated to the west, D. Brutus wished to pursue him, but young Caesar refused to cooperate with one of his father's assassins and allowed Antony to move away unhindered. D. Brutus tried to intervene in the withdrawal but was unsuccessful, and by May Antony was in Transalpine Gaul. In April, Plancus had marched to help the Republicans against Antony, but he halted his advance when he learned of Antony's defeat. Lepidus told Plancus that he would oppose Antony, and Plancus waited for the arrival of D. Brutus. On May 30, however, he learned that when Lepidus's and Antony's armies met, the troops refused to fight each other and that the two generals were now reconciled. It is hard not to suspect that the encounter between Lepidus and Antony was only a show and that Lepidus was now glad to reach an agreement with Antony as a form of protection against the victorious Republicans.

In June, Plancus and Decimus joined forces, but these were inadequate to attack Antony and Lepidus, and they remained inactive. Lepidus was declared a public enemy by the senate on June 30, but there was not much the Republicans could do against him.

Republican Attempts to Put Young Caesar in His Place

Antony had warned young Caesar that the Republicans were merely using him as a pawn and would discard him when it suited them. This now seemed to be the case. Even before the battle of Bononia, Hirtius had already insisted that young Caesar turn over to him the legions that had defected from Antony (a valid position from a legal point of view, but hardly a tactful one). After the victory over Antony, the attempt to put young Caesar in his place went on. Whereas he was granted only an ovation (a minor form of triumph), D. Brutus was voted a full triumph and to him was given command of the continued prosecution of the war as well as the dead consuls' legions. The senate also reduced the rewards previously voted to the legionaries and did not appoint young Caesar to the commission that was to distribute the rewards. As a final insult, the envoys who brought news of the rewards attempted to address the troops directly, sidestepping their general. Ominously, the troops refused to tolerate this insult, and young Caesar retained his army.

The external situation also seemed to favor the Republicans. The position of Brutus and Cassius was finally legitimized, and when Sex. Pompeius – the son of Pompey who had remained in armed opposition in Spain since the defeat at Munda and would be no friend of young Caesar – offered his services in defense of the state, he was rewarded with the novel position of "commander of the fleet and seashore" (*praefectus classis et orae maritimae*). Now the senate had sufficient military force under the command of the dictator's enemies and assassins to suppress his heir. Indeed, young Caesar got wind of a pun made by Cicero that could be taken to mean that the young man should be "praised, honored, and disposed of."[5] Self-preservation, if nothing else, suggested that young Caesar needed to find new friends. In any case, his Republican allies in Rome had served their purpose by allowing him to establish his own position and make himself someone whom Antony could not contemptuously push to the side. Now it was time to put the senate in its place.

Divided Counsel among the Republicans

After the battle at Bononia, a certain inertia set in at Rome. No new consuls were elected, and there were rumors that Cicero and young Caesar would hold the office. Certainly, young Caesar's ambitions lay in this direction. Cicero, who was still enthralled with the notion of acting as

---

[5] Cicero supposedly said, *laudandus, ornandus, tollendus est.* The first two verbal forms unambiguously mean, "he should be praised, honored," and in the context it would be most natural to take the last as meaning "and exalted." The verb *tollere* literally means to "raise up" and has two extended meanings: "exalt (with praise)" and "(raise up and) get rid of" (hence the pun). As it was, Cicero denied making the statement, but even if he did not make up the joke himself, it clearly reflected senatorial sentiment at the time.

young Caesar's mentor, continued to advocate all-out war against Antony and called upon Brutus to come to Italy's rescue with his Macedonian army. This Brutus refused to do. He saw accurately that Caesar was a greater long-term threat to the Republic than was Antony and refused to prosecute the war. Indeed, Brutus's half-sister was married to Lepidus, and to Cicero's annoyance, he tried to mitigate the sanctions against his brother-in-law. While Cicero had nothing to lose and wished to hound Antony and his associates to their deaths in alliance with the young Caesar, Brutus was not willing to burn his bridges yet.

Cicero's subservient attitude toward young Caesar was taken by Brutus and other Republicans to be tantamount to setting up a new despot, and they refused to go along. By June, it was clear that young Caesar wanted the consulship, but Cicero still refused to see the folly of his previous actions. In July, an embassy of centurions came from young Caesar to demand rewards for themselves and the consulship for young Caesar. When they were refused, one centurion pointed to his sword and said that this would grant their desires. And indeed it would.

Young Caesar's March on Rome

With his request denied, young Caesar marched on Rome in July. At first, the senate caved in, but upon learning that two legions had arrived from Africa as reinforcements, the senators rescinded their concessions to young Caesar. He now quickly marched to capture the city in order to protect his mother and sister. Resistance promptly collapsed (the only bloodshed was a praetor's suicide), and young Caesar took up the consulship along with his cousin Q. Pedius (son of the dictator's older sister). To preserve legal niceties, young Caesar forebore to enter the city with his troops, and on August 20 he was "legally" elected. Pedius passed a special law authorizing a capital quaestio to try those who had murdered Caesar. So much for any further alliance with the Republicans. Young Caesar also seized the treasury to give rewards to his troops. (For a coin minted at this time that advertises young Caesar's reconciliation with Antony, see Coin 26.)

Reconciliation of the Caesarians and Formation of the Triumvirate

Meanwhile, the governor of Further Spain came to join Lepidus and Antony and brought about the reconciliation of Plancus and Antony. Despite his willingness until now to fight on behalf of the Republic, Plancus must have concluded that with Spain and the rest of Gaul in the hands of Antony's allies and with young Caesar thwarting the Republicans in Italy, he had little choice but to yield to circumstances. Later in the coming civil wars, he would switch allegiance from Antony to Caesar, and his successful ability to change sides earned him the designation "horse jumper (*desultator*) of the civil war."[6] As the proverb has it, he must needs go that the devil drives!

Now that Plancus had gone over to Antony, D. Brutus's position in Gaul was completely untenable, and he had no choice but to flee. In his attempt to reach M. Brutus in Macedonia by a northern route to avoid Italy he was captured by a Gallic chieftain and executed on Antony's order.

For his part, young Caesar was in a perilous position. Though he had seized Rome and the consulship, he was technically still at war with Antony, who together with Lepidus controlled a greatly superior military force and could have crushed young Caesar. Yet, Antony and his friends had need of young Caesar's prestige, and a reconciliation was in everyone's interest. Young Caesar therefore traveled north and met with his former enemies on a river island near Bononia. The decisions reached there show the relative position of the conferees. Young Caesar was obliged to give up his newly won consulship. Though Antony had abolished the dictatorship, a new form of dictatorship was created. Antony, Lepidus and young Caesar were to be elected *tresviri rei publicae constituendae* ("board of three for setting the state in order") for a period of five years. This official board, which was established by the tribunician *lex Titia* of November 27, held wide-ranging powers to control the state. The traditional offices continued to be elected, but the triumvirs made sure that only their candidates were returned (the consulships were assigned down to 40 B.C.) and that the magistrates all acted in their interest. The consuls operated by virtue of their own imperium, governing provinces and celebrating triumphs, but they were basically no more than senior generals working for the triumvirs. The once proud consulship, which had been the senior magistracy in the Republican constitution for centuries, would never again be the most important office in the state. The triumvirs themselves received provinces. Antony retained Cisalpine Gaul and Gallia Comata, while Lepidus received all of Spain and Narbonensis; it was a mark of his inferior position that young Caesar received Africa and the islands of Sicily, Sardinia, and Corsica (Africa, which was in chaos at this point, would have to be conquered by arms, and as it turned out, Sex. Pompeius seized the islands). (For a coin minted by Antony right after the formation of the triumvirate

---

6   A *desultator* was a sort of circus performer who would leap back and forth between two galloping horses.

that tries to associate him with the assassinated dictator, see Coin 25; for a joint coinage of Antony and young Caesar, see less Coin 26.)

In typical aristocratic fashion, the alliance was sealed with a marriage bond. Antony divorced Clodius's widow Fulvia and agreed to marry Caesar's sister Octavia (this would not happen for several years), while Caesar himself married Claudia, Fulvia's daughter by Clodius and hence Antony's stepdaughter (one can imagine how Cicero reacted to this). In addition, as they needed both money and an excuse to get rid of their enemies, the triumvirs now revived Sulla's dreaded invention, the proscriptions.

PROSCRIPTION

The proscribed could be killed with impunity and their property confiscated. As with Sulla's proscriptions, the sources disagree on the numbers proscribed. A reasonable evaluation of the evidence gives a total of about 300 men proscribed, divided more or less equally between senators and equites. The triumvirs sacrificed their own blood relations (Antony allowed his uncle L. Caesar cos. 64 to be entered onto the lists, while Lepidus gave up his own brother, the consul of 50 B.C.), but these men survived and the only consular who was actually killed was Cicero. He met his end on December 7 after contrary winds prevented him from setting sail for Greece. His head and hands were cut off and displayed on the speakers's platform (*rostra*) in the Forum. In this way, the great orator paid the price for his foolhardy policies. (The ancient sources try to exculpate young Caesar, that is, the later emperor Caesar Augustus, by claiming that the responsibility for Cicero's death was all Antony's, but young Caesar did nothing to save the old orator and presumably was happy enough to acquiesce in his death.) Cicero's brother Quintus and nephew were also killed. The amount of money realized from the confiscations proved disappointing (apparently, property bought at auction under such circumstances was considered an unwise investment given the threat posed by the armies of Brutus and Cassius). In retaliation, Brutus had Antony's brother Gaius executed. The alliance of the triumvirs was thus sealed by marriage and blood, and the final showdown with Brutus and Cassius awaited.

REPUBLICANS CONSOLIDATE THEIR
CONTROL OF THE EAST

In 43 B.C., while events in the west played themselves out in the aftermath of the battle of Bononia and the anti-Republican alliance eventually seized control of Italy, Brutus refused to get involved, since he and Cassius were occupied with consolidating their hold on the East.

First, Cassius had to deal with Dolabella, who had moved on to take possession of Syria after murdering Trebonius in Asia. This was a foolish move on Dolabella's part, since the forces loyal to Cassius, who had been established in Syria since late 44 B.C., were far superior. Dolabella failed to take Antioch, the capital of Syria, and was forced to withdraw to nearby Laodicea. Seeing that his situation was hopeless – he could expect no mercy from Cassius after his brutal treatment of Trebonius – he committed suicide. To raise a war chest, Cassius set about imposing very large fines on towns in Syria and Cilicia that he viewed as hostile. Since Cleopatra, the queen of Egypt, had attempted to send aid to Dolabella, Cassius wished to wage war on her in revenge, but Brutus persuaded him to wait until after the triumvirs had been dealt with.

In mid 43 B.C., Brutus waged a campaign in northern Macedonia and Thrace to assure the quiescence of the tribes to the north (and to season his army). Then, seeing that the triumvirs were in no position to invade yet, he crossed over to Asia to cooperate with Cassius in subduing this area, which had until then remained loyal to Dolabella. While Brutus brought Lycia (an area in southwestern Asia Minor) under control, Cassius attacked the island of Rhodes, which had greatly aided Dolabella by providing him with a fleet. After successfully invading the island, Cassius seized its fleet, looted all the money he could lay his hands on, and killed all the leading men. He then demanded that Asia pay in one year all the tribute due for the next ten years. Cassius clearly realized that keeping the loyalty of his troops, most of whom had served under the dictator Caesar, would cost a lot of money. Brutus subdued Lycia with similar ferocity. (For a coin minted by Brutus that heralds his role in the assassination of the dictator, see Coin 27.)

Brutus and Cassius stayed in Asia until September 42 B.C., when they crossed the Hellespont with their large army to meet the triumvirs in Greece.

SEX. POMPEIUS/MAGNUS PIUS

In addition to the Republicans in the East, the triumvirs had Sex. Pompeius to deal with. In early 43 B.C., he had been put in charge of the fleet by the senate, and toward the end of the year he learned that he had been proscribed by the triumvirs. He sailed to Sicily, where the governor A. Pompeius Bithynicus (a distant relation) refused to submit to him but soon acquiesced in his presence on the island (later in the year Sextus had him executed).

Around this time, Sextus adopted the peculiar name Magnus Pius. Magnus ("Great," which sounded like "The Great" in Latin) was his father's adopted (and not always recognized) cognomen that recalled the name of Alexander the Great, while Pius was reminiscent of the title that Q. Caecilius Metellus cos. 80 had received because of his devotion to his own father (see Chapter 6). Thus, Sextus's new name both recalled his father's glory and suggested that those who revered the father should remain loyal to his dutiful son. This name was a strange use of certain trends in regular nomenclature and served to distinguish the mighty warlord from normal humans. (For a coin that illustrates Sextus's new self-presentation, see Coin 28.)

Though Sextus may have had some deficiencies in character, he was the only alternative in the west to the triumvirs, and the proscribed and others who were dissatisfied with the situation in Italy fled to him. In 43 B.C., young Caesar sent one of his major supporters, his boyhood friend Q. Salvidienus Rufus, against him, but Sextus defeated Rufus, and he would continue to cause trouble for many years with his large fleet based in Sicily.

SITUATION IN 42 B.C.

By the start of 42 B.C., the Roman world was divided among hostile armies commanded by charismatic leaders. The Republicans under Brutus and Cassius were in possession of the East from Macedonia to Syria, the triumvirs held Europe from Italy to the Atlantic, and Sex. Pompeius controlled the islands of the western Mediterranean with his fleet (disorder continued in Africa). Clearly, warfare was soon to break out among these factions, and by the end of the year the triumvirs had defeated the Republicans and were in general control of the empire, though the relationship among themselves was far from settled and Sex. Pompeius continued to be a problem.

On January 1, 42 B.C., not only did the senate swear an oath to uphold the acts of the dead dictator, but he was officially enrolled among the gods of the Roman state with the title *Divus Julius* (the "Divine Julius"). His heir could now style himself as *Divi filius* ("son of the deified one"). Given his pressing need for personal prestige, becoming the son of a god was no doubt a welcome boon for young Caesar.

PHILIPPI

While Lepidus stayed in Rome, Antony and young Caesar managed to transfer their army across the Adriatic despite Republican naval superiority. After leaving troops behind to maintain their position in the west, they had twenty-eight legions to deal with the Republicans. Brutus and Cassius arrived in the fall with nineteen legions. Knowing the way to maintain the allegiance of their (largely Caesarian) troops, the Republican leaders distributed among them the plunder that they had amassed in Asia, and their troops remained loyal.

The two armies camped near each other by the Macedonian city of Philippi. Given the isolation of the triumvirs from their home base, it was in the interest of the Republicans to delay battle and weaken their foes. After a certain amount of maneuvering, Antony provoked the Republican forces into giving battle on October 23. Cassius commanded the Republican left and Brutus the right. Cassius's forces were defeated by Antony's, and Cassius rashly committed suicide, unaware that Brutus had triumphed over young Caesar. Brutus now took over sole command of the forces but was not the general that Cassius had been. He offered battle in mid November and was completely defeated. He committed suicide the next day, reciting a line from an unknown Greek tragedy ("Oh wretched virtue, it turns out you were just a name. I used to cultivate you as a fact, but you were the slave of fortune").

Brutus is sometimes called the "last of the Romans (meaning 'last Republican')." It is debatable when exactly the Republic ended, but certainly the battle of Philippi was a blood bath for the nobility. Most of the prominent men from the period before Caesar were already dead, but large numbers of their descendants died at Philippi (for example, the sons of Lucullus, Cato, and the orator Hortensius all met their end there). Those who had taken part in Caesar's assassination or been proscribed committed suicide. A number of others managed to escape, joining either the Republican fleets that remained in operation or Sex. Pompeius in Sicily. In a certain sense, the last real Republican leaders were Caesar's creations, the consuls Hirtius and Pansa, who dutifully led the legitimate forces of the senate and magistrates to battle. Never again would military force be used overtly in the name of the Republican form of government.

QUESTIONS FOR STUDY AND REFLECTION

1. What did the assassins of Caesar expect to happen once the dictator was dead? What prevented the regular constitution from resuming its normal operation?

2. What did it mean to be a "Caesarian" in the period immediately after the dictator's death? Were Caesarians naturally opposed to the old Republic?

3. What was Antony's position at the death of the dictator? What were his motives? What attitude did he adopt toward the assassins? Did this change?

4. What was young Caesar's status when he became the heir of Caesar? What resources did he have in his bid for power? What was his attitude toward the Republicans? toward the assassins? toward Antony? toward Cicero? How constitutionally did he conduct himself?

5. What was Cicero's attitude toward Antony? toward young Caesar? What was his main intention in the year and a half after the dictator's death? What was peculiar about his methods?

6. What was D. Brutus's constitutional position in Cisalpine Gaul? What claim did Antony have against him?

7. Why did young Caesar ally himself with the senate in 44 B.C.? What was the senate's reason for accepting his services?

8. Why did relations sour between young Caesar and the senate after the battle at Bononia? What was his goal at this point?

9. Why did the governors of Gaul and Spain join forces with Antony? Why did all of them in turn ally themselves with young Caesar?

10. What was the constitutional function of the triumvirate?

11. What was the constitutional status of Brutus and Cassius as governors? What was their attitude toward Antony? toward young Caesar? What was their ultimate intention? How constitutional were their actions?

12. What was Sex. Pompeius's position during this period? What was he fighting for?

22

STRUGGLE OF THE WARLORDS

ARRANGEMENTS AFTER PHILIPPI

In the aftermath of their victory at Philippi, Antony and young Caesar made a minor readjustment of their provinces in the west. In addition, while Antony would go to the East and settle the provinces that had been held by the Republicans, young Caesar was to return to Italy to oversee the settlement of large numbers of their veterans. Antony was to help with money, and he imposed on Asia another payment of nine years' tribute within two years (since Cassius had already imposed a ten-year payment, one wonders how they managed).

CAESAR IN ITALY

By 41 B.C., young Caesar was back in Italy, carrying out the thankless job of distributing land to the veterans. They were never satisfied with what they got, while the dispossessed were obviously aggrieved. The full extent of land confiscation is not known, but large amounts were needed. Antony's brother L. Antonius and his wife Fulvia played a rather dishonest game in trying to undermine young Caesar. While they championed the cause of the dispossessed, they also tried to stir up indignation at young Caesar's handling of Antony's veterans by claiming that he was short-changing them and acting against Antony's interests. Some of Antony's troops sent envoys to discuss the matter with young Caesar, and they arranged a meeting between Caesar and L. Antonius at a small town outside of Rome. When each sent troops ahead to ascertain the security of the place, a fight broke out, and it seemed that war was inevitable.

PERUSINE WAR

L. Antonius marched on Rome, and young Caesar withdrew to Etruria. L. Antonius soon left the city and moved northward to join Antony's generals in Cisalpine Gaul. On the way, young Caesar forced him to seek refuge in the Etruscan city of Perusia (modern Perugia). L. Antonius expected help from the forces to the north and from Antony in the East. In this he was mistaken. The Antonian generals were half-hearted in their efforts and did not manage to cooperate with either the Republican admirals or Sex. Pompeius. In late February, 40 B.C., L. Antonius was finally forced to surrender through hunger. He was pardoned, but Caesar ordered the execution of not only captured senators and equites who were his enemies but also the town councilors (apart from one who had had the good fortune of having voted as a juror in Rome to condemn Caesar's assassins).

A famous anecdote holds that the executions were carried out by an altar dedicated to Caesar the dictator on the anniversary of his assassination. While young Caesar may have thought that this act would please the shade of his adoptive father, such an interpretation is belied by his generally mild personality in the later stages of his career, when his political position was not under threat. It seems more likely that this gruesome sacrifice had an immediate tactical purpose and was meant to serve as a stark warning for those who opposed his control of Italy. Given his tenuous hold on power, young Caesar was showing in a fearsome manner how he was prepared to deal with anyone who stood in his way.

Antony's apparently indifferent attitude is hard to fathom. While there may have been difficulties of communication during winter, he must still have been aware of the turmoil in Italy and of his brother's and his wife's role in fomenting it, and he could have intervened more decisively before the denouement in Perusia. The explanation in antiquity was that he was besotted by Cleopatra, whom he met at Alexandria in 41 B.C. But he did not see her until the strife in Italy was well advanced, and in any case he could not have been that smitten with her, since he did leave and would not see her for another four years. Presumably, he was content to let his brother act independently against young Caesar. That way he could gain much if L. Antonius succeeded while he could deny any responsibility in the event of failure. But if this was his plan, he gained nothing in the end.

ANTONY FLIRTS WITH THE REPUBLICANS

AND MAGNUS PIUS

In early 40 B.C., things looked bad for young Caesar. Though he held Italy, Magnus Pius's (to give Sex. Pompeius his new name) control of the sea threatened to starve the capital, and his own control of other areas of the west was contested. Young Caesar felt sufficiently threatened by the possibility of an alliance between Antony and Magnus that he divorced Claudia (Antony's stepdaughter) and married the daughter of Magnus's father-in-law.[1] Luckily for young Caesar, Antony's man in Gaul died, and his son was induced to turn his forces over to young Caesar, who went there himself in the summer to settle affairs. When he returned to Italy in the late summer, young Caesar found that Antony was back in Italy. Antony had become reconciled with the Republican general Cn. Domitius Ahenobarbus (son of Caesar the dictator's inveterate enemy L. Domitius Ahenobarbus cos. 54) and had landed at Brundisium in southern Italy. When young Caesar's commander refused Antony entry, Antony placed the city under siege.

The overall situation was desperate for young Caesar, who was recognized by no one of importance. He had betrayed his Republican allies in 43 B.C. and was responsible for the devastation of Italy in 41 B.C. Antony had just made an accommodation with the Republican navy under Ahenobarbus and was cooperating with Magnus Pius, who had provided refuge for most surviving Republicans. Now it seemed that Antony was in a position to crush young Caesar. But it was not to be. (For a coin issued by Ahenobarbus in the aftermath of Philippi, see Coin 29.)

TREATY OF BRUNDISIUM

When young Caesar arrived to confront Antony at Brundisium, Antony's Caesarian troops were once more unwilling to fight Caesar's heir and forced him to come to a new agreement with young Caesar. By the pact of Brundisium, the two warlords agreed to a reconciliation. Antony sent away Ahenobarbus (suspected of complicity in Caesar's murder) and told Magnus Pius to stop his attacks on the Italian coast. Antony and young

---

[1] By her he had his only child, his daughter Julia, who would cause him much grief in later years.

Caesar agreed to divide the Roman world basically in two at the northern border of Macedonia: Antony had what lay to the east, young Caesar Europe to the west. Italy was controlled by young Caesar, but Antony was allowed to recruit troops there. Magnus Pius was left in possession of Sicily, and Lepidus was given the insignificant province of Africa. At this point, Fulvia conveniently died, and Antony finally took young Caesar's sister Octavia as his wife. There were great hopes for this marriage, but as it turned out, the children were daughters and the marriage was a failure.[2]

Demotion of Lepidus

The Treaty of Brundisium made it perfectly clear that Lepidus was no longer of any importance. Back in 43 B.C. when Antony was retreating into Gaul after his defeat at Bononia, Lepidus temporarily held the balance of power because of his control of Narbonensis. His membership in the triumvirate maintained his prominence for some time, but his actual power did not live up to his title. Once Antony and young Caesar reconciled and the Republicans were defeated at Philippi, Lepidus's importance rapidly declined. While young Caesar could call upon the loyalty that many retained toward the dead dictator and Antony was able to rally those who felt uncomfortable with young Caesar, Lepidus simply did not possess the stature or force of personality necessary to compete with the other two triumvirs, and his being shunted aside to Africa is a sign that he definitely held an inferior position compared to his supposed colleagues. He would remain in this diminished status for half a decade until he attempted to displace young Caesar in an abortive effort that would show how totally outclassed he was.

Suffect Consulships

The year 40 B.C. saw a development in the holding of the consulship that would eventually set the pattern for the place of the office in a senatorial career during the Imperial period. In every year for the rest of the

---

[2] Virgil wrote his *Fourth Eclogue* in celebration of this wedding. In the poem, he describes the drawn of a new era to be ushered in by the birth of a boy whose parents are not specified. In its historical context, the poem shows the great (and ultimately vain) expectations that were held about the marriage. Later, the vagueness of the child's lineage led to the poem's being interpreted by early Christians as a prophecy of the birth of Jesus; for this reason, Virgil had a reputation as something of a wizard in the Middle Ages.

triumviral period, the two ordinary (regular) consuls who began the year would resign before the end of their term, and their places would be taken by a pair of suffect (replacement) consuls. The point of this procedure was to provide a larger number of men with the honor of the consulship (in particular, the suffect consuls were new men who had risen to prominence through their service to the triumvirs and would not otherwise be likely to reach the consulship). At the same time, the consular imperium would give such men the power to hold provinces and command armies without the constitutional irregularity of the triumvirs simply parceling out imperium on their own authority, as Caesar the dictator had done. This practice would continue until young Caesar's ostensible restoration of the Republic in 27 B.C., when the normal practice of electing two consuls for the entire year was brought back into usage. (Eventually, the system of electing suffects on a regular basis had to be revived; see Chapter 24.)

CONTINUING PROBLEMS WITH MAGNUS PIUS

The Treaty of Brundisium was supposed to end the problem of Magnus Pius's depredations in Italy and his interference with the grain supply to Rome, but it turned out not to be so easy to control him. He was dissatisfied with the agreement and promptly resumed his operations. He even regained control of Sardinia, which a lieutenant of young Caesar had captured. Though there had been rejoicing at Rome when news of the agreement arrived, it soon became apparent that the city would once again be threatened with famine, and rioting broke out. Hence, it was imperative to reach a permanent arrangement with him, and after an abortive attempt at negotiations, a meeting was held in 39 B.C. at Misenum on the Bay of Naples (one source says Puteoli, a town located a little to the north east).

TREATY OF MISENUM (PUTEOLI)

Magnus Pius had imagined that he would be made a triumvir in place of the ineffectual Lepidus. In this he was mistaken, but he was given public honors in the treaty that was negotiated at Misenum. In addition to a position in the college of augurs, he was to be consul in the next year, and he was allowed to retain control of Sardinia, Sicily, and the Peloponnese peninsula of Greece for five years. The position of his supporters (apart from legally condemned assassins of Caesar the dictator) was regularized. Exiles were allowed to return to Italy, and the proscribed would get back a quarter of their property. Slaves in his military service were to be given their freedom, while free soldiers would receive the same rewards upon their discharge as those of the triumvirs. At the same time, the consulships for the next five years were assigned in advance, as Antony was preparing to go to the East to deal with the serious situation involving the Parthians.

Renewal of Hostilities

The agreement with Magnus Pius was short-lived. Young Caesar had no interest in maintaining Magnus's position, while little benefit would accrue to Magnus from the now powerless consulship. There was also a dispute about the Peloponnesus: Magnus claimed it was to be his without condition, but young Caesar asserted that the taxes were to be collected for Antony first (one source claims that Antony intentionally ruined the region to diminish its value to Magnus). For his part, Magnus did not allow much grain to reach the capital, and young Caesar claimed that captured pirates admitted to working for Magnus. Finally, one of Magnus's lieutenants who held Sardinia defected to Caesar, returning control of the island to him. Young Caesar was resolved upon war, and in the spring of 38 B.C. he summoned Antony to Brundisium. Arriving from Greece, where he had been staying to keep an eye on events in Italy, Antony used the excuse that the Parthian threat demanded his immediate presence to leave for the East before young Caesar could show up, sending him the advice not to break the agreement with Magnus. Clearly, it was in Antony's interest for Magnus to remain a threat to keep young Caesar occupied. It was equally obvious that it was in young Caesar's interest to eliminate Magnus, whose control of the sea endangered his hold on Italy and the capital.

Decline in Position of Magnus Pius

The recognition given to the exiles by the Treaty of Misenum did nothing to help Magnus. Many of his followers were tired of their exile in Sicily, and in any case it was reasonably clear by now that Magnus was little more than a brigand who had little chance of assuming any official capacity in Italy. Though many influential Romans had fled to him in Sicily, he increasingly relied on the services of Greeks as his military subordinates (he ordered the assassination of one of the major Republican admirals who had gone over to him). While Caesar clearly had risen in prestige, it was Antony who received the lion's share of those who abandoned Magnus, especially those who had been opposed to Caesar the dictator. Even the admiral Cn. Ahenobarbus (Cato's nephew and grandson) and

L. Calpurnius Bibulus (the son of Caesar's consular colleague in 59 B.C.) took service with Antony.

Rise in Young Caesar's Status

At the time of his march into history in 44 B.C., C. Octavius (soon to be young Caesar) had few senatorial supporters apart from his relations and relied upon his small-town friends, who betrayed their non-Roman origin with their nomenclature. Q. Salvidienus Rufus was an important general, but during the Perusine War he entered into treasonous negotiations with Antony, and after his reconciliation with young Caesar in 40 B.C. Antony betrayed Rufus's treachery to young Caesar, who had him executed. A much more important friend in the long run was M. Vipsanius Agrippa, who eventually became young Caesar's heir and son-in-law and whose descendants played an important role in the dynastic squabbles of the Early Empire. Agrippa was embarrassed by his lowly nomen, and in a practice characteristic of the aristocracy he dispensed with it.[3] Agrippa would serve as young Caesar's right-hand man for decades, but he was fully aware that he was nothing without young Caesar, and he made sure that his own glory was always second to young Caesar's. (For a coin issued by Agrippa that illustrates his deference to young Caesar, see Coin 30.) Finally, C. Maecenas was an eques Romanus descended from the kings of Etruria. He never took senatorial office but served as a kind of personal agent for young Caesar until he eventually fell from grace for reasons not entirely clear.[4] In addition to these prominent figures, young Caesar's ascent to power was accompanied by the rise of a number of men from the municipalities of Italy. These men belonged to families that either had not been important in the politics of the free Republic or were entirely new to public office in Rome, and their later prominence in the senate would be one of the things in which the Early Empire differed noticeably from the Late Republic.

The reason why young Caesar had to rely on his lowly friends is that at the beginning of his career he himself was clearly a lowly upstart who had nothing to commend him but his inherited name, which he exploited to win the sympathy of the dead dictator's followers (especially his veterans). Hence, young Caesar had to rely at first on the brutal exercise of force to compel men to obey his wishes and yield to his demands (remember the slaughter

---

[3] Even today, the form M. Agrippa can still be seen on the entablature of the Pantheon in Rome. The present-day building dates to the reign of Hadrian (A.D. 117–138), but the dedication of the original building was modestly reinscribed on the new structure.

[4] Maecenas is most famous for his patronage of poets, and in certain modern European language his name is used to mean "patron of the arts."

of the captives at Perusia). The dictator had been assassinated because of his disregard of upper-class sensibilities in general and of traditional constitutional practice in particular, and it is thus hardly surprising that at first the obscure upstart who was his adopted heir was shunned by respectable society. Indeed, young Caesar's early actions marked him as the murderous enemy of the established order. As often happens, however, longevity in power bestowed respectability. By the early 30s B.C., it was clear that young Caesar was going to be a permanent feature of the political scene, and many members of the older aristocracy took advantage of the Treaty of Misenum to make their peace with him. The upstart now began to add some of the prestigious names from the past to his roster of supporters.

New Name for Young Caesar

In the year 38 B.C. at the latest, Caesar (like Sex. Pompeius) adopted a new form of nomenclature. In that year, he is attested on a coin as *Imp. Caesar Divi f.*: "General Caesar son of the deified one." Though there was some basis for this name in aristocratic nomenclature, no one had ever used the title imperator ("victorious general") as a personal name. With this strange new name, Caesar emphasized not only his connection with the late dictator but also his military prestige. He needed to enhance his reputation among the soldiery at the time that he was about to challenge Magnus Pius in Sicily without the help of any of his triumviral colleagues. The new name also served to distinguish him from normal human beings. (To mark his new stature, young Caesar will be referred to from now on as Imp. Caesar.)

Initial Failure in the War with Magnus Pius

Despite the lack of support from Antony, Imp. Caesar went on with his war in 38 B.C. When Imp. Caesar attempted to invade Sicily, Magnus Pius was having the better of things when a storm intervened, destroying much of Imp. Caesar's fleet and forcing him to give up the operation. Maecenas was sent to gain Antony's agreement to assist in the campaign, and he succeeded. In 37 B.C., Agrippa (now consul) gathered a great fleet for Imp. Caesar, and on the Bay of Naples he built a massive artificial harbor to contain it during training.

New Agreement with Antony

In the spring of 37 B.C., Antony showed up with his fleet at Tarentum in southern Italy. Imp. Caesar at first refused the aid, presumably preferring to defeat Magnus on his own. A rupture between the two triumvirs was averted through the intervention of Octavia, Imp. Caesar's sister and Antony's wife, and a new agreement was made between them. Antony promised to help in the war with Magnus, who was stripped of his consulship. Imp. Caesar accepted the loan of 120 ships and some admirals (including L. Calpurnius Bibulus, son of the dictator's consular colleague and enemy) and promised to lend Antony 20,000 troops for his Parthian war. To seal the alliance with more marriages, Caesar's infant daughter Julia was betrothed to Antony's elder son by Fulvia.

Renewal of the Triumvirate

The triumvirate had legally expired at the end of 38 B.C., and now it was renewed retroactively to last from January 1, 37, to December 31, 33 B.C. It is indicative of the extent to which legal niceties were now irrelevant that the triumvirs had in the interim continued to hold the same powers as before, even though the office upon which their power was theoretically based had lapsed. The feebleness of this pretence at constitutional propriety shows how low any regard for Republican sentiment had sunk after so many brutal years of conflict among the competing warlords. The fiction of the legal justification for their exercise of military power could not be dispensed with altogether, but if the constitutional charade faltered for a short while, no matter. The troops still obeyed their generals, and that was the crucial thing.

Defeat of Magnus Pius

After meticulous preparations, the war against Magnus Pius began on July 1, 36 B.C. Agrippa was admiral-in-chief, and there was to be a threefold invasion of Sicily, with two fleets coming from Italy, while Lepidus invaded from Africa. After various setbacks encountered during the invasion, Agrippa finally made an end of Magnus's pretensions at the battle of Naulochus on September 3. Using the technique of grappling the enemy ships to overcome their superiority in maneuverability, Agrippa defeated Magnus, who fled with the remains of his fleet to Asia. There, the ever-resilient Magnus reestablished himself and entered into negotiations with both Antony and the king of Parthia. Eventually, his fleet was destroyed by one of Antony's generals in 35 B.C., and Magnus was finally executed (the exact circumstances are a little unclear). In honor of his victory, Imp. Caesar was voted the sacrosancticity of a tribune of the plebs.

End of Lepidus

Lepidus brought his forces to Sicily to take part in the campaign against Magnus Pius, and eventually he had eighteen legions under his control. When Magnus's land forces, which Lepidus was besieging, learned of the defeat at Naulochus, they wished to surrender to him. Imp. Caesar forbade this, but Lepidus accepted their surrender anyway, and feeling that it was time to assert himself, he demanded that Caesar leave the island to him. Imp. Caesar entered Lepidus's camp, and his prestige was so great that Lepidus's troops went over to him. It seems that Imp. Caesar had already decided that it was time to remove the third triumvir, and this little drama had already been arranged beforehand through the bribery of Lepidus's troops, who apparently did not think much of their commander. Lepidus, who had been given the position of pontifex maximus upon the death of Caesar the dictator, was allowed to retain his priestly dignity, and he lived out the twenty-three years remaining to his life in exile in a small Italian town. Now the only major military leaders left were Imp. Caesar in control of Italy and the territory to the west, and Antony in the East.

Given Imp. Caesar's earlier ferocity, his lenient treatment of Lepidus may at first seem surprising. But Imp. Caesar's genius lay in his accurate assessment of political realities and his ability to manipulate them. This forms a noticeable contrast with the behavior of his adoptive father, whose disregard of senatorial opinion had cost him his life. Seeing that a showdown with Antony was inevitable after the removal of Lepidus, Caesar knew that he had to shed his intimidating image as a man who was ready and willing to use violence to get his way and that he had to acquire instead a permanent position on the basis of popular acceptance of his control of the state. His forbearance toward Lepidus shows that already several years before the victory at Actium that made him the uncontested ruler of the Roman world, Imp. Caesar was laying the foundations for his transformation into the man who alone could provide and guarantee the peace that was the main desire of so many people after fifteen years of disorder, violence, and bloodshed.

Antony in the East

Now that we have seen Imp. Caesar finally establish his sole control of the west, it is time to backtrack and recount Antony's activities in the East. After the victory at Philippi, Antony had assumed the task of subduing the areas that had been under the control of the Republicans. This he did without too much trouble in 41 B.C., spending the winter of

41/40 B.C. in Alexandria with Cleopatra while his brother Lucius contested unsuccessfully for control of Italy. In 40 B.C., however, the Parthians seized the opportunity to invade.

Parthian Invasion

In the period before Philippi, C. Cassius had sent Q. Labienus (son of the T. Labienus who had been Caesar the dictator's lieutenant in Gaul and then his opponent during the civil war) to Parthia to solicit the assistance of the king. In early 40 B.C., Parthian forces invaded Syria under the command of Labienus and Pacorus, the son of King Orodes (Pacorus had led the abortive invasion of Syria back in 51 B.C.). Labienus struck coins under the name Q. *Labienus Parthicus imperator* (see Coin 31). Though some Greek sources take this to mean "Parthian general," the prima facie interpretation would be "conqueror of the Parthians, general." If so, Labienus was posing as a conqueror of the Parthians who was using Parthian auxiliary troops. Presumably, he was portraying his military activity as a Roman attempt to liberate Roman territory from oppression at the hands of an illegitimate faction (i.e., the triumvirs). Certainly, the garrison of Syria, once loyal to Cassius, went over to him, and while Pacorus remained in Syria, Labienus invaded Asia Minor, reaching as far as the Roman province of Asia. At this time Antony was in Egypt, but instead of attacking Labienus, he sailed to Athens (stopping along the way at Tyre, which was holding out against Labienus) to deal with Imp. Caesar and Magnus Pius.

While he was himself occupied in the west, where he was waiting for an opportunity to undermine Imp. Caesar, Antony sent his general P. Ventidius Bassus against Labienus. (Ventidius had been one of the generals who failed to come to L. Antonius's aid during the Perusine war.) Ventidius proved a good choice, and in 39 B.C. he defeated Labienus in three battles in Asia Minor as he was withdrawing toward Syria. Labienus fell while fleeing after the third battle, and Pacorus abandoned Syria. In 38 B.C., Pacorus again invaded Syria, which Ventidius had reoccupied in the meanwhile, and on June 9 (the anniversary of the battle of Carrhae), Ventidius annihilated the Parthians at the battle of Gindarus in northern Mesopotamia, killing Pacorus himself. Antony arrived at this point, taking over command from Ventidius, who celebrated a triumph in 37 B.C. It is ironic that in his childhood fifty-one years earlier, Ventidius himself had been paraded through Rome in the triumph of Cn. Pompeius Strabo cos. 89 during the Social War (see Chapter 6). (It is also symbolic of the assimilation of non-Roman Italy into the Roman political system that one of Ventidius's lieutenants was a Poppaedius Silo, clearly a relative of one of the major leaders of the Italians during the Social War.) Antony achieved nothing of consequence, and by 37 B.C. he was back in Italy to deal once more with the problems of Imp. Caesar and Magnus. It was not until 36 B.C. that Antony could resume the war against Parthia.

Reorganization of the East

The invasion of 40 B.C. showed the unreliability of the system of client states set up by Pompey in western Asia Minor and Syria more than twenty years earlier (see Chapter 13). The kings mostly showed themselves to be disloyal or incompetent. After the reconquest, Antony carried out a general reorganization in the interest of four major kings. Now that the pirate problem was finally settled, he decided that there was no longer any need for the sprawling province of Cilicia and instead divided up the unruly areas of eastern Asia Minor between the kings of Cappadocia and Galatia. Southern Syria he left in the control of Herod, whose father had been a senior administrator in the moribund Hasmonean dynasty of Judaea. It was easier for these local kings to deal with the intractable problems of the recalcitrant locals.

Cleopatra

The final monarch to benefit from Antony's reorganization was Cleopatra, the Ptolemaic queen of Egypt. He had met her in 41 B.C., and by him she had twins (a son and a daughter). After the defeat of the Parthians, he strengthened the Egyptian kingdom by giving Cleopatra control of certain areas in southern Syria, a town in Cilicia, and the island of Cyprus (these territories had belonged to the Ptolemaic dynasty in the past). Later, after Imp. Caesar used Cleopatra as an excuse to wage war on Antony, it was alleged that he was completely under her sway and that these gifts were an outrage. In fact, the gifts were not all that extensive, and in any case it was to remain a common policy over the next century for the Romans to place unmanageable territories in the East under the rule of local kings ("client kings"). Furthermore, Antony was by no means completely besotted with Cleopatra, as he refused on several occasions to accede to her requests at the expense of Herod, the ruler of Judaea.

Nonetheless, like Caesar the dictator before him, Antony did to some extent fall under the thrall of Cleopatra. When he moved east from Italy in 37 B.C., he took along with him his lawful Roman wife, Imp. Caesar's sister Octavia, who was to bear him two children, but he soon sent her back on the pretext that the Parthian War made it too dangerous for her to stay in the East. Around this time, he recognized the paternity of the two children born to him by Cleopatra in 40 B.C., and she bore him another son in 36 B.C. When in 35 B.C. Octavia accompanied reinforcements being sent to Antony by her brother, he ordered her to return to Italy. Perhaps things might have turned out differently if Octavia had had boys, but both her children by Antony were daughters.[5] (Oddly enough, Octavia continued to be loyal to Antony, and even after his death she would act as mother to Antony's children by his previous wife Fulvia and, even more surprisingly, by Cleopatra.)

DISASTROUS CAMPAIGN AGAINST PARTHIA

King Orodes of Parthia was saddened by the death of his son Pacorus, and abdicated in favor of his son Phraates, who proceeded to murder his father and brothers and to drive various noblemen from the country. Antony decided that this was an opportune time to invade the country. In 37 B.C., he sent generals to attack tribes in the Caucasus to ensure peace in that direction, just as Pompey had done thirty years earlier (Chapter 13). In 36 B.C., he invaded Parthia itself, and his plan shows that the lessons of Crassus's debacle had been learned. Instead of marching directly south into Mesopotamia, he took a northerly route along the foothills of the Armenian mountains. He received help from King Artavastes of Armenia and intended to invade Media, an Iranian territory to the east of Mesopotamia. As he advanced along rough terrain, he decided to move on quickly with most of his troops, leaving the baggage train and siege engines to follow behind at a slower pace. While Antony besieged Phraaspes, the capital of Media, the Parthians overwhelmed his train, which had been left in the lurch by Artavastes. Antony at first decided to continue with the siege, but as it seemed that he had little chance of quick success without his siege engines, at the approach of winter he decided to withdraw. Unlike Crassus, he showed himself to be an effective leader of men during defeat (just as he had during the withdrawal from Mutina back in 43 B.C.). Though he managed to extricate his army intact, something like a quarter of the troops were lost.

In 35 B.C., Antony entered into an alliance with the king of Media (confusingly also named Artavastes), a subordinate of the king of Parthia

---

5   The elder Antonia later married L. Domitius Ahenobarbus cos. 16 and was the grand-mother of the emperor Nero (his birth name was L. Domitius Ahenobarbus), and the younger Antonia married Imp. Caesar's stepson Drusus Claudius Nero (the son of his wife Livia) and gave birth to the emperor Claudius.

who was disgruntled about the way the plunder taken from Antony had been divided. Antony's plan to attack Armenia was cut short by his need to meet Octavia, who had shown up again in Syria. In 34 B.C., Antony was finally able to launch his attack on Armenia, and he somewhat restored his reputation by deposing the disloyal king of Armenia. Now there were only two military leaders left in the Roman world, Imp. Caesar and M. Antonius, and a showdown between them was all but inevitable.

QUESTIONS FOR STUDY AND REFLECTION

1. What course of action did the surviving Republicans take after their defeat at Philippi?
2. What was the relationship between young Caesar and Antony after the battle of Philippi? What were their relative strengths and weaknesses, and how did they attempt to exploit these? What kept forcing them to reconcile despite their differences?
3. What was L. Antonius's purpose in provoking conflict with young Caesar? Why did he fail? Why did Antony not help?
4. What was Sex. Pompeius/Magnus Pius's position? What were his intentions? Why did he begin to lose support after the treaty of Misenum?
5. How did the political position of young Caesar change in the early 30s B.C.? What was the basis of his power at first? How did public opinion about him change?
6. Why did Lepidus soon lose importance after the establishment of the triumvirate? What led his forces to defect to young Caesar in Sicily? Why did young Caesar not have him killed?
7. What was the constitutional position of Q. Labienus, and what did he intend to achieve with his invasion of Syria?
8. Why did young Caesar and Sex. Pompeius adopt the respective names of Imp. Caesar and Magnus Pius? What was distinctive about their new nomenclature?
9. What was Antony's relationship with Cleopatra? What was the point of giving her territory outside of Egypt?

23

FINAL SHOWDOWN

IMP. CAESAR'S ILLYRIAN CAMPAIGN

After finally eliminating Magnus Pius in 36 B.C., Imp. Caesar spent the years 35 and 34 B.C. subduing the northern coast of Illyricum. The Romans had been involved in the affairs of Illyricum to some extent for the previous two hundred years, but only from the time of Caesar's consulship in 59 B.C. is it attested as a province. Since there was no immediately pressing problem in the area at this time, it is reasonable to conjecture that the purpose of the campaign was to keep Imp. Caesar's troops in training and to win him further military prestige on the cheap. It is worth noting that in 84 B.C. Cinna attempted to undertake an Illyrian campaign to prepare his troops for the final encounter with Sulla (see Chapter 10). In 33 B.C., Imp. Caesar used the plunder for some major building projects in Rome, and while he abstained from celebrating a triumph himself, he granted that distinction to some of his generals. It must have been obvious that with Lepidus out of the way, a final showdown between Imp. Caesar and Antony was imminent.

THE "DONATIONS"

In 34 B.C., Antony attempted to restore his military reputation by invading Armenia and deposing Artavastes of Armenia, who had left him in the lurch during the unsuccessful campaign of 36 B.C. When he returned to Alexandria, Antony celebrated the semblance of a Roman triumph. Soon thereafter, he carried out a thoroughgoing rearrangement of the East that was received poorly in Italy. By now, he had become inseparably involved with Cleopatra, and in this eastern settlement he made a number of grants (known as "donations") for the benefit of Cleopatra and her children.

1. Cleopatra herself was given the Oriental title "queen of kings," which suggested sovereignty over other monarchs outside of Egypt. Coele Syria ("Hollow Syria," i.e., basically Judaea) and Cyprus – territories that had been held by the Ptolemaic dynasty in the past – were transferred from Roman to Egyptian control.

2. Her child Caesarion was recognized as the son of Caesar the dictator and as Cleopatra's coregent in Egypt. This was an affront to Imp. Caesar, who not unnaturally disputed the child's paternity (as did many others).

3. Cleopatra's six-year-old son by Antony, Alexander Helios ("the Sun"), was proclaimed king of Armenia, Media, and Parthia. At the time, only Armenia was under Antony's control, with Parthia remaining completely independent. Since Alexander was already betrothed to the daughter of Antony's ally, the king of Media, the intention must have been that Armenia and Parthia were to be added to Alexander's territories once he came to control Media. Thus, this proclamation can only be taken as indicating the intention to wage a major campaign of conquest in the East. Presumably, the association of the child with the great Macedonian conqueror by virtue of his name was the reason for giving Antony and Cleopatra's elder son this rather provisional kingdom.

4. Alexander's sister Cleopatra was made queen of Cyrene, an area that had once belonged to the Ptolemaic kingdom and after being bequeathed by its last king to the Roman People in 96 B.C. was turned into a province in 75 B.C. (see Chapters 8 and 12).

5. Antony and Cleopatra's two-year-old son Ptolemy Philadelphus received a vast kingdom in the Roman East comprising Syria, Phoenicia, and Cilicia.[1] This was appropriate for a child named after the founder of the Macedonian dynasty of Egypt, who had greatly expanded the amount of territory he held outside of Egypt. The existing client kings of Asia Minor were to be subordinate to the mighty two-year-old.

While there was nothing unheard-of in giving Roman territory to Eastern potentates, the extent of these grants was unprecedented. Furthermore, Roman client kings were normally proven men who could serve the Roman interest in some way, but these grants to minors were clearly dynastic in purpose, benefiting as they did the Ptolemies of Egypt, who now had the blood of Roman generals in their veins.

---

[1] This is the description of the territory given by Plutarch (*Life of Antony* 54.7). Dio describes it much more expansively as stretching from the Euphrates to the Hellespont (i.e., he adds in all of Asia Minor). Plutarch's version is to be preferred as being more specific and less inflammatory. It is unclear how Herod of Judaea, who had been recognized as king by Antony and Caesar in 37 B.C., was affected by the grant of Phoenicia.

ANTONY'S INTENTIONS

To some extent, it is difficult to understand exactly what Antony was up to because the preserved accounts are fairly hostile. It seems that from 37 B.C. on he was increasingly operating in the guise of a Greek monarch. He claimed to be the incarnation of the god Dionysus (Hellenistic kings often associated themselves with some specific deity). At the same time, his quasi-spouse Cleopatra posed as Aphrodite. From the Egyptian perspective, these choices were very appropriate, since Dionysus and Aphrodite were the Greek gods equated with the Egyptian pair of divine sibling spouses Osiris and Isis (who were also associated with the kings and queens of Egypt). In the Greco-Roman context, Antony's choice of divinity left something to be desired, since the cult of Dionysus was associated with drunken revelry and Antony himself had something of a reputation as a heavy drinker. In any case, while in the eyes of Roman law any marriage with a foreigner was invalid, he became increasing attached to Cleopatra (literally and metaphorically) in the mid 30s B.C. Though he did not divorce Octavia officially until 32 B.C., he seems to have married Cleopatra before this (either in 33 or 32 B.C.). Seemingly, Antony was simply advancing further down the path that Caesar the dictator had begun in that he was adopting the trappings of Hellenistic royalty while at the same time maintaining his status as a Roman imperator. As the dictator's experience had indicated, and the developments of the next few years would confirm, this was not a viable policy for establishing permanent power in the Roman context. Not only was the notion of having an Eastern king not particularly appealing to Roman opinion in its own right, but the very idea would allow Imp. Caesar to pose as the defender of chaste and proper Italy against the threat of eastern tyranny. The initial offense caused to Roman sensibilities by Antony's eastern policies was probably exaggerated after his defeat, and it seems not to have caused immediate alienation among his supporters. Nonetheless, in the struggle for popular acceptance, Imp. Caesar would have a distinct advantage over his eastern rival, and once it became a distinct possibility that Antony would suffer military defeat, his supporters began to defect in droves. There is no way to know how Antony's attempt to set up a mixed Greco-Roman dynasty would have fared if he had been the one to emerge victorious from the showdown with Imp. Caesar. Certainly, Caesar the dictator had failed with his efforts along these lines, and Imp. Caesar's successful establishment of a personal autocracy eschewed any such eastern associations and was based on quite different principles. (For a coin that associates Antony with Cleopatra and downplays his Roman honors, see Coin 32.)

As for his intentions toward Imp. Caesar at the time of the donations, Antony's military dispositions as well as the dynastic arrangements indicate that his mind was fixed on campaigning to the East and not on a final conflict with Imp. Caesar. As late as 33 B.C., Antony had large numbers of troops in Armenia, and it seems that he was eager to consolidate his hold on Armenia and campaign with his ally the king of Media against the Parthians. Imp. Caesar, however, had other plans, which cut short Antony's dreams of conquering the East and setting up his family as a sort of eastern dynasty.

Rupture between Imp. Caesar and Antony

The triumvirate legally expired on the last day of 33 B.C., and this time there was no reason to renew the office. Antony was seemingly bent on basing his power on the principles of Hellenistic monarchy, and for his part Imp. Caesar had good reason to abandon the title. In the first place, it was associated with his old alliance with the man who was now his sole surviving rival. Furthermore, the triumvirate symbolized the unconstitutional nature of Imp. Caesar's rise to power, and since he would pose as the defender of tradition in the coming struggle, it was necessary to divest himself of this very untraditional office.

The consuls for 32 B.C., Cn. Domitius Ahenobarbus and C. Sosius, were both partisans of Antony. They had documents from Antony in which he sought official recognition of his dispositions in the East, and Imp. Caesar wished these to be made public in order to discredit Antony. After a certain amount of negotiation about this, Sosius attacked Imp. Caesar in the senate in early 32 B.C. At this point, Imp. Caesar convened the senate himself, though he no longer had any official position. Sitting in his seat between the consuls, Imp. Caesar attacked both Antony and Sosius. No one dared raise a voice against Imp. Caesar, and the consuls promptly left Rome to join Antony in the East. Three hundred senators followed them. Clearly, the person of Imp. Caesar was all-powerful in Rome, despite the expiration of his triumviral office.

Imp. Caesar was now in a bit of a quandary. It was obvious that war would soon follow, but he needed to rally public opinion in Italy first. He made no move against those who went east to join Antony, clearly wishing to distance himself from the murderous reputation that he had acquired in the past. (This effort fits in with his leniency toward Lepidus back in 35 B.C.; see Chapter 22.) Soon after the departure of Antony's supporters, Imp. Caesar made a speech whose contents are not known but which caused Antony to divorce Octavia in the late spring. (She left his house and took with her all his Roman children, apart from the eldest, who was in the East with his father.)

Antony's Will

Imp. Caesar received the necessary grounds for war in the form of information brought by two defectors from Antony. L. Munatius Plancus, whom we last saw as governor of Gallia Comata at the time of the battle of Bononia in 43 B.C. (see Chapter 21), and his nephew M. Titius (who had put Magnus Pius to death) decided to abandon ship in time, and when they fled from Antony to Imp. Caesar, they brought news about an incriminating will that Antony had had deposited with the Vestal Virgins in Rome (Plancus and Titius were witnesses to the will). Imp. Caesar had to remove the will from the reluctant Virgins' possession himself, and then read it to the senate. In his will, Antony

- recognized Caesarion as Caesar's son
- left large legacies to his children by Cleopatra
- directed that he was to be buried alongside Cleopatra in Alexandria.

People claimed to be shocked by these provisions. Substantively, it is hard to see why. The first provision had no legal significance at all. The second seems not unreasonable, though in conjunction with the third it could be taken as signifying an abandonment of Italy for the East. Certainly, that is how the official line took it: the drunken, degenerate Antony had now completely fallen under the sway of the wanton queen of Egypt. She was presented as the antithesis of the chaste and modest values of sober Italy, which had to defend its liberty against this threat of decadent eastern despotism. Another rumor also went around that Antony intended to make Cleopatra the queen of Rome and to move the capital of the empire to Alexandria. This will is so pointless and detrimental to Antony's interests that some modern scholars believe it was a forgery, though there is no evidence for this. Presumably, his long sojourn in the East had made Antony lose touch with political realities in Italy.

Antony was stripped of the consulship that he was to hold in the next year with Imp. Caesar as his colleague, but he was not declared a public enemy (hostis). Such a declaration would have meant an overt war against Antony, something that Imp. Caesar wished to avoid. It made sense in terms of rallying public opinion to portray the matter as simply a war against the foreigner Cleopatra. This policy also brought practical benefits with it. By rejecting the declaration of Antony as a public enemy, Imp. Caesar avoided difficulties in welcoming supporters of Antony who defected to him, and it would also be easier to reconcile Antonian loyalists after the anticipated victory.

Oath of Allegiance to the "Leader"

Italy was in turmoil. While Imp. Caesar's interpretation of events was clear, many still supported Antony or at any rate had no great desire to go to war again simply for Caesar's sake. Imp. Caesar, who, to judge by the staged takeover of Lepidus's legions in 35 B.C. (see Chapter 22), had a flair for public drama, hit upon the idea of turning the drummed-up outrage felt about Antony into a national cause. By now, it was such a long-standing practice for the votes of the assemblies in Rome to be determined through the use of force that they counted for little as a real indication of popular opinion. Instead, an outpouring of supposedly voluntary expressions of support from the municipalities of Italy could serve to indicate the will of the Roman People. Such mass declarations had taken place before – for instance, to demand Cicero's recall from exile in 57 B.C. (see Chapter 18) and to express well wishes for Pompey during a serious illness in 50 B.C. Now all of Italy swore a personal oath of allegiance to Imp. Caesar and demanded that he act as their "leader" (*dux*) in the upcoming struggle. The term "Roman People" now signified much more than simply the population of the city on the Tiber, and the oath, which was administered not just in Italy but throughout the western provinces, gave Imp. Caesar the necessary legitimacy to lead them in a final war that was supposedly directed against Egypt but would give Imp. Caesar undisputed control of the Roman world.

The terms of the oath are not known, but several oaths from the early Empire are preserved in which all provincials swear to

- hold the same personal enemies as the emperor
- pursue those enemies until they paid the penalty
- hold his life as dear as their own.

It is noteworthy that the text uses the word *inimici* to express "enemies." This word literally means "non-friends" in Latin, and signifies personal enemies within society, as distinct from hostes, who were foreign military enemies. Thus, the citizens of the Roman state obligated themselves to support Imp. Caesar in his hostilities with citizen opponents. In effect, Imp. Caesar's personal adversaries were being converted into public enemies, whom all Romans were obliged to fight to the death.

While Imp. Caesar made out that the oath was taken by the Roman citizens in areas under his control as a spontaneous expression of loyalty, it is reasonably clear that the whole affair was orchestrated. Imp. Caesar ostentatiously excused the people of Bononia (modern Bologna) from taking the oath on account of their traditional ties to the house of the Antonii, but this indicates that compulsion was normal. Certainly, after the war some municipalities of Italy were harmed during the distribution of land to the numerous discharged veterans, and it is an easy conjecture that those who had shown reluctance in taking the oath were being punished.

This oath not only served as an excuse for the war and a rallying point, but it also gave Imp. Caesar a (nonofficial) political position that would simultaneously legitimize and mask the fact that his power was ultimately based on his control of the military. With this outpouring of "national" support for the coming showdown with the East, Imp. Caesar had war declared on Cleopatra in the fall of 32 B.C. Conveniently enough, Imp. Caesar had previously been designated as consul for 31 B.C., and thus he could lead the war in the East as the holder of the traditional chief magistracy. This would add further luster to his stance as the defender of Roman virtue against eastern despotism.

Campaign in Greece

Antony's total army is said to have numbered 100,000, but large numbers had to be left in the East as garrisons. It is known that many client kings contributed contingents, which indicates that after the many years with Imp. Caesar in control of Italy, Antony's legions were depleted. Geography forced Antony to adopt a basically defensive strategy. Whereas the Aegean shore of Greece has numerous good anchorages, the only major ports in the southeast of Italy are Tarentum and Brundisium. Thus, while Imp. Caesar could easily block the few landing areas in Italy, Antony could hardly prevent Imp. Caesar from establishing himself somewhere in Greece, and he had to wait for Imp. Caesar to make the first move. Accordingly, he posted detachments in outlying ports to find out where the invasion would arrive and held his main force back in readiness in the centrally located town of Patrae in the Gulf of Corinth, from which he could sally forth once Imp. Caesar's invasion plan became clear. Under the circumstances, this was a reasonable strategy, but it failed in practice. (For a coin that was minted with the purpose of maintaining the loyalty of Antony's legions, see Coin 33.)

Already in the fall of 32 B.C., Imp. Caesar concentrated his forces in Brundisium and then attempted to cross the Adriatic. After he had made it as far as the island of Corcyra, a storm forced the fleet to return to

Italy, and the end of the sailing season meant that the invasion had to be postponed until the next year. In the spring of 31 B.C., Agrippa, who was once more acting as Imp. Caesar's admiral, launched a major raid on the western coast of the Peloponnesus. After storming the town of Methone, he used it as a base from which to seize a number of Antony's supply ships and to make further raids in Greece. Presumably, this was a feint meant to throw Antony off guard. Encouraged by this success, Imp. Caesar decided to embark his main force of eight legions once again. This time, he managed to seize the island of Corcyra, from which he threatened the Ambracian Gulf (modern Gulf of Arta). He took the promontory of Actium at the entrance to the gulf and established an armed camp there, while Antony's forces retained control of the strongly fortified gulf itself.

Word of Imp. Caesar's arrival was quickly sent to Antony, and in response he hastened to the rescue with his whole fleet. Once Antony's main force was committed at Actium, Agrippa seized the initiative by destroying a fleet of Antony's at Leucas and capturing his major base at Patrae. Antony found himself stuck in a very disadvantageous situation. A stalemate ensued during the summer, with Imp. Caesar refusing to give battle on land, where Antony probably held the advantage, while Antony, who had little experience in naval warfare, was unwilling to fight at sea. With his main lines of communication cut off by Imp. Caesar's naval superiority, Antony's situation progressively deteriorated. His troops were weakened through malaria (his camp was placed on unhealthy ground), and his supporters – both Romans and client kings – began to go over to Imp. Caesar. By late summer, only three consulars remained with Antony (even Cn. Ahenobarbus cos. 32, whose father had been such an inveterate enemy of Caesar the dictator and who had himself fought the dictator's heir for more than a decade, seized the opportunity of a disagreement with Cleopatra to go over to Imp. Caesar). By late August, it was clear that Antony was outmaneuvered both politically and militarily and that only drastic action could save him.

Battle of Actium

On September 2, 31 B.C., Antony's fleet sailed forth from the bay near the promontory of Actium, which closes off the entrance to the bay (and gives its name to the battle). There is much confusion in the sources as to his intentions, but it seems that he had decided to fight his way out of the trap into which he had fallen and then withdraw with such forces as he could extricate to the East, where he would regroup his land forces. Given his naval inferiority, this plan was a gamble, but it was the best option available. As it turned out, Antony's large ships were defeated by the smaller vessels and better trained crews of Imp. Caesar's fleet, which was commanded by Agrippa. Cleopatra kept her ships in reserve, and when an opening appeared in Imp. Caesar's line, she fled through it. This maneuver led to accusations that she betrayed Antony, but nothing in her later behavior lends credibility to this interpretation. When he saw her leave, Antony abandoned his fleet, which was clearly being defeated, and sailed after her with a few ships that managed to disengage. The commander of Antony's land forces in Greece, who had been ordered to bring them to Asia, abandoned the troops, and they promptly went over to Imp. Caesar. While the battle of Actium may not itself have been a major military engagement, it was politically decisive. Though it took another year to get rid of Antony and Cleopatra, they were already finished. Imp. Caesar began his pursuit and had gotten as far as the island of Samos in the Aegean when troubles with veterans in Italy forced him to turn back, the invasion of Egypt being postponed until the following year.

Like a good Hellenistic monarch, Imp. Caesar founded a city at the site of his camp above the battle site. Nicopolis (the "City of Victory") was created by forcibly transferring the population of a number of surrounding towns in Epirus. (Pompey had given the same name to the city that he founded to commemorate his victory over Mithridates; see Chapter 13).

END OF ANTONY AND CLEOPATRA

While Cleopatra sailed back to Egypt, Antony made for Cyrene, where he had collected an army. The commander (L. Pinarius Scarpus, a descendant of Caesar the dictator's elder sister) defected to Imp. Caesar and refused Antony admission. Antony almost decided to commit suicide, but instead he joined Cleopatra in Egypt, where they spent nearly a year awaiting Imp. Caesar's arrival.

By the summer of 30 B.C., Imp. Caesar was bringing a force to Egypt through Judaea, while the troops in Cyrene were invading from the west. On July 31, Antony enjoyed a final (minor) victory by routing some of Imp. Caesar's cavalry on the outskirts of Alexandria, but the next day his position became untenable when his cavalry and fleet surrendered to Imp. Caesar. His infantry then followed suit, and Alexandria capitulated.

Cleopatra fled to a mausoleum that she had recently had built for herself. Antony attempted suicide by stabbing himself in the belly but was not entirely successful (he lived long enough to be brought to Cleopatra before his death). Cleopatra herself entered into negotiations for surrender with Caesar. What exactly he wanted is not clear, but on August 9 she committed suicide, perhaps to avoid appearing in the victor's triumph in Rome. On August 29, Caesar was proclaimed pharaoh, though legally Egypt became a possession of the Roman People.

Antony's troops were taken into Imp. Caesar's service. A few of Antony's Roman supporters were executed, though a number were granted clemency. Of Cleopatra's children, only the eldest (Caesarion), the putative son of the dictator, was killed (the younger children by Antony were too young to be a danger and appeared with a statue of Cleopatra in Imp. Caesar's triumph). Of Antony's two sons by Fulvia, the eldest was executed, but the younger one, named Jullus, was favored by Imp. Caesar. He received as his wife his stepmother Octavia's daughter by an earlier marriage (and thus Imp. Caesar's niece), and reached the consulship in 10 B.C. (He eventually got back at Caesar by committing adultery with his lascivious daughter Julia and was executed for this outrage when the news of Julia's behavior broke out in scandal in 2 B.C.)

Imp. Caesar was now the undisputed ruler of the Roman world and its chosen leader. It remained to be seen how Imp. Caesar would conduct himself in victory. His adoptive father the dictator had gotten himself assassinated because of his inability to reconcile the reality of his autocratic powers with senatorial attachment to the traditional constitution. Imp. Caesar's recent attempts to shed his reputation for bloodshed show that he was aware of the problem and was preparing the way for establishing his control of the state on the basis of popular consent rather than naked force. His success at reconciling the seemingly irreconcilable would establish a new form of government that would endure with little (and mostly organic) modification for two and a half centuries.

QUESTIONS FOR STUDY AND REFLECTION

1. In what way did Antony try to achieve glory for himself in terms of being either a Roman general or a Hellenistic monarch? What was his purpose in his extensive campaigning against Armenia and Parthia?

2. What was Antony's relationship with Cleopatra? What was the purpose of the "donations"? What was the reaction to them in Rome?

3. How did Imp. Caesar and Antony differ in their attempts to seek legitimacy for their power?

4. What steps did Imp. Caesar take to present himself as a man of peace in the years leading up to the battle of Actium?

5. What was Imp. Caesar's excuse for going to war? Why did he choose to present the war in this light? How did he treat Antony's supporters?

6. What was the significance of the oath taken to Imp. Caesar at the start of the war? What position did he assume as leader of the war?
7. What was Antony's strategy in the war with Imp. Caesar? Why did it fail?
8. How did Imp. Caesar deal with Antony's and Cleopatra's offspring after Actium? Did he treat different children differently? Why?

24

THE AUGUSTAN SETTLEMENT AND THE "RESTORED" REPUBLIC

AUGUSTAN SETTLEMENT: END OF THE REPUBLIC?

With the defeat of Antony and Cleopatra at Actium and the annexation of Egypt, Imp. Caesar was the sole and undisputed power in the Roman state and the question was, now what? The constitutional arrangements by which various powers were granted to Imp. Caesar took place over the course of several decades. (As we shall soon see, Imp. Caesar would receive the new title Augustus for his role in "restoring" the Republic; this is discussed later in the chapter.) The final result of the new constitutional system was inherited by Augustus's stepson Tiberius with no dispute after his own death, and these arrangements, known as the Augustan settlement, would provide the basis of the Imperial government for the next 250 years.

With the benefit of hindsight, we can see that the new arrangements of Augustus marked the foundation of the Roman Empire. Indeed, his "reign" is generally dated from the year 27 B.C., when the first attempt at a permanent solution was made. At the time, however, exactly the opposite was supposedly going on. So far from establishing himself as emperor, Imp. Caesar claimed to be *restoring* the Republic, and in recognition of this act he was granted the title of Augustus. Thus, our perspective is entirely different from that of contemporaries. And the failure to realize that a new (and autocratic) form of government had been set up – or at least to understand that the old Republican institutions could no longer be restored to their previous operation – persisted for generations under the Julio-Claudian dynasty (such being the designation of the Imperial house established by Augustus). To some extent, this failure to grasp what appears to us to be the self-evident demise of the Republic can be ascribed to the ingenious way that Augustus acquired full legitimacy for his political supremacy in the state through a supposed restoration of the institutions of the Republic while at the same time assuming for himself unprecedented powers that allowed him to manipulate the entire political system and retain full control of the military. But the real question is, did Augustus intend – either at the beginning of his constitutional settlement or as time went on – to establish what we recognize as the Imperial form of government? The answer is almost assuredly no. It is a basically teleological interpretation to view historical developments as inherently and intentionally leading up to a later historical reality that grew out of those developments. When Augustus began his initial efforts in the later 30s and early 20s B.C. to arrange a permanent constitutional settlement that would allow him to retain control of the political scene in Rome and of the armies stationed in the provinces while at the same time accommodating and assuaging the general assumption that the old Republican form of government was to be restored, he had no way of knowing that he would live for more than four more decades, much less that over the years he would gradually acquire powers that would be exercised by a series of successors over the course of centuries. At the time, what he knew was simply the chaos and violence of the preceding decades, and he made a series of ad hoc efforts to remedy this situation. As it was, he enjoyed a success in this endeavor that fully justified the gratitude of his contemporaries. This sense of gratitude, coupled with Augustus's care in avoiding insult to traditional sensibilities and concealing the untraditional nature of his new powers and the new institutions that he set up, made it possible for contemporaries to be unaware of the long-term implications of the new system.

This chapter is intended not to look at the developments under Augustus in terms of how they created the Imperial system of government that lay in the future. Instead, we will examine the way in which they were either based on Republican precedents (however distorted) or represented novel solutions to the conglomeration of institutional and political factors that contributed to the breakdown of the Late Republic. In effect, we will not consider the system set up by Augustus retrospectively from the perspective of the future Empire. Rather, the development of the Augustan system will be analyzed as a response to specific problems of the Late Republic that had to be solved if peace was to be put on a permanent footing (and Augustus himself was to be spared the fate of his adoptive father).

It must be borne in mind that the powers that Augustus accumulated were not granted in one fell swoop. Instead, over the years he received more and more honors. Since he lived for so long – forty-one years after the supposed restoration of the Republic – by the time of his death he had in effect assumed so much power and taken over so many public functions that without anyone really noticing, he had in many ways become the personification of the state. In exercising these powers he eventually set up a permanent central government – something that the old Republican constitution had so signally failed to provide – and as a consequence, upon his death there was no alternative but to fill his position with a successor.

We are not interested here in a full picture of Augustus's career. Instead, the discussion is organized around three themes: the personal powers granted to Augustus, the new administrative apparatus that he set up, and the military structure that he established and the strategic planning that he implemented with it.

PRELIMINARY SETTLEMENT

The first thing to deal with after the defeat of Antony and Cleopatra was the soldiery. Having taken over Antony's troops, Imp. Caesar now had about a half million men under arms. He dismissed around 300,000, providing land for them through both distributions in Italy and the establishment of numerous colonies abroad. By confiscating the treasury of the Egyptian kings he had a huge amount of money available, which made it rather easier to acquire all this land without bloodshed. He broke up a number of legions and retained twenty-eight in service. (For a coin minted in the period directly after the victory at Actium, see Coin 34.)

After spending two years in the East settling its affairs, Imp. Caesar returned to Italy in late 29 B.C. and celebrated a lavish triumph, in which vast sums were distributed to the troops and inhabitants of the city. Upon his arrival, he promptly set about giving up some of his untraditional powers. Apparently, he had previously held the right to twenty-four lictors.[1] As consuls of 28 B.C., Imp. Caesar and his close friend and general M. Agrippa each had the traditional twelve lictors. They also held the census, since the division of the citizenry into the five census classes was a necessity for the functioning of the centuriate assembly, but no census had been carried out in decades. In their capacity as censors, Imp. Caesar and Agrippa also removed from the senate some unsavory characters who had gained entry during the preceding period of civil war. All this was a lead-up to a first attempt at a permanent settlement. Imp. Caesar was also empowered by law to create new patricians (patricians were needed to fill certain priesthoods, and their numbers had been rather depleted during

---

[1] Each consul normally had twelve lictors as a symbol of his imperium. Since the consuls' hierarchical superiority over praetors was marked by their having twice as many lictors as the six normally serving each praetor, Caesar's twenty-four showed that he was the superior of any consul and thus in full control of the state.

the civil wars). (For a visual representation of Imp. Caesar's restoration of traditional procedures, see Coin 35.)

Constitutional Settlement

of January, 27 B.C.

Imp. Caesar was faced with a seemingly insoluble political problem. His adoptive father the dictator had ended the previous civil war by defeating his enemies and taking sole control of the military, but he had then been assassinated for refusing to restore the old political system and adopting the trappings of royalty and divinity. On the other hand, recent history had shown that if the armies were left in the control of the annual magistrates, someone would inevitably undertake to use his troops to try and seize power. Many thousands had died during the civil wars, and clearly there was no going back to the Republic. The military could not be kept under control without someone assuming such extensive powers as to preclude any restoration of the Republic. It was a mark of Imp. Caesar's genius that he found a way to take up autocratic powers that allowed him to maintain control over the army while at the same time seeming to restore the old Republican system of elective office.

In January of 27 B.C., Imp. Caesar ostentatiously restored the Republic. We have his own account of this act in his *Res Gestae*, a sort of memorandum composed in his old age in which he looked back (at times rather tendentiously) on his public accomplishments (which is what the title signifies in Latin):

> In my sixth and seventh consulships [in 28 and 27 B.C.], having become master of everything by universal consent after I had put an end to the civil wars, I transferred the Republic from my power to the control of the senate and People of Rome. (section 34)

The historian Velleius Paterculus wrote the following assessment of the same event in the collection of historical biographies that he wrote in A.D. 30, more than halfway through the reign of Augustus's successor Tiberius:

> After twenty years, the civil wars were ended, foreign wars buried, peace revived, the fury of arms everywhere lulled to sleep; force was restored to the laws, authority to the courts, and its majesty to the senate, and the rule of the magistrates was returned to its old forms (except two praetors were added to the eight). The ancient, original form of the Republic was brought back. (2.89.3)

The Republican constitutional order was ostensibly restored: the old magistracies regained their full vigor, and in particular the consulship resumed its traditional primacy in that the practice of electing suffect consuls every year was given up. The number of praetors was fixed at ten (later raised to twelve, which was still a reduction from the sixteen elected under Caesar the dictator), and they were to preside over the public courts in the traditional manner.

To the extent that the old offices regained their functions, the old constitution was in fact restored. But looks can be deceiving. What actually took place was a carefully orchestrated piece of showmanship. Imp. Caesar first went before the senate and laid down all his powers. Though this was undoubtedly what any good member of the senate would theoretically desire, everyone must have known that such a move would only lead to a renewal of the civil wars that had cost so many lives during the preceding two decades. Therefore, a compromise was proposed whereby the old system would be restored in a limited way, but Imp. Caesar would retain great power, particularly control of the military. Imp. Caesar must have had the details worked out in advance and coached various senators in the proposals they were to make once he ostensibly gave up all his powers. Thus, whereas Caesar the dictator was assassinated for not restoring the Republic and for assuming monarchical powers in defiance of senatorial wishes, his heir did restore the Republic and was then granted powers that nullified that restoration by a senate that feared a return of bloodshed. As a reward for this restoration, Imp. Caesar was voted the title Augustus. (For a coin that is emblematic of the supposed restoration of the traditional governmental order, see Coin 36.)

Control of the Military

How was it possible for Augustus to possess such powers while still ostensibly restoring the functions of the Republic? The answer is through the retention of military force. Virtually all provinces that had legions in them were assigned to Augustus. While the peaceful, ungarrisoned provinces had a senatorial proconsul, the unruly internal ones and those along the border were commanded by Augustus through legates. The precedent for this procedure dates back to Pompey's extraordinary commands. The practice had started in 67 B.C., when the lex Gabinia granted Pompey the right to appoint legates with propraetorian imperium to assist him in the war against the pirates, and the precedent was set in the late 50s B.C. when for several years he had used legates in the same way to govern the two provinces of Spain without ever setting foot in them. Now, Augustus was authorized to use a similar system to administer all the provinces that had legions (with a few minor exceptions). The initial grant was for a ten-year period, and these provincial assignments were renewed whenever the old grants expired. Not surprisingly, Augustus makes no mention in the *Res Gestae* of these extraordinary provincial commands, which were at complete variance – in terms of both their duration and their extent – with the spirit of the Republican constitution. Furthermore, since the troops had sworn allegiance to him personally, all the legions (with one exception)[2] were likewise commanded by a legate appointed by Augustus. Thus, there could be no possibility of civil war resuming since virtually no one commanded troops apart from Augustus and his representatives, and in any case all the troops were bound by their oath to Augustus.

Technically, Augustus would merely be a senatorial governor like any other (though his command was unusually extensive), and his legates would be inferior in rank to the other senatorial governors. Two constitutional practices were formalized to reflect this hierarchical distinction. Augustus's legates were allowed only five lictors, whereas the senatorial promagistrates possessed six. In this way, the traditional governors seemed to outrank the legates, but in practice no senatorial governor would have the right (or temerity) to meddle with Augustus's provinces or the men that he had placed in charge of them. In addition, the senatorial governors were all called proconsuls, even if they were technically propraetors, and in this way the ex-praetor who governed a minor province like Crete and Cyrene with the title of proconsul was given formal precedence over the senior consular put in charge of a major military province like Syria with its garrison of several legions. In practical terms, however, the latter was far more important, and it was this sort of intentional concealment of effective power through misleading constitutional arrangements that obscured the new political realities and made the restoration of the old Republic credible.

Since Augustus now held the ultimate command over all troops, the legates who commanded them were not technically in command (the "auspices" belonged to him). For this reason, the legates' victories were ascribed to him, and it was he who was hailed imperator (in the old sense of "victorious general").[3] Later, the route of the triumph would be shifted

---

[2] See note 18.

[3] Under Augustus and Tiberius, certain senators were allowed to celebrate triumphs in the traditional manner, but this right would eventually be reserved for the emperor and his relations (victorious generals were granted no more than the ovation, a lesser form of triumph under the Republic, but they were sometimes granted the right to wear the insignia appropriate for someone who had celebrated a triumph).

in a way to emphasize Augustus's control of the military: instead of winding up in the precinct of Jupiter Optimus Maximus on the Capitoline Hill, as had been the practice under the Republic, the triumphal procession (see Chapter 3 n. 21) led to the Temple of Mars Ultor in the new forum that Augustus built.[4]

GRANT OF THE TITLE AUGUSTUS

In recognition of his restoration of the Republic in January 27 B.C., the senate voted to bestow on Imp. Caesar the title *Augustus*. This honorific was proposed by L. Munatius Plancus, the man whose shifting loyalties during the civil wars after the death of Caesar the dictator had earned him the nickname "horse jumper" (see Chapter 21 n. 6). (No doubt Augustus himself arranged for Plancus to make this proposal, just as all the other proposals of that month were carefully worked out in advance.) The title Augustus was very cleverly chosen. Some of his advisors had suggested that he be called Romulus as the new founder of Rome, but this was rejected because of its monarchical associations (Romulus was the first king of Rome as well as its founder). Based on the Latin adjective from which the English word "august" is borrowed, the new title means basically the same thing. The word is related to the verb *augere* (to "grow") and in origin meant something like "magnified," and hence designated something or someone as being "exalted." While grand sounding with its religious overtones, the new title had the advantage of lacking any specific political signification. In this way, the leading man of the state acquired a title that set him apart from everyone else without really indicating the nature of his preeminence or suggesting that his lofty position was in any way at variance with the traditional constitution. All later emperors adopted this honorific, and along with the title pontifex maximus, it was the only element in the Imperial titulature that was reserved solely for the ruling emperor (all other titles could be bestowed on the heir apparent). Augustus now comes to be known formally as Imp. Caesar Augustus.

[4] The construction of this temple in commemoration of his avenging Caesar the dictator's murder (Ultor means "the Avenger") had been vowed by young Caesar in his youth at the battle of Philippi back in 42 B.C., and it is indicative of the extent to which Augustus wished to set aside his image as a man of violence and portray himself instead as the upholder of peace that the temple was not dedicated until 2 B.C. (After Actium, Augustus generally deemphasized his connection with his adoptive father the dictator, who had destroyed the Republic.)

Princeps

In recognition of his dominant position in the state, Augustus was often referred to with the unofficial title *princeps*. This is a Latin word meaning "eminent person" and had several different senses under the Republic. It could be applied to any of the most politically important individuals of a state (this sense was expressed more fully as *princeps civitatis* or "leading man of the citizenry"). More specifically, it could refer to the leading ex-consul whose opinion was asked first in the senate (the *princeps senatus*). The vague use of princeps without any specification indicated Augustus's preeminent position in a general way but at the same time implied that as the "first among equals" he had no particular powers that distinguished him from the other leading men of the restored Republic. Like the title Augustus, the informal designation princeps was adopted with the intention of indicating Augustus's special position in the state while at the same time denying it substance. In particular, the new title had civilian connotations of leadership in a free political system, and was generally preferred to the military sounding imperator. Princeps became a favored designation of Augustus's successors, and for this reason the early Imperial government is known as the Principate.[5]

New Arrangements in 23 b.c.

To retain control over the newly restored Republic, Augustus held the consulship every year from 27 until 23 b.c. At the same time, the constitutional irregularity of electing two suffect consuls every year, which had been regular practice since 40 b.c. (see Chapter 22), was abandoned with the restoration of the Republic in 27 b.c. While this development had the intended effect of heightening the impression that the old constitution was once more in operation, it greatly reduced access to the consulship if Augustus held the office every year. Such a situation would cause obvious problems in the long run. It was the ambition of any self-respecting Roman senator to become consul – and those with illustrious consular ancestors considered it their right – but if Augustus had to hold the office every year to maintain his control over the state, the aspirations of many

---

[5] During his lifetime, Augustus was addressed as imperator, and this title was already becoming a general term for his official position, but his successor Tiberius never used the title in his titulature, presumably because of its connotations of unconstitutional power. It nonetheless remained in common use, and in the reign of Nero it began to be placed at times at the beginning of the emperor's name, and this practice then became invariable from the Flavian period on.

members of the old Republican families would necessarily be thwarted. Furthermore, during the 20s B.C., Augustus's consular colleagues had for the most part been of comparatively lowly background rather than from the leading families of the past. Thus, there was every reason to fear that some unhappy oligarchs might try to solve the problem through assassination.

An old scholarly theory held that the decision to cease holding the consulship was reached as a result of a conspiracy against Augustus that was entered into by one of the consuls of 24 B.C. When the senatorial proconsul of Macedonia was brought up on charges of treason (*maiestas*) for having waged a war against a Thracian tribe without senatorial authorization, he cited instructions from Augustus in his defense. Augustus was in attendance at the trial, and when questioned by the presiding magistrate, he denied having given such orders. The defendant's advocate in this case was named Varro Murena, and he entered into a conspiracy against Augustus's life with another senator named Fannius Caepio. It used to be thought that this Varro was also a consul who was removed from the list of consuls (*fasti*) before holding office in 24 B.C., and from this it was conjectured that it was this course of events that led to the new constitutional arrangements in the following year. It has since been shown, however, that the conspirator is likely to be a separate individual so that there is no necessary connection between the conspiracy and the change in Augustus's official status (and the exact chronological relationship between the conspiracy and the new arrangements remains unclear).[6] Nonetheless, the conspiracy was indicative of dissatisfaction in senatorial circles, and the defense used by the proconsul of Macedonia showed that uncertainty about the relative powers of Augustus as permanent consul on the one hand and the regular senatorial proconsuls on the other could cause uncertainty and complications. In effect, holding the consulship could easily result in conflict with the proconsuls while at the same time leaving Augustus responsible for decisions that he did not actually make.

The solution was to give Augustus a novel position that allowed him to interfere in activities in Rome while sparing him the invidious burden of regular administration, which would be left to the consuls. Augustus

---

[6] The fragmentary Capitoline fasti (the most authoritative ancient list of magistrates) show that L. Calpurnius Piso replaced an A. Terentius Varro Murena as ordinary consul. Since he is not mentioned in any of the other lists of consuls, Varro Murena presumably died while still designate, a fact noted in the official record but ignored in the lists made for practical purposes, which cared only about who the actual consuls were. The conspirator turns out to have been L. Licinius Varro Murena, who may well have been the brother of the consul.

would cease to hold the consulship on a regular basis and would be given tribunician power instead. As the traditional defenders of the plebs, the ten tribunes were sacrosanct, and Imp. Caesar had already been granted the sacrosanctity of the tribunes back in the 30s B.C. Now, as holder of a tribune's powers on permanent basis, Augustus could preside over the senate and quash the actions of any magistrate.[7]

At the same time, an attempt was made to assuage senatorial opinion by ostensibly enhancing the prestige of the consulship. Augustus's consular colleague at the start of 23 B.C. was a prominent member of the Republican nobility, L. Calpurnius Piso, who had fought with Brutus and Cassius at Philippi, and once Augustus resigned, his place was taken as suffect consul by another man with strong Republican credentials, L. Sestius, whose father had helped Milo in combating P. Clodius back in the early 50s B.C. and who for his own part had not only served as Brutus's quaestor but continued to cherish a statue of the fallen assassin of Caesar the dictator. In addition, the consulship came to be held for next two decades by many members of the famous senatorial families of the past. Thus, someone who was judging the political situation in 23 B.C. on the basis of external appearances without understanding that the true basis of Augustus's power was his control of the military would assume that the old Republic really was back in operation. In addition, to further lessen the appearance of personal autocracy, Augustus had his long-time associate M. Agrippa granted consular and provincial imperium equal to his own (the implications of this grant are discussed later in the chapter). In the *Res Gestae* Augustus makes much of the fact that he always had a colleague in his powers, but of course the colleagues were of his own choosing, and in any case since they were closely linked to Augustus, this "sharing" of power did nothing to lessen or restrict his own supremacy.

Furthermore, the apparent reduction of Augustus's powers in Rome was accompanied by two measures that assured his continued control of the provinces, where the real (military) power lay. First, he was exempted from the traditional principle whereby a promagistrate lost his imperium once he crossed back over the pomerium into the city. The practice had originally been intended to prevent the long-term tenure of imperium in the center of civic life in Rome, and Augustus's position would have been undercut if he could never return to the city without forfeiting his provincial commands. In addition, his imperium was made superior to that of any other governor (this was technically called *maius* or "greater"

---

[7] The grant of tribunician power had to be renewed every five or ten years like his provincial commands, but this was a formality.

imperium), a move which ensured that he would retain control of all provinces, including those that had supposedly been turned over to administration by the ex-magistrates of the restored Republic back in 27 B.C. Thus, even while Augustus gave up his obtrusive control of the political system in Rome by abandoning his constant tenure in the consulship, he confirmed and strengthened his less noticeable but more significant domination of the provincial administration.

As the next few years would prove, the regular consuls were not capable of managing affairs in Rome without assistance from Augustus, and this would result in his being granted greater powers. Thus, in the long run, the tribunician power turned out to be more symbolic than functional. In effect, it lent formal legitimacy to Augustus's interference in the regular operations of the senate and magistrates and thus helped to conceal the autocratic nature of his position in the Republic. Augustus (and all subsequent emperors) would list in their titulature an indication of the year of their tribunician power, which thus became a sort of regnal year. From now on, Augustus (and his successors in the Julio-Claudian dynasty) held the consulship only on special occasions, leaving the old chief magistracy to the most important members of the senate.[8]

Electoral Strife Underscores Augustus's Role as Guarantor of Order

If the intention in the settlement of 23 B.C. was to allow the consuls to assume more administrative responsibilities while Augustus still retained overall control of the senate and magistrates, the next few years would show that any substantive return to the old system was impossible. In 22 B.C., popular feeling against Augustus's relinquishing of the consulship was exacerbated by natural disasters including a grain shortage. The result was popular demonstrations at the senate house demanding that Augustus be appointed either perpetual consul or (what amounted to the same thing) dictator, and that he be made censor and given control of the grain supply. Augustus defused the situation by taking over control of the grain supply, but the event demonstrated that Augustus's personal prestige was such that

---

[8] Augustus's Julio-Claudian successors possessed enough legitimacy through their dynastic relationship with him that they had no particular need to hold the old Republican offices. The consulship would not be held frequently by members of the Imperial family until the Julio-Claudians were replaced by the Flavians, whose dynastic insecurity impelled them to seek prestige through the accumulation of old-fashioned civic honors.

the general populace would insist on a prominent position for him under any circumstances, and they were inclined to entrust him with permanent control of public functions. This attitude manifested itself again the following year when Augustus was away settling affairs in Sicily. When Augustus refused to stand for the consulship, the electorate insisted on electing only one consul, hoping thereby to compel Augustus to assume the other position. Augustus refused to intervene (perhaps to underline the senate's and the magistrates' inability to control the political situation without him). Eventually a second consul was chosen, but the same problem arose in the following year (21 B.C.) when Augustus had to send Agrippa to supervise the elections. As Augustus's representative, Agrippa succeeded in conducting the elections, but in 20 B.C. renewed disturbances resulted yet again in the election of a single consul in the hope that Augustus would accept the second position. The election that this sole consul presided over in 19 B.C. became even more turbulent. First, candidates for the quaestorship whom he had rejected as unsuitable continued to run for the office, so that he had to threaten them with force. Even more troubling was the case of Egnatius Rufus, who had won popular acclaim as aedile in the previous year and gained election as praetor for the present year. Wishing to build upon his illegal acquisition of one office directly after another, he now sought the consulship. The situation became so serious that the senate passed the senatus consultum ultimum, and Rufus was executed. Continued disturbances caused the senate to send an embassy to Augustus requesting his return. Instead, he nominated a member of the embassy (Q. Lucretius, who had been proscribed back in 43 B.C.), who was duly made the second consul (presumably through election).

The motives of the obstreperous candidates are hard to divine, but presumably they really believed that the chaotic electoral practices of the Late Republic had been restored and that they could gain office through popular acclaim despite the disapproval of the consul and magistrates. This drummed home the message that without oversight from Augustus the electoral system was dysfunctional: the assemblies would be dominated by the turbulent populace of Rome and were in any case determined to give Augustus powers that would be uncongenial to the senate. To rectify this situation, Augustus was given additional powers that more or less gave final form to his position in the state.

FURTHER GRANT OF IMPERIUM IN 19 B.C.

On October 12, 20 B.C., Augustus finally reentered the city from Spain and restored order. In recognition of how his return had been necessary for public order, the senate declared that the date should henceforth be celebrated as a holiday and voted for the construction of special altar to Fortuna Redux (the divine personification of "Restored Good Fortune") as a memorial. An addition to Augustus's constitutional powers was also granted in recognition of the fact that order could not be maintained in Rome without his personal intervention. The years since he had given up the consulship back in 23 B.C. had shown repeatedly that the populace was insistent that he should receive some sort of permanent position in Rome, and in any case the electoral process had failed on numerous occasions and could be carried out only after he (or his representative) took charge of the situation. To facilitate his oversight of Rome, he was granted consular imperium for life and the right to sit in a curule seat between the consuls. In effect, he now held the imperium of a consul in Rome without actually holding the consulship. Once more, this very untraditional power goes unmentioned in the *Res Gestae*. In any case, although the electoral process was not perfect, from this point on there was to be no more interruption of the elections through rioting.

FURTHER TITLES AND HONORS

As Augustus's unassuming and indirect control of public life continued, he received further honors that underlined his preeminent position. In 12 B.C., M. Aemilius Lepidus, Augustus's old colleague as triumvir, finally died. Lepidus had held the post of pontifex maximus, and he retained it throughout his long years of disgrace. After his death, the post needed to be filled, and as an expression of loyalty, people from all across Italy came to Rome to elect Augustus to the position. (This title was always bestowed upon subsequent emperors.) In 2 B.C., Augustus was acclaimed pater patriae ("father of the fatherland") by the plebs, equestrian order, and senate, and apart from his immediate successor Tiberius, all later emperors adopted this title. Once more, Augustus received a distinction that proclaimed his prominence while not directly indicating any unprecedented domination of the state.

AUGUSTUS AND DIVINE HONORS

One of the ways in which Caesar the dictator had caused the resentment that resulted in his assassination was his adoption of the quasi-divine honors associated with the kings of the Hellenistic world. Augustus went out of his way to avoid such honors in Rome, but he allowed himself to be worshipped outside of Italy and to be treated in an implicitly divine way in Rome. This is another form of personal prestige that goes unmentioned in the *Res Gestae*.

In the triumviral period, Imp. Caesar was conceived of popularly as a godlike figure (the poets Virgil and Horace both speak of him as a god). Yet, there was no official recognition of his divinity, and Imp. Caesar was clearly aware of the dangers of offending senatorial sentiment as his adoptive father had done. When he attempted to make a permanent settlement with his pseudo-restoration of the Republic in 27 B.C., he rejected the title "Romulus" because of its unfortunate regal associations and instead chose the vaguely religious "Augustus," which suggested something divine without making it clear how exactly the "August" one was associated with the gods. From this time on, he also consistently downplayed his relationship with the Deified Julius.

Yet, this is not to say that he did not receive quasi-divine honors in Rome. In 8 B.C., the month of August was renamed in his honor. The custom of naming months after kings was associated with Hellenistic kings, but to downplay this aspect of the grant the month chosen was not that of his birth (September) but the one in which he had first assumed imperium in 43 B.C. and finalized the conquest of Egypt in 30 B.C., which gave the renaming a certain "public" character. Altars were set up in honor of his return from abroad (both the altar to Fortuna Redux and the surviving altar of the Augustan Peace). Not only were annual sacrifices associated with these altars, but the former had a public festival (*Augustalia*) connected with it.

In the last decade B.C., a reform of a certain early cultic practice provided yet another vehicle for associating Augustus with the divine. An old spring festival called the *Compitalia* that had been particularly patronized by the lower classes was revived as a way to allow such residents of Rome to offer sacrifice to him in a subtle way, this rite being carried out publicly by the local organizations of the 265 "neighborhoods" (*vici*) into which Rome was divided in the years from 12 to 5 B.C. In this new festival, Augustus was treated as a sort of national father figure, and official sacrifice was made to his *genius* (a sort of guardian spirit) and *lares* (hearth gods) by the neighborhood officials. In this way, the inhabitants of the city were given a form of honoring the princeps that did not exactly look like a ruler cult and thus could avoid offending upperclass sensibilities.

In the cities of Italy, Augustus set up boards of six freedmen (*Augustales*) to carry out honors to the princeps. This was a way of allowing a form of public service to wealthy freedmen, who were otherwise barred from holding office. These boards then spread to the Romanized communities of the west.

While subterfuge was necessary to conceal divine honors for the princeps in Rome, this was not the case in the East, where it was the common practice for the expression of loyalty to the ruler to take the form of offering him divine worship. Even here, however, Augustus showed due caution, generally insisting that he be worshipped alongside the goddess Roma, who had received sporadic worship in the East during the Republic as the personification of Roman power.

In the west, Augustus encouraged the establishment of similar cults in areas that had not been influenced by eastern ruler worship as a way of securing loyalty to the dynasty. The most famous example of this is the great altar of Rome and Augustus that was established in Lugdunum (modern Lyon) in Gallia Narbonensis by his stepson Drusus in 12 B.C. (a similar altar was set up in the newly conquered region of northwestern Spain).

In addition to the quasi-divine honors given to the princeps himself, his household (the *domus Augusta*) was treated with a respect that bordered on the godlike. All of this association of Augustus and his family with the divine gave him a form of prestige and political legitimacy that had nothing to do with the old elective offices of the Republic.

WEALTH

Another extraconstitutional factor that assured Augustus a dominant position in the years after Actium was his personal control of a vast amount of wealth. He had received a huge inheritance from Caesar the dictator, more sums wound up in his control from the proscriptions, the wealthy would frequently leave bequests to him, and he had seized the royal treasury of the Ptolemies after the death of Cleopatra. In the *Res Gestae*, Augustus notes with pride the huge sums that he spent on providing for the physical adornment of the city of Rome and the entertainment of its populace, and throughout the Principate the emperors would continue to be obliged to shower similar largesse on the capital. In terms of the establishment of his personal control, an equally important expenditure was the provision of discharge benefits for the soldiery, who were thus personally beholden to the princeps. Eventually, even Augustus's wealth proved unequal to this ongoing burden, and in A.D. 6 a special "military treasury" (*aerarium militare*) had to be established to administer the proceeds from special taxes dedicated to this purpose. By this time, however, the soldiers had been serving under a personal oath to the princeps for an entire generation, so that the change to a more public mode of payment would not threaten their loyalty to him. In any case, the princeps continued to dispose of immense wealth, and Augustus boasts of having given large subventions to the public treasury. Under the circumstances, it is hardly surprising if people conceived of the princeps as a man of godlike qualities.

EGYPT

An additional element in Augustus's power were the anomalous arrangements made for Egypt. Although it was legally annexed by the Roman People, a special status was set up for this very wealthy region. No senator was allowed to set foot there without Augustus's permission, and it was administered in his name by a nonsenatorial governor (called a "praefect"). In Egypt, Augustus acted and was treated like a traditional local ruler, receiving all pharaonic honors. Augustus clearly felt that Egypt's geographical isolation and great wealth would make it an ideal base from which to launch an attack on Rome, and his administrative arrangements were designed to keep it firmly within his personal control. Later Imperial history would show that his fears were never to be realized (probably because of the province's peripheral location and its lack of an effective military establishment for such an endeavor).

In more practical terms, Augustus revived the strict regimentation of rural life that was characteristic of all previous regimes in Egypt. In immediate terms, this strict governmental control was necessitated by the complicated system of dykes and canals that preserved and dispersed the waters from the annual inundation of the Nile, thereby making Egypt the most fertile (and wealthy) area of the ancient Mediterranean basin. From a self-interested point of view, the wealth created by the Nile could be taxed for Augustus's benefit just as it had been for his pharaonic predecessors. This system had fallen into shambles during the last decades of Ptolemaic rule, and much work was necessary to restore Egypt to its full agricultural potential.

Augustus's treatment of Egypt is markedly different from the way that Pompey had organized Pontus back in the mid 60s B.C. The Pontic kingdom had had a similarly intrusive royal control of the countryside, but knowing that the Republican system of provincial administration could not handle the ongoing oversight and direction necessary to keep such a system in operation, Pompey had divided the countryside up among the previously stunted Greek city-states (see Chapter 13). In effect, in recognition of the administrative limitations inherent in the constant turnover of governors and lack of a permanent bureaucracy, he abandoned the old system, which was profitable but demanded a level of supervision that it was impossible for the Republican form of government to sustain. For

Augustus, the situation was different. By keeping the traditional Egyptian form of administration under his personal control, he could (through the praefects he appointed) provide the complex administrative apparatus that controlled all aspects of food production in the Nile Valley. In the process, Augustus would reap huge financial benefits, and the agricultural surpluses of Egypt would help provide the grain dole in Rome. Thus, by personally controlling state functions, Augustus could oversee the exercise of institutional powers in a way that would have been impossible under the Republic.[9]

LATER ELECTORAL PROCESS

Now it is time to consider the role of the senate in the new system. How the electoral process functioned in the 30s B.C. is not known. It would seem that upon the restoration of the Republic, the elections were held according to the regular procedures in the usual assemblies. Nonetheless, Augustus exerted control over the system in a number of ways. First, he could accept the names of candidates, and it was hard to imagine someone proceeding with a candidacy that Augustus had rejected. Second, he himself regularly attended the assemblies and exercised his right as an upper class Roman to "commend" to the People the candidates whom he supported.[10] From A.D. 8 on, declining health prevented his further atten-

---

[9] In the long run, the Roman administration with its constant exactions eventually ground down the economic prosperity of Egypt. Since in the initial reestablishment of the tax system, Augustus was, for the most part, merely retaining older levies collected under the Ptolemaic regime, the problem was probably not that the burden of Roman taxes was substantially greater than had previously been the case. Rather, what distinguished the Roman system from the previous one was its permanence and (comparative) efficiency. Whereas older pharaonic dynasties would periodically fall into chaos through disputed succession or the incompetence of individual rulers, the Roman government was unaffected by the quality of the rulers in Rome. The taxes were collected year after year, decade after decade, with monotonous regularity. Even if the traditional taxes were only slightly more than the economy could bear, after a long period of marginally excessive taxation, the countryside became exhausted (an extensive edict issued by the praefect of Egypt Ti. Julius Alexander in A.D. 68 shows that the economic situation of the province had already become critical by the end of the Julio-Claudian dynasty).

[10] Augustus is said to have "given" the consulship in 19 B.C. to one member of the senatorial commission that requested his return to Rome (Dio 54.10.2), and the same phraseology is used by Tacitus (*Annals* 3.75) to describe his offer of the consulship to Labeo (see n. 16) as if it were in his gift to bestow. This terminology has led to some confusion, but presumably all it means is that Augustus could more or less guarantee election to a man whose candidacy he would openly support ("commend"). Dio also informs us (55.34.2) that in A.D. 7 Augustus "appointed" all the magistrates because

dance at the assemblies, and instead he published a list of candidates that he favored. It came to be the regular procedure that those who appeared on these lists were automatically elected (they were termed *candidati Caesaris* or "candidates of Caesar"). The number of men elected in this way for the lower magistracies is not known, but Augustus established the custom of commending four of the twelve praetors.

He also had to intervene to make sure that the full list of offices was filled. While there continued to be keen competition for the consulship and praetorship, which still had important functions to carry out and also served as prerequisites for the Imperial legateships that bestowed senior military command, the junior offices sank in importance, and at times Augustus had to take various ad hoc steps to provide enough aediles, quaestors, tribunes, and more junior elective officials.

Return of Suffect Consulships

Back in the 30s B.C., there had been numerous suffect consulships, with the ordinary consuls resigning to allow others to gain the prestige of the office and to hold the imperium necessary for military command. These voluntary resignations to allow for extra consulships ceased after Actium. Once Augustus gave up holding the consulship regularly in 23 B.C., the office reverted to its old pattern, and for nearly two decades only two consuls were elected each year, mainly from the old nobility of the Republic but there were also some new men being rewarded for meritorious service. The year 5 B.C. saw the return of suffect consulships (and perhaps in an effort to conceal or at least mitigate this deviation from traditional practice, Augustus himself held the ordinary consulship that year with the portentously named L. Cornelius Sulla, a descendant of the dictator). For the rest of Augustus's life and for most of his successor Tiberius's reign, the ordinary consuls with whom a given year started would resign in midyear, to be replaced by a pair of suffect consuls. There were two reasons for this development. First, the number of Imperial appointments that needed to be filled by someone of consular rank simply outstripped the number of consulars that would be available if only two men held the office per year. In addition, if the two positions were held (as was frequently the case) by men from the old Republican nobility, then there would be little opportunity to reward (and make further use of) the talents of men with less distinguished backgrounds. Thus, suffect consulships could allow for the

of strife in the electoral assemblies. Again, this presumably means that he used his personal prestige to "commend" a full slate of candidates, who were duly returned.

rise of new men while at the same time maintaining the apparent preeminence of the famous names of the past.[11]

New Men

A remarkable aspect of the restored Republic was the extent to which it gave ostentatious prominence to men of the old nobility while at the same time allowing the rise of new men from the municipalities of Italy.[12] In particular, while it would not do to deny senior commands to the old nobility, great use was made of competent new men who owed their promotion to their own merits, and who were loyal to the princeps and in any case lacked the prestige necessary to challenge him. Eventually, the members of the old nobility would die out (both through natural attrition due to high mortality rates and frequent prosecutions for treason under the Julio-Claudians), and by the end of the dynasty the senate would be dominated by families that came to prominence under Augustus and his successors. But this was hardly Augustus's intention.

Final Electoral Reform

The Imperial historian Tacitus baldly asserts (*Annals* 1.15.1) that the elections which took place in A.D. 14 after the death of Augustus marked the first time that the electoral process was transferred from the People to the senate, and certainly the evidence seems to indicate that under the Empire the magistrates were chosen in the senate, though these choices were then ratified by pro forma elections in the old Republican assemblies. However, a partially preserved inscription that was found in 1947 indicates that the development in electoral procedure is more complicated than Tacitus suggests.

---

[11] As a further token of the ostensible restoration of the Republic, Augustus managed to dredge up for senatorial office some descendants of celebrated men whose families had not been heard of for centuries. For instance, one of the consuls of A.D. 8 was M. Furius Camillus, whose homonymous forebear had famously captured the city of Veii back in about 390 B.C. (the family then sank into oblivion in the middle fourth century B.C.). A Sempronius Gracchus – perhaps the descendant of Gaius the tribune of 123–122 B.C. – was even found (though the upshot was unfortunate in that the man was exiled for committing adultery with Augustus's daughter). As already seen on several occasions, Augustus also promoted prominent Republicans from the civil war period.

[12] Interestingly, under the Empire, the term "noble" referred exclusively to those whose family had gained the consulship under the old Republic, and the term was not used for families that first reached the office under Augustus or his successors.

This inscription (the *tabula Hebana* from the year A.D. 19) preserves honors that were granted by the senate in memory of the emperor Tiberius's recently deceased adoptive son Germanicus, and among these were certain honors that paralleled ones that had been voted to Augustus's deceased adoptive sons L. and C. Caesar in A.D. 5. Since the inscription records only the modifications of the earlier honors, there is some uncertainty about details, but the general sense is clear. In A.D. 5, a special modification of the electoral procedure was instituted for voting in the centuriate assembly whereby all the senators and the equites Romani who were enrolled on the album for the public courts were to vote separately in ten special centuries, five named after Lucius and five after Gaius. The votes cast in these centuries were tabulated and announced before the voting of the other centuries in the regular elections, and the candidates returned in this fashion presumably enjoyed an advantage in the regular polling.[13] But how this procedure relates to Tacitus's statement about the exclusively senatorial vote in A.D. 14 is unclear. Certainly, the procedure of A.D. 5 with its special voting privilege for the equestrian jurors seems still to have been in operation in A.D. 14: if it had fallen into abeyance prior to A.D. 19, what would be the point of adding five new centuries named in honor of Germanicus? Furthermore, a further five centuries were added in the name of Tiberius's next heir, his natural son Drusus, after Drusus's death in A.D. 23. Certainly, this new procedure was (originally at any rate) compatible with regular electoral competition in the assemblies, since Dio tells us that in A.D. 7 Augustus had to "appoint" the magistrates because of strife in the assemblies.[14] In any case, whatever the exact method by which it eventually gave way to the exclusive selection of magistrates through the votes of the senate, this procedure indicates that even before the end of Augustus's life, the traditional principle of popular election of magistrates was giving way to self-selection by the senate (together, at first, with the equestrian jurors) under the oversight of the princeps. Even under the Republican procedure, the electors in the first census class had exercised a dominant influence on the outcome, but now the process was placed even more firmly under the control of those with the greatest wealth (the senators and equites Romani would possess far more than the 100,000 minimum property qualification for the old first census class).

---

[13] In a similar procedure in the centuriate assembly under the Republic, the vote of a single ("prerogative") century selected at random from the first census class was read out first, and its result had a strong influence on subsequent voting.

[14] See n. 10.

NEW ROLE FOR THE SENATE

The electoral difficulties of the 20s B.C. reemphasized the reality that the senate as a body was incapable of actually exercising authority; over the years its political impotence became clear, and attendance declined (Augustus was forced to make attendance obligatory and had a list of the senators displayed in the senate house in order to keep track of absences). In the old days, the debates had mainly served to set out the views of the senior consulars, and the junior senators for the most part decided which of these views to suppport. Now, this procedure made little sense in as much as the view of Augustus was the most important. In any case, the traditional method of conducting a debate in a body numbering several hundred was not very practical. Augustus tried a few variants on the procedure of selecting a board made up of a small number of senators with various levels of seniority to help draft legislation and to deal with administrative matters, but this practice did not outlive Augustus (and in any case undermined the authority of the senate as a whole, which would then only serve to rubber-stamp the board's decisions). On one of the few occasions when the senate was consulted on a major issue (the need to fund the retirement bonuses of retiring soldiers once Augustus's personal fortune was no longer up to the task), he forced the senate to accept his own proposal, which it found disagreeable. As for the passage of legislation, Augustus for the most part got the consuls to propose laws that he favored.

While the senate's role in determining major policy was at an end, the development in the relationship between the senate and the princeps set the stage for a new role in the state for the senatorial order. The senators no longer needed to court public popularity for office, and instead the senate became a self-regulating institution under the oversight of the princeps. The senate was given jurisdiction to try accusations against senators (the details are unknown, but presumably this was provided for by law) and lost interest in the public courts, the control of which had been such a bone of contention with the equestrian order, for the previous century. The matters left to the senate's decisions may not have been as exciting as the issues it had dealt with under the old Republic, but its decisions about such legal and administrative issues would eventually acquire the force of law (though this development took decades to work itself out). Augustus also began the practice of giving social privileges and legal obligations to both senators and their descendants that would make senatorial rank a hereditary status. In effect, the senate was no longer the body in which those who had managed to secure election met. Instead, it was the hereditary meeting place of the rich individuals who choose to enter public life by holding the highest offices from the past in order to serve in major military and administrative positions under the leadership of the princeps. Such certainly was the thrust of developments from the time of Augustus on, but undoubtedly few were perspicacious enough to fully grasp the new situation at the time.

SENATORIAL OPPOSITION

Though Augustus's domination of the state must have been displeasing to some senators if they considered the matter in the abstract, he was remarkably successful in concealing the autocratic nature of his powers, so that the appearance of Republican norms was satisfactory to most people. The only major conspiracy against his life was the one in 24 B.C. that preceded his relinquishing the consulship.[15] There was the occasional hitch in Augustus's attempts to use traditional institutions in quite untraditional ways. When he was about to set off for Spain in 25 B.C., Augustus wished to appoint M. Valerius Messalla Corvinus (member of a patrician family and Augustus's consular colleague in 31 B.C.) to the post of urban praefect (discussed later the chapter). Corvinus at first accepted but then resigned within a few days on the grounds that the appointment was "unconstitutional" (*contra morem maiorum* or "contrary to ancestral custom"). Presumably, it was only when he took up the post that he realized that it entailed functions (perhaps police powers within the city) that had no precedent. In any case, Corvinus eventually lost his Republican scruples over the course of time, as he was to become the first (unprecedented) curator of the city's aqueducts. There are also a few instances of men who withdrew from public life out of disenchantment with the situation, but they were few and their example was not indicative of a widespread sense of alienation from the new political order.[16] In any case, Augustus was

---

[15] At a later date, a conspiracy of L. Cornelius Cinna, a descendant of Sulla's opponent in the 80s B.C. and of one of Caesar the dictator's assassins, was revealed to Augustus, who was so far from feeling threatened by the plot that he actually raised Cinna to the consulship of A.D. 5 (conceivably the year after the conspiracy, though its date is not secure).

[16] C. Asinius Pollio had been a supporter of the dictator Caesar who had Republican sensibilities, and in 43 B.C. he wrote to Cicero that as a governor in Gaul he would have preferred to back the Republicans. The force of circumstances, however, compelled him to go over to the triumvirs. Pollio's retirement from public life in the mid-triumviral period (he became a literary patron and wrote an influential history of the civil war that is not preserved) cannot betoken unhappiness with the Augustan settlement, but his persistent refusal to take part in political life even after Actium may have had

occasionally heckled when leaving the senate with the complaint that the senate was not actually allowed to enter into substantive debates, but such instances were no doubt uncommon.

Establishment of a Permanent Administrative System

Augustus gradually came to assume many governmental functions. Under the Republic, comparable functions had often been carried out by various magistracies, but for the most part in an uncoordinated, ad hoc manner (the aedileship in particular was stripped of its most important functions, which contributed to the inability to find candidates for the post). The process by which these new permanent functions were established was a protracted one that spanned many decades, and by the time of Augustus's death, the princeps directly or indirectly oversaw a large number of operations, which made good the lack of any sort of permanent bureaucracy under the Republic. Some of the more prominent functions in Rome and Italy were entrusted to senior senators, but a whole host of new functions were carried out by men of equestrian rank, and even by the slaves and freedmen of the princeps. Not only did these operations allow for administrative continuity and long-term planning, but they also provided the princeps with a form of control over important governmental functions. These functionaries appointed at the discretion of the princeps held positions of great authority that would never have been open to them under the old Republic, and they were naturally loyal to him. Not surprisingly this new system with its complete lack of precedent in Republican administrative practice finds no mention in the *Res Gestae*.

Senatorial Curatorships

For the most part, senior senators were appointed with the title of curator to preside on a long-term basis over operations in and around Rome that would be noticeable to the general public: the public works in Rome, maintenance of the city's aqueduct system and the road network in Italy, and the distribution of the grain dole in the city (all consular positions

broader significance. In any case, it is directly attested (Pomponius in *Digest* 1.2.2.47 and Tacitus, *Annals* 3.75) that the talented jurist M. Antistius Labeo, whose father had died fighting for the Republic, refused to accept the consulship when Augustus offered it (and that his career suffered on account of his attachment to the Republic, in contrast to the success of the obsequious jurist C. Ateius Capito).

apart from the last one, which ex-praetors exercised). While the appointment of the permanent curators may have seemed to reflect senatorial control of important governmental functions, the senatorial curators were no less Imperial appointees than Augustus's provincial legates were. In any case, the staff to carry out the operations on a day-to-day basis were slaves belonging to the princeps, to whom the curators were really responsible.

In this category was the initially abortive attempt to use the old position of praefect of the city to empower a senior consular to maintain order in the city. In the old days, a praefect of the city would be appointed by the consuls on a temporary basis to look after the city while they were absent for a short period, but the post had fallen into abeyance after the third century B.C., when the praetors (and traditional dictators in the earlier period) could act on behalf of the absent consuls. In 25 B.C., Augustus tried to use this post to keep order while he was away in Spain, but as we have seen, the first incumbent soon felt that the powers he was to exercise were unconstitutional. In A.D. 13, the post was accepted by a consular, and from then on the consular praefects of the city were responsible for maintaining order in Rome on a regular basis (generally for years on end).

ESTABLISHMENT OF A NEW BUREAUCRACY

A wealthy Roman was not expected to administer his property on a day-to-day basis. Instead, he employed a procurator ("manager") to run his affairs. These procurators could be of freeborn status, but they were commonly freedmen.[17] As the princeps came to bring more and more traditional functions under his personal control and to create entirely new ones, he not unnaturally used the normal administrative practices of wealthy Romans in administering these operations, which he treated as if they were part of his own household. These positions were instituted by

---

[17] This practice may seems odd to someone assuming the modern, racially based version of slavery, which intentionally demeaned the slaves and used them only for menial work, but it is consonant with the ancient institution, in which the main external sources for slaves were war captives and abandoned children of the lower classes whose parents were unable to support them. Thus, there was no inherent stigma attaching to slaves that prevented them from being used in intellectually demanding tasks, and slaves reared within the household could be examined carefully for talent and educated accordingly. Thus, it was possible for a master to train his own slaves (or to purchase ones already trained) for managerial tasks. Loyalty and efficiency could be encouraged with the prospect of eventual manumission (just as malfeasance could be severely punished), and those who were thus freed would still be beholden (and grateful) to their ex-master (and present benefactor).

Augustus, and thus they were appointed entirely at the princeps' discretion. In effect, Augustus began a process by which a permanent bureaucracy was established to exercise administrative responsibilities on a long-term basis, a procedure that had not been possible under the Republic's regime of annually changing magistrates.

The distinction between administrative appointments to be held by equites and those to be held by freedmen was hazy under the Julio-Claudians, and the only fixed differentiation was that those of servile origin could not command military units (though the navy at times formed an exemption). The power that accrued to well-placed freedmen in the Imperial household under Augustus's successors came to be bitterly resented by the senators, and by the second century A.D. the most senior positions in the new Imperial bureaucracy were reserved for freeborn men of equestrian standing.

Establishment of an Equestrian Career Pattern

Under the Republic, the whole point of the equestrian order was that it consisted of the wealthy men who had decided not to enter into politics by embarking on a senatorial career, though they did have military functions. Augustus's treatment of positions instituted by him as part of his household created an entirely separate administrative career pattern for men of equestrian status. Nominally, the equestrians ranked below the senators in census qualification and rank (the minimum property qualification for equites was fixed at 400,000, while the corresponding figure for senators was eventually settled, after some variation, at 1,000,000). In practice, however, some equestrians were richer than most senators, and in any case some men preferred to restrict themselves to an equestrian career, which dispensed with the public aspects of a senatorial career (like the need to curry popular favor and to pay for expensive public games) and gave more immediate access to the princeps.

Military Commands

As under the Republic, equestrian officers continued to command auxiliary units and to serve as legionary junior officers (military tribunes) under Augustus. (It was only toward the end of the Julio-Claudian dynasty that the lower career pattern became formalized.) In addition to this normal military service, the three legions stationed in Egypt were commanded by equestrians under the overall control of the praefect of Egypt.[18]

Procuratorships

The princeps came into the possession of a vast amount of property throughout the empire and employed procurators to manage his property in the provinces. These men also came to take a role in public administration, since the emperors could rely upon them as their own appointees. In Imperial provinces, the procurator performed the financial function of the quaestor in senatorial provinces, collecting revenues and paying the troops. This did not cause much friction, since both governor and procurator were Imperial appointees, and the superior rank of the former was clear. In senatorial provinces, the procurator simply managed the Imperial property. Since the procurator was a direct appointee of the princeps, however, there was a tendency for him to encroach on the jurisdiction of the transient senatorial governor. Lower rank procurators were put in charge of various individual estates. There were also procurators attached to the various curatorships of senatorial rank (like those overseeing the aqueducts) and the important equestrian prefectures (like the grain supply), as well as certain Imperial functions like the mint and the gladiatorial schools. (The permanent staff for these functions were placed under these subordinate procurators, and such posts tended to be filled by Imperial freedmen.)

Praefectures

Equites were employed as the primary administrators of certain Imperial functions under the title *praefectus* ("someone put in charge"). With this title, they served as the governors of smaller Imperial provinces (these minor governors later came to be called procurators). These were generally the provinces not considered worthy of an entire legion as a garrison (e.g., Judaea, the Balearic Islands, Raetia, Noricum). The major exception to this pattern is Egypt, which Augustus forbade senators even to set foot in and which was governed by equestrian praefects who acted in the name of Augustus in his capacity as pharaoh (as already noted, the legions

---

[18] Command of the one legion in the senatorial province of Africa would later be placed under an equestrian praefect, but under Augustus and Tiberius it remained the sole military unit in the hands of the senatorial proconsul.

stationed in Egypt were likewise commanded by equites). Under Augustus and his immediate successors, this was the most important equestrian position, but later it ranked second after the praetorian praefecture.

Men of equestrian rank were also employed to administer various activities taken over by the Emperor. Among these were the praefectures of

- The fleets (discussed later in the chapter). Under the Julio-Claudians, Imperial freedmen often served as fleet commanders, but afterward they were normally of equestrian rank.
- The *vigiles*. This was a force of slaves set up by Augustus as a fire brigade. Back in 22 B.C., he had put 600 publicly owned slaves at the disposal of the aediles for dealing with fires in Rome, but in A.D. 6 he instituted a large body of slaves that was organized along military lines and controlled by a praefect appointed by him. Eventually, this force came to assume policing functions as well.
- The *annona* ("grain supply"). In 22 B.C., Augustus also took over the *cura annonae* ("supervision of the grain supply"). 150,000 to 200,000 people in Rome were entitled to receive an allotment of grain several times a year, so providing enough grain, mainly from Africa and Egypt, was a major undertaking. For a long time, Augustus supervised the importation personally, while appointing senatorial praefects to carry out the distribution. At some time in about the last decade of his life, Augustus instituted an equestrian-rank praefect to manage the transportation of the grain to Rome and its storage, but he left the distribution in the care of the senatorial praefects.
- Praetorian Guard (discussed later in the chapter). The praetorian praefect had an extremely important role as the commander of the elite troops stationed near Rome. After the early Julio-Claudians, this was the senior equestrian position (previously it ranked in second place).
- Egypt. As already noted, this was initially considered the highest appointment for an equestrian administrator, but after Augustus it sank to second rank.

In terms of the operations in Rome, one can see two major periods of change. In 22 B.C., Augustus tried to regularize the administration of the city by boosting the powers of the senators (in the form of the aediles or senatorial praefects of grain distribution). In the last decade of his life, he delegated his responsibility for these tasks to equestrian praefects who were personally appointed by and accountable to him.

Public Courts

In connection with the role of the equites in the new administrative system, the final developments of the public court system should be mentioned.

Control of the jury panels had been a source of frequent strife in the period since C. Gracchus first put equites on the jury panels back in 123 B.C., and since 59 B.C. the jury panels had been evenly divided between senators and equites. As already noted, in a poorly understood development, the senate came to exercise jurisdiction over its own members under Augustus, and in any case, the senators had little grounds for interest in the courts, which no longer tried senior statesmen when accusations were lodged against them for political reasons. Such a potentially anarchic procedure had no place in the well-ordered state set up under Augustus, and the result was that the juries of the courts were given over entirely to the equites. Though the courts continued to function under Augustus's successor Tiberius, they would soon give way to the jurisdiction of the emperor (and his appointees). The old control of the judicial system by elected officials had no place under the new system, with governmental authority ultimately resting with the emperor.

Permanent Strategic Planning

Now that we have examined the administrative system by which positions of command were appointed, it is time to consider the military set up that formed the basis of Augustus's power. One advantage of the new system was that it made it possible to draw up and execute long-term policies regarding the expansion and defense of Rome's empire. Under the Republic, armies were raised and disbanded on an ad hoc basis. Perhaps in conjunction with the enrollment of the landless as permanent soldiers, the legions came to have a more permanent existence, though exactly how they were kept at full strength is not clear. In any case, the Republic certainly had no mechanism to maintain the forces under arms on a permanent basis, and there was no procedure to determine how many troops were needed and where to deploy them. (Such a determination did not even make sense under the Republic with its rapidly expanding territory, and a decision like this could be made only under the more settled circumstances of the Principate, when the borders became more or less permanently fixed.) Augustus's personal control of the military finally allowed a rational assessment of the strategic needs of the empire to be made in light of the resources available.

In the *Res Gestae*, Augustus mentions the fact that he dismissed from service some 300,000 troops. At the time of his defeat of Lepidus and Antony, he transferred their troops into his own service rather than discharging them ignominiously. After Actium, he did not simply retain his own troops and dismiss Antony's. Instead, he apparently released all those who wished to leave the service and kept some of Antony's units. On what basis he decided upon the number of troops to be retained in service is unknown.[19]

There is some doubt as to the exact number of legions he retained because of the peculiarities of the Roman method of numbering them, but the best evidence seems to be the report of Tacitus that in A.D. 23 there were twenty-five legions. On the (disputed but apparently correct) assumption that no new legions were raised after the loss of three at the Teutoberg Forest in A.D. 9 (discussed later in the chapter), Augustus decided to fix the number of legions at twenty-eight. These would amount to somewhat under 150,000 men. The total number of auxiliary units (i.e., those of non-Romans) is never recorded, and how Augustus deployed them is not known. Such evidence as there is indicates that the numbers of auxiliary troops on campaign generally equaled that of the legionaries. Thus, another 150,000 auxiliary troops may have existed at the time of Augustus. The later history of the Roman military indicates that the total number of troops chosen by Augustus was reasonably close to the necessary total.[20]

PRAETORIAN GUARD

In addition to his command over the troops in the provinces, Augustus also established a large corps of troops called the praetorian guard, who were permanently deployed in Italy. This corps arose from the traditional bodyguard of provincial governors but was much bigger than any earlier force. Nine cohorts of these troops (nearly the size of a whole legion) were created in 27 B.C., three being stationed near Rome and the rest scattered throughout Italy. This was a novelty since under the Republic there had been no permanent military or police force in Rome or Italy, and it may be conjectured that the decision to disperse these cohorts and not to gather them into a single legion as their numbers would warrant

[19] The extent to which there actually was any strategic planning under the Empire is a matter of dispute. While it may well be that there was no self-conscious policy making in the modern sense (with an overt review of the options available and a clear assessment of possible courses of action), certain decisions with strategic implications did have to be made, presumably on the basis of established tradition and experience. Whatever the method by which he reached his conclusions, Augustus must have had to decide after Actium how many troops to keep and how many to discharge, how many legions to retain, how many to disband, and where to deploy those that he did keep.

[20] As it turned out, Augustus somewhat underestimated future needs. The number of legions would gradually increase over the course of the Principate until the total reached thirty-three in the late second century A.D.

was intended to downplay the existence of this unprecedented military garrison in Italy. (In A.D. 23, the cohorts were finally united in a single camp close to Rome.) The praetorian guardsmen received better pay than the regular legionaries, and were presumably originally meant to act as an especially loyal corps that the princeps could use to maintain control in Italy. As it turned out, they were never needed in this capacity under Augustus (and very seldom later).

Augustus kept personal control of the praetorians until 2 B.C., when he established the position of praetorian praefect. This post had to be filled by someone especially trusted by the princeps, and for this reason the praetorian praefects came to be entrusted under the Principate with a number of administrative duties that went far beyond command over the troops. (Later emperors would always make sure to pamper the praetorian guard, and from their centrally located camp the guardsmen and their praefects were well placed to influence the succession in times of dynastic uncertainty.)

FLEET

One of the major faults of the old military establishment had been the lack of a permanent navy, and the Republic relied on vessels provided by allied maritime powers on an ad hoc basis. Augustus's trusty assistant Agrippa had assembled a major fleet in order to seize Sicily from Magnus Pius (Sex. Pompeius), and this fleet performed well at Actium (see Chapters 22 and 23). Afterward, two major fleets were established in Italy (one stationed at Misenum on the Bay of Naples and a second, somewhat smaller one at Ravenna at the head of the Adriatic) along with lesser provincial fleets. The main fleets saw little active service, serving mainly to deter piracy and facilitate occasional troop movements. They had the title "praetorian," which shows that they were technically a maritime equivalent of the praetorian guard.

WARS OF CONQUEST AND CONSOLIDATION

With the creation of this permanent military establishment, another role provided by the princeps was the development and execution of a coherent strategic policy to expand and consolidate Roman power. Augustus launched a number of aggressive military campaigns, some more successful than others. In the mid 20s B.C., he undertook the conquest of the northwestern Iberian peninsula. There were a few further small-scale revolts, but these were the last gasps of local resistance. Though under

Augustus there was a garrison of three legions in Spain, the number was soon reduced to one, as the process of Romanization quickly advanced and no further revolts broke out. In the mid 20s B.C., there were also two attempts to extend Roman territory southward from Egypt into the Arabian Peninsula and Ethiopia, but these proved to be abortive.

In the East, Augustus decided not to undertake any campaign of conquest at the expense of the Parthians. Despite the often expressed expectation of contemporary poets that he would be a latter-day Alexander, Augustus's actual goals were limited. Basically, he wished to secure the return of the military standards and prisoners captured by the Parthians as a result of Crassus's debacle at Carrhae and Antony's unsuccessful invasion and to restore Roman control over Armenia, whose king had regained his independence in the period after Antony's conquest in 34 B.C. Augustus must have decided that in light of Crassus's disaster, the risks involved in attempting to conquer the Parthians were too great. In any event, the threat of invasion compelled the Parthian king to give in, and he complied with Augustus's demands. Augustus then acted as if this diplomatic victory was a military one, celebrating a triumph and issuing coins that trumpeted the return of the standards and captives and proclaimed the recapture of Armenia.[21] In the case of Parthia, this attitude was rather a misrepresentation, and in the case of Armenia simply not true. Though the kings of Armenia did at times pay homage to Rome, they were often murdered by their nobles, and the Romans were incapable of asserting any effective control over the area, which remained a constant source of trouble both in its own right and in terms of Roman relations with Parthia.

Augustus adopted a rather different policy regarding the interior of the Balkans. After some troubles in the early 20s B.C. had been settled, an incursion into Roman territory made by northern tribes in 16 B.C. led to a major campaign of conquest in the years down to 9 B.C., when Roman territory was extended up the Danube and the new provinces of Pannonia and Illyricum were established. At approximately the same time, the area of the headwaters of the Danube in the northern Alps was annexed in the form of the provinces of Raetia and Noricum.

---

[21] The supposed victory led to the construction of a large triumphal arch, replacing a smaller one that had been built in the Roman Forum to commemorate the victory at Actium (see Coin 34). Presumably, the sham triumph over the Parthian king alone was considered more preferable grounds for permanent commemoration than the victory over Cleopatra and Egypt, which was difficult to dissociate from the defeat of Antony and his Roman supporters, however much it was officially viewed as a purely foreign war.

In the meanwhile, an effort was undertaken in 13 B.C. to extend Roman control eastward across the Rhine into Germany. In a series of campaigns that are reminiscent of Caesar the dictator's conquests in Gaul, the Romans quickly moved as far as the River Elbe but were never able to establish lasting control. Starting in A.D. 4, an effort was undertaken to crush a Germanic kingdom in the area between the upper Rhine and upper Danube, but at this point it became clear that the Romans had overextended themselves.

A large-scale revolt broke out in Pannonia in A.D. 6. Augustus encountered great reluctance to serve in the military when he tried to raise emergency reinforcements in Italy. Just when it seemed that this grave danger had been surmounted, news arrived of a fresh disaster in Germany, where three legions were destroyed in an ambush at the Teutoberg Forest. Following on the heels of the recruitment difficulties during the Pannonian revolt, this debacle, in which more than 10 percent of the total legionary force was wiped out, could not be made good, and the German conquests had to be abandoned.

Augustus's Injunction against Expansion

Augustus was now an old man and apparently took the loss badly. The prospects for the conquest of Germany that had seemed so bright only a few years earlier were now dashed. The Romans simply did not have sufficient resources to risk them in the attempt to conquer the undeveloped areas of Germany. While it was comparatively easy to control the settled agricultural populations around the Mediterranean, it was difficult for the Romans to impose their will among the comparatively primitive Germans.[22] A major factor in this failure was the fact that central Europe was at the time thickly covered with forests (these would not be removed until the Middle Ages). This situation meant that agricultural practices were less intensive, and the local inhabitants did not have much investment in the land they did cultivate. This low level of existence allowed them simply to move on if they found things disagreeable, and the Romans were reduced to moving their troops around from camp to camp without being able to establish permanent control over their newly acquired non-urbanized subjects. While the local commander may have been to blame for the immediate circumstances of the defeat at the Teutoberg Forest, nonetheless the task assigned to the Roman army was basically impossible

---

[22] Caesar the dictator had encountered a similar difficulty in his abortive attempt to subdue Britain back in 54 B.C.

to carry out. It was at this stage that Augustus wrote down instructions to his successors advising them not to extend the Empire, and with a few exceptions they complied until the second century.[23] The boundaries of the Empire would be the Atlantic in the west, the rivers Rhine and Danube to the north, the mountains of Armenia and the deserts lying to the west of Mesopotamia in the east, and the Sahara and the second cataract of the Nile in the south.

This sort of long-term institutional planning had been impossible under the Republic, which had no mechanism for regulating or coordinating the activities of the individual governors, much less drawing up and implementing any coherent strategic policy. The military and administrative structure set up by Augustus would prove to be well suited to the circumstances, and the Empire would enjoy two centuries of more or less undisturbed peace and stability.

CENTRALIZED COMMAND

A further area in which Augustus was able to correct a military problem that had plagued the Republic was the need to control the commanders in individual military campaigns. The conquests in Spain, the Balkans, and Germany were largely the work of his trusted lieutenant (and son-in-law) Agrippa, and his own stepsons Tiberius and Drusus, whose loyalty he could rely on without question. Tiberius played a major role in commanding the military force used to extort the capitulation of the Parthian king to Roman demands in 19 B.C., and both Agrippa and Augustus's adoptive grandson Gaius were dispatched with wide-ranging powers to operate independently in the East.[24] Even when campaigns were conducted by generals who were not related to Augustus, the commanders chosen were men who did not belong to the old nobility and lacked sufficient

---

[23] Starting with Trajan (A.D. 98–117), the Romans attempted to extend their border in the East by undertaking various invasions of Mesopotamia, and this effort would lead to persistent conflicts with the Parthian kings (and their Persian successors). Given the lack of any permanent gain that could outweigh the heavy cost of these campaigns and the not infrequent defeats that were suffered in them, it seems that the later emperors would have done well to have heeded Augustus's admonition.

[24] Some sources suggest that Agrippa was sent east to avoid conflict with Augustus's putative heir and nephew M. Claudius Marcellus in the 20s B.C., but this is absurd. If Augustus had not had complete faith in Agrippa's loyalty and reliability, it would have been out of the question to bestow such power on him. The ancient interpretation of Agrippa's missions illustrates how difficult it could be for ancient observers to divine the motives for decisions taken in secret by the emperor and his advisors.

personal prestige to challenge the princeps.[25] A similar situation under the old system would have posed a very immediate risk of armed rebellion.

IMPERIAL PEACE

In the many years after his victory at Actium, Augustus portrayed himself not as a conqueror but as the bringer and guarantor of peace. No doubt, there was an element of military might in this, and Augustus did wage extended campaigns of conquest, but in Rome he mainly promoted his image as the man who had restored peace and prosperity after the twenty bloody years of strife that followed Caesar's crossing of the Rubicon. He also actively promoted the idea that the continuation of his household (the domus Augusta) was necessary for the long-term maintenance of the peace.

In a famous summation of the means by which Augustus took over the state, the later historian Tacitus wryly notes that he "enticed everyone with the sweetness of peace" (*Annals* 1.2). It was no doubt easy for Tacitus, writing after more than a century of the peace that was brought about by the establishment of the Principate, to disparage the arrangement by which (as he saw it) the Roman People bought that peace at the price of their liberty, but the new arrangements must have seemed less disadvantageous to those who had lived through the bloodshed of the dying Republic. In any case, while Augustus's restoration of the old Republican forms and his concealment of the new institutions that allowed him to control public life (and maintain the peace) made the nature of the new government less obvious, the cessation of civil war was plain to see. Augustus, moreover, was not himself a tyrannical individual, so that his exercise of autocratic power was not inherently oppressive. It would take the experience of government under Augustus's successors to reveal the true nature of the autocracy that he had devised.

---

[25] In 29 B.C., M. Licinius Crassus, grandson of the old associate of Pompey and Caesar the dictator, had as the senatorial proconsul of Macedonia won the extraordinarily uncommon right to dedicate the *spolia opima* ("rich spoils") by personally killing the enemy commander, a feat that had been achieved only twice previously in Roman history (once by Romulus!). At this early stage of his career, Imp. Caesar did not feel sufficiently confident in his position to allow anyone else to win such prestige, and he used a dubious ruling on Crassus's status as commander to deny him the honor. Later, this problem could not have arisen in the first place, since a man of Crassus's background would not have been given such a command.

Questions for Study and Reflection

1. What was Augustus's constitutional position after 27 B.C.? How did this position change over the years?

2. Was the Republic really restored in 27 B.C.? Which aspects of the old constitution came back into force? What powers did Augustus retain?

3. What other actions could Imp. Caesar have taken to reestablish his authority in 27 B.C.? Do previous figures from the history of the Republic suggest different paths that he could have taken?

4. What was the difference between regular senatorial provinces and those of Augustus? On what basis did Augustus control his provinces, and how did he exercise this control in practice? What was unusual about the treatment of Egypt, and what was the reason for its unique status?

5. Why did Augustus stop holding the consulship in 23 B.C.? Why did the elections in the next few years not proceed in a smooth and effective manner? What was the purpose of Augustus's assumption of the tribunician power?

6. How did Augustus maintain control over the electoral process?

7. Which administrative practices or offices instituted by Augustus have no Republican precedent?

8. Why did Augustus institute a new set of positions to be held by men of equestrian rank? In what way did they provide for functions that had not been performed under the Republican constitution?

9. In what way did Augustus receive divine honors? Why did this not cause the same sort of resentment that had resulted when Caesar the dictator received similar honors? How did the divine worship of Augustus vary across the Empire?

10. How did Augustus maintain control of the military? Why was this so important?

11. In what way was it now possible to develop a coherent policy of military strategy? What was the overall purpose of the military campaigns carried out under Augustus? What failures did he meet? Why did he eventually counsel against further expansion?

12. Was Augustus a despot, and was his Principate a form of tyranny? Is there a significant difference between autocracy and tyranny?

EPILOGUE

AUGUSTUS'S DYNASTIC EFFORTS

Since Augustus held no single office and went out of his way to deny his vast accumulation of powers through various constitutional subterfuges, it was impossible for him to appoint an heir to a position that did not exist in law. Nonetheless, he of all people could hardly have failed to appreciate the importance of dynastic loyalty – his initial seizure of power had, after all, been based solely on his filial relationship with the assassinated dictator – and he strove to leave behind an heir from his own family who could succeed to his status as princeps. In this, he was hindered by his lack of a son and – ironically for someone who did not possess the most robust health – his own longevity.

While women in the Republic were not entirely bereft of influence, nonetheless they could not vote or hold public office, and thus a daughter was in no position to act officially. She could, however, serve to designate Augustus's heir through marriage: not only would the heir's political position be strengthened by this tie to Augustus but any son born to the marriage would have Augustus's blood in his veins. While Augustus enjoyed much luck in his life, fortune did not smile on his dynastic efforts. He left behind what today would be termed a dysfunctional family.

One after another, he married his daughter to a series of prospective successors: his nephew M. Claudius Marcellus (son of his sister Octavia), his faithful lieutenant M. Agrippa, and his stepson Ti. Claudius Nero (each new marriage being prompted by the death of the previous husband). By her second marriage, Julia had three sons, and Augustus adopted the eldest two as his own sons and heirs (they were then known as C. and L. Caesar). In the meanwhile, first Agrippa and then Tiberius were given imperium and tribunician power comparable to Augustus's own, the intention being that if Augustus should die in the interim, Agrippa or

Tiberius could manage affairs until the adoptive sons reached adulthood. In the meanwhile, the sons were favored with swift (and unconstitutional) advancement in the magistracies of the Republic, but their deaths in A.D. 2 (Lucius) and 4 (Gaius) compelled Augustus to associate Tiberius once more in his imperium and tribunician power.[1] Augustus's efforts to manage the succession during his own lifetime were not at an end. Despite the fact that Tiberius already had a son, he was obliged to adopt his own nephew Germanicus, who was married to Agrippina, the daughter of Julia and Agrippa. Germanicus's children were thus the great-grandchildren of Augustus, and Augustus would finally be succeeded by blood heirs after two generations.[2] (For illustration of Augustus's use of the coinage to promote his adoptive sons Gaius and Lucius, see Coin 37.)

SUCCESSION

At the time of his death, Augustus was supposedly nothing more than the leading man of the restored Republic, but the apparent functioning of the old magistracies was just a façade that concealed the personal autocracy he had built up over the years. He retained the loyalty of and command over all the soldiery, had legal control over half the provinces and the legal right to interfere in the rest, managed the magistrates and senate in Rome with his tribunician and consular power, oversaw the state religion as pontifex maximus, and possessed a form of personal prestige that equated him with the gods. Though no one ever consciously decided to establish a despotism, and indeed Augustus ostensibly restored the free Republic, Rome was in fact ruled by a man possessing autocratic powers, and when he died in A.D. 14, the vast extent of the new administrative apparatus that was overseen by the princeps (including the military establishment) made it impossible not to replace him. The demise of the Republic was not, however, so self-evident to contemporaries, and it took a certain amount of disturbing debate in the senate before the new princeps could be legitimized.

Genuine grief undoubtedly ensued after Augustus's demise. Thoughts quickly turned to the future, however, and first the consuls and then the major praefects in Rome swore an oath of loyalty to Tiberius, as did the

---

[1] Tiberius and Julia did not get along, and in 4 B.C. Tiberius had withdrawn from Rome in voluntary exile. He may also have wished to avoid conflict with Augustus's adoptive sons as they were reaching adulthood.

[2] As it turned out, the descent from Augustus would be generally fatal to these great-grandchildren. Most were killed as a result of dynastic machinations, but one (Gaius, who is not to be confused with Augustus's adopted son and is generally known by the nickname of Caligula) eventually succeeded Tiberius.

senate and general populace. This was entirely natural, as Tiberius at that time held all the substantive powers of his adoptive father, including the tribunician power and maius imperium (he lacked only the titles pontifex maximus and pater patriae). Tiberius himself was not so sure of his position and preferred to act through the consuls (though he summoned the senate by virtue of the tribunician power). The historian Tacitus notes that Tiberius continued to give the password to the praetorian guard and was accompanied by soldiers in the city, which he takes as a sign that Tiberius's hesitation was a fraud. Rather, Tiberius's continued command over the praetorian guard shows the inherent impossibility of restoring the functioning Republic. His status as the dominant figure in the state was definitely dubious in terms of the old constitution, and his deference to the consuls made sense within this context. But what right did they have to control the praetorian guard, whose sole loyalty was to the old princeps who had created the unit as his personal force? This question was of much broader significance, since the same issue arose with reference to both the entire military establishment together with its command structure and the huge administrative apparatus that Augustus had established without any precedent in Republican procedure. Whatever Tiberius thought of the system of Republican magistracies that Augustus had maintained to avoid offending the sensibilities of the senate, the new power structure was centered on the person of the princeps, and now that the old one was gone, a new one had to be found.

In the first session of the senate called by Tiberius, he resolved to deal with the honors to the dead Augustus, who among other things was deified, just as the dictator Caesar had been. Then the issue of Tiberius's own position arose. Now a fifty-six-year-old man (quite old by ancient standards), Tiberius claimed to be unequal to the task of administering everything, a burden that only Augustus had been capable of bearing, and he asserted that in a state which relied upon so many illustrious men, public affairs would be carried out better if the work was shared. What exactly he had in mind is unclear. Presumably, the point was to restore, in part at least, traditional senatorial control of governmental activities by entrusting the senate with the oversight of certain administrative functions, so that these would in practice be carried out by the illustrious men to whom Tiberius alluded (mostly the scions of the old senatorial oligarchy but also those whose families had first risen to prominence under Augustus). As it was, Tiberius never had the opportunity to spell out his intentions clearly, since he was immediately interrupted by shouts and prayers that he should exercise the same powers as had Augustus. In reply, he had a memorandum read aloud in which Augustus laid out the public resources and the military establishment (as well as his advice against expanding the borders). The purpose of this was to illustrate how great the burden of administering this vast system was, and he again asserted his inability to carry out the task but indicated his willingness to undertake whatever share in the burden was assigned to him. At this point, the senator C. Asinius Gallus (son of C. Asinius Pollio) asked which share he wanted, a question that immediately made clear the impossibility of Tiberius's entire proposal. After a stunned silence, Tiberius replied that it would be immodest of him to choose, and Gallus explained that his question was merely a rhetorical ploy to show that it was impossible to divide the functions of the state and that it had to be administered in its entirety by a single individual. And this was the heart of the matter. While Augustus had left the old magistracies in existence and given them certain limited powers to satisfy the ambitions and expectations of the senatorial order, he had at the same time gradually assumed control of a huge new administrative system that was totally unprecedented in terms of the Republican constitution and presupposed centralized control in the hands of one man. In effect, the traditional senatorial system to which Tiberius apparently wished to return had never been intended to deal with the present circumstances, and it was totally unsuited to administering the new structure set up by Augustus. Chief among the functions of this new system was control of the military establishment that had caused so much bloodshed in the past but was indispensable for the defense of the vast expanse of territory under Roman control. It is hard to see any way in which the new permanent bureaus such as the one in charge of Rome's grain supply could be distributed effectively among the old annual magistrates, and it was likewise impossible to dismantle the centralized control of the military without a return of civil wars fought among powerful magistrates. Though Tiberius still resisted, he was eventually persuaded to become the new princeps and to receive all the honors and privileges that Augustus had held.[3]

REIGN OF TIBERIUS

The further development of the Augustan Principate is basically the subject of Imperial rather than Republican history. Nonetheless, even after

---

[3] The only title that he refused was that of pater patriae. (He apparently did not feel himself entitled to this honor; later emperors felt no such compunction.) He never adopted the designation imperator within his own name, since this was clearly an indication of domination based on military power (he did continue to count among his honors the number of acclamations as imperator in the traditional sense of "victorious general" that he received on account of the victories won by his legates).

the problems raised by the senatorial debate about his powers, the realities of the situation were still unclear to the most important man concerned: the new princeps himself, who continued to act as if the senate should take substantive decisions and the magistrates should exercise independent command in the traditional manner. Given the paramount position of the princeps in the system, any such expectations were unrealistic, and the senate's refusal to act in the independent manner desired by Tiberius – which was fundamentally incompatible with his own powers – led him to exclaim in exasperation after leaving one session of the senate, "How suited these men are for slavery!" And in fact if one takes the political freedom enjoyed by the senate and the magistrates under the old constitution as the standard by which to judge the situation, the Principate did signify slavery to the will of the princeps. Though in his old age Augustus had become somewhat intolerant of criticism, he generally restrained the potentially tyrannical elements inherent in his autocratic powers. Such was not the case with the embittered old man Tiberius, who did not really grasp the implications of his position within the state and was manipulated by courtiers who did.

By the end of his reign, the despotism of Imperial rule was clear to all, and it was with relief that men greeted his death and with the highest hopes that they hailed the accession of his adoptive grandson Gaius, who was the great grandson of Augustus. But Gaius (better known by the nickname Caligula) was an unbalanced young man who would revel in the capricious exercise of untrammeled and irresponsible power. There could now be no doubting that the Republic was dead, as power passed through dynastic succession to various members of the house founded by Augustus.

THE REPUBLICAN IDEAL LIVES ON

And yet throughout the Julio-Claudian period, men continued to believe that the Principate had not entirely replaced the old Republic and that the old system could in fact be restored. As we have seen, Tiberius wished to share power with the senate. For his part, even the deranged Gaius made a disastrous attempt to free the electoral process in Rome from senatorial control and to restore it to its traditional form. (In the event, voting had no real significance for the inhabitants of the city, and the electoral assemblies simply degenerated into chaos amid bribery committed by the candidates.) Upon Gaius's assassination in A.D. 37, there was an abortive attempt on the part of the senate to restore the free Republic, but it soon became apparent that individuals within the senate were conspiring to seize power, and in any case, so long as there was someone related to Augustus, the prestige of his dynasty was such that a member of the Imperial house was bound to become the next princeps. The bloodshed within the dynasty during the previous two reigns meant that the only available adult was Claudius, the deformed son of the younger of Augustus's stepsons, who had already been hailed (apparently to his surprise) as emperor by the praetorian guard. The attempt to restore the Republic promptly gave way before the newly proclaimed princeps. When Nero, Claudius's successor and the last member of the benighted dynasty, finally lost control of the political scene through his own bungling, several governors proclaimed their loyalty to the "Roman People," as if this were a viable alternative to the establishment of a new dynasty. But any restoration of the Republic had long since become out of the question, and Galba, one of the governors who had gone into revolt in the name of the People, was recognized in Rome as the new emperor. Though the Republic lived on in the dreams of the unrealistic and the nostalgic, the administrative realities of the vast empire conquered under the Republic rendered the old constitution a thing of the past.

Questions for Study and Reflection

1.   Upon the death of Augustus, why was it necessary to appoint a successor to his powers?
2.   What was Tiberius's attitude toward accepting Augustus's powers?
3.   In what way did certain individuals in the Early Principate think that the Republic could be restored? What did they think this entailed, and why did this course of action prove impossible to carry out?

Questions for Study and Reflection about

the Failure of the Republic

1.   What exactly constituted the popularis tradition in Roman politics? What were major elements of popularis politics? Were these policies inherently antisenatorial? In what way were the two Gracchi, Saturninus, Marius, Pompey, and Caesar populares? Were their aims and methods the same?
2.   Why did the senate oppose the principles upheld by the populares? What policies did the optimates advocate? To what extent were the optimates and the senate as a whole equivalent?

3. How did the use of violence become acceptable in Roman politics? Who started its use? under what circumstances? for what purpose? How did its use change over time? What role was played in this development by the deaths of the Gracchi? by that of Saturninus and Glaucia? by that of M. Livius Drusus? by the senatus consultum ultimum? by the Social War? by the enrollment of landless soldiers?
4. How did the use of violence in the electoral assemblies affect the political process in Rome? What effect did this violence have on the legitimacy of the decisions reached in the assemblies?
5. Would it have been possible to make the electoral process in Rome representative of the greatly expanded citizen body after the enfranchisement of the Italian allies? Why was no effort undertaken to achieve this?
6. How did the military needs of the empire affect politics in Rome? In what ways did maintaining the empire conflict with the traditional constitution? Could the Republic have provided a permanent military establishment? How could the behavior of generals have been curbed to prevent them from acting against the political establishment in Rome?
7. What circumstances led to Sulla's seizure of power through military action? How was Caesar's seizure of power similar to or different from Sulla's?
8. How was the loyalty of the soldiery maintained during periods of civil war?
9. Which year marks the end of the Republic: 60 B.C., 59 B.C., 49 B.C., 44 B.C., 42 B.C., 31 B.C., 27 B.C., A.D. 14? Give evidence for and against each date.
10. What principles and institutions characterize the Republican form of government? When did these cease to function? Or were they superseded by other governmental forms and practices?
11. In what way did the Principate established by Augustus represent a break with the traditional constitution? In what ways did the Principate build upon Republican institutions?
12. Was the end of the Republic inevitable? Was the defeat of the Republicans at the hands of Caesar the dictator and the triumvirs merely happenstance? Could they have adopted different policies? What would Pompey and his allies or Brutus and Cassius have done if they had emerged victorious?
13. Was it possible for the Republican form of government to develop in such a way as to solve the sorts of administrative and political issues that were dealt with by Augustus's Principate? How could the Republican institutions have been adapted to meet the political and administrative needs of the Late Republic?

APPENDIX

Roman Nomenclature

The name of every Roman male had four obligatory elements and one optional one. The first three obligatory elements derived from a system of nomenclature that had been common throughout Italy since the Iron Age. First, there was a personal name (*praenomen*, pl. *praenomina*). The number of these was very limited; in the historical period, fewer than ten were at all common, and each had a uniformly used abbreviation:

A.=Aulus
C.=Gaius[1]
Cn.=Gnaeus[1]
D.=Decimus
L.=Lucius
M.=Marcus
M'.=Manius[2]
N.=Numerius
P.=Publius
Q.=Quintus
T.=Titus
Ti.=Tiberius.

In addition, there were a few old names that were restricted to a limited number of families.

---

[1] In the abbreviations "C." and "Cn." the use of the letter "C" to indicate the sound "g" reflects an archaic spelling. The Romans adapted their alphabet from the Etruscans, who did not distinguish the sounds "k" and "g." For this reason, the Romans used the letter "C" for both sounds in the earliest period, and the form "G" was a later development, with a bar added to "C" to differentiate the two usages. The abbreviations thus go back to a very early date, when the two sounds were not yet distinguished in the Roman script.

[2] The abbreviation is conventionally represented as an M followed by an apostrophe in modern works, but as written in Roman inscriptions the abbreviation consisted of a regular M with an additional upstroke at the end of it.

Ap.=Appius
Sp.=Spurius

Each boy would be given a different praenomen, and normally the eldest born was given his father's. Child mortality rates were high, however, and if the eldest child died the father's praenomen was often given to a child born later.

Next came *nomen* (pl. *nomina*), which indicated the clan (*gens*, pl. *gentes*) to which the man belonged. Theoretically, all the members of a given gens had a common origin in the very distant past, but even if there was some common origin (and it may well be that there were originally separate *gentes* that had a common name), the various families that shared the same nomen had long since ceased to have any sense of blood relationship (one might compare those who share some Scottish clan name but do not feel themselves to be related to everyone who bears that name). While some nomina were rather unusual, others such as Cornelius and Julius were held by large numbers of people. Roman nomina usually ended in –*ius*, and Roman citizens whose nomina did not have this ending were clearly of peregrine (non-Roman) origin (e.g., C. Norbanus cos. 83, C. Carrinas pr. 82). Etymology sometimes makes it clear that even certain nomina ending in –*ius* were not of Roman origin. For instance, Pompilius was an Oscan equivalent to the Latin Quinctilius (*pomp-* and *quin(c)t-* being derived from the respective developments of the Indo-European stem for "five").

The old Italic name was then closed with the patronymic ("filiation"), which indicated the man's paternity. Among certain Italian groups, this was represented only by the father's praenomen in the genitive case, but among the Romans the word *filius* "son" was added (always in the abbreviated form *f.*). Thus, an early Roman might have been named C. Marius C.f. ("Gaius Marius, the son of Gaius").

At an early date in the Republic, it became customary to add at the end of the traditional three-element name an indication of the voting tribe to which the man belonged on the basis of the location of his property. In the written form of a man's name, his tribe was indicated after his filiation with a three-letter abbreviation.[3]

---

[3] These names were really feminine adjectives modifying an implied noun *tribus* "tribe." Modern epigraphic works often supply the noun as if a Roman would have actually stated it explicitly in the spoken form of his name, but as far as I know, there is no Republican evidence that the personal name contained anything but the adjective (in the ablative case).

Urban tribes:

- Esq(uilina)
- Pal(atina)
- Qui(rinia)
- Sub(urana); Suc(usana) in inscriptions[4]

Rural tribes:

- Aem(ilia)
- Ani(ensis)
- Arn(ensis)
- Cam(illia)
- Cor(nelia)
- Cru(stumina)
- Fab(ia)
- Fal(erna)
- Gal(eria)
- Hor(atia)
- Lem(onia)
- Mae(cia)
- Men(enia)
- Ouf(entina)
- Pap(iria)
- Pob(lilia)
- Pol(lia)
- Pom(ptina)
- Rom(ilia)
- Sab(atina)
- Sca(ptia)
- Ser(gia)
- Ste(llatina)
- Ter(entina)
- Tro(mentina)
- Vel(ina)
- Vol(tinia)
- Vot(uria)

The voting tribe marked the end of the official name of a Roman until the first century B.C. Thus, someone like L. Domitius Ahenobarbus cos. 94 would appear in official documents as L. Domitius Cn.f. Fab. ("Lucius Domitius, the son of Gnaeus, enrolled in the Fabian tribe"). But where is the name Ahenobarbus?

---

4 The abbreviation apparently reflects an archaic variant of the tribe's name.

After the filiation came the last element of the official name, the *cog-nomen* (pl. *cognomina*). This element began as a personal nickname, but eventually such names came to be hereditary. Though there is some indication of a corporate identity for the members of the gens, this was supplanted at a very early stage by a unit that more or less corresponded to the nuclear family of two parents and their children. This unit was called the *Familia* and was indicated by the husband's cognomen.[5] The late development of the cognomen is reflected by its placement at the end of the name. It was not commonly used in official documents until the last century of the Republic. Not surprisingly, the nicknames that eventually turned into cognomina frequently referred to mental or physical charac-teristics, often in an unflattering manner: *ahenobarbus* "bronze beard," *brutus* "stupid," *caesar* "hairy," *capito* "big head," *cato* "smart guy," *catulus* "puppy," *cicero* "chickpea" (reference to a nose deformity), *cras-sus* "thick," *crispus* "curly," *luscus* "one-eyed" (a number of names refer to problems with the eyes), *metellus* "hireling," *naso* "big nose," *pulcher* "good-looking," *rufus* "red(-haired)," *scipio* "walking stick." (The mean-ing of some names, for instance, Gracchus, is unknown.) Certain cogno-mina came to be passed to the next generation and turned into more or less meaningless family names (i.e., the sense of the name had no direct rel-evance to its bearer). For instance, whatever the reason why some Tullius came to be called "chickpea," the name Cicero was borne not simply by the famous orator but also by his grandfather, father, brother, son, and nephew, none of whom had any noteworthy connection with chickpeas.

On rare occasions, the process by which a nickname turned into a cog-nomen can even be seen at work. The family of the consular Pompeii had no cognomen, but Cn. Pompeius cos. 89 acquired the cognomen Strabo, which means "squinter" in Greek, presumably as a result of a personal character-istic. His son Gnaeus, the consul of 70 B.C., did not inherit any cognomen, and made a cognomen for himself out of the adjective *magnus* ("the Great"). Given its associations with Alexander the Great, the name was routinely ignored by his oligarchic opponents, though his sons would use it. A mor-bid example of the adoption of a personal accomplishment is provided by a certain man with the nomen Lucretius who served as aedile in 133 B.C. He cleaned up after the rioting in which Ti. Gracchus and his supporters were killed, dumping the bodies into the Tiber (maintenance of the city was one of the jobs of the aediles). In commemoration of this task, he took on the

---

[5] Strictly speaking, a wife was not legally part of her husband's family according to the type of marriage that was most common in the Late Republic, but this legal technicality did not of course affect normal family relations.

name Vespillo, which means "undertaker." A Q. Lucretius Vespillo is later attested as fighting for Caesar during a civil war, and another descendant became consul in the year 19 B.C., none of these men having any personal connection with the events that gave rise to their cognomen.

The placement of the cognomen after the filiation and tribe shows that it was not originally recognized as a part of a Roman name.[6] Yet, in normal speech, the filiation and tribe would be left out, so that the proper name consisted of the praenomen, nomen, and cognomen. In fact, under the Empire, the possession of these *tria nomina* ("three names") was a distinction reserved for Roman citizens. Such a conception would have been impossible under the Late Republic, since many important senators (as well as many lesser individuals), still lacked one: C. Marius cos. 107, M. Antonius cos. 99 (and his descendants), Cn. Octavius cos. 87. The use of cognomen had become extremely common by the time of Augustus, yet even as late as the year of his death, both consuls lacked cognomina (Sex. Pompeius and Sex. Appuleius).

To give an example of a full Roman name, the dictator commonly known as Julius Caesar was officially styled C. Julius C.f. Fab. Caesar ("Gaius Julius Caesar, son of Gaius, enrolled in the Fabian tribe"). Such a name could in regular usage be varied in a number of ways. It was common practice to omit the nomen of a high-ranking individual if it was a widespread one, and so this same Caesar could be referred to simply as "C. Caesar." Since it was sometimes necessary to distinguish between separate branches of a family, the filiation could be placed after such a reduced form (e.g., Q. Metellus Q.f.), which makes the cognomen seem to take the place of the nomen. Another practice was to omit the rather indistinctive praenomen and refer to a man by his nomen and cognomen in inverted order. Thus, C. Asinius Pollio could be called Pollio Asinius. The ways in which Romans used their names in regular discourse varied a great deal, sometimes taking forms that seem to us counterintuitive. For instance, Cicero regularly referred to his son simply by his cognomen, which would thus have more of the feeling of a modern given name than a last name.[7]

---

[6] The failure to use the cognomen in lists of senators drawn up before the first century B.C. can cause problems of identification. For instance, the same praenomen and nomen can appear in different families; for example, someone identified merely as L. Cornelius could conceivably be a Balbus, Cinna, Dolabella, Lentulus, Scipio, Sisenna, or Sulla! Even when there is not such a large number of alternatives, the same pairing of praenomen and nomen can appear in successive generations or be borne by cousins in the same generation.

[7] In a development of the Empire, the rather colorless praenomen tended to be ignored in informal contexts, and this practice gives rise to forms that are common in English, such as "Julius Caesar." Another example is the Tiberian praefect of Judaea Pontius

If the cognomen began as a personal nickname, there was no reason that men who already had a cognomen could not acquire a nickname of their own. No doubt this was the case with men of lesser importance, and their nicknames died with them. But it sometimes happened that high-ranking families with a cognomen would acquire a second hereditary cognomen known as an *agnomen* (pl. *agnomina*), which served to distinguish the family descended from a famous individual from other branches of the family. For instance, the cognomen Scipio is attested in the fourth century B.C., but the family quickly found the need for distinctive agnomina, such as Asina, Barbatus, Calvus, and Hispallus. Most of these did not last long, but the name Scipio Nasica started in the late third century B.C. and lasted into the early first B.C. And members of this branch acquired personal nicknames of their own on top of their cognomen and agnomen, so that the consul of 138 B.C. was P. Cornelius Scipio Nasica Serapio – and his son (the consul of 111 B.C.) inherited the whole lot, including his father's nickname Serapio! But such an extravagant accumulation of names was rare. In the first century B.C., most men were content with one cognomen, and many still had none.

In the Middle Republic, Roman magistrates who subdued a region were often given a title based on the name of the region with the addition of the ending *–icus*. For example, to commemorate his defeat of the Macedonian rebels in 148 B.C., the praetor Q. Caecilius Metellus received the title Macedonicus, while L. Mummius cos. 146 earned the title Achaicus for defeating the Greeks of Achaea. In the Late Republic, such titles continued to be granted, but only to comparatively small-scale victors (Q. Caecilius Metellus Numidicus cos. 109, P. Servilius Vatia Isauricus cos. 79, Q. Caecilius Metellus Creticus cos. 69). On the other hand, despite their vast conquests, which generally dwarfed those of the generals of the Middle Republic, the major military figures of the last century of the Republic like Pompey and Caesar never adopted titles of victory formed in the traditional manner.

Adoption was a comparatively common phenomenon among the Romans, and left its mark in nomenclature. The adoptive son became a full-fledged member of his new family and from then on was responsible for the performance of its traditional religious ceremonies, especially the rites owed to the dead.[8] The Romans did not have much interest in the

---

Pilatus (anglicized as Pontius Pilate), whose praenomen is never used in the ancient sources. A fragmentary inscription discovered in the early 1960s contains his name, but unfortunately the beginning is broken, so his praenomen remains unknown.

[8] Apart from problems of infertility, child mortality was high. For instance, of the twelve children of Ti. Gracchus cos. 177, only three survived to adulthood: the tribunes of 133

bloodline as such and were much more keen on maintaining the family *name* in future generations. Hence, adoption provided a means by which a childless man could gain a son and perpetuate his family. The new son assumed the nomenclature of his adoptive father and added at the end an agnomen in the form of an adjective in *–anus* formed from his birth nomen. For instance, L. Aemilius Paullus cos. 182 enjoyed the good fortune of having four sons survive into adulthood, and he gave away two for adoption into prominent families without an heir of their own. One became P. Cornelius Scipio Aemilianus cos. 147 and the other Q. Fabius Maximus Aemilianus cos. 145. In effect, the latter name meant "the Q. Fabius Maximus who originated in the Aemilian gens." Normally, the adopted son used his adoptive father's praenomen in his filiation, but sometimes it was felt clearer to indicate the man by the use of his birth father's cognomen in the filiation. The son of an adopted father could then assume an adjective in *–inus* based on his father's birth cognomen, and this could in turn become inheritable. Thus, a branch of the Cornelii Lentuli sported the agnomen Marcellinus, which went back to a man who identified himself on coins he minted as *Lent(ulus) Mar(celli) f.* (that is, a Cornelius Lentulus who began life as a Claudius Marcellus).

In the late Republic, alternative methods of adoptive nomenclature arose. The man born as M. Junius Brutus (the tyrannicide) changed his name as a result of being adopted by the will of a member of his mother's family. She was the granddaughter of Q. Servilius Caepio cos. 106, and by adoption her son became officially Q. Servilius Caepio Brutus. The motivation for this new procedure was presumably the same as the one that led the moneyer to use his father's cognomen in his filiation, namely, a much more specific indication of the birth family through use of the distinctive cognomen in place of the rather vague adjective from the nomen (Claudianus and Junianus, respectively, in the cases of Marcellus and Brutus). Presumably, the agnomen Brutus would have been inherited if the tyrannicide had left behind a son. In any case, even after adoption he seems to have been known in familiar usage by his birth name. Oddly enough, the other tyrannicide named Brutus was also adopted but seems to have used the opposite procedure. Greek authors indicate that his name was D. Brutus Albinus, and a coin apparently minted by him bears the legend "Albinus Bruti f." This is usually interpreted as meaning that he was a Junius Brutus by birth and was adopted by a Postumius Albinus (perhaps the son of A. Albinus cos. 110). Thus, Decimus kept his birth

---

and 123 B.C. and their sister. She married her adoptive cousin P. Scipio Aemilianus cos. 147, but this proved to be another infertile union.

name and added the cognomen of his adoptive father, while Marcus's new name worked the other way around.

In the Middle Republic, the nomenclature for women was very simple. There is evidence for the use of female versions of praenomina in the earliest period, but this practiced soon died out and a woman was known only by the female version of her father's nomen (e.g., Caesar's daughter was simply called Julia). To avoid confusion when there were multiple daughters, they were distinguished with *maior* "the elder" and *minor* "the younger" in the case of only two, and with ordinal numbers if there were more, such as *prima* ("the first") or *quarta* ("the fourth"). By the Late Republic, the use of the female version of the father's cognomen arose often in the form of a diminutive. For example, the daughter of M. Livius Drusus (the son of the tribune of 91) was named Livia Drusilla.[9]

---

[9] She would marry Imp. Caesar, and from the children of her previous marriage to Ti. Claudius Nero the names Livia, Livilla, Drusilla, and Drusus would enter the Imperial family.

CHRONOLOGY

All dates are B.C. unless otherwise noted.

ca. 507: Establishment of Republican form of government, with creation of consulship.

ca. 367: Plebeians admitted to higher office, formation begins of the patrician/plebeian nobility. Creation of the (urban) praetorship.

ca. 244: Creation of the second (peregrine) praetorship.

238: Seizure of Sicily and Sardinia.

227: Creation of two new praetorships to provide governors for Sicily and Sardinia.

198: Creation of two more praetorships to provide governors for two Spanish provinces.

181–ca. 175: Operation of lex Baebia, which provided for the election of four and six praetors in alternate years.

180: Lex Villia sets minimum age requirements for senior magistracies and provides for a two-year interval between offices.

153: Last legally repeated consulship before Marius.

149–146: Third Punic War. Revolt in Macedonia and Achaean War in Greece.

147: Dissatisfaction with conduct of Punic War results in illegal election of P. Scipio Aemilianus as under-age consul.

146: Creation of provinces of Macedonia and Africa.

139: Lex Gabinia sets up voting by ballot in elections for magistrates.

137: Lex Cassia sets up voting by ballot in all trials before the People except those for perduellio (treason). Consul C. Hostilius Mancinus forced to surrender to Numantines, release arranged by his quaestor Ti. Gracchus, and the resulting treaty rejected by senate.

135: Popular dissatisfaction with the handling of the war against Numantia leads to the illegal election of P. Cornelius Scipio Aemilianus as consul for next year.

133: Tribunate of Ti. Gracchus. M. Octavius removed as tribune. Lex Sempronia agraria passed, agrarian commission established. Inheritance of Attalid kingdom. During melee caused by his attempt at reelection, Gracchus is killed along with 300 supporters by a gang of senators led by the pontifex maximus P. Cornelius Scipio Nasica. Numantia captured by Scipio Aemilianus. Consul L. Calpurnius Piso Frugi continues suppression of slave revolt in Sicily.

132: Consuls P. Popilius Laenas and P. Rupilius conduct a quaestio into the behavior of Gracchus's supporters. Rupilius settles the affairs of Sicily in the aftermath of the slave revolt with the aid of ten-member senatorial commission. Nasica goes to Asia, soon dies.

131: Consul P. Licinius Crassus Mucianus receives command to suppress the revolt in Asia, is killed in battle.

130: Consul M. Perperna defeats the rebels in Asia.

ca. 130: Tribune C. Papirius Carbo unsuccessfully proposes bill legitimizing reelection to tribunate, passes another introducing voting by ballot in legislative elections.

129: Consul M'. Aquillius succeeds Perperna in Asia, spends several years settling the affairs of the new province. End of land distribution when allies' complaints lead to jurisdiction being transferred from the Gracchan agrarian commission to the consul C. Sempronius Tuditanus, who instead departs for a military campaign in southern Gaul.

126: Consul L. Aurelius Orestes sent to Sardinia to suppress a revolt; C. Gracchus accompanies him as quaestor. Aquillius celebrates his triumph from Asia.

125: Consul M. Fulvius Flaccus unsuccessfully tries to grant citizenship to the Italian allies; Fregellae revolts and is destroyed by the praetor L. Opimius. Flaccus then campaigns in southern Gaul. C. Gracchus returns from Sardinia before Orestes (who remains there until 122), is accused before the censors but acquitted.

124: Proconsul M. Flaccus and consul C. Sextius Calvinus continue war in Gaul.

123: First tribunate of C. Gracchus. Lex ne de capite civis Romani iniussu populi Romani passed, P. Laenas cos. 132 withdraws into exile. Lex Acilia reforms quaestio de pecuniis repetundis. Gracchus returned as tribune for next year.

122: Second tribunate of C. Gracchus, with M. Flaccus as colleague. Agrarian legislation revived, colonies established (lex Rubria sets up Junonia on old site of Carthage). The tribune M. Livius Drusus and consul C. Fannius undermine Gracchus; bill granting citizenship to Italian allies defeated. Gracchus loses bid for reelection. Consul Cn. Domitius Ahenobarbus campaigns in Gaul.

121: Consulship of L. Opimius. Violence breaks out during attempt to repeal lex Rubria, Gracchans seize Aventine Hill. Opimius has the senate pass SCU, then M. Flaccus, C. Gracchus, and thousands of supporters are killed when troops attack the Gracchan position on the

Aventine Hill. In conjunction with the proconsul Ahenobarbus, the consul Q. Fabius Maximus finally ends Gallic campaign, gains the title Allebrogicus.

120: Ahenobarbus organizes Narbonensis as a province in Transalpine Gaul.

118: Colony established at Narbo in Gaul. Death of King Micipsa of Numidia.

113: Consul Cn. Papirius Carbo defeated by Cimbri in Balkans

112: Jugurtha captures Cirta, whereupon he kills Adherbal and slaughters the Italian defenders.

111: Consul L. Calpurnius Bestia's campaign against Jugurtha. Tribune C. Memmius summons Jugurtha to Rome. Passage of epigraphically preserved lex agraria, which is perhaps the law that finally ended the last vestige of the Gracchan land program.

110: Consul Sp. Postumius Albinus's campaign against Jugurtha and the surrender of his brother and legate, Aulus.

109: Consul Q. Caecilius Metellus begins campaign against Jugurtha. Tribune C. Mamilius sets up quaestio Mamilia to investigate bribery. Consul M. Junius Silanus defeated by Cimbri in Gaul.

108: C. Marius elected consul.

107: Tribune T. Manlius Mancinus passes law granting Marius command against Jugurtha; Marius enrolls troops without regard for census qualification. Tribune C. Coelius Caldus passes law introducing voting by ballot in trials before the People for perduellio. Consul L. Cassius Longinus defeated by the Tigurini.

106: Consul Q. Servilius Caepio passes law adding senators to jury album, steals treasure at Tolosa in Gaul.

105: War in Africa ended when Jugurtha is surrendered to Sulla. Proconsul Caepio and consul Cn. Mallius Maximus suffer overwhelming defeat at Arausio in Gaul.

104–100: Marius's repeated consulships.

103: Tribune L. Appuleius Saturninus passes land law for veterans from Africa, sets up quaestio on maiestas minuta. Caepio, Mallius convicted of treason.

102: Marius wipes out Teutoni at Aquae Sextiae. Consul Q. Lutatius Catulus fails to prevent Cimbri from crossing Alps into Italy. L. Equitius unsuccessfully tries to be registered in census as son of Ti. Gracchus.

102–100: Praetor M. Antonius wages war against Cilician pirates.

101: Marius wipes out Cimbri at Vercellae. Saturninus elected tribune through murder of a candidate. Glaucia as tribune passes law restoring jury panels to equestrians and reforming the extortion court. Consul M'. Aquillius assigned to suppress slave revolt in Sicily. Passage of the epigraphically preserved law on praetorian assignments (or in next year?). Cilicia to become a permanent provincial assignment.

100: Saturninus passes grain law, land law for Marius's veterans. Q. Metellus Numidicus exiled for not swearing to uphold land law. C. Memmius killed during consular elections. Saturninus and Glaucia seize Aventine, surrender after passage of SCU; are murdered by mobs (with permission of Marius?).

ca. 98: Praetor L. Cornelius Sulla assigned Cilicia as province, establishes Ariobarzanes as king of Cappadocia, reaches first agreement with Parthians.

95: Consuls L. Licinius Crassus and Q. Mucius Scaevola establish quaestio to investigate usurpation of Roman citizenship by Italian allies.

92: Conviction of P. Rutilius Rufus for provincial extortion.

91: Tribunate of M. Livius Drusus the younger. He passes legislation through violence, and it is invalided by senate after death of L. Crassus. His citizenship bill is defeated, then he is assassinated.

90: Outbreak of Social War. Consul P. Rutilius Lupus killed, Marius treated shabbily. Legate Cn. Pompeius Strabo begins siege of Asculum. Consul L. Julius Caesar passes lex Julia granting citizenship to allies. Tribune Q. Varius institutes the quaestio Varia to investigate those responsible for causing outbreak of revolt among allies.

89: Consul Cn. Strabo seizes Asculum. Legate L. Sulla subdues southern front, gains consulship. Marius retires from service. Outbreak of war in Asia; M'. Aquillius overwhelmed by Mithridates, and he and Q. Cassius are captured.

88: Consul Sulla opposes plan of the tribune P. Sulpicius Rufus for enrolling new citizens. After a riot in which his son-in-law Q. Pompeius Rufus (son of the other consul) is killed and Sulla forced to seek refuge in Marius's house, Sulla is released after swearing an oath to Marius and P. Rufus. When Rufus passes a law establishing election for command of war against Mithridates and Marius is chosen, Sulla marches on Rome with his army. Rufus is killed, Marius flees; Sulla revokes laws he opposes. Cn. Strabo engineers death of consul Q. Pompeius Rufus, who was to take over Strabo's army. Mithridates's armies overrun Asia, Greece; many thousands of Romans slaughtered in Asia.

87: Bellum Octavianum. Consul L. Cornelius Cinna reneges on deal made with Sulla, is driven from Rome by his colleague Cn. Octavius. Cinna removed from office and replaced by L. Cornelius Merula, but he returns by force with C. Marius, Cn. Papirius Carbo, and Q. Sertorius. Consul Cn. Octavius and some leading senators killed. Sulla crosses over to Balkans, launches unsuccessful assault on Athens.

86: Marius, Cinna consuls; Marius soon dies, is replaced by L. Valerius Flaccus. Sulla defeats Mithridates's forces at Chaeronea, Orchomenos. Flaccus brings army to Balkans, is killed in mutiny instigated by C. Fimbria.

86–84: Three years of Cinna's "domination" with Cn. Carbo in Italy.

85: Fimbria crosses over to Asia, attacks Mithridatic forces. Sulla refuses to cooperate, concludes Peace of Dardanus with Mithridates. Sulla crosses to Asia and takes over army of Fimbria, who commits suicide.

84: Cinna killed by troops during crossing to Illyricum. Sulla abandons negotiations, decides on war.

83: Sulla invades Italy, reaches agreement with consul L. Scipio Asiagenus, who reneges.

82: Sulla conquers Italy, winning major victory at Colline Gate, is elected dictator. Consul C. Marius besieged in Praeneste, commits suicide before town surrenders. Cn. Carbo driven from northern Italy, flees to Africa. Cn. Pompeius ("Pompey") raises army for Sulla, captures Sicily, then Africa, kills consul Cn. Carbo.

81: Proscriptions.

80: Q. Sertorius seizes control in Spain. Sulla consul with Q. Metellus Pius, passes numerous laws reforming the government, including exclusive senatorial control of jury album and curbing the powers of the tribunate. Number of praetors raised to eight and that of quaestors to twenty.

79: Sulla resigns as dictator. Metellus Pius begins unsuccessful attack on Sertorius in Spain.

78: Consul L. Aemilius Lepidus rallies opposition to Sullan settlement, is opposed by his colleague Q. Lutatius Catulus. Lepidus assumes leadership of a revolt in northern Italy. Catulus's legate Pompey kills Lepidus's legate M. Junius Brutus in Cisalpine Gaul, then refuses to disband the army that he controls as legate and extorts proconsular command against Sertorius.

75: Consul L. Aurelius Cotta passes law once again allowing tribunes to seek other office. Quaestor P. Cornelius Lentulus Marcellinus sent to organize Cyrene as province.

74: Praetor M. Antonius granted imperium infinitum to combat pirates. Kingdom of Bithynia bequeathed to the Roman People. Consuls L. Licinius Lucullus and M. Aurelius Cotta given commands in East in anticipation of war with Mithridates.

73: Slave revolt of Spartacus starts. Third Mithridatic War breaks out. Sertorius assassinated.

72: Slaves defeat several commanders, including both consuls; M. Licinius Crassus takes command against them. Antonius defeated by pirates in Crete.

71: Crassus ends slave revolt. Lucullus conquers Pontus.

70: Joint consulship of M. Crassus and Pompey, tribunate restored to traditional powers. Praetor L. Aurelius Cotta passes law enrolling senators, equites, and tribuni aerarii on the jury album. M. Tullius Cicero successfully prosecutes C. Verres for corruption as governor of Sicily.

69: Lucullus invades Armenia. Consul Q. Metellus attacks Crete.

67: Roman campaign in east halted by Mithridates's victory at Zela. Election held under the lex Gabinia grants Pompey huge command against the pirates, whom he defeats in forty-nine days. Tribunate of C. Cornelius.

66: Pompey about to interfere with campaign of Q. Metellus cos. 69 against Crete when lex Manilia grants command against Mithridates to Pompey. P. Cornelius Sulla and P. Autronius Paetus returned as consuls for next year but are stripped of office when convicted of electoral corruption.

64: Pompey organizes the provinces of Bithynia and Pontus, annexes Syria as a province.

63: Consulship of Cicero, suppression of Catilinarian conspiracy.

62: Praetor C. Julius Caesar and tribune Q. Metellus Nepos stir up trouble, are stripped of office; Caesar promises to behave himself but Nepos flees to East. Pompey returns to Italy in December.

61–60: Vain attempts to secure land for Pompey's veterans, ratification of his eastern acta, and reduction of publicans' payment for taxes of Asia.

59: Consulship of Caesar. Two laws passed to distribute ager publicus in Campania. Lex Vatinia grants him five-year command in Cisalpine Gaul, Illyricum (Transalpine Gaul soon added by senate). Rash words of Cicero cause Caesar to allow adoption of P. Clodius by a plebeian.

58: Caesar offers to have senate review his acta, then departs for Gaul, where he defeats Helvetii, Ariovistus. P. Clodius's tribunate. Exile of Cicero.

57: Recall of Cicero from exile. Caesar conquers Belgae, Brittany in Gaul.

56: Conference at Luca. Rioting at Rome for the purpose of postponing elections until next year in order to improve the chances of Pompey and Crassus for the consulship. Caesar conquers Veneti, Aquitania in Gaul.

55: Second joint consulship of Pompey and Crassus. Lex Trebonia gives five-year command to Pompey in Spain and to Crassus in Syria. Caesar's command in Gaul extended for five years by lex Pompeia Licinia. Caesar crosses Rhine, then leads preliminary expedition to Britain.

54: Crassus begins campaigning against Parthia. Caesar launches abortive invasion of Britain, fifteen cohorts under L. Cotta, Q. Sabinus lost in Gaul. Massive electoral scandals in Rome.

53: Year begins with interregnum, as continued electoral disorders postpone election of the consuls until July. After Crassus suffers disaster at Carrhae, his quaestor C. Cassius Longinus organizes defense of Syria.

52: Year begins with interregnum. Death of P. Clodius during melee between his gang and T. Annius Milo's; ensuing riots result in election of Pompey as sole consul. Trial and conviction of Milo. Metellus Pius elected as Pompey's colleague. Law of ten tribunes allows Caesar to run for consulship in absentia. Lex Pompeia de magistratibus introduces major change in method of appointing governors. Large revolt in Gaul led by Vercingetorix eventually defeated at Alesia.

51: Attempt of consul M. Claudius Marcellus to start senatorial debate on the topic of replacing Caesar in Gaul halted on technicality. Cicero goes to Cilicia as governor.

50: Consul L. Aemilius Lepidus and tribune C. Scribonius Curio thwart discussion of replacing Caesar. In December, the consul M. Claudius Marcellus and the consul elect L. Cornelius Lentulus Crus hand Pompey a sword as a symbol of their entrusting the defense of Italy to him.

49: The tribunes M. Antonius and Q. Cassius Longinus block discussion of Caesar's replacement, then flee to Caesar after the SCU is passed. Outbreak of civil war. Caesar crosses the Rubicon, then enters into negotiations, but suddenly launches a full-scale assault on Italy in late January. Pompey withdraws to Greece. Caesar subdues Spain, is elected as dictator. C. Curio launches attack on Africa as Caesar's subordinate, suffers complete defeat.

48: Caesar defeats Pompey and Republicans at Pharsalus. Some Republicans make peace with Caesar, some join Republican forces in Africa. Pompey assassinated in Egypt; Caesar embroiled in events in Egypt, then vacations after making Cleopatra queen.

47: Caesar defeats king of Pontus at Zela, then finally returns to Italy.

46: Caesar defeats Republicans at Thapsus in Africa, receives extraordinary honors.

45: Caesar defeats Republicans at Munda in Spain, receives further honors.

44: Caesar appointed dictator for life, is assassinated; P. Cornelius Dolabella replaces him as consul. Consul M. Antonius (Antony) attempts to reconcile with assassins of Caesar, but is thwarted by the arrival of Caesar's heir (young Caesar). Tribunician law transfers Cisalpine Gaul to Antony and grants Syria to Dolabella, but Cisalpine Gaul is occupied by the governor appointed by Caesar, the tyrannicide D. Brutus. Caesar's heir attempts coup d'état in Rome but fails. His forces clash with Antony's; young Caesar withdraws to Etruria, Antony moves north to take over Cisalpine Gaul from D. Brutus by force. M. Brutus, C. Cassius given provinces of Crete and Cyrene, then seize Macedonia and Syria.

43: Proconsul Dolabella kills the tyrannicide C. Trebonius in Asia, then commits suicide after failure to take Syria from Cassius. Young Caesar cooperates with consuls in attacking Antony, who is pushed into Gaul. The consuls die in battle, then young Caesar's relations with the senate cool and he seizes the consulship. Young Caesar reconciles with Antony and Lepidus. Triumvirate established by lex Titia, proscriptions enacted, Cicero killed. Sex. Pompey appointed naval commander by senate, seizes major islands.

42: Brutus and Cassius subdue Asia. Antony and young Caesar defeat them at Philippi.

41: Perusine War.

40: Treaty of Brundisium. Parthian invasion of Syria, Asia Minor under Q. Labienus.

39: Treaty of Misenum. P. Ventidius throws back Parthians.

38: Another Parthian invasion of Syria decisively defeated by Ventidius. Young Caesar adopts the name Imp. Caesar.

37: Imp. Caesar launches unsuccessful attack on Magnus Pius (Sex. Pompey).

36: Imp. Caesar seizes Sicily from Magnus Pius. Lepidus's army goes over to Imp. Caesar, and Lepidus is sent into exile. Antony unsuccessfully invades Parthian territory.

34: Antony conquers Armenia. "Donations" to Cleopatra and her children.

33: Triumviral powers lapse, but Antony and Imp. Caesar retain power.

32: Final rupture between Imp. Caesar and Antony. Consuls and many senators flee to Antony in the East. War declared against Cleopatra; personal oath of loyalty sworn to Imp. Caesar in west.

31: Antony and Cleopatra defeated at Actium.

30: Imp. Caesar invades Egypt. Antony and Cleopatra commit suicide, Egypt annexed.

28: Imp. Caesar begins to give up some of his unconstitutional powers and prerogatives.

27: Imp. Caesar "restores" the Republic, but retains control over most militarily significant provinces, continues to hold the consulship every year. Grateful senate bestows title of Augustus upon him.

24: Abortive assassination attempt on Augustus's life.

23: Second major constitutional settlement, in which Augustus gives up the consulship, is granted the tribunician power.

19: Augustus receives consular imperium for life.

13: Upon Lepidus's death, Augustus elected pontifex maximus.

2: Augustus granted title pater patriae.

A.D. 4: Death of Augustus's adoptive son C. Caesar.

A.D. 6: Augustus adopts his stepson Tiberius, who is granted all his powers except for the titles pontifex maximus and Augustus.

A.D. 14: Succession of Tiberius to Principate. Start of the Imperial period.

SUGGESTIONS FOR FURTHER READING, ANCIENT AND MODERN

For each chapter, the suggested readings are divided into two parts. First come ancient sources. These are by no means meant to be all encompassing but should give some sense of the main sources. It is always strongly recommended that the reader first examine the ancient evidence. This is not infrequently inaccurate or misleading (and it should always be borne in mind that the interpretations and analyses of ancient sources have no more inherent claim to accuracy than do modern ones), but it is sensible to have a general idea of the evidence before reading modern treatments. (For those unfamiliar with ancient works, they have a system of references that goes back to the earliest printed edition. By this system, a work is divided first into the books, which have ancient authority, and each book is then divided into sections, which in turn are divided into individual sentences. Thus, Dio 38.2.1 indicates the first sentence of the second section of Book 38. The main numeration for the letters of Cicero refers to the chronological reordering given in the editions of D. R. Shackleton Bailey, and the parenthetical numbers that follow give the traditional order according to the books of the manuscripts.)

Next come modern works. Given the intended audience of this book, it seemed out of place to cite articles in obscure journals and foreign languages. Instead, the following short titles (the fuller form is given in the bibliography) should provide suggestions of where further discussion may be found (plus more detailed references if these are required). Also, the reader should always consult the elaborate chapters (covering both narrative and thematic topics) in vols. 9 (*The Last Age of the Roman Republic*) and 10 (*The Augustan Principate*) of the *Cambridge Ancient History*. These will give extensive academic bibliographies. For a good collection of essays that aim to give a general introduction to salient topics relating to the history of the Republic as a whole, see Morstein-Marx (2006). Needless to say, all these works may well present interpretations that differ from those given here.

Chapter One (Historical Background)

Modern works

Astin, *Scipio Aemilianus*
Badian, *Publicans and Sinners* (on the equites), *Foreign Clientelae* (patronage in foreign affairs)
Brunt, *Italian Manpower* (detailed exposition of traditional interpretation of the agrarian crisis)
Gelzer, *Nobility* (excellent short introduction to the nature and practice of aristocratic politics in Rome)
Gruen, *Trials*
Harris, *War and Imperialism* (needlessly judgmental but nonetheless useful exposition of the nature of war making in the Middle Republic)
Kallett-Marx, *Hegemony to Empire* (discussion of development in the nature of Roman domination in the Eastern Mediterranean)
Lintott, *Roman Constitution, Imperium Romanum* (discussion of Roman provincial administration)
Millar, *Crowd in Rome* (attempt to emphasize the "democratic" element in Roman politics)
Morstein-Marx, *Mass Oratory* (argument for serious involvement of the electorate in the political process)
Nicolet, *World of the Citizen* (examination of how regular citizens interacted with the political and administrative system)
Rosenstein, *Rome at War* (revisionist treatment of the agrarian crisis)
Ross Taylor, *Party Politics in the Age of Caesar* (a bit dated but still a good introduction to the general practice of politics)

Chapter Two (Ti. Gracchus)

Ancient sources

Appian, *Civil Wars* 1.7–20
Cicero, *Philippics* (on Mucianus's election to the campaign in Asia)
Dio fr. 83
Livy, *Epitome* 58
Plutarch, *Life of Tiberius Gracchus*
Velleius Paterculus 2.2–3

Modern works

Stockman, *The Gracchi* 6–86

Chapter Three (C. Gracchus)

Ancient sources

Appian, *Civil Wars* 1.21–27
Dio fr. 85
Livy, *Epitome* 60–61
Plutarch, *Life of C. Gracchus*
Velleius Paterculus 2.6–7

Modern sources

Badian, *Publicans and Sinners*
Keaveney, *Unification of Italy* 47–70
Stockman, *The Gracchi* 87–205

Chapter Four (Numidia, Senatorial Failures and the Rise of C. Marius)

Ancient sources

Dio frs. 90–91
Sallust, *Jugurthine War*
Plutarch, *Life of Marius* 1–10; *Life of Sulla* 1–3

Modern sources

Evans, *Marius* 1–78
Keaveney, *Sulla* 6–24

Chapter Five (Ascendancy of Marius)

Ancient sources

Appian, *Civil Wars* 1.28–33
Livy *Epitome* 67–69
Plutarch, *Life of Marius* 11–31; *Life of Sulla* 4

Valerius Maximus 3.2.18, 9.7.1
Velleius Paterculus 2.12

Modern works

Evans, *Marius* 78–127
Keaveney, *Sulla* 28–34, *Unification of Italy* 76–81

Chapter Six (M. Drusus and Social War)

Ancient sources

Appian, *Civil Wars* 1.35–53
Dio fr. 96–98
Livy, *Epitome* 70–76
Plutarch, *Life of Marius* 32–33, *Life of Sulla* 6
Velleius Paterculus 2.14–16

Modern works

Badian, *Publicans and Sinners* 87–94
Carney, *Marius* 51–56
Keaveney, *Sulla* 42–52, *Unification of Italy* 81–171

Chapter Seven (Sulla, Marius, and Civil War)

Ancient sources

Appian, *Civil Wars* 1.55–75
Dio fr. 102–104
Livy, *Epitome* 77
Plutarch, *Life of Marius* 34–46, *Life of Sulla* 7–10,
   Life of Sertorius 4–5
Velleius Paterculus 2.18–23.1

Modern works

Carney, *Marius* 57–71
Keaveney, *Sulla* 56–76, *Unification of Italy* 171–176
Seager, *Pompey* 20–24

Chapter Eight (Territorial Expansion)

Ancient sources

Appian, *Civil Wars* 1.116–120
Dio. 36.3, 9
Livy, *Epitome* 96–97
Plutarch, *Life of Crassus* 8–11

Modern works

Ebel, *Transalpine Gaul* 41–95
Keaveney, *Sulla* 34–42
Magie, *Roman Rule in Asia Minor* 3–52, 147–176
Sherwin-White, *Roman Foreign Policy in East* 80–92
Ward, *Crassus* 83–98 (on Spartacus)

Chapter Nine (First Mithridatic War)

Ancient sources

Appian, *Mithridatic War* 10–62
Plutarch, *Life of Sulla* 11–26, *Life of Cimon* 1–2, *Life of Lucullus* 2–4

Modern works

Keaveney, *Sulla* 78–117, *Lucullus* 15–31
Sherwin-White, *Roman Foreign Policy in East* 93–148

Chapter Ten (Sulla's Victory in Civil War)

Ancient sources

Appian, *Civil Wars* 1.76–95
Plutarch, *Life of Sulla* 27–32, *Life of Pompey* 3–15, *Life of Crassus* 1–7,
    Life of Sertorius 6
Velleius Paterculus 2.24.3–28.4

Modern works

Keaveney, *Sulla* 117–145
Lovano, *Cinna*

Seager, *Pompey* 25–30
Ward, *Crassus* 58–66

Chapter Eleven (Sulla's Settlement)

Ancient sources

Appian, *Civil Wars* 1.96–104
Cicero, *In Defense of Sex. Roscius of Ameria*
Plutarch, *Life of Cicero* 3, *Life of Sulla* 33–34

Modern works

Keaveney, *Sulla* 148–202

Chapter Twelve (70s b.c.)

Ancient works

Appian, *Civil Wars* 1.105–121
Cicero, *Divination against Caecilius, Against Verres*
Livy, *Epitome* 90–96
Plutarch, *Life of Sertorius* 2–3, 7–27, *Life of Pompey* 16–23, *Life of Crassus* 8–12, *Life of Cicero* 7–8.1

Modern works

Keaveney, *Sulla* 204–212, *Lucullus* 32–74
Rawson, *Cicero* 29–43
Seager, *Pompey* 30–39
Ward, *Crassus* 66–82, 99–109

Chapter Thirteen (Third Mithridatic War)

Ancient sources

Appian, *Mithridatic War* 63–121
Cicero, *On the Imperium of Cn. Pompeius*
Dio 36–37.23
Plutarch, *Life of Pompey* 24–42, *Life of Lucullus* 5–37

Modern works

Keaveney, *Lucullus* 75–128
Magie, *Roman Rule in Asia Minor* 232–378
Seager, *Pompey* 40–62
Sherwin-White, *Roman Foreign*
  Policy in East 149–234

Chapter Fourteen (60s b.c.)

Ancient sources

Asconius, *Commentary on the Pro Cornelio*
  and *on the Pro Milone*
Dio 36.20–25
Plutarch, *Life of Crassus* 13.1,
  Life of Cicero 9

Modern works

Rawson, *Cicero* 44–59
Seager, *Pompey* 63–66
Ward, *Crassus* 128–151

Chapter Fifteen (Consulship of Cicero)

Ancient sources

Cicero, *Catilinarian Orations, Orations against the Bill*
  of Rullus, In Defense of Murena, Letters to His Friends
  SB 1–3 (5.1, 2, 7)
Dio 37.25–41
Plutarch, *Life of Cicero* 1–22, *Life of Cato the Younger* 20–23,
  Life of Crassus 13.2–4
Sallust, *Catilinarian Conspiracy*

Modern works

Rawson, *Cicero* 1–88
Seager, *Pompey* 66–72
Ward, *Crassus* 151–192

Chapter Sixteen (Consulship of Caesar)

Ancient sources

Cicero, *Letters to Atticus* SB 12–14 (1.12–14), 16–23 (1.16–2.3), 41
    (2.21), 44 (2.24)
Dio 37.42–38.12
Plutarch, *Life of Caesar* 1–14, *Life of Pompey* 43–48.4, *Life of Cato the
    Younger* 1–19, 26–33, *Life of Cicero* 23, 28–29, *Life of Crassus* 14.1–3
Suetonius, *Life of the Deified Julius* 1–21

Modern works

Gelzer, *Caesar* 1–100
Rawson, *Cicero* 89–112
Seager, *Pompey* 75–100
Ward, *Crassus* 193–226

Chapter Seventeen (Caesar in Gaul)

Ancient sources

Caesar, *Gallic War*
Cicero, *Letters to His Friends* SB 26–31 (7.5–9, 17)
Dio 38.31–39.5; 39.40–59; 40.1–11, 31–44
Plutarch, *Life of Caesar* 15–20, 22–27
Suetonius, *Life of the Deified Julius* 22, 25

Modern works

Gelzer, *Caesar* 102–194
Goldsworthy, *Caesar* 380–489

Chapter Eighteen (50's b.c.)

Ancient sources

Appian, *Civil Wars* 2.15–32
Cicero, *In Defense of Sestius, On the Consular Provinces, Against
    Piso, On His House before the Haruspices, Thanks to the Senate
    and to the People, Against Piso, Letters to Atticus* SB 57 (3.12),
    68–69 (3.23–24), 73–75 (4.1–3), 90–92 (4.15, 17–18), 124 (7.1),

126–127 (7.3–4), 130–132 (7.7–9), *Letters to Brother Quintus*,
Letters to His Friends SB 20 (1.9), 77–98 (2.8–15; 8.1–14), 110–112
(15.4–6)

Dio 38.13–30; 39.6–39, 55–65; 40.12–30, 44–66

Plutarch, *Life of Pompey* 48.5–59.1, *Life of Caesar* 21, 28–30, *Life of
Cato the Younger* 34–51, *Life of Crassus* 14.4–33, *Life of Cicero*
30–36, *Life of Antony* 3, 5

Suetonius, *Life of the Deified Julius* 23–30

Modern works

Gruen, *Last Generation*
Rawson, *Cicero* 112–182
Seager, *Pompey* 101–151
Sherwin-White, *Roman Foreign Policy in East* 271–297
Tatum, *Tribune*
Ward, *Crassus* 231–288

CHAPTER NINETEEN (CIVIL WAR)

Ancient sources

Appian *Civil Wars*, 2.33–154
Cicero, *Letters to Atticus* SB 134–142 (7.11–18), 144–148 (7.20–24), 151–
153 (8.1–3), 158 (8.8), 160–174C (8.9a, 8.11–9.7C), 176–190 (9.9–10.1),
195 (10.4), 198–203 (10.7–12), 217 (11.6), 226 (11.5),
236 (11.21), *Letters to His Friends* SB 143, 146 (16.11–12),
149 (8.15), 151 (4.2), 153 (8.16), 157 (9.9), 174 (15.15), 183 (7.3), 230
(4.7), 234 (6.6)

Dio 41–43.14, 28–40

Plutarch, *Life of Pompey* 59.2–70, *Life of Caesar* 31–56, *Life of Cato
the Younger* 52–72, *Life of Brutus* 1–6, *Life of Antony* 7–11, *Life of
Cicero* 37–38

Suetonius, *Life of the Deified Julius* 31–36

Modern works

Gelzer, *Caesar* 195–271
Goldsworthy, *Caesar* 380–489
Rawson, *Cicero* 183–225
Seager, *Pompey* 152–168

Chapter Twenty (Caesar's Domination and Assassination)

Ancient sources

Cicero, *In Defense of Marcellus, In Defense of Ligarius*, and *In Defense of King Deiotarus, Letters to Atticus* SB 298–299 (13.27–28), 302 (13.31), 352–353 (13.47a, 52)

Dio 43.15–27; 43.4–44.22

Plutarch, *Life of Caesar* 55, 57–68, *Life of Brutus* 7–17, *Life of Antony* 11–13, *Life of Cicero* 39–42

Suetonius, *Life of the Deified Julius* 40–44.3

Modern works

Clarke, *Noblest Roman* 1–47 (on Brutus)

Fishwick, *Imperial Cult* 3–72

Gelzer, *Caesar* 272–333

Gradel, *Emperor Worship* 27–72

Rawson, *Cicero* 230–259

Syme, *Roman Revolution* 47–96

Chapter Twenty-One (Turmoil after the Ides)

Ancient sources

Appian, *Civil Wars* 3–4

Cicero, *Philippic Orations, Letters to Marcus Brutus, Letters to Atticus* SB 355 (14.1), 358 (14.4), 363–371A (14.9–17A), 376–379 (14.22–15.2), 383 (15.5), 389–390 (15.11–12), 411 (16.4), 415 (16.7), 418–419 (16.8–9), 426 (16.15), *Letters to His Friends* SB 325 (11.1), 329 (11.2), 336 (11.3), 342 (11.4), 345 (12.3), 346–347 (12.22–23), 349 (11.28), 363–365 (12.4, 10.28, 12.5), 368–371 (10.31, 27, 6, 8), 378 (10.30), 380 (11.9), 382 (10.11), 385 (11.10), 387–388 (12.12, 11.13), 390–391 (10.15, 21), 395–396 (10.18, 34), 401 (11.20), 405–406 (12.14–15), 408–409 (10.38, 33), 413–414 (11.14, 10.23), 419 (12.13)

Dio 44.23–47; 45–47

Plutarch, *Life of Antony* 1–2, 14–22, *Life of Brutus* 18–53, *Life of Cicero* 43–49

Suetonius, *Life of the Deified Augustus* 1–12

Modern works

Clarke, *Noblest Roman* 47–78 (on Brutus)
Fishwick, *Imperial Cult* 73–82
Jones, *Augustus* 23–43
Osgood, *Caesar's Legacy* 12–107
Rawson, *Cicero* 260–298
Southern, *Augustus* 1–65
Syme, *Roman Revolution* 97–206
Watkins, *Plancus* 52–91
Weigel, *Lepidus* 44–79

Chapter Twenty-two (Struggle of Warlords)

Ancient sources

Appian, *Civil Wars* 5
Dio 48–49.33
Plutarch, *Life of Antony* 23–52
Suetonius, *Life of the Deified Augustus* 13–16, 27

Modern works

Jones, *Augustus* 23–35
Osgood, *Caesar's Legacy* 108–349
Sherwin-White, *Roman Foreign Policy in East* 298–321
Southern, *Augustus* 65–87
Syme, *Roman Revolution* 206–275
Watkins, *Plancus* 52–91
Weigel, *Lepidus* 79–100

Chapter Twenty-three (Final Showdown)

Ancient sources

Dio 49.34–50.35
Orosius, *Against the Pagans* 6.19.3–13
Plutarch, *Life of Antony* 53–87
Suetonius, *Life of the Deified Augustus* 17–18

Modern works

Jones, *Augustus* 35–43
Osgood, *Caesar's Legacy* 350–384
Southern, *Augustus* 87–99
Syme, *Roman Revolution* 276–312

Chapter Twenty-four (Augustan Settlement)

Ancient sources

Augustus, *Res Gestae*
Dio 51–56
Suetonius, *Life of the Deified Augustus* 19–101
Tacitus, *Annals* 1.1–5

Modern works

Southern, *Augustus* 100–159
Fishwick, *Imperial Cult* 83–93
Gradel, *Emperor Worship* 109–139
Jones, *Augustus* 45–130
Syme, *Roman Revolution* 313–524

Epilogue

Ancient sources

Dio 57.1–2
Tacitus, *Annals* 1.6–15

Bibliography

Badian, Ernst. *Foreign Clientelae (264 B.C.–70 B.C.)* (Oxford: Clarendon Press, 1958).

Publicans and Sinners: Private Enterprise in the Service of the Roman Republic (Ithaca: Cornell University Press, 1983).

Brunt, P. A. *Italian Manpower: 225 B.C.-A.D. 14* (Oxford: Clarendon Press, 1987).

Carney, T. F. *A Biography of Gaius Marius*, 2nd ed. (Chicago: Argonaut, 1970).

Clarke, M. L. *The Noblest Roman: Marcus Brutus and His Reputation* (London: Thames and Hudson, 1981).

Crawford, Michael H. *Roman Republican Coinage*, corrected ed. (Cambridge: Cambridge University Press, 1983).

(ed.), *Roman Statutes* (London: Institute of Classical Studies, 1996).

Dittenberger, Wilhelm. *Orientis Graeci Inscriptiones Selectae* (rep., Hildesheim: Olms, 1960).

Ebel, Charles. *Transalpine Gaul: The Emergence of a Roman Province* (Leiden: E. J. Brill, 1976).

Fishwick, Duncan. *The Imperial Cult in the Latin West: Studies in the Ruler Cult of the Western Provinces of the Roman Empire*, vol. 1. (Leiden: Brill, 1987).

Gelzer, Matthias. *Roman Nobility*, ed. Robin Seager (Oxford: Blackwell, 1069).

Goldsworthy, Adrian. *Caesar: Life of a Colossus* (New Haven: Yale University Press, 2006).

Gradel, Ittai. *Emperor Worship and Roman Religion* (Oxford: Clarendon Press, 2002).

Grueber, H. A. *Coins of the Roman Republic in the British Museum* (London: British Museum, 1970).

Gruen, Erich. *Roman Politics and the Criminal Courts, 149–78 B.C.* (Cambridge: Harvard University Press, 1968).

The Last Generation of the Roman Republic (Berkeley: University of California Press, 1974).

Harris, W. V. *War and Imperialism in Republican Rome, 327–70 B.C.* (Oxford: Clarendon Press, 1979).

Kallett-Marx, Robert. *Hegemony to Empire: Development of the Roman Imperium in the East from 148 to 62 B.C.* (Berkeley: University of California Press, 1995).

Keaveney, Arthur. *Sulla: The Last Republican* (London: Croom Helm, 1982).

Rome and the Unification of Italy (London: Croom Helm, 1987).

Lucullus: A Life (London: Routledge, 1992).

The Army in the Roman Revolution (London: Routledge, 2007).

Jones, A. H. M. *Augustus* (New York: W. W. Norton, 1970).

Lintott, Andrew. *Imperium Romanum: Politics and Administration* (London: Routledge, 1993).

The Constitution of the Roman Republic (Oxford: Clarendon Press, 1999).

Lovano, Michael. *Age of Cinna: Crucible of Late Republican Rome* (Stuttgart: Franz Steiner Verlag, 2002).

Meier, Christian, *Caesar,* trans. by David McLintock (New York: Basic Books, 1995).

Millar, Fergus. *The Crowd in Rome in the Late Republic* (Ann Arbor: University of Michigan Press, 1998).

Morstein-Marx, Robert. *Mass Oratory and Political Power in the Late Roman Republic* (Cambridge: Cambridge University Press, 2004).

Morstein-Marx, Robert and Nathan Rosenstein (eds). *A Companion to the Roman Republic* (Oxford: Blackwell, 2006).

Nicolet, Claude. *The World of the Citizen in Ancient Rome,* trans. P. S. Falla (Berkeley: University of California Press, 1980).

Osgood, Josiah. *Caesar's Legacy: Civil War and the Emergence of the Roman Empire* (Cambridge: Cambridge University Press, 2006).

Rawson, Elizabeth. *Cicero: A Portrait* (London: Lane Allen, 1975).

Reynolds, Joyce. *Rome and Aphrodisias* (London: Society for the Promotion of Roman Studies, 1982).

Rosenstein, Nathan. *Rome at War: Farms, Families, and Death in the Middle Republic* (Chapel Hill: University of North Carolina Press, 2004).

Seager, Robin. *Pompey: A Political Biography,* 2nd ed. (Oxford: Blackwell, 2002).

Sherwin-White, A. N. *Roman Foreign Policy in the East: 168 B.C.–A.D. 1* (Norman: University of Oklahoma Press, 1983).

Southern, Pat. *Augustus* (London: Routledge, 1998).

Stockton, David. *The Gracchi* (Oxford: Clarendon Press, 1979).

Sutherland, C.H.V., *The Roman Imperial Coinage, vol. 1 (rev. ed.), from 31 BC to AD 69* (London: Spink & Son, 1984).

Syme, Ronald. *The Roman Revolution* (Oxford: Clarendon Press, 1939).

Tatum, W. Jeffrey. *The Patrician Tribune: Publius Clodius Pulcher* (Chapel Hill: University of North Carolina Press, 1999).

Watkins, Thomas H. *L. Munatius Plancus: Serving and Surviving in the Roman Republic* (Atlanta: Scholars Press, 1997).

Wiegel, Richard D. *Lepidus: The Tarnished Triumvir* (London: Routledge, 1992).

INDEX

CPSIA information can be obtained
at www.ICGtesting.com
Printed in the USA
LVHW042256280721
693950LV00017B/1298